The LITTON Adventure That Was

A Tribute to the Founder
Charles B. "Tex" Thornton

By Col. Barney Oldfield, USAF (Ret.)

2006
The Kinman-Oldfield Family Foundation

Published by:

Kinman-Oldfield
Family Foundation Trust
U.S. Bank N.A., Trustee
233 South 13th Street,
Lincoln, Nebraska 68508.

ISBN-13:978-0-615-14482-5
ISBN-10:0-615-14482-9

Other books by the author:
NEVER A SHOT IN ANGER, 1956
Those Wonderful Men in the Cactus Starfighter Squadron (Die
    Aussergewöhnlichen Männer der Kaktus Starfighter Staffel),
    Volume I, April 1976; Volume II, April 1986
OPERATION NARCISSUS, 1991
The Kid from Tecumseh, 2002
Plus, Contributor to Collections

The LITTON Adventure That Was

A Tribute to The Founder
CHARLES B. "TEX" THORNTON

Dedication

As Litton Industries' Founder Charles B. "Tex" Thornton often said that "people are more important than things", it is to people who worked with and for him to bring this company to its greatness, people who made all those smaller firms which were joined with Litton and came with them people who believed in and invested in this enterprise, people who stayed with it all or part of its way and sentimentally remember their Litton days, people who stood on the sidelines and only marveled about how an idea placed in hands of those who are mesmerized by it can be made to bloom and grow, and even people who were never a part of the Litton scene but who wished they could have been and know that they missed something and for all those who came afterward and wondered how the Litton Industries they encountered came to be, this book is dedicated.

Col. Barney Oldfield, USAF (Ret.)

TABLE OF CONTENTS

FORETHOUGHT

BOOK II: That Difficult Decade

BOOK III: The Baton Passes

Introduction

Story telling is one thing, but Col. Barney Oldfield, USAF (ret.), was lucky enough to be a close-up and often good friend with the people he wrote about. His range was wide and diverse—newspaper man, radio commentator, military officer, businessman, magazine contributor, scriptor and gallivantor who lived, worked and had assignments in 81 countries on every continent. He and his wife, Vada, married nearly 64 years, were that rare package, a "military couple," she one of the original WAACs (forerunner of the Women's Army Corps), and he was in class 23 of the Parachute School at Ft. Benning, GA, making him a pioneer paratrooper. Both served overseas in WWII, she as a teletype operator with Hq. 12th Air Force across North Africa, Sicily and Italy, he in northern Europe and in the Korean "police action" in 1950.

A Warner Brothers film studio publicist, he had charges named Errol Flynn, Ann Sheridan, Janis Paige, Jane Wyman and a sports announcer who would become the 40th President of the U.S., Ronald Reagan (for whom he wrote jokes for over 40 years).

For one film, he worked with a teen named Elizabeth Taylor.

There were 1,828 war correspondents accredited by the U.S. in WWII, and he knew most of them. He wrote the Tables of Organization and equipment for their so-called Press Camps to which they were assigned while following field armies liberating a continent. A press officer with General Dwight D. Eisenhower pre-Normandy, when NATO began in 1949, he was his advance man as the common-purpose linked 12 nations were given military teeth.

On retirement in 1962, he was brought into 10 year old Litton Industries as a confidante to the firm's founder, Charles Bates (Tex) Thornton, served as director of Foreign Relations and did a breakthrough of the Iron Curtain by imaginative use of commemorative postage stamps. When the company took on a contract to teach high school dropouts employable skills, among them a teenage juvenile delinquent he was assigned to counsel, George Foreman, the great heavyweight boxer. Forbes Magazine would later call George the best salesman in the world—under that tutelage he had gone from a dysfunctional communicator using less than 50 words to nearly a billionaire in net worth.

When Thornton was diagnosed as dying of cancer (he left us on Nov. 24, 1981), he was one of four Tex sent for and told he would be calling him all hours of the day and night giving him personal instructions to carry out when he was no longer able to do so.

The author called President Reagan to suggest to him as worthy of the Presidential Medal of Freedom, which was awarded him two months before cancer took him. After he was taken to be given full military honors at Arlington Cemetery for his WWII setting up the office of Strategic Control. He had dictated two letters the last day he'd been able to work—one to his friend Art Linkletter, and one to Col. Barney Oldfield—the fact that they were unsigned making them more touching. Incredible man was Tex Thornton, and this book tries to tell a reader why this is so.

SPECIAL SITUATION #1

STANDOFF ON PARK AVENUE

An idea can take a man to strange doorsteps.

It was nothing like the dusty streets of Haskell, Texas, this 300 Park Avenue address. Charles B. "Tex" Thornton had an appointment on the 9th floor of the building. There had been many such one-on-one meetings. Some had gone well. Others had been a waste of time, except that he had learned something from each of them. He was leaving no possibilities unchecked. This meant he was shopping his idea around. Money men said that was wrong, but he didn't believe it was good advice in his case. The idea Tex Thornton had was so fascinating to him, he thought exposure to it would cause the support he needed to catch fire. It was that combustible enthusiasm he sought. As the elevator crept upward he had reason to believe what Fred Allen, the comedian, had said in jest was very true. There is nothing so nervous, Fred declared, as a million dollars. Tex Thornton needed at least $1,200,000 to buy a small company. He would use it as the cornerstone for a corporate edifice which could reach all directions benefiting and profiting from the likelihood that electronics would revolutionize the world's industries.

The man he was about to see was one who could turn such ideas into the required money to lubricate and nurture them any day he felt like it. At one point, he made overtures to buy the Brooklyn Dodgers so he could give the ball club to his son, who would be its president. What Tex Thornton had in mind was in no way as ephemeral as batting averages, throwing arms, and shoestring catches on which to stake a future claim.

This was no casual call, hat in hand. It had begun with a conversation with his friend, Dr. Edmund P. Learned, the Harvard professor. Learned said professors didn't know many rich men, but that Boston had at least one. The way to 300 Park Avenue had been prepared very carefully. At Brown Brothers, Harriman at 59 Wall Street, Harold Barry knew Tex Thornton well, and he also worked with a colleague named Herbert Shriver. Shriver's brother, Sargent, headed Chicago's huge and sprawling Merchandise Mart. He was married to Eunice Kennedy, daughter of the Boston, Hyannisport, New York and Hollywood Joseph P. Kennedy. It was Barry who suggested contact be made first with Sargent Shriver. If he was impressed with Tex Thornton and his idea, he could suggest that his father-in-law give the proposal a hearing.

The call on Sargent Shriver in the Windy City went extremely well. The two men not only liked each other, they bolstered each other's infectuousness. There was talk that if the deal jelled, Shriver might participate in the management at a high level, or at least would come on the board of directors of the new company. Shriver was sufficiently high on the idea that he wanted nothing to block receptiveness at 300 Park Avenue. He counseled Tex that all his father-in-law's key advisors be brought up to speed on all the ramifications. "Be especially sure that Bart Brickley knows every detail," Shriver said. Brickley was the Boston lawyer who had drafted all the Joseph P. Kennedy trust programs. That advice had been taken. Kennedy was the learned "rich man."

The elevator leveled with the 9th floor. As Tex Thornton stepped into the corridor, he knew that every one of those advisors including Sargent Shriver and Bart Brickley, had made recommendations and said he had a potential investment of great merit. No detail had been overlooked. Only this imminent and crucial face-to-face size-up remained. The elevator door slid silently shut behind him as he looked at the numbers on the apartment doors.[1] This was not an office building. It was used as living quarters. The door Tex Thornton was seeking for this milestone moment was no different from the others fronting on the corridor, nor did it have even as much traffic. There were no casual drop-ins as none came there unbidden or without invitation. He touched the button and heard the soft buzz inside.

He was admitted into the hallway by Paul Murphy, an old Kennedy family retainer and bookkeeper. "I'm Tex Thornton," he said. "I'm a little early for an appointment with Mr. Kennedy."

"Oh, yes," Murphy told him, while taking his coat. "You are expected. He'll be with you in a moment."

The reception area, such as it was, had been a parlor or dining room. It accommodated the desk Murphy used, and his filing cabi-

---

1. 300 Park Avenue in New York today is the Colgate Palmolive Building. The old apartment house came down in 1954 and the new structure on the site opened in 1956.

nets, Tex seated himself on a sofa, and surveyed the austerity with which he was confronted. The location was on the 50th Street side of the building. As Kennedy lived in the Waldorf Towers not far from the apartment of Ex-President Herbert Hoover, and had no wish to conduct business where he lived, he had chosen 300 Park Avenue as convenient and sufficient for the kinds of activities which interested him. There were two rooms that had once been equipped with beds, but one was now for files and the other Kennedy used as his base of operations. In it were desks and telephones, and a Wall Street ticker which chattered along discreetly. Tex could hear the Kennedy end of the conversation on one phone only faintly. Murphy indicated he was talking to a broker in New York. There was a Washington call holding. When these were over and done with, Kennedy would see him. Murphy's instructions were to hold all other calls until their meeting was over.

Tex Thornton was the kind of man who could focus intently to the exclusion of everything else on whatever situation he chose to deal with. He used his waiting time for that concentration. Joseph P. Kennedy, in another time, had been a man on the move, too. Sharp trader, they said. Wheeler-dealer, they said. President Roosevelt made him head of the Securities & Exchange Commission because he thought it akin to the British custom of making a successful poacher gamekeeper. How better could the job of policing be done than by one who knew all the sharp practices? As a film producer he made the fourth Tarzan movie. He had been a controversial Ambassador to the Court of St. James's. The British thought he marked them down as of no consequence to resist Adolph Hitler's preparation for showdown in Europe.

Tex Thornton wisely assumed his idea and its appeal had been well established, or he never would have been asked to come in for this chat.

Kennedy would be making that all-important personal assessment: Could the man who had the dream make it materialize into substance? Forty years before J. Pierpont Morgan had been asked by a Congressional committee if commercial credit was not based on money or property, and he had said No, the first thing was character. "A man I do not trust," he said, "could not get money from me for all the bonds in Christendom." The man from Haskell, Texas thought he had built a course record which would cover that portion of the judgment.

He had two points, however, and on those two he could not yield. They had been troublesome before, one of them always. That one was that no matter who put up the money, or how much, Tex Thornton had to have control. He had more experience than he ever wished to have again with decision making, or worse yet, decision withholding being other than in his own hands beyond his instincts and intuition. It wasn't enough that an entrepreneur could grow ulcers that way, it was more sinful than that it was time-wasting. Napoleon Bonaparte had once flayed his planners with the statement that they could ask him for anything but time. Time to a Tex Thornton was more important than money. Wisely expended one needed never to overtake it because time's sparing user would always be ahead. Control meant everything to the enterprise.

The second standpat point was that whatever else this firm did, it had to participate in military contracts. The people who wrote military requirements had ravenous, wide-ranging technological appetites. Being professionals who worked in environments where being first equated with survival of men and nations, they literally shot for the moon in their specifications. They not only paid well those who responded with the hardware they asked for, there were myriad commercial, consumer applications which could be developed from those findings. Being at the outer reaches of such technologies assured a company lead time in selection and types of such applications which could appeal to the general public. And sell.

"Mr. Kennedy will see you now," Paul Murphy said, and showed him in.

The elder Kennedy's handshake was warm. His Irish ancestors had assured him of copious supplies of graciousness and charm. He was in command of his world. He knew he could reach as far as he wished, any time he wished. Life, once hard and scrambling and requiring steely toughness, was a game he could play now by his own rules.

After the amenities, the ease making, he got right down to business. He had already made up his mind what kind of individual this Tex Thornton would be in the thoroughness with which he had knocked on all the doors prior to his own. He had submitted himself to scrutinies of men whose judgments Kennedy respected. Finally, it was nitty-gritty time, and Kennedy turned to the subject closest to his heart, his family.

"You probably know," he said, "that I lost a son in World War II. Another one was wounded pretty badly in one of those PT boats. The loss of the son, Joe, our oldest, was a blow to Mrs. Kennedy and myself. The other son, Jack, is now a young congressman down in Washington. I was just talking to him on the phone. I believe he has a future in politics, has a flair for it."

It had been Joseph P. Kennedy, Jr. who was the personality boy, the first born, who had been expected to assume that role. As a Navy flier he had been killed over the English Channel. The family was clearly in a fallback position, and the John Fitzgerald Kennedy for whom his father had tried to buy the Brooklyn Dodgers, was the surrogate for his adored brother. Tex Thornton was following the Kennedy recollections closely, genuinely interested and sympathetic. Momentarily it seemed off the mark in so far as why he was there. Suddenly, it wasn't at all.

Kennedy was saying he had to be careful about his investments because of his son, Jack. "I would not want to be a backer of a firm which was engaged in military contracting," he said. "I would never want Jack, on any vote he might have to make, to be put in the position where the Pentagon was concerned in seeming to have voted one way or the other to protect his father's investment."

He said it matter of factly. He had been around. He knew the insatiable hunger of the press for an angle. It was not a tastebud he wished to gratify. In Tex Thornton's ears, he heard the rattling sound of the drawbridge chains as they tightened and started the hoist which would separate him with a deep moat from the Kennedy treasury. Kennedy was not through, either.

"I have never been interested in minority positions," he told Tex. "What you're asking for (a million or so) isn't all that much, but I'd have to have 51% of the stock."

The two "hold-fast" positions Tex had vowed could not be breached were unacceptable. He could only thank the Kennedy dynasty's head and part in a friendly way. Later Kennedy told Shriver that he was mightily taken with the Thornton confidence and competence. He felt the proposal was an exceptionally good one. He had

5

his rules about participation, though. The line was drawn just as firmly as Tex had enunciated his, hence the standoff.

As Tex went along the corridor to the elevator, he reviewed his situation. He was empty handed, yes, but he was still convinced that he was right. He had to have a place in the military contract picture. He had to have control. And from Joseph P. Kennedy he had seen a warning flag waving the specter of politics at home and abroad; would always be riding beside him. Once down at street level on Park Avenue, he felt his buoyancy coming back. Kennedy, one of the most astute business opportunists in America, had liked everything about his idea so much that he wanted to control it.

Charles Bates Tex Thornton of Haskell, Texas, might have been unable to get the backing he sought from Kennedy, but everything about their encounter had been reassuring as to the rightness of what he was doing. His spirits lifted with every step as he strode along Park Avenue. He had not been stopped.

And Joseph P. Kennedy, the man who'd said, "NO," was condemned to hear for the rest of his life that he'd allowed "the big one to get away."

SPECIAL SITUATION #2

"TEX" THORNTON AND HOW HE GREW

The very air smelled of intrigue and adventure.

The tall, slender, smartly dressed man, standing in Genoa, Italy that morning was no ordinary traveler. But then, 1940's summer was no routine moment in world history either. The greenish-gray uniforms of the *Wehrmacht* were all over Paris. Fully a third of metropolitan France (the part President Roosevelt had accused Mussolini of stabbing in the back) was about to be Vichyfied. The world beyond the Axis powers was between tears for losses suffered and apprehension as to where the next strike would be. Even though the man waiting for his passport to be checked had an urbane air about him, he was Huntsville, Texas born. The passport in his hand, which he tapped lightly with his fingers was one of the last four of its kind. It permitted him to land in Genoa, transit quickly to Switzerland. When his work was done there, he was to exit via Milan and return to his offices at 59 Wall Street. Over that entrance the sign said: Brown Brothers Harriman. It was the firm's business he was about that day.

Investment bankers in the U.S. had to do a great deal of adjusting as one European state after another was menaced by Hitler. His *anschluss* had swallowed Austria in 1938, and it opened the Brenner Pass access to Italy. Switzerland on the north, east and south had the Axis at its borders. Then, in June of 1940, France had been crushed. Switzerland was now a geographic, and political island. Brown Brothers Harriman had many Swiss bank relationships and clients with numbered accounts there. The question was: What moves could be made protectively for the responsibilities entrusted to them should Hitler's rampant territorial appetite make an *hors d'oeuvre* of that small, rich land?

That is why Robert Abercrombie Lovett was in Genoa. In whatever time that remained, and as alternatives were decreasing by the hour, he had to get on the scene and make crucial investment banker decisions. Passport *Kontrolle* signaled for him to step forward. He was to get special attention. In the ways of bureaucracy, the regular scrutiny of his documents was not enough. The uniformed man who reached for the packet took his time about leafing through it all. When he reached the passport photo, his eyes flicked upward to match it with the face before him. Two others joined him, each in the corroborating ritual. Then there was some whispered counsel. Finally came the double thump of the hand stamp, first on the inkpad and then squarely on the visa. All the papers were handed back. He was escorted to his waiting transportation, proceeding to Switzerland via Geneva to Zurich.

While there, through that special communications conduit which is available to money men, he heard analytical reports of the military colossus the *Fuehrer* had thrown against the West on May 10, 1940. First the lowland countries (the Netherlands and Belgium). Next was the end run around France's arthritic Maginot Line, found quickly to be more immobile than invincible. The *Wehrmacht*, with its overwhelming *Luftwaffe* support of dive-bombing and strafing lightningbolts, had emerged not even breathing hard from its exertions. Robert Lovett may have been well known as a respected banker, financial counselor, and sage adviser in many matters, but he had extra dimension beyond all that. In World War I he had been with Great Britain's RAS (Royal Air Service), the forerunner of the RAF (Royal Air Force) which was about to be in "the Battle of Britain." His focus was sharpest on how Hitler had used his air power. Between the wars, Lovett had gotten to know such early German aces as Ernst Udet.[1] Udet had once done his favorite show-off trick, the one in which he would walk out in the middle of the airfield and make a small pyramid of a dropped handkerchief. Boarding his aircraft, Udet took it aloft, made a turn, then flipped upside down to come ripping along barely above the grass. At the right moment, just as a rodeo cowboy in Texas might run down and grab a sprinting chicken, Udet reached out and retrieved the handkerchief. Lovett knew that a nation which had produced fliers such as these in an earlier generation could be expected to be even more formidable when it was *lebensraum* (living room) oriented with a power mad helmsman in Berlin's Reichschancellory. When he thought of the military situation in the America he had left so recently, he said it literally made his "hair stand on end."

He was a company man, however. Brown Brothers Harriman partners were entitled to know what he heard and felt, and he would

---

1. Udet, who lived a life of derring-do, was among the many high-rankers made scapegoats by Hitler. He shot himself on November 17, 1941.

tell them. In his heart he had the sensation that no matter what political exhortations there might be to the contrary, the United States could not escape involvement sooner or later.

Congress easily passed the Selective Service Act in 1940. In 1941, Congress extended the time to be served from one year to 2 1/2 years. This was passed by one vote. Procurement was limping along so poorly that when Roosevelt mentioned in his campaign oratory the thousands of rifles which were "on order," his adversary, Wendall Willkie said scathingly that no doughboy ever made the mistake of firing a rifle which was "*on order.*"

Robert Lovett enroute home, wrote a wide-ranging informative memorandum which was addressed to all the Brown Brothers Harriman, offices. He weighted it heavily with air power significance. He assayed the Army Air Corps predicaments as woefully inadequate to the challenge it might face. To him it was a mishmash of misconceptions, uncoordinated and whimsical headings, and misunderstood training requirements. Lack of cohesion was self-defeating and dangerous, as well as pure folly in many cases. It was intended as an "in-house" memorandum and sent to the Brown Brothers Harriman "brotherhood." He had had his say, and went on about his business.

As that unprecedented "third term" political Punch and Judy show wore on, Roosevelt restated that he had no intention of sending Americans to fight in any foreign wars. A copy of the Lovett memorandum fell into the hands of a young White House staffer named James Forrestal. Roosevelt had recently made the move toward bipartisanship in his cabinet by appointing two Republicans, Col. Henry L. Stimson, Secretary of War, and Col. Frank Knox, Secretary of the Navy. Forrestal told Stimson about the Lovett situation analyses. Stimson found it especially well reasoned and the conclusion stark and realistic. He instructed Forrestal to have his friend, Lovett, come to Washington to see him.

When Lovett picked up the phone that day and heard the invitation, he wasn't sure what it was about. Telephone calls to and from Washington were veiled and highly guarded. Even though he hadn't much to go on, Lovett went to Stimson's office. The reason was not long in coming.

"I want you to come down here," Stimson said. "I want you to help me. You'll be Assistant Secretary of War for Air."

Lovett may have had the "cool" of a banker on the outside, but his pulses pounded. Washington was beginning to get the right vibrations, was sensing the enormity of the forces arrayed against America, and its traditional allies. The old Army axiom was still true (OK, you complained about the mess hall, you're the new mess officer!). The conversation indicated he would have to take a leave of absence from Brown Brothers Harriman, of course, but only for "about a year." He saw no problem in that. It was to be a very very long year!

Almost at once, on being assigned an office, Robert Lovett found he missed something. At 59 Wall Street every morning, when he arrived at work he started by reviewing a neat summary of the status of Brown Brothers Harriman that sunup—deposits, loans in force, cash on hand, interest accruals, that comprehensive picture of the business health and well-being. There was no such compilation ready for him each 24 hours, covering the U.S. Army Air Corps. In one conversation, he was told the number of B-17s was up to 57. From another, there was a "best guess" that there were about 26,000 officers and more than 100,000 enlisted men. There had been 1,650 officers who were rated when Hitler teed off against Poland in 1939, along with 850 reservists, and the total strength was 22,500. Lovett knew the eventual numbers had to be huge (there would be 380,000 officers alone by 1945).

What he had to start with was as vague as the state of training. How to match the various disgorging materiel pipelines was foggy. Facilities expansion programs were piecemeal and spasmodic. Current statuses were impossible to finger. The overall strategy for an Army Air Corps could hardly be drafted with readiness factors so gauzy. The only contingency plan anyone could come up with, and that reluctantly, was a paper on the air defense of New York City!

The orderliness of his banker's soul was violated. It could be better, he said, and it was going to be. After all, as a banker, one handled money which had a designated value. The designator of that value was the country through which this medium of exchange trafficked, and its obligations abroad were met. Therefore, if a nation could be defeated, or destroyed, the whole edifice would crumble. A nation's resources to protect its integrities and its guarantees had to be as equally and accurately known as any bank's funds.

The LITTON Adventure That Was

It is one of the fascinating sides of history that certain men and women, usually from unexpected quarters and more often than not, from small towns, just seem to be standing there to walk on stage when called. None is more surprised than they are. At this very peak of Robert Abercrombie Lovett's frustrations, he was making a search for the "right" individual to reduce the unknowns and lessen the chaos. He kept thinking it would have to be a man in his late 40s or early 50s, but for one reason or another the intuitive needle within him kept swinging back to a mufti-clad $4,600-a-year civil servant who'd been in the U.S. Housing Authority. A RIF (Reduction In Force) there made a move necessary. He wasn't even in the Munitions Building environs of Robert Lovett. But the things he had done were intriguing to the Assistant Secretary of the War for Air.

He was young, but he had started on the lowest rung of the Washington ladder on November 1, 1934 as a junior clerk, CAF-1 in the Agricultural Adjustment Administration at a none-to-Princely $1,260 annual wage. He had taken off fast. Within two weeks he joined the Federal Surplus Relief Corporation with a raise. He was going to night school and to George Washington and Columbus Universities to get his degree in business administration. He was studying for and had gotten a reserve commission in the Army. By 1938, he had parlayed this into promotion to Assistant Statistician at the Housing Authority. He had acquired an agencies-wide reputation for being able to wade the bureaucracy mire, isolate the significant items, and make sensible analysis of how to attack a problem. He worked for certified curmudgeons, among time servers and refused to be bogged down by outdated frames of reference and he could argue, and did. Contrary to some who only assumed the role of Devil's Advocate, this young Turk had deep convictions about directions to take, methods that would work, shortcuts, and best of all, had a way of being right most of the time. But, he was only in his 20s. Lovett saw around him great numbers of senior people who were twice his age. Could he cut it? He was from a small Texas town called Haskell, which lay in the Congressman George H. Mahon 19th District. Haskell was about half the size of Lovett's hometown of Huntsville. His youthful prospect had attended Texas Tech before coming to Washington. The name on the card Lovett studied and restudied was Charles Bates Thornton.

Lovett decided age didn't have much to do with it; it was the approach to the task he had before him which was conclusive. When Thornton came to see Lovett he was told that he wanted him to come to work for him. Every morning he wanted to know what was in the Army Air Corps corral. It was to be a summary on paper which would tell him the status of people, locations, aircraft in commission, munitions, fuel and lubricants, specialties in which men were being schooled, and their state of training, projections in personnel and production—a true air power "world at a glance."

"Can you do it?" Lovett asked him, watching closely for reaction as he did so.

"I'm sure I can," Tex said cheerfully.

His confidence in himself made a deep impression on Lovett. He didn't talk a small situation to death, didn't waste his time or that of other people. He had had enough related experience factors in government that he knew the form. He had been talking for many years about statistical analysis and how it could work. He was ready to give this one his best shot.

It was only one of those eyelid flickers on any given day in Washington, but one which would have incredible reach and implications. From that day in 1941, the U.S. Army Air Corps began to find itself literally, to know what and where it was and what it could do on any given day in the face of the girded enemies lined up against free peoples around the globe. The insights Tex Thornton would acquire there in the management of men and resources would give him the breadth to deal with the technological revolution rushing onstage. But, first things first.

Before Lovett's interest in him, Tex Thornton was being described as a "comer." Anybody who refused to float on the civil service sea, and who made a wave now and then riveted attention. One who made the wave wash away debris and indecision attracted admiration from his bosses and unless very careful, it also provoked concern among his colleagues followed by the sickness with which people so easily become afflicted—envy. Tex was somehow effective in every milieu. Where he came from explained a lot about why he performed as he did, the measures he would take, and where his bulldog tenacity originated.

The LITTON Adventure That Was

If Tex Thornton had a fetish about control, he came by it honestly. His parents (said by the Texas people who knew them both to be "a dab too much for each other") were married when she, Sarah Alice Bates was 18, and he, Word Augustus Thornton was 20. She had been the belle of her own family of an even dozen, of which she had been the 11th to come on the roster. As often happens when new arrivals have become commonplace, she learned assertiveness early, how to carve out an identity for herself, and this translated into a steely will. She would have her own way, and she did in matters of church, children—all of it seasoned with her own rigidness about what was proper and right.

Her husband was known early around the oilfields as "Tex," a "shooter" who could take on great and destructible blazes and "blow them out." He had left his Mississippi birthplace which he considered sedentary alongside the freebooting atmosphere of Texas to the west. The wedding day was July 13, 1912 and their son, who was called Charles Bates Thornton was born one year plus nine days later.[2] One thing the elder Thornton could not stand was enclosure, denial of the right to roam. This coupled with the restrictions associated with living at the start with her family led to strong words between them when he would take off in response to some distant cry for help. To get away, he would go looking. When the jobs were over for which he was sometimes paid in the $10,000 range, he would stay overlong at the scene celebrating and being profligate with the earnings.

The Thorntons, without going public with the admission of strain, slid into separation around the time their son was five years old. She had believed—nay, insisted that when people got married, a nest was built in which both parents lived and offsprings were a shared responsibility. Their son was first a little boy with an occasional father, and as he grew, the father figure receded while this mother was always and overwhelmingly present. Such was her difficulty in accepting part of

---

2. That son on innumerable occasions later delighted in telling a story of an oilfield volunteer firefighting crew which ran right up into searing flames. The fire out, the townspeople collected $7,000 which was given to the crew in appreciation. When the spokesman for the unit was asked what they were going to do with the money, he said: "One thing for damn sure, we're going to get them brakes on the fire truck fixed." As Tex told it, one could almost feel the presence of that redoubtable father in the background, because from the depth of his son's admiration one gathered that the elder Tex would have driven in close on purpose!

the blame for her husband's running free, she took her anxieties out on the youngster.

This was unsettling to young Tex. He loved them both. Added to that, he admired them both. This disturbed relationship in the umbrella over his life could have developed a monumental insecurity in him. His mother, unable to sleep because of her inner turmoil, often came to awaken him in the middle of the night and talk about where she was right and his father was wrong. Fuzzy with interrupted slumber, her outpourings caused him agitation paralleling that of his mother. Later in life, people awakened Tex Thornton from a deep sleep at their peril. He would come up swinging. And then he found it difficult to sleep after 3 a.m. As long as he was wide awake, it often led to the shocking experience for some key member of his staff of being called at such an hour and asked to express an opinion on some complicated problem. Tex often heard pillow-muffled rejoinders, usually accompanied by the next bed voice of an outraged wife saying that either the phone was to be hung up or they would hereafter sleep in separate rooms.

So, that polite word "separation" had come first. Then, the elder Thornton admitted there was "another woman." Immediately, divorce action was taken that put a period at the end of their marital sentence. The son found himself elevated to "man of the house." He was not yet six years old. He was the kid in town whose mother was divorced. They lived with his aunt. It was a roof overhead; it wasn't their own home. Inside a house they might be, but they were outsiders and felt it.

One thing left that his mother could do was zero in on him, and she surely did. He was going somewhere and amount to something. He was going to be what his father had not been in her view—responsible. He was going to be a great success in a proper career, which would not include oilfield roughnecks and barroom roisterers. How it was all going to happen remained a mystery, but there was conviction enough there in his mother's mind. Her fervor was intense, and being a devoutly religious woman, she had her prayers for additional reinforcement. Over and over she told him he had to do better than his peers. They would work together on it. There was nothing subliminal about it; it was all head on. She issued the orders by which he would march and they had to do with deportment and personal conduct, his studies, etiquette, the clothes he would wear, respect for his elders and teachers, all of it poured from his possessive and possessed mother.

When Tex went to school, he was teased for being "fatherless." He gravitated to friends who had fathers in residence. He was very small, but he threw himself into the toughest kinds of athletic competition. He loved the roughness of it, the exhilaration of knocking people down in football. He'd show 'em and he did. He alternated unlikely roles such as center, tackle and linebacker. He cracked his opponents much harder than his featherweight seemed capable of doing. He was the prototype of the touring vaudevillian's tale of having been in a fight with one of small stature. "He only came up to here," he said, indicating his chin, "but God, he came up often."

When he was still in Haskell high school, his mother encouraged him to buy nearby land at 25¢ an acre. He had his own checking account. She urged him to take out small loans to get into opportunity areas, and work off their payment. He did some door to door selling. When it came to college time, the two of them moved to Lubbock which was the location of Texas Tech for him. For his mother, there was a dry goods store and running a boarding house for young women attending business college. It was all precarious brinkmanship on making ends meet.

His mother remarried a Dr. A.J. Lewis, a veterinarian, an easy-going homebody in direct contrast to her first husband. She had other children. Although Dr. Lewis included Tex with his own brood, it was forming up in the youngster's mind that it was time to strike out on his own.

Texas Tech was important to him, but no matter how much sentiment and ties and memories it held, which were high within him always, he knew it was not the kind of base on which to survey what the future held nor from which to grab the brass ring of the world's merry-go-round.

That merry-go-round was still stalled by the Great Depression. If it was to restart he thought it was a national paralysis which had to be treated and that action would be in Washington for some time to come. All this was swirling in his head in 1934. The new president might be barely into his term and bound to a wheelchair, but the wheels spinning in the presidential head intrigued Tex Thornton. The Plymouth automobile agency he tried had failed, and he was looking.

There had been a development a year before when the Texas state legislature had created four new Congressional districts. One of them was the 19th which was made by cutting approximately in half the one represented by Chairman Marvin Jones of Amarillo who headed the House Committee on Agriculture. The district attorney for 32nd Judicial District who lived in Colorado City, Texas, barely eight miles within the new boundaries decided to run for Congress and make his appeal to the 200,000 who lived within those confines. It was conservative, hard working country where it was not yet respectable to be a registered Republican, nor to be too liberal a Democrat. George H. Mahon fit the mold. When he talked in Haskell, one of his hearers was Charles Bates Thornton. Since both men were thinking Washington, but not the same access route, Tex decided to visit the office seeker at his home.

Mahon remembered that moment after Tex so nattily dressed presented himself at the screen door to wish him well in his quest, and to tell him that he, too, was going to Washington. He hoped they would meet there. He didn't ask him for help, but said when they both were in the nation's capital, they would not lose touch. "It was a most delightful visit," Mahon recalled, and "that's when our friendship began."

A fellow townsman, Bob Herron, lent Tex $50 "get away money." Tex went on before the votes were cast in Texas, and on November 1, 1934, he got that first job with the Agricultural Adjustment Administration. The first Tuesday after the first Monday in that same November, the 19th district of cotton growing, oil, grain and small businesses, put George H. Mahon in his Congressional seat which he would hold 43 years—a lot of it as Chairman of the House Appropriations Committee. By the time he got to Washington to take that seat in January, 1935, Tex Thornton had gone to a better job and had his salary raised, and wore a homburg hat. To Mahon's secretary or administrative assistant, Lloyd Croslin, he seemed to be a replica of the Watkins Remedy Man who was best dressed, had the freshly painted vehicle, and was up on all the news that gossipy District of Columbia produced far in excess of legislation. When Tex called on them, they were the newcomers and he was the old hand and probably the most elegantly dressed Texan in town.

A new Congressman even then was not all that imposing and most of the people Mahon and Croslin knew well were back in the 19th district. Tex was with them often and participated in the organization known as "the little Congress." These were people in roles adjacent to power such as Croslin and his contemporaries, and those with agencies related to the interests of particular constituencies and that included Tex Thornton. They tended to be about the same age, had varying degrees of ambitions, and the nation's capital and its workings fascinated them to a man. Croslin was a sort of resident Tom Sawyer restricted in what he could do with a staff of four, but in this grouping which assembled in Mahon's outer office every weekend, he had other willing types.

Mahon knew the 25 counties he represented as he did the veins in his hand, and the people who voted there. He paid them perpetual court with all the gallantry of a passionate suitor. No bride known to him in the 19th went without the present of a cookbook sent her almost as she was being carried over the threshold, or her stove was being installed in the kitchen. No baby was born unnoticed without suitable acknowledgement by a well wishing card. The "little Congress" was much a part of all that because with Croslin as a team leader, Tex Thornton and others did feverish wrapping and mailing after study of the daily and weekly newspapers.

There was a new boy in town, too, who came over to talk and address and wrap as he was a clerk on Congressman Dick Kleberg's staff. By the things he said and his total enmeshing in the Washington razzle-dazzle it was obvious he would not leave it willingly while he lived. His name was Lyndon Baines Johnson. The "little Congress" was only one of many small groups which attracted Tex Thornton, to which he gave himself freely, and years later would meet him at some other crossroads.

He was not one to overlook much, but at Texas Tech, he had attended a church where there was a soloist named Flora Laney. Apparently they never made much of an impression on each other. But in Washington when she showed up to visit her sister who worked in the same office that Tex did, a dinner one evening brought them together for the first time. She had a career on her mind, singing in shows or dress design, and that meant New York. He had numbers in his head, and knew how to negotiate the Washington bureaucratic ladder. It wasn't what you would call a sunny romance, but it finally wound up at the altar on April 10, 1937. Only then as many brides do did Flora confront the enormously complex man she had married. A long range planner herself, she saw hm as one who acted on impulse, could be all systems GO one minute and equally NO GO the next. She measured such things as disappointments, he saw them as being flexible. She was one to look at the moon, he was one to shoot for it. Everybody liked them, as they were "full of beans," and the Mahons who attended their wedding had them over frequently. Flora sorted the debris of many of her well laid projections, and Tex weighed the opportunities.

This was the man who stood before Robert Abercrombie Lovett that day in 1941.

SPECIAL SITUATION #3

"COUNT OFF!"

It wasn't exactly a beehive that Tex Thornton stepped into that day in Robert Lovett's office but there was a lot of stinging going on. On June 20, 1941, air power in the American military picture made its first sturdy step upward when Major Gen. H.H. "Hap" Arnold was made chief of the newly named Army Air Forces. That picayune bumping of airmen in the old Army Air Corps was over. Then there was that hectic fortnight right after Hitler socked it to his erstwhile non-aggression treaty partner, the Soviet Union, two days later. The British could relax a little after Adolf's hot breath had been on them since the Low countries and France had fallen a year earlier. There was some time, but none knew how much.

On July 9th, both Secretary of War, Col. Henry L. Stimson, and his Navy opposite number, former publisher Frank Knox, had been handed urgent inquiring letters with first morning light, signed by third term President Franklin D. Roosevelt. He wanted and—right now—an estimate of what it would take in overall production requirements "to defeat our potential enemies." There was no longer the luxury of such makeshift toy playing as Lend-Lease of overage destroyers. No matter what he'd said in the recent campaign about having no intention of committing America's youth to foreign wars, he wasn't about to be waylaid in some international dark alley. There it was, black and white "to defeat our potential enemies." He didn't need any flashing neon signs to tell him who they were, nor that the attack on the Soviet Union was any halter on the *Wilhelmstrasse* or *Piazza Venezia*, or their Japanese counterparts who'd been working over Asia even before he'd taken office the first time. Roosevelt was saying the kind of response he wanted was the backup required if America had to "go for broke"—all out war. There was no indication that he would share this knowledge widely. That's a prerogative of political leaders, as orchestration of public opinion is their special business as is timing as to when the baton-waving begins. Before anything else, he needed, baldly and starkly, the American predicament as a first priority on which to organize what he had to do.

A part of the accounting of the Secretary of War was the state of the Army Air Forces, the domain of his Assistant Secretary of War for

Air, Robert Lovett. It rang of Shakespeare's line for Brutus: "On such a full sea we are now afloat, and we must take the current when it serves or lose our ventures." Military service chiefs when summoned to major staff conferences tended to answer off the tops of their heads with guesstimates. There were as many answers as there were people present, none of them likely to be right. It was not conscious misrepresentation, but scarcity of accurate information. The Army Air Forces was so small then, that in all of 1941 it would train 8,500 men for its air and ground crews. Commanders, those with varying sizes of responsibilities, vouched for "personal contact" as the means of knowing what was going on. The accuracy of reporting was flawed even in the small numbers of the period. This same Army Air Forces was enroute to being deployed all over the globe, eventually to have a strength of 2,500,000 men and women at its peak and cost more than $75,000,000,000!

With hostilities on the doorstep, there was need for harder, more substantial information. A young officer then, later to become an Air Force Chief of Staff, Thomas Dresser White, said: "Information is the most essential link between wise leadership and purposeful action." Therefore, a President who was about to become almost totally engaged in the role of Commander-in-Chief, had to know what he had and what he needed.

There was a wide difference of opinion on this. One review board listened to contention that the Army Air Forces should have 100 groups on the one hand, and 350 groups on the other; that it needed 50,000 planes, or 100,000 planes. Personnel numbers, clothing, procurement, housing, training sites—everything—the indecisiveness of direction reflected in the variances. That board was so incensed when it wound up its questioning, it reported with some bitterness to the White House that the Army Air Forces was lacking in "foresight and coordinated planning." The result was the order by Roosevelt to Harry Hopkins to keep him personally advised of the "Air Force progress and its relationship to the mosaic of total warfare." Hopkins read the disturbing paper, then turned to Robert Lovett.

"I want," Hopkins said, "a complete Army Air Forces program covering at least a 12-month period." If his unhappiness was any reflection of the Oval Office, and everyone assumed it was, something constructive was on order. At once.

The LITTON Adventure That Was

Those early conversations between Lovett and Tex Thornton had been filled with references to the use of "a bank type statement", a simplistic variety of accounting. What he was looking for was a working procedure or plan so designed that anyone, whether he understood Air Force technicalities or not, could clearly get the picture and the broadness of the scope of the program.

They ticked off the critical holes to fill which were: "What do we have on hand? What we will need one year from now? That's an increase of how much? What do we expect to lose? What have we got to have? What did we previously plan to produce? And, we should increase production by how much?" The initial use of the form was pointed at aircraft requirements, of course, but on that primitive stem and its success, grew similar tabulating of units, by type, for the projected Army Air Forces personnel program, combat crews and the service specialties within them.

Tex Thornton had started the Pentagon chapter as a civil servant, then with Pearl Harbor hit by surprise attack, reverted to uniform as a reserve second lieutenant with a pay cut! There weren't very many lieutenants ever seen in Washington, let alone around the bowers of the mighty and powerful, but Lovett thought that rare as his rank might be around there, he was a remarkably well fitted recruit to solve some of the burgeoning entanglements which could result from inability to keep track. Besides, he was to be the most momentary of second lieutenants. The Thornton promotions came faster than he had time, on a couple of the occasions, to buy the new insignia. He skipped ownership of a couple of them completely. But the suggested means he gave enabled Lovett to have knowledge at his fingertips. That so pleased the Secretary, Lovett added his name to the title of the paper: The Thornton-Lovett Study. Not many young officers ever know the dizzying experience of having the boss take second billing, yet insist on being there to emphasize the importance of what's contained therein and why it should be paid attention.

Five times in one week, Tex Thornton was asked to present it. Lovett was the host for senior people in his office for one, to convey his blessings and complete buyoff. Then there was a run through for General H.H. "Hap" Arnold, and the senior members of the Air Staff. The exposure of the means and the purpose of the reporting mechanism, as an assist for all the planning then in motion, was increasingly seen as valuable and necessary. The method showed the parallels required for aircraft production, other procurements, training infrastructure and its capability to produce skilled people, plus the additional times and places for meshing into combat crews. General Arnold himself sat through it five times, saying to every audience: "That's the finest staff study made in this headquarters since I've been here."

The test was Harry Hopkins, and how it would hit him. He read it over and his reaction was quick. "It's the best program in any of the military services," he said.

It is not as celebrated in history as the Magna Charta, but as documents go, was far reaching. Hidden away in Air Force historical files is the statement: "From this original document, the Army Air Forces program was born. Everything that Mr. Lovett has done with the Army Air Forces program has found its basis in the original Thornton-Lovett Study."

Ah, but it had to work. The hopes of high headquarters often get dismembered by translation through the various layers, or echelons which exist from on high to the lowest units. In olden days, zealots arrayed themselves against the Roman Empire; there had to be some similar dedications of deeply indoctrinated personnel on which to rely, so the Thornton-Lovett Study, could escape bureaucracy inertia, take its own wings and fly. In November of 1941, as the Japanese carrier task force sailed out of the home islands bound for Pearl Harbor, the Army Air Forces had not had an overall strength return for seven months. So much for "personal contact" as a command mechanism.

Washington's "elephant numbers" were not awesome to either Lovett or Thornton, Lovett's having to do with the dollars of investment banking, Thornton's with congressionally authorized national programs with ponderous price tags. There was more to this than money. Tex had been turning over in his mind the many ways statistics were applicable to large tasks. They could be made to serve, he thought, both as persuasion and even as the tie breaker in councils where applicable numbers, trends and characteristics were important weapons. The Air Forces personnel mushroom was one which had to grow to eye popping proportions. It was a monitoring requirement of significance whatever was to come, the people factor would be decisive. There was the big Officers Candidate School in Miami Beach where leadership was given courses and processed in droves into commissioned ranks. Technical schools across the country took re-enlistees into expertise in radio, gunnery, mechanical and maintenance support. The MOS (Military Occupational Specialty) numbered categories were fastened to all individuals at the end of this training as tightly as the serial numbers assigned to them. The program had to have the trappings to make sure that everyone was able to do his share of pulling at the same whiffle-tree that made operations possible.

Tex Thornton had to take the crystal ball out of the action, and provide forecasts compatible with realities. Logistics—the movements, the pipelines—were so demanding because everything—people, petrol, oil, lubrication, rations, materiel and munitions—had to be synchronized on a timetable from origins to the battlefields. Putting a handle on this veritable Cornucopia of supplies pouring from what President Roosevelt called his "Arsenal of Democracy" had to insure delivery at proper destinations in quantity and readiness. Out ahead was another mountainous and diverse task—combat statistics, which included destruction of men and machines—from those losses the kind of replacements in men and materiel and what levels could be figured. There was even an allowance of percentages for aircraft, which for dubious reasons, would turn back short of the target run and head for a neutral country seeking internment. There were such chinks in the courage armor of pilots and crews, particularly when the missions numbers piled on and morale sank while other squadron mates were being shot down or crashing. As the unit leader of antiquity always said: "Count Off!" Tex Thornton found himself at the helm of the biggest numbers game of all, the difference being that not only was the U.S. national security dependent upon it, but the hopes of beleaguered allies as well.

There was something astir in an unlikely place: the Harvard Business School tucked off in Cambridge, Mass. Its Dr. Edmund P. Learned had been invited to a special Army orientation short course at Fort Leavenworth Kansas. Some 35 business leaders and representatives of academia attended. They were told at the end of the first month, November, they would hear from General George C. Marshall himself. The Army Air Forces, and to some degree its Army parent, were beginning to believe there should be inputs from sectors hitherto held at arm's length. Marshall wore no West Point ring, being a dark horse out of Virginia Military Institute, and having wisdom enough to know the "Hell on the Hudson" could have been a mite too insular in its leadership courses. The range of problems which went with the military submission to the multiplication table had to be addressed by the required competence wherever it could be found.

Surprisingly, at the last moment, General Marshall cancelled. He sent General Hap Arnold in his stead, because Arnold was on his way to San Francisco anyway to see the flight of B-17s off to Hawaii. Nothing was said about the Japanese codes having been broken, and that war was thought imminent. Learned took Arnold to his plane on December 6th. He took a train to Chicago. It was in Chicago that he and his travelling companion, Robert Stevens (later to be Secretary of the Army), were told of the Pearl Harbor catastrophe—and that they should divert to Washington to see General Marshall himself. In the midst of all the turmoil swirling to accommodate that newly existing "state of war", Marshall talked to them of the size of the challenge, how there would have to be reliance for special expertise on people who had never worn uniforms—that they should think what such placings might be. Learned could not get over how calmly he organized his day as Chief of Staff. There was nothing on the top of his desk!

For awhile, the only happenings were an occasional visit to the Harvard Business School by one or two colonels. The conversations were inconclusive, frustrating Dr. Learned mightily. Sensing this one day, one of the visitors suggested to Dr. Learned that he really should get down to Washington and "make contact with a First Lieutenant Thornton in Secretary Lovett's office." His world largely populated by generals and colonels, admirals and captains, being sent all that distance to hold court with a lieutenant who would brief him on what lay on the opportunity horizon, inform him and lay down contractual requirements was not his idea of a sparkling prospect, but Learned eventually took the advice.

In Washington, Learned found his man in a cubbyhole of an office, shielded by a secretary in equally small quarters. The occupant, he found, was already a major and moving fast. Before that secretary would allow him entry, all papers on the major's desk had to be covered. Learned was chafed further by this, as after all, he had a very high security clearance himself—but not up there far enough without these covered precautions in this office. His ruffled feathers were immediately relaxed when Tex Thornton greeted him warmly. He told him how glad he was to have him there where they could talk. From the procession of interruptions, the calls he was getting, the summonses to the offices of Lovett and Arnold, Learned knew at last he was in the presence of the answer man he'd been looking for and not finding. Their rapport was instant, and Tex had only just gotten what he called "the Statistical Control division" established officially on March 9, 1942.[1]

He explained what he had been charged with:

The planning of the organization and functions of the division and to direct its activities as well.

Represent the Army Air Forces in all matters pertaining to the Air Forces' statistics and act as liaison with the Army's Ground Forces, Services of Supply, the General Staff, the War Production Board and other offices and agencies concerned.

Provide through initiation, development and operations of a standardized statistical reporting system, all types of statistical material to be used by the Air Staff and the operating directorates for planning control purposes.

Prepare statistical analysis and studies required by Headquarters in the formulation of plans, of the Army Air Forces.

Establish and regulate Statistical Control units in the commands of all Air Forces to collect and report, in accordance with the prescribed respective headquarters directives and to Washington.

Dr. Learned felt his scalp prickle—all that, loaded on one brand new major! The key things for that moment were the planning of the organization and functions of the division and directing its activities and personnel—it would go only with the right kind of people, having the right aptitudes and inclinations, especially trained.[2] With an as-

---

1. The Statistical Control Division had to be accommodated on the Headquarters chart. It was placed under the Management Controls wing, then headed by Gen. Byron "Hungry" Gates. The day after Pearl Harbor, the Thornton civil service career had ended abruptly. He went into uniform as a Lieutenant and began immediately to bring his burgeoning activities into Statistical Control divisional status. All the way along, Thornton was carried as Chief, Office of Statistical Control.

2. Things in dimension was a Thornton talent. Stat control was barely in being when he reached to England for a young lieutenant named Edward R. Finch who had been engaged in early training action with the Royal Air Force. Thornton saw an upcoming appetite for more than just U.S. Air Force data. He asked Finch to give him OB (Order of Battle) information on the British, Canadian and Australians which he incorporated in his reporting for Gen. Arnold. Arnold liked it, passed it to the Ameri-

tuteness which accompanied Tex Thornton's fetish about "control" he had already locked the gate to his enclosure using that new Army device, the Military Occupational Specialty (or MOS), a number which designated for those relatively new IBM punch-cards a certified specialty. Tex had not only gotten MOS 6402 for his Stat Control types, but none could have it unless so qualified by him—and no commander at any level could assign such 6402s other than in his reporting apparatus. Many tried, the favorite alternative being to designate them as mess officers, but such malpractices were usually quickly remedied when the offending commander learned what kind of high level support the Statistical Control action had.

Tex Thornton talked earnestly to Dr. Learned about setting up a Stat control Officers' course at the Harvard business School. It was a fateful step not only for the Army Air Forces, but for the future of the U.S. which would have to take the biggest hand in restoration of a destroyed and destabilized world left in the wake of the war, and for the future management of colossal business enterprises. MOS 6402, in its way, because of the talents it attracted, refined and gave a worldwide laboratory in which to work under pressure, became a "numbered account" on which America would draw for three or four decades for leadership in trade, manufacture and management techniques.

While it has been politically popular to deride taciturn Calvin Coolidge, as early as 1924 he had seen wisdom in giving Army Officers time off for attendance at the Harvard Business School. In the bizarre bureaucratic world, precedent means everything—if it was earlier wisdom, it could be again. Learned moved in. When he said the Harvard business School would do this, he went back to tell his colleagues with some excitement that they were off the flat wheel of indecision at last. Anticipation heightened each day as they waited. Dean Don David began calling in young professors asking them if they would be interested in working on an Air Force contract if the school got one. The dean was sensitive to changes of relationship of the school to society, a large portion of that society about to be engaged in military and associated endeavors. One of those young pedagogues, wore glasses, combed his straight hair back with a middle

---

can Joint chiefs, and the international Combined Chiefs of Staff. Finch later became U.S. Ambassador to Panama.

part, had no goal throwing a shadow longer than getting tenure and an improvement on his $5,000-a-year salary. His name was Robert Strange NcNamara. He said he would like that very much.

May 8th, the telephone in Dr. Learned's office jingled. His secretary was out. He picked it up himself.

"This is Tex Thornton, in Washington," the caller said. "I'd like you to pick 10 to 12 men from your Business School teaching staff, and bring them to Washington for an intensive training course. You will then begin the conduct of an Air Force Statistical Officers Candidate School there at Harvard in June." There had to be a lot of trust in those days, as all this preliminary action was being done without a formal contract; in fact, it took Harvard months to get that piece of paper—but they got it. It was walked through, office to office by James O. Wright.[3]

To outsiders, it looked so easy. This junior officer named Thornton saying something would be done, and it got done. Dr. Learned knew better. It was a firm Thornton thesis that while within the circle of power, one stayed there by somehow getting responsibilities attended to, not by taking his problem to his superiors, only pointing fingers and distributing blame for shortfalls in delivery. The Lovetts and the Arnolds were last resort if there were impasses. It went against the Thornton grain to admit to an impasse. Later Tex Thornton was to recognize those people who thought likewise and solved things on their own; then he was the power center and they were the underlings. It was testing, testing, testing all the time to see who would break first. It surely helped if there was an understanding and trusted friend somewhere on whom he could play his difficulties, consult for means of end running or circumventing obstacles erected by combinations of stubbornness and tradition. This part was played once weekly by Dr. Learned, who flew down to Washington in his consultant role.

---

3. Wright had been a statistician in the Housing Authority in the same office with Tex Thornton and was lured into the Pentagon by him. A soft spoken Virginian, he became Thornton's executive officer. None was better than he at coaxing signatures on the appropriate dotted lines. When anything innovative confronts a bureaucracy, persuasiveness has to make up for lack of precedent. Wright was a past master, and for Thornton, the indispensable man.

The ritual was always the same. Dinner with Flora, Tex Thornton's very pregnant wife, then the drive to Bolling Field. While awaiting the Boston plane, the two would leave Flora curled up in the car, and go into what was known to them as the Learned-Thornton promenade. It was a stroll around a small circle during which they whispered of the TOP SECRET related affairs with which they were dealing. The hurdles for the Statistical Control operations were war gamed. "I really believe," Learned said later, "that it was only the fact of Bob Lovett and me—that Tex could always count on our backing and reassurance—that he was able to stay the course."[4]

Dr. Learned was endlessly engrossed in how many business parallels there were to the military requirements. The intelligence estimate whether for the grand strategy or a battle plan resembled the diagnosis a businessman would make of opportunities for solving situations or serving his customers. A battle plan and a sales drive had many similarities, requiring preparatory actions, commitment and reinforcement of success. There were even times for cutting losses and to withdraw saving for campaigns to assault anew from a new direction.

There were ten on the Dr. Learned roster who came to Washington from the Harvard Business School, that pioneering ten on whose backs the Air Force Statistical Control Officers Candidate School was erected. They were Assistant Dean Fraser, who was to do all the Harvard contractual negotiations as the agreement grew in size and additions were made; Dr. Learned, of course; Dan T. Smith, an observer who already had consultant status with the Army's Quartermaster General; Dr. Myles Mace, newly graduated from the Quartermaster Officers Candidate School; Thomas Carroll, whose commitment to serve in the Navy removed him early and didn't permit him to teach a course; George Lombard, and experienced author of case studies, plus Vigo Nielsen, John Desmond Glover, Lynn Hollinger and the studious Robert S. McNamara. Some of what they were given was Washington time so that power center wouldn't intimidate them. A lot of their

---

4. Those Thornton revered names—Lovett and Learned—caused Tex Thornton to become the prime mover in the endowment of a Learned-Lovett chair in the Harvard Business School. Many of the Stat Control types, the MOS 6402s—were contributors, but the bulk of the endowment was provided by Thornton himself.

days and nights were also in travel to the many outlying supply and training command appended facilities.

Dr. Learned was always the scholastic ringmaster, and Jim Wright, their "den mother." When Learned asked his crew to state their preferences for specialization, McNamara and Mace immediately opted for the supply mechanisms which procured and distributed the materials of war making. The military was adamant about not letting go of one rigid position—that requirement for the 13-week basic training course be met. Only after that could they go into specialties.

It was again trusty Jim Wright who maneuvered to speed up the action, getting permission for half the time to be in the Miami Beach Air Force Officers Candidate School with the rest of the time spent at Harvard—and then the award of commissions. Thornton sent Wright to Miami Beach to check the files for recruits who merited being lifted out for the rest of their honing at Harvard. Every man who interested him was personally interviewed with his aptitudes carefully checked and if thought to have the intelligence level and pertinent characteristics, a thumbs up signal from Wright had them on the way to Cambridge. All types, save one, that is—he could not have any weathermen. For all those places the Army Air Forces expected to fly and fight where climatic vagaries and caprice could help or hinder missions, expertise in weather forecasting was one of the highest priority. Also, shut off was the shanghaiing direct from civilian careers into direct commissions. They would be in the Army Air Forces first, then whatever—including Stat Control Officers. Wright and his seekers in Miami Beach had no reason to complain, the GCT (General Classification Text) average was 119 and those selected for Harvard averaged out at 138. A cerebral crop, indeed!

Facing them all was the paper known as ABC-1 (American-British Conference No. 1) early in 1941, which was midway into that U.S. not yet at war contingency planning for offensives against German military power, supplemented by air offensives *against other regions under enemy control*; to support a final offensive if it became necessary to invade the European continent. The major targets indicated to throttle Germany were her electric power sources, the railways which carried 72% of all transported military and consumer goods, petroleum as long as it lasted including synthetic oil. And there were AWPD-1 (Air War Plans Division No. 1) which asked for nearly

63,000 operational aircraft, 180,000 officers, and 1,920,000 enlisted people—a total of 2,200,000. It was to that target the Army Air Forces Statistical Control division had to address its efforts; this all being before Japan tried to prove that the sun could rise from the west and move east.

There were some monumental battles which developed over Col. Thornton's numbers. He insisted that they meant what they said. One of his most notable adversaries was Maj. Gen. Bennie Meyers, who bossed the Air Materiel command in Dayton. Meyers wanted to count an aircraft in inventory when it was paid for, which was when it was committed for assembly on the floor of some plant somewhere. Such a plane could neither take part in training, nor in operations, being as it were in the fetus stage. General Arnold had to resolve that one, in favor of the procurement and production allowance of gestation period—which supported Col. Thornton. Meyers didn't like it, but accepted it grumbling all the way back to Dayton. Accepting is not the same as enjoying being foxed by a junior officer. Meyers was to have bigger troubles than the Office of Statistical control, being summoned for congressional investigation and eventually doing time for conflict of interest practices.

Less related to sensation in the public mind, but sensational nonetheless, were some of the big decisions founded on those Office of Statistical Control findings. They told when to direct curtailment of construction of bomb production facilities as the war progressed, the number of flying hours pilots and crews should have before being slipped into formation for combat, and frequency of bombing missions tolerable in terms of crew morale. They provided the superior qualities of the B-25 over the B-26 in terms of flying safety, which caused upping of B-25 production and cutback in the B-26s.

Similar comparisons put the B-17 Flying Fortresses well ahead of the B-24 Liberators, even though the B-17s absorbed greater damages. They were generally given the longer missions extending their time over hostile, flak-frequent landscape. The B-24 missions tended to be shorter, penetrating enemy territory less deeply. The B-24 production was lopped and plans were initiated to convert the surviving crews into the B-29s shellacking the island routes to Imperial Japan. The B-17s were expected to be the staple of all overseas air forces, but they, too, stumbled over the Office of Stat Control numbers which wigwagged an ominous message—that the B-29s, capable of superior bomb tonnages, were ten times more effective that the B-17s. Decision: Down the B-17 production pace and utilize it for B-29s. Always those dreadful numbers trod on the sentiments of men who had grown attached to one weapons system or another. But on reflection, the saltiest, most opinionated Air Force leader went with the decision of the Stat Control jury. To do otherwise was Russian roulette.

MOS (Military Occupational Specialty) numbering of everyone in the Army Air Forces tied to the punch card accounting machinery and the parallel development of the sophisticated teletypewriter, were combined with the then best known means of rapid communications. One uniform system became possible for both continental and overseas force status reporting. As result of all this innovative insertion into the maw of war, it was possible for Washington to know its continental strengths within 48 hours of an effective reporting data, and from all the dispositions around the globe within a month. Better assignments relating to an individual's skills were one dividend. It was the thread all the way through training, procurement, and an influence on strategies as it could all be combed from these data accumulations. If Col. Thornton were asked for the complete operational history of the Army Air Forces in W.W.II, it could be had on 700,000 punch cards.

Behind that number were all the mission reports which included tonnages of bombs dropped (2,057,244), rounds of ammunition expended (459,750,000), personnel and aircraft losses, destruction inflicted on enemy targets, circumstances under which attacks were ordered and where they took place. By analysis of those stats, efficiency of various bombing methods was determined. Nearly 700,000 punch cards dealt with numbers and whereabouts of equipment balances in the Air Technical Service Command's eleven great depots. These were totaled monthly for transmission to Washington.

The lone eagle, however much admired, how shining in song and story and how much his courage gave to ultimate victory, was on those punch cards a sortie maker in this mighty overview of war, which, after all, is an organized effort in which there are parts to play. To insure that the lone eagle's sorties had translation into eventually delivering the winning difference, leadership needed to know what were intelligent decisions for his unleashing. Policies generated arose from three areas: The experience of individual members of a staff including their educational background, judgment, or common sense. And the facts. The Office of Statistical Control—this Thornton-Lovett brainchild—provided one of these—the *facts*. To get to that accounting, there had had to be summaries of Zone of the Interior units and bulk allotments, preactivation trainees, committed units, combat crew personnel in training sequencing with aircraft production deliveries, elements overseas, combat losses and replacement requirements of men, machines and munitions.

The Army Air Forces Statistical control system was the largest centrally coordinated installation of mechanical accounting equipment and private wire teletype networks on earth. There were 66 major Stat Control units manned by 3,000 Harvard trained statistical officers, plus some 15,000 enlisted men. Two of these who had scored a high 138 in the GCT in Miami Beach were J. Edward Lundy and right along with him Arjay Miller. Another who had served well and attracted attention for his intellectual capacities and wide ranging mind when at Harvard was asked to come back to attend the Harvard Business School formal courses for a degree—even though he did not have the required undergraduate preparation. He, with his wife and their youngster, did go back to Cambridge postwar on $91.00 monthly in GI Bill funds, from which he took $11.20 a week to live on while he was developing his cerebral creases. Gastronomically it was near starvation, but was an exciting classroom diet on which he thrived. He graduated an honor Baker scholar. His name was Roy Lawrence Ash.

As the war ground down, particularly after V-E Day, Col. Tex Thornton was eyeing the future. He was recommended for promotion to Brigadier General,[5] and such was the level of his sponsorship, he could undoubtedly have done better than that in the cadence of military affairs. The Air Force, in peacetime, didn't make his adrenaline

---

5. Although he didn't stay around for the promotion, when Tex Thornton was barely settled in his Ford Motor company office, he had a telegram from Washington telling him the Statistical Control Division he had created had not been forgotten. War Department General Order No. 66, dated July 8, 1946, awarded him the nation's highest military non-combat decoration, the Distinguished Service Medal. A month later, when he was in Washington, the medal was presented to him officially by General Carl A. "Tooey" Spaatz, who was slated 13 months later to become the first Chief of Staff of the newly created separate Air Force.

jump. He had conceived of something different, not merely employ-ment for himself, but to offer up a package of executive talents, all young, all confident, all experienced in the big time beyond their years. The Statistical Control Division had amassed a great many de-tails about various industries through its procurement and production tracking. He knew the ones which were good and were getting better. He also knew the business Neanderthals suffering with hardening of executive arteries, infighting, and all the intramural cutting and slash-ing trying to line up for succession to the thrones.

Tex had some conversation with young Henry Ford II. He was about to be the inheritor, after all those years of his grandfather's ex-ceptional production genius but often quirky management. In these conversations, Tex talked of his firm conviction that management and command were synonymous, except that business did not have what the military did: discipline and control. He said the military forces had first to become big business before evolving into an effective fighting machine. "The Air Force Officers I know," Tex told him, "were probably the best educated technically and as tactical profes-sional in all the world, but their backgrounds and knowledge of big business principles are wholly lacking. Cost in time, effort, materiel, lives and casualties during this past war were incalculable. The appli-cations of these statistical control trained officers to business and busi-ness principles will be the easiest postwar transition of all—and their experiences can be priceless to a business which needs an infusion of new blood and ideas." He cautioned that he was championing no in-flexible principles, as conditions change and call for new measures. He said his group would be an ideal gamble for the Ford Motor Company.

General Arnold was ill at war's end. Lt. Gen. Ira C. Eaker was his deputy chief, and in effect was running the day-to-day Army Air force action. He had been one of the first overseas commanders to inherit some Stat Control types, after arriving with a handful of men on February 20, 1942 to organize and build the magnificent 8th Air Force.[6] Even with surrender on the doorstep now, Eaker knew there

---

6. The two nominees for Stat Control officers for the 8th Air Force were to two Harvard professors—McNamara and Mace. Eaker was not enthused about the Stat Control idea, but he knew Arnold was high on it. McNamara and Mace got the full "treatment" and on arrival in England were lodged in a replacement depot full of

would be a tremendous amount of adding up, numbers such as the U.S. Strategic Bombing Survey findings to deal with the effectiveness of all those incendiary and explosive tonnages sorting out the significance. He was not happy when he learned that young Henry Ford II was evidencing interest, waving him off at first. By that time, though Col. Thornton knew how to work the Pentagon E-Ring, and Washington, and how people could "organize themselves out of a job." He talked earnestly to the ones he wanted to be a part of that "package" he proposed to sell to Ford—Arjay Miller, F. D. "Jack" Reith, George E. Moore, James O. Wright, Wilbur Anderson, Charles E. Bosworth, Ben D. Mills, J. Edward Lundy and the most reluctant and disinterested of them all, Robert S. McNamara. McNamara wanted only to go back to Harvard, resume his professional direction, get tenure and teach for life in what he felt was his field and expertise, financial management.

Tex Thornton was dismayed. "Bob," he told McNamara in his best Dutch uncle manner, "you can't go back to Harvard. Your wife is ill, has polio, you're in debt, and will have all those medical bills. On what they'll pay you, you can't make it. At least, do us the courtesy of going with us to Ford when they talk with us. If you still aren't interested, you can always go back to Harvard. You owe it to yourself to look this Ford opportunity over." Not enthusiastic, and in fact, shamed into it, McNamara went to Detroit. There Tex had an intellectual trap all set for him, putting him in proximity to Ford's most depressing statistic—in the first eight months of that year, Ford had a hemorrhage of $58,000,000 in losses. That trial run financial appraisal put such a tie on McNamara, Harvard knew him as a staff member no more. That group, later to be known as "the whiz kids"[7]

Section Eight types with mental problems. Thornton thought they could only be effective if in uniform and sought direct commissions for them from Eaker. Eventually they were captains. Properly uniformed they found they were to see Eaker in person. McNamara wanted to report impeccably as a prescribed in the "Soldier's Handbook". He came up before Eaker's desk, cracked his heels together and rendered a smart salute saying: "Captain Robert McNamara reporting as ordered." General Eaker almost fell off his chair as nobody in the Army Air Forces had been as formal or as precise as that as long as he could remember.

7. The "Quiz Kids" were an NBC radio network replacement for blind pianist Alec Templeton on June 28, 1940 and were a durable six years old when the Thornton personnel package knocked on the Ford gates. Created by ad man Louis G. Cowan, he started with a precocious 6-year old Gerard Darrow and an old "National Barn

of business legend and a talent vein of gold was taken on enmasse by Henry Ford II. The one he selected to give them the Ford overview and orientation was a splashdash and rollicking 26 year old, one Crosby Moyer Kelly, who was not at all awed by his audience or what might come of it.

Of the group, only Tex Thornton had an office on the Ford Motor Company "Mahogany row". The rest were put into questioning roles throughout company staffs. Query they did as to how things had come to be done the way they were, whether another way had been tried, what had worked and improved, what had not and worsened situations. It was intelligent curiosity, which was grudgingly admitted, but it was prone to make people uneasy who had had safe seats during the long reign of the founder. The Thornton ear was open to all those men who had been in the automobile business for all of its history, or who had known people who had been there when Henry Ford himself was considered a failure, and William Crapo Durant was the supposed architect of the horseless buggy's future.

Ford was the dedicated centralizer, suffocatingly so; Durant, a delegator, who let men and their imaginations run free. The same Detroit that Tex Thornton now found himself had been the centerpiece of the American business miracle, a place where imagination had gone hand in hand with engineering, and put the world on wheels. Often at night he pondered these stories and studied these men, the giants of another time. There was a kind of reassurance in the fact that they had all started from scratch. But what was pale to Tex Thornton was that

---

Dance" master of ceremonies, Joe Kelly. Other juvenile joiners were such smarties as Joan Bishop, Cynthia Cline, Mary Ann Anderson, Charles Schwartz, Joel Kupperman and Richard Williams. Van Dyke Tiers for spelling, Ruth Duskin on Shakespeare, Jack Lucal on politics, Harve Fischman and Claude Brenner. The Thornton group reversed the technique in that it asked questions of penetrating nature addressing the Ford management. Their first Ford label was, sometimes derisively, "the quiz kids". McNamara, the most disinterested initially, rose to the Ford Presidency, leaving that office to become Secretary of Defense for Presidents John F. Kennedy and Lyndon B. Johnson and after that heading the World Bank. Arjay Miller was another Ford President who on retiring became Dean of the Stanford School of Business. Lundy and Wright were both Ford executive vice presidents—Lundy for finance and Wright over all car, truck and assembly divisions. It was the record set by such as these that coined the term "Thornton Tech" as the brand of executives than those who had gone to any single business school.

the Detroit empires had been built, and mending was the mood of the time. It was not as interesting as he thought it would be.

In 1947, Lt. Gen. Ira C. Eaker, who had been on every hot seat America could find for him and in every instance had done well, decided to retire and hang his uniform in the closet. He had seen an Army Air Corps of 1,600 officers and 18,000 enlisted men with 1,700 planes in 1939 when Hitler struck Poland and had seen its rise to 2,500,000 soldiers use 231,000 aircraft of all types to help mold the victory, and then squeeze it all back to around 400,000 men and women in the two post war years. The swords and spears into plowshares and pruning hooks mood was on the land. The General Electrics and the Lockheeds favored refrigerators and commercial air transport, and did not want to be bothered about defense items until there was another war. General K. B. Wolfe, the logistics chief of the Air Staff, told Eaker that the new needle nosed fighters, the 100-series, needed modern radar and fire control equipment. There was nobody to whom they could turn for this expertise. Eaker had just joined the staff of the Hughes Tool Company in Houston. One of the special watchdog areas assigned to him was Hughes Aircraft in Culver City, California. It housed all those 800 people who had helped Howard Hughes design his famous "Spruce Goose", the huge wooden transport. Hughes wanted nothing to happen to them. He asked Eaker to survey the place and recommend to him what might be done with it. Eaker told Hughes about the Air Force dilemma, the disinterest in most companies in defense work. Hughes cocked an ear. What would it take, he wanted to know? Eaker told him they would have to recruit some scientific and engineering talents, cluster them in Culver City, and bid on the contract.

"How much?" said Hughes.

"Probably you'd have to sink from $15,000,000 and $20,000,000 in it before you'd see anything coming back," Eaker guessed.

"Let's try it," Hughes said, and went on about his other interests.

Ford was not the blooming rose Thornton had thought; it was an established edifice, set in its ways. He thought it was the electronics revolution which would contain the ingredient of excitement he was seeking. Eaker told him what was going on, what Hughes Aircraft had to have. As he talked he convinced himself that Tex Thornton

36

was tailored to not only set up what was required but to interface with the Pentagon. The 1948 Hughes Aircraft roster of 800 grew to 25,000[8] and Hughes fire control equipment was on board every manufactured fighter in the country's growing air defenses. The Thornton position was vice president and general manager, and although retired Lt. Gen. Harold George was titular head of the company, Tex rendered the necessary protocol touches in the relationship but he did run the unit— and General George was glad he did. It was no new thing for Tex, when he had been a lieutenant in the pentagon, a colonel was in charge but only as a figurehead. It was tougher than that at Hughes. First, there was the man himself, Hughes, who liked it better at RKO, the film studio at Melrose and Gower Streets in Hollywood, where he made his offices. He wouldn't give a total charter to anyone to run one of his enterprises, and be answered to in terms of success or failure; he had to have look-in and certain decision rights—yet he was the hardest of men to find when something was urgent. Either Eaker or Tex could be rousted from their beds at 3 to 5 a.m., instructed to come to the studio because he was now ready to see them. On arrival, because he had a pathological fear of his hotel, home or office being bugged and his secrets learned, he loaded either or both of them in his ancient Chevrolet and drove around the Hollywood Hills while such matters were discussed and the NO or GO given. And he had some altar boys, who were always trying to carve up a portion of the realm, and encroachment on such territorial stakeouts was the game to play. Tex Thornton was only 36 years old[9] when all this was happening to

---

8. Always futures oriented, one of the Thornton programs was the hiring of a block of 100 UCLA students who worked 25 hours a week at Hughes and simultaneously sought masters degrees. One of those was Orion L. Hoch. One of the orientation speakers for the group was Tex Thornton, of course. Hoch never actually met Thornton during the Hughes hiatus, but they were never off each other's wave-lengths after that. A time would come when Orie Hoch would represent a "futures projection" for Litton Industries itself.

9. After his 1948 start at Hughes Aircraft, Tex Thornton had a family tragedy on his hands. His father, Word Augustus Thornton, who he had always admired from afar, was murdered on June 22, 1949. He had picked up two hitchhikers, Evald and Diana Johnson, and he was beaten up and choked to death in a roadside motel. His son, and his father's second wife, Sarah Troxell Thornton, sat through the trial in an Amarillo court and unbelievingly saw Johnson released. Since he had stolen the Thornton car and taken it over a state line, Johnson was retried in a Federal court

him, and as young men will, he grew restive and began looking around again. His credentials were formidable by then. Hughes Aircraft Co. started at the $8,900,000 sales level in 1949 when Tex Thornton had his hand on the magic of electronics, a knowledge he could take anywhere—or better yet, go anywhere he wanted to on his own, given financial backing. The Korean war had shown that forces in being were what an America had to fight with. Contractors poised and at the ready who could deliver to specifications quickly, were today's dependencies. Mobilization was too slow a word, and time lost too dangerous. Rumors ricocheted around the Hughes' Culver City premises, one being that Hughes wanted to sell it off. This caused a small ray of hope to buoy the top staff, but it was short lived.

Tex Thornton had taken Hughes at his word and sought backing in Wall Street to buy the beleaguered place which had such great potential if it could be pried from the mire of internecine warfare and lethargy in decision making. The group was formed involving Lehman Brothers; Bear, Stearns, and Pennroad Corp.'s Ben Pepper, and Hughes Aircraft management. Each would have equity fractions which was something Hughes himself had never permitted. It all came to naught. It was a long, hot, acrimonious, charging and counter-charged summer and fall and on September 14, 1953 Tex Thornton sent his resignation to the Hughes Office at 7000 Romaine in Hollywood. He was unemployed but he was on to something else.

---

which dealt with him less sympathetically. Having been a pioneer nitro "shooter" who invented the asbestos protective suit he wore as an oilfield conflagration squelcher who lived among rough men all his life, the elder Thornton had been "on velvet" for a long time—and his string ran out. In the tawdriness of the trial, some wondered in Tex's business circles why he put himself through it all. "After all," said Word Augustus' son, "he was my father." Loyalty was a pronounced characteristic in Tex Thornton as long as he lived. During the trial, he formed a sour opinion about the legal profession which stayed with him all his life.

SPECIAL SITUATION #4

THE STARTING POINT AND WHY

The hiring interview was conducted in the front seat of a Ford convertible overlooking the garbage dump of Redwood City, California.

It was smelly. A lazy pall of smoke issued from one smoldering corner and chose to tarry rather than dissipate. The prospect was being told that a manager was needed at a small electronic plant in nearby San Carlos. The founder was doing the interview.

He engaged and fired about ten managers in ten years, he said. He had picked the garbage dump site deliberately as it was symbolic of the dead end which could well lie ahead if his offer was accepted. The six feet three inches of 140-pound wraith of a man slumped under the wheel was making sure his candidate knew he was talking to a certified SOB. He had to be endured rather than endeared. He wanted no false impressions about that. At one point, looking him straight in the eye when he said it, he stated this candidate was probably the 11th who would be tossed out as unsatisfactory. Only the future could tell either of them if it would be so.

As threatening and shady as it seemed, Dr. Norman Moore agreed to run the mine-strewn gauntlet and find out. As they sat there that evening in the summer of 1948, Moore kept thinking that the author, Washington Irving, could have designed his new employer. His exterior appearance duplicated the awkward and laughable Ichabod Crane of "Legend of Sleepy Hollow." Clothes hung loosely on him and he didn't care. It was what was on and in his mind that counted. The man in the driver's seat, as was always the case with him, was Charles V. Litton, founder and sole owner of Litton Engineering Laboratories, which contained within it an entity called Litton Industries of California. His enterprise had been constructed with exacting care around his fascination with the versatility of the vacuum, and the electronic wizardry which could be accomplished by enclosing it in glass tubes making a smooth highway through which currents could pass. He could literally "think" himself into the personality characteristics of the electron stream and predict what its behavior would be in an atmosphere-free environment. He understood microwaves so well that few were his equal in that field.

39

Special Situation #4

It was fateful decision time for them both. Neither knew it then, but dating from that summer night, Moore was to stay longer on the premises of the company than the man who put him on its payroll and, in terms of stock value, would leave the place wealthier. He not only survived all the abrasiveness, the intimidations, often demeaning and belittling tirades Litton could deal out, he balanced all that off against the benefits of proximity to the technical smarts and insights which went with it. He was never sorry for having made the tradeoff. Just five years further along, Moore was to be the transitional linchpin when Charles Litton sold his Litton Industries of California unit to a young Turk ready to charge — Charles Bates "Tex" Thornton, with two action-oriented flankers at his elbow, Roy Lawrence Ash and Hugh William Jamieson. He was slated to be a key consideration in that package because he had learned his lessons so well.

Litton had always loved and romanced his machines, those predictable, dependable, delicately responding lathes. Under his hands they turned out products for which there was great respect and a ready market. They dovetailed completely with his workaholic lifestyle. A longtime bachelor, he much preferred these lathes to the ladies, as they did his bidding. The women who he knew were not all that dependable. The buying trio saw what he had so reverently done as a remarkably apt cornerstone for a business empire. In the new dimension Thornton foresaw, it could impact on the whole world and its future.

Dr. Norman Moore was out of Oberlin in 1938, with a doctorate from Massachusetts Institute of Technology in 1941, and teaching experience at both MIT and Stanford. He started absorbing the hard way just what he'd gotten himself into — a significant part of it being piecing and stringing the endless personal foibles which bagged together were Charlie Litton. For although Charlie Litton agreed to give him going in what he would pay a manager of his whole business, he was to begin at the very bottom. He would have his mettle tested in ways which Torquemada would have ruled fitting for the Spanish Inquisition. Moore, no matter what his eventual role, was told to run a lathe. For openers he would know what could or could not be made on one. From that point, he could graduate to a drill press, into shop tools, thence to the foundry to learn how to make patterns and castings. His sense of progress would be an assignment on the glass lathes and the learning experience of refining oil for his own vacuum box. At that point, Charlie Litton would turn the whole engineering supervisory task over to him. If that were handled to Litton's satisfaction, he would shift into the general manager's chair for the whole lot.

Moore went to work on a December Monday morning in 1948, and 6-day weeks were the mode. On Saturday, he saw the other four men in the model shop with him close down their machines in late afternoon. Each man got himself a bucket, a brush, soap, and wax. Each went to his knees to scrub the asphalt tile floors and wax them. The machines were wiped to mint fresh condition. Nobody had to tell Moore that if he expected to be there the next Monday, he had better do likewise whether he had a hat full of University degrees or not. Get to it he did. He even went a step further and labeled various machine parts with "open", "close", "on", "off", "up", "down", "high" and "low" and so on. He was stunned when Litton came by, said absolutely nothing about the freshening of the premises, but rebuked him for the labels.

"Dammit, take those notations off," he said. "If you understand what you're doing, you don't need them; if you don't know what you're doing, you shouldn't be using the machine!" Having so said, he stomped out.

It took Moore two years of this and similar happenings to get to the title of Director of Engineering. He had not only calluses on his hands, but on his soul as well.

It was a decision about windows and ventilation that won it all for him four years after the Redwood City dump hiring interview. The dormer windows were in the quonset hut second floor shop, where the engineering department was wedged in between the arched roof in a tight 30 x 60 feet of linear spread. On sunny days, it was a veritable furnace. Litton had convinced himself that a suction fan at one end and a blower at the other was sufficient air flow. He had decreed that the windows remain shut tight. People working there did so shirtless, and perspiration poured from them. One day Moore ordered the windows opened to augment the laboring, whirring blades. The workers objected saying Litton had strict orders about keeping the windows closed. Moore said to hell with that, and that he would assume the responsibility. The windows came open and the place was immediately more liveable. One day soon after, Litton came along at his usual loping gait and spied the windows ajar. He stopped short and asked who'd countermanded his orders. Moore said he was the one. Everyone else in the place was riveted on his task, ears distended to catch what would surely happen. "Hmm!" said Charlie, turned his back and stalked out. Moore expected to be sacked, as these were the minor kinds of confrontations which led to terminations. The next week he was made General Manger and had it all. It had taken him from 1948 to 1952 on the calendar and maybe ten years of his life.

Litton was a second generation American. His grandfather, a rough and tumble ships captain,[1] had come around the Horn of Scotland. He decided that 19th Century Sonoma County in California beat any bridge on any ship he had ever known. Once he saw the interesting and abundant landscape, the seas knew him no more. A village called Lytton grew up around him. Nobody ever knew how the "y" got in there. It had always been "i" in the family records. Perhaps it was because most of the people who were in California when he came were renowned more for ruggedness of fist and resolve than they were for schooling and spelling. When his son was born, he grew up to become one of the pioneer dentists practicing in San Francisco. It was more of a pain-inducing than pain-killing profession then, and being smooth mouthed early in life was commonplace. It was one of those generational pendulum swings — a father tough enough to knock the teeth out of an unruly crew with a belaying pin if need be; yet a son dedicated to maintaining the oral integrity of his patients for as long as possible. There was a greater difference than that. The dentist was a confirmed tinkerer. He had an aversion to sending out orders to laboratories when denture manufacture was called for, because he liked to mold, form, fit and grind make-do bite-and-chew items. He built his own laboratory and did this kind of labor himself. While his tools of extraction might be strewn over one table, at another he savored a growing familiarity with gold-copper and silver-copper alloys.

When the attending family doctor announced the old captain had a grandson, and the dentist a son, the new arrival came with a ready

---

1. He "a triangular tradesman", had cargoed slaves and rum in his time; slaves over to the Caribbean, rum on the return to the British Isles. The Emancipation Proclamation and the Union win of the War Between the States demolished part of the circuit. When he arrived in San Francisco, he sold his ship for gold and immediately bought most of the Alexander Valley; as his timing was bad before, it was again in that valley before the grapes took it over. His investment there foundered, too.

made heritage. Being an only child, he had the focus of full attention. Charles Vincent Litton, they called him. He didn't care much for the screams that came from those who sat in the dentist's chair. He was no more enthused about that wing of his father's occupation than anyone else would be in his right mind. He saw it as a last resort. His father could have all that and welcome to it. The laboratory was quite another matter. It became young Vinnie's playpen, Vinnie being what the family used as the pet name for him. With big round eyes he watched the wonders worked with the gadgetry his father stocked in his lab. As soon as he started separating an occasional word from the rest of his babyish babble, his lips formed more "whys" than a hive has bees. Many a parent would have despaired of the scope of his curiosity, grunted a lot of monosyllables, and hollered for help from the distaff side. Better that he be off crayoning the walls or indulging in some other suitable means of expression to stem the avalanche of questions. Not so, Dr. Litton. Stereotype family stories abound of the new father on hearing of his first born goes addlepated and rushes off to buy a horse, a car, or tries for early registration in Harvard Law School all before the infant has a full working knowledge of a nipple.

Well before the clubbiness of his teens, Dr. Litton bought him a metal lathe of his own, powered by a foot pedal. His parents urged him to have all the kids who were his contemporaries join him and play with the machine. The lathe gave him a sense of precision which never left him. He once confessed to his longtime colleague, Paul W. Crapuchetts, that it was this collection of friends which gave him an early appreciation of group action. Certainly, when it came to foot powering a lathe, anyone not lending his weight was immediately noticed by all the others. Litton rather quickly added an electric motor. Some of his frolicsome playmates had a short attention span for machines and a much longer one for the swimming hole.

With this kind of running start at Stanford University, Charlie Litton emerged a Phi Beta Kappa engineer in 1925. That was a heady time.

Lee DeForest, one of the men he most admired, had people listening to him at last. He had founded Federal Telephone and Radio. America was on the verge of long distance telephone service, large numbers of radio stations and even networks; also the sound-equipped talking screen because of DeForest and his audion, or amplifier tube and its derivatives. The jungle of disinterest and lethargy about new technologies through which he had had to wade had all but strangled him, but he always managed to slip through. As early as 1910, his radio expertise had attracted the great Enrico Caruso. He did a singing broadcast for him. Six years later, DeForest had presented the first news broadcast. His was the initial showing of sound on film applications in 1923, with a couple of black artists, Eubie Blake and Noble Sissle.[2]

The year following Litton's graduation, the process was to be introduced commercially by Warner Brothers with a film called "The Adventures of Don Juan" starring John Barrymore. It was followed a year later by the blockbuster, "The Jazz Singer" with Al Jolson.

The aging but much respected Thomas Alva Edison was still around, he was a powerful stimulus to those who could not only dream but had engineering skills to bring devices into being. He had found the means in 1878 of enclosing filament in a vacuum where it would remain intact and produce electric light. By the time Litton was born, 20,000,000 electric lights were in use.

None of this was lost on Charles V. Litton. He first went to work for Bell Laboratories, but that was too sedentary and pale for him. After two years he returned to the west and worked up to chief engineer of the Federal Telephone and Radio branch in Palo Alto. As often happens, the least imaginative of all corporate departments — accounting — came to a conclusion that had the most to do with Litton seeking a new direction. The suggestion by the accountant was that Federal needed to be closer to its money. That meant removal to the East. Federal in Palo Alto was to be closed. The man sent to do it was St. George Lafitte a seasoned and respected businessman who had known and liked Litton. He disliked seeing Federal abandon its western ship-to-shore communications business, but his orders were clear.

Federal wanted him to somehow hold onto Litton, even though California was his home, and he felt more comfortable in that environment. It carried with it an attitude on which he thrived. Less hidebound, structured, and fenced, it always seemed more adventurous and daring. The east was for collectives, the west for loners. Litton had

---

2. Also in that DeForest "talkie" film were Eddie Cantor, Weber & Fields, Phil Baker, Eva Puck & Sammy White, and Conchita Piquir.

even known people in Manhattan to whom the right bank of the Hudson was "west!" In contrast, the Pacific Ocean in all its vastness was just over the rolling hills, stretching beyond view where it inspired properly prepared minds to range widely. Such was the nature of Litton's contract with Federal, he was only to work on the west coast and if Federal no longer had an interest in the ship-to-shore business, it could buy back the rest of his contract. When he was watching Lafitte box up and batten the doors in Palo Alto, he asked as part of this contract settlement to have first search on equipment; he thought he could use it for an enterprise he had in mind. Lafitte OK'd it. Litton got the best of everything he thought he needed. That was better than any payoff in money. Federal asked for a string on him as a consultant assuring him he would only have to take a couple of trips east annually.

Litton, a man who was not to marry until much later in life, had been living with his parents on Eton Avenue in what is now San Carlos. It was then a 10-acre expanse of fruit trees. Litton, as part of their agreement, built a 3200 square feet, 3-room building, with cellar, later to become the "glory hole" where metals were melted and molded. It was as a "mom & pop's store" as one could find, except the parents contributed only land, tolerance and encouragement. Lone hand Vinnie gave the premises technological life. He had a reputation not far removed from Darmstadt's Dr. Viktor Frankenstein whose monster made him famous.

Some of the strange noises which came from his lab were not reassuring to the townsfolk. There was cracker-barrel talk about his mysterious behavior. An inventor wasn't a normal, every day citizen. Litton proved that. One of the youngsters who was bug-eyed about what might be happening there was Roy Woenne. He had graduated from Redwood City's Sequoia High School where he had taken architectural drawing. His interest was half-and-half, partly the doings in the lab, and partly stealing cherries in season, which brought him to the attention of Litton's mother and father. It was the mother who finally suggested that her son needed some help. Roy Woenne became his first fulltime employee.

In that July 1935, America was limping from severe economic wounds. Wall Street prices were not too far from their deepest markdowns. It was as if the great American show had closed and there was only winter in the spirits of everyone. Not Charles Vincent Litton, though. The electronics industry still needed what he could give it in unmatched quality. He was a small enough operator that he could tailor his vacuum tubes with his own intuition, expertise, and secrets added.

None, the biggies or the smalls, could equal him. He could read a patent as a general reads terrain. He invariably could come up with something better than the current average, and avoid infringing on that which was protectively guarded for others. The fact that he could get along, Napoleon-like, with four hours sleep, and sometimes would stay at the lathe alone for 72 hours in sequence, made him hard to compete with, and few tried.

He and Roy Woenne were an odd twosome. Instead of "Take a letter, Miss Jones" routine as in other offices, Charlie was always asking Roy to "take a drawing". Litton himself was skilled in the transfer of an idea to paper. He always did it with precision, often getting a very complicated device on a neat and easy to follow single sheet. Roy Woenne brought in steno pads by the dozen. Page after page was filled with the specifications and designs of seeking buyers. Their needs were often exotic and bizarre. For years before there would be a formal architectural drafting unit, what were Litton Engineering Laboratories' technical archives were these bulging steno pads indexed and tabbed for easy reference by Roy Woenne. They were pulled out when reorders came in. Although light years primitive from the computer pattern printouts which were to come, they performed the same guideline and standardizing functions. The glass lathe, the sealing machines, spot welders, bell jars, induction heating work applications, hydrogen furnaces, and vacuum pumps all were identified as necessities and had their places in those steno pads.

"Charlie would sit all night," Roy Woenne said, "designing such things. He was extremely good technically. There was first a San Jose pattern maker that he used, who had a little foundry where the patterns could be refined and made into castings. He'd then bring them to our shop, machine them, and put them together." Later, Litton preempted his father's garage and did all this kind of work there. Once he had the raw materials, then his was the ultimate vertical integration because all the way to a finished product, it never left his hands.

The LITTON Adventure That Was

Albert Einstein once said of himself: ". . .never has the world so honored a man who only originated a thought!" He was speaking late in life, and understating because the theory of relativity was hardly a fleeting or whimsical occurrence. In the case of Charles V. Litton, his thought turned him in the direction of what he called "the praying pig". It was a vacuum tube, made of glass, about 14 inches long and four inches in diameter. It was in electronic parlance, a high frequency triode — anode, cathode and grid. There was a snout-like connection at one end, and a curlycue of copper at the other. In order to stabilize it and keep it from rolling, there were four short, bent legs for support, as if kneeling. This high powered triode was to be a key element in radar and communications. It unlocked a quarter of a million dollars investment money from American Trust's Ransom Cook. He looked it over warily when Charlie showed it to him. He said he didn't understand it. He did understand Charlie Litton's account with him, however, as it was fat and constant and its replenishment steady. A late blooming Dr. Frankenstein he might be in the neighborhood, but what Charlie Litton was doing seemed to be a license to coin money. Ransom Cook had no trouble backing his needs for a couple of additional 60x100 foot buildings which were crowded into the orchard.

Late in World War II, there was a great scare in the Pacific. American forces overran a Japanese held island and found what appeared to be a German style magnetron of the type Hitler was trying to rush into service to jam the highly effective radar which Sir Robert Watson-Watt had perfected. Military intelligence was anguished that this might mean the Japanese had the technology, too. The subduing of Japan was the last of the strategies enunciated at the Cairo Conference for conduct of the war, and if true, this could mean the Japanese home islands would be tougher than ever to take.

Litton took on magnetron manufacture. At war's end, the Japanese were found never to have had this capability. The mystery of the find was never solved. The Litton magnetrons were never built in time for use in the war — but the magnetron had found a roost in the Litton reference books as a technology ripe for possible commercial applications.

With the war over, quonset huts could be had for a song. Litton moved into a budding San Carlos industrial development area in that kind of housing. St. George Lafitte had never lost touch with Litton. When he retired from Federal Telephone and Radio in 1949, Litton remembered what a leg-up Lafitte had given him, so he brought him on the roster as a financial administrator. It wasn't all a matter of past favors, because Litton was at his wit's end about government contracting and regulations, contract renegotiations and tax problems. He hated it all. Especially annoying to him was the certain knowledge that government tended to reward inefficiency (lesser quality products costing more) rather than efficiency (better products costing less to produce, but priced comparably). And there was all the general knowledge that he could handle his technologies better than anyone else. This made him a more popular walk-in point for the careful and sophisticated purchasing agents. Life was getting too cumbersome taking him away from the machines he loved and the laboratories which housed them. He was having to use more time for ledgers and journals and fine print. He didn't like it at all, none of it.

Hughes Aircraft in Culver City, California was highly pleased with the products bought from him. Hughes had Hugh William Jamieson, a first class engineer. He was constantly on the search for vendors who were reliable and known for established quality workmanship over time. Hughes was blessed with a series of progressively more sophisticated contracts for fire-control systems, which would perform collision course rocket launches from North American's F-86Ds, Northrop's F-89Js and Lockheed's F-94Cs. With fittings in the next generation of aircraft allocated, Hughes had an assured aerospace defense role. Litton's product was an admirable fit. The viciousness of the air battles and ground actions in Korea were chilling the political bloodstreams of Western Europe. If it was likely that the Soviet Union was peering over the North Pole for softnesses in North Americans readiness, an aerospace defense system was a necessity. These all-weather fighter aircraft and fire-control systems, plus the distant early warning and other radar, cried out for various high powered microwave tubes. The "seeing eye" for fire control systems was microwave energy which could only be generated in sufficient power by the magnetron.

Generalissimo Josef Stalin was aging. He found his geriatric advance haunted with suspicions, and preemptive strikes against this or that member of his palace guard (the do-him-before-he-does-you syndrome) were as regular as each new day. There was a body of opinion that he licked his lips over the vision of what power he would command if by subversion or conquest, he could get under his wing the huge industrial potential of Japan and Western Europe. Had he this addition, what remained of the world would be menaced as it had never been. The United States enunciated policy was that it would never strike a first blow. What if Stalin or a successor who was his clone elected to attack North America? There were too many examples of frustrated ambitions where the production capacity of America was left alone to pump weapons and in time its own blood into the fray to make the difference between victory and defeat. The thin margin remaining for the West — the capacity to make a Stalin pause — lay in warning time. This was tied to detection as near the origin of any strike as could be managed. Those electron tubes which Litton manufactured so well were a key element of radar sites, large and small.

The requirements of air defense indicated that the machine gun or small cannon mounts in aircraft were inadequate for a fleet of incoming nuclear weapon laden bombers advancing on bomb release sites named Indianapolis, Seattle, Boston, Minneapolis, and Kansas City. Rockets were the answer. The Air Force took three of the top jet aces with experience in Korea to Yuma, Arizona to spearhead the transition from guns to rockets — Major James Jabara, the first jet ace, Major Vermont Garrison, the world's only double double ace (more than 10 in prop aircraft in WWII, more than 10 in jets in Korea), and Major Ralph Parr, who had shot down the last aircraft in the Korean War. (Unfortunately, it was at a wrong curve in the Yalu which had it technically over Manchuria at the moment with some Soviets aboard). If anyone could make the rocket work, they could. It called for a new technique, abandoning the chase for a 90-degree angle approach. The fire control system released the rockets which on collision course would bag the intruder in North American air space. The magnetron, a copperish bit of metal in a rising sun configuration rode in every air defense plane. That microwave emitter was a critical element in the performance of the tattletail function for the computer to spot where the target was and its speed for allowances in lead time to assure the rockets came in with unerring accuracy.

Special Situation #4

In 1952, Jamieson had started spending social time with Litton, both in San Carlos and in his Grass Valley Jackson Lake mountain retreat. He was there when the Jackson Lake Lodge was opened in the summer. It gave them a lot of conversational opportunity. The topics were many. Litton aired his predicament as a sole owner of the research and manufacturing facility, what a tax jolt it would inflict on his estate, and the size of the operational headaches he was encountering daily. This was because his experience coincided so directly with the intelligence of the West and the countering weapons systems that were needed. At one point, he asked Jamieson if Hughes Aircraft might not be interested in buying him out. After all, they seemed to respect his product. Why not bring it all comfortably together?

But Jamieson knew that Hughes Aircraft was unwell. There was revolt in the air. Being as close to Howard Hughes as he was, and in on many of the private quirks of the man, he knew the stubbornness of which he was capable. He could loiter interminably over a decision. He also knew that whatever other boxes there were passing for organization, the key individual and the repository of the vision of what could be, was resident in Tex Thornton, listed there as an assistant general manager and vice president.

Howard Hughes was serene in his knowledge that he never had to do anything if he didn't wish to do so. He knew the atmosphere was sulfuric, but even if everyone left him on the morrow, let 'em go. He could throw his money out to a new batch of brains, who could occupy the chairs of the departed. He could do some fast shuffling along the Pentagon corridors with appropriate excuses. What was his would still function. He was one of the few who hadn't abandoned military contracting when it was no longer patriotic and fashionable, in favor of the huge consumer appetites awaiting for cars, radios, TV sets, suits, dresses and nylons. Just for hanging in there, the Defense Department owed him an excuse or two.

Jamieson knew that Tex Thornton had gotten Hughes to agree at one point to being bought out for around $40,000,000. Midway in the hunt for backing, Tex was stalled when Howard reneged. The prevailing mood for everyone was to "get out of there." Jamieson had told Tex about Charlie Litton, what he had, what his own problems were, and Tex was highly interested. When Hughes heard about the Litton availability from Jamieson he said "No", insofar as it being a Hughes acquisition. He countered by offering Jamieson $25,000 a year, guaranteed for five years if he would stay. If he was determined to leave, he would back Jamieson to make the buy himself. By that time, Jamieson was too well acquainted with Howard's vagueness about yesterday's promises. He told him he had already put something in another oven. He couldn't take either of Hughes suggestions, he said.

Roy Ash was Tex's numbers man in the controller's office. He could chart more direction for dollars than a Hydra had heads. Everything about the Litton packet rang right with him; it was a treasury menaced by the tax man. IRS could be headed off at the pass if it were invested in ventures and technologies which had appeal and promise. The annual income was steady and formidable with no end in sight. It was one of those "best of everything for everybody" possibilities. Litton could have the money he needed to carry him through all he wanted to do for the rest of his life. He could retain the Litton Engineering Laboratories where his heart and mind were stored. Tex had told Hughes and his buffer, Noah Dietrich, that he was leaving. There was no secret about that.

Bill Jamieson made a reservation at the Ben Franklin Hotel in San Mateo for Tex and himself. He told Charlie Litton they were coming up for a chat with him. This was the initial get together for Tex and Charlie, complete with the usual parrying and fencing. Ballpark figures were mentioned, each trying to mask eagerness. On his side, Litton was abandoning his baby, his brainchild. As savagely as he had sometimes treated them, he wanted the assurance that his employees would transfer to the hands of sensitive ownership instead of rapacious ogres which were known to plunder and run. Tex and Jamieson made him rest easy in that regard, but just to let him know he was in the running and not their only prospect they casually mentioned that they were also sizing up Bill Jack's scientific instruments in Solano Beach. That meeting did not break up until it was time to catch the last flight around midnight back to Los Angeles.

As they parted, Litton gave Tex his financial statement. Sitting there with it in his lap on that midnight ride, Tex Thornton needed no longer to control excitement as he studied exactly what a bonanza Litton Industries of California really was. Like some reincarnation of Paul Revere it was — not shouting that the British were coming, but the opportunity of a lifetime. He knew it.

SPECIAL SITUATION #5

THE SEARCH FOR BACKING

Neither knew of the other's existence, but when Joseph Thomas was born in Texas on September 27, 1906, it was almost day and date with Lehman Brothers' decision to convert their cotton brokering firm into investment banking.[1]

It would be two Lehman Brothers' checks—No. 2265 for $5,250 and No. 2266 for $1,460,000 signed by an obscure senior clerk, Melville Bertschy, and certified by the Bankers Trust Company—which got a new company known temporarily as the Electro-Dynamics Corporation out of the idea stage and into serious action. The company name came from a "bull session" encounter involving Thornton, Ash and Jamieson with Phil Klass, the Aviation Week magazine writer. Klass suggested it. It was time for prefixes, "nuc" and suffixes, "onics" "amics" in company names. Such things were so seriously con-

---

1. The Lehmans were originally from the small Bavarian village, Rimpar (1,200 pop.) in Germany. Henry, first over the Atlantic in 1844, settled in the cotton trade in Montgomery, Alabama with meager stocks on bare shelving in an old candles-and-whale-oil-lighted warehouse. When his brother Emanuel followed three years later, the sign at their 17 Court Street location stated: "Lehman & Bro." It's now the site of the skyscraper housing First National Bank. A third brother, Mayer, joined them in 1850. By then they were not only in cotton, but groceries, general commodities and consumer goods which made them pillars in the business community in that quarter of the bustling south. Their first tragedy came when Henry contracted yellow fever on a New Orleans business trip and died in 1855 at the age of 33. They felt a second ominous presence in the air about them as secession fever was everywhere, no less a potential destroyer than Henry's physical affliction. As so much of cotton belt economics depended on buyers in New York for textile mills of the U.S. northeast as well as those of Great Britain, Emanuel opened the Gotham office of Lehman Brothers at 119 Liberty Street in 1858.

What had worked for the Rothschilds in the strifes of Europe now worked for the Lehmans—Emanuel was a northern patriot and Mayer, loyal to the Confederacy (When it was over it would be Mayer's son Herbert H. Lehman who would be a New York governor and senator). The Lehman Brothers shared in America's family quarrel from both sides. When carpetbaggers swarmed southward after "Mr. Lincoln's war", Emanuel was foundationed on cement-solid currency in contrast to the valueless paper of the defeated, dispirited and demoralized Confederacy. As a family, their adjustment post-war was easier, but as the 19th century gave up its final days, the Lehmans began looking for a better course. They saw it in association with Goldman Sachs as their sighting and aiming device identifying investment opportunities. They became investment bankers.

sidered their inclusion was said to be worth 5 to 10 points in a stock's price! Dated on December 4, 1953, the Lehman checks could not have been written without Joe Thomas' persuasion of his partners and his signal to go ahead.

Even when he was on his deathbed, Joe Thomas had high roller and high fallutin' ways about him. Callers summoned to his side at his home often found him under his oxygen tent, chewing an unlit black cigar and taking occasional nips of his favorite bourbon and soda. He had brought north with him from Fort Worth some wild and woolly lifestyle characteristics. Only those who viewed him from a distance saw a kind of cowboy roughness and brashness as all there was to him. Closer contact quickly revealed trimmings of Yale and the Harvard Business School added to an already gifted and adventuring mind. He was a "deal maker", proud of it, proven at it. He roamed widely in thinking. He saw possibilities and angles others more orthodox ignored or hadn't the gambler's stomach for. When he needed to do so because his partners were stubborn or cautious for whatever reason, he could be as fractious as a stallion impatient at the snorting pole who feared a teased mare might be denied him.

Thomas was no starter-at-the-top. His first year's pay in 1928 was $2,000. By the time he came along, all the founding Lehmans were gone. They would have loved him, though. He was a kind of flamboyant head of steam seeking and finding channels for locomotion. He was also indefatigable. He worked hard, played late, drank deeply and lived up life until it spilled over. He knew racehorses by pedigree, once had a percentage of the professional football Rams and got into backings of prizefighters such as that young and personable Cassius Clay, who had been one of the most charismatic and incandescent of the U.S. Olympic Team in Rome. Nobody, but nobody, was ever going to stand at Joe's graveside and make woeful expressions of sorrow about what he had missed while alive! Even as Joe Thomas rounded 40, he had done it all and was repeating the same course with equal zest.

Thomas had been in the Navy while Tex Thornton was in the Air Force. They had no encounter then. It was when Tex was stewing in the juices of indecision caused by the ephemeral Howard Hughes that put them on intersecting lines. The only common happenstance they had was both being Texans. As the Thornton reputation was growing

The LITTON Adventure That Was

in the electronics field, Thomas was on a firm foundation of demonstrating financing successes. As an avid admirer and user of its waves, he had sprung the first post-1929 stock market crash turnaround of Schenley. Proving he was no one-shot phenomenon with that one, he accomplished a similar revitalization of American Export Lines. And there were others where his ministrations profited them.

It was when Tex Thornton had been encouraged to believe by Howard Hughes that he would say *yes* to him as an individual, or as the leader of a group, should he be able to raise the backing to buy Hughes Aircraft in Culver City that they met. As a connection, the Thornton choice was an old friend, Don G. Mitchell. He was the electronics systems adviser to Secretary of the Air Force Thomas K. Finletter. He counseled Tex to put what he had in mind down on paper, a plan, and then go see one Joe Thomas at Lehman Brothers in New York. It was that time-honored "splicing" action, so common in business, involving people whose respect for each other 's judgments introduce a stranger into the confidence of the other.

Tex had that Hughes price tag: $40,000,000. That was in 1951. They, the Thornton-Thomas combination, were instantly compatible. With Thornton, anything dreamable and well-thought-through was possible. With Thomas, anything clearly envisioned that made sense was financeable. Of course, the Lehman Brothers were not the only checkpoint on the Thornton trek. That intense time did a lot to establish him as someone who knew what he was about. He was transparently eager to get something and run it. General opinion in the Wall Street neighborhood was that he should be watched and listened to politely, because he was no flash in the pan. He might just have something. There were memories of such men who came with a burning idea. When they got the money those who had decided to risk for them basked in a share of their sunshine. As was so often the case where the last word was Howard Hughes', he shied away from the sale. That Thornton-Thomas first try lived for such a short while, it was only a conversational might-have-been. The Hughes Aircraft sale could hardly have been said to have gotten far enough along to have its demise described as "stillborn".

One thing was leading to another, and fast, in Culver City. Scientific and managerial talents were in wholesale exodus, draining the Hughes swamp. Joe Thomas found Tex Thornton back on his old One

55

William Street stoop in yet another request for money. There was a difference this time—Thornton had a man with a wish to sell.

The Thornton credentials were substantial and belied his youth. Joe Thomas had shaken his head often as he was approached with big ideas needing Lehman Brothers' nod and bankroll. He liked this thought route that Thornton was taking—his wish to get a small company that had a product, promising exploitable technologies, a firm foothold in the marketplace, a future—and an access to horizons for expansion.

Thomas wasn't the only Wall Streeter who heard the Thornton story. Roy Ash said it was talked around so much everyone in lower Manhattan knew about it. There were bets afloat[2] that rather than holding tight to one sponsor and instead declaring open season, all hopes for any serious financing were dashed. Hearers were varied such as Joseph P. Kennedy, the Boston financier, and Clarke-Dodge who could join in Lehman Brothers action. Its head man, Arthur Choate, had strongly supported advice from Guerney Dyer, a member of his staff. Dyer was one of those Statistical Control Military Occupational Specialty 6402 types in his Air Force days. "Anything Tex Thornton touches," he told Choate, "will go!" What was being sketched by Tex Thornton was the outright buying of an ongoing company, not only a strong, productive and healthy one and a profit maker of itself, but also a springboard to bigger, grander things.

Thomas tuned in closely as Charles V. Litton's wholly owned Litton Industries of California in the San Francisco Bay area was described. It seemed to have everything—the family ownership insured against any dissident or holdout shares. The founder was annoyed by the size and complexities in his life introduced by his success. There was a well-priced product line and no resistance to potential rewards. The asking figure was less than the forecast for three years earnings as the going concern it undoubtedly was. It was turning an easy annual

---

2. One scoffer was Charles Allen, of the H. Allen & Co. financial house. He bet Roy Ash "the best dinner in town" that talking to any and everybody to get money was a Wall Street "no-no". He declared the backing would never be forthcoming. Ash never stuck him with that dinner check, but let him rest in history with his reputation as a flawed prophet. Allen was only one of many in the long parade of financial experts to come up wrong about Litton Industries.

56

profit of nearly $400,000. The hazards were minimal for any investment house or individual. It was a financial fail-safe.

Thomas was not uncomfortable with the Thornton fetish about control. "Tex" wanted 60% of the holding to rest with management, and 40% to ride with the "money". Wall Street did it the other way. Others at Lehman Brothers were shaken up by this leniency on Thomas' part for such loose tethering. Thomas read in the Thornton profile that he was so confident of his control of the decision making process it was in itself an incentive to prove his point—and reward his backers plus vindicating their judgment. The "money" was not accustomed to being generous with leeway (Joseph P. Kennedy had said the money wasn't much, but he wasn't interested in minority positions). Thomas pointed to the Litton annual report of earnings. What Lehman Brothers were risking was peanuts for almost a sure thing.

The "shirtsleeves" assistants to the two men were busy in the backroom and on plane flights—William "Bill" Osborn for Thomas, and Roy L. Ash for Tex Thornton. Ash was current on every conceivable figures combination pertaining to the worth of the Litton facility. Tex had him do an exhaustive analysis for Hughes Aircraft, when it could have been a possible add-on if Hughes really meant what he said when he indicated willingness to sell for $40,000,000. No matter that Hughes had backed away, that same Ash analysis was valid, in hand, and made unnecessary any further time consuming study. As a reference resource in the Lehman Brothers talks, all responses could be quick and precise. But Thomas and the Lehman Brothers wanted corroboration. Thomas told Osborn to saddle up and ride into the sunset—to San Francisco, and look over the Litton facility in detail. Osborn did, and was met by Bill Jamieson in his "company car", a 1946 bent and battered Chevrolet from which he alternated as "finder" and "chauffeur". Osborn was introduced to Charlie Litton, but beyond that was mostly under the guidance of Dr. Norm Moore.

"My bags stayed at Rickey's Motel," Osborn said, "but I never seemed to leave the blasted plant." He was there 48 intensive, observing, note-taking hours. Osborn worked for Joe Thomas, but he had heard the mutterings in the Lehman hallways which led him to believe that Tex Thornton was a really controversial subject of concern. The key thing Osborn was to nail down was the Litton treasury replenishment pattern ($375,000-plus annually). He marveled at how great a deal it was and returned to Rickey's. He retrieved his still packed bags on the fly. Jamieson drove to the airport. He had all the reassuring information Joe Thomas needed.

It was at a leisurely dinner meeting that Joe Thomas scratched out in pencil the financial design to produce the bundle Tex Thornton had to have. It worked out on the back of an old envelope which Thomas took from his inside coat pocket. The envelope had been used before to list two horses of interest in some Jamaica gallop. Whether they had been bet or had won was not disclosed. No matter, new business was at hand. Fifty units, he wrote, worth $29,200 each. Then he broke them down into categories: 20 debentures with price tags of $1,200, 50 shares of $100 preferred, and 2,000 of 10-cent par common. When sold, the amount would total $1,460,000. Off there in San Carlos California, three zones away, Charlie Litton was saying he wanted $1,050,000 cash. The Thornton option to buy had to be exercised with nearly a third of that amount. It would buy 90 days during which final unit sale could be accomplished. The two operatives, Osborn and Ash, worked out the details of the prospectus in a Lehman corner office going late into sleepless nights.

With all that in motion, Joe Thomas had to get to other pressing matters—including those which took him out of New York.[3] No sooner did his shadow cross the door when Lehman Brothers' other staffers moved in with questions. One of them, a soft spoken North Carolinian, Ray Rummisel, had been with the legal end of the Securities & Exchange Commission for years. He was a nitpicker, in love with regulations and the questions they entitled him to ask. There were nights when Tex Thornton and his old friend Glen McDaniel, of the Lundgren, Lincoln & McDaniel Wall Street law firm would walk more than 40 blocks to the upper midsection of Manhattan where McDaniel lived. There was real tension in the air. Tex felt the deal might become unstuck with the hemming and hawing delays thrown up

---

3. The Thornton-Ash billet during all this was a loaned apartment belonging to a friend, Bob Brunson, at Sutton Place, in New York, rent free. The driving pair ate at Nedick's and other corner fast food places. After one particularly grueling day, both of them dog-tired, and everything seeming to go badly, Tex ordered a milkshake. When he had sucked noisily on the straw and got to the bottom of it—there was a dead fly! It gave them a perspective on the state of their affairs at the beginning of the dream that came true. It lasted all their lives.

when Joe Thomas was out of reach. Then late one night, an urgent call came from Bill Jamieson on the West Coast.

"I think Charlie Litton is cooling off," he told Tex. There were about a half dozen big, established companies which were making him proposals. At first, he was fearful of their very size. They would eat his small operation alive, which could impact adversely his people at the plant. But a deal was a deal, after all. The money for the option was slow in coming. It could all blow up, just as the Howard Hughes back-off had done earlier. Without telling anybody where he was going or what he was doing, Tex Thornton flew to San Francisco on a night plane. He was almost desperate. Litton had mentioned a banker he knew named Cook, and Tex made up his mind to see him.

As soon as the American Trust Company opened the next morning he was in the office of the Vice President, Ransom Cook. He told him he needed about $300,000 to exercise the option to buy Litton Industries of California, the Charles V. Litton plant complex near Redwood. Cook knew it was turning an annual profit greater than the loan and its prospects were substantial. After hearing Tex, Cook placed a call to his American Trust branch manager in Redwood City, where Litton had his account.

"I don't understand what he manufactures," the manager said "but he sure rakes in money. The stuff pours in and his account is always rock solid, and flush." Cook made some other calls. Nearly all the comments were reassuring, heavily enough weighted to satisfy him.

Ransom Cook had all he needed to know. He advanced $300,000, the option price. "Tex" Thornton immediately paid Litton. The 90 day option was working. The leverage he needed for Lehman Brothers was in his hands.[4] The Thornton demeanor approximated a

---

4. The key participants in the backing drama were never to be forgotten by Tex Thornton as long as he lived. Joe Thomas, the Lehman Brothers grubstaker, went on the Litton board of directors in 1955. Ransom Cook, who orchestrated the option money at American Trust, went with it when it was merged with Wells Fargo. When he completed his Wells Fargo time, there was no longer any conflict of interest. Thornton called him the very next day, asking him to go on Litton's board of directors in 1967. Don G. Mitchell, who told Tex to put what he had in mind down on paper— a plan—then go to a moneyed listener named Joe Thomas, was brought on the board in 1973. Good as his advice had been in getting the Thomas-Thornton hitchup, it backfired on him initially. Mitchell was electronic systems adviser to Air Force Sec-

cat that had fallen into a pan of cream. Although the night's passage coming west had been fretful and sleepless he slept soundly all the way to New York. Let them dawdle now if they wished, he was committed and had the lock on. He had no subsequent payments to make until 1954. They couldn't let his clock run down any longer and squeeze him for concessions. He had negotiated the deal with Litton. Charlie was at ease.

Dr. Norman Moore, Roy Woenne, St. George Lafitte[5] and Paul Crapuchetts had also been in a state of suspense at the plant. That was ended abruptly when from his retreat in Grass Valley, Charlie Litton got Moore on his one-way radio—he could talk and Moore could only listen. No matter how much he might want to, he could not talk back to his boss.

"Call all those other companies," Litton told Moore. "Tell them I have decided to go with Tex Thornton. We've shaken hands on it. It's a deal." Even though Litton couldn't hear, Moore did talk back to him. He shuddered at the prospect of slamming the doors on all those other carefully worded proposals and on the proposers who had put time and effort into them. Moore had his orders; call them he did. In those calls, two way conversation was possible. Each of the responses was vituperative enough to burn the phone wires. Eventually they accepted the turn-off for the very good reason that there was no alternative left. Litton stayed up in Grass Valley assured now that he would get his $1,050,000 in cash, and the five years consultancy agreement at $75,000 annually. He was not intimidated by later accounts of the disappointments he had caused. He translated it all into the ultimate flattery it was—that what he had built with his own hands was so all fired attractive to so many good judges of quality merchandise.

When "Tex" Thornton resumed his Lehman Brothers conversation in Manhattan, he was the picture of serenity: loose, interested and the tenseness gone. He waited them out. Finally the option matter was broached. He smiled, and softly said: "I've already laid the

---

retary Thomas K. Finletter when he instructed Tex to do it. When he left the Air Force, he went to Sylvania. Sylvania was a spirited bidder for Litton's company, but lost out to Thornton. Mitchell never wearied of telling how excellent his counsel had been in advancing the Thornton scheme, but also the dangers of giving good advice to people who just might take it!

5. He was the great grandson of that other Lafitte, Jean the pirate.

money down for that. I have exercised the option." Jaws dropped all around the negotiating table. In the backroom of Lehman Brothers Bill Osborn and Roy Ash, hurried the final prospectus drafting to accompany the 50 "units" of debentures, preferred and common stocks which were to be offered by Lehman Brothers and Clarke-Dodge. The centerpiece for their labors was the old envelope on which Joe Thomas had scribbled the essentials for packaging ingredients.

The sale of the "units" was the burden of Lehman Brothers with 55% of the action, and Clarke-Dodge, with 45%. Thornton had misgivings about a one house offering. Besides, he had two strong believers in Arthur Choate and Gurney Dyer at Clarke-Dodge. "With a man like Thornton," said Choate, "one has to sit and think with him. I was told as a young man that if I could learn to detect the difference between two individuals who looked the same, I'd have a happy and successful life. It took me a lifetime to figure out what that advice meant—but the difference is character and strength, a desire to work, a target to aim for and a knowledge about how to manipulate people. *Genius* is what I call it. Tex had the gift, had it all, wrote the book."

There were myriad papers to sign. A questioning Charlie Litton and his legal counsel, Bert Currie, had to be appeased and reassured. Many required actions on both coasts called for hours on airplanes, long lunches in restaurants and off the corner of desks, dinners into the night, and breakfasts at the first pinking of dawn. In getting it all done, whoever among the trio of Thornton, Ash and Jamieson, or any combination thereof, produced fountain pens to sign any needed document. For one short period, by one of those signatures, Roy Ash owned it all.

Very early in November 1953, Tex Thornton squired Joe Thomas to the Litton facility, where Jamieson met them in the company's Chevy along with Dr. Norm Moore functioning again as guide and answer man. The Osborn fact finding was so complete, Joe Thomas knew every question to ask and did. Everyone on the acquiring side was so well up on the Litton property, it was easy to be responsive and complete about it. None of the trio even thought about it then, or the world's implications, as it was about five years off that a business publication would refer to them as "founders", or "cofounders". In reality, Jamieson was the "finder", the one who knew and zeroed in on Litton and his property and told Tex about it. Roy Ash was the fast man with the stats in a money sense, the wordsmith of the prospectus. The visionary, though, the maneuverer, the one who shored up and called the turns, the decision maker every step of the way was Charles Bates Thornton. There was no doubt at either Lehman Brothers or Clarke-Dodge about the key figure, as the ever cautious Lehman legal hand, Rusmisel saw it. He insisted on an "If I die" letter which was signed by "Tex" Thornton indicating the protective direction for the Litton property to take in case of his demise!

With that ever present Thornton concern about control, he immediately purchased 375,000 shares of the then Electro-Dynamics 10-cent stock. He mortgaged his home to get the cashier's check to be used for the transaction. Of this, 60,000 shares were kept by Thornton personally with 20,000 each going to Ash and Jamieson. The remaining 275,000 shares were transferred to the Electro-Dynamics Stock Trust Fund, as it was called, an equally participating partnership of the Thornton-Ash-Jamieson trio. Thornton also purchased an option to buy an addition 275,000 shares of common stock, it being the Thornton-Lehman Brothers wish that such holdings would be available through stock options as an incentive offering above salary for superlative executives performance. The stipulation was that this right of participation not be closely held, and within the reach of no less than 25 of the company's stalwarts along management row.

Glen McDaniel, of the Wall Street Lundgren, Lincoln and McDaniel law offices, was part-time legal counsel. He had written the company's articles of incorporation. Suddenly he had a phone call from one of his ex-Navy friends who was now retired and berthed with General Dynamics, Admiral Laurence "Dick" Richardson.

"You have a problem," Richardson said. "General Dynamics has a division in New Jersey—our Electro-Dynamics unit. It's in electronics. There's bound to be confusion with what you call yourselves. Do you rename your outfit, or do we sue?"[6] McDaniel said he'd get back to him.

---

6. Litton Engineering Laborites operates on a modest sized mountain top above Grass Valley, California. It was still owned by the Litton family (the widow, Mrs. Lucy Litton Griffin; daughter, Alice, sons Larry and Charles V. Jr.). President and general manager, was Charlie Litton, Jr. It's not far from where the notorious Countess of Landsfeldt who had been the mistress of the King of Bavaria conducted her last salons (she being better known there as Lola Montez, who taught Lotta Crabtree to

The LITTON Adventure That Was

"I've been liking the sound of Litton Industries[7] for us better all the time," Thornton told him. "Let me talk to Norm Moore about it." Norm Moore said he'd be flattered if that became the corporation name. There was a pause. Moore could almost hear the wheels turning. Being quickly perceptive, he asked if his being president of Litton in San Carlos would cause a problem. The Thornton relief was almost transmitted over the phone, on the indication it could be worked out so agreeable.

"Hell", said Moore, "I'm not hung up on the title. You should be president of Litton Industries and I'll be a vice president and run this operation". So it was worked out. McDaniel called Admiral Richardson to tell him the conflicting name problem was cleared up without firing a legal shot.

On August 16, 1954, the new company had a new name— Litton Industries, Inc. The excitement, though, was as closely held as were the shares in the company.

---

dance!). Charles, Jr. gives one the spooky feeling of being a duplicate of his parent in every physical detail, the same beanpole figure and standing 6 feet four inches. Both sons then asked for one word most-memorable-characteristic of their father spoke almost in unison: "Impatience!"

7. Precision multi-turn wire-wound potentiometers, a necessary ingredient of inertial navigation systems, sent Litton early to the Birklan Corporation, an unlikely site nestled between two Mt. Vernon hills in New York, roofed over by a railway trestle. It became Litton's Potentiometer division and met its inertial navigation requirements squarely. It was acquired for $44,000 on May 27, 1954. Potentiometer has always been the "Mayflower" of Litton as it was brought in when the company was still named Electro-Dynamics. The papers which were signed bore Charles B. Thornton's signatures as President, and Roy L. Ash's as Secretary. It also produced one Justin Oppenheimer, who was to be a profit maker in every position Litton placed him.

SPECIAL SITUATION #6

THE CAST OF CHARACTERS

No massive swoop into place characterized the arrival of Litton's movers, shapers, and shakers. More of a desultory trickle.

It was assembled as a free form enterprise from the first. Pedigrees were not their long suit. Most of what became pillars of the structure weren't there at the beginning, nor did any of them even expect they might be key figures. They were scattered all over the landscape—in businesses, in laboratories, in government service as if waiting for that mutual catalyst which was to bring them together in whatever configuration it might be. Some were lured in. Others walked on or were homegrown. There were the roamers, uneasy about taking root and, after a smattering of the Litton experience, would hurry on. There was an acronym for them: LIDOs (Litton Industries Drop Outs). It was inaccurate as a description as they were mostly gravity defiers, in that they tended to do better, or drop UP. "Thornton Tech," the place was called, and rightly so because as many major corporate heads were to have Thornton or Litton associations as any single business school could claim as alumni.

There were awesome ambitions among them. Egos were often larger than one finds in the theater. Some had incredible imaginative and conceptual abilities. Others turned out to be pretenders and were shown the door. Litton executives fascinated a generation and were envied widely. Litton became a headhunter's poaching ground of grand proportions. Recruiters stalked the top and middle range personalities on social and after hours occasions. They were sidled up to in the watering places. Whispered and seducing words were exchanged about all the glittering opportunities off the Litton reservation.

The first-named corporate body—Electro-Dynamics—was temporarily housed at 2301 Purdue Avenue. It was neither an impressive neighborhood nor address, cheek-to-jowl where Los Angeles begins to give way to Santa Monica, California. The first girl hired, Jean Randall, learned quickly that she was the factor of dependence for an accurate whereabouts head count on the lot of them. She was the locater, the coordinator of movements, recordkeeper and even custodian of the daybook in which Roy Ash made entries in his neat but stilted handwriting. He didn't have much money action to track in those startup days, but he paid elaborate attention to such details. No matter that the numbers were smaller than those he had dealt with at the Bank of America and Hughes Aircraft, or the Army Air Corps before that, they were very personal numbers locked to him and his future.

The "Randall roster" showed Charles B. Thornton, Roy L. Ash and Hugh William Jamieson as the troika.

Jamieson had been the one who convinced her to sign on over a single cup of coffee. Tex Thornton quite obviously was first in the pecking order. Then there was his administrative assistant and secretary, Jack Fairburn; Foster Campbell, the first to move into components manufacture; Charles "Chuck" Abrams, an Ash financial coworker and master of digital dialogue; James McCullough, an accountant; William Harriss, a writer, quipster, resident court jester good at breaking the strain of tense moments; Ray Krogh, John Carlson, Bob Denton, Teck Wilson, all engineers; Dawson Bray, a Thornton friend from Texas in industrial relations; Grafton P. Tanquary, III, a Harvard Business School graduate and buzzword lexicographer who worked with Abrams and Emmett Steele. Steele's province was customer relations and marketing. He was to become eventually a Litton legal storm center because he persisted in assigning himself a role as one of the company founders with entitlements to match, producing a wrangle which dragged on for a decade.[1] None will ever know the

---

1. In 1959, Emmett Steele sued Litton Thornton, Ash, Jamieson and the Electro-Dynamics Stock Trust Fund based on two claimed obligations—an alleged oral promise by Thornton in 1953 that Steele would be permitted to purchase an amount of Litton stock equal to that granted Ash and Jamieson, and an alleged repetition of that promise said to have been made by Thornton in 1958. The jury voted for the rightness of Steele's claim on the group, but didn't find for the so-called 1953 promise. Superior Court Judge Frederick W. Mahl set the whole verdict aside when the jury chose to accept that the declaration of 1953 was non-existent but was remade in 1958. Judge Mahl did grant a new trial, saying evidence had been insufficient in the first one. Through complications of Steele's death in 1971, some 600 of the defendants' exhibits being inadvertently destroyed by the court clerk, Judge Arthur K. Marshall told the defendants to settle with the Steele widow and children which they did for $2,400,000. The original contention had been for $7,600,000. Had it been allowed to stand, with accrued interest, the defendants would have had to ante more than $10,000,000. Steele had actually sold participations in the outcome of the legal struggle, and his attorney's fees amounted to $960,000. Judge Marshall later became much

depth of distractions in executive thought and frustration this cost the company.

The swinging entrepreneur, the risk taker extraordinary and the moon shooter later to be associated with Litton in legend weren't much in evidence then for good reason. Among other nitty gritty of that hard beginning which had carried the Thornton idea along was the stark reality that he had to subsist through that gap from the Hughes payroll termination until late November insertion of himself, Ash, Jamieson and Fairburn on the Litton Industries books in San Carlos. That $35,000 mortgage on his home was being gnawed away rapidly. Almost as the ink was drying on that new pay window affiliation, Ash appeared on Dr. Norman Moore's doorstep in San Carlos, somewhat embarrassed. He was there to ask for an advance on his own $15,000 a year salary. He said both he and Tex could use a loan of $500 apiece for "grocery money." The monetary meanness of getting under way was never forgotten. Who could blame them for remembering just how bleak it was?

Jean Randall, the "Jacqueline of all trades," was the office antenna and control center. With a mind like a blotter and tied to sensitive ears, she was the splicer and verifier. The place was in too much of a hurry for memos. Who had a conversation with whom and about what often required inputs from Jean Randall. It was known from the first that the Thornton philosophy frowned on high salaries, relying on the incentive of stock options to goad key people. She was the interface with the designated crown princes eligible to purchase their shares in whatever agreed numbers for much less than the market price. Electro-Dynamics and 2301 Purdue were but a short rest stop. On March 15, 1954 the people constituting corporate headquarters shifted to 336 North Foothill Road in Beverly Hills, a glamorous post office address but a haphazard structure which had once housed a White Sewing Machine factory.

The Electro-Dynamics name trouble was behind them. Norm Moore had seen the high arcing ball as to the presidency and had fielded it well. Later when there were lots of vice presidents and they got together, Moore was often asked why Tex Thornton and Roy Ash

---

more famous in the Hollywood style "palimony" suit brought against actor Lee Marvin by sometime actress/singer Michelle Triola who sought a portion of his income for boudoir and pillow counsel over an extended period.

left him pretty much alone while always leaning a little on the others. "I have several advantages," Moore explained. "I stay 400 miles away. I always send money 'home' and never ask for any." All very true, but he never mentioned those early understanding gestures such as "grocery loans," or his easy surrender of his hard-won title, or that he had endured indignity and temper tantrums and long hours of perspiration, or that he was a consistent producer. Having performed well enough to please Charlie Litton—no small record—he enjoyed frolicking in the vastly different, freer, exhilarating atmosphere his new bosses created and extended its running room to him. He relished being given his relatively unrestricted, unbridled technological bluegrass in which to romp and gallop with neither rein nor halter. Charlie Litton predictably didn't like it when he heard it was his name which was not going to umbrella the whole thing. He claimed that was not part of his deal, but it was a harbinger of things down the pike. The owners of names merged into the company usually wanted guarantees of enhancement and that the original family builders' identity would remain once they were merged. In that respect, Charlie Vincent Litton surely got his wish.[2]

---

2. Litton upscaled to the empty corporate headquarters of that entertainment giant, the Music Corporation of America. Jules Stein, while in the University of Chicago learning to be an ophthalmologist, continued what he had done in off hours, playing saxophone and violin in college bands. One night, he had a disaster on his hands—found his orchestra booked for two separate dance dates. He asked his friend, a piano player named (unbelievably) William Goodheart, to collect some other musicians and play the other date. On that small stem was to grow MCA, established in 1924. It went big time in 1928 signing Guy Lombardo. It became a colossus, set its eyes on the vulnerabililty of the old studio and star system and moved in on Hollywood in 1937. He did well rounding up stars for representation (one of them a fellow named Ronald Reagan). Its landmark intrusion on the movie moguls was when Jimmy Stewart was sprung from his contractual obligations. He made his own deal with MCA help for the film, "Winchester" and became a millionaire. Stein headed into TV with his Revue Production in 1949 and eventually bought Universal Studios for its production home. Decca Records came in, too. It was on instruction of Attorney General Robert Kennedy that the Department of Justice set about to reduce the MCA clout by stating it could be in talent representation, or production, but not in both. MCA chose production and moved to Universal City.

Tex Thornton made a deal for the flossy address in Beverly Hills. Stein had commissioned Paul Williams, the black architect, to design the English Tudor style building. When it was decided to expand into a three building Litton complex in 1966, Williams was called again and made everything match. The office suite occupied by Thornton-Ash, Thornton-O'Green had a small space for their two secretaries.

The LITTON Adventure That Was

Where they all were when Litton was born as a full fledged company was something often recalled later, laughed about sometimes, and sentimentally regarded.

Several did show on Litton's premises in the early months. One was a graduate of the Massachusetts Institute of Technology. Computers had engaged him then, but he found himself "out back" at Autonetics, working on navigation upgrading. His budget was fourth class. There wasn't much discernible enthusiasm for what he was doing where he was—tinkering with inertial navigation. It was one of those "far out" technologies for which there was no immediate customer interest or demand, no readily identifiable futures market, a hard row to hoe in stony ground all the way. Tex Thornton was intrigued with his direction. They couldn't safely meet in public places such as a restaurant, as suspicions would be aroused. They could only "run into each other" as if by accident, talk rapidly in low tones feeling each other out. When both were satisfied, the hiring was actually done near a bus stop under a tree in the Westwood section of Los Angeles. None could have assessed an iota of the implications then. That simple binding handshake and subsequent transfer from one pay window to another opened the way to Litton's biggest, persisting, internal growth. It improved Free World security immeasurably and brought about safer, more economical operations of more than 100 of the world's airlines. That "new hire" was Dr. Henry Singleton. He was to stay six years, point Litton toward an excess of $3,000,000,000 in sales for various versions of that one item in the company's first quarter century.

A second was George Kosmetsky.[3] He had been working on book, subsequently published and called "Electronic Computers & Management Controls." An alumnus of Hughes Aircraft, he had left in September of 1953 when its "brain drain" dam burst. He first

---

It was in that office that a screen actor who seemed to have no movie future had been signed to be the TV host for "GE Theater." He went on to make speeches for GE and become the 40th President of the United States!

3. By Litton's 30th year, only Dr. Henry Singleton and George Kosmetsky had made FORBES magazine's *400 Richest* list. Singleton was said to have "at least $450,000,000" which ranked him 60th and Kosmetsky was estimated at $185,000,000 and 200th in line. Teledyne, which was founded by them, had about 28% of Litton's common stock.

flirted with a Robert McNamara job offer at Ford. He then gravitated to Chrysler which was more troubled, therefore more challenging, eager to listen. But his book had a hold on him, driving him to seek some place where he could develop applications of what he had been thinking and writing.

His strategy was to lay on a "Russian dinner" which he prepared himself, inviting Flora and Tex Thornton to join him. They barely got on the other side of their beet red *borscht* first course when Kosmetsky laid down his spoon to launch into how he wanted some place as a base to develop specialized computers. From that moment on only his wife and Flora paid attention to what they were eating. Kosmetsky found the Thornton enthusiasm matching his own. Before the evening was half over, he was told there was a place for him at Litton. That Kosmetsky foot in the door, his subsequent identification of a scientist named Floyd George Steele as a talent MUST for Litton, and that base being enlarged upon by Jack Connolly provided a capability so specialized yet so vast in scope that after they were all gone the created division would be sought by a nation. That was Saudi Arabia which entered into a $1,640,000,000 contract to design and build its whole air defense system. The concentrated effort was labeled the Data Systems Division. It became a significant economic and employment factor in Van Nuys, Calif., Colorado Springs, Colo., Salt Lake City, Utah, Lubbock, Texas and New Orleans, LA. The Saudi Arabia contract, much later caused it to spin off a whole new Litton Data Command Systems division in Agoura, Calif.

Both Singleton and Kosmetsky were frequently at odds with Roy Ash. When each had $225,000 in pocket, they took off for their own adventure which became Teledyne, Inc. Having had monumental influence on the direction of Litton Industries, they went into monument building themselves—and with great success.

Also, in that first 365 days, there was a walk-on in the austere Ash office in Beverly Hills. He came from about as prosaic and improbable a background as could be imagined. A wartime infantry captain out of Milledgeville Corners, Georgia, his first job after being demobilized was selling Dodge trucks. He went on to Greyhound, the bus company, but in its most static department, moving and storage. New ideas had hard going there. He had heard a rumor about Litton's stock option executive incentive plan wherein especially anointed people who demonstrated a capability to contribute to the firm's profit growth would get stock options below the market prices. He liked that better than perfunctory pats on the back and plaques on the wall. He tried a similar suggestion at Greyhound; its management seemed to be wearing earplugs when he talked. This new and eager entrant on Litton's scene was Harry J. Gray, a self urging, determined individual who had no doubts about what he wanted—what he wanted was all he could get. His scenario, as played page by page, had him as the Littonite who would not only run hard but range widest—components, business systems and equipment, ship-building, machine tools, material handling, and who would stand nearest the Thornton-Ash pinnacle as a Senior Executive Vice President. He was a very visible and authoritative spokesman. Stay with Litton two decades, he would, but the lack of maneuver room at the top eventually caused him to bolt for the ailing, old, sedate United Aircraft which was in hard times. He took it through a reincarnation as United Technologies. He came on as Litton's 200th employee hourly rate, $5.78. As CEO of UTC he was later listed as America's most highly compensated executive.

The fact of Litton's existence was of little moment to an adventuring married couple. More on their mind was what they saw around them driving from Washington for a job with Carboundum in Niagara Falls. The driver had topped out as a civil servant in Washington and had decided to go outward and upward in industry. He knew the workings of the nation's capital, its personages large and small, and he had a wide acquaintance with power sources. They were on the brink of a whole new lifestyle. Not only that, northern New York was in the grasp of its early winter stormy worst. As they drove by Niagara Falls, which seemed in low spirits that day, Mildred mournfully and accusingly looked at her husband, Joseph Imirie. "We never even came to Niagara Falls when we got married—what are we doing here now," she said. Imirie, a professional Irishman, had been what he described as "everybody's chief clerk" as the key civilian in the Army Air Force's A-3, or Operations staff. Shoulder to shoulder with him in th beginning had been a spate of young majors named Hoyt S. Vandenberg, Nathan F. Twining and Frank Armstrong. He had met that "numbers" fellow down the hall in the Statistical Control division. It made no strong dent in his consciousness except that people said he seemed to be promoted another rank every morning—that Col.

Charles B. Thornton. It never crossed his mind that fate would put himself and that same Thornton-in-a-hurry on meeting paths. There was an interim modicum of pinball dodging—first, the election of John F. Kennedy to the presidency which found Imirie offered the position of Assistant Secretary of the Air Force for Materiel. He was happy to be back in Washington. Nearly everyone he knew had blossomed from two to four stars on his shoulders. He exulted in their successes and in his good luck to be once more among them.

At an American Management Association meeting, Joe Imirie and Tex Thornton found themselves on the same panel. While dawdling through the chicken fricassee, he was told that Litton believed there was a place in its organizational structure for a "professional group," a means of harnessing specialty areas and expertise having to do with practically everything important to the human race. This time the setting—if he went back to business and industry—was to be California. It wasn't hard to say yes. In no time he saw himself riding almost as many different horses as he had in the Pentagon—geophysical exploration, medical products, specialty paper, microwave cooking, frozen foods, a string of restaurants and inns and magazine and book publishing.

George Scharffenberger[4] was a case of dual needsmanship. He saw nothing ahead of him that was exciting, promising or rewarding at International Telephone and Telegraph. His usual bubbling enthusiasms were going flat. Rather than burden his wife Marian with most of this unsettlement he was feeling, he found himself talking to his dog. This was to see how it sounded, and he was sure his dog wouldn't rumor his dilemma about. Finally, he told Marian one night he thought they should make a move. He had hardly done so when the phone rang. It was Glen McDaniel, Litton's legal counsel. He had known Scharffenberger a long time, dating from his own similar position as a troubleshooter for General David Sarnoff at RCA. McDaniel came right to the point. He needed someone to run a newly acquired

---

4. A Scharffenberger first move was to put retired Army Signal Corps General W. Preston (Red) Corderman on top of Westrex, and he later ran the Litton Washington office. Corderman was already a historical artifact, as having been a long-time member of the U.S. Army's Signal Intelligence Service, it was in his domain that both the German and Japanese codes had been broken during WW II.

activity. There was a whole world to step into from it. Coming as close to his "let's make a move" talks with his wife as it did, Scharffenberger was almost convinced there was such a thing as Extra Sensory Perception. He got all he bargained for, and more—not only a division—as he was soon running all of Litton's defense and space commitments.

The alumni records of Ball State University in Muncie, Indiana show them as having been impressed by one of their football tight ends. Right out of college, he started working in Huntington for a transformer manufacturer, Utah Radio. It was a part of Merritt, Chapman & Scott, the corporate fortress structure from which Louis Wolfson, a notorious corporate predator, would sally forth to do battle for promising properties. He was about to advance on the castle of his next target, crusty Sewell Avery and his Montgomery Ward.

Wolfson needed to accumulate cash to buy Montgomery Ward stock. He decided to sell various subsidiaries of his company—Merritt, Chapman & Scott. Among them was Utah Radio, UTRAD for short.

Arnie Kaufman was the general manager of UTRAD. When he learned of Wolfson's plan he decided to make an offer to buy UTRAD. He sounded out some others and they came up with enough cash, which added to his own, might be enough to make the purchase. But his biggest obstacle was an audience with Wolfson who seldom met with managers at Kaufman's level. But Arnie had a door-opener.

Frank Leahy was a member of Wolfson's board of directors. Leahy had been a renowned lineman for the legendary Four Horsemen of Notre Dame in the 1920s and later he became the head coach at Notre Dame where he established awesome records of wins and national championships. As a member of the parent company's board of directors, Leahy would make inspections of the UTRAD operation. His inspections happened to coincide with Notre Dame home games at South Bend, a short distance from Huntington. Arnie often lunched and dined with Leahy and naturally accorded him all the courtesies due a board member.

Kaufman called Leahy, told him of his plan to buy UTRAD and asked him to intercede with Wolfson. Leahy was happy to do so, and

Arnie got his audience. That led to his purchase of UTRAD and his sale of UTRAD to Litton and to his outstanding career with Litton.

Two to be caught on the fly much later were well off in the boondocks, not even dark horses or tardy starters. As Litton was being christened, one was at the Naval Ordnance Laboratory in Silver Springs, Maryland. He got there via a degree in engineering from Iowa State University, where he had once played clarinet in its Ames symphony. He had resisted private industry until electrical engineers were beckoned by contractors playing about the edges of space. When it came to program management, and particularly out there at the uncharted and mysterious extremes, he was a recognized whiz. Perhaps such status wasn't all that unusual for a clarinet player, but it was downright phenomenal in the case of Fred W. O'Green. Son of an immigrant mailman in Mason City, Iowa, it pained him to see his father dig down for that half dollar each clarinet lesson cost. After a dozen lessons or so, he became a Tom Sawyer type tootler—and started giving lessons to neighborhood kids for a half dollar each. That relieved his father of that 50 cents a week obligation producing a situation wherein he could pay his own way, learn, and show a profit. He grew up in a family and time when everyone, as soon as possible, was expected to pitch in and work hard. An early pragmatist, he had great confidence in himself, was nearly unerring in his evaluations of people, was accurate in analysis of problems and could make recommendations that brought about solutions.

Lockheed shoehorned him out of civil service and into its Missiles and Space division at Sunnyvale, California. The X-7, the first reentry type missile; the surveillances MIDAS and SAMOS systems and that standard satellite payload propulsion system, the Agena,[5] were all his babies. Agena put more payloads into orbit than any other

---

5. Lockheed's head man, Dan Haughton, and also C.L. "Kelly" Johnson, saw a company interest in the Agena project. Fred O'Green gave them a 90-minute presentation on all the problems—leading to his strong recommendation that Lockheed not get into it. Casually, as they walked along to lunch in the executive dining room, the project was given the go-ahead, and O'Green was assigned the program. Their reasoning was that since he had such a comprehension of the difficulties, he was the best man to lick them. He did—and in less than a year! Had he not done so, America would have been even farther back of the Russians at the inception of the space race.

Pegasus-like devices. His colleague, Ray Kent, said Fred's forte was to recognize capabilities of people and build on them.

By 1964, General Bernard A. Schriever of the U.S. Air Force Ballistic Missile Division gave him its first major award officially recognizing his key importance in the space catch-up action after the Soviet's Sputnik I aroused an incredulous America to the fact that it was trailing in the celestial sphere.

His Swedish ancestors spelled the family name Augren. Ellis Island was so full of immigrant Irish, the classifier wrote the name phonetically—O'Green. Fred's grandfather saw no reason to argue and O'Green stayed. The moment would come when he would be made the iron man at Litton's rudder as Roy Ash departed under pressure.

The top executive at Landis was Milburn "Metz" Hollengreen who was grafted on the machine tool business in 1926 by the Landis brothers. He was a man who built with care, a statesman in his field. He operated as well offshore as in country, and he planned well. It was in his best laid plan, the carefully prepared succession after him that Fate intervened cruelly. To sort out his life he sold the company to Litton who thereby acquired what was called "the Cadillac" of them all, the Landis Tool Company in Waynesboro, Pa., in England and France. It was Litton that gave him an avenue to rebuild and leave his heritage in good hands.

Almost in tandem beyond the horizon was a perturbed former president of the Machine Tool Builders Association. Well up in the superstructure of the Sundstrand Corporation, he was at odds frequently with some of his bosses about their decisions, and particularly the moves they had made while he was off attending to overall association business. His dismay was mounting in direct parallel with Litton's rising belief in the electronic potential of numerical controls in the machine tools field. He was Burnell Gustafson, the offstage answer to Litton's need.

When he left his old employers with no reluctance, he joined his new one with alacrity. Under his expert guidance, when Litton would be asked where it stood in the machine tool field, he could be evasive and say "somewhere in the top ten," but the truth was, Litton was nearly always in the top five.

75

There were actually jillions of electronics companies. They were hard to remember for their individual strengths. Some didn't last past one or two widgets which gave them limited life. The ones at the lower end of the spectrum were hard to recall even by name. Once Litton was in motion, the problem of how to stick its head up over the crowd was by no means small. Yet, attracting that standout kind of a company personality was critical for many reasons. In order to be paid attention, there had to be someone who would not only tell why, but convince hearers it was important. First, it was Tex Thornton who did most of it. Then Roy Ash got in the swing of it as a panel member, talking to trade publications, participation in the right professional societies and associations. It needed more constancy of attention. A hard economic fact of life away off in Cuba was about to make an indelible imprint on Litton. Out of the disaster of a failed automobile agency in Havana, Crosby M. Kelly[6] wandered westward across the U.S. In Los Angeles at a convivial barfly encounter session somebody mentioned that there was a new corporate enterprise on the Southern California scene called Litton Industries. Kelly wondered aloud who was heading it, and was told. A light went on in his head! Could it be the same Thornton who had brought all those Whiz Kids from the

---

6. Crosby Kelly hired the author, who signed in Jan. 2, 1963. He said he had no idea what his role would be, to sit around, talk with, study and come up with suggestions—if Litton liked, that's what he'd do. The resulting title was a corporate nonesuch, Corporate Director, Special Missions and Projects. Litton would be 10 years old, come fall. My suggestion was a TIME cover. "Ten years," scoffed Kelly, "what's that? I've been chasing a TIME cover for two years!" But was there ever suggestion that Litton's growth curve was so straight up it would make a top-to-bottom single column to show it? Kelly's jaw dropped, phoned Marshall Berges, TIME's bureau chief in Los Angeles. He called his editor and Tex Thornton was the cover story. He asked for a ghost-written article about Tex for a military publication drum-beating inertial navigation, which was done. Two days later Thornton himself came to my cubbyhole office article in hand asking "Will you work with me on a lot of special things, speeches and such? I love the way you write." When at 25th anniversary time in 1978, Board members Ransom Cook proposed and Dr. Jayne B. Spain seconded, "there should be a book about Litton, Fred O'Green said there was no need to seek an outside writer, that it could be given to me! My longevity stretch as a Litton employee was 27 years. I was allowed to work on my 80th birthday in 1989 setting a geriatric record never equaled, and when Tex Thornton died on Nov. 24, 1981, it was said that there was no special relationship our equal! When given a 65th birthday bash, he came and handed me a letter demanding that I read it. It said: "Come to work tomorrow as if this birthday never happened. You can work as long as you wish or until you drop dead, whichever comes soonest!"

Pentagon to the Ford Motor Co. in Detroit? Tex would overlook that he had failed with an automobile dealership. Kelly called the next day. He and Tex caught up on each other. It was a fast developing Thornton conviction that here was exactly the media minstrel he needed, one who could bedazzle, articulate, excite, even spellbind.

This led to the Crosby Kelly odyssey, providing Litton Industries with an oral orchestrator of elegance. It gave him a stage from which to glow and shine—and, ahem, provide him with a needed novelty in his life then, weekly compensation. There might have been an electronic company here, and another there, but Kelly, a vocal virtuoso, was to have most to do with the verbalizing and convincing as to the Litton merits. George Scharffenberger once said, and seriously, that he thought a dozen of Litton's early stock value points were because of Crosby Kelly and the way he made the promise ring true to a listener. The listener could be a journalist, analyst, or a cocktail conversationalist. It wasn't all an act by any means—Kelly correctly saw what the dimensions might be, and rhetorically asked why not? Why not, indeed? He believed and made others do the same.

The money man who would chase Litton's fortunes and bring them to columns of figures longer than anyone else was in a most unusual setting. Litton would have 3,500 accounts in 400 offshore banking institutions. It had to be adept in as many as 30 or more currencies, as well as their always changing value relationship to each other. This future keeper of the cash box on Litton's natal day had been a student in Fordham University, and also a part-time "private eye" for the Thoroughbred Racing Association. The job called for him to lurk about the stables on the far side of the tracks from the grandstand. He policed not only the stalls but paddocks attempting to ferret out unsavory Nathan Detroits, who held far less charm for his employers than they did for Damon Runyon. They were not above tampering with the diets and bloodstreams of the horses to insure alluring odds, yet alter the running speeds enough to protect the bookies from being plundered by some wagering oversight. This horseshoe and currycomb environment was not his choice for a life's work. As quickly as he could, he grabbed his Fordham diploma and ran for the respected accounting house, Touche, Ross. That meant that the first glimpse of Litton by red haired Joseph T. Casey was Litton balance sheet in a file folder in that office. No horse ever gave its jockey a rougher, or more demanding ride than the one Casey was to know when Litton went into its troubled decade. He was to experience cash flow distresses and staggering interest charges. He had to field and answer all those barbed questions which came at him from every compass point. Some of them, in times of stress, he even asked himself.

In Cincinnati, Ohio a near miracle was homing in on Litton, a blonde woman executive who was too busy with her own unbelievable challenge to look to the left or right. While Hughes was having the full Thornton attention, she, by inheritance, came into possession of an old company called Alvey-Ferguson. It was founded on the unwillingness of men to wrestle beer barrels; it had evolved into the most sophisticated variety mover of unit handling of vast inventories by item and category. The bankers, once the will was read, implored her to sell. As she wavered, all the old time employees begged her not to do so. "You run it," they told her. "And we'll help you."

Because of her belief in handicapped people as a usually overlooked resource, more than 40 of those who pleaded with her to stay were wheelchair bound, or without an arm or a leg, or blind and deaf. They were not sure how a new owner would react to them, or if it would be as compassionate as she. After all, it was she who insisted that one in every ten of them should be recruited from among the physically impaired. Jayne Baker Spain set her jaw and elected to take the front office.

Litton waited until January of 1966 to see materials and unit handling as a prime place for electronics to be added. In those fifteen years, Jayne B. Spain, an on-the-job training neophyte rose to great stature in her industry, never failed to profit in any of those years, and exhibited herself as a social conscience-oriented executive in more than 20 countries of the world. She was an Elizabeth Arden devotee who was never seen other than impeccably dressed or coifed. She became Litton's first female division president and its first woman member of the firm's board of directors. She always said her principal contribution to the executive suite was that she cleaned up the language, but she had remarkable effect on thought processes, too. In the time of the "token woman" and the "token ethnic," she was a formidable rebuttal. She had proven herself as a business executive first, then all the rest of it followed. She was one of several from Litton's top shelf sent for by Washington. In her case she was to be the Vice Chairman of the Civil Service Commission. Her role: To make possible more high level positions for women in government. She was skillful in both opening career doors as well as lifting promotional ceilings.

Hardly anyone looked less like a revolutionary than Monroe's homegrown comer. He had been there early enough to merit only $14 a week at the pay window. But he was a good observer, gave right answers when asked and started up the responsibility ladder. One of the things he observed was a company principal that resented rather than applauded the commissions eager and dedicated salesmen were able to reap. Another item he witnessed was where the company's stock was owned, and how brusquely, even ruthlessly that ownership was treated. The biggest block was a voting prerogative of the founder's son, and a substantial amount could be put alongside it by a cousin. The cousins didn't know each other well, were separated by residences in Kalamazoo, Michigan and New Jersey, but at a company meeting the suggestion was made that they room together. That led to a long night of conversations between Malcolm Monroe and cousin George from out west. They decided to go for broke and overthrow the front office.

While many in the company sympathized, they were fearful the cousins wouldn't win and their jobs would be jeopardized. But Fred Sullivan was young, knew what they were doing was for the good of the enterprise. He threw in with them. If the palace coup failed, he could always go elsewhere. It didn't fail, when the fog of battle cleared, Fred Sullivan would be in the saddle. He had more ideas than shingles on the roof. One of them was to spread Monroe over the business machines field. His trouble was that while the New Jersey cousin saw him as the company's man-on-horseback, the Michigan one saw him on a Shetland pony. They both agreed eventually that they couldn't go-it-alone—they had to be a part of some company. And that led to Litton.

How to do that walk through the minefield of conflicting opinions and figures and come up with a working recommendation time after time takes a special breed of cat. He is the perennial "fixer." In a highly diversified company, he gets all the work he can handle, gets to know airline schedules as well as commuters are familiar with inter-urban buses, seldom sees his wife and children. Usually he is never sent for until all the alibis have been exhausted or found wanting and the situation is about as bad as it can be. Grady Warwick, out of Denver University, and an accountant in the backroom of Kistler's, a stationery house, hurdled financial problems and solutions barriers higher than the mountains he grew up in. He could see through whatever it was, explain it in the detail required, offer sensible remedial suggestions and make the hardest decisions palatable because they were logical and worked. He and Fred O'Green converged at Litton's Guidance & Control Systems division the same year—1962. Wherever Fred went after that, so did Grady Warwick. And when Litton was in the valley of its troubles, wherever the sores were most evident, Grady Warwick had ticket, did travel.

It was something he did half defiantly in June of 1919 that was to make an Explorers Club member an authentic museum piece.

He filed incorporation papers in Wilmington, Delaware for something he called The Aero Service Company. That filing date gave World War I pilot Virgil Kauffman both satisfaction and amusement. It caused KLM, the Royal Dutch Airlines, much discomfort and required an amendment of its claims. Kauffman, on a transatlantic KLM flight to Johannesburg, South Africa, post WW II, gently rebuked the Dutch stewardess serving him drinks. He showed her his paper napkin which stated KLM was the *world's oldest flying company*. Kauffman told her it wasn't true. She was sufficiently distressed to call the captain from his cockpit. He said sternly it was well known that a young Netherlander, Lt. Albert Plesman, had gotten from Queen Wilhelmina herself a blessing for "the first of the world's flying companies, when Koninklijke (Royal Dutch) Luchvaart Maatschapik KLM was founded on October 7, 1919."

"Wrong," said Kauffman stubbornly, "my Aero Service Company was incorporated in *June*, 1919."

Word of this pioneering one-upsmanship shook the mighty KLM headquarters at Schiphol in Amsterman which was then serving 227,230 miles to 109 cities in 72 countries. Since then, KLM revised its claim to read "the world's first commercial airline." Kauffman didn't like to dwell on the airline business too much as whatever he had done on aerial surveying of the world, he too had wanted to establish the first passenger service, and in that he had failed. On the other hand, had it been a success, Litton would never have interested him, nor would it have been interested in him.

The Dutch apple pie recipe that was to turn into a good genie for Litton was the handiwork of motherly Mahala Stouffer. She first wrought the miracle for her two boys, Vernon and Gordon, then went public with it at a small lunch counter she started in downtown Cleveland. It was hard for workmen within a mile of the place to resist and whatever else they ate there, topping it off with a generous slice of that pie.

Her son, Vernon, an industrious dynamo with big ideas, took it from there into a string of restaurants, hotels and into frozen foods. He was a man of parts, had a yacht, and once owned the Cleveland Indians baseball team. He was unnerved by a decision he couldn't make—the selection of a talented and able son-in-law over his own son. A merger, he decided, could fatten his personal treasury, and the surviving company would have to make the decision about continuance of the management in the right hands. The trail from the Dutch apple pie recipe to the merger with Litton was accomplished just a few days before Litton's highest stock price was reached. Litton opted for the son-in-law, and from its perspective, it was the only choice. To Vernon, it had always been the hard choice; for Litton, it was easy.

When one's customers are the likes of Radio Free Europe beaming programs to all the Soviet Union's satellite countries, the Voice of America reaching for a world, and even Evita Peron for voice of hope transmissions, nothing should be surprising. And if one is reared in a family of affluence, known nothing but the best schools and finds himself trying to put a saddle on one of America's most troublesome problems—heading the high school dropouts away from being unskilled and unemployable pointed for a lifetime of welfare ties—he should be immune to shock as well. Yet they were coming together when the Litton ferment was on, and they, with a weapons systems conceptualizer who had done sparkling, imaginative time in both industry and government were to see Litton in the market for sociological contracting and the knowledge industry.

Alfred Strogoff at Adler Electronics in New Rochelle, N.Y. was a builder of transportable UHF, VHP and other communications systems. It came into Litton by merger in 1963. Dr. S.S. Uslan was recruited in 1960 to set up the training for assemblers for Litton's inertial navigation systems, which required a highly specialized in-house skill training course. And John Rubel, alumnus of Hughes Aircraft and General Electric, was talked off his chair as Deputy Director, Research and Engineering in the Department of Defense, and into a Litton task of technical planning. They converged under Litton auspices, joined forces and brainstorming tendencies and took the company off in many directions—controversial directions, tumultuous directions getting Litton headlines, deep involvements, profits, but very little credit in public quarters. They were a triad which provided Litton with a caring stance—when caring was not supposed to be a characteristic of businesses or their leadership.

Bob Lentz was best prepared mentally for what he would encounter in Litton. As an infantryman in Europe, he switched to the 533rd Combat Engineers. The 97th Infantry Division he was in went home. He was sent with his unit to the Pacific and New Guinea. When orders were written for the land invasion of Japan, that unit was to be in the lead and suffer major punishment on the Japanese southern island of Kyushu. It was to draw down Nippon's defenses, reducing the opposition of the main island of Honshu. At least a 50% loss was anticipated—and then, President Truman elected going atomic into Hiroshima and Nagasaki. Robert Lentz made up his mind that he had reason to be calm about everything after that—a needed characteristic for a corporate legal counsel.

Insiders knew a special relationship dated from times well before Litton's formation. There was an unspoken but real "three man club at the top, which no one else was asked to join, and if anyone leaves, he will not be replaced." Two of them, of course, were Tex Thornton and Roy Ash, whose acquaintance time dated from the Army Air Corps Statistical Control days in the Pentagon. The third member was Glen McDaniel. From a boyhood in Seymour, Texas, he transitioned through Southern Methodist University in Dallas and Columbia Law School in New York, into the Manhattan offices of Sullivan & Cromwell. He had played fullback on the Seymour High "Panthers," where he was the despair of old Coach Gerald. He was a slow starter in the backfield. "Creepin' Jesus," he was called, because of his tardiness after the snap which invited bumps for him on the line of scrimmage.

One of the high spirited rival elevens was Haskell. That team had 140 pounds of pugnacious energy, sometimes a tackle and others a linebacker, named "Bates" (a designation still used by old cronies) Thornton. He had delighted in limiting McDaniel's running game. They really didn't know each other then, except that Haskell was frequently discomfited when Seymour had to punt or try field goals. McDaniel was unfailingly precise about that, obviously one who delighted in set piece encounter rather than being a broken field dazzler.

From his earliest moments at his books, he was thought a sure thing to become a lawyer. His father was a judge and his mother a school teacher. There was a neatness and orderliness born in him, along with a hearty respect for words and their polished use. When youthful Glen McDaniel dreamed, though, he did not see himself involved in the drama of persuading a jury; in that sugar plum world, he saw himself as an actor. He might be in law school, but he sought every extracurricular opportunity to comport onstage. Then one night in New York, he had a Gothamized version of Gethsemane—he let his head rule him. His choice was to turn his back on the shakiness of the footlights for the steadiness of fanfolds and briefs. He decided to use his forensic skills on juries and became very effective as a trial lawyer. Not many corporate legal practitioners were. For what Litton was about to be, he was a carefully shaped asset.

World War II saw him in the Navy. He finished as Chairman of the Navy Board of Contract Appeals. He became especially adept in untangling hastily drawn contractual messes.

His intention to return to Sullivan & Cromwell was altered by RCA's General David Sarnoff who tested him through several corporate positions into eventually running RCA's Washington office. That was when the U.S. Congress was finding the RCA effort for TV an inviting target for excess profit taxes. Before the Radio Manufacturers Association, McDaniel delivered an impassioned plea for that body to oppose mightily such measures with all its resources. A whole loose bag of fast developing and not too well understood varieties of American manufacturing got together in the RMA successor organization, the Electronic Industries Association—and McDaniel became its first fulltime president. From that vantage point, he knew everyone in the business, and they knew him—the large, medium, the small, even the miniscule. McDaniel was a walking encyclopedia on the electronics business. This, plus law and his courting of the acting Muse made him formidable for both the Litton then and to be.

Out of New Britain, Pa., a town of less than 400, Len Erb graduated from the Valley Forge Military Academy, and won nomination to the U.S. Naval Academy. He graduated as a young Naval officer in 1942 into a succession of submarines and destroyers. Len Erb knew what it was like in rough seas, playing hide and seek with those who would sink and kill him if they could. He knew that one depended on people, team spirit, and strong resolve when one's butt was in a sling. He applied the same principles wherever he was to be after that.

Finishing by skippering the POLARIS submarine U.S.S. Abraham Lincoln into 1963, he retired and a year later joined Litton's Guidance and Control Systems division. He rose to VP for business development.

The Ingalls Shipbuilding operations by then had seen a succession of chiefs. He spent a year as the top hand at Amecom, in Maryland, adjacent to Washington. He had heard the thunder and lightning being thrown from the capital's many vocal critics of Litton's ship manufacturing. By then, he knew well the people being complained about. His Navy sources being good, he was hearing that side with poopdeck and fantail profanity at its raunchiest for emphasis of their displeasure.

When his time came in 1974—the Presidency of Ingalls Shipbuilding—his approach to its hemorrhaging was pure Len Erb. Not one to devote full time ever to the fo'c's'le, he sought to let every worker on the Ingalls roster know who he was. He walked among them. He made the headquarters staff serve among them. He could see in short order what the problems were in the yard. He could tell the Navy all the ways they weren't helping. From that point he steered a course through all the reefs, submerged and showing. Man of the hour, no, man willing to give the course long, carefully directed and meaningful hours, he was.

The cast of characters ran on and on. Some were headliners to be, others vital middle managers, but one thing sure—those who lasted and counted and will always be remembered were tempted in, tempered and taught not in a business school, but at that demanding regiment of "Thornton Tech." The composer, Harry Warren, wrote a song called "I Found a Million Dollar Baby in a 5-and-10 Cent Store." That's about the only place Tex Thornton didn't see as a recruitment source. "Million Dollar Baby" was a hit, and so, over time, would his Litton Industries be.

SPECIAL SITUATION #7

EVOLUTION BY EMBRACE

After the first decision — the acquisition of Litton Industries of California — a second had to be made fast. It was to obligate the company's prospective cash flow to the several high technology sectors which seemed to coincide with the direction they had taken.

It was done quickly. From early conversations, selections were made on technologies which appeared promising. Their potential could be swollen by both internal effort and merger. Those selections were military and aircraft electronics such as inertial navigation, industrial controls or specialized computers, electron tubes and radar, business machines, x-ray and electronic components.

It was almost as if they were in such a hurry, so impressed by the time factor, they couldn't wait a full twelve months to let it be known how well they were doing and why they thought they had such a hold on the future. They set July 31, 1954 as the end of the *fiscal year*, a year they were barely nine months into.

While an Abraham Lincoln could mistake yet another mournful memorial occasion as of momentary and only passing importance when he wrote the remarks he'd used at Gettysburg, Tex Thornton took no such chance. What Lincoln said went into schoolbooks, history, and in some places was chiseled in marble. The Thornton feeling was that if what he had in mind worked out, he should have what his original intentions were down in black and white. He had a definite concern about how what they were doing would look on paper in years to come. He labored over the first annual report text himself. He wanted it written his way. And in such a way that those who came later into the company or who would look in from the outside could sense the certainty and confidence Litton directed. It probably never occurred to him what an attractive bull's eye he might be making of himself if his approach faltered. If that was to be the case, the "I told you so" chorus was always tuned up and ready to be vocal.

His second paragraph zeroed in.

"From the outset," he wrote in his firm, forward slanted longhand, "the company's management *planned* first to establish a base of profitable operations in advanced electronic development and manufacturing. Using this base, the plan contemplates building a major electronics company by developing new and advanced programs and by acquiring others having potential in complementing fields. The *plan* calls for research and development utilizing revenues from operations in those directions which will allow us to achieve substantial quality production and additional significant profits. The plan is designed to establish strong proprietary product values and a 'broad base' on which to grown — a profitable balance between commercial and military customers and an integrated but diversified line of electronic products. Your company has followed this plan."

Five times in that declarative paragraph he made reference to a *plan*. He sought to convey there was firm direction and a clear picture at the top as to how to proceed and what the appearance and conduct of Litton's growth would be.

In the highly successful musical, "Finian's Rainbow", for which E.Y. "Yip" Harburgh did the book and Burton Lane the music, they had Finian as a sentimental Irishman who talked endlessly of a favorite place he called Glocca Morra. There was a touching and often reprised song, "How Are Things in Glocca Morra?" As the *play* lilted along to its close, Finian's daughter is finally asked the whereabouts of Glocca Morra. She explains that it doesn't exist — except in her father's head. In parallel with that show's long run on Broadway at the 46th Street Theater in the late '40s, what was to be Litton was just a niggling, needling, haunting, taunting sort of mirage which was chasing around in Thornton's thoughts. It was a mental plaything to which he resorted for contrast and comfort when at Ford and Hughes Aircraft. He sensed a better day. His clock was running and a treadmill at his feet exercised him, but it was taking him nowhere. Decisions cried out to be made but they were beyond his charter to make. Opportunities were lost daily from inaction. Horizons beckoned to be explored. He couldn't get investors' interest. Worse yet, on occasion he was told flatly not to pursue such will o'wisps. His "Glocca Morra" was a fleeting rainbow end off yonder where he could provide an atmosphere and an environment which would turn him and others on, not off.

Now it was in his hands.

The plan was always a conversation piece. There were those who actually believed it was handwritten on a piece of parchment locked away in some Litton version of Ft. Knox. It conjured up cameos of "Tex" Thornton, Roy Ash and Bill Jamieson — the trio listed as the board of directors in that first annual report — pulling out this Holy Writ[1] as a mariner would his charts in a reef-infested ocean. From it was determined whether to give a little right or left rudder, or add some sail. Of course, it was nothing like that, but who gains from knocking charming legends when they grow, don't hurt and serve well?

There were several outlines of the plan, one of the earliest being Roy Ash's which had at its hub "Leadership in Electronics". The sections were labeled industrial controls, business machines, military electronics, aircraft electronics, electron tubes, radar, x-ray, electronic components and communications equipment.

Beyond that were names of companies eligible to be sought which would both fit and complement. In a way it was a reverse spin on Ralph Waldo Emerson's discourse on building a better mousetrap.[2] Ash saw several firms around that were picking up one product companies that were leaders in a field, but which did not progress. He reasoned that it was not the better mousetrap which made the best sense, but the companies which had the pathways to widening markets and could be built on, expanded and could develop a range of products to meet special demands. That is what made Charlie Litton's small company so attractive. Even though it was pre-eminent in electron tube technology, it contained proprietary resources and many other exploitable product directions. His established product excellence entitled him to a hearing on any new proposal. It was from that analysis

---

1. PLAN became Tex Thornton's ubiquitous "four letter" word. It was said almost as often as he breathed. A mini-legend grew, that there was, indeed, a mapped direction, an outline kept in the office safe, always consulted, read and re-re-read prior to making a move. At a dining-in meeting of old faithful at Guidance & Control in Woodland Hills, Roy Ash was asked point-blank how big a document it must be, what it set forth, could he tell them? Roy said, straight-facedly that it existed. "Before coming here tonight, I went to our safe, took the dial in my hand, did the combination known only to Tex and me. When the door swung open, I looked to the right and left to be sure I was alone, and read it. It didn't take long, only a single line was written there, I suppose I can trust you?" He paused, and his audience was about to bust its collective blood vessels. A chorus of PLEASE, PLEASE came in a wave toward him. It says: "When in doubt, do the right thing."

2. Emerson said: "If a man write a better book, preach a better sermon, or make a better mousetrap than his neighbor, though he build his house in the woods, the world will make a beaten path to his door."

that decisions were made to focus initially on components, specialized computers, inertial navigation, x-ray and radar.

The essence of entrepreneurship[3] is to organize, manage and assume risks of a business or enterprise. That was the diet on which they fed. The assumption of risk was the adventure. Organizing the effort meant selection of people for roles who had heads full of ideas and who could steer with imagination to sensible applications. The "managing" had to be there to choose best courses, targets, allocations of responsibilities to right hands, and coming up with necessary financing. From all these nuances, the firm's portrait would be brush stroked into bold relief. The *plan* was an umbrella in whose shade there was room for interpretation and technological maneuverability to cross fertilize where appropriate. The founder was wise enough to know that in bringing together what had been separate companies — some of which had competed fiercely when on their own — would take a while to adjust, associate and cooperate. Ash saw no reason to hurry or harry them from above.

How differently does man perceive things! But then, perception is very personal, part of one's baggage, making him hostage to his experience. The way the philosopher Eric Hoffer saw the period in which Litton's meteor-like blazing skyward took place was that — "we are all condemned to death at birth, and life is a bus ride to the place of execution. All of our struggling and vying is about seats on the bus and the ride is over before we know it!" In other words, not much time is available to individual human beings. A Tex Thornton not only knew that, but was determined to make the most of his allotment. Not for him to sit on a bench somewhere, feed squirrels and

---

3. The Ash description of an entrepreneur likened him to a hunter of big game. He doesn't exactly know what's coming, or what he's going to do about it, but he has confidence that he'll figure out something when the time comes and will ultimately conquer. He also allowed that being an entrepreneur was not too much different from a Las Vegas trip for high stakes play — he must learn as he goes, or he'll not survive. Entrepreneurs are restless by nature, Ash says. It's hard to keep them around. They want money. They like the entrepreneurial work environment which lets them rule their particular roost. They want to be able to fail as well as succeed as long as the latter happens more often. They aim to be measured for effectiveness as well as efficiency. They have a desire to practice the art of spending money rather than the skill of saving money (he says bureaucrats tend to try to save money, but don't know what to do with it after they've saved it. Entrepreneurs invest their way out of their problems rather than conserve their way out).

lament about the portion of the calendar which he'd already used up. He liked more the attitude of Thomas Edison, the inventor, who declared that — "nothing works by itself! *You've got to make* the damned thing work!" And when one of Edison's employees asked him about rules in his shop, he was told sharply, "Hell, there ain't no rules around here."

At Litton Industries, what a bus ride it was. Everyone was trying to outthink, outdo, outshine and outreach. They all were collected in a kind of venturesome talent pool which could be turned off and on at will. The "Off" option didn't occur very often. Coming of age as he had in those depressed turbulent, discontented '30s had instilled within Tex Thornton cautions and warnings about the folly of trying to fly without wings. He had reverence though, for new ideas and appreciation for the sort of people who could produce and carry them out. He saw the way to have a Litton Industries attract these special people.

Initial growth would come by careful seeking of companies already in existence with such people demonstrably meeting a need in the marketplace that commanded for them respect, compensation and profits. Having studied the automobile industry from youthful participation in a not-too-successful dealership all the way to "mahogany row" of the Ford Motor Company, he marveled at the virulence of the fever which had once been conjured up by automobiles — their assembly, their ownership, their effect on lifestyle and progress. A kind of enduring homage to that first inventor of the wheel, it was. Hundreds of companies, large and small, were said to have added their strengths to what became General Motors. Alone, most of them had been weak, suffering from malnutrition or disinterest, and vulnerable to crumbling with the first signs of adversity.

The electronics industry was taking multiple routes to its inheritance. It was experiencing rough road it its early stage. In Tex Thornton's assessment of the prospects, he felt one could only be in it with strength and diversity to survive. Instead of waiting for small companies' frailties to become apparent, he determined on courtship when those being courted were looking their best. He wanted them to see and savor the rewards he could offer: securities appreciation for their holdings given in exchange for ownership, stock options for shares available well below the market prices, the management positions held prior to acquisition, and continue building. When needed, he could dangle financing from Litton's treasury. He offered other carrots or enhancements, such as the assurance that he would join them with complementary enterprises, either acquired or developed. He would even graft new life on units stalled or stagnant. It was a sparkling prospect indeed. And he wanted the decision to join Litton to be theirs, that they come happily anticipating better things.

Never far from his thoughts, though, was that this sustained building ordeal would demand that he penalize himself the most. After that, in order, his family, his close associates and all the way down to rank and file employees in terms of long hours, absences from home, and mindsets which made it difficult for others to break in on their concentrations. Those around him were even uncomfortable when thinking of taking an earned holiday to which they were entitled. Working weekends were normal, as was making do with five hours sleep or less. Tex himself would get up at 3 a.m., go to the hanger in Van Nuys where his own plane was held in perpetual readiness. He would take off eastward to meet the rising sun and escort it in as if fearful it would dawdle without his coercion. He did some of his best, uninterrupted thinking under such circumstances. When he wanted company to bounce ideas around, he would make random calls to snoozing executives who were asked to join him. A kind of nocturnal Russian roulette, their wives said.

Flying was an ever present mode at Litton. "Red eye" aerial crossings of continents and oceans were much favored. People who once believed themselves incapable of sleep on planes found out they could, usually from sheer exhaustion as commitments telescoped one day into another. Those in Litton harness who did such things could work a full day before taking off on either end of the line. It rumpled the suit, but it saved a hotel bill. Everything was right out of Ben Franklin's "Poor Richard's Almanac" (he said a penny saved was a penny earned). The Litton custom saved not only money but time.

Roy Lawrence Ash was the "inside" man, a reinforcement to the Thornton "outside" tendencies. In Ash's garden grew numbers, currencies, sums and balances. The Thornton milieu was visionary as to goals, talents which excited him, the marketing and selling of ideas, and innovations however identified and benefiting the corporate health. Bill Jamieson, with his electrical engineering orientation, was of pure technological bent, gadget and widget minded. His lab was the altar at which he worshipped.

With Thornton, every day was a fertility rite, ideas-a-borning. Ash, the money man, fenced it all into manageable proportions. Thornton wandered conceptual pathways, embroidering them with his own gut feelings. He seldom found himself fazed for workable solutions. Ash weighed the discomforting details, facilities and funding. If vaudeville had one-liner jokes, Ash had one-liners which were pokes and prods to getting things done. If he were going to be out of the office, the list was handed to Tex who could both follow through and add on. They covered a wide field — purchase of building sites, tax adjustment on acquisitions, plant visits, board meetings, employee profit sharing,[4] stock distribution to key personnel, financial information to customers, or pricing guideline.

Ash was assigned the "logical mind" among other descriptions. As cash flow generation assumed greater and greater importance, he was widely admired for his mind's quickness in such matters. Wizardry in money handling was quickly identified as Litton's very bloodstream, almost from Day ONE. Ash was uneasy with engineers and marketers on the upper corporate shelf. People such as Singleton,

---

4. Litton employee participation in the company's success ranged from stock options available at less than the market price for executives to the stock purchase plan for those who could have 4% taken from their paychecks to which Litton would add enough to make purchases at 80% of the market price. Any raise which went above $25,000 had to be cleared at the top. Thornton contributed his share to the "lean and hungry" legends by being notorious among his peers for never having any money in his pocket when it came time to pick up the check. He was ganged up on one night at Club "21" in New York. All ten attendees at a lavish dinner came without money and instructed the waiter to give the check to Tex. He didn't have it. George Scharffenberger, who had plotted it all had to leave the rest of the diners — including Tex — as hostages while he went back to his hotel and retrieved his wallet to bail everyone out.

Jack Benny always made a public spectacle of himself as a skinflint which was a comedy ploy, but Thornton used his empty pockets to project Litton as a careful place about money. He, like Benny, could be privately generous and was — but not with the lights on. When Robert Berry was head of Litton's Washington office and Thornton stayed at the Madison Hotel when in town, Berry had the Bell Captain keep track of Thornton "shorts" in tipping, which he corrected after Tex left town. Thornton always told people he loved to stay at the Madison because it wasn't one of those places where ". . .everybody has his hand out." He was always very well treated. He never did know that Berry came along behind him making financial amends.

Kosmetsky, Sullivan and others had their reasons for concerns about this, each in his own time. They made no bones about wanting their tie or "special relationship" to be direct to Tex Thornton bypassing the stringencies Ash might impose on them and their sectors of interest. It worked awhile that way, but could not endure and they knew it.

Ash was every Littonite's fascination piece, so sharp, so questioning, so penetrating, so difficult to fathom. Gordon Murphy, who was to pass through Data Systems, and the Litton International Development Corporation said: "I don't know why it is, but every time Ash calls me my palms sweat." Cool he was, and then some. Some said he was downright cold, one who considered other men as insertable and disposable parts in the corporate machine. They were "known quantities", or "capabilities" who could be matched with requirements. Yet as a family man, he had a genuine commitment to himself. A ritualistic iron resolve which was almost a fetish, made him sure he would be in his own home for Sunday morning breakfast with his wife, Lila, and their five children. Saturdays, too, if possible. He thought nothing of flying all night from the other side of the world where he was carrying on negotiations and meetings. It appealed to him greatly in a time managing sense that when returning from the Orient, the international dateline worked in his favor as the routing from west to east used the same day twice! At least half of Litton's management was in motion all the time. There was little inclination to write things down. Memorandums were for the lawyers who had to have records. People at all levels were always accessible, talked face to face in hallways, sorted over ideas during wolfed lunches. They were occupationally enchained by telephone connections. It was doubted that anyone had a door which could be closed if privacy were needed. "Free form", it was called.

In spite of demands and inroads on individuals which seemed excessive, for Litton types with Roy Ash whipping them on, there was a game to it all — a game they all wanted to play and did. Ash saw Litton as a kind of privileged horse race where it was not always necessary to place the company's bets when jockeys and their mounts were in the paddock or even at the starting gate. The way he visualized Litton was that money could still be put down when the horses, or technologies, were far down the backstretch, developing positions in the far turn, then coming into the stretch fresh and sprinting.

The LITTON Adventure That Was

While he and Tex had played against each other in high school, it was a conversation with Robert Tate, who headed Stromberg-Carlson, that brought in the third man who was to have a lion's share in the Litton Industries shaping and shoring up. Glen McDaniel, then President of the Electronic Industries Association, needed to recruit members on the west coast. "When you get to California," Tate told him during a Washington conversation, "go straight to see Tex Thornton at Hughes Aircraft. He runs the outfit. He perceives better than anyone else in industry what you're wanting to talk about. There will be big developments in the field of military and industrial electronics, revolutionary in every sense. He's the man, I think, who can open the doors for you. He'll lead you in favorably recommended to those tradition bound airframe manufacturers who won't want to cooperate. He will."

It was good advice. With similar Texas and Washington experiences, they hit it off well in their first encounter. It had been a fortuitous moment for both. Tex was on a great crest of industry attention in 1951 at the expense of General Electric. He had run an adversary campaign in his recruiting, attempting to separate GE from some of its best engineers asking them to displace to Hughes. He placed his appeal right under their noses as GE had a brochure which asked for 40 years of faithful service, after which they could retire under a palm tree somewhere. Tex Thornton suggested the engineer come to work for Hughes, where he could have his own palm tree to sit under on weekends, so why wait in Cleveland or Schenectady or Cincinnati? So many of GE's hands bit on this, that Dr. W.G.R. Baker, one of the GE giants in the industry, harrumphed and growled a lot whenever the Thornton name came up. Tex, delighted with how well it had worked, was expansive and promised assistance to McDaniel in increasing his association membership. It was not many months after their meeting that Litton was born. It was only natural that McDaniel would be leaned on for advice. Although he did not immediately come on the payroll, he had been very much a Thornton confidante in the preliminaries. This continued afterward. It made good sense as the focus was on electronics, government contracting and considerable military involvements. The McDaniel knowledge in such things was extensive making him a common sense reliance point, a substantial factor in the blossoming of the Thornton idea.

A persisting Thornton belief was that a technology in one area, whether it was the result of research or merger, could have application in another. The "pie chart" originally had "Leadership in Electronics" for its centerpiece, but in other later applications had a big T for Technology, as its center. In that case, Tex and Bill Jamieson would draw their circle, sectionalize it outwards from the T. Checkmarks were all around the circumference indicating plants or divisions or labs, with lines drawn across the enclosed space showing how capabilities learned and working in one area could augment and help in another. He needed verification of that assumption because it was a key ingredient for internal growth. Acquisition of existing, performing, profit-making companies was one side of what he had to do. The true test of whether Litton was well managed by knowing leadership lay in significant part in what it could grow in its own hothouse. He had to have well-picked inputs, and an in-house mushroom bed for evidence to serve up for inspection by analysts and investors.

Bill Jamieson hankered for doing his own thing, his way. His engineering background, his gregariousness, plus all-around acquaintance in electronics pressed him into that thinking. The corporate headquarters in his view should have the atmosphere of an engineering lab. He saw it turning into a counting house. Many of the new directions were foreign to his thought processes. Litton was not only changing, it was changing fast but he was not. He was out of step.

From the moment Harry J. Gray walked in the door, he knew there was a strong wish to diversify into quarters not entirely dependent on government contracting. Tex had written plainly and obviously meant what the *plan* said was desired ". . .a profitable balance between *commercial* and military customers." When Gray became a part of the picture, his first impression was that Litton was a bar-less cage variety of zoo. Everyone seemed to be on his own. He could crane his neck and look around, paw the premises assigned him, and it was too pleasant to even think of escape. Gray brought with him a background in commercial and industrial activities. He knew little of electronics. He talked at length with Ash, not so much with Thornton. They thought his background could vault that existing gap in the versatilities essential to bridging those commercial applications. As Litton was then, no job was clearly defined. Gray found one assignment could lead to another and to additional responsibilities without dropping any.

"When I joined Litton in 1954," Gray reflected later, "all kinds of things were going on in all corners of the building. One could spend a whole day visiting one activity after another, ask questions, have a very interesting time."

Gray became Litton's faithful burro from his first day. He had more different things loaded on him than an old time prospector freshly grubstaked would put on his animal as he headed for the hills. For a while, he was the official aye or nay sayer. As identifier of market potentials he could deliver the "kill order." When he questioned a proposed fire retardant which would increase safety in Christmas tree usage as unlikely to be profitable, because there was insufficient allowance of time for advertising and distribution to sales outlets, he wound up not only believed, but with the public relations and advertising portfolio in his lap! When it became evident the drive to collect an assortment of component firms was being undertaken, Gray was given the whole group — with exception of Litton's Electron Tube. Dr. Norman Moore did not fancy his high technology and superior product coming under Harry Gray, so recently an incomer from a pedestrian company such as Greyhound! It led to the oft stated Tex Thornton contention that one of the major tests of management is to somehow bring out of situations where talented people who can barely abide each other, a running, successful enterprise. That "loose rein" atmosphere of Litton called more frequently than most for organizing around personality clashes and incompatibilities.

Harry Gray was a dog-faithful company man, so much so that he once set up a Litton product press conference day and date with the expected birth of his first daughter. He got the room arranged and the product displayed. He went out to the hospital so his wife would see him as she was taken to the delivery room, waited to hear the baby's first cry, then rushed back in time for the media encounter. His wife was still in a fuzzy state when he reappeared but she was not amused. The Litton view was that he was well organized, dependable, could handle many things well, and had his priorities in proper order. Gray, once badly injured in a motorcycle accident and thought to be crippled for life, had his office moved into his hospital room, then into his home. In the 8 months required for convalescence, he never missed a day's work.

The Thornton natural graciousness and boyish eagerness made him the ideal "white knight" for the acquisitional thrust. He was there from the first analysis of prospects, checking them for their conformation characteristics, the quality of their management, the profit and loss records, the likely longevity of the technologies in which each was strong, and their overall rightness.

"Rightness" was often interchangeable with how hungry Litton was to get them in the portfolio. Some had already been picked off before he started talking to Harry Gray about his ideas in depth — his basic believe that components were both a short and long-range best bet. Litton, he said, would begin its structure by merger. Wisdom in plucking candidates set up some of the pins for internal growth. The mergers would bring with them packets of researchers in technological tandems, already meshed and assembled, along with leadership and marketing know-how, patents of proprietary worth, the means and already in place locations of distribution facilities — all of which were functioning and would so continue avoiding time loss or break in momentum for the inheritor, Litton Industries, Inc.

The first judgment had to be that the unit would fit, that it could be resuscitated if floundering and extended into the future. Its management had to be amenable to being bolted into place for as little or as much of a transitional period — up to five years — as would serve the corporate destiny.

There were governing words, *barter* and *formula*. Barter, of course, meant exactly what it said, the trading or exchanging of one thing — stock— for another — the firm being wooed. This is distinct from sale or purchase in which money is paid for transfer of ownership. Formula indicated the payout schedule, the increments determined by profitable operations after the merger had been declared final.

Money is usually described as a medium of exchange, with a measure of value, an officially coined or stamped or printed on paper convenience sanctified by issuing governments or banks. Securities, representing ownership of a business, have no pegged or decreed worth except in the estimation of traders sophisticated in such assessments. Enthusiasm for an enterprise will find its share values bid up. Disdain for its prospects may be shown by traders standing on the sidelines or offering no interest at all in their possession.

As Litton had little money to make any formidable outright purchases, in some acquisitions it had to get prices for its securities verified. The formula was a means to keep the management in place. It discouraged those who would be clever by seeking to get their profit levels up quickly by drastic staff reductions, cutting research and development, then making a run for it in a couple of years, leaving behind a shell, shattered morale, and a shambles. The longer the timeclock ran with contemplated appreciation in the stock values, the less the total in shares necessary to complete the absorption into Litton. It diminished chances of games playing with earnings of the merged unit by those who knew it best and who could do all those things which operatives skilled with numbers can do to achieve a runup. The five-year formula tended to bequeath stability and avert wrecking what was a Litton division to arrive at a short-term bonanza for the sellers.

Swept up into Litton in 270 feverish days were:
- the San Carlos cornerstone, Litton Industries of California;
- a corporate headquarters and plant location in Beverly Hills;
- three related precision resistor companies in Colorado;
- the Birklan Corporation which was a potentiometer manufacturer and developer in New York;
- the I.E.S. Corporation;
- Digital Control Systems for its key personnel and expertise in computers;
- West Coast Electronics, for communications and navigation, and
- U.S. Engineering, to get its electronic hardware and printed circuitry capability.

The first of these was genuinely big money for the Thornton team — the $1,050,000 to Charles V. Litton for his 1,239 shares of Litton Industries of California — $816,414 for all his capital stock, and $233,586 for his patents, applications and other proprietary disclosures including those Roy Woenne stenopads of primitive drawings. That was the high cost part of the inventory made possible by the Lehman Brothers backing. The low one was almost laughable — that three element Precision Products of Colorado, which was nearly bankrupt, but contained film potentiometer technology. Roy Ash wrote the check for it, $163.60 — a penny a share. The film resistor was intriguing because it differed from the usual wire wound elements. It was a bargain as to price, had some loss records for tax purposes, but it had never gone anywhere. Its purchase raised expectancies in one shareholder, then disappointed him. He became a hostile whenever Litton had Congressional contact. He was Peter Dominick, later to be the senator from Colorado for many years.

That 270 days generated $2,980,051 in sales. Operations were in ten buildings with a quarter million square feet of floor space on ten acres of land in six cities. Five were in California, one in New York. Neat it was, but hardly gaudy. The I.E.S. Corporation went down as a first error in judgement. It was quickly shouldered off into deserved oblivion.

The 270 days were also revealing in the temptations which were there in the "loose rein" realm. The Litton leadership was similar to officers who win battlefield commissions after years of common soldiering. The Litton toppers knew most of the stories and excuses by heart. They sensed dodges and the possibilities of a question producing less than the truth when someone was pinned for an answer which could only be embarrassing. They understood, too, how men were prone to claim a glorious future to gloss over a present that wasn't too shiny.

George Kosmetsky by conviction and inclination buried himself in specialized computers. He urged the buy of Digital Control Systems, mostly to get Floyd George Steele. The smallest of actions then seemed to have major significance. Steele was a brain phenomenon, as bright as an unshaded 1,000 watt bulb. Many thought him absolutely mad, or at least, too far out to touch. He slept odd hours, choosing to work all night which relieved him from necessity to associate with the nine-to-five plodders. In the case of one warm-up Navy contract proposal solicitation, Litton had refused to bid, saying it had no applicable expertise. The Navy extended the bidding time, asked Litton to bid, and assured them that they would get the job because the Navy wanted Floyd Steele to work on it![5]

The first annual report didn't mention that the "chip" was forming in the minds of Steele and Jack Thorn. Steele was sure that computer banks in sizes and numbers it would take barns to hold would soon come down to razor-thin silicon repositories for photographic registration of beams and lasers. Wiped out would be those millions of electrical circuits first thought necessary and needing high power wattage to function. People who were around Floyd George Steele were in awe of his confidence and the intensity with which he pursued his beliefs and ideas. Some he rubbed the wrong way. Military officers tended to like him very much. He held Pentagon top brass entranced for nearly two hours with his scenario for World War III and weaponry with which it would be fought! When there was a complicated problem, there was always a search to get him. In the end, he was usually right. For Litton, he brought in the digital differential analyzer.[6] That became the basic root of Litton's Data Systems Division. It was a smaller version of digital and analog models then being used for scientific calculations and for solving complex industrial control problems.

Dr. Harry Singleton hunched over and anguished about inertial navigation. He was commissioned somehow to worry it down from its initial tonnages and huge cubage demands into something small enough to slide into those sylph-like oncoming military fighter aircraft without losing reliability in the process. He was initially the most persistent, and seemingly unpromising leak for Litton's sparse trea-

---

5. Navy Commander George Hoover was after the means of redoing all the airborne cockpit instrumentation in aircraft. He had known Steele when he was at Northrop and closing in on the digital differential analyzer. Hoover was impressed that Steele could not only do anything, but could also explain it in its most simplified form, a rare human being, indeed! In those days, Steele went by his middle name as he was apprehensive that where his first name came from might somehow interfere with the way he was viewed by colleagues. The Floyd name came from his mother's brother, that formidable financier, Floyd Odlum!

6. John Von Neumann, of Princeton's Institute for Advanced Study School of Mathematics, described the digital differential analyzer as a ". . . most remarkable and promising instrument. . . established the principles for a whole family of very new and most useful instruments." Steele's item became the computer of choice in the fields of vehicle navigation and control.

sury. The tenacity with which he pursued that challenge in the face of almost non-existent market or interest stood as a 20th Century update of Horatio Alger's "Bound to Succeed."

John Clark was the x-ray reliance and hope, and Sid Frankel, the gamble for Litton to crowd in for a larger share of the radar picture to which it had so long been a respected contributor.

Major systems contracts were attractive to shoot for, and had sizeable pricetags for the winner. Tex Thornton cautioned everyone at their stage of organizational life NOT to win because considerable effort and investment could destroy a small company. Overextending that way could be similar to a crap shooter letting it all ride on a single roll. Worse than the money loss it could also be destructive on employee morale.

"But if we're in components," he told Harry Gray, "we always have a chance of selling components to whoever does win."

Gray[7] heard this over and over as he went through several chairs — manager of commercial planning, public relations, advertising. These way-station stops gave him chances to see the company from a higher perspective. The radar and x-ray commitments weren't cooking very well. Then the day came when the decision was made that Gray take the whole components bundle, 14 listed areas with eight lines of product, and point to what it was to be. Along with it, he was given the right to decide about the x-ray situation. Litton had a genuine "take charge" type on its hands in Gray's former Silver Star decorated infantryman. The thulium x-ray made possible by thulium irradiated isotopes, could be an independent and portable energy source with no need to plug in some wall socket. This back-packed version, encased in a leaden shield, had an aperture which registered x-ray pictures of battle casualties or police emergencies on the scene. It sounded fine in theory, but battlefield memories told Harry Gray that actual locales of wounding, peace or war, were no place for x-ray taking. It was his first corporate *coup-de-grace*. The x-ray did persist

---

7. Gray's components group office was located in the West Coast Electronics unit, the one he liked least. Only because Litton's corporate secretary, Dick Loewe, "knew somebody" could he even get to work and park his car. Access was through the Carnation Co. parking lot, and Loewe through a Carnation friend, got him a visa of sorts.

in Litton thinking, to surface in more orthodox form, much later and differently.

"I was told to develop a good marketing program to sell a lot of components throughout the electronics industry," Gray said. "Many might be competing with Litton when it got ready to try for major systems contracts, but no matter. I thought it was a sound idea then. I still think so." He was asked to evaluate all the components in residence. He took Litton out of the precision resistor business. His reasoning was that Litton was so imperceptibly small and the marketing costs so excessive, it made no sense at all from Litton's tail-end-Charlie position. Radar, in spite of the best efforts of Sid Frankel, wilted at that juncture and phased down. In that early commitment of the Litton intent, three of the five directions were promising — components, computers and inertial navigation — which momentarily two faded, x-ray and radar. Three out of the five in Roy Ash's mind was not bad at all. Radar and x-ray were due for revival later.

The accommodations at 336 North Foothill Road in Beverly Hills, California were far from impressive. When Litton moved in, it was mindful of one of those typical movie sets in nearby Hollywood. The few people up front thinned quickly into empty spreads of floor space on which temporary, separating walls were erected. When or if a project ended, the walls came down like a struck circus tent to be pitched in some new form somewhere else on the premises. With those Litton "firsts" on the payroll, it was the Thornton custom to give them the goldfish bowl treatment as he took visitors around introducing them and talking of their involvements. He never tried to hide the vacant panorama of floor space. In an assured, if understated way, he said it would be right there that things were planned to happen which would take Litton up to $100,000,000 in annual sales in a few years. Such tour takers were always goggle-eyed as they departed, accepting that they had indeed been on the ground floor on which the Litton edifice was a-building and where the next industrial miracle would occur. Grafton P. Tanquary, III, an early name on the corporate payroll, used Thornton description when he was the designated tour leader. He marveled about the willingness to accept the dream as outlined, even second hand.

Litton Industries was only 545 days old when it set out to get that fix on the real value of its stock.[8] On June 1, 1955, it was offered OTC (Over The Counter). Not bad, either. The BID was $11.875. The ASKED, $13.00. That's where its barter potential was first assessed as the Litton leadership tested the water. A couple of other things had been going on quietly within the staff, which taken together were to add up to the biggest noisemakers loosed on financial headwaters in that area. At first, Thornton and Ash attended to mergers in a highly personal, face-to-face and secretive way. As there was more to running a company than just augmenting it, they became involved more and more to running a company than to augmenting it.

The 85th employee badge number had gone to a patent attorney, Seymour Rosenberg.[9] He surmised rather soon that however important proprietary knowledge protection and patents were and would be, that wasn't where the action was. It circled, rose, fell, went upwards from Roy Ash's office. He decided he wanted to work in that environment in some way, some day. It evolved eventually as an advance planning element, and he, with Don Greene and Pat Lyons, did studies, analyses, and made projections of possible acquisitions. It had as many as 50 to 100 company profiles in folders constantly being updated and under some degree of active consideration for merger. With it supplying detail, and Glen McDaniel for easy reference because of his own electronics industry knowledge, it was as up on the state of and what was moving in that fast changing world as a claims office once was in registration of mining properties.

In that same time frame of the establishment of the stock price, Crosby Moyer Kelly had been talked on, or talked himself on the Litton premises. As both Thornton and Ash had pulled back from the details of mergers to devote more time to management, they also had

---

8. The first sale of Litton shares was by Roy Ash in February 1954, at an arbitrarily fixed price of $5. There were one or two others who got similar prices in the same time period, but the general mood there was to hold as the future promise was so fixed in their minds.

9. Rosenberg and the other Seymour, "Si" Scholnick, coming as they did from the patent orientation, were always highly aware of Thornton's "proprietary" concerns. When they were scouting, they picked up on key people as much as companies. They were the ones who saw Digital Control Systems as a "people package", principally to get Floyd George Steele, who in early years contributed more to Litton's patent roster than any other employee.

to have a fulltime articulator of what Litton was doing. Whatever the differences in a Litton Industries from all those other electronics companies, with Crosby Kelly as the resident oracle, it was the contrast of a downtown lamp post with the Statue of Liberty! The No. 1 plank in Litton's *plan* as enunciated by Kelly was a floral and perfumed version of his own. He did it with variations hundreds of times for the next decade and more. He described Litton almost lyrically as seeking ". . .to build a major industrial entity which would have at its heart and core an ever increasing capability in the changing technologies — strength, not size, integration, not diversification." As the company's spokesman, he rose to the status of not merely a vice president, but a princeling. Through him, electronics dulled by the pedestrian jargon of its artisans and engineers, took on a kind of poetic quality, a glamour of sorts and a mystique. Hearing him, a listener could close his eyes and see him as Columbus talking Isabella out of her crown jewels for his voyage of discovery. In the bottom line potential of extraordinary dimensions he attributed to Litton's careful search for capabilities, he fried it all up in the deep fat of excitement and invited his listeners to savor the flavor of it all. Analysts, media reps, formal audiences, or just anyone who would encourage him by standing nearby were sure to be mentally kidnapped by him and reluctant to leave him when released.

He was a flamboyant word and phrase coiner and charmer, capable of making an evening out both a social and professionally memorable experience. In all startups, there is a time for explanation, perhaps even a kind of evangelism, then enumeration of opportunities — and realization. Some people can fit only one mode. Others can transition from one to another and grow with each new set of requirements. Some become enamored of "the way it was" and become dead weights on progress. That "major industrial entity" as Kelly parsed it was never meant to be read "the biggest". It was technological biceps Tex Thornton was after, not an iron-pumping hulk. "Major" meant he was in control of Litton's destiny. "Industrial" conveyed product applications and their manufacture, as well as offering services such as the location of natural resources from which products could be realized. Litton was a structure, not a haphazard collection. Rather than compensate for a bad economic cycle, Ash would say, why be in such a business at all.

Kelly invited his hearers in, a kind of privileged entry. He masterfully showed them what he wanted them to see. It was wrong, he said, for them to read or write or say that Thornton was merely "acquiring companies" as Tex said his goal was "acquiring time". He meant it. Thornton's *time* was somebody else' investment of money, weeks, months, years. By the simple act of merging, Litton was given immediate market position and presence as well as inheriting the ongoing contracts or products and access to more of the same. So much of what was to be was converging on Litton as a place for it to happen. The company was still young in 1955 when there was a machine tools convention in Chicago. The subject of the impact of numerical controls began to enter the trade's conversations. Since nothing really happens in industry without machine tools to make it possible, Litton's specialized computer development and what its electronics could add caused some cerebral note taking. Litton was forever seeing and picking up on things like that. None of it seemed an impossible dream. It was just that few thought about it quite that way, or that Litton probably had something going which would provide an answer.

The books showed on January 24, 1956 that something remarkable had happened to the Litton dream: The company just crossed the $1,000,000 profit line! That very night at the Gourmet Restaurant in Beverly Hills, a substantial break from the diet of "roach coach" sandwiches and muddy coffee was engineered as a Thornton surprise. The gang around him had put together a framed scroll which said: "This is to certify that Charles Bates Thornton is hereby awarded the first and only charter membership in LITTON'S FIRST MILLION, a fraternity of people banded together to make a profit within the framework of the principles of American enterprise. This award to the man who has been our captain is made on the completion of Litton Industries' first $1,000,000 of net profit, after taxes, an expression of appreciation for his vision, his leadership, his ability, his consecration to his responsibilities and for the confidence he has expressed in those who have joined his team."[10]

---

10. The signers of the scroll were Charles R. Abrams, Roy L. Ash, Foster Campbell, J. Ray Donahue, Jr., Sid Frankel, Fred Gagnan, Jr., Harry J. Gray, Sig Hansen, Gerry Heath, H.W. Jamieson, Alvin L. Johnson, Tom Keene, Crosby M. Kelly, George Kosmetsky, Richard Loewe, Myles Mace, Phil Phillips, Dick Roche, Seymour

The LITTON Adventure That Was

It was at a meeting of the Board of Directors on February 24th — Chairman Charles B. Thornton, Roy Ash, H.W. Jamieson, Dr. Myles Mace, General Carl A. "Tooey" Spaatz, USAF (ret.) and Joseph Thomas — that the resolution was passed to list Litton Industries on both the American (AMEX) and the Los Angeles (later Pacific) Stock Exchanges. It actually happened seven months later on September 24th. AMEX moved only 1,700 shares that day with a $27.75 high, and a low of $27.375. It finished at $27.50. On the Los Angeles mart, 475 shares changed hands ranging from a high of $27.75 to a low of $27.125 where it closed. Litton had more than doubled in investor esteem in a year, was a part of the action and in the record books to stay. The Big Board, the New York Stock Exchange (NYSE) was

Mortimer Marcus (trading specialist), Tex Thornton & Keith Funston (NYSE President) look at first ticket tape on July 30, 1957

Rosenberg, A.S. Scoles, Henry Singleton, Marvin Skoller, Emmett Steele, Vaughn Thompson and Bruce Worcester. The reviews hadn't been written yet, but they were all sure they had a "hit" on their hands.

well aware of this fast moving newcomer and the "personality" which seemed to ride with it. That flashy quality caused NYSE President Keith Funston to invite Litton Industries to its exalted domain.

Litton moved across that NYSE tape for its big-time bow on July 30, 1957. There were only 3,100 shares traded in that baptismal offering. The higher taker got his for $52.25, the lowest, $50.25, and at the end of it strengthened to $50.75. A heady moment, Tex Thornton was on the stock exchange floor for that initiation rite with Roy Ash and Glen McDaniel, plus Mortimer Marcus, the trading specialist for the new stock and Funston. It was a quantum jump from those Haskell, Texas beginnings and Thornton's eyes moistened a little as he saw LIT flashed up there over the heads of traders. A quick calculation told him that Litton's issued and outstanding 1,193,986 common shares in the possession of 4500 individuals and organizations were worth nearly $60,000,000. Those retained in Litton's treasury had a verified value and could be bartered in terms of their futures prospects, or terms of their futures prospects, or rising price/earnings ratio for needed acquisitions. Those 10-cent shares in the original 50 "investment packages" as designed by Lehman Brothers' Joe Thomas were really climbing and had made several paper millionaires — all in less than five years.

It didn't just happen. It is seldom that anything ever does on its own. One has to look in the woodwork for a clue sometimes, but Litton was as overt as it was outward bound — and upwards headed.

It had never really wanted for curiosity as insiders were always wondering where Tex Thornton's hand would be raised next. As the pace accelerated following those initial Litton months, the media microscopes came out in force. The trade publications were first at the door, and then general interest media hands looked in on Litton to find out why it was different, why was it in many conversations — and what a difference it might make. All of the Litton people, as if by rote, declared repetitively and simply — parroting Thornton — that any merger candidate had to dovetail with the company's product and market planning, must have strong management — and the price — after projections of probable return on investment — had to be right. The glitter of the corporation's short but exotic history and its golden touch softened the toughest resistance into selling itself on being a part of it. Tex Thornton was saying on every oral encounter that he was a buyer and a builder of companies, and holding onto them, not in near term burnishing and resale. He recognized that many he was collecting might have problems, could develop even greater ones and that the remedial steps could be extensive in effort and doctoring. One that was available now might not seem to make sense, nor fit snugly into the current picture, but could be joined and re-enforced by others. He excused the taking of something new as rising to an opportunity, or the corporate version of drawing to an inside straight. It made more sense in company building than in Hoyle, as there were so many wild cards in electronics' almost unlimited deck. Many of the smaller firms had staked it all on a winning widget of one kind or another, but were having trouble staying in the pot awaiting interest in what they had. They often had a consuming desire as much to be right in their technological convictions being upheld as in the compensation in money or stock that might be offered.

"We are builders, not promoters," was a Thornton declaration. "If we buy a company, we hold it. What's more, we live with it." He often startled his listeners by saying the targeting on merger candidates was how they corresponded with long range plans, whether they were immediately profitable or not. He would even forego hope of rapid improvements just so long as the new element offered that potential ladder run on which to step. He was forever emphasizing technical research as significant in making overall profits probable, therefore adding to the attractiveness of the sought enterprise. Both he and Roy Ash stated they would cold shoulder anything which was merely a money maker unless it was technologically eye popping as well. Ash said they were after coherence in divisional relationships. Mergers, which would only increase the magnitude of Litton holdings, were out.[11]

---

11. Floyd George Steele helped Litton into the "big time" in a non-laboratory way. When the business doyen, FORTUNE, got interested, it sent one of its best writers, William Harriss, to check Litton out. After his preliminary encounters with the Thornton-Ash-Jamieson trio he was a little dizzied by what they said they saw out there in the future. He'd had a troubled youth, and was semi-reared in Colorado by Steele's father, so had known Floyd George from away back. "Your father was about the most honest man I ever knew," he said, "and I believe some of it had to have rubbed off on you. Tell me if these Litton guys are for real!" Steele said they were, and why he thought so. Harriss went ape and FORTUNE blossomed in April, 1958 with several pages, the company's first big ink. Harriss insisted that one of the pic-

The components bead stringing never wavered. In 1955, Ahrendt-Automatic Seriograph in College Park, Maryland, a designer of electronic and electromechanical servomechanism equipment, was the first substantial and well-located east coast acquisition of that facility on Washington's[12] doorstep. U.S. Engineering Company, one of the very largest suppliers of etched circuitry and electronic hardware in the country was the next buy.

The worth of Litton's Over The Counter stock action begun that June 1, and appreciation thereafter illustrated the benefits of barter and formula. Litton had set aside 340,000 shares of its common stock to compensate for these two entries as the cash equivalent when the talks started. The value had risen so much by the conclusion of the agreements and the closing, only about 75,000 of the shares were called in for the deal's sealing.

Getting more than is bargained for in the wildest of circumstances can happen in business sometimes. Litton encountered such a situation in an odd string of events, one seeming not to bear in any way on the other.

---

tures be of Steele, and the editors went along. For the financial pooh-bahs of the period, it was a signal that Litton had, indeed, arrived.

12. Ahrendt, joined with the 1958 acquisition of Maryland (MEMCO) Electronics from Bill Morris just across the street, became Litton Amecom division. It was the main Litton residence of RF (radio frequency) technology. That's the basic root of electronic warfare systems, radio navigation such as OMEGA and LORAN and other products including receivers, ship communications electronics and voice switching systems. Ahrendt was attractive as it was in the medical electronics field and was the builder of the Sanchez Perez Seriograph, a machine capable of holding a stack of x-ray cassettes. They could be chain driven and get x-ray photos in sequence as rapidly as 15 per minute. This amounted almost to a slow motion movie of bodily functions. Bill Ahrendt, very soon after selling the company which was built on his renown in control engineering and servomechanisms, was killed in a South American plane crash. Maryland Electronics had a small group of research engineers headed by Charles Fink. It was almost an electronics candy store including not only medical electronics, but microwave antenna, oceanographic instrumentation, passive and active electronic warfare and radar. There were so many name changes of the College Park activities, there was some joking suspicion that they couldn't pay the rent. Amecom it ultimately became, and Charlie Fink, who worked all the way up from the "candy store" lab, became its President and took it into its big money-making years. Some of the others went to Applied Sciences in Minneapolis and worked on the 2-man exploration deep diving submarine, ALVIN. Later, some moved into Litton's microwave oven effort.

The LITTON Adventure That Was

Louis Wolfson was an ambitious raider and plunger. He owned Merritt Chapman & Scott, a company that manufactured speakers, transformers and TV cabinets. The bull's eye in the sights of Wolfson was Montgomery Ward. He needed a sizeable sum of money for that takeover contest. He felt he could raise some of it by putting Merritt Chapman & Scott on the block, in whole or in part. When word of this got out, Frank Pyle, who ran Wolfson's speaker division, quickly countered by putting together an investor group to buy the speaker business. Adolph Schenkel, an uncle of the TV sports commentator, Chris Schenkel, bought the cabinet manufacturing portion. All eyes then swung to a ruddy-faced, canny, quiet and shy former football player out of Muncie, Indiana—Arnie Kaufman.

Arnie was built along measurements that made coaches' mouths water. Once set, he was as immovable as an oak stump. On the run, he was intimidating. The Ball fruit jar family's endowed school (Ball State University) still considers him one of its most illustrious graduates. Kaufman had been running Utah Radio (UTRAD); its principal product was transformers. He was the logical one to purchase it.

A problem developed. The other two buyers of divisions had swallowed up monies available around Huntington, Indiana. Kaufman set out for New York, ostensibly to attend the Institute of Radio Engineers convention, but really to seek backing. Kaufman ran into Lewis Howard of TRIAD in Venice, California. Howard and his two partners knew Kaufman well and liked him. Each said that he would advance him $10,000. One of them, Oz Perry, stayed with agreement all the way, but Tom Walker changed his mind and backed out. Other increments of $10,000 each came from Dick Wetherford and Elmer Fige, and other manufacturers' representatives. Arnie anted his life's savings of $10,000. He had $90,000 to face Wolfson and make an offer. Wolfson rebuffed him—he was too busy to make time for small fry and small offerings. Kaufman decided the time had come to cash in on a "brownie point" with Frank Leahy, the former football coach of Notre Dame, and one of the "Seven Mules" of its famous "Four Horsemen" era.

Leahy was the head coach from 1941 through 1943 and again in 1946 through 1953 with a record of 87 wins, 11 losses, and 9 ties. On autumn Saturdays, he had a compulsion to return to South Bend for the home games. He was a businessman on Wolfson's staff, so he would arrive early Saturday morning in Huntington to "inspect UTRAD" and be "brought up to date." That took about ten munutes. After a cup of coffee where he would give Arnie betting counsel, Leahy would go 60 miles up the road to South Bend to see the game.

Now Kaufman confronted Leahy to tell him he wanted to buy UTRAD and beseeched him to intercede personally with Wolfson. Kaufman quickly gained Wolfson's presence and offered him $50,000 for the Merritt Chapman & Scott transformer division.

"Peanuts!" said Wolfson. His assessment of inventory and machinery put the division's worth at $400,000. "I can liquidate it for at least $200,000, easy." The interview was over as far as Wolfson was concerned.

Arnie quickly made him aware of an unfinished U.S. Army Signal Corps contract which involved UTRAD. If not fulfilled, it had heavy penalty clauses. Wolfson paused, asked Kaufman to wait outside for a few minutes. He needed to think over the implications of a black mark against him for non-delivery on a government contract commitment. A minute later, he called Kaufman back.

"It's a deal for $50,000," he said. They shook hands on it. Within a fortnight, Kaufman had to move UTRAD under another roof. He did it. His first six months were highly profitable. He outgrew his emergency facility and rented more space. He made an agreement to buy a new plant.

Lew Howard, who had helped him raise the money for the buyout, called him one day. "There's a west coast company called Litton Industries," he said. "They're about $28,000,000 in annual sales, have a A-B rating. We're thinking about selling to them. We'd like you to go along."

Kaufman was not interested at all, and said so. He liked it just the way he had it. He had his very own money tree — but he only had $10,000 of it. All those other $10,000 pieces were Litton-minded. Dragging his feet, feeling abused and muttering a lot about the vicissitudes of life, his UTRAD went in the Litton collection in September, 1956 part of a TRIAD/UTRAD packet of transformer manufacturers. Litton was suddenly 20% larger than it had been the day before.

Lew Howard had neglected to tell Kaufman about the way the formula payout arrangement worked, and the pertinent profit levels and how they were computed. Ash inadvertently let him know by congratulating him about how UTRAD's performance alone in six months with Litton would guarantee the TRIAD people their formula rewards. Kaufman, not in on this, was naturally furious, threatening to resign and start over somewhere else. Ash daubed his wound with liberal stock option arrangements over the next four years. By Ash handling the situation as he did, he not only quieted a potentially explosive situation, but Litton got the benefits of wisdom, management expertise and in-depth knowledge of components which were all bound up with Arnold Kaufman. He was money in the bank, and unlike so many with Litton then, he found a home and stayed the course.

Lew Howard left Litton before long. Harry Gray became a Litton vice president with the mission of increasing the components cluster. TRIAD was always sluggish, but Kaufman's UTRAD went merrily upward in sales and earnings.

Ex-New York architect and Virginia "Colonel" James Pandapas was paid nearly $2,000,000 for his Poly-Scientific in Blacksburg, VA in August 1962. Their major product was sliprings, which were key elements in search movements or radar, and in gimbals for inertial navigation. In 1963, in March, Winchester Electronics in Oakville, Connecticut, and in December, Clifton Precision Products in Clifton Heights, Pa. were added.

In the Harry Gray regime, the components scope and enrichment process found Litton constantly bettering its position to get substantial subcontracts in important programs. Rising from about $20,000,000 in annual sales when the Gray custodial era started, he carried it to around $90,000,000. At that juncture, Crosby M. Kelly left Litton to bedazzle for other clients and causes.

Gray was then made a Senior Vice President for Finance and Administration, which included Investor Relations. On the Thornton conviction that components was the surest footing for the company to get under way and grow richer, Gray now found himself in what his one-time Milledgeville Corners neighbors would call corporate high cotton. It was easy for him to appear to be the company's No. 3 figure even though none had said so out loud. He was in that spokesman seat, which led to being quoted a lot. This gave him the highest profile of his life up to that time and he rose to the occasion.

Jack Connolly was pulled from his No. 1 situation as headman at Data Systems Division to take over the components Group. He nursed its momentum in the traditional Litton way — taking in Jefferson Electric[13] in Bellwood, Illinois in February 1967. It was a leader in ballast production for fluorescent and mercury illumination of industrial, commercial and outdoor lighting systems. With significant assistance from UTRAD's Arnie Kaufman — Kester Solder — aging Frank C. Engelhart's[14] Chicago, Illinois producer of flux for cleaning metal surfaces of oxides and particles to permit soldering, as well as resin residue removers, protective coatings and solvents, cast its future with Litton. Kester had more than 200,000 soldering products with the greatest range of any manufacturer of this line. It had markets in 60 countries.

During Connolly's time as group Executive Dr. Norman Moore was off after the futures of the microwave oven field. John McCullough had taken Moore's chair at Litton Electron Tube, which at long last was eased into the components domain where it properly belonged. Between 1966 and 1969, Connolly and his components' colleagues, generated a money waterfall into the Litton treasury finally getting to a $155,000,000 annual sales level. Then Connolly signed

---

13. Jefferson Electric, Bellwood, Ill., started in 1915 as a manufacturer of small transformers used in doorbells, chimes and toys. It grew into applications for oil burner ignition, machine tools, and luminous tubes as well as ballasts to operate fluorescent and high intensity discharge lamps, clocks and hospital isolation panels. In June 1973, it began satellite plant operations in Athens, Ohio and in April 1977, in Williamstown, Ky. Each of these satellite facilities increased local employment opportunities for women in areas where vocational training had always favored male skills.

14. Arnie Kaufman had sallied forth to talk with Frank C. Engelhart on several occasions. He had a split family and lived alone in his big house. He liked to take steam baths. It was in a steam bath that Kaufman, dressed in a towel, joined him. With perspiration pouring, he talked with him about the size of the credit or Litton preference shares he could command. Engelhart didn't know what to do with the money. Kaufman suggested giving some to his alma mater, the University of Michigan. He said he wasn't interested. Kaufman mentioned nearby Northwestern University in his town of Evanston. Part of the $8,775,000 worth of Litton Preference stock he was paid found its way to establishing Northwestern's Englehart Library. This so irked his second in command, Ferdinand Kaiser, who figured the employees should have been the beneficiaries, one being himself, he could hardly wait for the closing papers to be signed to tell Engelhart to vacate his office. "But what will I do for an office?" Englehart asked, figuring he was entitled to that courtesy as long as he lived. "Go down to Northwestern University and ask them for an office," Kaiser told him through his teeth. Englehart did that — and officed at Northwestern as long as he lived.

out to go his own way. He'd made his mark and wanted to swing his own bat.

Like an old movie script, the summons went out to becalmed, sleepy and leisurely Huntington, Indiana for the man who had fought UTRAD going into the Litton fold in the first place, and who had almost left in a huff — Arnold Kaufman. He was first to say it was nearly incredible. Among the Litton population then, saturated as it was with conversational swingers, he was almost a silent Sam. A good listener when sense was being made, his neck would redden and he'd become a laughing scoffer when it was not. He could diagnose a bad decision with the unerring case of a professional linebacker. He cauterized rather than patted where he detected Litton bleeding. He left the whereas and the rhetoric to lawyers, and sought clear explanation rather than excuses. He depended on earthy people such as Alex Owen, of Arkansas and with the disposition of a razorback when signing some stupidity and who knew how to price for profit; Phil Lynn, who matured in industrial relations arenas; Don Krueger, so pat with his accounting he not only knew the whereabouts of the next dollar but could set the time on his wristwatch for it to show up; Charlie Gallagher, who made a comprehensive and competent computer product team of the advanced Circuitry Division in Springfield, Missouri; U.S. Engineering of Glendale, California and Dumont Aviation (Litton Fastening Systems) in Lakewood, California; and that uncut and brusque jewel, Julius "Jules" Vetter, a production expert. He was recruited by Kaufman from Norden, and quickly assessed the ailing Jefferson Electric as a production problem. Then, after a year there, he was whisked to Louis Allis in Milwaukee behind Paul Brunton to continue the turn-around process.

At Litton's quarter century milestone, Kaufman was on a pedestal all his own. All that troubled decade, 1968-1978 components and whatever else was assigned him worked right, grew, and profited. It would be Kaufman who would see components engage 18,000 Litton employees, and his group's sales went over $1,000,000,000 annually.

It was everybody's bonanza. The Litton top leadership was vindicated. Kaufman's divisions and plants were flushed with success. Arnie Kaufman himself, who started his long march into Litton Corporation history with $10,000 it had taken him 34 years to save, became better remembered at Litton than in the alumni records of Ball

State University back in Indiana. But where would he be today if somebody had questioned Frank Leahy UTRAD "'inspection trip" expense accounts when Notre Dame was playing in South Bend on autumn Saturdays?

SPECIAL SITUATION #8

THE GREAT 1958

Litton was about to be entitled to five candles on its birthday cake.

Neither Tex Thornton nor Roy Ash were inclined to stay up to escort the clock hands across the midnight demarcation line that New Year's even, glasses hoisted and full of bubbly. If they didn't sleep well as 1957 surrendered its waning minutes, they had good reason. They were at the parting of the ways with their associate Bill Jamieson. Both sides were glad of it. Their stopwatches were not really synchronized any more, if indeed they ever had been. It was a thing that happened to partnerships, athletic teams and marriages. The Thornton-Ash focus didn't hover long over that. Getting a good grip on 1958 was what they had to do.

Litton, in that allotment of 365 24-hour days, became a vastly different corporate animal which ran well with the Wall Street bulls in their wish to jump Dow Jones barriers upward whenever encountered. Litton would know three times the dollar numbers in annual sales when laid alongside the previous twelve months. Via acquisition and corresponding interior development it improved its equilibrium and became less vulnerable to cyclical swings of defense spending. Some of the most venturesome and courageous technological bets paid off. It became, in one action, an international company. Critics had used disparaging words such as "opportunists" as dismissal for Litton's previously stated pretensions. Now they awakened to the thought that Litton was wooing a sort of technological infinity which stretched broadly over the horizon—and bravely into space itself.

America was emerging, in fact had been startled from its giant-sized complacency cocoon. The previous August, TASS, the Soviet Union's official news agency, announced the successful launch of a "super" long-range intercontinental, multi-stage ballistic "rocket". Undoubtedly based on German World War II V-2 tests and data, the exploit testified eloquently that the Soviets had not only listened to the captured talents from the rocket resourcefulness and experiences of

Hitler's Peenemuende[1] on the Baltic, but were urging them onward—and outward—with the highest priorities placed on their efforts.

Space was a nonsensical no-no with the Congressional wisdom of the early '50s. Air Force budgets were scrutinized closely to see if any monies for such purposes were cached in accounting nooks and crannies with innocent sounding labels. The Air Force was restive under these harassments and restrictions. Its far-out thinkers were sure that beyond the atmosphere lay a logical extension of its roles and missions. These translated into legitimate requirements that space be viewed and explored from the special perspective of national and international security.

"Studies in deceleration" was one of the tolerated research sectors as long as it was tied tightly to pilot survival after ejection at great altitudes, or from crashed high performance aircraft. This became one of the most exciting "stretch" areas for experimentation. On December 10, 1954, Lt. Col. John Stapp rode a rocket driven sled along a 3,350-foot Holloman Air Force Base track at a velocity of 937 feet per second. His impact and precipitous stop in a water trough at the run's end found he had registered between 35 and 40 times negative gravity! It was the culmination of tests with monkeys and bears[2] who paved the way by participation in such tolerance probes. It was unspoken that the major meaning of this applied knowledge lay in the human capacity to endure the positive Gs of a rocket takeoff with astronauts

---

1. Peenemuende, a vast German military research center on the Baltic, when commanded by Generalmajor Walter Dornberger, produced an operational rocket Propaganda Minister Josef Goebbels named *Vergeltungswaffe zwei* (Vengeance Weapon No. 2), the V-2. A total of 3,745 were fired against targets on the European continent and in England. Their effect was slight, but the shadow they cast over the human race will be there forever. The Soviets captured only a handful, but the allies came up with most of the space talent riches. "This is absolutely intolerable," Soviet Generalissimo Josef Stalin barked at an unfortunate Lt. Col. G.A. Tokaty, one of his rocket experts. "We defeated the Nazi armies, we occupied *Berlin* and *Peenemuende*; but the Americans got the rocket engineers." Complain he might, but Stalin didn't do badly as the Russians bagged hundreds of technicians, the laboratories, the assembly plant and the lists of component suppliers. The Soviets interrogated their captives, but did not allow them any shoulder-to-shoulder association with their later experiments. The Americans depended on their Peenemuende experts for leadership, there were such people as Hermann Oberth, Ernest Stuhlinger, Wernher von Braun and Eberhard Rees. Dornberger later worked for Bell Aircraft and instigated their rocket launched glider concept.

2. The Litton Bionetics Research Laboratories came out of this experimentation.

aboard, or the negative Gs the same astronauts would have greeting them when penetrating the atmosphere returning to earth from space exploration and missions. The quality and array of the findings were a serendipity success story in aiding Air Force to forecast spatial headings and equipment necessities. Inclusion of Man with his judgment and decision making skills in the man-machine system was considered an imperative.

Quietly, some months before, the U.S. Air Force Office of Scientific Research encouraged the fledgling Litton to develop a unique facility for the study of the associated physical phenomena that would accommodate Man in simulated conditions of ultra high altitude well beyond the reach of manned aircraft. This was done by imaginative Sig Hansen, a Hughes Aircraft alumnus, who had remarkable similarities in thought processes to those of Charles V. Litton where the vacuum was involved. Stan Webber, one of the long timers with Litton Electron Tube, said that both men could mentally "insert themselves in the environment of the vacuum and often talked of what it would be like to labor there". Hansen was the one picked to determine the feasibility and set up the mechanics—the construction of a chamber capable of interior reduction to one billionth of an atmosphere. Once that was achieved, a human being suitably outfitted in a Litton Industries conceptualized and designed "garment" had to be placed in that forbidding and hostile environment to both observe and control experiments, as well as function competently in the performance of assigned tasks and movements—and live!

And then it happened, that startler. On October 4, 1957, the Soviet Union lofted the very first artificial earth satellite—an instrument-packed, 184-pound package called SPUTNIK (Fellow traveler of the Earth). In 1954, 3 years before SPUTNIK, the Ramo-Wooldridge Corporation, in El Segundo, CA. obtained a rare blank check contract to build the Atlas intercontinental ballistic missile. There was the usual spluttering and tracks-covering on the Potomac, one highly placed die-hard in the administration dismissing it was merely a "basketball in the sky". At the North American Air Defense Command press queries were answered with ". . .if they have the propulsion to put such a thing up there with precision over our heads today, why not on our heads tomorrow?" The White House preferred the momentary politically reassuring stance that it was of "no military importance."[3] There was reason for some comfort among the insiders. They knew how many places halters on appropriate research and testing had been slipped to allow for freer running in the labs. As was so often the case, the logic of forward-looking was nowhere as powerful a stimulus for America and the West as were demonstrated Soviet moves and accomplishments and the fears they conjured.

A month later they threw up a space sequel, a SPUTNIK II, also heavily instrumented. The payload increased to 1,120 pounds and part of that was a frisky mongrel dog, Laika. Litton industries found itself, as it often would later, THE reliance point for exotic technological emergencies. The pressure chamber and the protective garb with which it had had some experimental success evolved into the first contract for ". . .the Mark I USAF Model: Extra-vehicular and lunar surface suit."[4] Space was a no-no no more. Dark statements were being made about how far ahead of the American the Russians were. Commentators in voice and print moaned of "the missile gap". A whole era of new attitudes was born. This was the exciting entry into 1958. Litton was also closing fast on a substantial and solid added ingredient for its future infrastructure.

Business firms of all kinds were being formed in the thousands, not only in the U.S. but in Western Europe and the Orient. Office buildings were towering to dizzy heights on the bomb rubble of city centers abroad. It was as if the recent world conflict had been a step toward urban renewal. The commercial organisms and the operatives quartered in such office blocks hungered for advanced machines and materials. Electronics seemed to be urgently needed in them all.

---

3. Four days later, President Eisenhower stated ". . .there is real military significance to these launchings . . . evidenced by the powerful propulsion equipment necessarily used." There were still tendencies around the Washington waterholes to make light of the Soviet accomplishment, but Eisenhower signaled the necessity to shift gears and take what had happened seriously.

4. That Mark I Model is today in the U.S. Air Force Museum at Wright-Patterson Air Force Base, Ohio. Next to an Apollo Command module, it is captioned as the "Great, Great Grand-daddy of the Moon Suits" in which astronauts eventually walked on the Moon. The historic appraiser described it as ". . .equivalent of one of the Columbus' discovery ships, the potters' wheel, or the chariot used by Caesar when he crossed the Rubicon."

The LITTON Adventure That Was

Business schools were in their heyday turning out sharp management diploma carriers who were considered to be in their starting blocks in running for the money. Mechanization and depersonalization were becoming cultish. Buzzwords abounded. All those old family names so reverently attached to firms by their founders were coded into acronyms or initials, often the very symbols under which the companies' stocks were traded on the various exchanges. What was once "the big boss" became more and more the 'executive suite". The international language would never be Esperanto, yet all languages would have to move over for the computer. Ambitious young men were to take on the world as in an earlier time they had tamed the Western frontier. There were self-styled Merlins among them whose incantations were advertised as able to make money dance, multiply and do miracles. Acrobatic accountants hawked skills in making paper pyramids in the manner of old Hollywood that marched the same dozen Indians around one rock enough times that the camera made them appear to be a war-painted horde. No matter, they were all in business, and they needed modern accoutrements to operate, or impress, or both.[5]

Words and numbers processing were not just terms. They assumed the proportions of overwhelming facts of life. The potential for service and profit in feeding this appetite seemed enormous. Companies that had a long relationship with trade and its conduct were often finding themselves uncomfortable. Perhaps, they mused, they had grown old-fashioned, hidebound, tradition plagued, sluggish, idea resistant, and even Neanderthal enough to be an endangered species crying necessity for electronics technology to be added if they were to be able to stay competitive, keep their management shelves intact, and

---

5. Samuel Kalow, lecturer and author on business and office technology, says, ". . .the major reason for any change in the office was productivity. Technology has affected the office only twice before in history. The Egyptian Pharoahs, Julius Caesar and Abraham Lincoln used office systems in exactly the same way. No technology existed to help people use the office system after writing was invented. If Abraham Lincoln needed a copy, somebody had to make a copy the same way someone did for Julius Caesar. The technology that first affected the office was electricity. With the invention of the telephone in 1876, the office system changed and continued to change rapidly. In 1877 Edison invented the dictating machine. Herman Hollerith was working in the Census Bureau in 1880, and it took years to count the 1880 census. He then invented the punch card equipment which was used for the Census of 1890, and it became the foundation of today's computing equipment. . ."

strike out again for leads in their fields which they had either lost or were in the process of losing.

One of these companies approached Lehman Brothers' Joe Thomas who had owned IBM shares for along time, and was entranced by that company. In 1939, Thomas Watson, Sr., the IBM high priest, had tried to buy out the family ownership in the Monroe Calculating Machine Company. Jay Randolph Monroe, its founder, had shied from telling Watson he couldn't "sell out" men who had worked shoulder-to-shoulder with him to build the business. Joe Thomas' visitor was George Monroe, and he wondered if IBM might still have an interest. Thomas heard him out. He really didn't have to, except as a courtesy. He had been over that road many times before and knew the Monroe plight well. As he was hearing the recount, Thomas knew that IBM would have an antitrust problem with Monroe and was not likely to seek mergers with such companies. Besides the very heart of Monroe was its sales and service field force, all of which would be downgraded unless the right company could be found, one which would need Monroe as much as Monroe needed it. As Thomas listened he was sure he had just the prospect in mind, and it would be a better solution than IBM. Thomas saw Monroe as one of those classic family owned situations where there were as many positions, opinions and points of view as there were shareholding members of the clan. The Lehman Brothers also knew that old Rothschild advice and respected it—that very good deals could be made when someone wants to sell very badly, or buy very badly.

George Monroe, son of S.B. Monroe, came from Kalamazoo, Michigan. He'd been to the Harvard Business School. He thought he saw the future more clearly than anyone else in the Monroe Calculating Machine Company which was established in 1912 by his father's cousin, Jay Randolph Monroe. Jay, as a young man, had been magnetized by the patents of Frank S. Baldwin, some of them dating fro 1874. All of them had to do with calculating or reckoning machines. The very first one won the Franklin Institute Gold Medal at its beginning as the most meritorious invention. Like so many way-out ideas, nothing happened.

When Jay Monroe first saw the model, it was retrieved for him from under Baldwin's bed where it had gathered dust for four decades. He was immediately obsessed with the idea that he saw a wave of the future. Baldwin, caught up in the enthusiasm of Jay Monroe, practically gave it to his young and admiring acolyte. He had run out of gas himself. He knew if his idea was to materialize, he had to trust a surrogate. Jay Monroe had not only the vision of what could be, he also had need of a product. In that crude junk pile in the old man's bedroom, he saw an answer to both. If he could put a keyboard on the machine and cut down the brute force requirement to operate it, he could cast himself as a boon to all those people who had to do sums, yet were no more accurate about it than he was. He wanted to build a manufacturing plant somewhere in New Jersey in proximity to Gotham as the blossoming business center. There he would pursue a career.

Needing money to get on with it, he sent his brother-in-law William Penn Breeding, to speak for him to S.B. Monroe and his equally prosperous associate in Michigan, Alfred B. Connable. They had farms, properties and banks. So well placed were they that Connable had once been Mayor of Kalamazoo. When Breeding told S.B. Monroe what Jay had in mind, the midwest relative moved his chair a little farther away and observed him for a moment incredulously. When he sensed that Breeding was genuinely serious, he exploded a statement that this was the stupidest idea he'd heard lately. That quick reaction was because S.B. Monroe was a whiz with numbers, one of those people capable of running his eyes quickly down a column of four or five digit figures producing the correct total at the bottom—at once—and with ease. Breeding said that he and Jay Monroe were not so blessed. What Jay had in mind could handle that deficiency in lightning-like calculations for everyone, making tallying less tedious and make them all lots of money.

The Kalamazoo moneybags, whether out of tolerance or in the hope that it would keep Jay occupied in the East where he would be no greater family embarrassment than he was, advanced the funds. He was given quantities of stock in what was called the Monroe Calculating Machine Company. None was more surprised when it caught on than the Kalamazoo wing of the Monroes and the Connables who together controlled about 32% of the firm. Income rights to certain quantities of these shares were assigned to various family members at Christmastime. The primary interest of these beneficiaries was dividend disbursements, and never in running the entity which made them possible.

The Kalamazoo backing, proffered so lightheartedly in 1912, was to have a great deal to do with the ability of a building, seam-bursting America being able to cope with and account for itself. Imagine anyone dreaming of a 16th Amendment in 1913 which brought in federal progressive income tax as the law of the land, or a Social Security Act 22 years later, had there been no calculators!

Jay Randolph Monroe visualized how the future might shape up more clearly than most of his countrymen who were opting for insulation in the disillusionments of post-World War I. As up front as 1919, he appointed W.R. Cummings his foreign sales manager and sent him abroad repeatedly, once even around the world with instructions to select dealers in all significant or promising markets. Two years later, the first oversees sales subsidiary, Monroe Calculating Machine Co., Ltd., was put in operation in London, England. Swiss-born George Schmucki, after having been a successful sales executive and helper in setting up Monroe's pride and joy—its sales and maintenance organization—was sent to England to monitor all the United Kingdom and European selling.

It was in this time Monroe shared many important dealers with the Royal Typewriter people as they were in noncompetitive lines. That intimacy and acquaintance with Royal long before there was a Litton Industries was to have far reaching implications separate and apart from offices in common. After the UK, Europe was quick to lay out a welcome mat as far to the east as Poland, Czechoslovakia and Yugoslavia. Belgian Congo and South Africa followed. China, Japan and Australia tied in from across the Pacific. Canada extended its latchstring on the north, and Mexico, Venezuela and Argentina to the south.

It was on April 29, 1937 that the first cat was thrown among the Monroe chickens. At 54, Jay Randolph Monroe died suddenly. The founder and president, the molder and strategiest, was gone. There had never been any necessity for one so young, so he thought, to engage in future planning in a successor or estate sense. There had been conversations, yes. There was a line in his will to the effect that he hoped his son, Malcolm, would one day succeed to the company's management chair. At age 28, Malcolm was to be granted sole right to vote stock in testamentary trust funds. One such fund held 44% of the Monroe securities. The other, which Jay had given to his second wife, Ethlyn after their 1932 marriage, had 10%.

In Jay Monroe's chats, he had seemed always to favor W.G. Zaenglein, his sales vice president. He was the one with the personality and management characteristics for the interim until Malcolm, only 20 at Jay's death, could absorb the experience needed for the helm. The other candidate was Edwin Franklin Britten, the manufacturing vice president. Britten knew that Jay's first wife, pregnant with Malcolm at the time he was being interviewed, had advised against employing him. Malcolm, he knew, wouldn't vote for him to be janitor. Britten took his case to the 32-percenters in Michigan and said he had the toughness the Monroe Calculating Machine Company needed after the long tenure of the easy-going founder. S.B. Monroe and Alfred B. Connable picked Britten, and the battle began to form.

Shortly afterward, with World War II on America's doorstep, Malcolm found himself in the 66th Infantry Division's 262nd Infantry as a jeep courier. That job, not without hazards, didn't seem too different from his experiences in corporate life. It was when his Division was drawn up before the French ports of *Lorient* and *St. Nazaire*, which housed pockets of diehard Germans denying those harbors from use in easing allied logistics, that he found in the pouch thrown in his jeep a communication just for him. There in a French rainstorm, water dripping off his helmet, he had a five-page telegram. It said if there was no answer from him before a date which was already passed by three weeks when he received it, certain takeover moves would be made.

Being executor of the Monroe estate, Britten had great advantages which he exercised with surgical skill. The Monroe family was forced through Orphan's Court of Esses County, New Jersey to sell enough of its shares to deny the Monroe family control. With Malcolm off dodging from hillock to hedgerow in France, Britten was able to corral those securities. It was as beautifully done as a Prof. Moriarty would have conceived for a face-off with Sherlock Holmes.

There was no fatted calf for Malcolm Monroe when he returned home, but there was one who sympathized with him, that onetime $14-a-week accountant who had worked his way up through the corporate thickets. He was suave, expert in handling people, and his

name was Fred Sullivan. He had been on the Monroe scene for decades, knew everybody, buried and otherwise, every skeleton and
where it was and of what importance. He was held in high esteem by
the vast spread of Monroe sales and service people. While Britten
chafed that the no-salary, all commission arrangement often produced
sales that gave people in the field greater pay than top executives,
Sullivan saw it as the beat kind of an incentive system for their complicated world.[6] The sales force was at a strength of more than 2,000.
There were 2,700 service employees ready to jump when there was
emergency or routine action needed. Sullivan had a flair for people,
their motivation, their sense of team and fraternity. Respect for
Monroe product rode on their backs. Relationships with customers
made a shining flame among the dark doings of the time. Under his
influence, Monroe had been able to hold even with the two main competitors, Friden and Marchant, but dissension and unsettlement was
dropping Monroe to about a fourth of the market share.

It was Sullivan who put the two cousins Malcolm and George in
the same room at a Monroe meeting. That night was long and sleepless and full of talk. How were they to marshal forces and resources
for a 'Palace revolution'? In April, 1947, it was finally mounted.
Malcolm, allied with Harold M. Connable, Alfred's youngest son, was
assigned to convince his father and brothers. It worked—the sweep
took out E.F. Britten, Jr., his brother, Clarence, and the son, E.F. Britten, III. They lost their company officer status, and a new management team came in with W.G. Zaenglein as president. Sullivan, who
had played that quiet but supportive key role, became the company's
president six years later. Instantly, now that something could be done,
there were conversations about how the family control, newly restored, could continue without being endangered again in the future.

---

6. Don McMahon was an example of how the straight commission selling
worked at Monroe. When his parents died as he turned 16, he quit high school and
became a Monroe sales trainee. By 1958 when Litton acquired Monroe he was national sales manager. In 1965 he was made President of Monroe, and corporate vice
president of Litton. His first year, he drew commissions of more than $25,000. "I
thought I had died and gone to heaven," he said. Once Tex Thornton told him if he
were to write five names on a piece of paper of those who might one day head Litton
that McMahon's would be one of the five. But executive searchers took him out of
the Litton promotional traffic pattern, first to head Baker Industries, and then to become President and Chief Executive Officer of the Royal Crown Companies, Inc.

Malcolm himself was first to have misgivings about how far beyond the grave a hand could be maintained at the tiller—and whether it was even wise. Herman Kahn, a Lehman Brothers partner, told him once: "Ashes to ashes, dust to dust, you will be a public corporation, or you will go bust!" George, sensitive as always, didn't try to sell his cousin Malcolm on one course over another, but did tell him: "After all, your father founded and operated this company for 25 years. You are his heir. You now have to search your soul and make up your mind about what to do."

It was to correct the error of his father and Connable in the Britten selection, plus the feeling of Sullivan that only with electronics assistance could Monroe get back into competition, that brought George Monroe to Joe Thomas' office at Lehman Brothers. Participation in Harvard Business School theory and philosophy told him that Monroe had to have some new technological teeth. George was talking from only his 12% of the 300,000 outstanding shares. Both Malcolm and Sullivan were on his side. He, as they, felt to their shoe soles that unless Monroe quickly fielded an electronic calculator and all those new product lines that could attend such a development, the family enterprise might well be doomed. It was lost on none of them that being merely in calculating machines was but a small fraction of the business market. If they were to build other office products, or acquire companies which did, it could hardly be managed by Monroe standing alone. It would take a hugh investment. The family wouldn't like inroads on those dividends grown accustomed to and enjoyed.

Merger was impossible because their stock was not traded nor was it listed on any exchange. However, while no merger candidates would find them attractive in the lead position, a company already listed on some exchange might be cajoled and won successfully. It was readily apparent that a suitable partner in harness, or merger, beckoned as the only way to jimmy the window of their family prison allowing escape into that frothy outer corporate world. It was where managers really ran things, had handfuls of stock options and bonuses. Those heavy, disinterested remote, inhibiting and indecisive restraints would no longer pester and be a brake on actions.

Could George Monroe, Joe Thomas asked, convince the many splinters of the family and its adversaries to manage enough shares in favor of a merger consideration? George wasn't sure, but he said he would try. It was then that Joe Thomas, who had helped Tex Thornton bring about Litton Industries in the first place, suggested that rather than IBM that Litton was the way to approach a solution. Litton's stock, Thomas said, had been in the 30's lately and had maintained a climbing attitude through 1957. That would be the boudoir in which to consummate this marriage of convenience. It had bountiful electronic credentials and a need Monroe might just fill beautifully. Thomas spoke with the assurance of being a Litton board member, one who knew how precarious it was for Litton to be on a one legged milk stool of government contract. The Thornton plan said Litton wanted to serve both commercial and military customers. How better than this, then, an ideal situation beneficial for both parties?

Later it was referred to as the "battle of the Biltmore" a name given by George Monroe. That was the New York hotel where Connable, Malcolm Monroe, Fred Sullivan and George were quartered. Tex Thornton, Roy Ash and Glen McDaniel, the Litton trio, were a few blocks further uptown at the Barclay.

Early on, it developed that Connable was going to be the sticky one. He looked like a board chairman. He enjoyed being one, with all the entitlements in respect, honor and status. It was bigger than being the Mayor of Kalamazoo. Having a fist-full of Litton shares in exchange for all that grandeur seemed a pale bargain to him.

Diminutive George Monroe had a rubbery physiognomy capable of more expressions than the great Lon Chaney had achieved in faces with the help of skilled makeup. He effected whatever of them was required by any of the situations as the negotiations proceeded. To Tex Thornton he portrayed his colleagues at the Biltmore as unreasonable tribal chieftains difficult and wary, hard to charm and convince. After getting some concession from Tex he would go back to his brood, telling them he could report that Scrooge was both real and hard of heart a.k.a. Tex Thornton. "I made so many trips back and forth," George said, "I had a deal with this one taxi driver. He hauled me between those two hotels for fifty cents a trip, each way. No tips. He made out on volume."

Finally, the skirmishing was over. Monroe shareholders got 1½ shares of Litton common for each of their own units of Monroe, or ½ of one share of Litton voting preferred, or a combination of both. In

The LITTON Adventure That Was

1957, the fiscal year ending July 31, Litton had sales of $28,130,603 and Monroe booked twice that. When the last "i" was dotted and "t" crossed right after the New Year began, the way ahead looked rosy. On January 2, Litton stock closed at $41.875. All the Monroes and the Connables had a genuine barometer reading as to their net worth. The electronics horses were galloping to the rescue. Fred Sullivan had no obstructions to expand and built a business machines enclave. That office products field which had haunted him as the makings of dreams only, was at his fingertips—and he was a member in good standing on Litton's board of directors. Litton from its side looked out upon three times its previous year's sales volume.

Analysts were titillated by how remarkable it all was. Growth by explosion, so to speak. The old "defense contractor" plague sign and cyclical dismissal so long present when Litton was considered disappeared overnight. Litton in that one stroke was ready for description as a multi-industry company. With Monroe Rekenmachinen in Holland, it was flirting with being a multi-national, too. As would be the case, so many times afterward, Litton was also a way out of a family problem—in this instance a merciless Internal Revenue Service which lurked outside the door as an uninvited guest at the funerals of shareholder members converting estate values at arbitrary government pricing.

By July 31, 1958, the Litton sales total bounded to $83,133,473! Synergism—cooperative action between elements being such that the total effect becomes greater than the sum of two efforts taken independently—was not only an intellectual mouthful, it was bankable. Litton, so very young, had those great expectations but an even greater potential for their realization. George Monroe, who also came on Litton's board, was everybody's hero. He had been the wily contortionist, sword swallower, grand illusionist and zealous chameleon—all things to all parties. He was as pleased as everyone else with his handiwork. His cousin, Malcolm, scion of the one who had started it all, and who had known demeaning and insulting treatment at the hands of his father's successors, was serene at last. Tex Thornton and Glen McDaniel had sensed one of his gnawing concerns, his wish that this new division which bore the Monroe family name, would not only keep it but would have its integrity as an operating unit maintained.

That fast track was really in view now.

Litton's real "key" to the bigger world of opportunity was achieved on the back of yet another's trouble, albeit of a different kind. The American Telephone & Telegraph's Western Electric subsidiary had to make a move—divest itself of its Westrex element. Westrex came into being originally in an association of Western Electric/Bell Laboratories with the film making Warner Brothers. One of those brothers, Sam, was gadget minded and loved to tinker. At one juncture he talked his whole family in Youngstown, Ohio into emptying all pockets on the table to go into hock because he needed $1,000. There was a broken movie projection machine, he said, which was a bargain because he could fix it, and with it would come a few reels of film called "The Great Train Robbery".

The Warner family head had a butcher shop and a meat wagon to make deliveries. The power element was a horse named Bob. Their father wouldn't put up the butcher shop, but he did allow them to give old Bob as collateral. This launched the family in show business. They traveled about eastern Ohio and Western Pennsylvania seeking warehouses which could be transformed into makeshift theaters by setting up chairs borrowed from local undertakers between funerals. Every town in the region got to know Harry, Albert, Sam and Jack and their sister, Rose, who sold tickets. Sam, forecasting where his interests would lead them, was always the projectionist.

That same Lee DeForest for whom Charles V. Litton would later work came into the early 20s with one of his parade of inventions, the audion tube. Drumming up interest for it wasn't easy, which seemed incredible later. It was the technical bridge to long distance telephony, telegraph extension, the broadcasting networks and sound on film in the movies. Western Electric finally bit, and Sam Warner enthusiastically insisted to his skeptical family that through this they could steal the march on the rest of Hollywood. Sam had enough of the con man in him to pull it off.

The Warners and Western Electric joined in a togetherness pact. Their original venture was called Electrical Research Products, Inc. (ERPI). ERPI evolved into Westrex.[7]

---

7. One of the Wextrex addresses was 120 Avenue *des Champs-Elyeès* in Paris. It was there in an earlier time that James Gordon Bennett, the founder of the Paris edition of the Herald-Tribune, a great boozer and *bon vivant* played a memorable scene. Stark nekkid and happily swizzled, he drove a coach and four up that magnifi-

The LITTON Adventure That Was

For years wherever sound and talk were added to films anywhere in the world's studios and projected in the world's theaters, it was for the most part due to Westrex technology and the product line. The magnetism inspired by the movies around the globe meant that Westrex had to be within quick and easy reach for maintenance and repair of its equipment which was for the most part leased with promise of technical and instant service being ingredients of the package. Westrex had a large technical international presence with offices and staffs in major markets and remote quarters of the earth. Monroe had put Litton into the United Kingdom and Holland and into dealerships in many nations, but Westrex could open wider additional marketing doorways. It had established respect, acceptance and professional expertise wherever it was. Through those same portals Litton could walk with whatever it had additionally to offer, and as an indigenous business citizen rather than as an outsider trying to drum up attention and credibility.

Seymour Rosenberg was asked by Tex Thornton to write a rationale supporting the Westrex acquisition. Considering that the established direction of Litton was heavy focus on components, it baffled Rosenberg who couldn't see it as logical at all. He went over all the obvious things. In puzzlement, he approached the front office for added guidance. He ticked off what Litton was and what Westrex had. There was one item of dimension he had overlooked, one that was most important of all to Tex Thornton—the fact that Westrex was one of Ma Bell's offspring's and proud achievements. Faced with the order to divest, Westrex still had to think of all those loyal employees— about 3,000 of them all over the globe—and all of its own excellence stamped on the product itself. Long after Westrex left the Western Electric Fold, memories would still assign Westrex and what it was to MaBell. In no way would it ever shed this off to just anybody. If a convincing case could be made for this Westrex to pass to Litton Industries—the very biggest in the business world transferring an ele-

---

cent thoroughfare at a gallop in the wee hours of the morning. He turned sharply into the enclosed court of No. 120, and banged his head on the low entrance archway, which toppled him to the street with serious injuries. Litton was never able to equal that exploit which became the talk of Paris, but it was the most trafficked address abroad, the location of the busiest Telex machine other than Zurich for Littonites on the move in Europe.

ment of itself to the newest, it would be a statement that Litton was sensitive to the technologies involved. It would also confer a mantle of instant responsibility and respectability on the new foster parent. Rosenberg suddenly saw a big light in another window, and it was no longer difficult to see a mesh.

In that single acquisition, Litton was enriched internationally by long standing addresses in 35 countries,[8] and branches in another 15. Those sales and service branches extended Litton into every major industrial market outside the Communist bloc. Before the shades were drawn on 1958, in addition to the traditional clients Westrex had served so long and well, those same offices were also distributing Litton developed instrument landing systems, radar antennas, communicating equipment and medical X-ray elements. Westrex had more than 1,000 of its employees abroad, at least a quarter of them with 20 years of service. Many of them were at the Westrex manufacturing facility in a London suburb in England.

Litton's initial thrust—components—was being vindicated daily. They were on 21 of the U.S. missile arsenal. Airtron, Inc. owned by David Ingalls, was showing superior craftsmanship in specialized microwave components and equipment for radar. It had other possibilities too.[9] This gave Harry Gray an itch to have the Morris Plains, N.J.

---

8. AT&T, confronted by antitrust consent decree requirements to divest Westrex, was not having an easy time finding a buyer who would not have similar anti-trust problems. Frederick R. Lack, Westrex exec VP, had known Tex Thornton from his Air Force days and told Glen McDaniel once that he knew no one who had the vision in the electronics field that Tex had. McDaniel put together an elaborate, album-like presentation of Litton's antitrust spotlessness as a Westrex buyer. Westrex president Arthur B. Goetze O.K.'d the sale. Litton got the 14,000 shares of $100 per preferred, and 14,000 shares of $100 per common of Westrex with all its internationally placed wholly-owned subsidiaries for $2,400,000 cash, payments made in installments over five years. Closing date was July 15, 1958.

9. Airtron, a laser grower (laser being the acronym for "light amplification stimulated emission of radiation"), had far more in it than that careful appraiser, Harry Gray, surmised. He knew it for flexible waveguides, conduits and leads for jet engines, microwave components such as amplifiers, antenna arrays, attenuators, circulators, isolators, mixer-duplexers, delay lines, dummy loads, harmonic frequency generators, hybrid junctions, multipliers, phase shifters and switches—and more.

From laser crystals to artificial gems turned out to be an easy jump, first with very high quality garnets, and then on to "diamonds", clear and unflawed, which could be sold for around $50 a carat. These artificials came from chemical wedding of Zirconia Oxide and Yttrium Oxide, both opaque white ores which could be melted

operation. It was easily brought about, and with missiles fast being assigned a duality of roles—national security and propulsion systems for space exploration—the number of items in Litton's catalog was each day greater than the day before. It would have been opium smoking then to have seen Litton Industries with more than 200 different participations in the Mercury and Apollo space programs, but this would be a later fact and make the firm a footnoter to history. Litton was to be no bystander when it came to shooting for the moon. It was no longer unexpected of this precocious 5-year-old.

It was on December 6, in 1958, that Litton was really ablaze. That was St. Nicholas Day in Europe. What happened couldn't have been a better gift. The decision was made in Bonn by Minister of Defense Franz Josef Strauss that the Lockheed F-104 "Starfighter" would be for the Federal Republic of Germany its ". . .basic interceptor, fighter-bomber and reconnaissance aircraft."

One of the first allocations to research and development from that initially acquired Charles V. Litton cash flow, which would otherwise have gone to the tax collector, had matured into first rank importance in the defenses of the West.

Every one of Litton's 8,600 employees and 5,800 shareholders celebrated the New Year's eve of 1958, as well they should have. The stock which had sold a year earlier for $$41.875 closed at $83.125. All the Monroe contingent that Christmas had a finer sense of "appreciation" than their single dividends had ever given them before. None in Litton or elsewhere associated the Westrex arrival with a long ago, but most appropriate remark made by Al Jolson. His "Jazz Singer" role brought about the first special award for "best sound" by the Academy of Motion Picture Arts & Sciences given to Westrex. In that

---

together resulting in an amazingly brilliant clear crystal. Dean Mitchell, who headed Airtron in the late '60s, consulted with Saks Fifth Avenue which was intrigued by its potential and urged him on. There was an in-house contest for a name, and Joseph J. LoSchiavo, executive VP of Airtron suggested Diamonair. That spin-off technology became the basis for nearly a quarter of Airtron's profit. Diamonairs achieved a hardness of 8.60 to a natural diamond's 10.

For Airtron, Litton gave 19,947 of Litton common and 7,700 voting preferred shares to Ingalls, J.W. Anderson, Robert Carr, J.W. Hamilton, William Scott Bernard Leroe, Tore Anderson, Ernest Wantuch, Lillian Feciuch and Emanuel Margulies. Tex Thornton said it ". . .extended Litton's position as one of the most complete of any company in the microwave field."

movie, 30 years earlier, he had startled theatergoers when speaking to them from the screen he said: "You ain't heard nothin' yet."

Litton Industries could say the same!

SPECIAL SITUATION #9

THE DRAMA OF INTERNAL GROWTH

Roy Ash said it was the fourth most important decision made in getting Litton Industries under way.

The scope of what German Defense Minister Strauss had brought about was so huge and so full of implications for Western Europe that what it was to mean to Litton was hardly perceptible. Only Littonites knew how big it was to them.

Strauss had cast the Federal Republic as the lead participant in a consortium that included three other continental states—Italy, the Netherlands and Belgium. The news was released in the first week of December, 1958. It cast a long and comforting shadow on Litton through the whole Christmas season. Together, the four countries would buy 1,521 Lockheed-built F-104 "Starfighters" as the basic interceptor, fighter-bomber and reconnaissance aircraft for the air arm of their arc of NATO defenses. Litton's LN-3 had the nod for the inertial navigation system in this ". . .missile with a man in it" concept.

The road to that moment had been tortuous. Shortcomings in inertial navigation capabilities had already altered history. When the German scientists and engineers clustered around Wernher von Braun in Hitler's time, their instructions were as clear as they were hurried. Germany had need of the "mystery weapons", later known as the V-1 and V-2. The guidance systems were so faulty that the pilotless putt-putting V-1 and the rocketing V-2 were only fired at London and Antwerp, two large areas. Hitler harassed the Peenemuende group so much that they finally settled for cosmetics rather than accuracy. The nature of the effort showed up in Royal Air Force reconnaissance flights as early as May of 1943. By 1944, Hitler had 96 launch sites plotted along the English Channel coast. The RAF crippled 75 of these in varying degrees with bombing and strafing runs. Prime Minister Winston Churchill set his teeth deep in his succession of cigars, chewing sternly while 2,734 of the V-1s[1] were fired the first month they went in operation after D-Day. More than 8,000 of them crossed the watery moat between the continent and England. Of these, only

---

1. The V-1, a primitive cruise missile, was a technology that would one day reach for Litton's sophisticated inertial navigation when the U. S. opted for that means of adding longer legs to its strategic weaponry.

2,300 got through. The others were blasted out of the sky or went astray to explode harmlessly in some meadow or in the North Sea.

The V-2 was even sorrier. About 1,000 went off fiery-tailed in the direction of London. These were from sites in Holland. Half of them made it, but the rest dug "divots", mostly around Norwich. The memories of these navigational shortcomings, came to America with von Braun and his colleagues in "Operation Paperclip". These key individuals with exotic credentials constituted a colossal brain bank culled from the debris of the Third Reich.

In their debriefing, the nature of the inertial guidance that Hitler had rushed them into using without adequate refinement was revealed as entirely missile-oriented. Aircraft applications had never been tried nor seriously considered. The device was an air-supported, shell-encased, gyro. Multiple jets spurted air to support the gyro. They had tried to make the gyros strong and powerful enough within themselves to be stable for the relatively short post-launch time in which the course was set.

One of those tuned in on these debriefings and endless discussions was an authentic old, bold pilot, self taught in a World War I Jenny. His interest in instrumentation for aircraft went back to the very early '20s. He was Dr. Charles Stark Draper of the Massachusetts Institute of Technology. Shaking his head as he listened, he knew only too well that gyroscopes for inertial navigation suitable for aircraft would have to be several orders of magnitude better in terms of accuracy!

Draper had a partial finger on it by then. He had been on the U.S. Air Force C-45 flying from Flint, Michigan to Dayton, Ohio when the radio band the crew was listening to revealed that the Japanese had just surrendered. Lt. Col. Leighton I. Davis, who was at the controls that night was also head of the Army Air Force Armament Laboratory. Draper had been working with him for some time on gyro gunsights. He remembered some unused snakebite remedy in his gear, and not being involved in the flying, set about celebrating. He also did some fast thinking.

At some 8,000 feet he approached Davis with his quickly arrived at conclusion: There was no longer any pressing need for improvements in weapons sighting, and now was the time to strike with some funding for the development of a blind bombing system. The critical

The LITTON Adventure That Was

German Defense Minister Dr. Franz Josef Strauss in Munich. He brought about the consortium which bought the F-104-G STARFIGHTER, with Litton's LN-3 inertial navigation, and literally standardized nine of NATO's national Air Forces major weapons systems.

thing was to get the funds contractually committed before the victory euphoria passed and freezes were put on procurement monies. By the touchdown of the C-45 at Dayton on the Wright Patterson air Force Base runway, Davis thought well enough of Draper's course record to go along with him. The contract was written. The money came from what was earmarked for "production of bomb shackles". It asked Draper for a completely inertial bombing system which would use no outside references.

137

On a cross country trip, President Gerald Ford asked during a stop at Luke Air Force base in Arizona that a few minutes be set aside for a chat with a Luftwaffe pilot in training there.

Lieutenant Juergen Dessau and his wife Beate told him: "Mr. President, it is a great honor to meet you, but besides that for me to tell you in person for all of us in the Luftwaffe who have enjoyed the hospitality of this American and that through you we wish to thank the American people for having made this our second home—and such a well-remembered one."

Draper was a "long looker" as well as a considerable doer.[2] He had diagnosed the trouble that the French 75mm artillery had against

---

2. When Dr. Charles Stark Draper was enshrined in 1981 in the Aviation Hall of Fame, former NASA Administrator James E. Webb said of him, "He has often been called the super hero of science. No one better than he used the educational process to harness knowledge with propelling power in the era of exploding technologies. He is a man who personifies the incredible thrust of the 20th Century, exciting those within his reach . . . On behalf of quantum jumps in Man's achievements both here and in the infinite space which surrounds our sphere of earth."

Chairman Charles B. "Tex" Thornton was a diehard believer in inertial navigation, Fred O'Green, the production 'whiz' who proved it.

Germany's fast moving *panzers* during the fall of France, and the sluggish inability of the British pom-pom antiaircraft guns that went down with the Prince of Wales and the Repulse. Those mighty ships were sunk because the guns were unable to line up on the darting Japanese Zeroes. The gyro link with gunsights had engaged him throughout the war. If what he had found did a better job of laying on a target, why not by similar means extend the technology to insure on-the-button positioning of planes in flight and of bombs at target.

What Draper came up with was an awesome bit of apparatus. It worked, yes, but it weighed about 4,000 pounds. His innovation was a viscous liquid-floated, fully-housed gyroscope which reduced the impact of both friction and acceleration. He was driven to find acceptable equipment for the new aircraft now on the drawing boards. He demonstrated what he had, first in 1949, and by 1953 he had it down to 2,000 pounds. He mounted it in a B-29, and tested it on a 12-hour flight from Boston to Los Angeles. That successful flight made a deep dent in the thinking of Tex Thornton.

Litton Industries was "wheels up", ready to fly. Part of the cash flow bequeathed by Charles V. Litton in the first acquisition had to be put to work, or the heavy hand of the IRS would be in the till. Inertial navigation had been engaging to General Motors-Delco, to North American-Autonetics, Northrop, Sperry, Kearfott, and ARMA, but

139

Fred O'Green was a followthrough executive, there for the first delivery of inertial navigation for the Luftwaffe F-104G 'Starfighter' and for the 10,000th which was for the US Navy Carrier Inertial Navigation (CAINS) System, and for the 15,000th on the McDonnell F-18 Hornet, and for the 20,000th for the A-310 Airbus for the Air Force.

most of the thought processes were tied to missiles. The Thornton sixth sense told him that there was an overlooked opportunity for aircraft. He had also been watching the pages of contemporary history.

Back when he'd been getting Hughes Aircraft into a manageable operational and production unit, he visited Washington frequently.

On October 19, 1950, President Harry Truman had a bad day. There were intelligence reports on his disk from Korea that "volunteers" wearing the quilted jackets of the People's Republic of China were on the North Korean side of the Yalu river. He had to do something about improving the political and military muscle tone of Western Europe, and most of the nations there being signatories of the

Litton's Donald P. Wisgirda showing the LN-3 "undressed" to Luftwaffe student pilot Stuffz Bemd Branzow.

North Atlantic Treaty. Every one of the continental armies, navies and air forces had been defeated except those of the Soviet Union, which was feeling its oats. He had dictated a letter earlier to the president of Columbia University. When it came to him to sign, he wrote a postscript in his own hand. It said: "First time you're in town, I wish you'd come to see me. If I send for you, we'll start the speculators to work." Having written it, he licked and sealed the letter, placing the stamp on it himself.

On October 28, retired General Dwight D. Eisenhower came as bidden to the Oval Office. Truman said he wanted him to come out of retirement because he intended to nominate him to become NATO's Supreme Allied Commander. His task: To assemble from that coalition of contributed forces a cheek-to-jaw confrontation capability to face the USSR and its satellites along 4,800 miles of land and water frontier. The NATO Treaty had been in effect since April 4, 1949. It was time for biceps—in fact, past time. The Treaty had not only been

One good monument deserved another. Litton president, Roland Peterson, and the author at the monument at Luke Air Force Base in Arizona where it all began.

signed in ink, but in an atmosphere of common fear of the loneliness of being outside such an alliance.

Eisenhower had grown to manhood on the litany of West Point—"Duty, Honor, Country", felt it, believed it, could never have said no to a commander-in-Chief. In his mind though must have lurked the thought that Napoleon might not be entirely wrong when he said a coalition was always the easiest to vanquish. He'd been right every time except the last, at Waterloo. In agreeing to be the Supreme Allied Commander, Europe, though, he did say with great conviction that some way had to be found quickly to include West Germany's industrial and military potential. It didn't make sense to attempt to defend Western Europe without them. They corked the bottle of the traditional invasion route. In defense of their soil, they would be tougher than anyone and therefore the alliance would be served better. That was a harsh political peapod to shell, emotions being easily stoked by even a hint of half soiling what were once Nazi jackboots.

Eisenhower was nominated, and one by one, the 11 governments accepted him. As he and his wife, Mamie, were sifting through items to take with them which were symbolic of home, word came from

142

Korea on November 12 of a significant happening. USAF Lt. Russell Brown hopped suddenly on an unsuspecting North Korean pilot in a never before seen aircraft. Brown's F-80 didn't have much staying time. In a brief flurry of action, the North Korean went down.

This had been the first appearance of that versatile, highly maneuverable and lethal rover aloft. Named for its designer, Maj. Gen Artem Ivanovich Mikoyan, it was the MIG-15. It was the first jet fight.

Lt. Brown knew he was lucky that day. As time passed and the performance statistics accumulated, he grew to know even more just how fortunate he had been. North American built F-86 Sabrejets were rushed in quickly. In all, 39 air Force pilots were to become jet aces—five or more kills—and 811 MIG-152 were knocked down. No North Korean lived long enough, even in this incredibly agile plane, to become an enemy ace.

The Pentagon—where Tex Thornton moved among old friends who shared confidences with him—was concerned. The most disturbing feature came in the reports of Maj. Gen. Earle E. Partridge, the South Korean based 5th Air Force commander. The MIG-15s, the said, seemed, to be able to get as much as 10,000 feet higher than the laboring F-86s. Undoubtedly Soviet advisers sometimes sat "upstairs" at those safe altitudes, counseling beleaguered North Koreans to break off and "come on up" to safety. Some did go, and from that commanding plateau could survey the scene below and pick when to dive on the backs of vulnerable American lower down.

While General Eisenhower was making the first swings through NATO countries to perk up the war-shriveled spirits of their political and military leaders, Lockheed's Clarence W. "Kelly" Johnson and others were asked to go to Korea at once. They were to make determinations as to what kind of an aircraft it was going to take to match in every category from speed to climb not only the MIG-15, but its probable next generations. If the MIG-15 was in Korea, it could be used against NATO. The Pentagon even allocated rockets to Johnson so he could put wings on their slim fuselages, fire them, get a feel for how far he could to in cutting down wing requirements while still retaining control near projectile speeds with a man aboard. Air Force Chief of Staff General Hoyt S. Vandenberg kept saying: "We want a plane that'll go like hell, one that a pilot can yo-yo up and down like crazy."

Johnson, as always, retired to his "skunk works" in Burbank, California, walled in with secrecy and security.

One day, Lockheed's top test pilot, Tony Levier, was summoned. He was handed a memo which said he would engage in "in-flight dynamic simulation" of a new concept. He was sent to the Ames Research Center at Moffett Field in Sunnyvale, California. They wrung him out a bit in the simulator to be sure he was up to what was in the schedule for him. There were three different simulation configurations—wings straight (no dihedral[3]) wings five degrees dihedral, and wings ten degrees dihedral. The latter was the wing-droop desired. It was on it that he was questioned, but he had one of his own first: "What the hell kind of a plane would fly like this?" His question and his amazement were greeted with silence. Only a few knew then that this is what ultimately determined the high T tail, fighting cock mien that became the F-104G "Starfighter". The tail added an important factor of control to make up for the lack of wing structure. It led to a $5,000,000,000 contract, which produced more than 2,700 planes for the Air Forces of 15 countries which 8,000 pilots flew.

At the time of these airframe determinations, nobody was thinking about avionics to any serious degree, especially not inertial navigation. Tex Thornton had known Henry Singleton at Hughes Aircraft before Henry went to North American, where he was at work on the technology for the Navajo missile. The Navajo missile's future was clouded, and the Autonetics division's urgency for what he was doing was reflected in a small budget.

Thornton's hunch grew that there was a prize for a company which could miniaturize this part of the avionics package to fit the small space available in those needle nosed and slimish fighter aircraft. He began conversations with Singleton. Singleton sensed an excited climate might be there for him at Litton, a contrast in high degree with where he was. It led to that under-a-Westwood-tree agreement for Singleton to leave Autonetics and become a part of the Litton payroll—and its high hopes.

If there are reincarnations of the zealots of old, or lookalikes only, Dr. Henry Singleton was whichever one the beholder perceived. What he believed, he believed with intensity. He could make a labo-

---

3. Dihedral is the angle formed between the airplane wings and the fuselage.

ratory vibrate. When he left North American though, his departure wasn't judged significant enough to fly the company flag at half-mast. The aerospace industry had more Gypsies than ancient Romany anyway. Engineers had similarities to violinists in orchestras—easily replaced. But Singleton brought several much-needed characteristics with him. He had razor sharp thought processing, and an uncanny ability to sort out the unnecessary and to miniaturize the crucial. He was no technical pack rat addicted to adding on. He traveled with the barest of requirements for the trip, which included under-population in staff and minimal payroll.

Tex Thornton and the Litton top shelf was that way, too. They were not only putting their scarce money on a technology, but on an individual who seemed to have a special appropriateness for the unmapped task at hand. At MIT he had never been near inertial navigation at all, although he had met Dr. Draper many times. His specialty then had been computers, those applicable to communications. An especially critical part of what he had to do for Litton was to get a workable computer dwarfed well below any existing specimens.

The missileers were the VIPs of the era. They were not easy company to keep. Anyone still thinking about something with a cockpit in it was trying to rationalize flight pay continuance, or was going geriatric. The missileers had languages of their own, egos of their own, and prejudices which were evident to all who sought to intrude on their domain. They were the new Philistines, who could be dealt with only by modern zealotry. Even among the airframe manufacturers the best that could be managed was a willingness or the courtesy to listen.

Singleton flushed some early serious contacts among the fraternity. They said he'd have to get his inertial navigation package, complete, functional, reduced in cubage and weighing less than 100 pounds! Only then would those makers of those reed like fighter aircraft want to talk further. In no time, Singleton's nerves were raw and his temper short. He was watching Litton's meager funds dwindle. "Down a rat hole," as he put it. There were frequent meetings in Litton's first and second year about whether to give up on the whole idea of inertial guidance.

Doppler inertial navigation was based on findings of the Austrian physicist, Charles Johann Doppler, that there were shifts in frequency when approaching or receding from sound sources. Doppler navigation was available, but was spotty and ragged. A 30-degree bank placed the antennae at such an angle that distorted readings came back. Over rough water or undulating terrain, it wasn't dependable.

Resurgent West Germany was becoming more real every day. Disjointed occurrences suddenly began to relate. Reports of the aerial combat over "MIG Alley" in Korea had NATO airmen uneasy in early 1952. General Lauris Norstad, Allied Air Forces Central Europe Commander, said he urgently needed the son of a Wichita, Kansas grocer to join him in Europe. Air Force Chief Vandenberg agreed and dispatched Major James Jabara[4] to him for two months temporary duty. Jabara, on a previous October's afternoon in his F-86 on the last mission before he was to be reassigned and with a dangling wing tip tank that refused to jettison, closed quickly on not one but two MIG-15s. Both were demolished. He became the world's first jet ace with six kills! It was from this special eminence and perspective that Norstad wanted him to lecture and answer the questions of NATO pilots from Stavanger, Norway, to Erzerum, Turkey on the quality of American-furnished aircraft and pilots. There was quite a difference in the F-84Es and Fs of NATO from the F-86s in Korea, but the statistics of the 15-to-one kill ratio favoring the west said that piloting could make the winning margin even when the equipment match was unequal.

Jabara, a first generation American whose father had migrated from Lebanon, was diminutive and smoked great black cigars. He was at his ingratiating and professional best, country after country around the NATO circuit. He had particularly looked forward to the halfway mark—an appearance at the old German base, Fuerstenfeldbruck, near Munich. A lot of his old Air Force cronies were there on occupation duty. There would be relaxation, drinking, hangar flying and who knows what all? When he landed, they told him there would be some "German civilians" in the listening group that night. Jabara was jaunty about it, probably one of those "community relations things." He thought the "German civilians" were unimpressed and he soon found out why. Poorly dressed they might be, but they gave him

---

4. Floyd George Steele said nothing was harder than to get the "aluminum benders" (airframe types) to see that electronics represented the future's big money. And they always graduated to the management positions where they erected layers of stumbling blocks, impeding that realization.

the grilling of his life, boring in for details he had encountered no-where else. One of them was former Luftwaffe Oberstle;utnant, Guenther Rall, who had 275 kills in World War II! He and his once

Lt. Genther Rall, German ace, had 275 air victories. Here he comes to Arizona for training in the Litton inertial guidance system.

well decorated colleagues were working on airbases in proximity to modern aircraft that they were forbidden to fly—to keep current. Once there was a peace treaty, a new military force would lock them in as a NATO contributor. In his audience that night were not only Luftwaffe Super-Super-ace, Maj. Erich Hartmann but four future Luftwaffe chiefs.

In 1957, 15 of those who had been Jabara's audience better dressed but still in civilian clothes, stepped down at Sky Harbor airport in Phoenix, Arizona enroute to Luke Air Force Base. Named as it was for the World War I balloon buster, Lt. Frank Luke, a German nemesis, they were a part of the parade of political paradoxes. They had all had some flying hours in those bronco-like German jets.

One of them, Johannes Steinhoff,[5] had to have his face entirely rebuilt after having the flesh burned from the bones when his jet exploded on the runway during takeoff. Major Erich Hartmann had 352 victories. Capt. Friedrich Obleser had blasted 127 and Lt. Col. Guenther Rall was credited with 275. Along with them were Capt. Paul Schauder, Capt. Fritz Wegner who knocked down 19, Major Walter Grasemann, Capt. Dieter Bernhard and so on. Rall and Obleser were also slated for the F-104G "Starfighter" test team. Those 15 constituted the first German Air Force America-trained class.

Germany was keenly interested in a way to jump over 11 years of enforced grounding after the 1945 unconditional surrender. They had to get into the forefront of technology and associated capabilities against what they knew the Soviet Union and its Warsaw Pact bloc

---

5. As the post World War I Treaty of Versailles forbade Germany military aviation, pilot training was fudged in glider flying clubs. One of the von Braun team being debriefed after coming to the U. S. was Dr. Ernst Steinhoff, who had worked on inertial navigation's potential as a glider autopilot as early as 1931 at the Institute of Motorless Flight in Darmstadt. The equipment had been tested on small powered aircraft, too. He transitioned to rockets at Peenemeunde for the V-1 and V-2 programs. Stationed at the Arbor Vitae complex of the U. S. Ballastic Missile division later, Steinhoff visited Litton and knew Dr. Henry Singleton. It was his cousin, Oberst Johannes Steinhoff, who would come in that first group of 15 to Luke Air Force Base and enthuse about having the Litton LN-3 inertial platform on their version of the F-104G "Starfighter"—and then go on to head the Luftwaffe and eventually NATO's Military Committee.

had beyond the barbed wire which halved what had once been their country.

Henry Singleton, though restive that progress was slow and apprehensive about costs, was proving himself a genuine engineering "shrinker". There were sharp disappointments, but he'd finally gotten his prototype down to 87 pounds. These acceptable proportions in weight and cubage supported a stable platform, and also assured constant equilibrium in gyroscopes with two degrees of freedom and sensitive accelerometer and a tiny computer to calculate the earth's rotation and distance traveled.[6]

The platform kept a constancy of reference with coordinates during airborne movement. The accelerometer transmitted the computer information revealing velocity and position.

A man Singleton had once worked for—H.R. "Dutch" Kindelberger, a premier figure among "aluminum benders" who headed North American Aviation—had poked fun at early computers in a speech when he said: ". . . as sophisticated as the manufacturers of machines have become, they still can't match the reproductive powers of a woman who by the simple act of giving birth encloses in a baby's head what can grow to be 10,000,000,000 binary systems or decision making elements it would take 65,000 IBM machines to duplicate. Since we can mass produce these items with unskilled labor, we would be foolish not to use them!" He was, of course, making a podium case for the man-machine system and to get a chuckle from his audience. Singleton was after no slick rhetoric or laughs. He had to make up for that same Man deficiency by producing an instrument which couldn't be much larger than a man's head. This was the only way it could qualify as to weight restraints, yet perform to rigid, demanding and lightning-like specifications. No more to be tolerated

---

6. Patent attorney Bob Lentz was called in one Monday morning by Henry Singleton and Hal Erdley. They had it at last. For a long time they had been working on inertial navigation platforms using three single degrees of freedom gyros, and on that morning they explained the concept of the two-degrees-of-freedom gyro, which reduced size and reduced the cross coupling servo-mechanisms to eliminate error. They'd worked day and night that whole weekend. This was the revelation which walked Litton into its inertial navigation heritage. Of the many patents tracked into fruition by Lentz, this one became a model for a Litton trophy to be given on special occasions. Lentz kept the one given to him on his desk as a reminder of a historic moment and his being "the first to know".

was the pilot response to the Bolling Air Force Base control tower when at 30,000 feet, he was asked for position saying if looking down on the right "Over Washington". Or, if looking down on the left— "Over Baltimore". Inertial navigation of the kind Singleton was bringing in would say for him that he was over the southwest corner of Seth Gaither's farm in Maryland. It was that precise.

The strong conviction held by Tex Thornton about electronics and the transformations to come because of it, never flagged. He had to live with his decisions. He wanted to force time to serve him, not intimidate him. If he had any misgivings, he kept them to himself. Henry Singleton said that this was ". . .a most significant thing".

"He had confidence in us. Trust in us. He knew we were determined to lick this," Singleton said. "He had nothing other than his evaluation of us to go on. He continued to fund the project."

Singleton, above all, knew how prone any industry, the aerospace one especially, could be in instant enthusiasms and be equally quick to abandon them as frustrations and costs mounted.

"A lot of people in Tex Thornton's shoes," he declared, "would have said '. . .to hell with it,' and would have written it off." It was the only one of many times in Litton's history that the Thornton doggedness would show, and it was probably his first and biggest test.

Litton was bucking two distinct disadvantages. Others had been chasing the elusive inertial navigation commercial solution for years, and Litton was but another new boy in town. Litton was really untried except that it had taken a brainy first step in its initial acquisition. No matter how much Tex Thornton bragged about the cerebral types he was gathering around him, the company's development credentials weren't obvious. Singleton's best shot had been an approach to Bell Laboratories, where he got several million dollars for a study on inertial navigation and how to accomplish it. The Air Force Tactical Air Command was scouting about for what it was labeling a tactical bomber. Singleton screwed up his courage and took on more people. He had barely gotten seriously in motion on the project when Bell Labs called with shattering news that the contract was cancelled. Singleton, as if struck in the solar plexus, gritted his teeth and walked heavy footed to the Thornton office to tell him they'd hit yet another stone wall. Jack Fairburn told him Thornton was at the Pan Pacific

Auditorium looking over the exhibits of the Institute of Electronic and Electrical Engineers convention then in progress.

Singleton didn't believe the bad news could wait, so he got in his car and drove to the auditorium. As he strolled along one of the aisles, he suddenly spotted Tex standing alone peering intently at one of the exhibits. Singleton could almost sense his wheels turning about possible applications or extensions into the future. Penetrating that dreamy concentration made what he had to do all that more difficult as he knew how tight an enclosure Thornton could draw around him fencing everything else out.

"Hi," Singleton finally said softly.

"Hi, yourself," was the cheery greeting, "What's up?"

Singleton told him about the cancellation.

Forever, that moment remained indelibly etched in Singleton's mind. Whatever sinking feeling he might have caused, it was kept behind a serene and unruffled mask.

"Perhaps there's still some way we can get somebody to keep our part of it alive," said Thornton matter of factly. "Let's go to Washington and see what we can do."

Singleton is not sure whether it was stated in that offhand way to lift him from his depression, or if there was really hope for continuance. What Thornton suggested turned out to be right,[7] because there were some definite undercurrents of Air Force interest.

A young fighter pilot named Col. Gordon Graham, was a believer. His thoughtfulness was respected on the inertial navigation subject. He was talking up a previously unheard of role for it—that it could play a critical part in atomic weapons delivery. One supporter does not a contract make, however, and Singleton learned how often Dr. Charles Stark Draper was asked for advice by the Pentagon. He knew Draper was often scathing about inertial directions others were taking. There was concern on Singleton's part that there might be more than friendly difference of opinion in his remarks, because first conceptualizers are known to find it difficult to surrender to other

---

7. In that tense time period, though, some meager money turned up in an unexpected quarter—the Army. It was a contract for the first LN-1 for a little more than $100,000. The Army was exploring inertial navigation for its small airplane fleet at Ft. Huachuca, Arizona.

hands what they feel belongs to them. Graham suggested that some time be devoted to making sure that if Draper did not go along with the new tacks by competing firms that he would not oppose or knock these departures from his "true faith".

He was a formidable father figure in the technology. Military consultations with him were frequent. The services were pleased with the prospects of self containment of a system with no radiation or radio waves being produced to clue an enemy weapons system as to the whereabout of the speeding target in which it was a passenger. But on Draper's side, uppermost in his mind was that he needed all the disciples he could get, people who understood "Draperese" (his special brand of oral shorthand terminology). He wanted those as driven as he was to make inertial navigation respected, accepted, and capable of performing its function. He assigned value to the learning benefits of "blind alleys" as he had been up more than a few in his own researching. Some had not been the *cul-de-sacs* they appeared to be.

The Federal Republic of Germany had quietly assigned its Luftwaffe future to the expert judgments of Rall and Obleser. Members of the Luke Air Force Base pioneer German 57-T class often traveled with them on their exploratory trips. Once they had gotten jet training at Luke, there was some test flying arranged for them at Palmdale in California. Because they were that near, the German contingent decided to visit the 336 North Foothill Road Litton Industries' location in Beverly Hills. They showed up in their sharp new Luftwaffe uniforms

Two of the men sent to escort them were J. Ray Donahue and C.V. "Mac" Meconis. As an American Air corps lieutenant flying a B-24 Liberator from Attlebridge RAF station in England for 33 missions "Mac" Meconis had fought against men such as these. On seeing them at close range and even that long after, the hair at the nape of the neck tingled. With all those "kills" with which they were credited, one of them might well have been Meconis. Donahue found that Oberst Johannes Steinhoff and himself had actually been clobbered the same day and hour over Anzio in Italy. They tried to match details to see if they'd done each other in, but were never able to prove it.

Everyone with war memories including times and places pondered how many occasions all of them in the room had once shared the same agitated air space. It was an instant lesson in how

Man must be able to adjust to the phenomenon called politics and the alliances it creates. Not unlike sports, it was like being traded to another team for what leadership had decided can be the next winning combination. This was the truly big league, where the play was for international security rather than pennants and cups and playoff shares.

Henry Singleton discussed Litton's inertial navigation with them thoroughly. He knew these were men who had chafed for years in their dungeon of defeat, made even deeper because they were denied any right or access to flight, hitherto their total lifestyle and preoccupation. They had been the superstars and had ranked with the best. He could sense their wish to have not only that feeling again, but to catch up on that had developed while they had been in neutral. They looked for ways to span that awful gulf of 11 wingless years, but in rebirth, they wanted to come on the scene brand new in every technological way.

Oberstleutnant Rall immediately grabbed the knobs on the Litton model. As he played with them, the others looked on with excitement. Singleton noticed he had a make-do thumb on one hand. What Singleton didn't know then was that Rall, for all his 257 victories, had been shot down eight times. He was lucky to have anything left of him at all. His first back-to-earth had been in JU-52 in the Soviet Union in 1941. Carried away from the crash of his ME-09, his back was broken in three places. During nine months in various hospitals, one of them in Vienna, he courted, won and married one of the lady physicians. Even though they said he would never fly again, he was soon back on the Russian Front doing his missions and averaging 20 kills a month. He had to perform with a cushion at his back and another under one leg, but fly he did. It was clear that when he made up his mind nothing would be whimsical about it.

The Federal Republic of Germany had a special problem—it was only 15 jet minutes wide and 20 jet minutes long. Border patrolling at high speeds required great care to prevent inadvertent overflights of the German Democratic Republic as all the Communist bloc countries were mightily exercised by "air space violations". An exact fix over homeland geography had diplomatic significance.

No decision was made that day of first encounter. J. Ray Donahue was assigned to monitor closely the various foreign teams that were engaging in flight tests at Palmdale. Among the aircraft involved was the F-104. Probably because of the developing German interest in it, Lockheed's on-scene test pilot, Lou Schalk, asked Donahue if Litton would allow one of its LN-3 inertial navigation systems to be placed on the F-104 permanently and participate fully in the tests. Singleton had been doing his own massaging of Lockheed. Perhaps this was the long awaited glimmer of hope.

J. Ray Donahue was the corporate Litton clone of the 19th century "drummer", the traveling salesman who knew every customer from foibles to faith to family tree. As a onetime Air Force pilot, he had been shot down into a belly flop landing in the Mediterranean. Post-war he lived to become one of those most glamorous of all airmen—a project test pilot for North American Aviation. His head was full of names, associations, records, professional calibers, conversational minutiae on myriad subjects, and in some way could summon one or all to coincide with the right moment. He had known Singleton at North American and Tex Thornton from when he was the pilot assigned to Hughes Aircraft Company for trials. Scientist or engineer he was not, but when it came to finding a sales opening few were his equal. He relayed Schalk's request to Dr. Harold Bell and Allen Orbuch who were with Singleton's unit. What Schalk was suggesting amounted to a laying on of the hands to Litton's crown jewels. Donahue was given two LN-3s and Lane Wright, a field engineer, to insure the systems were kept in top form.

Having two systems was important. Any aircraft being tested, has a regimen to follow. At that time there was head-to-head competition between Northrop's F-5 and Lockheed's F-104. On the return from each aerial joust, the moment wheels touched the runway, a meter flag went down. Thirty minutes were available to taxi, refuel, reload bombs, turnout, and take off. Donahue and Wright wanted protection if an installed LN-3 gave a flawed performance, then the second one could replace it during that half-hour ground time. Lockheed didn't like the hazard of possible interference with its own movements during the scant 30 minutes, but agreed.

At lunch one day, Donahue sat down with the Royal Canadian Air Force Wing Commander Robert Christy, who had been flying F-11s for his government. He was distracted and seemed to have his mind on other things. He picked at his sandwich, not at all his usual ravenous self. "I can't eat with you for awhile", he told Donahue suddenly. "We've been instructed to fly back to Canada tomorrow."

Donahue started thinking. Both Canada and the Germans had been giving the F-104s a stiff going over. Donahue that morning had noticed that the Germans were gone.

"Sounds as though somebody has made a decision," Donahue said.

"I can't tell you anything," Christy told him poker faced.

J. Ray Donahue had guessed right. The Germans had made their choice.

Defense Minister Strauss said: "The decision to select the Starfighter for the Luftwaffe was the conclusion of a long process of investigation and was the unanimous recommendation *in all aspects.*" One of the aspects was Litton's inertial navigation.

It was exactly eight years after Eisenhower had told Truman some way should be found to include West Germany in the defenses of Western Europe and Air Force Lt. Russell Brown's first victory over a MIG-15 in Korea. Nine of NATO's air forces would ultimately have the answer "MIG Alley" over North Korea had signaled so urgently—and all of them would have Litton's inertial navigation in the avionics packet.[8]

There was no stopping now. Some hands were shaken in token appreciation of the great meaning this conveyed about Litton. From a scratch start, in five years it had produced an up-front technology. Several governments searching for security upgrading and balance now lined up to buy Litton's concept and product. Prototype models had to give way to assembly lines not only in the U.S. but offshore. Employees in industries with skills in precision work were about to be retrained to not only manufacture inertial navigation systems, but also to repair and maintain them.

There was some undercurrent of disquiet in U.S. Military circles that NATO air forces were about to be better in instrumentation and

---

8. Bob Lentz had to go after a large parade of patent applications dealing with inertial navigation as each new step was taken. Years later, at a Litton Advanced Technology Achievement Awards dinner, he was given the prestigious G-200 gyroscope-topped award. Those key patents he secured in Litton's infancy were illustrative of what Tex Thornton had said in his original plan about the aim being to "establish strong proprietary product values."

avionics. General Curtis LeMay, the Chief of Staff, heard a lot of advice that inertial navigation was not to be taken too seriously. He had great respect for a Reserve Navy Captain Charles Blair, which was heightened when Blair used a sextant and flew over the North Pole in an old P-51. That kind of thing took savvy, a lot of confidence in one's ability—guts, too. At first he, too, was cool on inertial, but he began sharing time and conversations with Col. Gordon Graham, LeMay's first chief of the Tactical Division for the USAF Deputy Chief of Staff/Operations. Little by little, Blair came around and wanted to see it tried out.

Col. Graham was sent to Palmdale to personally fly the F-104. The constituency that was open-minded about inertial navigation was still minuscule. If Graham was going to have the Litton system with him, he would have to "borrow" it from some other country's plane at Palmdale. He did that. Allies did such loanouts then, a thing nigh impossible now. When he appeared in his flight gear, he told J. Ray Donahue grimly that he thought the success or failure of the system on his missions would be ". . .the proof of the pudding." He was taut when he said it as he was carrying his own baggage of his perpetually expressed convictions about inertial navigation merits.

As they walked out to the F-104, Donahue looked back. Lane Wright, the field engineer, held both thumbs up indicating the equipment on board was aligned and ready, as was the holdout model to sub it. The flight plan called for a simulated "bomb run" to the southern tip of Death Valley taking off from Palmdale, dog-legging to Bishop, letting down to minimum levels over the intervening mountains and valleys, making "bomb drop", then asking Litton's inertial navigation to take the plane back to Palmdale.

The 12,000 foot plus Telescope mountain peak was in the way, blocking the as-the-crow-flies return so inertial navigation had to avoid it, recover its course and get home. As Col. Graham scooted off and upwards, Lane Wright began warming the second system as if it were some high school freshman squirming for the coach to send him in. The round trip for Graham was 450 miles. A half-hour later the plane was back on the Palmdale concrete. He told Donahue as soon as he came on the apron that the system hadn't worked well at all. Nimble as a surgeon, Lane Wright had the original package out of its slot and the second one in place. Graham took off again. On that return, he had both arms up, thumbs extended, saying it had worked like a jeweled watch! Charlie Blair now moved all-out into Graham's corner and told LeMay and others he believed inertial navigation should be seriously pursued.

The U.S. Navy was even more reluctant than the U.S. Air Force about this type of avionics. Under strong pressure from Dr. Harold Bell of Litton, it was finally decided to give it a roughhouse going over on the U. S. S. Bennington aircraft carrier. Originally, the Grumann WF-2s were only to give suitability check-outs in a series of takeoffs and landings. A total of 86 of these were set up for the WF-2 performance under duress. To that number, an additional five missions were decreed to focus on what Litton then called its Pitch-Roll-Azimuth-Reference-Systems mercifully acronymed to PRARS.

Dr. Bell and his associates, T.J. Rickords and Jerry Frownfelter, boarded the U.S.S. Bennington on July 5, 1959. They were met by the Navy's project officer a dedicated, serious Lt. Lawrence Richard Allen who knew there were many "wagging tongues" in the Navy about how this test had been made so rugged it would put an end to any pretensions that inertial navigation had a place in the fleet air arm. No matter, Allen had no feelings one way or another—he just wanted a better, more capable Navy and hoped his findings would help that.

While he did the 86 required takeoffs and landings the Litton crew used the time to conduct careful alignment measures through July 6th next day. When aircraft #211 catapulted off the Bennington five times on July 8th, whatever happened, that would be it. The tone and finality of the way it was phrased was hardly heartening to the Litton team, as if judgments had already been made that failure was certain, and to steel themselves for a disaster.

From the first to the last of that five missions, the #211 would leave with a swoosh, the plane transforming quickly into a dot, then disappearing in the distance. Each time #211 came back, it would settle in like some aerodynamic claw hammer, the claw down to catch the barrier across the Bennington deck. Each was a real slammer, but Allen would stand up in the cockpit and V-sign the Littonites excitedly. PRARS worked![9]

---

9. Navy Lt. Commander Lawrence Richard Allen was later a 1963 KIA (killed in action) in Vietnam.

Whatever else happened on those two separate Air Force and Navy occasions, they were natal moments for Litton's right to claim ultimately for itself that it was the inertial navigation capital of the world. There were continuing struggles, but the Luftwaffe decision, the Palmdale, and U.S.S. Bennington findings were the delivery rooms for Litton's bouncing high technology baby.

The Air Force was in its period of acute disillusionment about its commitment to Republic's F-105. A ponderous aircraft, it was irreverently dubbed by its pilots "the lead sled." Fifteen wings of them were on the Air Force plate. As will happen, Col. Gordon Graham, who had done all the pioneering inertial navigation tests including tight loops and barrel rolls which neither disturbed nor baffled Litton's inertial navigation on the F-104F, drew the first F-105 squadron, and with that 'honor' his first experience in his life of having to make a flameout landing. Tactical Air Command's General Cameron Sweeney didn't like the F-104, which he said was too short-legged in range, too limited in its ability to bear armament.

Litton decided to pass the F-105, because McDonnell had a zinger coming down its lines which the Navy called the F-4C "Phantom." Hard though it usually is for one service to see merit in the materiel of another, roles and missions being different, as well as carrier and land based operations vastly dissimilar, the F-4C, or the F-110-A, as the Air Force nomenclatured it, was a very versatile beaut for its time. Blistering fast, durable, it could also go distance. While other interceptor thinking might be fast off-and-up, short fighting stay, and down due to proximity of attack bases and defense runways, it could manage that, too.

The Tactical Air Command had the kind of assignment for which the F-110-A was a match. McDonnell netted an initial production contract for ten. Litton's strategists recognized that if there was a way to get onto an Air Force program that was going somewhere, the F-110-A had to be it. Munday Peale, Republic's head who had sold all those F-105s, had said he didn't think the Air Force was ready for inertial navigation. Litton didn't argue. It was just as happy not to be included in that one. The F-4C and the F-110-A were causing lights to dance in the eyes of two military services.

Dr. Harold Bell, Allen Orbuch and J. Ray Donahue were at McDonnell for a meeting with Robert Little, Charlie Forsyth, Sandy Mc-

Donnell, who was old "Mac's" nephew and heir apparent, and Frank Christofferson. One after another, the "Phantoms" were coming down the line and Litton hadn't made an indent yet. Suddenly, they were talking about No. 9. The No. 9 member of any such flock was usually the one to which the avionics systems were tied. Donahue heard Christofferson saying that as director of all flight test operations they would like a Litton system for that plane. Donahue was sure that this was because there was lots more Air Force chatter about inertial navigation coming of age, that overseas air forces were more modern than the USAF, and Christofferson was ready to take the chance. Donahue also knew that all the inertial systems of Litton were contractually committed. The question had been to Orbuch, the Litton marketeer, and Donahue was afraid he'd give the correct answer—that what systems Litton had belonged to others. Fearful of what such a response might trigger, Donahue broke in.

"Allen," he heard himself saying ever so carefully, "don't you think we could get them a system in a couple of weeks? Maybe 18 days or so?"

Orbuch's mouth dropped open, but before he could get anything out, the McDonnell people said that would be fine as they were going to test No. 9 in about 21 days. If Litton could install one of its systems within that 21-day period, it would ride on all the tests. Donahue, once the meeting was breaking up, expected to be taken to the woodshed by his superiors for having made that time squeezing commitment. But they gulped gamely and went along. The promised system was at McDonnell's plant in St. Louis within a fortnight, and flew on the 17th day after that conversation. The Germans and the Canadians were both looking ahead to the potential of the "Phantom". It was they who permitted the "borrowing" of the two of their Litton inertial navigation systems for this Americanization chapter.

The test crew, McDonnell and Litton paired, went to Langley Air Force Base, Virginia in February. Weather at that time of year is from frivolous to frolicsome to fraught with peril around Langley and subject to change without notice. February finds it at its most capricious. McDonnell's test pilot was a seasoned ex-Navy hand, no stranger to elements gone foul, but if he could have had his choices some setting less unpredictable than Langley would have been his preference. But that's where the U.S. Air Force's Tactical Air Command is located.

The McDonnell man, Emery "Bud" Murray, arrived in his hall-mark fedora which he always wore except when in the cockpit, and with him was an aircraft called the F-4H with a Litton LN-3 in it.

Some short flights went well. Then with a painstakingly in-structed Col. John Gregory riding as observer, the teeth-gritter course was laid. They would fly from Langley, via Flat Rock and Charleston to Louisville, Kentucky, and return. The date of the adventure was Washington's birthday. It was to be a moment of truth, indeed, over 1,036 nautical miles east to west, and west to east. There was scut-tlebutt that inertial navigation worked well on north/south and south/north courses, but not east/west and west/east.

"We were seriously in need of a navigation system for our tacti-cal forces because we were becoming global in mission, flying oceans nonstop," said Gregory. "We had to make weapons deliveries in all weather conditions, at night, and we needed an ultra-reliable platform so we could do this with accuracy in addition to supplying data for cockpit instrumentation. Inertial navigation had this potential. We were dependent then on Doppler. This worked all right in larger air-craft which had room for complementary support such as Doppler re-quired. Fighter aircraft had too many space limitations for that. First, we had to convince ourselves about inertial, then the Air Staff, who in turn had to get it through the civilian secretariat in the Department of Defense—as well as the money from Congress. Always these kinds of things start with the working, the using people, the ones called on to perform the missions."

The F-4H scampered down the runway, climbed and went off to the west. Within minutes, a weather front placed itself across the path of the plane's return. With the 180-degree bank over Louisville, "Bud" Murray and Col. Gregory came back into that front south of Washington. TACAN, (Tactical Air Navigation) went temperamental and dropped them. Their LN-3 was now their major reliance. There were 33,000 feet involved in the letdown, and it was a hairy time. The calmest item in the plane was the LN-3. When Langley finally showed through the scudding clouds, after 1,036 nautical miles, the LN-3 had placed them within .74 or 3/4 of a mile from the control tower.

With such ammunition, the Air Force sent Maj. Gen. William Momyer to testify before the House Armed Services committee in behalf of inertial navigation over Doppler. Inertial navigation had a price-tag at least a dozen times greater than the cost of a good Doppler system. That was very disturbing to a conservative Congressman from Michigan. He argued against going for something which only had a great promise and cost a lot and dropping something old whose shortcomings were understood but he thought could be lived with. His name was Gerald Ford.

But even opposing congressmen wilted before the severely contrasting findings: Litton's inertial navigation not only bettered Doppler, but was non-radiating and sent no invitations for enemy weaponry to accept. It was capable of jam-proof operation, had more accurate navigation and had a reliability factor of 200 hours operation, MTBF (Mean Time Between Failure) in contrast with Doppler's 45 hours. It provided precise outputs of acceleration and verticality required for reconnaissance sensors. It was unaffected by turbulence of seas or rough terrain beneath it. It was insensitive to aircraft maneuvers, no matter how violent, and no memory mode was necessary. The last line of the test report said it all: "The F-110-A with the Litton inertial navigation system will provide superior navigation for all missions of the F-110-A to make the most effective all purpose attack/fighter aircraft in the free world today."

When General Momyer did that crossroads testimony before Congress, he was not only arguing an Air Force position which eventually won, he was making a modernization step from which he would be a beneficiary. The implications were unknown to him then, but when he later commanded the 7th Air Force in Vietnam, he had more inertial navigation equipped aircraft in combat than any other military leader, all the systems Litton-manufactured. The "Phantom" production line turned out more than 5,000 of the various F-4 models before having to pinch off to assign a new major effort to the F-15. All except those "Phantoms" sold to the British Royal Air Force had Litton inertial navigation system.

Then came the test of Tex Thornton's main thesis, that initial resolve about having a company which would participate in military contracts and the new, fresh, outreaching technologies that international security demanded. In them he firmly believed, were all kinds of commercial applications which would extend their blessings to the general public. He was sure that inertial navigation had a place in the airline and private aircraft industries that could make a safety contribution, and its disciplined accuracy would be an energy saver.

Not one to shrink from a challenge, the penetration into passenger and cargo service fleets came about under the banner of a test contract with Pan Am. Their Boeing 747s on the Atlantic run to London, Frankfurt and Paris were outfitted with the Litton LN-12s, the model which had evolved for the "Phantom", the cost being about $100,000 per system. It was inevitable that the airlines, would go with some company's system. The alternative in their case was to recruit navigators, as many were required for one transoceanic crossing. If a black box would do it, requiring no on-board man-power, it made sense. but for all their rationale and belief, Litton knew rebuff again.

Charlie Bridge, one of the pioneers dating from Singleton's time and who held many of the Litton patents himself,[10] knew the sleeplessness of being on call for troubles of one kind, or another in all the time zones Pan Am served. Boeing shook Litton by deciding to take a relatively untried competitor, AC-Delco's "Carousel". It was one of those "buy-in" things, a bid so low and with a guarantee of Mean Time Between Failure (MTBF) so long that Litton believed it impossi-

---

10. Parcel to the developments in Europe was the German decision to buy into the U. S. Air Force Training command facilities in America, paying $250,000 per graduated Luftwaffe pilot into the U. S. Treasury. It was a reverse gold flow of nearly $700,000,000 over 25 years, but more than that produced, because of the two year student pilot residence, a professional generation who became and are the most pro-American voices in Western Europe.

This required that the prime contractor, Lockheed, and principal sub-contractors such as Litton be on the flight line at Luke Air Force Base, AZ, to be sure all equipment was fine tooled. Litton published a book about the program in which about 40 of its people were employed, and the sale of the book produced the endowment base of what is called the Luftwaffe/US Air Force International Friendship Foundation. It makes disbursements to Arizona boys and girls clubs and other charities annually, and will do so forever as a living, working monument to a successful and historic international project which was accomplished there.

One Litton employee, Tom Rhone, took more than 35,000 individual photographs of that training, which were drawn on heavily for the book. The Germans called him, with affection and respect, *Unser Mann in Arizon* (Our Man in Arizona). The International Friendship Foundation intent and purpose is now an exchange scholarship Fund at the Arizona State University Foundation in Tempe, AZ, the endowment at Millennium 2000 grown to $311,000. A Luftwaffe offspring at Albert-Ludwigs-Universitat in Freiburg, Germany gives a year at ASU, and a USAF dependent at ASU a year in Freiburg. What began as military instruction has evolved into an annual scholarship experience in knowing each country's people and culture better.

Barney Oldfield and Tom Rhone, who trained German pilots in Arizona.

ble to maintain. It was a Litton-wide corporate shock. Nonetheless, when the counter selection word came out Litton felt it could afford to wait—a contract just for contract's sake in no way equated with making a profit, nor with satisfying a customer.

It was eventually an American Airlines requirement for its military charter flights to Southeast Asia which resulted in Litton being invited to the party, and Litton came. They called the Litton global-server the LTN-51. The main reliance for the project was faithful, indefatigable Dr. Charles Bridge, later to become Litton's chief scien-

Barney Oldfield's book in German about the training of German pilots in
Arizona.

tist.[11] American was spanning ten time zones with its contract, but he'd had his rehearsals during the Pan Am relationship.

No new experience or application is ever without glitches in performance or surprises, nor was the American bow-in. Overall, though, it filled a pressing demand impressively. It opened other doors. McDonnell-Douglas had DC-10s, and Lockheed the L-1011s for which they'd let their airline customers choose the inertial systems, and so eventually did Boeing when 747s going to Continental and a growing parade of other buyers went with Litton's commercial inertial navigation systems on them.

More than 100 of the world's airlines voted in favor of the Thornton conviction about how a basic technology could spread and serve, no matter how demanding the clientele might be. As inertial navigation orders grew, and applications increased, sales treated him to not only the pleasantness of being right, but the profitability of it, too.

It was only the first dramatic evidence that a technology given its head could run. It was to be an old, so wonderfully old story at Litton Industries.[12]

---

11. In 1969 it was obvious to Dr. Charles Bridge at Guidance and Control Division that the Aero Products section which was pointed at commercial inertial navigation sales was ready to stand alone, and it became a division. In 1971, he coaxed Charles "Chuck" Hofflund over from Lockheed and into its presidency. From that toeing the mark start, in a decade it was running at $100,000,000 in annual sales.

12. Dr. Henry Singleton who miniaturized inertial navigation for fighter aircraft did few things small after that, as he founded Teledyne after he left Litton in 1960.

The two Germans who were major believers and subsequently persuaders in the selection of the F-104—Oberstleutnant Gunther Rall and Major Friedrich Obleser—both became chiefs of the Luftwaffe, the LN-3 being a major factor in their professional careers and leadership roles.

Lt. Col. Leighton I. Davis became an Air Force Lieutenant General commanding the U. S. Missile Ranges during the Mercury and Apollo projections of man into the edges of the universe. His prescience never left him, nor did respect for his judgment after that C-45 night flight from Flint, Michigan to Dayton, Ohio when his traveling companion talked him into giving him a contract which led to the first principles of inertial navigation and a working model. Davis was the one President Kennedy sought to tell him how great the odds were that America's astronauts would live through their experiences. He didn't believe NASA for some reason and wanted it face-to-face from Davis. Davis said Col. John Glenn had a 1,000-to-1 likelihood of success, but that the next astronaut would have 5,000-to-1 odds on his side—all because the test firings had been so carefully done. Kennedy said he wanted to believe him, but was afraid to do so. Davis turned out to be right one more time.

Dr. Charles Blair retired from Pan Am and founded the largest seaplane airline, Antilles Aire Boats, which grew to 23 planes and $5,000,000 in annual sales from a borrowed cash start of $50,000. For a while after his crash death, his wife, screen star Maureen O'Hara ran it, then sold it to Resorts International for stock worth $2,700,000.

That renowned man of MIT, Dr. Charles Draper, attracted millions of dollars in MIT grants just because he was a proponent of the inertial guidance system. Paradoxically, some of that money was used to hire professors who differed with him and voted against him over and over again during the Vietnam war. They considered his 8-story lab a suitable target for outrage because some of its work was weapons related. He reflected in relaxed retrospect that so many of those things he came up with—including inertial navigation—served a whole world well. What if it does hurt a little that those professors whose positions he made possible opposed him? There on the building at 555 Technology Square at the Massachusetts Institute of Technology in Cambridge is his name—and none of theirs.

SPECIAL SITUATION #10

THE MAKINGS OF A MULTI-NATIONAL

Technology transfer! It sounded a ring of hope, revival of the spirits, a transfusion to sagging economies, the ticket to nationhood itself.

The very letters which formed the two words were like matching pearls which when strung become rich necklaces. One U.S. Senate Select Committee in its prose described technology as ". . . the process matching solutions in the form of existing science and engineering knowledge to problems of commerce and private programs." Litton Industries had three products that fit this definition. Each of the items weighed less than 100 pounds, or less than 50 kilograms if one wanted to state it metrically, which Litton had to do. The disparate trio included inertial navigation systems, calculating machines, and cash registers. Of these, Litton's inertial navigation was the high technology leader.

While "technology transfer" among American chauvinists might have been thought to have been all one way, from the U.S. to wherever, Litton never bought that foolishness. It knew technology comes from inventiveness, ambition, eagerness, imagination and competitive pressures, and has neither nationality nor patriotism. Just as America was learning it was fast becoming short in strategic materials, sole source dreams about technology were even more illusory. Litton not only wanted but needed a technological two-way street, and made no bones about it. Cash registers, for openers, were an example.

Inertial navigation was a whole new approach to making one's airborne vocation accurately known at great speeds and heights. The total package to accomplish this weighed 87 pounds and cost about $100,000 per copy. Its electro-mechanical element was called a platform; the electronic portion, a computer. The platform gimbaled or hinged the two incorporated gyroscopes and insured the vertical axis stayed fixed on the earth's center of gravity. That vertical axis alignment put the mounting frame for the accelerometers precisely in position to measure east-west and north-south acceleration components.

Dr. Henry Singleton and his crew had reduced the gyros to 3-inch diameter widths. Their temperatures had been stabilized. They were floated to spin at the dizzying rate of 24,000 revolutions per minute.

By this device, a pilot even in a supersonic aircraft could read with remarkable exactness his location at any moment. After an hour's flying at breakneck speeds and altered course he could arrive at the destination with less than two miles error. This had acute meaning for Norway, for the Federal Republic of Germany, for Italy, Greece and Turkey, countries chock-a-block with Communist states.

How to bring all this about was Litton's problem.

A country cracker-barrel wit once said that some names were just too long to paint on a rural mailbox, and had to be written down the post which held it. He may or may not have tied this to George Thomas Scharffenberger, but for what Litton had in mind for him that last name was right on the mark, as if minted for the occasion. Under him, in those startup years, Litton was to plant many of its roots abroad. True, Glen McDaniel recruited him for a current and pressing problem, the running of the Westrex acquisition but along with him came all his ITT-acquired knowledge about global political and financial quicksands. McDaniel had had a quick learning experience about the right person for the job, because on Litton's pickup of Westrex, he'd sent Myles Mace to check it out. Mace did a quickie sampling of the some 3,000 Westrex employees scattered over the world. He returned not at all impressed. To him, they were phlegmatic time-servers. He recommended firing them all! McDaniel couldn't accept that as a solution, and baited the hook for Scharffenberger. He came with the full knowledge that in foreign climes it is not unusual that it takes twice as long to do half as much.

Litton was not a strange place to Scharffenberger, either. He had known Tex Thornton for a long time, being one of those who counseled him on the rightness of the original acquisition of Charles V. Litton's San Carlos plant in 1953. They had even talked some of that growing specter—business enterprises already so big that their annual sales were greater than the Gross National Product of countries where they had plants, or in which they hoped to build and expand. Political concerns were being aroused. Not only were companies being thought of as multi-nationals, there were fears that perhaps they sought and often had supranational status as well. Roy Ash, Litton's loquacious and often quoted No. 2 man once said—and only partly in fun—that the ideal headquarters site for globe encircling commercial organisms would be the moon![1]

Philosophically, questions were being phrased in many countries about whether such huge economic empires more powerful than individual nations, or at least of intimidating size, were a good thing. On the other side of the doubters were the known towering demands for employment and other problem-solving that called for entities with strength and versatility to reinvigorate and build. Should such extraterritorial capabilities be feared, fought and somehow curbed, or should they be welcomed, urged on and given cooperation? It was hardly enough to be thinking of taking orders and delivering products of high to medium technology manufacture, and pocketing the profits. The Litton leadership sensed that from its first offshore moment. There was that other important factor, too, positioning—and that meant politically as well as marketing—for realization of long stay for future opportunities. Sometimes this could make an acquisition appear a bonanza from one vantagepoint, but from another, a poor alloy flecked by foreign substances. That could make it a bad fit for any dedicated free enterpriser's mode of operation and politically and monetarily hazardous as well. The first decision usually dealt with whether a move was worth it, and then whether even greater rewards were there for staying the course; if the answer was NO, shed the vulnerability prospect quickly. As Litton was to grow internally and collect outside companies, nearly always there was an international consideration.

---

1. It was Thomas Jefferson who said: "Merchants have no country of their own. Wherever they may be they have no ties with the soil. All they are interested in is the source of their profits." He also said: "Americans are possessing a chosen country with room enough for our descendants to the thousandth and thousandth generations." All of which goes to prove that a sage isn't always right—only quotable on proper occasion. Roy Ash was saying ". . . the world corporation will be a new species . . . it will consider the whole world its production place as well as its market and will move factors of production to wherever they can most optimally be combined . . . its ownership will be transnational; its management will be transnational. Its freely mobile management, technology and capital, the modern agents for stepped up economic growth will transcend individual national boundaries. In practice, it will be devoid of any single national identity or home, figuratively, its headquarters could be on the moon. *It will be domestic in every place, foreign in none—a true corporate citizen of the world.*"

In some countries, only recently freed from colonialism, the multinational didn't look all that much different from the vividly recalled trappings of the British Empire. Its commercial forms were well known in India, Hong Kong, Singapore, South Africa, Rhodesia and Hudson's Bay. They had laid the conduits for raw materials to industrial centers in the United Kingdom for the manufacturing processes which sent them back products marked up and costly. Why go the distance when raw material sources might be wedded to production within national borders? Litton wasn't big enough then to be a target for politicians or polemicists, but it was big enough in the scheme of technological things to be useful, and small enough to cause no real fear. It didn't want for invitations or interest either at home or elsewhere and while some companies were just that—ordinary, plodding, single-product specialists—Litton had more colorations than Joseph's Coat. Where it showed up, excitement had a way of not being far behind.

The same America which had in its infancy been the product of investment and development effort financed largely by European and British money had been returning the favor for some years. Major opportunity probings increased post WW-II. There were inviting vacuums everywhere. When the misgivings set in, they were hardly restricted to small, emerging, newly christened sovereignties. The older powers, having been made into production paraplegics by the recent conflict, had misgivings, too. However grandly Americans felt about it at home, the Marshall Plan, flailed by the whole Communist propaganda apparatus, was never viewed offshore quite as altruistically as it was in the U.S.

In France, *croissant* conversationalists bracketed their dunking and dialogue and concluded it was just a handy political device for unloading the excesses of U.S. assembly lines on prostrate countries. It kept employment levels high in the U.S., they mused ruefully, as they watched goods and machinery unloaded at LeHavre, Cherbourg and Marseilles. Over their *vin rouge*, the same cynical Frenchmen decided they were being had as much as helped. Being uncomfortable with the generosity of an ally anyway, they accepted what came, but wanted no one to believe they were fooled by it all.

The appetite in the newly shaping Federal Republic of Germany, truncated by the Soviet Union having sliced off its eastern half, was ravenous for modern technology and the plant structure to make products that could compete in the world markets—and sell. They were intense about regaining their industrial status because so much had been destroyed, they wanted to come up new and renewed in one sweeping sustained action.

Greece and Portugal, the two poorest nations of Europe, yearned for monetary and foreign exchange respectability.

Italy had droves of technically trained young people who wanted a life more rewarding than that of their ancestors. Italians might densely populate a narrow, spiny finger of land hanging like a pendulum from the continent, but they were a varied people. Eager and ambitious in the north, in the south they perennially fought off poverty and slept each night with expectancy of some new disaster on the morrow. Italians practiced the politics of seduction so well on themselves, they were delighted to find it worked even better on foreigners.

Great Britain was suffering from withdrawal pains, veritable agony in having to let go in great chunks of its long and strong diet of world greatness and rule.

Three Scandinavian lands—Norway, Denmark and Finland—had been bloodied in the war. A fourth, Sweden, its politics steeped in socialism on the march, had managed the tightrope of being neutral in its pronouncements during WW-II but had bent agreeably when pressured by the Third Reich for rights of passage for the *Wehrmacht* to strike Scandinavian cousins. Rich now and unblemished, Sweden was financially healthy, vigorous and ready to plunge as an international merchandiser and trader.

Holland's ports of Amsterdam and Rotterdam, always competitive with Germany's Bremen and Hamburg, had been a first priority *blitzkrieg* target and were paralyzed and starved by long residence of hostile occupiers. Its border sharer, Belgium, also under the boot, had been governed by a less severe military regime, but was badly shackled economically. It was busy taking inventory of its old self-respect.

Centerpiece to it all was that ancient Alpine sanctuary, Switzerland. Its heavy winter snows thawed each spring to trickle down in all directions feeding the many rivers that did so much writing of European history. Its banks and financial houses were obese with the currencies of all nations. Conversions could be arranged there into its own impeccable francs, providing safe havens for countries and rulers whose foundations were shaky and futures uncertain.

The Orient was crowded with eager and semiskilled labor masses whose services were temptingly priced.

South America and Africa were for the most part economic nightmares, and their people were intoxicated with unsupportable dreams of overnight stature, unaccompanied by either substance or development for their accomplishments. Confidence was in the air, though, after long absence.

In Beverly Hills, Litton strategy put most of that world on "hold" and concentrated on Western Europe.[2] Litton International S.A. and Litton World Trade were organized, and ushered into existence in Zurich, Switzerland. Everybody intent on dealing in Europe, Africa and the Middle East tended to take that kind of first step—the implied respectability and the certification of financial heft of a Swiss address, and Swiss accounts. William Reynolds, once corporate Secretary, was selected to move to Switzerland and run it.

Technical purists will always assign Litton's first multinational credentials to the acquisition of the Monroe Calculating Machine company in Litton's rambunctious fifth year. In a personnel sense, this made milestones of two ex-Japanese prisoners of war, Ralf Daniel and Rens Blauboer. Daniel, a pygmy-sized East Prussian Jew, had been well known in calculating machine marketing circles, but had to run for his life from Germany in 1933 when Hitler came to power. First, he sought refuge in Holland, then went even farther away to Java in the Dutch East Indies. He and his partner, Blauboer, did very well there, so well they stretched their luck and overstayed into a miscalculation. They suddenly found themselves hemmed in with all escape routes blocked by Nippon Premier Hideki Tojo's rampaging Imperial Japanese Army. It was advancing smartly to achieve what Tojo called his Greater East Asia Co-Prosperity Sphere. It was especially parched

---

2. There was one tentative action elsewhere when Litton stuck a toe in Oriental waters with a Technical and Licensing Agreement with T. Kogyo Corp. in 1960 for electron tube manufacturing in Japan. Ultimately Litton would have ties and agreements with more than 20 of the mighty industrial empires in Japan. Roy Ash became co-chairman with Fuji Bank head, Yoshizane Iwasa, of a Japan-California Association effort to include business exchanges generally and perhaps Litton's as well.

for the sustenance of oil and rice rich Southeast Asia and the Indies. Having served their prison time, on being released as the war ended in the Pacific, they surmised correctly that continuance of colonial status was hardly going to wear well. They went back to Amsterdam.

Daniel and Blauboer became part of Litton's international underpinnings. Monroe, of course, had been in Great Britain from the opening of its first overseas sales office in London in 1921. Its European market and respect for its product had fanned out from that time. Malcolm "Mac" Monroe, who was given the international development portfolio after the overthrow of the old management, decided in 1949 that the moment had come for a manufacturing facility outside of the U.S. It was to be one which took that Atlantic moat away as a barrier to the United Kingdom and continental clients. He first favored Britain. Monroe already had a long and old-shoe-comfortable sales association in England. The pleasant commercial atmosphere combined with sociability in which business was transacted in England was a lure of its own. When "Mac" Monroe made those beginning overtures, however, he was dismayed and not a little surprised by the Labor Government's attitude. Not only was it negative, it was excessively suspicious and restrictive. Transoceanic phone calls, endless correspondence, nitpicking and a series of inconclusive London visits were so fruitless and the British so uncooperative he suddenly decided to point for Holland—and Ralf Daniel.

He had known him for years. He saw in him just the stalking horse he needed to arrive at some compatible arrangement with the Dutch Government in The Hague that would permit the manufacture of the Monroe line in The Netherlands. Holland was swollen almost to the bursting point by its colonial domain's shrinkage. The people once deployed there were returning to that already jammed lowlands country. Anyone who trotted out a suggestion which held the promise of employment of people and turned out products which would represent foreign exchange money flow—and particularly if the proposer had been a *bona fide* POW—was given not only audience but every possible assistance. There could have been no better choice than Daniel. He had everything going for him. Monroe Calculating Machine Co., Holland, N.V., became a plant on the outskirts of Amsterdam. It was the Netherlands' gain, Britain's loss. The official opening in 1950 was cause for celebration on both sides of the Atlantic. The filing papers listed Malcolm as President *Commissaries* and Ralf *Directeur*.

"It was a success from the first," Monroe declared. "That was because I was never carried away by my high sounding title, nor silly enough to overrule decisions made by our highly responsible Ralf Daniel."

For several reasons, one of them being that it made good business sense, Litton wanted to retain offshore managements which came with properties. This saved many an Excedrin migraine. It didn't always work, but it did more often than not. It ran counter to the practices of many American firms who were inclined to have "an American at the top."[3] This often made resident and deserving nationals grind their teeth, snicker behind their hands about gaffes they saw coming and let the Yankee make. More ominously, it set more politically abrasive wheels spinning than anyone could ever want—or afford. The quirk invited dilettantism on the part of many American managers who fancied themselves as more worldly hep than their peers in international matters. It rarely worked well, either for the company sponsoring such policies, or for the individual whose career often ran into a stonewall, or worsened to the degree that his resumes were soon flooding the mails.

The Westrex division, the one which collared Scharffenberger, was instantly dramatic on a global scale for Litton. Fifty countries had Westrex operating as both a respected and glamorous technology proponent. Its sound-on-film and recording systems were in both movie studios and theatres. All those voices of the "beautiful people," the stars of the cinema, the noises of adventure from far places came via Westrex to the lowliest of ticket holders wherever they faced screens supported and enhanced by this extra dimensional equipment. Westrex was in a special niche and on a pedestal. It was an exotic stage from which its new parent was introduced, all suited up and shiny.

---

3. A persisting exception within Litton was the onetime project engineer at Litton's Guidance & Control systems division, Richard T. "Dick" Hopman. He signed on in Woodland Hills, California on June 22, 1959, transferred to Litton Technische Werke in Freiburg on June 16, 1964, was made its management head. He was expert in Litton's inertial navigation, and provided the Litton desired protectiveness for that infant technology.

The LITTON Adventure That Was

When Scharffenberger was barely signing in at Litton, portals were swinging wide for the company into new and old cultures. Countries were in varying hues of economic development. All kinds of banking practices were in association with often mercurial monies. Locations of commercial enterprises needed not only renewal but wider horizons. They had to be armed with the requirements to go out into the unknown cold to lay infrastructure for the travelling technologies.

All of it being so rapidly and extensively done, it could have been unnerving if there had been too much time to ponder. Anticipation overrode threats and dangers. There was a plethora of laws, duties, regulations, tolls and bewildering protectionist ploys. The "Yankee trader" tendencies which were imbedded in entrepreneurs had to learn to get along, or accommodate to all types of commercial climates. Governments were often deeply hand-in-hand with businesses on their own turf. This quickly produced knowledge of special tax forgiveness and easy border crossings where technologies were in demand. Such access could often be just as easily barred where the technologies were unwanted, competitive, or were subject to signals called by the indigenous power structure.

Both Monroe and Westrex were convenient shoehorns as they were part of the U.S. corporate extension. When they took the Litton banner under which to march, nothing really changed in their appearances. Both companies had learned well over the years and had gone through all the phases to meet legal residence and marketing modes. Their charters were unchallenged as long as they abided by local and regional rules. In that sense, Litton building on the run, was luckier in many ways than most of the new incomers. This is not the same as saying that Litton came away unmarked in its various encounters with customs and bureaucratic bramble bushes, nor unchastened by the memories.[4]

---

4. Forgiveness of taxes and imports of equipment without money penalties contribute to euphorics when entering customs, traditions and lifestyles of other peoples. Fierceness with which old ways are defended is rooted in past wars, centuries of bitter competition, international suspicions of good intentions and vulnerability of man to insecurities.

For any company whose base is offshore there is a complex learning curve— how to turn out a product with the overhead of social contracts and their punitive provisions. Americans tend to consider themselves as super-marketers forgetting that it was adventurers searching for new commercial opportunities who discovered the

Some of what Litton was to be was already in place abroad. The list of beginning technologies which Litton dangled before other nations was imposing—electronics, inertial navigation, components, office equipment and accessories, geophysical exploration, medical products and specialty paper. It had skill training and retraining capabilities nimble enough to jump national boundaries and language barriers. Wherever Litton elected to go, there were assurances of increased job availabilities. Foreign sales for those countries increased in greater quantities and range than was the case before Litton came.

Once the selected direction for concentration was Europe, it ballooned suddenly as the major action area. Fred Sullivan was on the march with Monroe unleashed to enlarge the business systems and equipment penetration in world trade.[5] The Federal Republic of Germany, heading the consortium of Italy, Holland and Belgium, had made the many-sided $2,014,000,000 contractual commitment to buy the Lockheed "Starfighter." Litton's inertial navigation, the LN-3 was in its avionics package. Dr. Henry Singleton's original Electronic Equipment Division was popping its seams. When he, with Dr. George Kosmetsky, left to set up their Teledyne, Inc., it transitioned into a superstructure or group. Scharffenberger became its top executive,[6] which gave him a mixed bag but not entirely unrelated bundle of

---

North and South American continents. Unlike America, where the government regulates, restrains and plays adversary to trading enterprises, in nearly every other country around the globe, governments work hand-in-mitten with their commercial forces. In their success comes foreign exchange and wider markets for the products of labor. Whatever any government extended in inducements to lure investment has to be understood as a momentary advantage. Through laws and regulations after the incomer is committed and lodged, a country can get it all back and more. Litton's toppers were aware of all this and that whatever the military requirements of NATO, the strategy of the alliance countries was to get technology and investment. Europe is a periodic battleground for warring nations. When it seeks restoration of its commercial life and well being, not all the minefields and booby-traps have been cleared. Knowing that, one can proceed; ignoring that, one can lose his *derriere*.

5. Monroe had gone abroad to buy the Swiss Oerlicon, manufacturers of a 10-key calculator which was difficult to make but a superior machine. The assembly line for that model was already in the Amsterdam Monroe facility at the time of the Litton merger.

6. Besides Scharffenberger, Fred O'Green, James Mellor and Joseph Caligiuri headed that group in its perpetual profit making trek through Litton's first three decades.

navigation, command and control applications, radio frequency and sound-on-film expertise. He was a man on the move, and a minder of all those precious and all purpose technologies in which Tex Thornton had placed so much of his faith for Litton's future—where it would first prove that Litton was not solely dependent on acquisitions and mergers for growth, but could develop a favorable traffic to its door through perceptive internal strides.

Teeth cutting and mettle testing exercises were on the Litton threshold. It was one tactic to go after growth by picking up companies which had already laid claim to geography afield of the U.S. It was a lot different when seeking to carve out a presence offshore where there was no existing foundation and the rules varied from one country to another. Litton found itself headed into two such big ad ventures almost simultaneously. It was to free himself for one of these that Glen McDaniel had so promptly hitched Scharffenberger to the comet. The other was the Fred Sullivan desire to bring into Litton the staid old Swedish Dataregister, A.B.

Scharffenberger was overseeing the placing of a manufacturing, overhaul and repair capability in Europe which would support the inertial navigation equipping of the "Starfighter." The "Starfighter" was more than technology transfer. That action required going metric for every drawing board item originally in inches, feet and pounds. The marketing and legal representatives found entanglements tended to in crease far beyond the multiplicity of languages and measurements into negotiating tactics and goals.

Svenska Dataregister, A.B. was tucked away in the Stockholm suburb of Solna. Principally interested individuals were Yacob and Marcus Wallenberg. Tall and handsomely gray, they had connections everywhere in banking that the Swedish *krone* was respected. This was everywhere in the world that money was understood as a medium of exchange. They were on boards of dozens of Swedish companies. Svenska Dataregister, A.B., the manufacturer of the Sweda line of cash registers was only one among many. The Wallenbergs, though, treated each in a caring and protective way. Such widespread presence did nothing to dilute their detailed attentiveness to the well being of the many corporate bodies, nor did it make them casual or careless about any of them.

In the beginning, the Wallenbergs were uneasy about Litton as it was too young, too untried. It became necessary for them to talk with Thornton himself. That was to be on their ground, in Stockholm, but not at their Enskilda Bank. That was too formal and the meeting was arranged for Yacob Wallenberg's yacht at anchor in the Baltic. From the dock to the yacht, Thornton was to be taken to his waiting hosts in a small boat. He arrived impeccably dressed, waved jauntily, stepped into the boat, and it promptly overturned dumping him in the icy water. He was rescued and was finally on the deck. His hosts solicitously wrapped him in a towel-like blanket. They fussed over him far more than they probably would have had he come to them dry. In their conversations hunting for a mutual acquaintance, respected by both, the Wallenbergs learned that Thornton was a onetime "protege" of Robert Abercrombie Lovett. They knew Lovett well, and Brown Brothers Harriman, too, so their misgivings subsided. They indicated they were ready to begin serious negotiations. Later Tex Thornton ruefully would recall his dousing as having been a warning of sorts. If he'd been superstitious, he would have paddled back to shore and gone home without proceeding further and he would have avoided involvement with ships in all their dimensions.

Svenska Dataregister, A.B., was tightly held. All of its 6,000 shares were controlled by so few people they could be gathered around a small restaurant table. For Litton to have the majority it desired, it was necessary to corral 3,010 of those shares. The obstacle was that after getting 15% of the total shares a door swung open permitting a severe, confiscatory tax being levied on the sellers. They all cringed from that burden, no matter if the remaining portions they retained would give them participation in what could happen under the new Litton auspices. In the negotiations, several tax avoidance measures were toyed with including the stretch over five years to final conclusion. The initial talks were in New York. Every conceivable angle was worried with, haggled over, and myriad avenues explored all the way from ownership and management control to the means of cash register distribution via Litton-owned sales and services offices, 310 distributors in 75 countries throughout the world.

McDaniel found quickly that he had to suppress any signs of overeagerness to get on with it, that fatal and so vulnerable American dickering impatience in board room jockeying. It took six long weeks which generated more whereases and conditions and qualifications by far than it did any verbs which suggested forward motion and hope of a satisfactory array of common interests. Finally, the papers were thought to be in sufficiently good order to shift the scene to Stockholm for any amendments. Signatures could then activate the document. The Wallenbergs side had been chaired by Count Archibald Douglas, called "Ibo" from babyhood. He'd come from a long line descended from a Scot mercenary who had hired out to an ancient Swedish King then took residence and title in Sweden when proffered for services rendered. Douglas was a meticulous and impressive explorer for advantage. He had the full confidence of the Wallenbergs. He wanted nothing to shake that. For this reason, the Douglas concurrence in shifting to the Swedish capital for the final act led McDaniel to believe his time spent and his patience were about to pay off.

That very next morning after SAS had delivered the negotiators to Stockholm, McDaniel was instructed to come to Enskilda Bank. He was in for a "learning experience." Barely clearing the Bank's entrance, he saw a distraught Count Douglas. He said the Wallenbergs were mightily displeased. Yacob himself had registered his disgust by tossing the sheaf of carefully drafted papers in the air, not caring particularly where they landed as they could be swept out later by a janitor. Douglas was summarily withdrawn from the Litton project. Everything had to start over. McDaniel, who had thought his ordeal would end in less than a week at the most, hurried to the phone to get a message to Tex Thornton about the unexpected snag.

"Stay with it, Glen," counseled the voice from Beverly Hills. "There has to be some way to work it out."

A Plan No. 1 evolved. A Plan No. 2. A Plan No. 3, and so on. None were acceptable. The Wallenbergs went off to sun themselves on the Riviera telling their conferring minions to carry on. Each approach was shot down by the Wallenbergs personally, or someone instructed by them. That blood sucking Swedish tax threat was always nesting in the rafters. McDaniel, with a pushing and urging Fred Sullivan as an ally on site, talked early and late of new strategies or new sides of older ones. Their Swedish counterparts, exasperating and draggy during the hours at the conference table, were transformed once out of the boardroom. Unfailingly and perpetually hospitable after hours, they entertained lavishly in their own homes.

Unfortunately, the only identifiable tangibles were increased trencherman girths for their guests and a sharpening of their toasting excellence and eloquence. But no progress. Then McDaniel made up his mind and voiced a desperate statement.

"Let's skip all the intervening alternatives," he said. "Let's go straight to Plan No. 51."

There was no plan with that number as such. McDaniel simply told the Swedes that Litton would up the bidding enough to protect the sellers against the Swedish tax bite! On that basis and after nine long weeks in Stockholm, the impasse showed signs of breaking. There was an urgent call to the Riviera. The Scandinavian negotiators began tentative counter-suggesting to give time for the Wallenbergs to get out of their sun gear in Cannes and fly home. Fred Sullivan had long since given up and had returned to New Jersey. The Swedes rubbed their chins, pondered, slightly viewed with alarm and entertained reservations about a clause here and there.

Once Yacob Wallenberg was in his Enskilda Bank chair he said he had one final point which was a problem for him—selection of an arbitrator should there be difference of opinion as to the intent of some portion of the agreement when it was finally consummated. McDaniel, having been elaborately fair in his own mind, had thought he had covered that point adequately when he had gotten assurances from no less than the Swedish Supreme Court Chief Justice to serve in that role! The matter was stalled again. That broke not only the dromedary's back but the straw as well. McDaniel closed his briefcase and said he was leaving for Beverly Hills the next day. He stalked out.

Overnight, the Wallenbergs, perhaps realizing their cats had played with the McDaniel Litton mouse long enough, asked McDaniel to come by the Enskilda Bank early the next morning. McDaniel, his bags with him in the taxi and with a sour taste in his mouth and his airline ticket in his inside coat pocket, went one last time. He asked the taxi to wait with the meter running. Almost as he came into the Wallenberg presence, it was as if they had brought him a gift wrapped package of the Riviera sun. They wanted the deal to go through, they said. But wise old Yacob had his one small "reservation" about the five year period and any refereeing which might intrude. He didn't think that Swedish Court Justice was enough.

"If the Justice were to die or become incapacitated for any reason," he asked, "what would we do then?" McDaniel could hardly believe what he was hearing. Courtesy or not, he was about to tip his hat and be gone. What did the Wallenbergs want in addition? The answer almost caused McDaniel to fall off his chair—the Wallenbergs' nomination as an acceptable standby was none other than Brown Brothers, Harriman's man, Robert Abercrombe Lovett! At that point McDaniel would have taken the Abominable Snow Man, but here he had only to agree to the Lovett suggestion. That was an easy one, one McDaniel could do without reference to Beverly Hills, as Lovett had always considered Thornton his star protege. The deal in hand at long last, a happy McDaniel sped off to catch his SAS flight which he'd expected to board empty handed with a big international failure on his record. He was even glad to pay the astronomical number of Swedish *krones* the taxi meter showed him owing. The 3,010 shares of Svenska Dataregister, A.B. marched obediently into Litton's scheme for its growing business systems and equipment group.[7]

While it was by no means the last headache Litton would know with the Solna property, it was still too early to say whether Litton had "won the day," or had gotten something far more valuable—schooling in survival of negotiations. The Svenska Dataregister, A.B. dangle-and-dally technique was one Europeans delighted in using with Americans. They knew them to be poor hagglers, short of patience, driving to finish whatever was at issue. Time, it seemed, was more valuable

---

7. Of the Svenska Dataregister 6,000 par value 1,000 Swedish krone shares, Johan Grönberg owned 1,250; Sture Edvard Werner, 300; Anders Reuben Torbjorn, 300; and two corporations, Aktiebolaget Investor, 2,700 and Aktiebolaget Thisbe, 650. Grönberk, Werner and Thrustrup, were willing to sell all their holdings, with Investor offering 900 and Thisbe, 260. That made the required 3,010 shares to insure Litton control. The price was $2,090 for each share of Svenska Data Register, which could be had in dollars, or in Litton common shares then valued at $110.40. The pact forbade any holder to sell his shares to anyone except others already in the small owning circle, this insuring Litton would eventually pick them up. At one of the nightly receptions at the home of the Swedish participants, during the toasting a host disclosed that McDaniel had been in Sweden so long he had "fallen in love." This startled McDaniel as he'd done nothing but glue himself to the stacks of worked and reworked papers all the time he'd been there. When all eyes swung to his host awaiting full disclosure, the host explained that he had "fallen in love with Plan No. 51." It was the one which eventually won the day—along with the additional seasoning of the McDaniel threat to leave Stockholm unless the palavering ceased.

than substance, and from Litton's point of view that was a critical factor. One thing for sure, Svenska Dataregister, A.B. was a working, producing, marketing and ongoing company which had only to be converted to divisional status now had a strong arm holding new opportunity gates ajar.[8] It was a significant, many faceted introduction for Litton to the warts and sores of international growth.

In the same time on Litton's tray was the quite different requirement which up to then was the biggest of Litton's offshore encounter sessions—how to get rigged for the 4-country consortium intake of Litton's LN-3 inertial navigation system.

Dr. William Jacoby, an able engineer, had never thought of himself as a modern day Daniel but he was in a lion's den nonetheless. When Singleton hired him, the job they talked about was technical marketing including the writing of proposals for the inertial navigation systems the Singleton crew was shriveling dimensions. Almost from his first Litton day, Singleton had haunted and ingratiated himself on Lockheed hoping for some part of their very secret and aeronautically sensational aircraft whose promise had the western world abuzz. Now that the LN-3 was on the "Starfighter" with other avionics bright hopes such as refined radar and fire control systems, it dictated having facilities nearer the buyers and users.

Maintenance expertise and other competencies were not easy to come by. Handwriting was not only on the wall, but more to the mark

---

8. Sweda, No. 2 in the American market, was behind National Cash Register (NCR), which had about 90% of the market. It came on the U.S. scene in 1950 when Erik Walquist arrived from Solna carrying two Sweda model 46 cash registers in a little bag. Paul R. Cates had been asked by Sweda to research for an NCR vulnerability to penetrate into its domination. He suggested a mechanical punch tape as a cheaper counter to NCR's electric. The discount houses grabbed it, and Sweda was in. Right behind Walquist came Arnie Meyer, a training specialist, and Ehrling Engell, a technician. Walquist set up offices in Chicago and in California. He surmised at once that Sweda could never compete with the service and sales offices of NCR all over the country except by casting its lot with independent cash register dealers. That produced mixed results, and was one of the things which made the bridge into Monroe's already existing centers most attractive. No sooner was the Litton ownership established than 440 Sweda cash registers were shipped by freighter from Solna to New York. As a result, Litton's first block "sale" package was to an insurance company, because all 440 of the cash registers were lost when the freighter sank during a violent North Sea storm.

was in the contractual print that a sizeable portion of that manning had to come from populations of participating nations. The barrier to acceptance of inertial navigation which had drained and demanded of its proponents so long while it was tested exhaustively was behind Jacoby. Yet its lion's den was some retained apprehension on Lockheed's part about whether the LN-3 would really work. Was Litton too technologically thin to manage the jump from hand built prototypes by top engineers to the assembly line in the new home of what was called Litton's Guidance and Control Systems division in Woodland Hills, California?[9] There was also that edgy consortium partnership in Europe. The Germans in particular had to be kept reassured that everything was on schedule. Jacoby was meeting himself going and coming over the Atlantic. He had to seem to be on both ends of the flight simultaneously, and he almost was.

In Europe, he organized a Litton, GmbH[10] office in Munich for the early interfacing. Nomadically, he decamped it to Hamburg when the German manufacturing sites topped his priority list, and ultimately, to the Rhine at Bonn as the contractual interpretations became the No. 1 concern. German's *Bundesministerium für Verteidigung* (Ministry of Defense) was a short taxi ride away, as was the *Bundestag* (the Parliament).

As the consortium leader, Germany was to get 917 of the thunderbolt fast, needle-nosed, fighter bomber configured F-104s for its reborn *Luftwaffe*. Belgium was down for 112 for its *Force Aerienne Belgique*. The Royal Netherlands *Luchtmacht Staf* had orders for 138, and the *Aeronautica Militare Italiana* allotment was 354. Each of

---

9. The backroom shop in the rear of the corporate Beverly Hills location went to the San Fernando Valley. It was now the Guidance and Control Systems division in Woodland Hills. It was on a part of acreage that once was the Warner Brothers film studio's ranch, site of innumerable stagecoach and good-guy-bad-guy chases on film. Data systems division went to Van Nuys. Each required expansion into satellite plants in Salt Lake City, Lubbock and Duluth.

10. Litton GmbH, born in 1961, was headed by Dr. Frank Moothart, with K.J. Hettich as his assistant. On staff were P.R. Hill, manager of plans and programs; W.W. Dunn, for special assignments; Henry Rathe, once in the *Luftwaffe* himself, for customer relations; Dr. H.L. Monauni, contracts; D. Buchmann, controller; R.P. Janssen, manufacturing, overhaul and repair; Harold D. Gillman, product support; G.S. Mayner, engineering and C.A. Harvey, quality assurance. While it was located in Germany, it tended to be the way station and clearing house for all European phases of the LN-3 program.

these countries been fought over, devastated, and occupied. Their own once proud aeronautical traditions had all but disappeared because of subjugation or surrender.[11]

All four of the countries wanted more than just being on the receiving end of the U.S. assembly lines. They desired, in fact demanded, that they have more than exterior trappings of power. They needed substance of it in industrial base and technical skills of their own to manufacture. Their goals were not security alone, but technicians recruited, trained, updated from their own populations and resources. By various kinds of training and familiarization included in this vast program, each country saw the re-creation of an aerospace labor force of its own. About 950 of those aircraft were specified as *not* to be built in the U.S. They were to come off four separate assembly lines during the first five years of the agreement—Messerschmitt in Germany, FIAT in Italy, Fokker in Holland and SABCA in Belgium. In Germany alone, the contract was to result in more than 500 principal subcontractors and 16,000 suppliers from all over NATO Europe, many of them starting from scratch. It was a magnificent example of technological transfer given marching orders, each with something to give and everyone benefiting in the process.

It was known that under provisions of the U.S. Military Assistance Program (MAP) that Norway, Denmark, Greece and Turkey were to get F-104s, too. Canada also would have them in its arsenal designated as the CF-104. It was one of the most staggering standardization measures ever to be achieved in a military coalition. The capability in each receiving country for maintenance and support had main reliance on the U.S., an ocean away. Henry Rathe, once a member of the World War II *Luftwaffe*, had graduated to *maitre d'* at the Neroberger, Officers Club HQs, United States Air Force, Europe in Wiesbaden. He caught the fancy of Scharffenberger and Jacoby as the ideal "customer relations" recruit. He knew all the key officers in the U.S. headquarters downtown on *Luisenstrasse* and at Camp Lindsey, as well as the celebrated figures of the old *Luftwaffe* on whom the

---

11. Germany was first to fly a jet aircraft on Aug. 27, 1938, one developed by Dr. Ernst Heinkel. It was an He-178 monoplane with a 26-foot wingspan, powered by an He-S-3B jet engine. On Nov. 30, 1941, an Italian pilot, Col. Mario de Bernardi flew a "pulsejet" or rocket plane at 130 miles an hour over a 295-mile Milan-Rome-Milan course.

revived Germany would depend. His access was total, and with names such as Scharffenberger and Jacoby to put forward whose origins were locally identifiable, Rathe was a substantial crutch to high and low level conversations, a way-smoother *par excellence*. The officer corps and their supporting bureaucratic chieftains in Germany, were well known to him.

Litton had to decide where to lay on the hands first, where to sink its mooring posts and how to carry out its responsibilities. Canada, not only closest but a convenient rehearsal example, was where the first actual LN-3 step was taken beyond the U.S. border. Litton needed a small Canadian company which already had credibility in that country's government contracting, knew the score and was so minor league anything that happened to it could only be an improvement. A firm called Servo-Mechanisms, Ltd. appeared to be just about right. It had 40 employees, a few small contracts all of which were in trouble, and it was losing money. In Rexdale, near Toronto, it was almost pathetically willing to sell when Litton said it would assume its production contracts and absorb its debts outstanding. In April, 1960, the discussions were completed and pens whispered across agreement papers which erased Servo-Mechanisms, Ltd. from its precarious existence. Something called Litton Systems Canada, Ltd. was in business on its old premises. It was an extension of Litton's Guidance and Control Systems division which justified the move because it had to have a good secondary location for inertial navigation production as well as a site on which to attend to the CF-104 "Starfighter." Canada was to get 238 of the Litton LN-3s first ordered. It was not only a good sense move, it was politically graceful.

When the Canada company was acquired, it was projected to have 260 on its payroll. It would do final assemblies with gyros and accelerometers sent to them from California. It would also have repair and overhaul contracts. In two years they had shouldered themselves into the world market when Military Assistance Programs began in Scandinavia and the Eastern Mediterranean. They strode confidently into export trade, there to stay and grow. Canada went rapidly into a "win" position. Litton was soon on its way to being the 30th largest employer in the greater Toronto area, and a principal employer in Canada itself.

There was further merit to it because of the marketing strength of its head man, J.M. "Monty" Bridgman, a volatile and well known ex-Royal Canadian Air Force officer of technical and procurement renown. He not only ran Litton Systems Canada, Ltd. with a verve, he was also capable of conducting a two-front war and did—one with the bureaucrats in Ottawa, and one to break restraints of his new parent in Southern California.

In a way, Canada was but a sideshow. Europe was the main event. It was time consuming and cumbersome. Jacoby felt he was the centerpiece in an Eric Ambler paperback novel. There were days when he was uncertain whether his costume should be a business suit with a ballpoint or a cloak and dagger in the breast pocket. There were outrageous stories none of which seemed safely ignored, yet were too ridiculous on their faces to be believed. Mostly they had to do with shifting decision powers, who was listening to whom, or the latest nuance signaled in a bar conversation where marketers gathered and swapped what passed for intelligence. A lot of it was time wasting, and time was what Jacoby had little of and it seemed to be running out. Jacoby felt himself a twin of Sisyphus, the legendary King of Corinth, who was sentenced to a lifetime of rolling a heavy stone up a hill only to see it roll down the other slope where he had to start rolling it up again.

The seasoned old *Luftwaffe* veterans being returned in the new, smart uniforms to leadership positions had done their sky warring without inertial navigation although in planes admittedly more than 1,000 miles an hour slower. They openly scoffed at the LN-3. This created a careless and cavalier attitude among the first young pilots. The "Starfighter" as a most demanding and jealous aircraft, couldn't forgive and didn't. Casualties mounted. The plane was quickly dubbed a "widow maker." Anyone who was a part of it as Litton was, caught some of the flak.

Jacoby unearthed another basic truth right away—there were no manufacturing facilities in Western Europe where inertial navigation could be easily introduced by license or joint venture agreement. This was contrary to how comfortably an airframe builder such as Lockheed could arrange its ties with old and respected continental firms similarly engaged for decades. When Jacoby heard the Germans talking about licensing agreements, he pretended not to understand. He

had no wish to hand off so delicate and new a technology to inexperi-
enced and even hostile stewardship. He had many after hours conversations stretching into the German dawn in the old Königshof hotel in
Bonn with his colleague, Roy E. Woenne.

Woenne had been pulled away from his San Carlos vacuum tube
regimen to massage the European entry, and develop alternatives. He
lived in Europe in 1960 and 1961 making all kinds of evaluations as to
how this huge Litton undertaking could be carried out. It was
Woenne's opinion, seconded by Jacoby and agreed to and signed off
by Thornton that there were no qualified persons, or means of qualify-
ing subcontractors for part of the LN-3 assemblies in Europe.[12]
Woenne's conclusion? Litton must either acquire adaptable companies in Europe, or that Litton had to build from the ground up its own
plant complexes to serve its own ends.

Once there was determination to bring German firms into Litton,
Jacoby quickly narrowed his choices to two. One was Fritz Hellige,
GmbH. Nestled in the 150,000 population university town of Freiburg
in Breisgau at the edge of the Black Forest, it was near both Switzerland and France. An esteemed medical electronics manufacturer, Hellige was a good trademark not only on its homeland, but on both sides
of the Iron Curtain in Europe. It was dreaming of a U.S. market, too.
The Litton antenna always there for the move today which could
translate into other options later caught signals beyond Jacoby's
needs. Even though Litton's thulium X-ray warm-up had died, the
blooming worldwide health market was still there and growing and
Litton was not unaware of its potential.[13]

---

12. While Thornton was strongly supported in this move by Singleton and Mc-
Daniel, it was against all the advice of Wall Street expertise and consultants having
Litton access and ears at that time. That counsel was that Littonites were neophytes
bucking the European establishment, and to be effective Litton could not do that. It
was Thornton's feel for "strong proprietary product values," and his instincts told him
what was wanted most abroad was access to the company's technology. He was right.

13. Roy Ash was a sort of "Lone Hand Luke" in that he negotiated the C. Plath,
Fritz Hellige and G.A. Henke moves into Litton on his own. Hellige was Litton's
starting point in Europe in its drive for the health care market. This led on March 29,
1965 to Henke, GmbH, in Tuttlingen, Germany for $2,200,000. Its products included
hypodermic disposable syringes and needles, endoscopes and allied medical instruments. It was to be a broadener of Hellige's already strong, but specialized position in
X-ray, laboratory and nuclear instrumentation. By Henke time, Litton had added

But first things first. One June 6, 1960, the 16th anniversary of D-Day, Litton International, S.A. in Zurich scored an important beach-head of a quite different variety. In this instance, after one of the important owners, His Highness Friederich Prinz aû Fürstenberg blessed the action, and 75.62% of Hellige came into Litton hands for 1,250,000 Deutschemarks. The Prince ranked second only in owner-ship to Franz Morat, who engineered the deal, but promised to stay only for a short transitional period. Germany, pre-war, was a leading exporter of electro-medical equipment and though depressed by long occupation, Morat sensed substantial comeback possibilities. He wasn't comfortable with being an umbrella for a sizeable subdivision in a totally different kind of electronics, this new inertial navigation which Jacoby had explained to him. On that Hellige stem, however, was grafted Litton Technische Werke (LITEF), a new stalwart on Ger-man soil to be highly valued by the *Bundesministerium für Ver-eidiaung in Bonn.*

The other was C. Plath & Co., GmbH, in Hamburg, almost at the Elbe river bank where that stream widens and deepens for its long corridor for shipping with a mouth on the North Sea. From 1862, when Carl Christian Plath developed his first special advanced sex-tant, C. Plath became and remained a most trusted house for marine navigational devices.

Hamburg, once a favorite bombing target of the British Royal Air Force which had almost obliterated most of it, was now a sturdy and hustling conservative city of 1,900,000. It was also the birthplace of Heinrich Hertz, which made it a sort of homage homecoming. Hertz, the talented physicist, in his too short lifetime demonstrated experi-mentally the existence of electromagnetic waves. The very begin-nings of Litton, its vacuum tube manufacture, could hardly have happened without Hertz' findings, nor could microwave ovens, radar and much, much more to which Litton had technological ties. But urgency allowed no time for sentimentality, and gyro manufacture was easily the sphere of this company which was within a year of celebrat-ing its centennial. It had already produced its sextant numbered 50,000.

Profexray in Des Plainest Ill. in the U.S. It was all so Litton-typical, a real time solution for a pressing purpose, and a long look ahead.

The LITTON Adventure That Was

The Tex Thornton exhilaration about acquiring C. Plath was expressed when he labeled the cash transaction as adding ". . . an important member of the European industrial team that Litton is forming to handle the production of inertial navigation equipment for the NATO countries."

It was a long, long way down through history from Plath's monumental disinterest in Latin studies in favor of becoming a precision mechanic. The St. Michael's suburb where he lived was adjacent to the Elbe river basin where more than 5,000 ships a year called. He found they all had need for quality nautical instruments. It was in his small Stubbenhuk shop that he'd made the sextant he marked No. 1. Now, on June 2, 1961, C. Plath & Co. GmbH, for an outlay of 2,500,000 Deutschemarks was brought in by Litton International, S.A. in Zurich. Johannes Boysen had 15% of the ownership. His separate and wholly owned Johannes Boysen Compass came along for an additional DM 125,000. Jacoby, the corporate gypsy, finally had the German infrastructure he needed.

Present in the takeover contract was a political paradox—a stipulation that for at least two years, Walter Clasen would stay as the resident managing director. He had been one of the highly decorated ex-submariners under German Grand Admiral Karl Dönitz. He had once sailed from Hamburg to gather in "wolf packs" at sea to torpedo allied shipping. But that was yesterday. Hellige and Plath gave Litton a wealth of related skills to draw on. Litton might be inclined to think of itself as young, but C. Plath had greater age with its 1862 origins. The German presence also brought with it something called "Codetermination" which Litton had to live with.[14]

---

14. Historic codetermination roots were in Germany where as early as 1835 three University of Tubingen professors, von Mohl, Roscher and Hildebrand said there should be "workers committees" in business and industry. The Marx-Engels "Communist Manifesto" was published 13 years later, and that same year Germany knew its first elected Parliament which set about legislating labor seats in management structures. It failed to pass, but socialism was on the move.

The 1919 Constitution, nurtured in the turmoil of defeat in World War I, had an Article 165 which said ". . . earning and salaried employees are called upon to cooperate, with equal rights and in community with the entrepreneurs on regulation of wage and working conditions . . ." The Montan Act of 1951 (covering iron, coal and steel) led to codetermination with shareholders and employees given an equal number of positions for company supervision and one outside member added for tie breaking.

With Litton's track laid in Germany, Italy was next in line. Having Westrex there made it less of a problem. Westrex-Italia, S.P.A. was created to meet the response requirement of the *Aeronautica Militare Italiana*. One of the Scharffenberger staff in Rome, who knew Italy as only a native son can, was Claudio Romagnoli. It was his idea that there should be this rump fixture on the Westrex root, separated to go into the task immediately. Given the go-ahead he didn't seek to be underground, but as close to that as possible by renting the basements of three newly constructed apartment buildings just off the Appian Way and almost within the Vatican's shadows. Romagnoli, as Litton's "man on the Tiber," was ever-present as Ash, Scharffenberger and Jacoby had their continuing talks with the Italian government.[15]

Whatever else he knew, he knew all about the *Mezzogiorno*.[16]

The Works Constitution Act of 1952 was a more conservative version, but all that braking action was lost with the Codetermination Act of 1976, a big win for the German trade unions. It applied to all companies with more than 2,000 employees (nearly 500 concerns were affected). It stated that each is required to have a governing board of 12 of which six are employee affiliated holder-backed. Larger concerns can have as many as 20, equally divided. The elected chairman votes when deadlock develops. The management worries included the necessity to disclose intentions that the worker members could take back to their constituency to use for advancing its own interests. It feared that the tendency of workers would to think short term in the span of their own employment rather than favoring decisions leading to growth and strength and endurability of the company or workers would induce no-risk clauses in wages and benefits of employees and offload all penalties for bad decisions on the company's investors. Texas A. & M. University Center for Free Enterprise Dr. Steve Pejovich summarized "The major purpose of codetermination is to bring about redistribution of income. Emotion charged terms such as "industrial democracy" and "labor participation" are merely code words for using the political system to secure wealth transfer."

15. Italy produced a comedy of expressions of incredulity in these negotiations, according to Roy Woenne, who was with Roy Ash in Rome. The Italians counseled Ash that there should be a 10–12% budget overage for "under the table" use, and Ash's jaw dropped. "No," he said, "Litton doesn't operate that way." The Italians' jaws dropped even farther!

16. The Mezzogiorno included the regions of Sardinia, Sicily, Calabria, Basilicata, Apulia, Abruzzi, Molise and Campania. The population of 20,000,000 people constitute more than a third of the nation's total living on 41% of the country's land. The average income was a little more than half that of the rest of Italy. It was also the region of that Third Century B.C. time when old King Pyrrhus of Epicus was invited in to drive off the looting and pillaging Romans, a battle he won but at such great cost the area never recovered and history was given the term of "Pyrrhic victory."

Litton's real estate operative, Jack Cogan, counseled that Litton should go along with a few other sharp companies in making the *Mezzogiorno* move. With all the uncertainties, mind-changing, backing and filling emanating from the Italian Ministry of Defense headed by Giulio Andreotti and the Italian Air Force Chief, General Aldo Remondino, plus the cognizant agencies which would combine into a new Ministry of Industry and Commerce, Romagnoli said it made both political and economic sense to ride alongside *Casa per il Mezzogiorno*. Lockheed and many of the others subcontractors made their ties with Italian firms in the Milan-Turino section of the north.[17]

Litton-Italia, S.P.A. didn't have to hook onto any existing entity. It had the flexibility for real estate selection and location. Wariness dictated not going too far below the *Mezzogiorno* north border. It was Italy's desperate attempt to do something helpful and constructive about that poverty stricken, bleak lower extremity of the peninsula where living was precarious and employment opportunities rare. The *Mezzogiorno* border Romagnoli explained, was a line drawn directly across the waist of Italy from a point about 20 kilometers south of Rome all the way over to the Adriatic. When with Westrex, Romagnoli often enjoyed the companionable presence of the movie makers along the Tiber and elsewhere in Italy. He had seen the mercurial move of Dino DeLaurentiis Cinematografica, S.p.A. to a location designated as Via Potina 23 (23 km from Rome's EUR district), a bare few steps south of the *Mezzogiorno* line, but far enough to qualify him. Those few paces entitled DeLaurentiis to a whole bundle of tax benefits and earned him the gratitude of Italian politicos. He was a very visible "good example" of a quick study in Italian expediency and a true patriot. Anyone, as Romagnoli put it, who went

---

17. The Italian scene stemming from the impact of the F-104 version alone had Talley, Firestone, Kelsman, R.C. Allen, American Brakeshoe, Clary, Hamilton-Standard, Hydro-aire, Irving Air Chute, Haskell Engineering, Lear-Siegler, Loud and Wiggins Oil Tool (of the U.S.). Participating for Italy were OMI, Pirelli, Salmoiraghi, Nardo, Microtecnice and Magnaghi, Secundo Mona, Aerostatica, FIAT, Macchi, Aerfer, Piaggio, Siai-Marchetti and SACA, for the airframe; General Electric US and FIAT (Italy) for the engines; Autonetica, Sperry, Airesearch, Raytheon, Bendix, Computer Devices of Canada, Litton Industries, RCA, ITT, all US in electronics, plus the Italians FIAR, Salmoiraghi, Microtacnice, Selenia, OMI, Litton-Italia, SITS and FACE (of Italy). It was a busy time, a reversal of Columbus, America discovering Italy not as tourists to visit churches, museums, art galleries and crumbled stone of the ages, but with a vitality struggling for rebirth.

similarly south of the *Mezzogiorno* line and there constructed a plant which employed Italian citizens could only be read as a good friend of Italy. Romagnoli had his eye on the *commune* of Pomezia, in the center of which was a village by the same name, and at the 27th kilometer marker out of Rome on Via Pontina there was an innocent looking, sun drenched quiet peach orchard. He drooled over what a site it would be for Litton.

The Littonites listened, but didn't attach the same priority to moving fast as he suggested. They did want to set the Litton-Italia S.p.A. in motion, get it as an entity which was performing in Italian record books and show Italians working for Litton at their assigned benches assembling LN-3s. Romagnoli pestered Jacoby, who told him to back-burner it. He was to continue to operate as if they were a cluster of gophers in those basements making inertial navigation systems for Italy's F-104S "Starfighters" coming out of "air section" at FIAT in Milan and Turino.

Romagnoli pouted. He continued to talk stubbornly about the *Mezzogiorno* in every passing Litton ear. He cited the business coup it represented, naming each example of other companies making such plans. Jack Cogan was suddenly confronted in Beverly Hills with the responsibility for real estate with the telexed words that one of Scharffenberger's Westrex types had optioned a 20-acre peach orchard in Italy, acting on his own! It was annual meeting time in California. There, in response to a question, Roy Ash talked about various curious and engrossing actions which were bringing in sheaves of promising future harvest prospects for Litton. A hearer was Count Rossi, of the Italian vintners, Martini & Rossi. As the gathering adjourned, Count Rossi bounded up to Ash at the podium telling him how wise it would be for Litton to tune in on those *Mezzogiorno* advantages. The tax incentives and other goodies, he said, were most inviting. Ash went immediately to Litton's telex, and sent a terse message to Romagnoli:

"BUY POMEZIA!" it said.

Romagnoli, after all the disinterest he had been treated to for so long, was thunderstruck. Did this change of heart mean Litton now wanted the whole commune, or the peach orchard? Not able to reach anyone that weekend for confirmation or guidance, Romagnoli took the most conservative interpretation of the instructions. He bought the peach orchard.

Later it became one of the fun "might have been" real estate stories around Litton. Romagnoli had not only been right from the beginning about *Casa per il Mezzogiorno*, he couldn't have made a real estate buying error if he had tried. He had gone ahead with the flamboyant interpretation of the telex and bought the commune, village, orchard and all, it appreciated four times its value in less than a year! Litton now had the acreage, a piece of history, too. The land was once part of those old mosquito infested Pontine Marshes Duce Benito Mussolini had drained to convert to agriculture and orchards with great blasts of accompanying propaganda fanfare. Up to and after the plant was built and ceremonially opened in 1964,[18] Litton accountants always had to allow for miscellaneous, one of a kind, unusual income item besides the high technology inertial navigation system. The results of the fruit harvested each year generated for Litton a *lira* cash flow, too.

The Italian startup attracted very young people who had technical schooling, but until the emergence of Litton-Italia S.p.A. and companies like it hadn't much opportunity. The more than 400 employees in the Pomezia plant had an average age of 24.[19]

The Lockheed sale and delivery of the first 66 F-104G "Starfighter" to Germany drew an order on Litton for 66 LN-3s to go along. When it was time for the 67th, and after that, a direct Litton-German government splice was made. Litton had to change quickly

---

18. The Pomezia opening was attended by a Cardinal, Giuseppe Pizzardo and by Giulio Andreotti, who held several Ministerial portfolios and was Prime Minister later. Roy Ash not only participated in the ceremonies, but used the 1964 Pomezia christening as an excuse to convene Litton's very first "European Managers Meeting" for a morale rouser and casual exchange of views. While other Litton activities in Europe were housed in old and sometimes ramshackle buildings, Litton-Italia S.p.A. was bright and shiny new, a forecast of further face-lifting and building programs.

19. When motion is onward and upward in international actions, the "social contract" aspects of companies' extensions abroad do not appear particularly menacing. The mode is a hiring and expanding one. Such things as possible force reductions, plant idling or closings, all seem remote and improbable. The "social contract," binding on any firm when employee numbers are reduced and manufacturing facilities stand down to maintain profit levels, bristle with monetary penalties on an employer—months and years of severance pay, taxation for fringe benefits, downtime tolerances for obscure holidays. The very thought of cuts or closings or dismissals makes any manager who reads the fine print shudder, and treasuries groan. Litton would find out about that later.

from prototypes to a production line. Litton's Guidance and Control Systems division came of age almost overnight and was astride a colossal world market probability which, if the company had its way, would only become bigger, grander and more formidable.

It had a technology transfer agreement with only one non-Litton unit, BTM, in Antwerp, Belgium. It possessed and was adding new facilities in Germany, had the splinter off Westrex in Italy, while "Monty" Bridgman was in full cry after the LN-3 business for the four Military Assistance Program countries (Norway, Denmark, Greece and Turkey) as well as the Royal Canadian Air Force.

The people impact was significant. In Freiburg, with Morat and his staff continuing to expand in the medical electronics field, about $2,000,000 in annual sales were keeping 420 employees busy. A short distance off on *Lorracherstrasse* but still under the Hellige aegis Litton broke ground for inertial navigation manufacture, overhaul and repair. Called Plant II at first, it later became LITEF (Litton Technische Werke).[20]

Jacoby, in his talks with Scharffenberger told him the plight of the Black Forest watch-making industry. It appeared to be troubled, indeed seemed to be dying. How about inviting those precision-accustomed workmen in for retraining and new careers in Litton's variety of electronics? In about 50 of the cinema theaters in the picturesque Black Forest villages slides were shown at intermission suggesting that anyone who might be interested should check job opportunities

---

20. On April 29, 1964, at a press conference at the Hanover Fair, Litton Industries became a part of the German consciousness when the press heard from George Scharffenberger. It was there he introduced Dr. Hans Rudolph as the new general manager of Litton Technische Werke, and invited the journalists to visit the Litton booth at the nearby Hanover Air Show. At an employees meeting on May 4th, Dr. William Jacoby reported that the "Plant II" had started with 100 workers and was up to 700 in a little more than a year. The first accelerometer had been delivered in July, 1963, the first gyro a month later, and were now coming off at 73 and 75 a month, respectively. When Rudolph responded to Jacoby's discourse, he said the new facility would no longer be known as Hellige II, but from then on as Litton Technische Werke (LITEF). When my boss Crosby Kelly was asked for a firm name for "Hellige II," he called me. Just having read an English language magazine listing 100 top German firms my suggestion was that it be called "Litton Technische Werke," and buzzed Jacoby who said "That's it!" Kelly called back and asked "How do you do that?" No use telling a boss things like that so one professes embarrassment and never, NEVER confess how easy it was.

with Litton in Freiburg. Response was immediate and heavy. The new employees' retraining was carried on in parallel with the plant's construction.

A particularly quiet but enormously important personnel action took place almost unnoticed in the U.S. when all the Western Europe entrenchment was taking place. Jacoby needed no one to tell him he was spread too thin. He felt he had to do something about it. He turned to the head hunter, Reeve Darling. He said he needed a production specialist, a disciplinarian, one who was forthright, believable and adroit enough with people to fill in wherever Jacoby wasn't. Reeve Darling had been after one like that for several years, and had one in mind. Trouble was, his candidate liked it where he was—at Lockheed's Sunnyvale, California Missiles and Space Division. He had successfully managed the Agena-B, the power element which was the space program's work horse. His credentials showed him to be a production expert. Darling had been after Fred O'Green for five years, had once been told by Fred that the Lockheed job in Sunnyvale was a dream position, and not to call him for three years. Promptly three years later, he called and Fred was not happy, was ready to listen and did. Who was it this time? Litton, Darling said.

Jacoby interviewed him in Woodland Hills, hardly under the best of circumstances—the day his prospect showed on the doorstep, a power failure had darkened and idled the whole of Litton's Guidance and Control Systems division. It had all the appearances of a disaster area, people running around and about, and none solving anything. Rather than do the interview by candlelight, Jacoby drove him to Beverly Hills to introduce him around. The lights were on there. It was more impressive. When the prospect was ushered into George Scharffenberger's presence, George honey-worded him into submission. The offer was made and the answer was YES. Did he think Lockheed would resent this proselytizing? Maybe, for a little while, but they might also rationalize it as helpful to have someone they knew to talk to about their mutual concerns and one who knew how to conform to Lockheed expectations.

On August 28, 1962, there was a new employee on Litton's payroll—one of the most important recruitments the company ever made. The Litton newcomer was Fred W. O'Green. Not only were feet on the Litton floor to stay, but so were Litton's foundations in many countries by then. Another multinational had gone through birth, almost caesarian in a way, had done time as an incubator baby and was showing signs that more would be heard about it later.[21]

Depth in management talent was increasing too.

That old truism about mighty oaks growing from small acorns was about to be illustrated for Litton in a personnel sense by the same Fred O'Green.

---

21. In 1969 it was obvious to Dr. Charles Bridge at Guidance that the Aero Products section which was pointed at commercial inertial navigation sales was ready to stand alone, and it became a division. In 1971, he coaxed Charles "Chuck" Hofflund over from Lockheed and into its presidency. From that toeing-the-mark start, in a decade it was running at $100,000,000 in annual sales.

SPECIAL SITUATION #11

BURIED TREASURE — BY GOD!

Being multi-national in Litton's view meant more than buildings, exotic addresses and payrolls outside the U.S. It had to do with the abilities and technologies the company's minions could apply which translated into economic development.

When Tex Thornton's mother read her Bible to him as a boy, the implied dramatics of Genesis' first chapter saucered his eyes and conjured up wild pictures in his mind.

Never for a moment did he envision that he would be touched by it personally, but such was to be the case. Genesis, of course, says nothing about a Creation "conspiracy theory". In that broadly brushed account of our beginnings, it does hint at an elaborate, even divine concealment scheme.

The earth was without form and void, says that Biblical second verse. It was in a totally disoriented and highly unstable state. However and how long it took our 25,000-miles-in-circumference sphere to come reeling through time for our ancestors to inhabit and survive its hazards, beneath its surface were hidden treasures. While some might proclaim it blasphemy to suggest that the Creator had allowed some things to "fall between the desks," it is all right to suppose something else He had in mind was that man should have some problems to solve.

The ultimate locations, conversions, applications and worth of all those minerals, gases, fluids and other properties were certainly randomly placed for man in his own intellectual growth to harness to accompany him to his own destiny. The ecclesiastical cloning was all-encompassing enough to include in man greater intelligence and ability to think than was granted any other living organism. Part of man's instant inheritance was dominion over all. For reasons best known to Him, that so generous God held out on granting man divinity or infallibility. Man often tried for it only to have it elude his grasp. Anyone who could appoint corporate vice presidents often found this out. The sure thing was that Man was inventive, curious and adaptive. Certain necessities and prodding incentives had to be lined up to reduce the misses and shortfalls. Extravagant as had been the allocations of ingredients for minerals and hydrocarbons as the earth added its centuries and millennia, their enclosed capabilities for enriching and adding comfort to life were not immediately discernible.

Those hydrocarbons resulted from land areas such as the U.S. that once were seabed. The departed sea had accommodated plankton and other minute species who died in cycles and covered ocean floors. This fossilized sediment sometimes piled up to Himalayan heights and of its own tonnages was treated to pressures and heat which transitioned the mass into hydrocarbons. By natural processes through the ages, oil and natural gas resulted.

Application comprehension came haltingly. It was a brand of thunderbolt that caused fire when it struck a tree trunk in a forest probably 10,000 years ago and lured man to come timidly toward the flame to warm himself. Another was to reveal itself in a Philadelphia backyard in the mid-18th Century. That time it was coaxed down a kite string by Ben Franklin and sparks were bounced off his bare knuckle to entrapment in a Leiden jar as the first primitive step toward the electrical and electronic revolutions and revelations to come. A roaring campfire over some peculiar combinations in stone caused them to "bleed" something which was called "copper" 6,000 years before Christ. Other metals were flushed as accidentally and primitively.[1]

The imperatives and the romance of hydrocarbons first got to Tex Thornton through his devil-may-care father. He started life with the smell of it in his nostrils. The elder Thornton, it was said, was the inspiration for the character played by Clark Gable in the old Metro-Goldwyn-Mayer movie, "Boom Town". He came home often in crude-oil bespattered garb, the combat scars from actually grabbing a

---

1. When Venetian Marco Polo set off to the East from his Adriatic home, he had barely entered Asia when he wrote that ". . .spurting from the ground was such a quantity of oil that 100 ships would be needed to transport it; oil. . . not edible, is flammable and used to fuel lamps that lit houses and shops." This was today's Baku in Soviet Azerbaidzhan on the shores of the Caspian Sea in the late 13th Century. Marco Polo was not only ahead of his contemporaries as a finder, he possessed a sixth sense as to the worth of his discoveries. He was also an unstoppable talker in relating what he had seen, whether anyone believed him or not. He told of "salamander" which was heat resistant and a first encounter with what had led to asbestos. His tales of "black rocks" which burned in China's coal grates caused his hearers to have doubts about his sanity. Marco Polo foresaw well ahead of others. It would be 1881 before the first 2,500 tons of Azerbaidzhan oil were sold in European markets. It was not Russian money which developed those fields, but British pounds, Swedish *Krones* and American dollars.

blazing oil well at its throat and choking off the flames. He wore his blistering casually, yet with a kind of a swaggering pride. His eyebrows were always singed snug to his forehead. Seemingly invincible, he waited restively for the next emergency action. Always on him were the marks and scents of oil. His companions and co-workers knew no other way of life nor subjects of conversation.

The Texas of his son's birth was a late entry in drilling for oil, but soon caught on. It became the acknowledged leader over Pennsylvania, Ohio, West Virginia and California. That then-largest state throbbed with the adventure and tales of it, more real than embellished, of those hell for leather and roll of the dice optimists whose dreams were tied to enigmatic bottoms of deeply dug holes in search for deposits made there from 1,000,000 to 500,000,000 years before. Theirs was a risky milieu. Seven of eight borings ended up dry. Only one in 25 strikes returned enough to defray the costs of the effort. When the depths of their probes yielded nothing and money ran out, with a shrug and a sigh whole crews repaired to the nearest saloon. There they sought comfort in another kind of wetness which could assuage pain and disappointment and prime renewed courage to make another try somewhere.

During the Howard Hughes association Tex Thornton found himself back in the "old neighborhood". Hughes Tool Company was Howard's version of the "miraculous pitcher". Among other accoutrements of the diggings, it had a patented bit which brooked no resistance from the hardest of bedrock which barred the way to rich oil pools. Everyone had to have this Hughes Tool product. The money always had to be up front. Nothing chancy about that. All this was running in Tex Thornton's mind in 1959 and wouldn't go away.

By then, Litton's board of directors included retired 4-star Air Force General Carl A. "Tooey" Spaatz. He had been the one on June 8, 1944 who had sent down his famous World War II "Achilles heel" order ". . .Primary aim of the U.S. Strategic Air Forces is now to deny oil to enemy forces." He also had a jillion stories about dire needs for oil and gas. One of the not serious was nevertheless true stories of his own earlier Air Corps days when government was less generous with its uniformed employees at the pay table. "Tooey" and some other enterprising fellow officers were prone to toss a barrel of gas in a rear cockpit and fly off cross country a safe distance from the base. There

199

they augmented their meager wages by taking up Sunday passengers for a short aerial spin at $10 a head. From such plain and obvious awareness of hydrocarbon derivatives, he had gone on to see America's embargo of oil to Japan on July 28, 1941 make war in the Pacific a certainty. Nippon's precarious oil dependence was so total and desperate, the very survival of the Japanese Empire led it to an ultimate grab for the oil-soaked Malay Peninsula and East Indies. Oil was to the military machines what rations were to the human element of the forces. POL (petrol-oil-lubricants) were always one of the key stats Tex Thornton had had to assemble in the Pentagon for the strategists. Without that factor being in sufficient supply, mounting any sustained offensive was impossible. With the warring over, perpetuation of the lifestyles the affluent had come to enjoy and that lesser nations envied were hobbled without it. Any advance or planning not taking it into account was hardly worth the paper it was written on. It was transparently clear in the Thornton scheme of things that oil was never to be less important in peace or any drive by the human race toward "great expectations". The key to it all, he reasoned, was to be the finder-for-fee for such earth resources wherever they might be in the world. His studies told him electronics could have important applications and contributions to improve the quality and reliability of such searches. The pull of oil became particularly acute for him in August of 1959, that being the centennial of America's first oil drilling.[2]

---

2. In 1859, a self-ranked "Colonel" Edwin L. Drake, 40 years old, a retired and ailing railroad conductor, had taken up with a new idea — drilling for oil along Oil Creek in Titusville, Pa. He had found no oil. Water complicated his labors. His hole was too close to the creek. Water was flooding in. His investors were no more patient than money men ever are. They hoped that his hole was relief from American dependence on whale oil for the country's lamps. Nobody wanted to go back to flickering tallow candles. Drake begged for a little more time. He finally secured some 10-foot lengths of iron pipe which had 1 1/2 inch thick walls. These were driven into the ground until they hit the rock. That held off the water seepage. He consulted with the village blacksmith, "Uncle Billy" Smith, who hammered out a special bit for him. It could be dropped into that stacked length of pipe to chew away at the stone barrier below. It was tedious and not rewarding. As the day drew to a close, Drake told the crew to drop the bit once more and call it a day. They were down to 69 feet. Begrimed, dog-tired and pessimistic, everyone left the drilling site to go home to supper. After a night's rest, some expected to go to church the next morning. When the preacher was done "Uncle Billy" took his 16 year old son to the becalmed and disappointing diggings. As they peered down curiously into the shaft, they found them-

The LITTON Adventure That Was

When Litton was in swaddling clothes, the Shell Oil bosses of geophysicist M. King Hubbert were unhappy about a speech he was preparing to give before the American Petroleum Institute. He did it anyway. In those remarks, he said that in less than two decades America would be dependent more and more on oil sources off-shore and this reliance would be on regions and countries great distances removed for our lubricant and liquid fuel sustenance. He was right. When he made that declaration in the 50s, U.S. oil men were spending $2,000,000,000 annually in search and exploration alone and by the time of his predicted 1970 crunch, authoritative estimates said $75,000,000,000 would be spent in the next 15 years attempting to tap other locations of this vital commodity, anywhere and everywhere. The rest of the world was increasingly petroleum-hungry. New nations were born with little hope of ever being able to walk in the same company and councils of older, more sophisticated, richer countries unless they had some means of fingering hidden oil, minerals and natural gas, and in some cases, subterranean water. Perhaps, as their dreams played, they sat over such riches all unknowing. Disclosure of earth resources was the magic wand which could transform them. From their stunted perspective they could, via raw materials, rise to stature and status. Some gave concessions for development to oil firms, letting them conduct their own explorations and where good prospects gleamed the granting nations could collect a share. Some were canny enough not to want to surrender the surveying directly to the developers because such grants for their own good reasons might not wish to proceed with the same urgency a government's leadership would desire.[3] If the find was a nation's proprietary information, it

---

selves as first observers of as nearly a modern miracle as anyone had ever witnessed. The last plunge of "Uncle Billy's" makeshift bit had cracked the rock face, opened a crevice and the hole was filling with an oozing dark fluid — oil! The date was August 27, 1859. Drilling for oil from that moment was to be ceaseless. It was a bare decade after John Sutter's mill-race had discovered gold in California. Each was to have an important bearing on the speed and certainty with which the United States would mature into a world power.

3. The U.S. had great needs for such strategic minerals as selenium, columbium, tungsten, mercury, industrial diamonds, manganese, tantalum, bauxite, cobalt, zinc, cadmium, chromium, platinum, tin and asbestos. Brazil, Mexico and South America had to be relied upon for 100% of columbium, strontium and industrial diamonds. Manganese, tantalum, bauxite, cobalt, chromium and platinum came largely from France, Japan, South Africa, Thailand, Canada, Malaysia, Zaire, Belgium and the So-

could provide substantial leverage in negotiations with entrepreneurs trying to outbid each other. There were surveying and exploring companies available. The world's publics without seeming to know or touch a drop of it were using 11 pounds of oil per person every 24 hours! It was something like breathing, having one's blood circulate, or heart beat — none would notice until the rhythm of its constant availability was broken.

Search methodology was becoming more precise. Earlier there had been reliance on such dubious devices as divining rods and dowsing, spiritualistic seances, resort to fortunetellers and not-too-educated intuitive guessing. Geophysicists came on the scene only after the turn of the century. Oil companies began hiring them and listening to what they had to say. Word was getting around in geology and physics departments of universities that the petroleum industry could offer a lifetime career.

Two independent geophysical firms intrigued Tex Thornton and Roy Ash. The oldest of the two did overhead aerial passes using a magnetometer, which its geophysicist, Dr. Homer Jensen, had identified as a major technological crutch. It could cover great areas quickly. The other company focused on promising geological formations by using seismic means.

The Thornton antenna was sensitive to what he thought would be a formidable wedding of geophysical effort which could be in growing demand for a century or longer. As pressures would inevitably mount due to insatiable demands for earth resources, electronics would undoubtedly be an important factor. There was a rising body of expert opinion on this, such as Dr. William Rust, Jr., a respected geophysicist with Humble Oil. He wrote as part of the centennial milestone appraisals: "Electronics has played a key role in geophysical prospecting for oil — the seismograph represented the first application of the infant art of electronics to oil exploration at about the same time that electronics was making possible the first radio broadcasting stations. One of the most spectacular applications has been the airborne magnetometer. . ." The two geophysical concerns beckoning Litton Indus-

---

viet Union. A company called Aero Service by aerial surveys spotted one of the greatest bauxite deposits on earth, in Surinam's rain forests along the northern rim of South America, and mapped all of Brazil in one summer.

tries were certified leaders in these innovations referred to by Dr. Rust.

The oldest of the two and the most intriguing in terms of how accidentally and tortuously it had reached its eminence was the Aero Service Company (later Aero Service Corporation). Its origin was rooted in the persisting romantic notions of a World War I pilot named Virgil Kauffman. He was determined after living through combat in France and several crashes that when war no longer gave him an excuse to fly, he would be foolhardy and be a birdman anyway. He had a vague wish that he could somehow make ends meet. Not much of a living probably, but make expenses. He lived in Yardley, Pa., near Philadelphia, and in June, 1919, filed incorporation papers in Wilmington, Delaware for what he called grandly, Aero Service Company.

At first Kauffman barely subsisted by an occasional flight to Atlantic City for the view — those curvaceous cuties in bathing suits. There were also calls to hoist aloft nervy cameramen from the Philadelphia newspapers who wanted to get quickly to and from train wrecks, tornadoes and other disasters beyond the city limits. Such aerial chartering became Kauffman's bread and butter. He soon learned that passengers were few. Camera mounts and instruments in his plane did not turn green the way people did in rough weather and throw up in the cockpit. For a long time he was the last resort of news photographers. Once commissioned to lift some well above a cloud bank which was denying groundlings a view of an eclipse he had to go so high his passengers passed out! This meant Kauffman not only had the flying to do but their photos to take as well. Back on the ground when he revived them at the runway's end, he told them what it was like up there and what he'd seen. Exciting stories were written — eye-witness accounts to happenings which none of them had laid eyes on. This could well have been the inaugural of that much maligned journalistic fudge well known as "magic carpeting", the dateline indicating the reporter to have been eyeballing the scene he described when he had not.

Photo mapping was pioneered by Philadelphia-based Brock & Waymouth. Kauffman was often hired by them. The U.S. Geological Survey and the U.S. Army Corps of Engineers used mapping techniques not upgraded very much from the primitive overviews drawn by George Washington and later by Lewis & Clark. To propose *photo* mapping to those flat-table, line-drawing inheritors was considered a heresy, also job-endangering. The resistance was substantial. The privately contracted for aerial tasks were good when secured, but were neither steady nor dependable. Government orders were likely to be more frequently available, but the fees were small — good enough, though, Kauffman thought, that they could steady the payrolls of his expensive $200-a-month pilots and his $15-to-$18 a week field hands and photo processors.

The career engineers were tackling all kinds of projects to do with ports and rivers. A special sector of interest was huge funnel-like arrangement of the east-west and west-east flowing rivers and streams that joined to make the Mississippi which rushed toward the Gulf of Mexico at from 500,000 to nearly a million (when cresting) cubic feet of water per second. Between America's two great wars, travel was still difficult, roads mostly terrible, and distances great. Regions assuming importance were oftentimes not readily accessible. There were colossal errors in maps. Careful hand artistry covered up inaccuracies which stood out when it was possible to compare them with the earth's actual topography. The Army had two intense military preoccupations, greatly different, but both lending themselves to third dimensional solutions. One was the Panama-Cuba defense complex in the Caribbean as a Panama Canal protective. The other was the rampaging, destroying, often killing Tennessee river. For years, the interior waterway had fascinated official Washington which debated if it could be dammed and tamed rather than just damned and endured. Eventually it was harnessed as the Tennessee Valley Authority (TVA).

Kauffman believed there was a role he could play because of the quickness and accurate detail Aero Service could supply with its mapping. He was striking out on his own and more confident than he had ever been. The trouble was — he was being thrown out of decision making offices in Washington about as regularly as bouncers tossed trouble makers out of saloons.

He finally got to a tall and lanky Nebraskan, Capt. Herbert E. Loper. Loper not only listened but agreed that what Kauffman was telling him made sense. From that meeting of minds onwards, Aero Service went into a climbing professional status which never stopped.

204

Loper soon found it was easy to extend an innocent effort into intelligence gathering of great value. The Army had to be very careful about how close its identifying plane tail markings were to boundaries where other sovereignties were involved. Being too adjacent to the military facilities of others could be an international relations irritant.

Loper hooked small extras on regional mapping contracts. Not in writing, but word-of-mouth, such as ". . .as long as you're in the Caribbean, how about going up high as you can and getting us some pictures of Martinique and Antiqua?" Reason: After the Fall of France, a large part of the French fleet took anchor there. The U.S. was unsure as to its inclinations that close to the American shoreline — whether pro-German, anti-German, or just proud and hopeful Frenchmen available to join the Allies against the Axis when the time was right.

And there was another mysterious and urgent requirement to map the whole of the eastern side of Newfoundland. The Army Air Force unit assigned the mission had been unable to do it because of intensive and interfering perpetual deep cloud cover. After sitting there unproductive for a 3-month period, the uniformed crews thought it laughable when Aero's tiny Beechcraft showed up with the effrontery to say it was going to give it a try, anyway. Aero's pilots went up every day looking for holes in the clouds, found them, and were back within a week with the area coverage desired for study in Washington. This provided details of the Argentia scene where Roosevelt and Churchill met soon afterward to ponder initial strategy for unconditional surrender of the Axis.

"My people," Kauffman said, and he was right, "would go anywhere for me. They were all as high on flying as I was. They'd take 60-40 chances every day in the week to fulfill any contract."

Kauffman also stumbled onto a means of third dimensional mapping. The relief map, mountain and hills rising and valleys sinking between them resembling topographic undulations of the earth, helped people who were not so good at reading contours in pen and ink on a flat surface. Kauffman used a form of easily sculpted stone, which he perforated. Over it heated, wet acetate was drawn tightly by vacuum to conform. When dried, it held its shape. The Massachusetts Institute of Technology enlisted him at once for TOP SECRET work in connection with the revolutionary development called radar. He was asked to do relief maps of the approaches to Berlin, Bergtesgaden and Munich, as well as the Western Pacific's Okinawa and Tokyo Bay. This gave him the directions of attack in all major theaters of conflict and where the targets lay. When the war was over, he participated on many technological advances.

When Dr. Homer Jensen came to him with the magnetometer, he gave the go ahead quickly to incorporate it in Aero Service. Kauffman and Jensen felt this was the route to better sensing of the phrenology of the earthen crust on which so many walked to casually and of which they knew so little.

The magnetometer was the tool for making contact with the iron left in the earth's cooling processes ages ago when it emerged from the state of a molten mass, a part of that being igneous rock. The turbulence of earthquakes, eruptions and erosions caused formations of basins into which sedentary rocks settled or were forced — to await the prying and assaying geophysicists, geologists and their penetrating equipment which would not be denied. The magnetometer was able to do its sensing while being flown overhead at 400 miles per hour or faster. Its registrations were convertible into charts for study and detailed inspection. The magnetometer usually showed the promise of oil to be above that igneous rock barrier, perhaps 1,000 to 2,000 feet down. In the Persian Gulf area, the basis depths were often 35,000 feet or even more.

Aero Service had some extraordinary pilots. Ed Caulfield was a onetime barnstormer who had done bounty hunting and shooting from his plane. He could not only fly, but as was the case with so many of his vintage, he knew all about soldering, welding and emergency mechanical procedures. He installed the first Aero magnetometer[4] and flew it and demonstrated the magnitude of its promise for exploration.

---

4. The first airborne magnetometer geophysical flight was by Aero Service in 1944. It was a cooperative effort of Aero with the U.S. Geological Survey to which Aero contributed aircraft, equipment and crews. It was to determine whether the magnetometer which had been used in submarine detection had a commercial application. Morgantown, Pa. was known to have small deposits of magnetite and it showed up in the results of the first test flight. Aero Service and the magnetometer had possibilities in locating minerals. The first Aero Service try with the magnetometer for petroleum was in 1947 with a group of oil companies backing Kauffman for a survey over concessions they had around the Bahamas. Aero Service has flown in excess of 10,000,000 square kilometers in nearly every free world country and has devised al-

The LITTON Adventure That Was

In the same league with him was Charlie Stinchfield, a tall, quiet University of Maine graduate. He was born with a impeccable sense of direction. He could put his head into a pattern and hold it to razor-blade precision while on a long flight. He could take off and out over 600 miles of barren desert, move over ten miles and fly all the way back in an absolutely parallel line. His charts always fitted together like a tile floor. To do this his concentration was often so total and the tenseness of his holding his heading so tenacious, he would frequently have to be lifted from the cockpit at flight's end and carried to his tent. He delivered in a faultless, machine-like fashion. His assurance was awesome in that he was satisfied he would never have to repeat or recheck his findings and in that he was always right. He could do anything, Jensen said admiringly, when he set his mind to it. Kauffman asked him once during a flight over Saudi Arabia if he had ever played checkers, at which game Kauffman was no slouch. Stinchfield said off-handedly that he'd never tried the dumb game, but he was sure he could beat his boss. Kauffman challenged him. Stinchfield read a book about checkers the night before the contest — and Kauffman was vanquished! Litton's eventual prowess in inertial navigation reduced the requirement for this built-in sixth sense direction finding for geophysical exploration. Aero Service, by the time Litton became flirtatious, had worked in nearly every non-communist country — and the welcome mat was still out for it in every of them.[5]

---

most all the procedures and methods used in collection and processing of data which later became the standards of the industry. Among Aero Service's impressive "firsts" were in use of inertial guidance; the alkali-vapor, high sensitivity magnetometer, the vertical magnetic gradiometer, the gamma ray spectrometer, infrared scanners, the radar profiler, digital processing and computer interpretation. When highly classified side-looking airborne radar during the Vietnam war was finally pried out of its security state, Aero Service worked with Goodyear Aerospace corporation in Akron, Ohio and Litchfield Park, Arizona to get a commercial application. The same wide sweeping radar which had ridden U.S. RF-4C "Phantom" jets in Southeast Asia was mounted in this new role in an Aero Service Caravelle, and a remarkable new era in exploration began.

5. Litton moved Aero's Airborne Geophysical survey activities to Houston, Texas. That facility housed people and equipment technically supporting the seven company owned aircraft as well as providing data compilation, interpretation and processing. The data bank held more than 10,000,000 square kilometers of surveys conducted in the U.S. and all over the Free World. Aero's computer center responds when needed for geophysical, tax and utility mapping, is a digital graphic database and resource for general photogrammetric data.

The other company in which Litton was interested and which wanted first was 14 years younger than Aero Service.

One of the masters degree graduates of Columbia University in 1926 had been Rome-born Henry Salvatori. His field: Physics. The bulletin board in the Columbia physics department had a small card pinned there indicating a wish to interview members of the new class, inviting any and all to come to a small office down Broadway to meet Dr. John Karcher. Salvatori, not too enthusiastically or very much intrigued by it, decided to check it out. Karcher, he found, was a geophysicist for Amerada Petroleum. Salvatori asked Karcher more questions than were laid on him. The shrewdness of these inquiries appealed to his potential employer. A two sided rapport came about in that Broadway office. Salvatori asked if he might come on for a kind of shakedown cruise from which he could make a quick determination whether to stay or go elsewhere. Karcher thought he had the brightest of prospects in his hook. He began telling Salvatori about how generous, challenging and rewarding the petroleum fraternity was. Once drawn into the industry's orbit, Salvatori found that not only true but more engrossing by the day. Its sheer world scope was revealed. The sensitivity it took to weave refining, transportation and marketing into discovery and development attracted him.

Salvatori went through all the steps associated with earth resources probing. No matter how forbidding, he walked hip-to-neck deep in tree clogged Louisiana swamps to set dynamite charges for seismic recordings. He ducked arrows fired at him by unfriendly South American Indians. He had hair-raising encounters interfacing with slithering reptiles and assorted varmints with teeth, claws, poisons and mean dispositions. There were times when he observed if he had been there to do so he would have counseled Adam to go more carefully in following the rules in the Garden of Eden. After all, it only had one snake! From what he learned in those early encounters with Nature and how its properties and affairs were arranged, he formed his own Western Geophysical Company. He became a principal figure in the fathering of the reflective seismograph. It grew in use to be depended upon in 98% of geophysical seismographic activities. It was the device which senses shock waves detected from the strata by explosive charges, and by electronically controlled mechanical instruments. It sent them downward through various earth layers. An echo comes back. By the echo registration of depths of layers, there are also determinations of "salt domes" and "traps" which can "hold oil". "The trap may not contain any oil," Salvatori says with many a rueful memory of that basic truth, "but if one is to get oil, this formation has to be there."

Electronics were all-pervasive in both companies with more to be expected. Together with the inertial navigation precision Litton was laying claim to as an expertise nowhere else available in a high quality, the acquisitional altar was decked out for a uniting of effort.

Dr. Rust had certified the airborne magnetometer was the first geophysical survey technique to be available at moderate cost. It could peer to points below the earth's surface hitherto difficult to impossible to reach. There were new amplifiers which could jack up those signals 1,000,000 times. Recording machines, new microphones and geophones, and vacuum tubes were all finding their way in. Well ahead of magnetic tape recording, Western Geophysical — Salvation's company — was the only exploration firm able to use it on a large scale as means of picking up seismic velocity from reflection data. Even as Henry Salvatori and Tex Thornton began their talks, Western Geophysical already had in operation an in-house devised practical system for analog data processing to monitor 24 seismic channels simultaneously. The rest of the profession was still depending on individual channels only.

Western Geophysical also had an invaluable personnel asset in Carl H. Savit, its senior vice president for technology. He had just collared the decade's most important discovery — the "bright spot".[6] Itself a modification of the seismograph reflection technique, it was

---

6. Western Geophysical increased Litton's employee numbers by 1,000 and the annual sales by $15,000,000. The international credentials of Litton were expanded and the company's face freshened. Along with the U.S. dispositions came Western Ricerche Geofisiche in Milan and Pescara, Italy, started by Salvatori in the summer of 1939, then boarded up during WW II; the Western Geophysical Group of Canada in Alberta, plus the world-wide reduction centers in the Canary Islands and West Africa. As Western came into Litton, her crews were on site in Spanish Sahara in Africa, in the North Atlantic and the Argentine. It had a fleet of seismic cleared vessels prowling the seas. The ownership of Western Geophysical was 65% held by Henry Salvatori, 10% percent each by Dean Walling, V.E. Prestine and Booth Strange. Bank of America, for the estate of Michael A. Boccalery, had 5%. Among them was split 145,000 Litton common shares worth about $5,500,000.

vital not only within the trade but was truly a step to benefit every
human being. It was the security-minded industry's best kept secret
for a long time. The detail it showed the scientifically trained viewer
increased the success ratio of wildcat exploration by five times. As
always, there was initial reluctance to accept it for the improved discovery statistics it produced. In many instances it was because the
real significance was not quickly grasped. "It's like TV," the saying
went. "You don't have to understand it to enjoy it." The strategy was
to have Western Geophysical enter the Litton enclosure first. It did, in
February, 1960.[7]

Roy Ash was the seeker of Aero Service. There was a difference
about the way the two companies, for all their sharing of the geophysical field, came into Litton divisional status. Henry Salvatori was to
stay and run Western Geophysical for five years. The understanding
was that he was not to have any "corporate interference". He was
placed on Litton's Board of Directors as well. There was no such
prospect for Virgil Kauffman who was past 60. No matter what he
knew or the level of his experience, that was too far along in years for
him to be thought compatible with the young, lunging, vibrant, fast
moving, and chance-taking management of Litton then. Also, there
was the bottom line. The Ash ideas of romance were not in geographic kilometers and miles logged in far-away climes with dubious
financials, but were with those elephant numbers down at the lowest
part of the page in the annual reports. Virgil Kauffman, who had incorporated that very first aerial company, was asked in his deal to turn
over 600 employees and 30 planes of various sizes and models to one
of the boys, Tom O'Malley, who had previously headed Aero's Canadian operations.

---

7. Later on as the U.S. sought natural gas everywhere to relieve the shortages,
Litton's Western Geophysical and Aero Service were both involved in nearly every
discovery area — the fabulous "North Slope in Alaska; the Overthrust, that strip
where two ancient land masses bumped into each other from Mexico northward deep
into Canada, and is fattest and richest where Utah and Wyoming touch; the Tusca-
loosa Trend in upper Louisiana, which may be just as rich; the Texas-Oklahoma complex known as the Anadarko Basin; the Gulf of Mexico-Atlantic sea-board coral
entrapment of natural gas so extensive it reaches almost to Long Island. More than
100 years of natural gas sufficiency for the U.S. is probable. "We worked all those
areas," say Western's Carl H. Savit, "and more."

The LITTON Adventure That Was

When Kauffman's shadow crossed the threshold the last time, his crews were mapping earthquake damage in Chile, doing studies on land use and looking for mineral resources, mapping a new African nation's unknown 28,000-square miles of wilderness, looking for underground water and mineral resources in Turkey and Egypt, providing topographic maps for Jordan, searching for oil in Australia, covering 600,000 square miles of Manitoba, Saskatchewan and Quebec in Canada and had fixed — to the accuracy of a pencil line's width — exact positioning of a Telestar 160-foot tall radome (a plastic housing sheltering the antenna assembly of a radar set) and antenna, the means of keeping tabs on a Telestar satellite in orbit 3,000 miles off the earth's surface. Not bad as a mark to leave behind him, he thought, as he and his company's President George Strawbridge closed the deal on January 4, 1962. Instead of that pocketful of dirty and oil smudged aeronautical charts with which they'd lived, they whistled jauntily contemplating the price tag of $4,175,000. They received 16,105 Litton shares valued at $150.50 each, or $2,439,902.50 that day and on August 10, 1965, an additional $1,675,000, or 17,137 Litton common to wind it up.

As Aero Service Corporation absorption papers were being completed in November of 1961, one thing was sure — Tex Thornton, the son of the oilfield "shooter", was well positioned in an oil business catbird scat — and in it big.

J. Paul Getty might have his own formula for success. "Rise early," he said. "Work late. Strike oil." Tex Thorton thought he could make his shareholders very happy by the rewards which would come to Litton for helping others "strike oil".

One could say that Litton's geophysical commitment only made the company "nothing but money", gushers of it. That would be right, but not the whole picture by any means. It made Litton wanted in every country of the world, courted by every country. It had the technological clout to cause Littlon Industries to be respected everywhere it worked its special magic: The finding of those hidden earthly treasures — buried by God![8]

---

8. Few people know when riding those exquisite curves of the Autostrada in Northern Italy's spectacular Dolomites that the core borings to determine rock strengths for that high speed traffic were made by Western Ricerche Geofisische, the Italian part of Western Geophysical.

SPECIAL SITUATION #12

THE ANATOMY OF A MERGER

The way to sculpt an elephant, they say, is to take a block of wood or stone and chip away everything that doesn't look like an elephant. Bringing about a successful merger is not even that easy.

Fred Sullivan and William E. McKenna were walking in the twilight along the *Avenue des Champs-Elysees* in Paris. Their minds were on Litton's exasperating first attempt to pick up a foreign company, Svenska Dataregister, A.B. They were being rebuffed, and they didn't know why.

At *Rue Marbeuf* a shadowy figure stepped out of a doorway. This Frenchman was in a dirty suit, small enough to indicate he was not its first owner. A smelly *Gauloise* cigaret had burned down dangerously close to his dry lips. He hadn't used soap lately, and reeked of overripe body odors. Laying an arresting, unwashed paw on Sullivan's arm, he whispered furtively:

"*M'sieur!* How would you like to spend zee evening in bed wiz' zee mos' beootiful girl in Paree?"

Sullivan didn't change his serious expression nor break his step. "Ah, but *M'sieur*," he asked, "is she *sanitaire?*"

"*Absolument!*" declared the pimp with exaggerated conviction. "I use her myself!"

The incident is not only true, it's representative of the different points of view which are on opposite sides of the negotiating table. What may seem attractive and a bargain to one party may arouse serious questions as to worth and quality, or be completely uninteresting to the other side. As mergers are expected to be more enduring than dalliances, in no way can they be entered into casually.

A Minnesota mother once told her daughter about marriage, and said if she wanted a relatively carefree life, she should marry a wealthy, sterile orphan. No matter how desirable a marriage or merger may look going in, Litton attempted each one with care. Each had to be as clear a mesh as possible with Litton's market planning and the product lines the company had in mind. The incoming company had to have an able and strong leadership and staff, or failing that, the acquirer knowing how to remedy the weakness of the executive shelf by an infusion of Litton ideas and people. Once assured enough, Litton checked against its financial analysis yardsticks for pricing in ratio to probable return on investment, given the add-ons of technologies already owned or in the acquisitional traffic pattern. There was a requirement, too, to hold at bay all those waves of young lions who were forever finding their way into "watchdog" assignments in Washington. There was always a quote from Roy L. Ash in some speech which appeared in business publications that Litton was only interested in challengers, bypassing market leaders. It didn't always work, but none had done mergers better — nor with more flair than Litton. No one else has aroused a greater avalanche of approving adjectives.

In its first frenzied 15 years, Litton made 103 acquisitions, 86 of them domestic, and 17 foreign. More often than not, they were "family affairs". These were clustered in 50 divisions under ten operating groups and subgroups. Its internal growth record was equally substantial, but it was hard to get any of the observers to give that the attention it deserved. If there was an attempt that fizzled, or became troubled, the headlines were as generous about that as they were inclined to look elsewhere when successful examples were in evidence. Litton was such a supreme repository for merger knowledge and *savoir faire* in such accomplishments, it was picked along with ITT, Gulf & Western, Leasco, National General and Ling-Temco-Vought by the Anti-Trust Sub-Committee NO. 5, chaired by an aged and sometimes addled congressman Emanuel Celler of New York, in his "investigation of Conglomerate Corporations." This was in the 92nd Congress, first session. It was a paper commotion of monumental size, a time of intense introspection. The ones being investigated cited bigness to be necessary to get big things done. The inquisitors sought to prove that in bigness American democracy itself might well come undone. Merger by then, in 1969, was almost an art form. Litton was regarded as the patriarch.

A popular buzzword of the era was "people business". As a good Catholic at his Rosary goes quickly by the "Our Father" and the "Hail Marys" to get to the crux of prayerful concern, it was sometimes more of an automatic and ritualistic stance than real. But it was never not a consideration in Litton acquisitions. There were "people" employees who had to transition from old family companies into what they feared were huge, uncaring vehicles organized totally for getting on with profits and growth. That "people" factor hovered over the proceedings as ownership changed and often tarried for a long time afterward. The Litton record was spotty in managing this, but it was more because of being in a hurry than being heavy-handed.

None of the Litton acquisitions was ever exactly the same as another. This was because the motives of sellers, of those leadership people who agreed to merge, were seldom alike, and Litton's wish to acquire them varied the directions from which the company came to the table. Almost without exception, there was a "people" angle, sometimes bigger than all outdoors and larger than life itself. There were ghosts that walked, unbelievable individualists, family dissenters, bickerers, succession decisions hard to make, and dripping-fanged wolves at the door — you name it, Litton could probably cite a "for instance".[1]

A ghost stalked Tex Thornton for a long time, a situation of which he was unaware.

Legend has it that it was a kerosene lantern kicked over by Mrs. O'Leary's cow in Chicago on October 8, 1871 that produced the city's catastrophic $196,000,000 fire. Almost a century later that devastating flammable kerosene spit had its equivalent in a souvenir Zippo lighter Tex Thornton was carrying in his pocket one day in the Alabama industrial city of Birmingham. Some said later it was calculated on his part. Others claimed it was pure entrepreneurial seizure of an opportunity. If it was just an accident or coincidence hunting for a place to occur, it led to a decade-long trauma which eventually produced a pretax loss of $333,000,000 to be borne by Litton's shareholders. It brought about a management exercise which truly separated

---

1. In that cluster of talents in science and engineering Thornton gathered around him at Hughes Aircraft, there was a young physicist freshly graduated from Carnegie-Mellon University with a B.S. degree in physics. While working in research at Hughes, which was in turmoil, he added to his schooling with an M.S., also in physics, from UCLA. He went on to Stanford where he emerged with a Ph.D. in electrical engineering in 1957. He was an attractive, knowledgeable and cool one who met exactly the criteria Dr. Norman Moore had in mind for a Litton Electron Tube research engineer. He was taken on in 1957. "He became one of the best negotiators I ever knew," Moore said, "In business brinkmanship, none better." His name was Dr. Orion L. "Orie" Hoch. Of all the personnel choices Moore made over the years, he was never prouder than he was of that one. It took 25 years for it to dawn on others how key a personnel acquisition Hoch was.

men from boys, some from their jobs. It produced the most Litton column inches of newspaper and magazine type, the most broadcasting commentaries, called up more explanations and answers to inquiry any other Litton engagement. Congressmen became self-anointed admirals and shipbuilding experts. They never deigned to visit or inspect the facilities whose management they used as never ending targets for their hit-and-run press releases. These they lobbed in for Monday mornings when headline pickings and bulletin materials were slim and their coverage was wide. Yet from it came eventual realization that for all the hot coals and flagellation heaped on Litton, it emerged with a shipyard which was characterized as a "national asset". Tex Thornton always maintained that Ingalls Shipbuilding was "only one of many problems" Litton had to solve in its headlong rise and the accompanying growing pains. There is abundant evidence supporting this contention. There was a time, however, when none around Litton would have dared to say, "bottoms up" if a toast were being drunk as those two words described so closely prevailing fear that the dead weight of Ingalls might capsize the whole of Litton.

The coincidences which had been at work for so long bordered on the fantastic in terms of leading Tex Thornton to Birmingham. Almost as he was starting to get antsy about Hughes Aircraft's potentials and the lethargies he was running into preventing their realization in 1951 another drama was playing more than 2,000 miles away. The so-called "father of the soap opera", Robert Hardy Andrews,[2] kept ladies glued to their radios morning and afternoon by having everyone in his stories in so much trouble, listeners no matter how beset their own lives might be found solace. They were at least better off than those characters they'd been hearing about. The novelist, John

---

2. Andrews crossed Litton's path, too. He once was prolific enough as a writer that he kept *seven* radio "soap operas" in scripts five days a week. They included such as "Just Plain Bill", "Ma Perkins", "Romance of Helen Trent", and he invented "Jack Armstrong, the All-American Boy" who munched on Wheaties. Andrews coined the phrase "Breakfast of Champions" which is still used today. He wrote "If I Had a Million" for Paramount, and when the TV series "The Millionaire" took to the air it was judged so similar that Andrews was paid a hefty fee for each episode. His "Bataan" screenplay was nominated for an Academy Award, but didn't get the Oscar for that category. The house on Beverly Glen Boulevard where he did so many of these things later became the home of Litton's Mildred and Fred O'Green. O'Green was second Chairman and CEO of Litton after Tex Thornton died of cancer in 1981.

O'Hara, wrote of strong, embittered unfulfilled philandering movers and muscle men. Robert Ingersoll Ingalls would have captivated them both. His story ran almost as long as their greatest tales. The difference was that Ingalls was real. His life played out for all eyes in Dixie. A serious novelist could well have been afraid to write some of it down, as it was extreme, overdrawn, the recriminations brutal and the intramural family squabbling as volatile as nitroglycerin in a cocktail shaker. The endless charges and counter-charges were made in country clubs, on the streets, in banks and in the courts.

The Birmingham situation which was lining up on Tex Thornton, of which he was all unknowing, began in 1909 when Ingalls arrived down south from Ohio and Pennsylvania. With an old black man named Alec, a collar-sored mule and a busted crane, he set up a junkyard which used the 25th Street viaduct as a roof. He was brash enough to court a Southern belle named Ellen who was sufficiently smitten by him that she advanced him $5,000 at a crucial moment. From that grew the sizable and respected Ingalls Iron Works. Many of the Mississippi bridges and other structures in the south have as their main reliance for strength and durability sturdy Ingalls iron and steel. Ingalls himself was tougher than the toughest employee he ever had. He never sent a half dollar out that he didn't expect $2.50 back. He was generous with abuse, orally and otherwise, but never with praise. He would walk a mile or more from the Louisville & Nashville railway station carrying his bag rather than use a taxi, which he thought was a waste of money. With a trained junkman's eye, he could spot iron and steel scrap, retrieving it to wave in front of laborers as still useful. In 1938, his resident marketer, Monroe Lanier, talked him into setting up the ways for a shipbuilding complex on 55 acres of land on the east bank of the Singing River (so-called by the Indians who were entranced by the humming sound which came off the waters in summertime). The first ship built there was the Exchequer, a forbiddingly symbolic name as the shipyard was slated to give generations of treasurers long periods of bad times.

Ellen and Robert Ingersoll Ingalls had a son, Robert, Jr. The money his father and mother had piled up so carefully he treated as a passport to status, social life, power and frivolity. William Guest, Jr., whose father ran the shipyard in Pascagoula, Mississippi, grew up with the son and heir, knew him well. "He had his priorities in good order," Guest remembers. "They were pussy, whiskey and when he had time for it, business." The trouble was that he trained so hard on the first two, he was never prepared by his father or his mother, nor did he have any inclination toward a business career. Yet, he was made the figurehead president of the whole firm. By gifts from his father, he amassed 4,501 of the 15,000 shares. Robert, Jr. was about 6 feet 3 inches tall, slender, and he carelessly allowed his excesses to bulge him at the midriff. Once he did startle the family heads by the excellence of his judgment when he married a New York socialite, Eleanore Frick, who bore him two daughters, Elizabeth and Barbara. They were adored by their grandparents, and 5,750 shares of the company were in trust for them.

When family affairs became inflamed, the crusty old curmudgeon who put it all together, tried to get his son's shares back. He actually paraded more than $2,000,000 up to young Bob's chair in a bank cart, all in packets of paper money. Give up the shares, and it's yours, was the proposition. The son could be as cantankerous as the father and said NO. Court action eventually ensued. The parents at one point tried to have their offspring declared irresponsible and incompetent. In 1941, in a less strained moment, Old Bob had written a two page letter to the draft board asking for his son's exemption because he was vital to the war-related work of the company. Thad Holt, a longtime, well-placed citizen of Birmingham, was deputy chairman of that board and handled the case that lead to the exemption being granted. Then ten years later, the two generations were at each other's throats in court, and the son produced that old letter as rebuttal to the claims of incompetence and irresponsibility. When both sides had had their say, old man Ingalls was sure that he'd made his case before the jury and the verdict was in the bag. More elated than he had been in years, he went down to the river where his celebration bedecked houseboat was enlivened by presence of sympathetic friends invited to join him in a victory whoop-up. The party had barely begun when the jury trooped in and young Robert was the winner. Right there on the houseboat, Robert Ingersoll Ingalls, Sr. suffered a massive heart attack — and a fortnight later, was dead. Ill-equipped as he was, as disinclined to serious business as he was and as vindictive as he was, Robert Ingersoll Ingalls, Jr. was in charge.

He began pushing his father's old dependables — William Guest, Sr., who ran the shipyard, and Monroe Lonier, the marketer who had priceless contacts in Maritime and Navy circles. "Why don't you both retire, and let some younger blood come in?" he'd say. Younger blood for him meant swingers, the ones who equated a ship launch with aftermath bashes featuring compliant wenches and copious quantities of the spirits. Under his erratic behavior, two ships contracted for by the Moore-McCormack Lines produced an open, bleeding wound at the bank, a $17,000,000 loss. One of them, to make the delivery date in New Jersey, sailed from Pascagoula with nearly a thousand workmen on board who completed it enroute at sea.

The Ingalls board of directors, under urging of the widow and her granddaughters who sided with her and against their father, recruited an engineering graduate of Renssalaer Polytechnic in Troy, N.Y. named Fred Mayo. He was told to take over and run the shipyard. It was by far the biggest Ingalls involvement, both for potential profit, as well as its present predicament, losses. A Birmingham financier, William Hulsey, bought the 4,501 shares of the prodigal son. Even with the mountainous deficiency in the firm's funds, there was a short-lived period of relief. There was no doubt that a state of emergency existed, not only in Birmingham and Pascagoula, but in Washington as well. Ingalls had produced 189 high quality ships including nuclear submarines for the U.S. Navy, and was in fact, the fourth largest U.S. shipyard. The Navy was casting about for a modernized ship constructor with far more than hull expertise, as more than half of ship costs in the future were sure to be in the elaborate electronics systems scheduled to be on board.

Fred Mayo and Monroe Lanier were tipped in Washington to check Litton Industries,[3] and to feel out Tex Thornton for possible merger inclinations. Through him it was thought that the management could be stabilized and Litton's financial ability could bulwark the Gulf coast operations for the prodigious commitments future Navy contracts would entail. They did have extensive talks. Mayo and Lanier were frank about the debilitating inroads the family crisis had made on the shipyard. The paranoia of the Ingalls ownership had now shifted to the belief that there were dark conspiracies afoot to wrest

---

3. Besides suggesting Litton, the Navy told Mayo to knock on two other doors, Philco-Ford and Lockheed. He and Lanier liked Litton best of the trio of alternatives.

the property from Ingalls hands. These fears rattled family thinking and caused a reluctance to do what had to be done. Distorted versions of the likely consequences of actions to be taken dominated the atmosphere. It was finally agreed that Tex Thornton with Litton's treasurer, William E. McKenna, would go to Birmingham, exhibit themselves for family inspection and test the climate for severance of the Pascagoula ship manufacturing from Ingalls Iron Works for incorporation into Litton.

The two Littonites, when in Birmingham, went to Ingalls Iron Works at the appointed time. They were ushered into a conference room, took seats at the foot of the long table, and waited. Lodged in their minds was the admonition of Mayo and Lanier that the widow, Ellen Ingalls, had an antipathy to "Yankee money." Tex Thornton found himself wondering how much of his Lone Star State drawl he had left, as he might need it now. McKenna, out of Worcester, Mass., decided he would only nod and shake his head a lot as his accent would be a dead giveaway. He didn't expect to be in the conversations much. He hoped not. A half hour went by. Both began to feel apprehensive that Mrs. Ingalls had developed cold feet and wouldn't even see them. Then in a sudden flurry, in she came accompanied by her two granddaughters.

Perfunctory handshakes over with, she left no doubt about how she felt. She launched into her perspective of the whole matter. She voiced pride in the family enterprise, how much hard work and dedication and sacrifice it had taken to bring it all about, what an involvement — nay, possession it had all been to her deceased husband and to her. Her concern was also for the thousands of employees, almost retainers in her eyes. It was as if Scarlett O'Hara, reincarnated, was addressing carpetbaggers from the porticoed veranda of Tara, her beloved plantation. Finally she ran down and was contrite. She was in the Old South, after all, and of it. Her tone hadn't been very gracious. She didn't want to take any of what she'd said back, but she was relieved when she saw Tex Thornton smiling shyly and with an expression on his face which read as fully sympathetic with her position.

"Ma'am," and he said it swaybacked as if it were spelled 'Maauumm', "Ah can understand your feelins' completely. Ah had trouble like you're talkin' about jus' last week. We were visitin' another plant of ours in Bristol — up in Virginia, this fella and me." He

220

pointed to Bill McKenna, a sternness on his face which indicated the *faux pas* was not yet erased from his memory.

"What sort of trouble?" Mrs. Ingalls asked. Her granddaughters cocked their heads to one side, birdlike, giving their full attention, too. Mrs. Ingalls thought he seemed "such a gentleman" or as they would say below the Mason-Dixon line, "one who was raised right".

"When we went in the plant, ah wasn't happy with what ah saw. There was this ol' cannon left ovah from the woah between the states (he didn't say Civil war). Ah didn't like it one bit, because that cannon was pointed south! Ah made this Yankee here and some othuhs go right out there and change it, turn it around facin' north which was the way it should be." Mrs. Ingalls and Elizabeth and Barbara all laughed and the ice was thawed. The gathering turned into a conversation, about alternatives rather than declarations of standfast position. It took on a front porch rocking chair atmosphere.

Suddenly Mrs. Ingalls became flustered, struck by a thought she never believed would originate with her: That the sale of Ingalls Shipbuilding to those people there with her would answer all the problems she'd been bedeviled with so long and could be in the best interest of the estate and its beneficiaries. To give herself time, she fished in the depths of her purse for a cigarette. Finally coming up with a long one which she popped in her mouth, she hunted for a pad of matches, or some way to light up. For the first time since the meeting convened, Tex Thornton rose quickly from his chair and walked over to her. As he did so, he drew a lighter[4] from his pocket, clicked it on and lit it for her. The lighter had the Stars and bars of the old Confederacy across its face. When snapped on, it played *Dixie*! Mrs. Ingalls thought it both endearing and amusing.

---

4. Where did that lighter come from. Tex said "somebody gave it to him." Couldn't remember who. McKenna said he saw it happen and couldn't believe it had been planned, but that it was surely there opportunist evidence that Tex was some kind of up there opportunist. Personally I must have asked 20 people if they knew, and finally it hit *the*, hot buzzer in the interview with Harry Gray. "I gave it to him. I was born in Noonan, Georgia, and bought a batch of them for convention pass-outs below the Mason-Dixon line. Tex and I were talking about who was born the farthest South, and I gave him one. Not knowing how hazardous it might be for me if he knew I reminded him. For that, when the Ingalls Shipbuilding was in deep yogurt, he sent me to Pascagoula to run the damned place!"

For about $8,000,000 of which $3,000,000 was in debt assumption, Litton Industries overnight became the fourth largest shipbuilder in America and was the new holder of that Pascagoula 55 acres along the Singing River. The marital admonition ". . .may all your troubles be little ones. . ." is usually a forlorn hope and mergers are no different. Tex Thornton's lighter[5] had touched off a long, slow-burning fuse, one which sputtered, crinkled, twisted and was at times similar to some mythological snake which when stomped on promptly grew several other annoyances double the size and complexity of the one momentarily solved. For those who believe in ghosts , that inexorable shade of Robert Ingersoll Ingalls must have rubbed his hands in satisfaction over how it came out.[6]

There was always that "people factor". They made all the difference in how companies could be persuaded into the Litton collective. The abrasives of tender offers and proxy fights never had any appeal for Litton. It was as though they were some kind of corporate Casanovas who charmed rather than clawed and mutilated the objects of their acquisitional affections. Litton found ways to accommodate people ambitions, people frustrations and conflicts, people fears, people

---

5. That famous lighter with the Stars and Bars of the Confederacy on it, and that played "Dixie" also charmed one Senator John Cornelius Stennis, of DeKalb, Mississippi, longtime head of the Senate Armed Services Committee. That added to the news that Tex Thornton although born in Texas had lots of "family" or "cousins" in his state enthralled him. He knew the Navy and Admiral Rickover had great plans for Ingalls in Pascagoula under more responsible management, and this meant Ingalls family brawling and turbulence extended into Mississippi no longer. He got on the phone to Beverly Hills. "Mr. Thornton," he said, "I am so delighted that you have purchased Ingalls shipyard. I want you to know I'm in your corner now." Glen McDaniel was in the office with Tex Thornton when he took the call, and often thought later how true to that promise Stennis stayed, which is not always the case with a political declaration on the spur of the moment.

6. McKenna, as the years ground on after the January, 1962 Litton succession to ownership, ruefully remembered one point in the final negotiations where granddaughter Elizabeth was displeased with him. Beautiful as she was, she had hung around her grandfather long enough to have enriched profanity resources which would blanche a longshoreman. "Yesterday," she told McKenna, "you tried to squeeze my tit, and today, you're trying to screw me!" McKenna taken aback by the explicitness of her metaphor couldn't think of anything to say then. As Litton's headaches mounted he thought many times that the roles were reversed, that Ingalls interests had lavished Litton with a little bit of Marquis de Sade on the side.

quirks, their disappointments and shortcomings, even hatreds with impressive solutions. There were "people mergers" where one or a dozen individuals were the prize rather than the firm which packaged them. And there were combinations of all these. Once Litton got rolling Seymour Rosenberg and later Frank Slovak had stacks of a hundred or more company profiles of the vulnerable, the interesting and the possibilities. They were no less carefully guarded than Crown Jewels. Some were on the front burner and hot, some on track and moving at a measured pace to coincide with some developing plan, and others were on the siding waiting for their train to assemble. Those folders had a lot of people assessments, the ones who had "dug the well". And who had pumped it after them until Litton came along. With Monroe, Litton not only got a star in Fred Sullivan, but such others as McKenna, Slovak, Ludwig T. Smith, Jim Sheridan, Don McMahon and Ralph O'Brien. All were to have their innings of importance to Litton, some doing well and some not so well. Litton was a biological flip-flop, a case of the parent being younger than most of its progeny.

George Kosmetsky's $7,500 expenditure for a whole company in 1954 was primarily to get Floyd George Steele. Bruce Worcester had written him a memo about a small Digital Equipment Company which he said had "as much chance flying as a rock in the ocean." Kosmetsky's microscope showed him a kind of umbrella in whose shadow were some significant patents, some exciting people including Steele. Steele already had his mental orientation on computers, and "chips" and a multiplicity of ways they would be needed.

Later on, there was Bruder Stove in Cleveland. It was the purest and simplest of "people acquisitions", focused entirely on one individual, Robert Bruder. Unlike Steele who didn't stay long, Bruder blazed a spectacular trail of Litton experiences, standing at some of the most important crossroads for the company and unerringly selecting the right fork to turn into — not once but several times.

Bruder was surfaced by Dr. Norman Moore. Moore, who was running Litton Industries of California when Charles V. Litton sold it, had some of that highly special hue himself. He was sure that the old magnetron was a building block for Litton to get into microwave ovens and cooking. Tex Thornton finally let him have his head and the right to step beyond electron, or vacuum tube manufacture. Moore had known through his associate, Paul Craphuchettes, that people at Raytheon and General Electric in the late '30s had cooked food and popped corn using microwave energy which agitated molecular arrangements and generated heat.

One day in San Carlos, he found Truman Clark, Tappan's production manager, at the outer reception desk. He had come without an appointment all the way from Mansfield, Ohio because he didn't want to be talked out of his notion on the phone. He said unless he could find some source for a vacuum tube with greater reliability than the ones Tappan was getting, Tappan might as well get out of the microwave oven business entirely and forget it. By this time, he told Moore, the whole industry potential for profit and customer satisfaction depended entirely on a magnetron none had yet shown him. Clark said he had been to GE, RCA, Sylvania, Phillips and Westinghouse. At nearly every stop, he was told that each company would be interested in trying to do something for him only if Litton expressed NO wish to service his kind of product line!

Nobody had to drop a load of hay on Moore to get his attention. If the Litton excellence was that well recognized in the trade he had more lights flashing in his head than a Saturday night pinball arcade. The way Moore broke it down in that conversation, there was a short range opportunity to merely sell Tappan a needed component; it could be additionally a learning exercise leading Litton into microwave oven manufacture on its own. Moore, like a kid with a bagfull of marbles he'd won, emptied all these possibilities before Tex Thornton. He said the industry had learned that tubes worked and ovens worked, but when the interfacing was tried, the results were tricky, worrisome and disappointing. This led those who were trying to lick the problem straight into the most perilous of circumstances for this kind of consumer product — temperamental performance of family meal preparation. Moore said in his preliminary fencing with Tappan, that he would proceed only if there would be full engineering cooperation. If this encouraged Litton, he had asked Clark, to go all-out after the microwave oven market on its own, could he have the assurance that Tappan would in no way feel violated, grouse and sue.

"I told him we'd spend our own money," Moore bubbled on. "If we get a better tube and price-performance ratio than anyone else, then Tappan buys from us." Clark was amazed at such confidence, as he had a $100,000 development contract in his coat pocket to offer as an incentive. Nine months later, there was a tube and a quote. The tube and oven were tested. It was a promising match. As Moore relayed all this to Tex Thornton, he said it was completely irrational just to be selling tubes to Tappan when there was this yawning permissive door for Litton to be in the microwave oven business while others were still floundering around.

"Norm," his boss, teased to probe the depths and firmness of his convictions, "are you telling me now that Raytheon has dropped about $15,000,000 in the last 15 years chasing this microwave oven thing that this is something Litton should be in?" By that time, Norm had been around the new Litton management long enough to know it was excessively careful to sort out what might be just brainstorming superficially over an idea and something thought through with thoroughness. Moore was ready.

"Raytheon is selling the wrong oven to the wrong people at a wrong price," he declared. "They're doing a good job technically, but their oven is 30 inches long, 27 inches deep, takes 220 volts to operate — and will cook a turkey, but costs $2,700! And they're trying to sell it to the restaurant market which means they have to call on about 280,000 purchase decision points. The vending industry has just as many outlets, but less than 100 purchasing agents to be covered. That's the way to go."

Tex Thornton listened, seemed interested but didn't say yes. Moore stewed, fussed and came back the next year loaded for bear. It was fortunate for him that he came on both with momentum and supporting information because Roy Ash handled that interview. He had more questions than there are ants in a hill. Moore had been around eight years, had a good record, but he still hadn't won this case. As the meeting broke up, Tex took his arm and said quietly, "Norm, have another good year at the tube division in San Carlos, and we'll back you." Moore's spirits bounced as high as a golf ball hooked onto pavement in a country club driveway.

"What do you mean by a good year?"

He was told that a million in the profit column would qualify him. In that year, the unquenchable Moore racked up almost $1,700,000. On August 1, 1961, Litton's brand new Atherton division named for the town where Moore lived in northern California was christened to take Litton into the microwave oven realm. While he had waited and was being gnawed at by the delay, Moore hadn't let his motor idle. If he ever got that coveted "GO" signal, he wanted to zoom. He had found reinforcement for many of his opinions and was impressed by the credentials of their source — this man Robert Bruder.[7]

He was a walk-on. He was burdened with having to make a decision about his own small, but highly profitable family enterprise. Small? How else would one describe a unit which consisted of his wife, his brother in law, his secretary and an assembler? Their product line was a compact electric stove under the trademark "Heat-N-Eat", a sandwich warmer which had attained a lot of regional popularity around Cleveland. It only cost $100, which meant the profit was minimal. Bruder, being bright, eager and imaginative, thought he could do at least ten times as well if he entered something for the same purpose but not so restricted in usages which had a price tag of $1,000 or more. He was convinced that none of the microwave oven entries so far were really capable of producing a commercially appealing unit, because everyone at work on the project was engineer-oriented. Engineers designed models to be built by engineers and picked at by engineer critics hemmed in by erector-set mindsets. It was a rewrite of the old dog food story, in which a fancy ad agency was commissioned to come up with a dazzling campaign to market a new diet for old Bow-

---

7. Bob Bruder first came over the Litton horizon when he was trade-showing his infrared cooking equipment, and Reed Holiday, a Litton Electron Tube engineer, met and talked with him. Holiday had produced the Litton 3730 tube for Sears, which was in a go-go mood about microwave ovens and had invested about $500,000 in their development. The Holiday tube had a life of from 6 to 10 hours. Earlier, in 1959, Litton's Vin Carver decided he was going to bust a gut to get the Raytheon tube out of Tappan's ovens and replace them with his Litton model L-3189 which started with the first cathode from the original Charles V. Litton arsenal of patents. There was a fault in the ceramic part, and all 400 tubes produced for Tappan were returned as unsuitable. Litton quickly switched to the standard magnetron, which was more expensive but it worked, and in January 1961, began heavy production for Tappan — which satisfied Tappan. These were wild times because even when Norm Moore's wife got her car wheels over in their neighbor's yard in Atherton, and Norm went over to apologize, the neighbor named Wells was found to be a manufacturer. Moore not only came away with forgiveness, but a joint venture agreement where Wells would make the fabricated part and Litton the electronics for its early microwave oven.

ser. Graphic artists sketched an eye-catching container with supporting posters for supermarket display. There were broadcasting jingles in which a pooch arfarfed "God Bless America". Name stars endorsed it. Shelves were swept clean by eager buyers, but no repeat business. A consultant was called in, looked it over, then took a package of the goodies to a hungry dog in an alley. When the contents were spread before him, the dog took a bite, chewed, coughed and spit it up, then slunk away. They'd been selling the wrong public. Moore and Bruder believed microwave ovens were not being sold to the consumer.

Bruder had an option to commit Franklin Manufacturing in Minneapolis to build about 2,000 to 3,000 microwave ovens to his personal specifications, which would be do-it-yourself customer-attuned, and reasonable in price. Before he exercised that option, he asked Moore whether his Atherton division of Litton would sign a contract to make them to be marketed under the Bruder brand name. He'd heard about Tappan, and reasoned that Litton must have something special in the technology.

Bruder found Moore an entrancing character, who had his own theory of relativity — he always traveled with two shirts, wore one the first day on the road, the second for two days, then he'd switch to the first shirt which was cleaner. No matter how long the trip, he always arrived home with one shirt relatively cleaner than the other. Whatever his theory about shirts, Moore wanted to be tied in with Bruder's marketing mind and his sales style of matching customer expressed wants rather than dependence on engineering theory. When Bruder said he had only ten days left on the Franklin option, Moore startled him with a sudden proposal.

"I think Litton should buy Bruder Stove," he said. "That would take care of everything and everybody."

"There'd be no way Litton could do all the required things to take over my 'peanut-sized' company in the time I have left," Bruder said.

"Wanna bet?" Moore asked. It was Tuesday. They met with Roy Ash on Friday for ten minutes. Ash had another appointment and had to leave them, but said they could resume their chat later in the day. Bruder was pacing the floor. He'd only come to Norm Moore to ask him a question. Now he was on the verge of being bought — lock, stock and Bob Bruder, too.

"I'm not prepared for this," he said weakly. "I didn't think it could move this fast. I've got to sleep on it. I have to talk to my wife."

When Ash returned Bruder was given a firm offer. A respectable amount of Litton stock was waved under his nose. Bruder went home to Cleveland for the weekend, returned to Beverly Hills that next November Tuesday in 1963, and Bruder Stove was forthwith a Litton Division.

"We were buying Bob Bruder," Norm Moore said.

It was a far-reaching and insightful move for Litton. Bruder was to be a persisting, relentless, never-give-up force in Litton affairs. The Moore-Bruder relationship was congenial and close. Bruder remembers the day he signed with Litton. Moore was wearing a shirt which was well into its fifth day — and Bruder recalls that more clearly than how many shares of Litton stock he received to bind the transaction![8]

The evolvement from magnetrons to microwave ovens was only a first step in the great and flourishing technological waltz affecting all ramifications of food service. The "safety razor syndrome" was there. No use for Litton to be in the action as the oven, or "razor" provider only, when it was the "blade" or the food which had the reorder factor. There was some feeling from Electrolux, the Swedish company. If it became a part of Litton it could bring its capability and marketing clout gained in selling its high priced line door-to-door. Norm Moore always believed that door-to-door microwave oven selling would have produced a quicker, greater market share than the route taken — appliance departments and speciality shops. There was a flirt with Automatic Canteen, generally accepted as the best food distribution operation in the U.S. The "razor blade" theory pointed directly to frozen foods, which was Automatic Canteen's bailiwick. The third alternative was that there should be contact and conversation with Vernon Stouffer, who headed the spreading tentacles of Stouffer Foods, including restaurants and inns.

---

8. There were 250 shares of the Bruder Company, 250 shares of one called Heatronics, and a single patent application, No. 64,435 pertaining to what Bruder called the HEAT-N-EAT process, which slid into Litton's Atherton division for about $165,000 in Litton common shares. An indication of how important Bruder was showed in the granting to him of options to acquire 3,300 of Litton over a five year period. The Litton NYSE price then was $81.875 at closing.

Stouffer's was a matriarchal family endeavor, which remained highly personalized and had a carefully cultivated and warm visibility about it. Known as it was for having grown from the lip-smacking recipe of his mother's Dutch Apple Pie, she was forever stamped in some reverence. As each new Stouffer activity opened, a part of the ceremony was always the placing of Mrs. Mahala Stouffer's portrait right at the entrance where she would be seen by everyone on the way in. If Mahala Stouffer's kindly gaze was there looking out over it all, it was a certification of care and quality cuisine. The Stouffers were Clevelanders, as was Bruder. He knew a great deal about them. He also believed it was crucial to get food dispensing and vending concerns to install microwave ovens that their customers could operate. If microwave ovens were sold only to restaurants and institutions, they would be unseen by the general public, and their acceptance would be slow.

Bruder knew Vernon Stouffer was facing a big decision as the deep family roots gave him a problem. He had a son and a son-in-law. This was calling on him to make a modern day Solomon-like judgment whether to go with the bloodline or do what he instinctively knew was better for the business for the next generation of management. It so tortured Vernon Stouffer that he was often heard muttering on flights or in taxis, or even while walking in the street. It was always the same dilemma. He couldn't bring himself to make that choice between them. There was nothing really new about this dilemma as it has always been one of the oldest and often recurring sets of circumstances which pester founders when they hand off to inheritors. The sentimental attachments are deeply imbedded, not only stemming from the small and unlikely beginnings where everyone is in shirtsleeves but it is natural for parents to hope that one of their own will have both the desire and qualifications to handle the leadership. The catch is that sentiment is never enough where a business organism is involved in which investors have placed their money and their trust. There is even family expectancy and reason to want steady wisdom and success to accompany the enterprise into the future. That decision calls for objectivity rather than subjectivity. Bob Bruder knew of the Stouffer agonizing.

Cleveland was structured along the lines of many old American cities east of the Mississippi. It had a spectrum of tightly knit families, intermarried and cross-fertilized for extension of their fortunes—almost modern throwbacks to ancient European city states. It had a country club which leaked as much of the doings and feelings of its membership as a rusty bucket and where people were often forced to skirt warily around appearing to "take sides" as if a "war of roses" were blossoming anew.

Bruder worked with Vernon Stouffer and his son, Jim, in developing the Standard Oil (ESSO) stations' fast food service using Bruder Stove "Heat-N-Eat" warmers and Stouffer frozen packets. A motorist on the turnpike or the Interstate between Cleveland and Columbus could turn in for an oil change and lube job, or even for a full tank of gas and have time to treat himself to instant hot gourmet selections on the spot (no 19¢ hamburgers, but for $1.95). The enthusiasm this generated went well with that particular string of ESSO stations then handling the highest volume of traffic anywhere in the country. On those Saturdays when Ohio State had football games in Columbus it took about the same number of cattle to fill stomachs of the trafficking hordes as had populated old trail drives.

There was enough business respect going between Bruder and the Stouffers for Bruder to be the natural agent to accomplish a splice between microwave ovens and the rising frozen food trend. Statistics were pouring in about the numbers of working women on the increase. Households were crying for both reduction in the kitchen time and some means of coping with staggered eating schedules of family members.

There was almost a trysting place quality about the Bruder questing. The Stouffers, Vernon and Trudy, wintered at Camelback Inn near Scottsdale, Arizona, so Bruder was there a lot. As summer came, the scene shifted to the Stouffer yacht, which he had acquired from the Duke of Windsor. It was a handsome 65-footer made somewhat less royal by Vernon's favorite competition with his guests. Vernon loved watermelon. Bruder never came on board without a couple of big, fat, dull-to-the-thump specimens, a country twist of the wooer's traditional ploy of candy and flowers. Part of the game was that they sat under the awning shade at the stern to see who could spit watermelon seeds farthest out into the Lake Erie water. Bruder was careful never to win, and he never pushed the conversation in the direction of his own interest. He knew that Vernon, given time, would get around to his fixation — the designation of his successor. When he did he ticked off the strengths of the two Jims who were cluttering up his enjoyment of life — Jim Stouffer, the son, and Jim Biggar, his son-in-law — and his wondering whether they could both benefit and mature if they were fortunate enough to have time and guidance of people such as Tex Thornton and Roy Ash and Joe Imirie.

No innocent watermelon games were big enough to hide what was going on. When it was finally divined by the Stouffer Board of Directors and the 7,600 Stouffer shareholders that a pot was stirring the stock which was normally very quiet, went up $3 and a fraction on the strength of rumors. But not all were happy about what they were hearing. At first Vernon backed away even though he and his wife held 21% of the stock. Stouffer visited each member of the Stouffer board and when they regrouped with a favoring majority consensus they returned to Cleveland to begin serious outline of the merger agreement.

Tex Thornton headed Litton's team, which included Joe Imirie whose industrial systems and service group where Stouffer would report. Bruder had been operating under Imirie's charter, and now along with Seymour Rosenberg, the foursome represented Litton's welcoming committee. Judy Tragos, Bruder's secretary who was about nine months and 15 minutes pregnant, was in a room in the Hollenden Hotel where she typed and retyped the agreement. Her husband was allowed to stand by ready to rush her to the hospital if her set of labor pains peaked before those in the negotiating room did. Almost every hour on the hour, she had to redo the whole thing. As the clock hands worked up to midnight, fatigue was heightening. Tempers were becoming short.

"We're going back to California in the morning," Tex Thornton told Vernon. "You can continue to run your family business the way you want. We'll continue to look for some other kind of a food tie-in for our microwave ovens elsewhere."

Vernon's eyes followed him but he said nothing as Thornton left the room and went to bed. Imirie and Rosenberg stayed on to talk to Bruder about how it might still be pulled together. Having put this much effort into it, and convinced as they were it was right for Litton, they were reluctant to let go.

"We have to all remember that Vernon Stouffer is a proud man," Bruder said. "He has every right to be, considering what Stouffer's is today. He's being offered less shares than he was a year ago. Sure, I know the price of the stock has gone up on Littons side, but this disturbs him."

It was almost a $100,000,000 transaction they were assembling with each Stouffer share to get .312 of a Litton share in exchange. The Litton Corporation pilot, Lyle Estelle, had his instructions from Litton's chairman to be "wheels up" for the trip west at 6 a.m. The Litton foursome stood together morosely the next morning on the ramp. Thornton was drained and impatient about all the seesawing and lost time. Even if there was a deal now, he said, the Stouffer side — for dragging it out — would have to relinquish rights to the upcoming stock dividend on the allocated Litton securities involved in the trade. This meant that on their packet of 927,522 Litton shares, the Stouffer's would not qualify for an additional 23,188 in those dividend awards going to all other Litton holders. On that sour note, everybody but Bruder got on the airplane. He was left there lonely and forlorn on the runway's edge. His cohorts were leaning back in the company plane, dozing and putting distance between them and Cleveland.

His secretary, loyal to the end, didn't go in the delivery room until the haranguing was over. Bruder hadn't seen his wife in two weeks and his four kids were strangers to him. He had been in his suit so long he was sure it was tattooed on him. He drove slowly back into Cleveland and once he'd parked his car, called Bob Baker, Litton's public relations man in Chicago.

"Get on over here to Cleveland," Bruder said. "We've got to do something quickly to quiet the New York Stock Exchange's 'stock watch'. Stouffer's stock has been up to 28 for four days in a row anticipating the probability of a deal. This was the second time around, so they'll think surely all the roadblocks were demolished."

Baker said he was off and running for O'Hare airport. As Bruder waited for him, he sorted over the crumbs from the negotiations table. He knew Trudy Stouffer had great influence on Vernon. He'd gotten to know her quite well through all the ups and downs. He called Vernon to tell him he would need his OK on a joint press statement. It was Trudy who answered the phone in their Winton Place penthouse apartment which afforded a breathtaking view of the Lake Erie shore. He told her Baker was on the way in from Chicago, and as soon as he landed, they'd like to come over together after lunch to work out the details.

"I'm sick of the whole thing," Mrs. Stouffer said. "You can come if you like, but I'm going to bed for three days and nights."

Bruder was as sympathetic as an undertaker at the side of a bereaved family member. He said since he'd been away from home so constantly, he was going to bring his wife along. "Bring her," said Mrs. Stouffer, "but I'll be in bed." Bruder couldn't have that. He wanted her to be up and able to participate and reason with Vernon. He said he understood the tediousness of it all, but he now wanted to go home, have a bath, and be freshened by the time he and his wife got there. Bruder was sure that knowing his wife would be along would work, and it did. When Trudy Stouffer opened the door to greet them that afternoon, she had been coiffed and was dressed to the teeth, the gracious hostess in every way. If Bruder had gone there alone, he was sure that would not have been the case, but if there was to be another woman in her home the threat to be off and in bed could wait.

While the two men busied themselves, Jim Biggar — the son-in-law — joined in the conversation. He wanted no part of the merger. He wanted to be on record with his father-in-law with that position. Bruder was in an advanced state of relaxed numbness by then. He told them Bob Baker had a notice out which would go to the press the next morning at 9 a.m. Wearily he reminded them that they had to say something.

"I'll leave the room," Bruder said finally at 2 in the morning as the talk ground on. "You family members can talk it over. I'll come back in a few minutes. If you decide merger, then that's what we'll tell the press. If you decide not to, I'll tell them we thought we had a deal, but you've chosen to change your mind."

Bruder stepped out of the room, went to the big window and looked out over Lake Erie where he had lost all those watermelon seed spitting contests to Vernon. He toyed with the idea of putting on his coat, waking his wife who was asleep on the sofa. Vernon burst in the room suddenly, the papers in his hand.

"All right," he said, "it's a deal."

233

Trudy signed the letter of intent, and so did he. Bruder quickly added his signature for Litton. The closing date was October 4, 1967. Stouffer was quoted at $28.875, and Litton was at $106.375. Litton was up from its low of $79.50 on January 11th of that year, and was still climbing. Almost immediately the decision Vernon Stouffer couldn't bring himself to make was made by Litton. Jim Biggar, who had protested the merger so vehemently right down the wire, was named by the new parent firm to head the Stouffer division!

If there had been high drama getting Stouffer's into Litton, there was more — old holders of Stouffer's shares saw their new shares rise $14 in the next 16 days. Bruder persistence added far more than the long-hunted food service interlock with microwave ovens. The securing of this gastronomic giant would later make the difference between Litton's sturdy continuance, or whether it would become a corporate cripple and easy prey for wolves which lurk out there picking up scents and waiting to pounce.

Things people fear which lead them to a merger frame of mind are often strongest motivations to get into partner brokering. With the arrival of Ingalls Shipbuilding on the Litton premises in 1962, there were pros and cons about the advisability of Litton having a "transportation group". It would include everything from vehicles to complete systems for moving things and people — the manufacture as well as the operation.

Warehousing — both military and commercial cargo movement from ships to shore with continuance beyond piers to loading or offloading points; conduits from mines to transports and movements of items in ships' interiors; and conveyor systems with varying degrees of sophistication.

Some of the Navy orders for ships indicated that interior conveyor requirements would be substantial, and that electronics would have a larger participation in making it all possible. In Seymour Rosenberg's folders there were several conveyor companies, all of them family heirlooms in their ways. They were all inhibited by inability to raise the capital investments necessary for upgrading conversions, although they all tended to do well, or reasonably well. The margins were not generous and therefore their lines of credits at the banks were insufficient.

One was in Stamford, Connecticut. Hewitt-Robins had grown to eminence from an 1891 patent of an "idler", a spool-shaped roller in which a rubberized, endless, swaybacked belt rode without spilling earth, ore or coal on it. In its time it was a remarkable relief to men and beasts who otherwise would have had to lift, drag or haul these great weights from places of origin to destinations for consumption or further processing. Thomas Robins, Sr., of courtly bent and a gentleman of the old school, spent many an hour with Thomas A. Edison to their mutual advantage.[9] They were not only friends but similar run-of-mind congenials.

They were contemporaries if not companions of the fabulous James Buchanan "Diamond Jim" Brady who dazzled everybody with the jewels he lavished on the beauteous Lillian Russell. He always bought two seats down front for her openings, the extra seat being for a box of chocolates on which he nibbled throughout the performance. Brady, among other actions far more glamorous, had formed the Hewitt Rubber Company in Buffalo to make hose which he sold to the railroad barons of the era for their air brakes. He added other related product lines as he prospered. In the time of Thomas Robins, Jr., Hewitt Rubber was bought out because it was found that rubber had to be added to conveyor belting to give it more resilience and be better able to take the pounding and wear and tear which went with high speed use.

In Cincinnati, there was Alvey-Ferguson whose base was a 1902 U.S. Patent No. 714,432. That was for the first roller conveyor system that had ". . .for its objects to enable goods to be transferred from one point to another, as in a warehouse, expeditiously and with a minimum of hand labor and to allow the apparatus being adjusted to receive goods at different points as may be required. . . with certainty." Other patents were granted Benjamin Alvey in 1903 in France, Germany and

---

9. Thomas Edison invented a magnetic separator for concentration of low grade iron ore which was found in considerable quantities in Northern New Jersey and Eastern Pennsylvania. He also brought into being a new process for crushing and briquetting ore. At first, he thought handling the mined materials could be done with simple scrapers and gravity buckets, but when exceeding 200 tons of traffic they failed him. It was his friend, Thomas Robins, who suggested and manufactured the first belt conveyor for his Ogden Iron Mine in New Jersey in 1891. What became Hewitt-Robins was formed less than five years later to do things like that and more.

Great Britain, and in 1904 he was awarded a gold medal at the Louisiana Purchase Exposition. All this concealed that what he had had for his starting motive was some means of trundling barrels of beer, other than by hand. Alvey always did it with a little more nerve than his contemporaries. His company transitioned naturally into unit rather than the bulk handling concept, making it adaptable to computer inventory storage and controls.

By Litton's time, it had a unique "personality aspect" in that it had been run well since 1951 — by a woman, who had in her 15 years of managing it had never failed to show a profit. She, Mrs. Jayne Baker Spain, had come into its picture by inheritance. At one time, Austin Goodyear, who then headed Hewitt-Robins, had made overtures to acquire Alvey-Ferguson. Jayne Spain, as cagey as she was capable, didn't find that too charming a prospect. Bulk conveyor companies, she felt, were hod-carrying relatives to what she had, maybe as much as a generation to the rear in its technology. In Jayne Spain's view, unit handling was a classier evolvement for serving a more demanding clientele. She had her eyes on Litton, and in January 1966, it became a Litton division. As part of the deal she became the first woman president of a Litton unit for the next five years.[10]

---

10. One oddly original patent acquisition had to be the collection which came with George Von Gal Manufacturing in Montgomery, Alabama, a combination of folk lore and pallet making expertise joined with Alvey-Ferguson (now Litton Unit Handling).

When Gordon Palmer was recruited from Logan, another conveyor company, to function as a product developer, he and his colleague, Lloyd Robertson, told Jayne Spain and Austin Goodyear that Von Gal was just what unit handling needed. While not the first, it was undoubtedly the premier pallet loading and unloading equipment manufacturer. It was the result of a Connecticut Yankee named George Von Gal, who'd been a B-25 pilot in World War II who wanted to coast into an airline left hand seat but not sidetracked. He married Sue Bellengrath of the Montgomery and Alabama Coca Cola family. She wanted him around, so gave him a job back on the docks where 50-pound cases of Coke came off the line to be toted to outbound delivery trucks and stacked. It was hard enough to keep the roughest, most muscular employees because each at the end of the day had wrestled tons and felt like it. Vol Gal saw this incentive to invent a better way. With $4,000 he borrowed from his wife — which he later paid back — he and an associate names J.H. "Son" Thomas, built a machine to do all that toting, racking and stacking on a pallet. The whole pallet load could then be moved onto the assigned truck. For many years, he marketed only to the members of the soft drink bottler's fraternity, but when it was made a link in the whole Litton unit handling capability, everyone was suddenly better off. The price in

The specter of "fear" as the lubricant for the takeover process came soon after that. The pall fell over Jayne Spain's spurned suitor, Hewitt-Robins, no less!

Louisa, daughter of Thomas Robins, Jr., lived across the street from a fairly affluent family named Goodyear. The tall and gangly Goodyear son, Austin, grew up with her, carried her schoolbooks, and diagnosed his own bad case of puppy love as a kind of lingering, terminal affliction incurable over time — and so it was. Austin made a short detour after college into Wall Street and worked for Brown Brothers, Harriman. His noontime sport was to join others on the corner to watch the brass-burnished, chauffeured chariot of John Pierpont Morgan go by for his daily ritual lunch with his partners. Goodyear tried the Texas oilfields, too, but returned to marry Louisa, did his wartime stint in uniform, and afterward slid naturally into Hewitt-Robins proffered chairs which took him to its presidency. It was not that odd a story as old family companies went in America's northeast. He was closely supervised every step of the way under the watchful and conservative eyes of his father-in-law. Austin tended to lean over backward so much anticipating a likely negative reaction to any suggestions he might make that the staff measured him as even more conservative than his wife's father.

Austin, though, did like exuberance around him even if he had to turn it off more often than go with the ideas and proposals it generated. In that most bizarre of places, being on KP on New Year's Eve at Fort Dix, New Jersey, he met a fellow sufferer who managed to make a grand game of peeling the mountainous sacks of potatoes dumped in their vicinity that night by the on-duty mess sergeant. He wasn't very careful about saving very much of the potato he worked on, but he dealt with each one quickly and was a natural born expeditor if ever there was one. His name was Ellis Gardner. The war over, one of the first things Goodyear did was to convince his father-in-law

---

1968 was $600,000 in Litton shares, but the Von Gal royalty was to total $2,150,000 for those patents paid over a 10-year period. Of the Von Gal Company shares, 500 of the 10,000 were owned by "Son" Thomas who helped construct the original machine — and the understanding he could work there as long as he wished. If Von Gal's wife had given him an easy front office management job with liberal time off for the country club, he might never have played the important role he did in easing men's burdens — and adding another element of sophistication to the materials handling field.

that Gardner was needed at Hewitt-Robins. Gardner, then with General Electric, was not too enamored of his job and on switching to Hewitt-Robins rapidly climbed to executive vice president. He was feisty, had more ideas than there are squirrels in a cottonwood tree, and favored Hewitt-Robins growth by acquisition.

One he was bent on getting and did was Foote Brothers Gear Company in Chicago.

E. Lawrence "Larry" Gay, who had come to Hewitt-Robins from a New York law firm, was Hewitt-Robins' secretary-treasurer. He, as others numbed by the previous dullness, found the Gardner Roman-candle-added quotient picked up the spirits by these new signs of liveliness. Little did they know how lively it was about to be!

One of the principal shareholders in Foote brothers was an Englishman, David Brown, Sr., the founder of David Brown, Ltd., one of the world's foremost gear manufacturers. He had plants in Spain and in South Africa, so he'd gotten clued in on Hewitt-Robins from that far off perspective. One of the first of the Rhodes Scholars was an American named Ellis Robins,[11] a cousin of Thomas Robins, Sr. He became chief of staff to that old South African empire-builder, Sir Cecil Rhodes. Robins Conveyor South Africa, S.A. had been a natural development. That cousin on Rhodes' death became head of the British South Africa Company, was knighted, and wore the formidable title of Brigadier, the Lord Ellis Robins. With that kind of tie in high places, David Brown, whose own family base was several generations running in England, was mightily impressed by that 15% of Hewitt-Robins the exchange for old Foote Brothers gave him. He began to plan his own moves, even as Hewitt-Robins was celebrating having

---

11. Brigadier, the Lord Ellis Robins, out of the University of Pennsylvania and Philadelphia, entered Oxford in that first 1904 class of Rhodes Scholars. He became a luminous answer to the Cecil Rhodes dream; he became a British subject, married an English woman, and headed the British South Africa Company that Rhodes established. He drew up and ran the extensions into Rhodesia making investments in mining, farming and other developmental activities. Robins, the son of an American soldier and from the "rebellious colonies", served on Field Marshal Wavell's staff in India and was a kingpin in Conservative politics. He was often referred to as a prime example of one generation passing the torch to others to carry on as he became one of the chief projectors of the Rhodes ideas and ideals — and business interests. Robins died July 22, 1962. At Oxford, the records show he "read history." He made some, too.

Foote Brothers now with it. He never attended the Stamford board meetings, always sending his son, David Brown, Jr. with instructions. It was his son, in his 30s, who threw in that in ingredient of "fear".

Larry Gay was aware of it first. He heard a careening and brake screeching Aston-Martin hit the driveway fronting the 30-room Elizabethan Tudor mansion housing the small staff of Hewitt-Robins. It was 5 p.m. November 18, 1964 on a Wednesday. David Brown, Jr. dashed in and went directly to Austin Goodyear's office, closeting himself there for half an hour. When he left, Goodyear, ashen faced and in a state of near shock, called in his key associates — Gardner, Gay and Forrest Griffiths. He had been told, he said, that the financial press the next day would carry ads making a David Brown, Ltd. tender offer to acquire 51% of Hewitt-Robins stock.

"You mean he wants to reverse the numbers?" Gay asked. "From his 15% to 51%?" He said it in dry-throated awe, not in fun.

There were doleful remarks about doing the corporate version of hara-kiri, that if Brown's grab was successful that they would all resign *enmasse*. As always, there were the hotheads and the cool hands. Gardner liked a good fight, licked his chops and called Hugh Knowlton of Smith, Barney asking him for some fast countermove suggestions.

"Perhaps there's another possible merger opportunity, somebody who would like to have us," he said, reaching for a way to get John Bull, Jr. in a melee of china shop proportions and in the process dehorn him.

Gay offered to comb the 1,000-plus listings of traded stock in that day's Wall Street Journal to help locate possible dovetailing enterprises. He said he'd try for capital goods companies with records for being able to make quick decisions. Everyone was to assemble the next morning in New York to plot a course. The clock on the wall, Gay said, seemed to be ticking louder and more imperiously than he had ever noticed it doing before.

Everyone reporting in the next morning was worn and depressed indicating minimal sleep. Their New York gathering place began to hum almost as they hit the door, as each one was on the phone with a list which had been separated out by time zones. The first findings were nerve wracking. Decision-makers were out of town or out of reach. Knowlton said he had one he was saving for noontime, which would be 9 a.m. on the West Coast. Right on that noon hour where he sat faced with an unappetizing cold sandwich staring at him, and a disappointing list of crossed off company names, he placed his call to Area Code 213, dialing after that, 273-7860. The operator answered, he thought gaily, "Litton Industries!"

He asked for Roy Ash and when Jean Randall picked up the phone, she put him right through. Knowlton and Ash talked at length. When he rejoined the group, the pickings had been so universally bad, none even bothered to look up.

"Roy Ash at Litton seems to be interested," Knowlton said.

The room was suddenly transformed. "He not only seems interested, he also seems to know a little about Hewitt-Robins. Definitely yes, Litton does have an interest in this kind of industry. That's what he told me." Knowlton said that Ash had added that Hewitt-Robins was actually on Litton's list of acquisition nominees. Everybody in the room was pinching himself to be sure he was hearing what he thought he was hearing.

In California, Ash no sooner hung up when he sent for Seymour Rosenberg.

"Remember that file you've been making on Hewitt-Robins?" he said. "They're interested in coming with us, and it has to be fast. Give me an update on everything you have on them."

The Rosenberg folder showed Hewitt-Robins as having a well-established reputation at home and abroad, and a whole hatful of "firsts".[12] Bob Lentz, and then Roy Ash and Ludwig T. Smith were on planes for New York before the day was out. The scare was

---

12. Hewitt-Robins claimed many "firsts", not disputed by competitiors. They included the roughed belt conveyor, the rubber covered conveyor belt designed for the rough treatment which went along with moving heavy bulk materials, the stepped-ply conveyor belt, the initial practical foolproof airbrake hose (which had attracted the legendary Diamond Jim Brady), a fire hose chemically impregnated against mildew and dry rot, the portable vulcanizer for joining ends of conveyor belting on the job, the self-reversing tripper for belt conveyors, the boat unloading conveyor belt, the downhill power-generating conveyor, acid resistant hose, synthetic rubber gasoline hose, twin welding hose, mass produced self sealing fuel tanks for aircraft, shakeouts for railroad cars, conveyorized ship loading plants, the self feeding coke wharf, those important revolutionizing conveyors pioneering the way for handling stone, coal and copper ore, the first mechanical ore and coal blending systems, the tandem drive conveyor, a conveyor that would complement the work of a dredge, the belt feeder, rotary grizzly, the circle throw vibrating screen, the hoses for high pressure steam, for heavy

heightened by David Brown, Ltd; bidding 30% above the market price. For this, Roy Ash had a palliative, but first he wanted to meet the Hewitt-Robins' management face to face, to tell them what they'd be coming into at Litton and why that aggregation of fast movers was interested in their more pedestrian kind of industry. Afterward, it was said to have been a genuine *tour de force*. His presentation took about an hour. When he finished, he said he'd step outside so they could consider, converse and vote yea or nay. He was hardly out the door when he was asked back in to be told that being 100% into Litton was what they all wanted right then more than anything else in the world! The palliative Ash told them about was that their joining Litton could be in such a way — stock for stock — it could be tax-free. The David Brown Ltd. route would be a tax man's bonanza levied on individual shareholders.

Ellis Gardner ran the campaign for shareholder agreement like a Prussian field marshal. He personally called everyone who owned 25 or more shares. The vote at a special shareholders meeting in Buffalo was a surprise to all parties — David Brown, Jr. got only about 5% more of stock than it already had.[13] Afterward, in the ecstasy of celebration, Ellis Gardner was kidded a lot for causing all the work —

---

duty suction, propane-butane, and Navy suction and discharge roles and the first durable gaskets for pipelines.

There were other promising prospects in the offing. These included Union Chain in Sandusky, Ohio, Precision Gear in Chicago, and chainveyor Corporation in Los Angeles.

13. David Brown Corp., Ltd. owned 105,618 of the 699,411 shares of Hewitt-Robins common stock outstanding, about 15%. Its tender offer made Nov. 18, 1964 was for 240,000 more at $32.50, slightly above the market's quote of $29.125. Austin Goodyear sent a telegram to all H-R shareholders that same day stating it was ". . .grossly inadequate based on the company's earnings, dividends and prospects." In the course of 19 hours, Roy Ash, accompanied by his legal adviser, Ludwig T. Smith, not only expressed the desire to merge the Hewitt-Robins enterprise into Litton, he exchanged $4,860,000 of Litton stock for 15%, or 125,000 H-R shares. Ash had suggested the exchange as a "technical assistance agreement", one party to the accord to provide expertise to the other, that agreement to wash out when the merger became final. Much was made of that 125,000 H-R shares given as fee of sorts for that "technical assistance". It went all the way to the Supreme Court of the State of New York. At the special meeting of Hewitt-Robins stockholders Jan. 14, 1965, 516,000 shares voted for the merger with Litton, about 74% of the shares outstanding, but Litton's 125,000 shares were withheld from that tally by court decision. No matter, the required 2/3 approving was achieved.

after all, it had been his eagerness to get Foote Brothers Gear as part of Hewitt-Robins which had brought David Brown to the Hewitt-Robins door.[14]

The Litton acquisitional push for components which got them Clifton Precision Products in Pennsylvania in a Philadelphia suburb also got them a sort of "Grandma Moses of management", a supreme individualist named John P. Glass. He dallied about coming to work each day from the succession of rooming houses he occupied, getting there about 2 p.m. There was always a stop at the supermarket on the way, so he arrived with a fresh loaf of bread and a pound of bologna. At the door, he took off his shoes revealing white socks. In these he toured the plant all day in his badge of office — a torn, old sweater and with a pair of calipers dangling from his hip pocket. *Precision* was in the company's name. He was forever measuring to make sure that this was so. There was a reason for the white-sox-shoeless ritual, and a good one — he had an absolute fetish about spotless work premises, and the white sox told him how well his instructions were being followed by janitorial help. He had radiant heat in the floor so his feet told him whether it was working. The comedian, W.C. Fields, once

---

14. Hewitt-Robins multi-nationalized Litton by five new foreign addresses overnight — Amsterdam, Holland; London, England; Milan, Italy; Sao Paulo, Brazil and Johannesburg, South Africa. Africa, the angriest continent in the world, was made up of more than 40 countries which were most unstable, all in ferment, led most often by tribal tyrants who plundered and kept them in disarray after having sent previous colonial masters packing. The economic giant among them, foundationed on gold and diamonds and strategic position, was South Africa whose apartheid racial policies made it the bull's eye for target practice of those engaged in polemicist archery. It was the last hospitable climate and productive land far south of the equator where ships rounded to Cape of Good Hope with so many sustenance cargoes on which Europe and the Americas depended.

Robins Conveyors-South Africa, (pty.) Ltd. made Litton advance planner Frank Slovak pucker from the first, as it was so far away, had managers going in and out all the time, and had cyclical habits. However much South African based U.S. firms — and there were about 350 of them — past could cause movement by skill training and economic betterment for blacks, there was a chorus of heckling going on. Seven years after Hewitt-Robins came into Litton, Envirotech Corporation, which had extensive mining interests in South Africa decided it wanted the Litton fragment in Johannesburg — and Slovak arranged for them to have it. For good money. It tightened up Litton in terms of distances to its dispositions and lessened Litton's offshore presence by one country as well as one more political nettle weed patch.

immortalized the littered desk on which he and he alone could always reach for and find whatever paper was needed. John P. Glass not only had one such desk, but several because he never filed anything, just left it in piles. One secretary after another trooped in and out because they all tried to play mother hen, "Put things in order" and then he could find nothing.

Finally, a girl named Ruth Morgan came, who was smart enough to accept him and all his peculiarities. She never touched anything, but listened a lot, and she was there before Litton, a finder of inestimable value when the Harry Gray handholding was bearing fruit bringing Clifton into Litton. She accompanied Glass to his new, small office after he left. She, an old Royal typewriter Glass would never give up, and several loads of shoeboxes which had been stored under the paper-strewn tables all went along with him. He got more than $6,000,000 in Litton stock, which he sold at once. Litton got Clifton and his No. 1 disciple, old Arkansan, rough Alex Owen, who was a golden management asset who stayed and stayed and picked up more responsibilities all the time.

The shoeboxes? They contained his collection of $25,000 in silver dollars, which, being real silver, were worth about seven times that! His office was such a paper pile, it was rigged with shades which could be drawn to shield it from visitor's eyes. None but he knew the treasures of those old pasteboard containers. The typewriter was one he hocked over and over again when he was rattling around New York after graduating from Massachusetts Institute of Technology, not sure of where he would head into the future. And the quirkiness didn't end there. To complete the deal, he had to produce his 244,000 shares, the majority ownership. High and low, he looked, while Harry Gray paced. It had to be on one of those desks, somewhere. One high number certificate was nowhere to be found. He was finally left alone in the late evening to continue the search. All the others went grumbling off to bed. In his reaching in here and there in the stacks, some of the papers fell to the floor. As he was down on his hands and knees to retrieve them, he suddenly saw a space under one of the tables which was lighter for some unexplained reason. He turned his flashlight on it. And there it was — he had pasted the missing stock certificate on the bottom side of his desk for safekeeping. All the Littonites were relieved, but Alex Owen was surprised that Glass had waited so long before looking there. "Knowing John," he said, "that was the only logical place for that certificate to be!"

Significant as were the actual acquisitions for the shaping and sharpening of Litton Industries, Roy Ash's idea of the ten most important moves in the corporation's history included mergers and actions Litton did NOT take. Considered, they were, but nixed. There were four biggies that Litton passed by for one reason or another. Ash ran them off on the fingers of one hand, reflectively — Lockheed, Studebaker, Western Union and the American Broadcasting Company. And a semiconductor firm, the idea of Harper North.

Lockheed, usually standing very high among defense contractors, had occasional storms over its life, but, had to survive a veritable hurricane of hair-shirted hue and cry about ethical shortcomings, political hog-wallowing contests and federal loan guarantees (which it never had to use, and the government made money out of it).

The same campuses which produced the anti-business uproar in the temper tantrum politics of the period had a student body which reneged on government-extended educational loans in amounts four times greater than Lockheed had available but didn't use. Lockheed was not as good at placard painting and protest marching. When Lockheed's headman, Dan Haughton, was picked as the Greater Los Angeles Press Club's Business "Headliner of the Year" the nominee to 'roast' him was none other than Tex Thornton who had been in those talks about merging.

"Dan Haughton was too young to have been there when the Wright Brothers first flew," said Thornton to that big audience. "His father told him about it, and warned him that there'd never be any money in the airplane business. I know of no man who worked harder than Dan to prove his father was right."

When the talks had been on, Haughton said one of his problems was that as he opened the door on each new year, he had to put more than $70,000,000 in the Lockheed pension fund. This made a piker out of John Ringling North's explanation of the money side of the circus business which he said was essentially ". . .betting $35,000 every day that the sun will shine and ticket-buyers show up. We can never take a day off because everything about the circus eats."

Whatever — Lockheed would have added a few throbs to Litton's headaches.

Studebaker was mostly a courtesy call as it was up to its neck in miseries, but had several military contracts which the Pentagon had particular interest in being completed. The Department of Defense was looking for a way to insure those assembly lines taking care of its agreements would continue. Litton was asked to give it a once-over. When the rumor got out, the security analysts were on every phone plying Litton with questions. It got big enough that Walter Cronkite and Chet Huntley were asking if it was true and their respective big audience CBS and NBC news shows the same evening. Litton's George Scharffenberger and its news bureau chief, Charlie Carll, were sent on this stealth mission hoping to get on and off the Studebaker grounds unseen, they were startled that night in their motel room when Walter Cronkite and Huntley with stern and questioning faces appeared on their TV sets. Huntley had a tinge of dismay showing; he was a Litton shareholder. That NO came loud and firm — there was no such thing as a Studebaker in the Litton future, nor even an interim sliver of it.

Western Union was one of the most government regulated of all industries. It was headed by Russ McFall, a former Littonite who had gone there from the Amercom division in Maryland. One of its biggest moan-and-groan sectors was its unfunded pension plan, which McFall wrestled with for five years before a solution came. His old colleagues cheered him on, but it was one of those sideline things where they all chorused "better him than us!"

And on that Ash stand that Litton was only interested in challengers when it came to mergers, not leaders, a major case could be made for The American Broadcasting Company (ABC) along those lines. It was way behind CBS, which by Litton's natal year of 1953, had a quarter of a century of $5,000,000 or more in profits annually. There were 21,000,000 home-owned TV sets, and CBS seemed to have a more or less permanent dial-setting on most of them which was well-known to advertising timebuyers.

NBC, under the considerable spread of Radio Corporation of America, had once had a Red and Blue network, which the Department of Justice thought a little much. The old Blue network, the runt of the litter, was cast off and renamed ABC. It became a part of Leonard Goldenson's Paramount Theaters. While it was not exactly a monastery demanding a vow of poverty from its employees, it was characterized as among the corporate handicapped. While it was known to be available and Roy Ash talked some about it, it was never with any true warmth. Litton was already on that multinational wavelength. Owning ABC would have included both its ABC-TV and ABC-Radio news operations, too. With activists on the rise, any international story in a country, where Litton might have a division, could lead to an easy charge of news tampering, or censoring, or slanting, whether true or not and even if a rigid hands-off policy was in effect by decree and known to be. ABC had frailties enough without the plague-carrier aspects it brought with it.

Certainly, in the earliest days, Ash said the biggest constructive negative decision was for Litton to stay out of the semiconductor business. The talent available was headed by Dr. Harper North, and it would have required an immediate investment of $5,000,000. With the sparse funds available then, this would have made the whole enterprise vulnerable — and would probably have broken Litton before it was out of its eggshell.

The absolute oddest of Litton's acquisitional experience was about as low on any technological pole as one could get. Sturgis Newport was one of those crack-fillers, for the Business Systems and Equipment group.[15] Yet, it had the potential of touching a lot of peo-

---

15. Sturgis-Newport was the work of a self-made, stubborn, strong man named C.L. Spence, who descended from ancestors who had helped civilize the frontier and sensed a change in trade as the 20th century began. The merchant-customer relationship in shops and stores created buyer uneasiness. There were jokes about how butchers were not averse to weighing their thumbs or their bellies along with a joint of meat. All charge accounts were kept in dog-eared journals by merchants and all the entries were written there by them. On paydays, wives intercepted wage-earners on the way to the bar, lifted most of the pay packet and paid on the accounts around town in the family name. It was a definitely one-sided arrangement. Some who traded on tick thought there was occasional kiting or fudging to increase the profit.

In 1911, Spence gave the firm he started the grandiose name of National Carbon-Coated Paper Company. The principal product was carbonized paper which was used in sales books so both the buyer and the seller could have copies of transactions. When payoff time came, it was on the basis of matching those slips which the chargee had signed across the face.

Among fellow-citizens, Spence was surely ranked at least #9 on a scale of 1-to-10, maybe even higher. He was community-minded, paternalistic in his dealings with employees, had every member of families on his payroll. He had a company bowling

ple. The rational for it was Litton's idea that it should be the oasis for everything anybody could think of or ask for which would help in the conduct of a business or commercial activity. It was profitable in a small way and it was speciality paper based, making forms and sales books. It was in Sturgis, Michigan, but had out-lying arms in Hampton, Virginia; Birmingham, Alabama and Whitewater, Wisconsin.

Whether it had anything to do with the next ownership or not, those prosaic sales books led to a variation or two. Much of gambling was illegal and surreptitious. It was found that those sales books carrying innocent headings were ideal for bookies to note their "understandings" of the amounts of money at what odds which were riding on what the jockeys were riding at the tracks. There was even a suit brought against Sturgis for engaging, however inadvertently, in such sinful matters. Sturgis had a good lawyer who said pencil manufacturers should also be included in the court action if that inadvertence line was pursued on such an illogical basis. The judge agreed and the case was dismissed. Whether because of it, or just in coincidence with it, a rather surprising buyer prospect surfaced — Frederick Van Lennep, who owned Castleton, Inc. He probably only saw Sturgis as a steady money producer and a diversification when he bought it.

The old C.L. Spence office Van Lennep occupied at Sturgis went through a facelift about as foreign to the flat lands around that part of Michigan as one could imagine. No private eye was needed to divine where the Van Lennep true interests lay. The wallpaper in this seldom used cubicle enshrined horses and jockeys and sulky drivers who had figured from olden times in the "sport of kings".

Orhan Sadik-Kahn, who was part of the business and commercial products Litton action, had Sturgis-Newport in mind as well-laced in a rich neighborhood of substantial midwest individual as well as chain merchandising operations. He started talking with Van Lennep about Litton buying it. None will ever know whether he considered it very important to Litton, but it was a lot of fun running about after Van Lennep. He was a moving target. Some of the discussions were at Pompano Beach in Florida, a racetrack he ran. Some took place in the

---

alley, restaurant, and a ballroom-sized hall in which he staged an occasional company dance bringing in name bands such as Duke Ellington and Tex Beneke to provide the music. For 40 years, those sales books, register forms and continuous forms grew into a substantial product line and performed in many applications all over the country.

law offices of Roy Tolleson in Detroit who represented Van Lennep, and several were in Lexington, Kentucky where Van Lennep's Castleton Farms owned a succulent spread of prime bluegrass on which his pacers and trotters munched contentedly waiting until hitched up to run their hearts out for him.

In the fall of 1966, there was one week of hectic offers and counteroffers. Finally, on the Friday, Van Lennep turned chilly and broke off negotiations saying he'd decided not to sell. He seemed to be thinking of something else. The frazzled Litton contingent headed by Ludwig T. Smith, with Seymour Rosenberg, Frank Slovak and Sadik Khan flew back to Beverly Hills, grousing all the way.

Midday that Sunday, there was an urgent call from Van Lennep for them all to come back to Detroit for a meeting in Tolleson's office. He had to have as much of the $5,800,000 they were talking about in a cashier's check as soon as possible. Reason: He had bought one half share of a horse, and he had to pay by that Thursday, or he'd lose it! Frank Slovak was carrying a check for $1,968,391 made out to Castleton, Inc., when he got back on the aircraft. He had an authorization to write a purchase formula based on a profit showing over the first years of Litton ownership — with 26,320 of Litton's preference shares to be held by Van Lennep until the completed cash payment would retrieve them for Litton. The deal was concluded at 3 a.m. that deadline Thursday without any member having known a bed. At the end, Lou Smith was asleep in a chair, as was Rosenberg. Sadik Khan was muttering to himself, and Slovak wrote the concluding formula paragraphs in long hand. It was done and over with. The crew, grown blasé through many mergers, knew this one had been unusual. They shrugged their relief, and thought "to each his own". The anatomy of a merger could take many forms, and sometimes even the *Racing Form* could have a certain pertinence.

The records of the U.S. Trotting Association in Columbus, Ohio do indeed show that Castleton Farms did get a 50% interest in a pacer at that time for $1,000,000. The other half owner is shown as Richard Downing. The animal was ranked as "horse of the year" in 1963-1964-1965, the pacer, *Bret Hanover*. The stud fee: $12,500 per service, each colt guaranteed to stand and suckle. The mare traffic has been unabated over the years and considerable. Litton got a steady moneymaker, always corporate license to happiness. Frederick Van

Lennep was delighted with yet another sparkler in his horsey halo. And if all that stamping and sniffing which emanates from *Bren Hanover* as each mare is brought to the snorting pole can pass for an affirmative vote, *Bret Hanover* was happy too.[16]

---

16. The period from January 1965 to the end of 1967 was the time of talk about "Chinese money", securities seen not in the context of real time worth, but a promissory note quarantining hands in the futures' pockets. Litton common having been split two-for-one December 18, 1959, and August 15, 1962 closed at $94.75 on January 3, the first day of trading in 1965. A year later, it finished at $138, and on January 14, 1966, split two for one again. On January 3, 1967, it was skimming along at $81.37 and on December 29th that year stood at $104.75. That steadily rising stock value made the Litton shares the currency of spectacular muscle flexing, and companies literally poured into Litton over that 1,095 days. Some were small, some medium, some large.

The 1965 "class" included Sylvania Microwave Devices, Food Tech, Inc., Papeterie de Versoix in Switzerland, Magnuson X-Ray, Royal-McBee, U.S. Hewitt-Robins, Royal-McBee (Canada), Ltd., the Royal Typewriter Co., Wittenberg X-Ray, Georg A. Henke, GmbH in Germany, Professional Equipment, Inc., Dictating Equipment Corporation, Newport Printers, Inc., the Leupold Co., Plimpton's, Inc., Lehigh Furniture Corp., Fairchild Aerial Surveys, Fairchild Camera & Instrument Corp., Sweda (Australasia) Holdings, Pty., Ltd., Electra Motors, Datatax Corp., Valley Office Supply, and Bagley Stationery. The 1966 in-comers were Alvey-Ferguson, Everett-Waddey Co., Maverick-Clarke McCray Refrigerator Co., Inc., U.S. and McCray Canada, Ltd., Willy Feiler Zaehlenund Rechenwerke, GmbH, in Germany, Institute of Computer Management, Inc., Fenix Manufacturing, The Louis Allis Co and Control Center, Business Interiors, Automated Systems, International, Profexray of New Jersey, Sturgis-Newport, Twin City Tool Co., Gordon Webb & Co., Datalog, Ltd., and Imperial Typewriter Co., Ltd. (United Kingdom). The 1967 parade with marching orders into Litton were Wilson Marine Transit Co., Jefferson Electric Co., American Book Co., Auto Education Corp., McCormick-Mathers Publishing, Fester Solder, Saphier, Lerner & Schindler, Chicago Solder, International Fisheries and Fishmeal, Ltd., Gravure Engraving Corp., Marine Consultants & Designers, Inc., Ditran Corp., Rust Engineering in the U.S., Canada and Belgium, Indiana Display Promotions, Streater Store Fixtures, Inc., Chainveyor Corp., Eureka X-Ray Tube Corp., Personal Plane Services, Ltd., American X-Ray Corp., The Ardes Co., Burton Crescent Corp., Allen Hollander Co., Inc., The Dentists' Supply Co. of New York, and Stouffer Foods Corporation.

SPECIAL SITUATION #13

THE MECHANISMS OF BUSINESS

The ex-Yukon and Nome saloonkeeper always saw things differently than other people did.

Once he was living with the reigning "Madame" of Nome. The wit and latter-day writer, Wilson Mizner, was out walking off a hangover in their neighborhood. As he came even with their front porch on the frame house, a man half thrown and half running emerged. His galoshes were flying. He was only wearing one shoe. Right behind him, the roaring saloonkeeper came cursing and firing his pistol wildly in the general direction of his fleeing figure. He finally saw Mizner cowering there by the fence which was scant protection from either six-shooter or the inflamed temper. Mizner said nothing, only his eyes raising a question.

"That bastard!" the saloonkeeper said, putting his gun back in his belt and gesturing in the direction taken by the offender, "he insulted Nellie!"

Mizner, knowing well what indignities madames and their hired girls had to put up with in line of duty, was incredulous.

"*What* the hell did he do?" he said in some wonderment, as he thought Nellie was impervious to insult.

He never got a satisfactory answer, but the saloonkeeper's ideas of decorum were final insofar as he and Nellie were concerned.

On another day, years later, the same saloonkeeper, now otherwise engaged, was having his own dilemma. He was again seeing things that others didn't appreciate. His name was George "Tex" Rickard. He had abandoned the frigid gold fields for another kind of flamboyant enterprise in the "lower 48". Having established himself as a premier boxing promoter, he had pulled off that fisticuffs *first* of the "million-dollar-gate" in 1921 via a 4-round encounter session involving the Frenchman George Carpentier and Jack Dempsey. He was on the eve of the biggest of all five years later in Philadelphia, that city of "Brotherly love" about to be violated by the same Jack Dempsey, this time with Gene Tunney.

As he could interpret Madame Nellie as maligned by something being said in her presence, he was seeing another phenomenon of the early '20s in an odd way, too. It was called the wireless, or radio, or broadcasting. It was primitive with crackling static-infested earphones and its signal given to fading out and in. There was much public fascination with it. The mere possession of a set had all the earmarks of social position. Rickard equated that rising infatuation with a new technology as potentially constructive if it were associated with something he had an absolute lock on—the exclusivity of all rights to everything about that championship fight. He decided to test the market value of one of those rights, blow-by-blow description from ringside by broadcast for a price. People around him said he was a fool. This would allow the fight to be had by yokels for free and would cut into ticket sales. Rickard assessed it as a possible powerful new element of his promotional dazzle. He wanted to hedge his convictions a little, just in case, with something called sponsorship.

That day he was standing in the presence of the Hartford hierarchy of the Royal Typewriter Company. He had known Thomas Fortune Ryan in Alaska. Ryan was the one who saw merit in the inventions of Edward B. Hess and his partner, Lewis C. Myers. He backed them for the Royal venture. Royal, for its time and fledgling state, was a whoop-te-do merchandiser. In 1912, Royal had enlisted the old Gus Edwards vaudeville act which was playing Proctors theater in New York and the Fifth Avenue in Brooklyn, then toured a whole season all over the U.S. billed as "Gus Edwards and his Blond Stenographers". They worked the Royal typewriters in the routines of the act. It undoubtedly gave the era's "tired businesses" ideas about how to perk up the atmosphere of their dingy offices. By 1926, Royal had sold its 1,000,000th typewriter, but had somehow missed out on the portable market. In its desire to correct that, it went into promotional overdrive by buying a blue-and-gold Ford-Stout airplane with three Wright Whirlwind motors, capable of 120 miles an hour with a cruising range of 500 miles—and importantly, a cargo tote of 2,730 pounds. It was crewed by a pilot, a mechanic, two passengers and carried aloft 210 new Royal typewriters. As the plane flew along a zigzag course dictated by where dealerships were located, one by one the portables were dropped by parachute into waiting hands of ground-bound Royal men below. There was press in attendance able to certify the machines as durable when surviving this sensational delivery system. Royal increased its portable sales by twenty times in one year!

The LITTON Adventure That Was

But with all this coloratura credentials array, Rickard caused them to hesitate. He wanted $40,000. For that they could select some glib boxing buff to give a jab and hook account of the leathery exchanges.[1] In the minute between rounds that same commentator could squeeze in as much praise as he wished for Royal Typewriters. There would be a sea of them at ringside and for several rows back. Their clatter and the Western Union sounders transmitting to newspapers all over the world would easily vouch for uttered claims that Royal was best of all. That $40,000 was a lot of money for something untried and unorthodox. He chided them that the same could be said about Gus Edwards and the parachuting portables. Royal offered $15,000. Rickard put on his 10-gallon hat and headed for the door. Royal upped to $20,000, and he said they had a deal. Royal became that first milestone on the long, long trail into bonanza-sized figures which constitutes today's mountainous costs for broadcast and telecast sponsorship of both amateur and professional gaming and competition. Surely neither Richard nor Royal saw themselves by that 1926 Dempsey-Tunney square off as an extension into Howard Cosell, or that a third international language—a communications link to all people through sports—would result. Mathematics and music had been the only big boundary jumpers before.

Royal relished these things, and to be competitive, felt they made the difference. As America moved into the 20th Century, there were 89 separate typewriter companies. Royal had three very distinctive characteristics which gave it a formidable standing—a new idea in typewriter design which when keys were hit downward an arm with a letter to be imprinted flew up requiring only a light, fast touch where other brands functioned heavy-handedly; the zeal and perserverance and innovativeness of Edward Hess and his partner, Myers, and the financial support of Thomas Fortune Ryan.

Ryan had made his money in railroading, but he loved the Hess-Myers light touch machine, and the fact that the user could see there on the roller what he or she was committing to paper. Royal swung

---

1. In an earlier fight, with Luis Angel Firpo, the "wild bull of the pampas" hit Dempsey so hard he was knocked from the ring and landed on a sportswriter's Royal typewriter. It was aggravations from that fall which caused Dempsey later to have corrective surgery and hospital time and walk with a cane—all before Litton's becoming part of the Royal story.

out smartly and passed Remington, Corona, LC Smith, Monarch and Underwood. Also, Royal's portable came in many colors which pleased women. It had been in 1906 and 1910 that first attempts had been made to bring out electric typewriters. Each was a financial debacle. That had to wait until 1933, when International Business Machines[2]—thought to be mad by the rest of the trade—came into the market with an electric. It was instantly popular, and was the result of exhaustive R & D which has never stopped. Royal's pride was its manual which was so well accepted that the word *Royal* and the word *typewriter* were practically interchangeable. Through World War II, the Korean "police action" and on into the growing involvement in Vietnam, the manual's sales were being artificially held up. Those thousands of miles of logistics communications lines from both coasts into the battle zones were paved with word processors that needed no electric current to operate. Domestically, though, electric typewriters were in increasing demand, and the sales were zooming. That pioneer, scoffed in 1933—IBM— had 80% of the market. Royal's Fortune family, well salaried and reluctant to make the substantial R & D ante necessary to get them in striking distance with anything like a comparable product, was just rocking along.

Fred Sullivan and William McKenna were hardly into Litton with Monroe when typewriters were picked as the logical extension of the

---

2. The typewriter itself is an old idea. Henry Mill, an Englishman, filed the first patent in 1714. In newspaper parlance, especially in press boxes and galleries, a typewriter is referred to as a "mill" even to this day. The typewriter technology did not popularize quickly, nor was it considered a very realistic adjunct to the writing process. From Mill to the first commercially marketed machine there was a span of 160 years. Oddly enough, it was a politician who did it, the (then) Mayor of Milwaukee, Christopher Latham Sholes. He is credited with having sold the first working model as the culmination of his development efforts in 1874. What a Pandora's Box it was for his craft, because nothing quite equaled the typewriter in laying the lash on elected officials and public servants. Many years down the pike, a rather young Litton Industries would have reason to remember ruefully that it was an Englishman who started it all. The typewriter was a kind of octopus with which it would struggle. There was another parallel, too, in that it was an earlier weapons systems maker who used profits from its military sales to back the first commercial typewriter, Remington. There was another historical and important twist in that Royal was pressed into WW II munitions manufacture, but IBM was ordered to keep on its typewriter course. This gave IBM a big post-war lead that neither Royal nor any other like manufacturer could catch—a point which was made later before the Federal Trade Commission by Litton's antitrust lawyer, T.F. "Ted" Craver.

Litton reach into the business machines and office products field. Their counsel was that if there was to be a true widening of the base from their Monroe starting blocks, Litton had to have a typewriter line. It was as salt is to pepper in condiments. Their initial sashay was a flexing of plumage in the direction of Underwood in the early '60s. They were outmaneuvered by the Italian Olivetti. Either the Italians were more anxious about the Underwood doorway to the U.S. market, or Underwood felt it would have an easier adjustment with a company already engaged in the same line. Whatever the reason, Litton lucked out in that case. Joining Litton conjured up being in lockstep with a striding, throbbing giant totally without experience in their milieu. The rejection bugged Litton a little, and Seymour Rosenberg was instructed to engage in something Litton had been wary about before as it smacked of the takeover process in subduing resistance. The designated target: moribund Royal-McBee.

Tex Thornton had had some feeler talks with Allan A. Ryan, the current board chairman and had been waved off. There was no interest in any merger then as things stood when the talks ended. Litton felt it had to show serious intent, so fell back for a new tack. Rosenberg arranged for an agent to buy up 9.9% of the Royal-McBee shares, but no greater than that because a holder of 10% or more had to disclose identity under the SEC rules. Litton, once it had that big block, was able to renew the quest with the additional heft of being a serious, interested party that had substantial money up as a convincer. None at Litton other than Rosenberg knew the identity of the persistent purchaser, so any Littonite asked could honestly say he didn't know who was buying. Royal-McBee began to suspect that the consistent gathering of their stock was not whimsical. Because Lehman Brothers at One William Street in New York often helped Litton.[3] Allan Ryan

---

3. The Royal-McBee merger picked up vociferous critics, too, who would heckle and harangue Litton's leadership in annual meetings and by mail and phone from then on. These were the brothers Lewis and John Gilbert, who had 29 shares of Royal-McBee, and Evelyn Y. Davis, who had 10. Lewis, a skilled floor adversary, had a foghorn voice which would have been the envy of a Marine drill instructor. He never missed more than a couple of shareholder annual meetings thereafter. Evelyn Davis could wrest a microphone from Gargantua, and was on the leadership neck like Sinbad, the Sailor's "old man of the sea". At Royal-McBee's meeting, she demanded to know whether there was a Litton representative present, whereupon Ludwig T. Smith identified himself. She pounced on him wanting the Thornton and Ash home

called Joe Thomas to ask him if it might be Litton back of the detected surge of interest. Thomas said he didn't think so as he was on the Litton board and it had never been mentioned in his presence. That produced a situation of some anguish for Rosenberg, and he rushed to New York to tell Thomas what was happening. Shortly after that, Thornton did meet with Allan Ryan at his home in Palm Beach and the possibilities of merger assumed a warming trend. On September 18, 1964, Roy L. Ash wrote the letter of intent to acquire Royal-McBee.

The terms were that Litton would issue its $3 cumulative preferred stock to Royal-McBee shareholders on the basis of $17.25 of its worth for each share of Royal-McBee common.[4] At least 80% of the Royal-McBee ownership of its $4.50 series of cumulative preferred stock had to agree to a one-for-one exchange for the Litton $3 issue. And to call the outstanding 5½% convertible subordinated debentures, Litton loaned Royal-McBee $7,675,300. Royal-McBee's previous full year's earnings were $1.04 a share. In the first month of the year the merger was finalized, it lost 8¢ against a forecast downer of only 6¢. Litton, obviously, had achieved a goal of being in the typewriter business, but had its work cut out for it.

It was Fortune Peter Ryan, the Royal-McBee president, who had dual reasons to celebrate. The completed merger was the 30th anniversary present to him and a graceful way to bow out. The problems of his ailing company were now on other shoulders. Into the record books on October 20, 1964 went the Litton merger of Royal-McBee. Almost at once, it was reborn as five operating Litton divisions, one of them, McBee, a moneymaker then and since. It was the healthy one

---

addresses, their phone numbers, and how many shares of Litton each owned. Smith said he really didn't have that kind of information with him. "You don't know nuthin'," she said with a flounce. Smith came back to Beverly Hills with a new perception of the harassments of corporate life when a company goes public—and goes merging.

4. Tex Thornton felt the impact of Royal's arrival on the Litton scene when the "all Litton points" order was issued—IBMs out, Royals IN. The two most viable adherents to him were Jack Fairburn and Jean Randall, parked as they were right outside his office. Noting their new Royals in place before them as he came in one morning, he asked cheerily how they liked their new equipment. When he saw their clouded countenances looking back at him, he ducked in his office and closed the door before either could answer him.

of the litter among the frail and concentrated on development, manufacture and marketing of simplified equipment for accounting, data
processing, information storage and retrieval. From that one stem
would grow what Litton later described as its specialty paper, printing
and forms and the "one-stop shopping", or office product centers
theme had an important foundation stone.

Well before the fruition of the Royal-McBee haltering by Litton,
Fred Sullivan had succumbed to the siren songs of Walter Kidde &
Co., the fire extinguisher outfit that wanted some new spurring. He
had done quite well hewing to the structure outlined for a business
systems and equipment Litton commitment, but he began to get cross-
ways with Litton's President Roy Ash. All those questions, on top of
questions. He had to put Frank Slovak, still at Monroe, to work 7 days
before he'd make his weeklong monthly hiatus to the West Coast trying to outguess what the next flurry of inquiry would be on, and to be
sure they were up on every conceivable one with an answer.

Being blandished by Kidde, as fine tuned executives will, he began to see the quizzing as harassment. He told Slovak he didn't think
he wanted to make that much effort to "educate" Roy Ash in the business equipment and office products fields. Ash was pressuring him,
too, to move to California from New Jersey. He was not charmed by
the prospect of getting his mail in the perpetual sunshine. The "loose
rein" he had heard so much about appeared to be shortening all the
time. In December, 1963, when the effort began to crystallize to get
Royal-McBee, he was making himself a silent, mental New Year's
resolution. A week into 1964, he carried it out—and left Litton.

William E. McKenna, who had known Sullivan so well and so
long at Monroe, was by then on Litton's corporate roster as the financial vice president and treasurer. He was named to fill the Sullivan
shoes, take his place at the high stakes gaming table, and draw to fill
out the rest of the group's hand. Sullivan had told McKenna that the
electronics lift he had sought by association with Litton was not the
variety Monroe could use, nor did he believe that in Royal-McBee's
case, if Litton got it, it would help. The business product lines had to
be low cost and as maintenance free as possible. He said aerospace
industry electronics specialists were not used to working in such a
cost-squeeze environment.

McKenna had not only been at Monroe in Sullivan's time soaking up his ideas about extension into the whole gamut of business machines and office products, his space when he was tapped to take over was but a few steps down the austere corridor (where the rug stopped and wood flooring began) from Thornton and Ash. This gave him earshot distance from top corporate cerebral processes on a day-to-day basis. He knew where the really "loose reins" were and also those inflexible taboos, and the nature of the fast tract he was on now. The $113,376,000 in annual sales rung up that last year by Royal-McBee had to be increased—and quickly. Trying to get a satisfactory, workable electric typewriter had been a kind of Job's boils affliction for Royal as it sought to mount a motor on the basic manual which had been so good and had served their customers so well. McKenna knew he had to press for a solution, but it was only one of the plagues he had to attack in pursuit of new markets.

McKenna riffled through what he had at that moment.

Though Monroe had come to Litton in 1958, a lot of 1959 had been used to get Svenska Dataregister A.B. The 12 months of 1960 found the company focused on a geophysical exploration capability and into Canada for its inertial navigation manufacture. The very first stop in January of 1962 started to fill in the blanks on a true, general presence in the business world with its machines and products. A. Kimball and Kimball Systems, Ltd.,[5] the punch-tag marking and punch-tag reading equipment providers, had appeal for Sullivan and

---

5. Kimball was started in 1876 by Alonzo Kimball and Arthur Thompson. Its first product was a self-contained pin-ticket for price marking and consisted of paper and a staple joined together in one unit. These were first used by the great storekeepers, A.T. Stewart and John Wanamaker, who had previously done all price marking a piece at a time. Wanamaker introduced his slogan "one price for all"—which created need for a method of multiple imprinting. Kimball between 1900 and 1930 brought about many "firsts"—the folding pin-ticket, the bend over ticket, the security ticket and the self-locking ticket for sheer and delicate merchandise. By Litton's time, it was presenting a big line of price marking and imprinting machines which were used by Strawbridge & Clothier and Saks Fifth Avenue. Kimball really began to play the big time when it moved to automation in sales accounting and inventory control in 1951 with the Kimball Punch Mark "75", which was offered in connection with the firm's 75th anniversary. It was taken by the great volume merchandiser, Sears, Roebuck in Chicago. Practically every major retailer used Kimball Systems as in the mid 1970s it came forth with Optical Recognition, that electronics price reading method which gave it a lead never relinquished.

The LITTON Adventure That Was

Frank Ricciardi. It seemed like the other horse in calculating, Monroe for the office, and Kimball as the mechanical servant of department stores. It could not only label items with their prices, but read off those prices at the cash register checkout counter. It was an inventory control crutch as well as a means of detailed transaction recording. With all the many ways electronics could be adapted to it, whole point-of-sale systems seemed a reasonable realization woven around as tributaries to the cash register. Apart from the technology involved, there was that ever present requirement to sell the product. That same year the marketing arm had been given additional muscle by the Litton portfolio addition of London Office Machines, Ltd., it being the biggest distributor of cash registers in the British Isles. Part of its handle was Imperial Typewriter, a well established brand name, but an old fashioned machine which seemed to fight back at its users. It was an initial possibility that Litton and Imperial might be a future match, if no U.S. typewriter firm was available.

That same summer produced Simon Adhesive Products of Long Island City, N.Y., makers of high quality stick-on coatings for pressures sensitive labels. This was not only a respected line of materials making it a tailored supplier of basic needs for Kimball, it included a super salesman named Sandor Simon. Single handed, Sandy Simon kept the two dozen people who worked for him busy turning out the $2,200,000 or so in annual sales which he drummed up himself. Litton figured there was a $40,000,000 potential out there, and tried to get him to hire on two or three marketers besides himself, but he wasn't interested. Simon's range of acquaintances was varied and vast. He was Willie Loman updated. He floated on an ocean of first names worldwide. He was high voltage enough after hours to coax a Hoagy Carmichael to a piano in a Tokyo bar to accompany him singing well this side of Ezio Pinza—and his repertoire didn't even contain one Carmichael song! He had legendary expense accounts, rationalizing that it was unnecessary for him to employ a trio of additional salesmen at $20,000 a year plus expenses, when he could use the $60,000 plus and bring in twice the business the threesome would. He was a continuing shockwave to the Roy Ash "school of management", a non-Harvard Business School commercial variety of Halley's Comet. As spectacular as he was in business performance, he gave executive orthodoxy acute spells of discomfort. He was proud of having become a part of Litton, one of those originals often drawn there who lived and thrived on every minute of it. He was sentimentally and sophomorically in love with his wife Jeannie, but however many were his endearing charms, he was considered dangerous and caused uneasiness with his loose-leaf mannerisms. Frank Slovak said of him, "he was not understood nor used as well as Litton could have used him, nor was the fact that all doors were open to him valued as highly as it should have been." He may have flashed brightly but briefly, but well remembered he was and is.

That 1961 July, the Cole Steel Equipment Co., of York, Pa. was put on the Litton list. This corralled a quite different variety of performer in Tony Scheinman. He had a million square feet of manufacturing and storage space in York. He not only never went near it—he was proud of the fact that he did not. Scheinman was a "catalog man". He knew what he was doing and about 22,000 non-exclusive dealers plopped down all over the countryside. His forte was to come up with a desk or chair design, a credenza or a file, which he sent along to his manufacturing manager, Otto Lewin. Lewin had to make the cost-price analysis for which he was paid a salary, plus bonuses and profit participation which made him one of the highest paid people in all of Litton. The products were reasonable in the office furniture marketplace, durable, no-nonsense, utilitarian. And the marketplace loved Scheinman for his consistency and for being reliability attuned to what the traffic needed and would bear. The Scheinman catalogs were one-on-one works of art as art can be tied to sales. His furniture looked the part it was built to play. Scheinman was dependable. His judgment was trusted. His friendship was valued. He knew all those dealers who waited for each new issue of his precious catalogs as though they were blood brothers. His showroom in New York was a *must* stop if any of them were in Gotham. If good theater seats were needed, or ringside preference expressed, Scheinman could always manage. He was the introduction for Litton to two considerations—the huge warehousing requirements for the planned business equipment and office product centers, and the potential if facilities and capabilities were owned to turn out not only those catalogs but many other kinds of commercial printing in-house.

Were Litton to follow Roy L. Ash's theory that it should be ready and able to serve as much of the action as possible with sophisticated business equipment and products, it had to select from some 30,000 such accoutrements to lay hands on. A bare month after Cole Steel was made a part of Litton action, Litton reached for something which had its origin at least 5,000 years earlier—paper. It was the *specialty* paper aspect which was alluring to Litton, the expansion into coating and the "value-added" methods which would enter them in communications, recording and decorative fields.

It was a quiet place to begin, but in 1961, on a byroad called Dunham Drive in Dunmore, Pa., a suburb of Scranton, there was an unlikely enterprise. It actually "printed money", or a negotiable counterpart of it, trading stamps. In cramped quarters in an old schoolhouse was the Eureka Specialty Printing Co. It was up to its armpits in the nitty-gritty of selling, and the name of its street was a tribute to one James H. Dunham. He had taken the business from its start in April 27, 1905 to its eminence and industry dependence by a process which glue-coated safety or non-erasable paper on one side, color printing on the other and perforating it into squares, for easy tearing at great speeds. He gave the trading stamp its natal day and presented housewives notorious for saving string and coupons a rewarding new angle for their thriftiness. That small stickum stamp became an enormous sales stimulant for pharmacies, filling stations, department stores and neighborhood markets. More than 80% of all trading stamps—though Sperry & Hutchinson's was the main customer—were birthed at Eureka. In America alone, about 1/750th of the Gross National Product at retail prices changed hands via exchange of those little 10-cent denominational squares of paper. It was, surely, our "other money." Whatever finished form was assumed by the raw paper introduced into those Eureka presses it was converted by all the techniques and developments through several millennia to augment the buying stimulus. Eureka was the starting point, and however out of the way the address might be, paper was how Litton in a host of unexpected ways would get to people more than by any other means.

As McKenna saw it, it was not all rosy. It was cyclical and very vulnerable to state legislatures and city councils prone to enact punitive laws, regulations and restrictions on trading stamp use. This menace was not to Eureka directly, but to its clients who had to maintain skillful batteries of lawyers to attempt to impede, delay or modify these restraints. Any state or city which set itself against premium assistance to merchandising reduced the volume of Eureka printing orders, or could so so.

When Fred Sullivan had gotten his go-ahead from Roy Ash, a part of it was that there would be some breakout from Eureka's confined, heavily specialized—though industry dominating—segment, of the printing field. To do that Litton had to come up with the money for another building to house new web presses as well as the purchase of the presses themselves. Those high speed items were priced at about $1,500,000 each and there had to be two. None would contract to a firm which had but one. It might go down, making deadlines impossible to be met or guaranteed. The outlay was projected to be $8,000,000 on top of the acquisition itself. But there was the S & H need for about 35,000,000 stamp catalogs annually, the Cole Steel brochures and order books and all the other kinds of interior-to-Litton printing prospects. On top of the premium opportunities, the Third World needed a supplier of paper money, bonds, postage stamps and myriad other government printing besides. There were 26 such countries on Eureka's list of satisfied customers. The United Nations' halls buzzed as delegations from other lands talked about it as a source. There was excitement in the air, and the mood was to press on.[6]

Thornton wasn't very comfortable with it and condoned it reluctantly. No matter what anybody said, it didn't ring any resounding bells as high technology even if Eureka was in a formidable command position. It was capital intensive and inviting to assault by consumer activists who were sprouting up all over the place. He was pleased somewhat by the fact that it was evidence that Litton was taking a position well away from the U.S. governmental and military contract dependence. There was a big enough diet of electronics potential oc-

---

6. Eureka Specialty Printing Co., largely held by people who had grown up with it in the neighborhood in that Northeastern portion of the neighborhood in that Northeastern portion of the Keystone state, had 50,000 shares each of Class A and B stock, with 30,000 and 31,195 shares respectively issued and outstanding. The Litton offer took three of its common for one of either kind of the Eureka securities. In November, 1961, that exchange completed, Eureka's sellers exited the company at its productive crest. Litton marched into an atmosphere filled with the stench of printers ink to become an extraordinary paper doctorer, user and transformer. Kimball's tags, plus Simon Adhesive, plus Eureka's trading stamps made a neat daisy chain in linkage with the Sweda cash register giving Litton an input at every sales juncture. Besides, there were several complimentary merger prospects in the offing.

cupying his attentions to appease him, some of which could be applied to other paper outfits being sized up.

Fred Sullivan, similar to a Mother Goose's Jack Horner when in his corner of Litton had his hand in many pies. Whether it would come up all thumbs and no plums was to be seen later. What Sullivan had envisioned but could never attain in the Monroe strait-jacket was now becoming in Litton's collecting of enterprises a supreme test as to whether it could all be made to jell. No matter, there was no time to pause for heavy breathing after all the exertions.

Paper was anything but dramatic in itself, but only in what could be done with it. Records and records-keeping, continuous and other forms, check printing for all those banks popping up on every corner, sales books, coated paper, which would take and preserve electronic tracings for everything from electrocardiograph registrations to weather mapping, sterilization-treated surgical containers, photocopying,[7] color printing strippable wallpaper, wood grained imprints for

---

7. Copying, and even more important, character recognition, a potential derivative from wire photo and facsimile technology, came across Sullivan's searching antennae. The New York Times-owned firm, Times Facsimile Corp., or Timefax was decreed available by Publisher Arthur Hayes Sulzberger. Initial pricing was $4,000,000, but Thornton said he'd pay only $1,300,000 and take over a bank obligation of $1,000,000. Sulzberger accepted, and Litton got what had once been a sensational technological development and all its ramifications. It grew from a big difference of opinion with Western Electric on one side (who said it could not be done) and two MIT graduate students, Dr. William R. Hainsworth and his associate, Austin Cooley, who believed photos could be transmitted over telephone wires. Hainsworth soon diverted into gas refrigeration, but Cooley had some success with image transmission by radio, first with WOR and then a dozen or so stations in the 1926-29 period. In 1934, the New York Times wanted a picture transmission system for its Wide World Photos. Cooley took a contract to build a prototype transmitter and receiver which could operate over a phone line without a connection to the line— by inductively coupling the picture signals to the transformer in the bellbox. Cooley did it in six weeks. Cooley sent his aide, Garrett Dillenback, to San Francisco with a portable transmitter he stowed under his Pullman car seat. Just as he arrived on February 12, 1935 the dirigible Macon suffered a disastrous crash off Big Sur providing a wildly dramatic situation for that first transcontinental test movement of pictures by wire. From his room, Dillenback sent several of the photos of survivors which were front paged by the Times bulldog edition the evening of February 13th, and all editions next day! A huge success, generously acclaimed. A Times editorial chided Western Electric for its stubbornness. The U.S. Army Signal Corps sought equipment for its use, leading Sulzberger to set up a separate corporation to deal with that demanding customer and be its equipment supplier. The Times only wanted the pic-

home and office decor, bagasse from recycled sugar cane stalks[8] which made a durable all-purpose line, and on into stationery and greeting cards.

McKenna had watched Fred Sullivan as he cast covetous glances over the American scene "up east" from Scranton. Early paper mills had clustered there because that's where the hard woods were as well as the refuse rags of the textile mills—those woods being best for pulping, and the rags cookable into fiber, both first steps in paper manufacturing. A wealth of small streams powered the machinery and processes. Proximity to these raw materials and the Nashua River in the woody, hilly Massachusetts countryside caused the Wallace family to settle in Fitchburg. Their plant there led them to consider Fitchburg a part of them. They treated community obligations seriously and constructively. The name of George R. Wallace, Jr., in Fitchburg was about as renowned and colorful and adventurous as was that of old Confederate Gen. Nathan Bedford Forrest in Mississippi. (An Ole Miss student once said: "Wheah ah cum from, when Nathan Bedford Forrest's name is said out loud, all them who wuz raised right stands up and teks off theah hats!"). Wallace went from private to officer status faster than almost anyone else. For his gallantry and demonstrated courage in the bloodletting of the Meuse-Argonne offensive in World War I, he was cited by Gen. John J. Pershing himself. He raced cars, had airplanes which he flew, planted orchards that produced fruit which won prizes, built libraries and was probably the only man ever to attend the Massachusetts Institute of Technology "majoring in banjo". He was booted within a year because of his all-consuming interest as a strummer rather than in technology. But there was no

---

tures, and at war's end began to look for a buyer. In March, 1959, Times Facsimile Corp. became a Litton division in Melville on Long Island. Later known as LITCOM, then Datalog, it is now the Long Island Facility of Amecom. As a sentimental tribute to the Cooley facsimile pioneering, on his 80th birthday, his wife, Helene, gave him a special recognition—a license plate which puzzles his Reno, Nevada neighbors— FAX. A whole world might not know him now, but it benefits from what he did.

8. The bagasse pulp is made from fibrous residue of crushed sugar cane stalks from which sucrose has been removed. It was the specialty of the 1954 organized Valentine Pulp & Paper Co. in the Cajun country of Lockport, La. All those magazine coupons inserts inviting subscribers and many of the Internal Revenue Service tax manuals are printed on that kind of paper. Valentine came into Litton in April, 1970. It is probable that this Litton product enters more American homes than any other as it comes with every magazine.

fooling about the way he ran the family's business. When he detected that his son, George III, was not enthusiastic about tying himself forever to the third generation involvement, he began to study alternatives. He was much impressed with a young Virginia Polytechnic Institute engineer he had hired named John Grado, Jr. It relaxed him as he elevated him up through varying positions increasing his responsibility, eventually into that major authority, executive vice president. If it eased the father's burden, so did it answer the son's wish to be removed from all those immediate decisions the day-to-day throb of manufacturing dictated.

Wallace was intrigued by Grado. He was the first one he encountered in 50 years of the sameness which characterized the industry who saw it in terms of dollars rather than tons. Labor constituted about 15% of the paper-selling price. Grado began to find things which led to money saving that papermakers hadn't given much attention. But in those after hours talks with the elder Wallace, Grado knew the older man's sense of community was on him so strongly that in his early 70s, he wanted to engage in some philanthropies. He owned two-thirds of the Fitchburg Paper stock. It traded once in a great while over-the-counter. He knew if any sizeable chunk of it were given away, it could knock the Over-the-Counter price into a cocked hat. There were always tax consequences to think about, too. Merger began to stand tallest as the way to get what he wanted to do for the rest of his life. Through merger, his employees could benefit most.

Grado, just after graduating, worked for awhile at Monroe. He knew McKenna well. He remembered research being conducted there for office copiers using the electrostatic process. When he was about to broach this, Wallace preempted him by saying he had played gin rummy a lot in Florida during winter vacations with Bill McKnight, the Board Chairman of 3M (Minnesota Mining & Manufacturing). He'd like to see if there was 3M inclination to take on Fitchburg Paper. At that moment, 3M and Litton were at about $600,000,000 in annual sales. There was one big difference. Grado held his tongue and the visit to Minneapolis was made. Then he suggested Litton. That difference he counted on showed itself when Grado took the Fitchburg Paper party to Litton's old 336 North Foothill Road offices in Beverly Hills. Where 3M had a 14-floor office building with hundreds on staff, Litton had less than 150. If there was to be any hope that Fitchburg Paper could retain any of its old ways, which was a matter of deep Wallace concern, the lean Litton affiliation minimized chances of Mongol management hordes swarming Fitchburg from out of the West. Both Wallace and Grado, found it easy in a $15,500,000 transaction to surrender Fitchburg's 983,262 shares and the future of the enterprise to Litton as a division.

"Linkage" had not yet become the buzzword for negotiations strategy, hooking on appendages which one or the other of the parties considered related for understandings between nations, but Litton had its own version. Once having gotten importantly into supermarkets and other retailing outlets giving merchandising aids of various kinds, the birddogs flushed another out-of-the-way premier performer and leader, Streater Industries in Albert Lea, Minnesota. Nationally known for the quality of its display cases, their enhancing shelving and designs which helped tip the "buy" tendencies of shoppers, Streater seemed a natural to feed to those Sweda cash registers. It had been an evolvement from a lumber business owned by E.G. Streeter and his wife, Alma. Their price tag was $2,809,000 in Litton common and preferred shares, with the usual formula for additional payouts over a 5-year period if the business continued to grow and prospects were good that it would. The May 11, 1917-born enterprise without missing a beat along its stamping, cutting and painting assembly lines became a Litton division in September of 1964. All the leaves on all the maples and birches were massively turning color then in Minnesota, so Streater took on the hue of the big time, too. Howard Scott, a hot salesman who knew where the moves were being made and had even sold shelving to the drugstore in the Dakotas which was operated by Senator Hubert Humphrey's brother, was in the big chair to run it as a Litton division.[9]

---

9. Kimball came from United Shoe and Machinery in Brooklyn. That parent company still manufactured the machines Litton used. Early warnings were being registered that good as the Monroe sales force was in marketing and maintaining calculating machines, Sweda cash registers and Kimball machines sales and service were pointed at a quite different clientele. The coming togetherness in theory was slow in achievement in reality, not to be denied forever, probably, but running against Litton's most precious commodity—time. In Kimball and Simon Adhesive were Litton links to the credit card business.

The LITTON Adventure That Was

With that diversionary swing behind them, there was a further homing in on paper and printing—this time a San Francisco concern which had started up in 1852 in the wake of John Augustus Sutter's discovery of gold in his millrace. It reflected the notions of importance of the time when boundaries of claims were often disputed with firearms, it being a mapmaker and printer. Now in the third generation of tender care in the same family whose name it bore and with its knowledgeable chieftain, Burlington M. Carlisle, frustrated and uncertain, it was looking for a fix. Known universally as "Bud" throughout the printing fraternity, and once head of their association, he knew everybody and everything going on in his field. He needed help, and he knew it—whether new money or some kind of umbrella corporation arrangement which would bring him in from the financial Sahara. A. Carlisle & Co., big in what it didn't want to be— a general line printing house—had shifted more and more to the label, election forms and manifold business and for about three years had gloried in an area it really wanted to run with, check printing. Bud Carlisle had talked with LIFE magazine, and with Pandick Press, which was growing big by leaps in financial printing, both of which were hemming and hawing. As such rumors of availability will, the Carlisle search for succor got to the ears of Gordon McKenzie, who was peering about for opportunities for McKenna. When the talks began and all the way to the end, from Bud Carlisle's point of view, it was just the mood required to reassure him that he was giving the family name and what it represented to him into a caring, improving situation. Bud Carlisle always said he was never told until later that what Litton had really wanted was his check printing side. He remains sure to this day that had he known that, he could have sold off the uninteresting parts arriving as a Litton insider with a real accounting pleaser. His check printing had been running at more than 20% profit, but the rest of what he had was not doing well. McKenna as much as anything else was after Bud Carlisle. He was finding that just because he knew someone from his Monroe alma mater and thought well of him, such nominees did not transplant with any blazing success to the world of printing. No sooner was Bud Carlisle in Litton's yard than he found himself not only McKenna's man to run both his family's inheritance as a Litton division but to bring Eureka Specialty Printing into manageable proportions. Its old guard had pretty much melted away into the Pennsylvania boondocks.[10]

By the end of McKenna's first year, he had tethered to him the active credit card printing house, M & M Manufacturing in Montrose, Calif. Then in quick time in 1965, he was telescoping American Tag in Dayton, Ohio into Kimball, snatching up available stationery houses such as Atlas, Newport, Plimpton, Everett Waddey and Maverick-Clarke,[11] and in June, that office furniture business, the combine called Lehigh-Leopold in Burlington, Iowa. In June of 1966, it was business forms and Sturgis-Newport, in Sturgis, Mich.—all on the move into the Litton open door. It was almost in the same cadence as

---

10. With Streator, Litton inherited a bad memory in Grants Pass, Oregon. On a Josephine county site in the beautiful Rogue River Valley, Streator, on allure of what seemed to be a fat extended contract for its merchandising and display cases, erected a huge plant in proximity to the timber abounding around there. There were prospects that about 200-300 of the local citizenry would be hired. Instead, the contract was cancelled and the plant closed. When Litton acquired Streator, it was in the midst of a growing need for floor space to accommodate its electronic production lines. Litton's Guidance and Control Systems facility in Salt Lake City saw Grants Pass as ideal for a satellite operation. On January 21, 1975, it started up with 62 people and a hostile community still embittered by the previous disappointment associated with the plant. But as early as three weeks later, the first DD-963 cards assembled there were sent off to Ingalls Shipbuilding. The employee head count has grown to nearly 500. Josephine county with an ethnic population of only 2.3% has seen 9% of this category of people go on the total Litton payroll. Plant Manager Ron Silver and his Industrial relations chief, Bob Morrison finally erased that old "bad memory" completely. Between them they had nearly 40 years of Litton service which said something of them as "stayers."

11. What a bit of planning history was in Maverick-Clarke! It was Sam Maverick in 1876, then a respected and cantankerous San Antonio citizen who had its Maverick Bank and the Alamo Insurance Company which was the first of its kind in Texas. Along the way, he purchased what he called the Maverick Printing Co. Webster's dictionary calls him into its word lexicon as "the Texas cattle owner who did not brand his calves. An unbranded animal, especially a motherless calf, customarily claimed by the first one to brand it. A refractory or recalcitrant individual who bolts his party, or group, or initiates an independent course." All this came from that one Sam Maverick who hated fences. Robert Clarke, not so colorful or opinionated but a good printer, began his business in Galveston. When the two firms were pulled together, they had 12 wandering salesmen who covered Texas, Louisiana, Arkansas, New Mexico, Oklahoma and the Republic of Old Mexico. The Southwest Region of Litton Office Products in Houston, headed by an old Maverick hand, John C. Crawford, has satellite locations in Austin, Brownsville, Laredo, Corpus Christi and San Antonio. No competitor had been able to fence Maverick-Clarke out—or in, either.

Noah loading the Ark, except in some cases there were more than pairings and into multiples which could take care of whole territories and regions where the acquired names meant something to a geographic market.

The first McKenna chore, caught up by him on the fly, the Royal-McBee acquisition was stepping out with its newest electric and three home portable models. Only the Defense and Space Systems group was posting more sales. Nobody was paying any attention to the fact that it was Litton's 13th year. But it was in that year that some began to feel that there was a rising vulnerability of problems among its possessions. Harry Gray described it as part of the endangering atmosphere that people both inside and outside the company thought ". . .Litton can do anything." Litton was building that "shipyard of the future" with no big contract in sight. Its response to the federal government's request that it take on a skill training contract under the banner of "the war on poverty" had it being stud horse-type flogged in newspapers, great and small, because of the incident-prone population the contract had to address. The increasing requirements for "business in Washington" appearances had Thornton on committees and commissions. In the midst of all this, McKenna had developed big eyes for Imperial, which manufactured the typewriter of that brand in the grimy midlands towns of Leicester and Hull in England.

It was a poor machine, which he thought could be improved and restored in the market by certain Royal additives. Imperial had one of the best sales organizations in existence, carefully deployed over many years. Imperial was on the ropes, but in McKenna's analysis, had several hues of noteworthiness which could benefit Royal and Litton. There was no doubt that Imperial had a hand on all the world's door-knobs. While France was making snarling noises and DeGaulle was postering with his usual contrariness denying the British the Common Market membership which they wanted, McKenna strongly believed that the British were sufficiently formidable in foreign trade that when ready they would find a way in. Olympia and Triumph-Adler in Germany, Olivetti in Italy and Hermes in Switzerland were either in or surrounded by the Common Market already. In the acquisition of Royal-McBee, Fred C. Rummel, its chairman of the finance and executive committee, had fingered the declining sales as having been due to failures of Royal's *international* division to meet its forecasts and projections. McKenna believed Imperial might help staunch that ebbing wound, and also was an added visa stamp in Litton's passport for its typewriter globally.

Imperial knew in its hardened arteries that it had the ingredients of its own doom. It needed technological transfusion badly, and a new source of capital. Desperation was thick in the air. Britain's Secretary of State for Industry was pathetically eager for McKenna to be convincing in his efforts to sell Litton corporate types that Imperial, however forbidding it might look, synergistically had some sense making aspects to it. About 3,000 employees, technically skilled human beings, were tied up in all this needing and hoping among themselves for some means to extend the life span of the job.

McKenna, normally a slow moving and phlegmatic executive, got himself so committed and convinced, he was at an emotional peak about it. At the critical moment of decision as to whether to go ahead, the lid flew off McKenna's traditional self control. He was ticked off when Frank Slovak, the auditor, was one of the several tied on a conference call with McKenna talking from his London hotel to Roy Ash. Slovak, never reticent about expressing any strongly felt opinion, heard McKenna review his case, then broke in: "I know all about Imperial," he said. "I wouldn't touch it with a 10-foot pole." The phone wires hummed with McKenna's rebuttal.

"Slovak knows nothing about typewriters," McKenna told Ash. "All he sees are his damned columns of figures." Slovak was about to voice his rebuttal, when he was aware of someone standing beside him. It was Roy Ash. Without a word, Ash took the receiver out of his hand and hung it up. The McKenna conference call audience was lessened by one. When Ash picked up his phone, he was hearing McKenna say if Beverly Hills was not willing to condone his strategy, they could have his job. There was more talk, and McKenna was quieted with the word that Litton would go along with the Imperial acquisition.

The Imperial face-off was in one of those large English boardrooms that was centered with a long table. The Litton delegation was on one side. The Imperial principals with their legal retinue was on the other, with Roger M. Evans, Chairman and General Manager, their spokesman. Evans, 60-ish worn and tired, at ease in the City of London's financial district or in any London club, had to have this connection with Litton. He had run out of maneuver room. His face was a mask. The atmosphere of such a conclave in Britain is highly formal, traditional, rigid in its protocols, a picture of a caste system at work dominated by barristers who talk only after conferring in hushed whispers with clients. Evans was at the head of the table on his side. Slovak, the wampum watchdog for Litton, was at the foot of the long oaken expanse opposite. The proceedings began, positions were taken as to clauses in the contract, substitute wordings offered and accepted or rejected. The processes were dragging. Suddenly, that rasping Slovak voice penetrated all the walls of decorousness breaking not only the rules but the nearly sepulchral silence as the body pondered:

"Mr. Evans," Slovak was saying, "Why don't you and I go across the street to the pub We can work all this out."

"A fine idea," said Evans, coming alive. They left the tsk-tsk simply-isn't done chorus of disapproval behind them paying it no attention. Across to the pub they went.

Over a mild-and-bitter there, Slovak said if the price were corrected downward drastically, they would have a deal. How drastically, Evans asked. "About 1,750,000 British pounds less," Slovak estimated. They talked awhile longer, then with a relieved sigh, Evans agreed. The two of them paid the pub, went back to the boardroom and announced it.[12]

---

12. There were 3,063,000 ordinary (common) shares in Imperial, which had traded as high as 17 shillings, but hung around the 12-shilling level more constantly. R.M. Evans and seven other board members owned 89,319 shares. They all knew how thorny was the way ahead of them. Their notice to investors of the Litton interest in them said that ". . .your directors strongly recommend shareholders to accept (12-shilling and 6-pence offer), and will accept in respect to their holdings." It was a graveyard whistle to screw up courage in that the Imperial directors said Britain's economic climate for business in the Island Kingdom was "less favorable" and that the current operations of the company had become "less profitable". Imperial was in one of the most intensive labor lines and in a country which had more than 13,000,000 union members who loyally voted majorities sympathetic to its wishes into Parliamentary power. In that cockpit, it was always fair game to flagellate and penalize private ownership, pushing for government bounty and, if necessary in the short term, nationalization. Winston Churchill once turned his back when he found himself side-by-side at a urinal with his arch foe, Clement Atlee. He said he feared to expose himself in the W.C. (water closet) to his adversary because ". . .every time you see a big thing running smoothly, you want to nationalize it."

Special Situation #13

It was Alfred Lord Tennyson modernized. Litton was about to play a comparable role to "The Charge of the Light Brigade". The desire to prove that Imperial could be turned around was strong, and that Royal could help and be helped was even stronger. Although there were head shakings and disaster prophecies all around, pouring in and intimidating, it just might work. On the British side it was halleujah time and Imperial was voted into Litton by 84%of its shareholders who among them held 95.15% of the issued and outstanding securities.

McKenna was pushing on. He wanted a domain and he had one. He thought he had executives in the right places who would master any of the festering sores they found and cauterize them. Litton, from its overview of his group, saw it as a commerce collage, a collection of diverse and sometimes perilous fragments which it expected McKenna to frame into a workable composition. A combination of artist and artisan with his accounting experience weighed in, he had to be. The scene from McKenna's chair in Beverly Hills, which he had little chance to occupy as he ran from one dike plugging scene to the next, was a shark infested sea with bared teeth aplenty showing. Yet, in 1967 Litton saw Royal increase office electric typewriter sales by some 30% which it declared to be double the industry average. Monroe said its calculators sales were up 56%. Royfax was introducing its Model 1700 book copier and was casting for customers from a sales and service network of 127 locations. Sweda was showing itself bouncy as automation cash register takers were higher by 153%, and the Dataregister traffic doubled. That 1967 annual report was a famous one for the way it looked—jet black cover giving bold relief to a multicolored stained glass window. Harry Gray was playing one upsmanship with Crosby Kelly. It was fancier than any Kelly had done. On one page the copy read: "Litton lives on accurate, primary information—quickly and freely communicated. . ." and Gray had no trouble with the statement as it moved on into print with him not knowing he would be one of the first it would bite back.

At the Soviet Union's Systemmotechnica exhibition that same year, Soviet Minister Konstantin N. Rudnev came directly to the Svenska Data register booth. He asked abruptly why no proposal was being made to his Ministry of Instrument Building, Means of Automation and Control Systems to package the design and tooling for a cash register manufacturing facility somewhere in the U.S.S.R. After all, he said, consumer goods were becoming more plentiful which made it necessary for Soviets to expand in retailing. In Moscow's 3,600-room Hotel Rossiya (Russia), 26 of the Sweda machines were working well. Even though the cashiers checked them and their totals with their trusty abacuses, no errors were found. All the tourist hard currency Beriozhka shops using Swedas were pleased. Not only was the Sweda line doing well in the West, it now had appeal in several communist bloc countries. Those 26 Swedas in the Hotel Rossiya were less then 250 metres from the Kremlin walls. The one in the Beriozhka on the first floor of the old Hotel National was ringing up capitalist country monies merrily just below the meager and lean two-room suite #107 in which Lenin himself had taken residence when the Bolsheviks brought the seat of government from Petrograd to Moscow after the Revolution. With these money tabulating devices Litton was as close to the physical and philosophical heart of the communist version of socialism as any free enterprise could ever hope to be! If that barrier was coming down, and the Common Market was entering Litton's commercial picture by leaps, there was a prospect of a world market in truth. Litton was less visible than Napoleon had been among the Muscovites, but had better chance of staying the course. It was pleasant to bask there in all that sunshine of the moment, and promise a new portable electric typewriter before long for the growing list of Litton products. The Atlas-like burden on the Litton shoulder was that money-eating startup of Ingalls Shipbuilding's West Bank facility.

Of the $1,561,510,000 in 1967 sales, 31% were revenues generated by McKenna's units. Only Defense & Space Systems at 32% scored higher for the company till. Industrial Systems and Equipment took in 27%, and the remaining 10% was marshaled by Professional Products and Services. McKenna made a brave forecast to beat the previous blistering pace.

Old Sir Francis Bacon once said: "It's not what men eat that makes them strong, but what they digest." Litton was about to find out how right he was. Tex Rickard put the typewriter in his picture with a different perspective—as a broadcast sponsor. Rickard was one smart hombre. He didn't own a typewriter. Litton was about to wish it didn't.

SPECIAL SITUATION #14

THE KNOWLEDGE INDUSTRY

Of all the studies compiled about the 1968 XIX Olympiad at 7,000-foot high Mexico City, the quadrennial Olympic Games, one which didn't enter the official documentation was a prized claim only Litton Industries could make.

There were 113 nations which filed entries, and 109 provided the 6,082 athletes who were in the many competitions. Only seventeen of the nations brought home more gold medals than did employees of Litton! They were appropriately symbolic, of how Litton came about, partly by acquisition and partly by internal growth. It had to do with how Litton did a tentative step in the educational field sensed it immediately as a place to be and develop, and found itself in some of its highest drama along the way.

Imbedded in the Litton past was a custom. Youngsters who did well in machine shops of Sequoia High School in Redwood City, California were eagerly and selectively sought and taken for apprenticeship by Charlie Litton. He introduced them to his glass lathes in his San Carlos plant. As they progressed in skill, he made a very personal event of reviewing their increasing worth to his business. He was only interested in the bright, though, the very curious, ambitious and teacher recommended front runners. The time would come when the quality would change drastically. For other reasons Litton Industries was drawn to those who dropped out after a few grades in America's schools. That was well down the road. Roy Woenne, Charlie Litton's first fulltime employee, came to him from Sequoia High. Robert Holm, much later, went on his payroll after winning the machine shop medal in that school in his senior year. Holm, there with Litton Electron Tube, remembers how big the 80-cents an hour looked to him going in, and how important and how high his exhilaration was when Litton personally conducted his ritual review and upped his hourly rate to $1.10 ninety days later! Litton made a great deal more of such occasions than it being merely a pay raise. Holm never knew a father after his 12th birthday. He listened to many who said Charlie Litton was a demander and just as much a slaver as his grandfather had once been. Holm declares if he had had a choice for a surrogate parent, he could have done no better than Charlie.

"He could talk with you at your level," Holm remembers. "He could take you up with him, step by step." The uninitiated were toured through all the production processes by the boss personally. He delighted in letting them know he could do it all. The value of know-how, example setting, the thrill of solutions and achievements of a working widget were a special brand of excitement. Litton celebrated those moments when an individual found himself capable of more than he had ever dreamed he could do. This early tendency to enlist on-the-job training was because it was hard to get help that was already skilled—nay, impossible—because an out-front technology was involved. Raw personnel with applicable aptitudes was needed to wed to his machines. The rising need for skill training and retraining was shortly to have worldwide impact sprouting many offshoots, even engaging the body politic when increasing sociological problem awareness surfaced. It was not farfetched that in the original acquisition was a valid link with the educational field, where Litton Industries later sensed a significant role for itself.

It became a critical situation for Litton when some of the carefully contemplated cash flow in the treasury of the San Carlos firm was channeled into developing inertial navigation. While if ultimately selected as reliable and better than existing equipment for flight accuracy and safety, such systems presented a problem in mass production. That old yardstick—being able to take neophytes by instruction to a proper capability level—persisted as an essential ingredient. Dr. Stephen Uslan showed first on Litton's roster of employees in 1960. He was immediately confronted with an inertial navigation production model. How to assemble it had to be taught. And in several countries.

The first determination he had to make was what kinds of individuals should be recruited. Where was the most promising source? The engineer orientation of what was called Litton's Guidance and Control Systems division was a dominating factor. Working with Bruce Worcester and Hal Erdley, the so-called "IT" (for Inertial Instrument Trainees) campaign was started. Under it, Uslan was authorized to get 100 young people who had to have a year at least of junior college. Within Litton they were to take a full year-long course. During that training span they were to work on every phase of the equipment assembly. These intensively schooled selectees were slated to become a cadre of senior assemblers when Guidance and Control got seriously engaged in production in their newly constructed Litton building on Canoga Avenue in Woodland Hills, California.

Uslan felt he was almost a casting director. He went through some 400 applicants of both sexes. He met with the superintendents and principals of Los Angeles schools and with various labor union poobahs who ruled on apprenticeship requirements. In tandem with Uslan, Worcester and Erdley were cajoling and pushing the top engineering figures into breaking down a complete inertial navigation system into its parts and major components. The thinking was that the components separated out in this fashion could be more easily understood and later combined into their relationships, the total packaging left to those who knew the systems from start to finish. The statistics were dismaying to Uslan, even chilling. More than a thousand different steps were necessary to get a single assembled system—250 of those steps on the gyroscope alone! The overseer had to be able to track an individual system all the way from the first spring assembly right up to the point where it was couched in its gimbals. There were in excess of 500 inspections along the way. Far more intricate and involved than any country quilting bee, it called for small bits of minute electronic materials rather than scrap cloth to be brought into a pattern by the synchronization of many hands. The recruiting effort ground on. The model kept diminishing in size and numbers of actions. While those actions held fast in the area of a thousand, and labor intensive as it all was, Uslan finally thought it was manageable.

If there was ever anyone who saw only "the tip of the iceberg," it was Uslan—and to a lesser degree, the American educational cult training the hands. So pinned was Uslan into the immediacy of what was happening around him, he had no idea he was being tailored and tagged for one of Litton's most surprising directions—that uncharted realm of sociological change engineered under government contract. Everything about that first Litton task fitted him for what lay ahead as no other person at Litton. He personally interviewed every one of the assembler prospects. He did a psychological assessment. He gave them dexterity tests. The inertial navigation impact was not to be restricted to the U.S. Many of the prospects he saw before him came not from America alone, but Sweden, Switzerland, from Holland and Belgium, from Canada, from the Federal Republic of Germany's

Black Forest country and the old Pontine Marshes South of Rome in Italy.

As often happens, Uslan learned more himself about the size of the undertaking and its ramifications than anyone, much more than he bargained for and a lot of it was simple and basic. Engineers to the contrary, the real need was for eye, hand and finger dexterity. Most of the Europeans were former watchmakers, and from stagnant industries in their homelands. They were intelligent, though, and quick to adapt because of their technical backgrounds. While they sometimes had language difficulties, they could read diagrams and translate them into appropriate actions. They were the first to say that guidebooks and manuals so laboriously and technically weighted and worded by engineers were often obscure and obstructive rather than helpful. Not content to be critical only, they offered to aid with the writing of the procedural pamphlets. Out of this came eventually the knowledge that the search difficulties of going after college trained people for inclusion in such a program was also wrong. They were over-qualified. the repetitive and detailed nature of the work repelled them making a built-in retention problem. Experience let Uslan know at once that not only were the ones he'd been working on over-educated and subject to boredom, they certainly expected salaries to match their college credits. With inertial navigation's costs already considered staggering and the labor factor a substantial part of the pricing, being able to jettison any unnecessary compensation was significant.

When the cadre version of the manuals was done it was immediately apparent that high school graduates and women who had had seamstress and petit point credentials were not only adequate but capable of superior assembler performance. The ladies, in fact, were the very best. It was neither the first nor the last time that false professional pride—be it in engineering, science or whatever—would be found standing in the way of simplifying a task. All one needed was a version of the old football cliche ". . . a good pair of hands."

The engineers had to cope with other personnel comeuppance which gave them a hard time. They had to learn flexibility. It was rooted in this swing to women. Their work areas were so-called "clean rooms" which had to be sucked free of dust and floating foreign particles. Assembly was so intricate that it had to be done with the aid of microscopes. All this the women took in stride except that the "clean room" environment permitted no lipstick, nail polish, or cosmetics and they had to don smocks and booties. The women muttered and even rebelled about this saying it took away their femininity. As the resident Solomon, Uslan had to persuade industrial relations to allow them a quarter hour margin at the end of the shift to get "prettied up" before they walked out of the plant's door. If the production whizzes could resort to color coding wires for ease of harness and breadboard handiwork, and could pick colors strong enough to get around occasional employee color blindness, Uslan said they should be able to turn their backs on the clock for 15 minutes as a nicety to promote employee satisfaction and comfort. He won the day. Color coding was one of the hurdles used to jump the language barriers and the "cosmetics pit stop" in the race for the door at the end of a shift became an allowable. Because of the high technology direction of Litton, the company always had a one-for-one ratio—every outside employee with technical training the company policy matched with an in-house instructional package which produced that skill. That educational or vocational instruction capability grew and grew in Litton. In addition to Guidance and Control, the Data Systems Division in Van Nuys was mushrooming. It had such special personnel demands, too.

A few doors down the street from where author Edgar Rice Burroughs "Tarzan" and "Martian" exploits flowed from the mind and facile pen of one who gave the town of Tarzana its name, Litton established its own technical training school. this included development of manuals and visual aids which dealt with every aspect of its assembly work. Uslan had a staff of 14, and they were galley-slaves-in-residence. Self-imprisoned by their interest in and the challenge of their work, that facility became the focus for a substantial interior-to-Litton production of slides, charts, packets of aids for outlying plants, a corporate pool totally undismayed by whatever exotic personnel training demands that might be levied on it.

Uslan had his head down with the rest of them. It came up suddenly when there was a surprise tour of his Tarzana premises by Litton president Roy Ash, the navigational and command and control group head, George Scharffenberger, and the Guidance and Control boss, Dr. William Jacoby. They were closemouthed about it, but had something on their minds and it showed. It was a corner-turning of sorts. A promise had been made to Minnesota's senior Senator Hubert

Humphrey that Litton would assist in the relief of employment depressed Duluth, a part of his constituency. It was away off in the country's mid-north on the banks of Lake Superior. The promise seemed deliverable and the inspecting trio's spirits picked up noticeably as the walk through the Tarzana shop ended. Uslan, as he stood there in the doorway, was told to get on a plane at once for Duluth, touch base with the school people and the Minnesota Department of Labor which would give him an idea of the available work force.

California-born Uslan, in a summer suit, arrived just after Thanksgiving. He had never been that far north, nor did he know about the Great Lakes wind-chill factor. He could only guess what kind of skills he would find. Nearly all were males, former steel and dockhands, whose idea of fun was wrist wrestling in bars. The loser was lucky if his hand was only downed rather than being crammed through the bar top itself! The kind of technology Litton proposed to bring to town was micro-miniature assembly, electronic harness board manufacture and other similar packets to be fitted into the delicate systems Litton was contracted to provide. His most crushing information came when he visited the Duluth high schools and found the staffs had no real understanding of what he was talking about. They were still using open fire soldering irons which were actually cradled in a perpetual blaze and about as unwieldy as a blacksmith's hammer. When they heard the Litton assemblies were accomplished by people peering through several lenses, they were indeed baffled. The only solution appeared to be to bring the principals and appropriate manual training staffs of high and trade schools to Tarzana for a week to survey the needs, the approaches and the results which were attainable through these new disciplines. If they could have some of the packages of training materials at the end of the stay for familiarization, they believed they could do it. Uslan's last act before boarding his flight out of town was to walk through a former dock warehouse which could be converted into a plant site if everything else jelled.[1]

---

1. Humphrey was not the only concerned politician. In Connecticut Dr. Joseph Nerden, a teacher of 37 years and maverick Yale thinker where mention of vocational training was reason for a soapy oral scrubbing, contended that one in every two people in the state worked in the machine tool industry. He championed placing skill and technical training schools in proximity to people clusters as a job readying measure. One day in the late 50s he fielded a phone call from North Carolina asking him if he could work out something for that state. It was Governor Luther Hodges, so Nerden

Glumness filled the air when he rendered his report in Beverly Hills. It'll never work, some said, but Uslan had some Pollyanna in him and believed it would. Duluth, for one thing, was highly motivated to do something about its plight. If they had to switch from loading bunkers of ore to gossamer wiring that they would do. The schools having committed to perform the training asked Litton to provision them with all the equipment, all the models for people to practice on, and reciprocated by paying for two Litton instructors to take up residence. Thus, a new labor capability dictated by a new technology became a boon to a becalmed and isolated community. The media attention paid this activity and the purring of Senator Humphrey about what he had inspired Litton Industries to do for his state made this the test tube from which grew the Manpower Development and Training Act of 1962. This was a federally funded mechanism by which schools would be subsidized if they expanded their curriculum to include unemployed people which would ready them for roles in new industries.

On November 22, 1963, in Dallas, Texas, President John F. Kennedy was assassinated. Less than 24 hours later his successor, Lyndon B. Johnson, was catching up in great gulps some of the thoughts and proposed legislation with which the fallen idol had toyed. Walter Heller, Chairman of the President's Council of Economic Advisers, and Kermit Gordon, the Budget Bureau Director, had his ear about several

---

was in Raleigh on the next plane. With a cooperative Wade Martin, state head of vocational education, 58 such schools cropped up over North Carolina. What was good enough there was also for South Carolina, with Governor Fritz Hollings asking Nerden to join his "group of seven" (one from each Congressional district), chaired by politically powerful Stanley Smith of Columbia. Hollings called it his Technical Education Commission and sixteen technical training centers resulted. The Carolinas were bringing together a methodology by which they could go more than halfway to attract industry to their states by not only industrial parks and tax incentives to lift them from agricultural dependence, but creation of skills to order. They canvassed companies with plant startups in mind, asked the expertise needed. The technical school closest to the site gave the training. This had started in 1946 anbd was referred to as the "Connecticut pattern". After the Duluth case the Carolinas appealed to Litton. That's how Union/Butterfield Straight Line's twist drill plant landed outside Gaffney in 1970; Monroe in Lexington and Hewitt-Robins in Columbia in 1963, Carolina Gravure in Lexington ten years later, and Clifton Precision's presence in Murphy, N.C. Union/Butterfield's Bill Yesberg was actually met by 20 prospects, and 14 were hired including all eight minority applicants.

aspects of the Kennedy thinking. One was his desire to have some kind of anti-poverty program. Ricochets from civil rights battles and tax measures had so bedeviled him, he just hadn't gotten to it, they told LBJ. Litton's John Rubel had his own leg-up on all this. Heller had conversations with Kennedy's National Science Adviser, Jerome Wiesner. He said tax money was rolling in so strongly that there would be enough to entertain and fund a range of social programs. Johnson was a formidable clout combination as inheritor from a loved leader and a bare knuckled legislative strategist. He still rankled from the smart-ass treatment he felt he'd been given by Camelot which seemed to relegate him to the status of stable boy to hold horses of the retinue. He was canny enough to use what he had, and he'd show them all a thing or three. "They always said Kennedy had the style," he groused to friends, "but I got the damned bills passed." It was a speechwriter, Richard Goodwin, in a draft which was never used for the occasion intended, who first pecked out "Great Society" on his typewriter. Even if Johnson didn't use that speech, his blotter-like mind held tightly to those two words. He talked endlessly using the term over and over as a label he fancied for his administration. On January 8, 1964 in his State of the Union chat with the Congress, there was a declaration which was to impact on Litton Industries: "This administration, here and now," he said, "declares unconditional war on poverty."

He had said before and he often did afterward that there were good reasons for businessmen to be interested because they were perpetually engaged in skill matching and upgrading to meet job requirements. Nowhere was this more true than in high technology companies. Kennedy had never been poor, but Johnson had. So had Tex Thornton. Kennedy got his ideas about such things from books and advisers, while Johnson had dug in the gritty dirt and had wrestled cattle of necessity. There was some evidence of interest around Washington even before the Johnson declaration—J.P. Sundquist in the Department of Agriculture, who thought young people could be used in many ways to help food production; Daniel F. "Pat" Moynihan, in the Department of Labor who wanted all those who failed to pass the military draft questionnaires to be considered for vocational training.[2]

Johnson's way of putting the Kennedy stamp on the proceedings was to assign it to the Peace Corps chief, R. Sargent Shriver, a Kennedy brother-in-law. The worldwide Peace Corps activity gave him both Messianistic and idealistic credentials. The "war on poverty" was definitely in addition to his other duties in the Peace Corps, but with the clear understanding that Johnson was going to make it all a part of the Executive Office of the President. He knew too well how old cabinet or agency domains strangled newborn infant programs in their bureaucratic cradles particularly if visible and troublesome knots had to be untied. Shriver, in the Kennedy circle by marriage, was a bubbling, exhorting starter-upper even if not believed as sure handed at tending or administering. Johnson needed just such a catch-fire kind of personality, socially impeccable, one who could paddle the upstream current and maintain a momentum legislatively. Shriver had had success in Chicago when he lived there in putting together a group of "Businessmen for Kennedy." It had some impressive names. He also had been corralling some carriage trade industrialists as "Businessmen for Johnson." One had been Charles B. Thornton of Litton Industries.

Washington does its thing by task forces and commissions and boards. That summer of 1964, a task force was convened, a sizeable packet of diverse backgrounds who brainstormed under Shriver auspices. Litton had in being an Economic Development division, headed by Dr. William Jacoby who had left Guidance and Control Systems to Fred O'Green to run. Jacoby's was an idea-winging group, too. He had all kinds of suggestions bouncing off the walls in Beverly Hills—the possibility of stringing a series of African wild life preserves across the American south which people could "safari" through in their own automobiles. It was dropped as impractical for Litton, but its time came later in other hands. There was a combina-

---

2. Moynihan's paper, "One third of a Nation: A Report On Young Men Found Unqualified For Military Service" said 33% of 18-year olds were being rejected from military draft induction, one half of those for medical reasons, the remainder for mental test shortcomings — the major proportion the products of poverty. "They have inherited their situation from their parents," he wrote, "and unless the cycle is broken, they will almost surely transmit it to their children."

tion education and leadership package being suggested to (then) Belgian Congo black leader, Moshe Tshombe, which called for mounting educational TV transmitters in transport aircraft. The planes would be flown in a circular pattern allowing the beam to reach even the most inaccessible regions.[3] Tshombe, unfortunately, transitioned from customer to refugee to DOA (dead on arrival) all too soon.

Rubel and Uslan were part of the task force commitment by Litton to Washington. They listened as there was talk of reviving the old Civilian Conservation Corps, the CCC of Roosevelt's time. Senator Humphrey liked that but wanted it called a Youth Conservation Corps so it could be a collection point for young people whether rural or urban. There was substantial belief that the high school dropout was the greatest input source to welfare roles and hard core unemployment and that the schools should be given a part—until someone produced evidence that alarming numbers of the dropouts were caused by the schools, much of this due to shortage of vocational and skill training opportunities. Rubel and Uslan were quick to throw in the constancy of industry's capability to instruct taking raw and unprepared personnel to qualify them as entering level employes. Litton over its young life, Tex Thornton once told the Harvard Business School Association had trained ". . . more than 15,000 people in our first ten years." Why not, postulated Rubel and Uslan, contract out to American industry to run what would be called Urban Job Corps Centers? They could train in areas designated by the Bureau of Labor Statistics in the kinds of expertise in the services category needed over the next three to ten

---

3. Off in Litton's wings was Alfred Strogoff who was every day more intrigued by the possibilities of "the knowledge industry" although he had his hands full as the fair-haired boy at Adler Electronics. Benjamin Adler first had a communications laboratory in 1945 and in ten years incorporated Adler Electronics in New Rochelle, N.Y. That was the suburb made famous by George M. Cohan in "45 Minutes from Broadway." Its 252,625 shares were in less than a dozen hands. About 80% of its business was designing, developing, engineering and manufacturing advanced electronic communications systems and heterodyne repeater transmitting and receiving equipment for radio, TV and microwave for government agencies. It was clocked into Litton October 14, 1963 when Litton shares equal to $8,400,000 were exchanged for the Adler paper. There was an additional promise of $1,304,024 in Litton securities after January 1, 1965 to make the transaction final. As Al Strogoff was heading it as a Litton division, he had that "knowledge industry" glimmer in his eye. Adler was making a variety of items in demand as educational TV (ETV) was taking those first, uncertain baby steps.

years. They made a most plausible and attractive case, and if President Johnson could bring it off on Capitol Hill, Litton was about to take a hard road. Johnson's shadow across the Senate was still giant size and his anti-poverty legislation was having no obstacles thrown in its way there. He was not sure of himself in the House, but when the crucial vote came on August 7, 1964 the House okayed the measure 228 to 190.

There was no doubt then about the Johnson power in legislative affairs. He was awesome. He grabbed every lapel he could lay hands on. He called in old brownie points. He cast tantalizing pork barrel possibilities out there for the Congress to beam and dream about. His "Great Society," once a speechwriter's hearts and flowers rhetoric, left the New Deal, the Fair Deal and the New Frontier behind, shelved for history, and was launched with fanfare.

At the same time, the towering teenage son of a black lady barber in the bloody 5th ward of Houston's ghetto, decided to drop out of school. He was street smart and tough, a mugger, an alcoholic at 10, a street brawler at 11 who hung around poolhalls waiting for nights to fall to carry out plotted depredations of one kind or another. He was well known to every policeman. Once he had knocked out 200 windowpanes in succession before they caught up with him. That record was the talk of his old neighborhood and still is. Earlier in lower grades he had yearned to be noticed so much by his teachers he offered to stay after school to clean the blackboards, but the teachers didn't want to chance it alone with this big-for-his-age kid. He thought the Mother Goose "Georgie Porgie, Puddin' Pie" had been written about him, and was desolated when told that wasn't so. He decided he didn't need school. There were other ways to be an attention-getter.

Litton, whether it was because Tex Thornton was a "Businessman for Johnson," or memories of those long ago shared Saturdays when both Tex and LBJ[4] had been volunteer "clerks" in Congressman

---

4. Being a certified friend of L.B.J. could lead to all kinds of excitement Tex Thornton found. When his Majesty King Faisal Ibn al-Aziz Al-Saud, King of Saudi Arabia, made his State Visit to the U.S., June 21st-30th, 1966, his stand on Israel being an enemy made New York Mayor John Lindsay politically nervous. He cancelled participation in any of his Gotham time. This resulted in Litton's Tex Thornton being asked to "stand in" and be key performer at the function in honor of the Arab

George Mahon's outer office, or because Tex knew so well himself what it was like to be young and at loose ends, made one of the first proposals to set up, manage and run an Urban Job Corps Center. Those who have shared ordeals often have ties which bind them tightly and endure long. That Johnson statement about "war on poverty" now had wings of its own. There was an undoubted national necessity to get some kind of hammerlock on the problem and for the government to illuminate it as an open wound which had to be addressed with every resource available.

Washington is a city prone to revere precedents and terms of reference by which agencies are licensed, teamed, or telescoped into each other. There is a comforting recognition factor about an old legislative wayfarer even if there is an updating requirement and name change. All well and good as long as the antecedents can be traced and verified as having been useful and sanctioned—and yea, funded in another time. Washington watches acronyms chase each other into and out of town. Whole batteries of people sit in niches here and there thumb-sucking collections of high flown words which reduce to a set of three to five capital letters. The result of all these poverty directed deliberations was OEO (The Office of Economic Opportunity). That was the vehicle assigned to carry all poverty's baggage.

John Rubel, for Litton, was in his element. He had a bright mind and compelling oratorical persuasive powers, and was the kind of pro-

---

ruler at the Metropolitan Club. The affair was attended by such other American Industrialists as Chrysler's Lynn Townsend, Union Carbide's Birny Mason, Jr., Lockheed's Dan Haughton, Deere's William Hewitt, Olin Mathieson's Thomas S. Nichols, Douglas Aircraft's Donald Douglas, Jr., Union Oil's Fred Hartley, Raytheon's Charles Francis Adams, Avco's James R. Kerr, TWA's Charles C. Tillinghast, United California Bank's Frank King, General Time's Don G. Mitchell, National Bulk Carriers' D.K. Ludwig, plus such Littonites as Roy L. Ash, William E. McKenna, Austin Goodyear, Henry Salvatori, and Gale Livingston. Adnan Khashoggi, the suave and grand Arab deal maker, was there, too. As was so often the case, there was a relationship from time before there was a modern Litton — Aero Service had flown nearly 800,000 square miles of 1-to-60,000 scale aerial photography from 1949 to 1958 for which Saudi Arabia paid $8,000,000. Westrex from 1962 had all responsibility for operations and maintenance of the Dhahran air base communications center. In 1965, a joint venture called Industrial Development & Engineering Co. involving Litton and a Saudi group was created. It would be seven years and another ruler later which was to attach vast significance to this emergency Metropolitan Club happening, June 29, 1966.

posal maker audiences like to have on last. No matter how dull the day might have been, Rubel could put a match to it. His time around the Pentagon E Ring had introduced him to all the swing and sway waltzing of proposal making. He had a firm belief that American business had so much power that some of it was spilling over its edges and being wasted from sheer unawareness of its potential for application to such problems as OEO was bringing into blurred focus. This problem quarter was big, no doubt about it, but where and how and with what means to grip the monster was the mystery. Business not having gone this route before was no excuse to Rubel. He thought the very foundations of the free enterprise system were being allowed to erode at dangerous speed.

Litton then was a mere 11 years old. It was "feeling its oats" and had reason to believe it would be nudging a billion dollars in sales in its next 12-month period. Thornton thought it was a proper direction for the company to take. Roy Ash sought Uslan to give him a rationale for the Litton presence and warned him off of any "corporate conscience" wicket, or sociological arguments. Uslan said he saw it as a built-in laboratory which could pave Litton's way into what Al Strogoff was so high on—the "knowledge business"—with teaching machines, establishment of community colleges, owning textbook houses. What better way to test the materials which would apply than with this hardcore educational situation? Harry Gray was not at all happy with it, and said so. Shriver, of course was delighted with the Litton interest, because if he got American business in the swim with him it would take the "bleeding heart" onus off what he was doing. Thornton found himself walking with two people who had been at important crossroads of his life, Shriver having opened the door for him to his father-in-law, Joseph P. Kennedy, when he was hunting for money for Litton's initial backing, and Johnson, now the President of the U.S., with whom he had been friends from their Texas youth. The first of seven contracts for Urban Job Corps Centers was given to Litton Industries,[5] the largest of the lot. Expectancy was that on

---

5. Litton was also subcontractor to Westinghouse whose Urban Job Corps Center was placed at Camp Atterbury, Indiana. Litton, through Al Strogoff's creation, Litton Educational Systems in College Park, Maryland was drawn on for the educational and Vocational curriculum. It was never a happy association and in one year Litton was out and Westinghouse assumed total responsibility for that midwest operation.

whatever site Litton would bring this Center into being that its teenage population would vary from 2,000 to 2,600 drawn from every state.

Most of the Litton executive shelf was turned off by this commitment. Not that there was a chance for Litton to lose money, the contract insured there was no way that could happen. It was the old "what *will* people think?" and for "people," everyone substituted "security analysts" as they with their desktop and hand calculators had trouble equating skill instruction with P&L. It did no good to bring up the statistic that in another time there had been a sweeping government attempt to ease the national conscience for having interfered in the life preparatory agendas of men and women sent to World War II—the so-called GI Bill. It had helped the veteran back to the campus and into careers after the curtain wait of conflict. Even as Litton headed down this new and unmapped contractual avenue, more than 20 of its upper and middle management people had gotten all or part of their education via this GI Bill. That included Roy L. Ash, the President and one of the company's most promising legal lights, Robert H. Lentz. But that was different, Harry Gray insisted, as the defrocked soldiery was said to be "motivated." He shook his head forlornly about the slim chance of this possibility. It was his firm belief that there would be no way to either inspire or dangle an incentive before the young people so long on the outer margin of society and welfare-accustomed. They would see it only as another way to tap into the U.S. Treasury. Not all GI Bill participants had been wildly ambitious either, but the ones at Litton had been. It was so easy to generalize for the negative position, throw out "what if?" questions and get on the record as predictors that Litton would "rue the day."

John Rubel was skirted in the corridors. Dr. Steve Uslan wandered with growing concern from office to office trying to explain Litton's proposal, its direction and the purpose the Federal Government wanted served. Over and over, the crown princes poised on the executive suite ladder adjusted their lapels carefully, straightened their ties anxiously and invited him to leave forthwith. They wanted no part of it, and said so. Everything he was saying confirmed their worst scenario assessments. Thornton was holding firm and most of his associates humored him in his "folly." He was the "big boss," after all. He had all those "political entanglements" to contend with, the "old boy network" and "all that jazz." Whispered concern about the corporate image and buzzword barrages were thrown back and forth across the soft carpets as various ones would slip into other offices to talk anxiously about "our direction," the maybe effect on the P/E ratio, those precious multiples—all those variable and psychological quicksands on which their optioned share prices rested.

Thornton and his preachments about the "work ethic," it was said, might unhorse not only him but the company as well. In another time, Omaha's Father Flanagan of Boys Town had mouthed the platitude that "there's no such thing as a bad boy." That cleric had finally had to abandon that statement. It was proven conclusively to him that there were truly bad boys. Thornton was not naive and had no illusions about those who wore brass knuckles and switchblade ruffians, but intuitively, he thought if they could be moved into a new and teaching environment which gave them the means of working with their hands, an attitudinal change might be made. Getting follow-on employment and drawing a wage regularly for constructively expended effort could reach some and perhaps a great many arousing a deeply buried urge to extricate themselves from central city urban morasses. "Poverty," he said often, "is not so much a lack of money as it is shortcomings in employable skills." He knew that 69% of the black population of 21,500,000 had left the land for metropolitan life, and substantial numbers knew it was a very mean life. No jobs where they were caused great migrations to big cities where there were no jobs either for the untrained. It was only a change, and mostly for the worse.

Litton found quickly that addressing sociological ills might be considered necessary at the Washington seances, and even noble in the eyes of some who weren't going to do more than observe, but it was given a kind of community wide heave-ho rejection when scouting for locations for its Center. It snagged new nerves never before encountered. Duluth, Salt Lake City,[6] Lubbock and Woodland Hills which

---

6. Sharp contrasts were Salt Lake City where Mormon Church President McKay, no less, sent for Dr. Norman Moore, Roy Woenne, and the Litton resident manager, Vin Carver, then working out of an old downtown building at 225 East Broadway. He wanted to let them know that Litton was the kind of industry Utah wanted. Any fancied difficulty about suitable labor force disappeared overnight as applications flooded in from the east, particularly New England where many Brigham Young and University of Utah graduates had gotten employment after graduating in electrical engineering. They yearned for their old Utah haunts, families friends and religious

had shouted welcomes with their industrial development hearts going pitterpat had no counterparts to aid Litton in its quest for this residence. There were no lollipops such as community industrial parks with their inducements packaged as lures into or near population centers for this attack on America's societal open lesions.

The Office of Economic Opportunity had a partial solution to these community aversions. The General Services Administration had all those closed, or near abandoned military bases across the country. These were installations where there was a more or less pleasantly or tolerably remembered association. The Army, Navy, Air Force and Marine Corps, when using such premises, had worked with neighboring towns through cooperative committees made up of the power structure or its designated representatives. This reduced chances of surprise, and provided a vehicle for coordinating any changes such as base strength adjustments upward forecasting a housing crunch or diminishing personnel numbers with downside economic impact. All very tidy, well oiled and with time's passage such Federal acreage's slipped into local terminology as "our base" or "our facility." An old eyesore building downtown was usually given a bunting and banner treatment and new life as a USO (United Service Organizations) lounge. This was a rest and recreation stop for getting the weight off one's feet and enjoying a little hospitality for those in uniform when off the reservation. It was not exactly a substitute for the beckoning bars or the hookers, but it was a choice.

This was light years different. Patriotism was almost an unmentionable in the '60s, so none invoked that. Job Corpsmen weren't to be in uniform, anyway. Litton was not alone in being a lightning rod for hostilities. There were 16 other major industrial firms given contracts for Job Corps operations. All had the same kinds of plague signs to reckon with and at least partially remove. Litton was first sent to Camp San Luis Obispo in California, one of the most charming

---

roots. Lubbock being one of Thornton's old stamping grounds when he attended Texas Tech, overturned another sterotyped concern and proved it groundless. The prevailing labor was migrant, mostly Chicano, and suspected to have gypsy tendencies when cotton crops ripened. The training difficulties which Dr. Steve Uslan had to surmount were not so difficult, but the thing most feared, Cliff Scheffler remembers, never materialized at all. The Chicanos loved permanence and set remarkable records for retention, good and faithful service. It was an early breakthrough in demolishing a long held conviction.

locations in that big state. Less than 24 hours after Uslan had done his inspection walkthrough with the camp's custodial officer who he briefed on what Litton's plans were, Washington told them to look elsewhere. Uslan's escort had gone to a Kiwanis meeting downtown as soon as Uslan left, and with the movie "Asphalt Jungle" playing at the local theater to underscore the kind of "young hoodlums" who would come to Camp San Luis Obispo held let the membership know what was about to happen. Every phone in town sought a Washington connection, and the outcry was heeded.

OEO told Litton to look at old Parks Air Force Base, nestled south and east of Oakland with bedroom villages all around named Pleasanton, Livermore and Dublin. All of them were attractive to their residents for the very fact that they were retreats from the turmoils of metropolitan inner cities. The Santa Rita prison was just across the road from Pleasanton, largely peopled by the refuse of drug addiction and alcoholism, these short-termers once their needle holes had scabbed, their shakes lessened, and their interiors dried out and partially mended returned to their pushers and wino life to renew their pleasures. Santa Rita's clientele was bearable while there because they were secure during their sentences and took off immediately on the next bus for the bright lights when released. But a Job Corps Center, and all those terrible, pathetic youthful dregs? It was too much and the countryside erupted fire, brimstone and ash!

Here was the Federal Government, those Washington "do-gooders," using a surrogate—Litton Industries—which should have known better. Litton, like some sanitation district employee gone mad, was now licensed to go berserk and engage in wholesale littering of decent people's doorsteps with these culls and sore-beset. The kids were streetwise and carried concealed weapons. Barracks or dormitories sheltering them were ideal labs for youthful gang formation. Townspeople knew none of these things, but they feared them mightily. What they saw as their vision was enough. Their conversational get-togethers and neighborhood coffee klatching conjured up horror on horror.

Pleasanton, the nearest town had only one black among its 4,000 people. He was the librarian, and they sent him home at night, so with sundown it was all white there. Community duress and distress had not been much of the Washington think tank theorizing when Job

Corps was being conceived and regimentation—the very thought of it—was repugnant. All Job Corps trainees were "voluntary," not forced or to be rigidly tied to any center. They could stay or they could leave. There were to be no uniforms. Viet Nam was a rising campus concern and everybody said the smartest generation was now in the nation's higher learning experience. The Free Speech Movement was the Berkeley smudge pot just up the road. There was more ferment in the Bay Area than all the grapes in Napa Valley had known. Pleasanton, after protests which turned out nearly half its inhabitants in mass meetings of shaking fists and hurled imprecations, declared itself OFF LIMITS. The community quarantine sign went up. No matter who or what monstrosities the U.S. government rounded up to ship to that Litton Parks Job Corps Center, there would never be any of its trainee population crossing that busy, broad highway. The Litton proposal said it would teach the incoming youngsters automobile mechanics, business machine repair, electronics assembly, culinary arts, landscaping, building maintenance and custodial services. Parallel with the increasing decibels of uproar, Dr. Steve Uslan pulled a staff together, began the overhaul of the ramshackle and dilapidated buildings. Almost before they all know it, the day dawned for the first Job Corps trainees to arrive.

That was April 30, 1965. The Parks staff had been assembled with care, although the guidelines were vague. Washington said that there would be many surprises among the Job Corps youth. Some would be exceedingly intelligent. They had quit school for lack of challenge or some poor teacher experience or just a too intimidating environment. Litton and any other contractor had no right to take an advance peek at the trainees, or recruit or in any way select the incomers. It had to take whatever came by train, plane or bus, or even ferryboat. Often they should be expected to arrive without warning. Any place in the Bay region fed by some kind of passenger service had to have a Litton representative there to splice the incomers into transportation to the Parks Corps Center.

What would the first one be like? There was a ripple of prickly suspense as the bus rolled through the gates and up to the staff reception group. As whoever was first was a piece of history, still and movie cameras were at the ready, tape recording machines, newsmen and women. For better or for worse, whoever he was would be a milestone.

When he did come, the sight of him produced almost unbelievable relief. He was well dressed. He was black. He had a stunning, warm, wide smiling personality. His name was Griffin Braithwaite, III from Newark, N.J. He had long ago learned to play the "white man's game," Uslan said in retrospect. He knew how to be charming, friendly, and being small only five feet four became everyone's mascot. The cameras and tapes rolled, and the bulbs flashed. The tapes took his words about what an opportunity he believed Job Corps was for him. Copious notes were made on yellow ruled tablets about individual impressions and appraisals of him. When it was all explained to him that he was given this attention because he could well be a significant moment in history, he became almost slavishly eager to cooperate. That cheered everyone into thinking that making good was his desire. In that the staff erred. Not so much was making *good* on his mind, but making *out*. But he cheered everyone into thinking he was a heartening beginning and no matter how the numbers of Corpsmen grew, Griffin Braithwaite III from the first had an established, special identity which found him well regarded and trusted by both the staff and his peers.[7]

As the Parks Job Corps Center ranks swelled, findings were appalling. More than 30% had never seen a doctor in their lives, and 100% had no knowledge of dentistry. The biggest outpatient requirement was for the most unexpected of physical disabilities — circumci-

---

7. Griffin Braithewaite III turned himself in one day when the FBI was investigating mysterious fires in the old barracks, now dormitories. He told Steve Uslan he was the arsonist and that he needed medical help. He even said he had stolen the suit he was wearing that day he arrived as he had so wanted to make a good impression. "Why would you confess?" Uslan asked in wonderment. "Nobody would have ever suspected you." Griffin said it was because of the "corpsmen government" program taught at Parks wherein whose who had grown up only fending for themselves were asked to consider that their misbehavior reflected on others. It was a first primitive introduction to responsibility for most of the Job Corpsmen. "I saw all my friends being questioned," he said, "and it was my fault. I've come to you for help." He was put under psychiatric care and while he was in no way the "success story" everyone had been hoping for, he was one in his own way. When Uslan briefed the staff and the press on how it all came about, there were editorials commending the Parks success with its Corpsmen Government course and arson was only mentioned in passing. Consensus: Litton was doing somehting right!

sions. Some were in such pain from this, from teeth abscesses, from hernias it was impossible to hold or even get their attention. Dr. Vinnie Platt, who had been a parachuting medic with Tom Dooley in Laos, was the least surprised, probably, but surprised nonetheless. He was used to the cruelties and inhumanities of Asia, but for the U.S., it bothered him. One of the most touching happenings was to him because he affected a Yul Brynner-Telly Savalas coiffure, skinbald.

When his clinic was overrun, he recruited a dozen young blacks to do various tasks around the place. Each morning he checked them carefully for clean nails, required that they wash up, looked them over for general hygiene needs, and they went along with it. But then they began to see what he could do and interested themselves more and more in how he alleviated suffering, how he could make comfortable the chronically ailing, his no-nonsense man-to-man manner. After a fortnight with him, they all came to the clinic on the following Monday with their heads shaved, just as he was! They told him he was the first man they'd ever met that they really admired and by going skinbald, it was their way of showing him that they wanted to be like him in some way. It was the only thing they could think of doing.

What a range of differences the youngsters displayed. The one who came from some small midwestern town, or the country, or the Eskimo from Alaska on being thrown in with someone from Harlem, Chicago's South Side or Watts was never any match for the wiliness, the con game artistry or in the simplest survival tactics. Some had parents, some had one parent, and there were those with relatives whose tie was maintained only enough to share in the monetary allowance Job Corps gave them to send home. When one Job Corpsman was killed in a drowning accident, a priest was sent to inform his mother. He found her with a half-killed bottle of rotgut and told her of the death of her son. She waved him off drunkenly and said: "I never wanted him anyway."

On July 27, 1967 after America's major cities had been in flames and gunfire punctuated nights, President Johnson appointed a special commission on Civil Disorders.[8] That same summer the Houston Po-

---

8. Tex Thornton was on that Commission on Civil Disorders because of arm-twisting by LBJ himself. He wanted someone with a practical background who had credibility with Congress, a man sensitive, experienced and who could suggest courses politically realizable — that old "art of the possible." When the Commission

After winning his Olympic Gold Medal in Mexico City and with $50.57 in his pocket as an amateur, George turned pro in late 1968.
L to R: Barney Oldfield, George Foreman, Doc Broadus

lice Department had run out of patience with a young black. He had
been in a pool hall trying to set up a game when the raspy radio came
on with a couple of public service announcements. One was by
Johnny Unitas, the Baltimore Colt quarterback, and the other by the
bone crushing Jim Brown of the Cleveland Browns. Both spoke of the
chance being offered to disadvantaged young people in the Job Corps.
The policemen who talked to him said he was coming to the end of his
string — and his freedom. Prison was his next stop, unless he chose
some remedial action quickly. With his mother's consent, and her relief, he took the Job Corps alternative mostly because he was high on
both the sports figures who said it was a good idea, and iron bars did
appear to fit his immediate future if he continued his flawed deportment. He went first to the Center in Oregon[9] and then transferred to
the Parks Job Corps Center. He was a certified troublemaker. Parks
classification cards carried notations about his brutalizing tendencies.
He used less than 100 words getting people to do nearly everything he
wanted from them by merely frowning his displeasure at them. If an
argument went against him, he delivered a mule kicking fist to the jaw
of his annoyance. It was lights out, and that ended that. He broke
trays over the heads of people in the cafeteria line ahead of him. The
clinic had to deal with broken jaws caused by some displeasure and
accompanying melee. His peers learned to kowtow or else.

He was assigned to the electronic assembler course. He dawdled
over the transistor radio whose parts they gave him. He was told if he

---

formed, it included: Chairman. Otto Kerner, the Governor of Illinois; New York's
Mayor John Lindsay; Senators Fred Harris, Oklahoma and Edward Brooke of Massa-
chusetts; Congressmen James Corman of California and William McCulloch of Ohio;
I.W. Abel, President of the United Steel-workers of America (AFL-CIO); Roy Wilkins of the National Association for the Advancement of Colored People; Katherine
Graham Peden, Commissioner of Commerce of Kentucky and Chief of Police Herbert
Jenkins of Atlanta. There was some rhubarb about why the firebrands were left off
such as Stokely Carmichael, Martin Luther King and Floyd McKissick instead of
Wilkins who they considered an "Uncle Tom", or Brooke, obviously in their eyes as
"establishment figure." Or, some radical such as Tom Hayden to roil the water. The
group was first convened in the Indian Treaty Room of the Old State, Army and Navy
Building, the room where Eisenhower's press conferences were held and TV coverage
first permitted, where he had declared the Supreme Court's decision on school deseg-
regation was sufficient to get on with it and needed no Presidential endorsement as if
it were toothpaste.

9. Now Community College, it was then Fort Vanning.

Became a penniless preacher and counselor on the Triple L Youth Ranch which had been established by his friend, Litton's Charles B. Tex Thornton, Foreman regained his title, in 1994 was picked by Forbes Magazine as the 'greatest salesman in the world'. Here he puts a headlock on the author.

did it right and it worked, the radio was his. He didn't show much enthusiasm, but when it did work, and he came by its ownership as a reward for his own handiwork he was impressed. Little did Tex Thornton and the young and surly black know that they were going to run into each other. His name: George Foreman.[10]

It would make a deep impression on them both which would last them all their lives. The certified juvenile delinquent? George Foreman!

By the time Thornton started to serve on the Commission of Civil Disorders and based on the company's considerable wading in educational needs, Litton was on its way into Strogoff's "knowledge industry" invasion plan. So were other companies such as Raytheon, RCA and General Precision. Al Strogoff, who had come to Litton with the Adler Electronics merger and had subsequently run the East Coast-based Litton Amecom division which included Adler, Westrex, Emertron, McKiernan-Terry and Maryland Electronics, was close enough to Washington to hear all the rumbles and about educational shortfalls and how they were being viewed with concern. The air was full of talk of teaching machines, community and junior colleges being needed and all the towering demands for the software of vocational education. Parks Job Corps Center was a veritable pipeline flooding him with the statistics of training necessities and opportunities as he read them.

Strogoff developed a plan to place Litton right in the midst of educational publishing, first in the L-High (elementary and High school), which could be extended into the junior college market. It made good on Steve Uslan's earlier projection of the legitimacy of being in the Job Corps programming to provide just such leads and data on which to make seasoned judgments. Roy Ash bought off on it as he was relieved to see Parks had something going for it besides engaging Litton in a social program. No matter the extent of Tex

---

10. Tex had taken me with him that day. He was fascinated with George, told me to "get next to him, help him." "Boss," I said with some concern, "have you seen his rap sheet. He's Mayhem, Inc." But we did hit it off, and when he was picked as the heavyweight on the U.S. Olympic (1968) Boxing team I was sent along to keep him out of the Olympic village as much as possible and away from recruiters for Sports Activist Harry Edwards "black power movement." They never got to him. And he waved that American flag!

Thornton's obvious emotional involvement in the Parks Job Corps Center and the amounts of time he spent going there to watch the trainees at their benches and listen to their stories, Litton's President never went there during the life of the contract except by telephone.

Strogoff had an "L-High" starting block, the old American Book Company.[11] Originally begun in 1890, it was a leading publisher of textbooks and audio-visual materials. It was more than just a publishing firm — it was also Norvell B. Samuels, a statesman in the educational textbook field. If he came in, others Strogoff was interested in would surely be intrigued and open their doors for conversations and perhaps would RSVP the Litton invitation to the party. On March 31, 1967, American book came into Litton and was given divisional status for 211,197 shares of Litton common and 515,101 shares of the Litton preference issue.[12]

---

11. In quick time, July 24, 1968, D. Van Nostrand and July 31st, Chapman-Reinhold was the result of consolidation of medical Economics, Inc. and Reinhold Publishing Corp. in May 1966. By Litton time there were four subsidiaries, Medical Economics, Reinhold Publishing, Medical Economics Books and Chapman-Reinhold Nederland, N.V. It had a Medical Economics Foundation supported by company contributions furthering medical education through scholarships and grants. Chapman had 1,250,000 shares outstanding, 85% of it in a small group and the other 15% with employees. Chapman brought out periodicals, catalogs and compendia in the medical and dental professions as well architectural, chemical, engineering and design fields and texts for trade, technical and college use. The price: $33,400,000 in Litton common, or about 400,000 shares. D. Van Nostrand involved a two-step action totaling $5,000,000, the initial gesture $4,250,000 in preference shares, the share price determined over 8 of 11 trading days preceding the transfer, with $750,000 a year later also in preference shares. Van Nostrand had subsidiaries in Canada, England, Australia and India. D. (for David Van Nostrand got into publishing in 1886 bringing out memoirs of Generals such as William Tecumseh Sherman, H.W. Halleck, Silas Casey, Philip St. George Cooke, Hugh L. Scott and Phil Sheridan, as well as Napoleonia and Fredericana from Europe and was into three languages early on. It was all eased into American Book by Strogoff along with McCormick-Mathers, and a Litton division, American Book-Van Nostrand-Reinhold Co., with Craig T. Senft, Edward N. Crane, Jr., and Lawrence Jackel the big executive names. While all this was going on, Van Nostrand editor William Steinkraus was using his off-hours training, carrying water to his horse, "Snow Bound", preparing for his fourth Olympic competition in Mexico City, come October.

12. McKiernan-Terry, manufacturer of radar antennas and precision mechanical equipment with defense and industry applications, built the huge Andover, Mass. tracking antennae that linked A.T.&T. with Telstar. The structure itself weighed nearly 400 tons and all to "hold onto" the 35-inches in diameter satellite travelling more than 16,000 miles an hour. President Carl Shattuck had an encounter with the

The author did his first ghostwritten piece for Nation's Business in April 1973, for which he was paid $999.99. That article became the magazine world's most reprinted, 34,000,000 copies sent to 160 countries of the world by the U.S. Information Agency, and was picked up by six Congressmen for entry in the Congressional record.

On Pepperdine University graduation day in 1999, Foreman saw his daughter graduate with honors, himself given an honorary doctorate in laws, being introduced by the widow of Tex, Flora Thornton, whispered to me afterward he had just been told he had a net worth of $243,000,000 and growing. He took the author on his lap to do this after all they had been through together.

Special Situation #14

The Thornton credentials for presence on the Presidential Commission on Civil Disorders were weighted heavily by the fact that he alone was working the problem by effort, investment of time and money, and down at the earth's crust level. The Parks Job Corps Center was running and nearly 2,000 high school dropouts were there. Some had already graduated into jobs in the skills in which they had been instructed. He and his company were dealing day-to-day and with some success with what the Commission had to contemplate and, after pondering, make recommendations of actions to the Oval Office. Litton had that big and early continuing commitment to vocational instruction in-house, and now on the school scene itself owned the No. 2 textbook supplier. Tex saw *work* as a four letter word entitled to respect, and people who did it, similarly entitled. He had formidable weapons at his disposal for that "war on poverty." And Litton worldwide was employing more than 95,000 men and women. He was actually engaged in the solving, while the others were probing for answers. Whatever side he came down on, he was entitled to a hearing and got it.

---

fast paced Litton stock price, too, the talks starting with 27,500 Litton common shares the agreed amount and closing anticipated Sept. 20, 1962. Litton split, Aug. 15, two-for-one, but rather than that taking the price up to 55,000 shares, Litton reduced its outlay to 40,000 of the new shares "subject to adjustments for stock splits and stock dividends." With the upwards-unlimited attitude of Litton shares then, there was no reason to quibble on the M-T side — nor did they. Emertron, whose major products were altimeters, radar beacons, electronic counter-measures, airborne fire control computers and simulators had 2,316,044 shares outstanding of which 2,000,000 were beneficially owned by Emerson Radio & Phonograph and Benjamin Abrams, its President and a Director. The encouragement for Abrams was Litton's offer of 79,000 of its common, plus $3,200,000 in its 3 1/2% convertible subordinated debentures, plus entitlement to the next stock dividend. Emertron was a Jersey City, N.J. firm, but its research laboratory in Silver Spring, Maryland and Field Engineering division in Washington, D.C. made its gathering into Amecom easy and sensible. Both were Litton owned by November 1962, not without a couple of twists. Because of the debenture involvement it was necessary to have Securities & Exchange Commission approval, and SEC had been waiting a long time for that moment — Litton had nearly 10,000,000 shares by then, had been on OTC, AMEX, and the NYSE, and had never registered with SEC! The other was Joe Casey's endurance of many an Essex House breakfast in New York with Abrams, who loved to plunge his spoon into his grapefruit for point emphasis. "He never tried to pull the wool over my eyes," said Casey later,"just blind me with squirting grapefruit juice."

There were times when he despaired of Kerner and Lindsay, who kept talking massive spending as a first and highest priority measure, with all other suggestions around the corner and away back second. He grew to firm respect for Roy Wilkins. Nighttimes they took long walks together around Washington. He recognized how much flak Wilkins had borne over the years with his "advancement" efforts, how his critics accused him of snail's pace and cried out for speedups in the progress without seeming to know or credit him for getting his race a hearing in high places. Tex Thornton became so upset by the spending recommendations forming up that he started talking of a minority report which he would file separately along what he thought were more practical and solution-reaching approaches.

From that August to November 1967, 130 people appeared before the Commission on Public Disorders to air their opinions and be questioned about ideas they had. There were tours of the riot-rubbled 23 cities and 44 days of meetings, those proceedings resulting in 3,900 pages of transcripts. A second panel[13] was constituted under Thornton, an advisory group on private enterprise to ". . . assist the Commission and Staff and formulating recommendations for increasing employment opportunities." It wasn't the threatened minority report exactly, but it was attached to the main one to stand in bold relief. President Johnson had asked the Commission three questions: What happened? Why did it happen? What can be done to prevent it happening again? One point was staggering – 10,000,000 people were under-employed of which 6,500,000 worked fulltime for wages below the poverty line and half a million were "hard core" jobless in central cities lacking education and unable to hold steady jobs. This was in large part 18 to 25-year old black males. Blacks were found three times as likely to be relegated to unskilled, part-time seasonal, low-paying, "dead end" employment as whites. "Education," the report stated, "in a democratic society must equip children to develop their potential and participate in American life."

---

13. The National Advisory Panel on Private Enterprise, chaired by Charles B. Thornton, included John Leland Atwood, North American Rockwell Corp.; Martin Gainsbrugh, National Industrial Conference Board; Walter E. Hoadley, Bank of America; Louis F. Polk, General Mills, Inc., and Lawrence M. Stone, University of California, Berkeley.

As the Commission was scratching signatures on the report, Dr. Steve Uslan had a big problem on his hands at the Parks Job Corps Center. "That kid from, Houston," his irate staff told him to a man, "We have to get him out of here, get rid of him. He is a menace to all the others, and to the staff, too." As far off as Washington, R. Sargent Shriver was up to his backside in crocodiles politically anyway. He didn't need this. He had decreed that the Job Corps Centers should purge themselves, get rid of the troublemakers. They were giving Job Corps a bad name, OEO said. Usland listened to Washington and to his associates. Only he stood between them and his problem. "He should be in some jail somewhere," he was told, "Because he'll get there sooner or later."

"But that's what we're here for," Uslan reminded them. "It's no solution to hand problems like this off to some other agency. We're supposed to correct things like this. Let me talk with him."

Uslan sent out word for this Mayhem, Inc. to report to his office. Soon his door opened and the big, black, unshaven giant flopped in the chair by Uslan's desk. His head was hanging down. He'd been drinking. He didn't care what was going to happen to him. Most of what could occur had been on his lap before, yet he was not out of his teens for all his huge size. His great proportions had found him being hired at $1.25 an hour to unload trucks at warehouses, sometimes ten to twelve hour days. When he was paid, it was at a dollar an hour, the foreman on the job pocketing the rest. He might not look it, but he was still a kid. Uslan studied the dossier on his desk and told him it was his prerogative to dismiss him, send him packing, forget him, but he wasn't about to take that easy way out.

"Since you like to fight so much," Uslan said, "I've called 'Doc' Broadus down in the gym. I've told him to put the gloves on you and let every big guy we've got here beat on you until you're sick of it." The Houston corpsman shuffled out, not worried. He knew alleys and street brutalities and what fists were for — it wasn't even nominal punishment. The next thing Uslan knew, an excited Broadus was on the phone.

"This kid's got the makin's of a champion," he said.

"Oh, no," pleaded Uslan. "I wanted you to beat the fight *out* of him, not the other way around." But he had other things of a personal nature to deal with, as he had gotten caught in crossfire between

Strogoff and Harry Gray.[14] Uslan left the Job Corps and Litton. As he was going out the front gate, he heard that the black puncher, awkward and slow, had won in Golden Gloves competition in San Francisco. He was sent off to Milwaukee for the American Amateur Union, and he won. In Toledo, incredibly, he snagged the heavyweight berth on the U.S. Olympic Team bound for Mexico City. There, in the boxing finals in Arena Mexicana against a bloodied Soviet Iones Chepulis, that "kid from Houston" — George Foreman — won the Gold Medal. In the exuberance of being such a resounding winner which he had never known before, he waved a small American flag in the ring. That simple act was seen by satellite by 500,000,000 people all over the world.[15]

In all his Olympic Village time when George Foreman was being interviewed and asked where he was from, he always said: "Pleasanton, California." That's where Litton's Parks Job Corps Center was even if it had always been OFF LIMITS to him and his fellow Corpsmen.

What he had done was not lost on President Lyndon B. Johnson, either. Although he had said it was too cumbersome logistically to see the whole U.S. Olympic Team, he made an exception in the George Foreman case. He sent word for Foreman, along with Tex Thornton, and Eugene Allen, the Parks director who had replaced Uslan, to visit him in the White House so he could congratulate that particular Gold Medalist in person. Foreman could hardly believe it, all the people looking up to him. There was much dismay about other black Olympians who had used that sports platform as a "black power" preachment. Before going to Washington Foreman did something on

---

14. Dr. S.S. Uslan became a popular Pepperdine University School of Business and Management professor as well as busy consultant for industry and government agencies. His students respected him as they did few others as his "Litton laboratory experience" contrasted sharply with the usual podium prescriptions laced with theory. None in any of his classes ever sought employment in that great subsequent Harry Gray empire, United Technologies. His management style was too often used by Uslan as an example before his classes.

15. The 1968 Olympics fielded 312 boxers from 70 nations. Iones Chepulis, the Soviet entry, won the silver medal; Giorgio Bambini, of Italy, and Joaquin Rochat of Mexico, tied for the bronze. As Chepulis had taken out Rochas, the Mexican national hero, by the time he faced Foreman everyone in Mexico was cheering for Foreman.

his own, "Every time I see the President," he said vaguely, "he's always givin' somebody somethin'." He didn't say what it was.

George Foreman, the disinterested electronic assembler who had been "punished" by Steve Uslan by being sentenced to the Parks Job Corps center "rec" hall, was about to turn professional. Litton planned to keep him on as a "rec" hall assistant until he decided to leave the nest. There in the White House Oval Office, with more than 40 pressroom habitues including photographers watching, Foreman unwrapped a small plaque he had made for the occasion. In that special room which has an aura grand enough to dizzy heads of state, the former almost inarticulate ghetto castoff said: "Mr. President, I brought this little plaque for you. It says: "To Lyndon Baines Johnson, President of the United States from George Foreman 1968 Heavyweight Olympic Gold Medal winner . . . in appreciation for fathering the Job Corps, which gives young Americans like me a chance for hope dignity and self-respect!" That was too strong sentimental medicine for even a seasoned old political hand like LBJ, as he was being cuffed around a lot at that time about Viet Nam. A tear started down his left cheek. He got hold of himself quickly.

"Thank you, George," he said. "I think I'm going to add you to my staff here. You make these presentations a lot better than I do."

He waved the plaque toward the White House press corps so they could see it.

"I'm going to put it here right on the desk next to mine, where all these guys can see it. Every time they come in here from now on, it'll remind 'em that there's somebody somewhere who thinks I did something right."[16]

---

16. In all the magnificence of the Lyndon Baines Johnson Library on the campus of the University of Texas at Austin, visitors are barely inside the door when they see an edited typewritten manuscript page from his memoirs which reads: "When I left office government reports showed that 13,000,000 Americans who had lived in poverty in 1964 had been lifted out, not only because of the war on poverty, but also because of the expanding economy. People were coming out of poverty two and a half times faster than at any time in history. We started something in motion with the attack on poverty. Its effects were felt in the fields of education, law, medicine and social welfare, by business and industry, in civil and philanthropic life, in the labor movement and in religion. Poverty was one of the compelling issues of our time. Finally and firmly, it was brought to the conscience of the nation." Since President Johnson died only four hours before George Foreman won his heavy weight chan-

The LITTON Adventure That Was

Foreman was on a diet of that Jackie Gleason "how sweet it is!", but never abrasive about it. In Mexico City he had gotten out of the Olympic Village to visit the Litton Triad de Mexico plant in its rundown industrial neighborhood. More than 400 little girls had screamed their heads off, so flattered that an Olympic competitor had come to see them. They promised they'd watch him in every fight and they did. To do so, they had no TV sets of their own and had to scout neighborhood bars so they could stand in the street and cheer him. Chepulis, the Russian, had beaten the Mexican heavyweight in the semi-finals, so Foreman to them was also an avenger. So many people "looking up to me," George kept saying. But it was Pleasanton, the town which had been the noisiest in its demands that Litton not locate the Job Corps Center there, where it all came home to roost. The town decided that for the one who had claimed them publicly as fellow home towners they should do something, so swallowing hard they arranged a welcome for Foreman. He was their conquering hero and the town's No. 1 publicist. He'd put them on the map. Some of the civic leaders accompanied by about 50 white and small school children lined up at the flagpole near the Parks hilltop headquarters. Foreman was coming in from San Francisco by helicopter. The kids waited excitedly as the craft came overhead, circled, then settled down in a cloud of dust and cinders.

There he stood, proud, well dressed, tall and still in a tizzy inside by his transition. His Olympic Gold Medal hung around his neck. As he walked toward the flagpole, that chorus of little voices started singing "America the Beautiful"! Down the line of them he went, each of them feeling and admiring the gold medal. One of the Pleasanton elders afterward, his eyes still misted said: "I guess I never really heard

---

pionship in Jamaica, and George was the most famous Job Corps graduate, Mrs. Lyndon Johnson invited Foreman to give his memorabilia to the LBJ Library which makes him the first champion to become a part of a Presidential heritage. The Johnson inclusion of "business and industry" was a bow to the memory of those 'little Congress' days when he and Tex Thornton had helped Texas Congressman George Mahon keep in touch with his back home constituency in the '30s. In 1997, George Foreman, who used TV every which way endowed a George Foreman Tribute to Lyndon Johnson annual scholarship in the Radio & TV News Directors Foundation with a $100,000 Check. It is always to go to a University of Texas Journalism student who must visit George's memorabilia in the LBJ Library and have a picture taken.

the words to that song before." That line ". . . and crown thy good with brotherhood. . ." had gotten to him.

Strogoff was hotly after continuing education. For all the success story of a George Foreman, he knew that such things as the Jobs Corps were band-aids at best. There was that critical transition from elementary to high school, then college, and beyond that, renewal and updating in one's profession where the track is fast and it is easy to become passé! Entry into college and university level textbook publishing brought up several companies ripe for talks of merging. If Strogoff could pick up every one he had on his tick list, Litton in one year would be the No. 1 educational publisher. The heavy emphasis was on the medical field, hewing to Litton's long expressed interest in health care as a corporate place to be. In Chapman-Reinhold Litton had that, but there was Saunders Publishing, Richard Irwin, plus the college book lines of Academic Press among his "most desired". CBS, coming on fast with its big black eye on the "knowledge industry", got Saunders and Academic Press and Dow Jones, the social sciences and continuing education house, Richard Irwin. Litton's bartering paper was in steady decline. Strogoff found himself unable to quiet expressed fears on the other sides of the table.

On the very last day of the 1968 Olympics, that final Grand Prix Equestrienne event was won by D. Van Nostrand's[17] editor, William

---

17. The D. Van Nostrand catalog contained one especially historic asset, the plates of the original primer and six grades of William Holmes McGuffey's eclectic readers. McGuffey, born in 1800, ushered in a first printing of such books in 1836. Between that date and 1901, more than 122,000,000 of them were sold. As early as 1642 in America, Massachesetts legislators were first with concerns about whether Johnny and Jane could read. There was a law making it possible to fine any family head $25 if he didn't provide proper reading instruction for his growing children. McGuffey gave the publishing rights to a printer for $3,000. That was only monetary reward he received for arming the schoolteacher who brought learning to the frontier, reducing the ignorance and brutality with which any America that would progress had to cope. Between 1870 and 1890, the McGuffey Readers were the exclusive texts used in elementary schools in 37 states. McGuffey never looked back. He was a University of Virginia professor for the last 30 years of his life. He died there in 1873. That same year, his grateful publishers stopped their annual custom — which was to send him a barrel of hams each Christmas, that being the parallel with residuals of TV today. In 1977, after all the arguments about whither-goest-education in recent times, Mesdames Genevieve Clements and Laura Tyler came to Litton Industries and told Executive Vice President Joseph T. Imirie they wished to start a back-to-basics private learning center. They wanted to use the McGuffey Readers and call it "the

The LITTON Adventure That Was

Steinkraus, giving him an Olympic Gold Medal after 25 years of horse shows all over the world. Litton found itself sitting with an extraordinary sports metaphor — George Foreman, a truly symbolic "internal growth" specimen, and Steinkraus who came by acquisition — true to the mold of Litton and how it came to be. By their two rousing performances, Litton could claim more Gold Medals than 92 competing nations in the XIXth Olympiad!

That December's annual meeting in 1968 was bound to be a rough encounter session. The stock was away off. The size of the Ingalls Ship building obligations was dawning. Litton was well over the threshold of what would be its difficult decade. Corporate Secretary George Fenimore was compiling questions probably to be expected, so the answers could be processed ahead of time and be accurate and explanatory. No one wanted any off-the-top-of-the-head surmises that time. The numbers of possible queries grew to almost book size. Unnerving as it all might be there in the Santa Monica Auditorium, Tex Thornton wanted to do something before formally calling the meeting to order. He hoped it would be as special to the shareholders as it was to him, and that they could have a small rosy glow of satisfaction, too. For it, he secured the footage of the Litton Gold Medalists from ABC's Olympic coverage from Roone Arledge. He asked both William Steinkraus and George Foreman to attend. He showed the Steinkraus clip first, then introduced the impeccably tailored editor from best schools and right-side-of-the-tracks birth.

"I feel like Lee Marvin when he got that Academy Award for 'Cat Ballou'," Steindraus said with polished ease. "I owe at least half of this honor to the horse." There was a titter of polite laughter and applause. He was so seasoned, poised and sophisticated, a social celebrity for a quarter century.

A tension filled the huge hall, and the film sequence showed Foreman pulverizing the Soviet Union's pride, Chepulis. He was clumsy, but Foreman could hit. The audience could almost feel the denting impact of those murderous fists. It was the epitome of Man's oldest primitive struggle to survive. None ever wore it more truly into a ring than George Foreman. And there on film at the end, he did that

---

McGuffey School". He gave them permission, wished them well, and they started at 1071 South Fairfax in Los Angeles with a single student. By 1981, the McGuffey School had more than 100 students and growing steadily.

simple boyish thing, waving the American flag in victory as he bowed all directions from the ring. All of the Madison Avenue advice in the world could never have produced the spontaneity of what he'd done and the sentimental warmth it generated. Tex Thornton asked him to join him up there with the Board of Directors.

All six-feet-three of Foreman came out of his front row seat and with power radiating out from him, he strode to the podium. Once he may not have been handy with words, or what would be appropriate for an occasion, but that was behind him. Only he really sensed what an achievement he was. He knew all his alley-cat background where he said his idea of the future was wondering on waking each morning if he would go to bed that night without being cut. He gripped the sides of the lectern in those big hands, looking out at the sea of faces owned by people who were investors in a company he'd never heard of two years before. All of them were that anonymous "they" he and his streetwise friends had used as excuses for their plights and failures to do well. At that moment, he knew that wasn't true. They were all for him, proud of him, pleased that Litton whatever its misgivings had gone sociological as well as technological.

"Mr. Thornton, ladies and gentlemen," he said, "I want to thank you all for bein' the kind of company you are or you'd never have taken a chance on me!" That was all he said. But suddenly everybody in that big auditorium was on his or her feet, clapping, roaring, stomping — an ovation, no less. Charles R. "Doc" Broadus, the one who had gotten him for "punishment" in the Parks gym, was an ex-Army welterweight and watching all this from his front seat. He had gone with Foreman to the Olympics as his corner man. This was his moment, too. He had prophesied that George Foreman had the makings of a champion. Up there with the board of Directors was Lehman Brothers' Joe Thomas taking it all in. He had been in that investor group which had gotten behind a talkative and attractive Louisville, Kentucky-born Gold Medal winner in Rome 8 years before, Cassius Clay. When the meeting broke and the Board adjourned to the Thornton home for postmortems, the two medalists were on every tongue, especially Foreman.

"I couldn't believe it," said Glen McDaniel, who had been wary about how this all might have been too circusy for the annual meeting ritual. "I looked out at that audience and there was my wife, Marilyn.

310

She knows nothing about boxing, but there she was on her feet, tears in her eyes, applauding."

It was a big lesson for Litton that day, that there could be another side to a company besides its numbers which the shareholder family could find interesting.

The Parks Job Corps Center contract did more than get Litton Industries into the "knowledge" business.[18] Over four years and two months, 14,000 youngsters from every state spent training time there. George Foreman was the most famous and identifiable Job Corpsman of them all. He was far from alone in finding a way into trades and professions. He was just more visible. Litton's Parks experience began with arsonist Griffin Braithewaite, Ill on April 30, 1965, and the last Corpsman went out the gate when it closed on June 19, 1969 with a junior college scholarship in hand.[19] The first left for medical and

---

18. The last to leave Litton's Parks Job Corps Center was Waymond B. Long, an 18-year old Florida youth. He had been one of 2,089 of the roster to get his General Educational Development (GED) certificate, the equivalent of a high school diploma and accepted as such by most employers. Long was one of Litton's 700 corpsmen alumni who had a scholarship, and did go on to a junior college. (Then) Center Director Eugene V. Allen expressed his appreciation to "thousands of people who gave unselfishly of time, money and goodwill in behalf of many of these young people who came as strangers and left with memories of close friends." On the 4th anniversary of the arrival of the first trainee who was a psychiatric case and an arsonist, the Center records showed 7,078 as certified placed employees, which grew to nearly 9,500, when all the reports were in.

19. Litton's Parks Job Corps Center alumni are found today as chefs in good restaurants, mechanics wiwth Volkswagen and Ford, business machine repairmen, McDonald's and Col. Sanders franchise owners, teachers, park and recreation empoyees, a few are doctors and one is the groundskeeper at Hollywood's last stop for the famous, Forest Lawn Memorial Park. Some were losers when they came and left as losers, too. It was costing the State of California $8,000 a year to institutionalize Santa Rita prison inmates just over the fence from the Jobs Corpsmen who were nicking the federal government about $6,000 each anually while in training. George Foreman cost the U.S. Government $9,000 for his Job Corps stay, and for the fight in which he lost the championship — against Muhammad Ali in Zaire, he paid IRS about $2,500,000. Not a bad return on *investment*. When TIME, April 14, 1980 did its feature about the "socially responsible" corporate chieftains, Marshall Loeb who wrote it ticked off the "activists" in what he called "the Class of the '70s". They included Irving Shapiro, DuPont; Reginald Jones, GE; Citicorp's Walter Wriston and AT&T's John DeButts, but there was no mention of Tex Thornton. He had taken his lumps for being "ahead of the pack" in the 1960s. He had been to Washington first and knew it well, the others were businessmen who went to Washington in what was called "enlightened self-defense". Going into the '70s, Tex made that million-plus

psychiatric reasons after being a firebug, the last with his eye on continuing his education.

The biggest postscript of all was the Ingalls Shipbuilding requirement to grow to an employee level of more than 25,000 for the LHA and DD-963 contracts. Pascagoula, Mississippi was not a locale in high favor with shipyard labor. The alternative was to set up a vocational training establishment on the site by the Gulf of Mexico and take anyone who came to the gates expressing an interest in employment. They were put through intensive instruction in all the appropriate skills to become painters, metal workers, shipfitters, electricians and all the kinds of specialties needed to take a ship from blueprint to being floated. The recruiting was concentrated in the 20 southern Mississippi and 15 Alabama countries which came to provide 95% of Ingalls labor. More than 20,000 were trained there, and it became truly the "skill school" for America's whole shipbuilding industry. What's more, Litton was by this time at ease with minority labor and fully a third were from the ample resources in the area. It was the population which otherwise could have been frustrated for lack of field and day work into migrating to inner cities of the north and west to further swell and complicate the teeming ghettos. By long expertize and experience with skill instruction, retraining methods and upgrading on the job, Litton Industries not only built the finest ships of the line but provided the means of economic mobility for thousands.

The Thornton thesis, which he outlined once before the Harvard Business School Association, was that ". . . free enterprise is based on the individual, so all individuals must be developed to a greater potential if we are to get the best from our system. As the principal element is industry, it should take an even greater part in this development process." He had good reasons to mean what he said.

Litton had been a proving ground.

---

personal gift of what became the 3,200-acre Triple L Youth Ranch in Center, Colorado as a child-caring haven for court-awarded, troubled youngsters. To a man such as Tex Thornton, that kind of youth would always show in society, and some means of giving it a hand should be there, one way or another. George Foreman, who'd lost his heavyweight title to Muhammad Ali in 1974, was having an identity crisis and Tex Thornton, put him on its board of directors.

SPECIAL SITUATION #15

THE LONG REACH OF A TECHNOLOGY

A technical method of achieving a practical purpose is what technology is; the totality of means employed to provide objects necessary for human sustenance and comfort as well as safety and security.

Josh Billings, that old and homely philosopher, said: "There ain't nothin' easy to write as poetry—if you know how." Technology, particularly with the preceding qualifier of *high*, came into the American consciousness and value system as the outer edge of what nations had, or needed to have, to enjoy a seat on this spinning earth when World War II ended. America was wallowing rich in technologies and was inclined to be generous with them. Technologies had been around a long time before that, spottily over the geography, but it burst as some holiday fireworks display with the arrival of peace. American business and industry were its principal igniters to usher in the last half of the 20th Century. A global conflict had gone into the hands of the victors because the United States in its remoteness from bombing and cannon range had mobilized its assembly lines and its technological wealth, while other countries had called up their birthrates and in many cases had sacrificed them. All things were possible, as Josh Billings said, if one knows how and has the means, the imagination, and the motivation.

Electronics was into its heyday. With electronics providing coupling, seven league boots were no longer the props of fairy tales. There were means of propulsion which made men able to move faster than the speed of sound while earth orbits and escape from gravity were attainable.

Litton from its earliest days had its hands on such technologies as microwave, numerical controls, specialized computers, inertial navigation, health care,[1] food preparation, educational aids, geophysical ex-

---

1. Profexray came into Litton August 1, 1964 for $590,000 in cash and $2,400,000 in Litton preferred stock. The sellers wee the Rosadel S. Vatz Trust Funds, whose trustees were Theodore H. Vatz, C. William Vatz, Theodore Zekman and Max Robert Schrayer and the Barbara Vatz Trust Fund, for which Zekman and Schrayer were trustees. It was a family affair, a small firm faced off against the bigger manufacturers such as General Electric and Westinghouse. To be competitive, the management was faced with a requirement to expand. It had no wish to put the clan's money back into the business to bring it up to a competitive level. Merger was

ploration, the components capability, radio frequency, word processing, command and control systems, machine tools, specialty paper, inventory control and accounting systems, conveyors and shipbuilding. The Litton leadership was certain that some of these had endless and enduring extensions, not only those already indicated and evolving, but the ones on which there would be serendipity stumblings. In some, of course, the record would finally show the company had only stumbled. But it was so right, excitingly right, and in some cases extravagantly right far more often than it came a-cropper. Rather than the quick "out," it hung on unbelievably long rather than take accountant's advice—cut loose early and board up the doors of the misfits—because there were people involved. It was Tex Thornton's oft-stated position that he was in the "people business." It was people who ripened a technology, adapted it, extended it and they were entitled to consideration as a most important company asset.

Soviet Academician Nikolay G. Basov, 1964 Nobel Prize Winner for fundamental work in quantum electronics, questioned Tex Thornton in great detail in Moscow at the Lebedev Institute of Physics. How he arrived at decisions as an industrialist of first rank on convertibility of research to products? Basov said that 70% of his effort was devoted to keeping research aimed at specific stated objectives of the recurring 5-year plans, while 30% was his allowance for straying into interesting avenues hoping to mine something from some beckoning promise or another. Thornton had no idea what it must be like in that Soviet controlled society, but he could visualize it as something like sliding down a picket fence. Chairman Vladimir A. Kirillin of the State Committee on Science and Technology sat with Prime Minister Aleksei Kosygin and their Council of Ministers, those Ministers heading the various industrial and professional empires for the whole country. It made him shudder to think how tortuous it must be to swim an idea upwards through all those layers of bureaucracy toward a stamp

---

decided to be the answer. Quickly picked up were several distributors of x-ray equipment such as Heether, in Jacksonville, Florida; Hamer in Minneapolis; Magnuson in Los Angeles; Wittenberg in New York; Finnegan in Menlo Park, Calif. and the Twin City Tool Co. in Grandview, Mo., which Profexray used as an equipment manufacturer. Starting in 1967, a series of Dental Supply houses were added. The biggest health move of all was in 1968, the acquisition of Bionetics Research Laboratories. This put the company into a research mode relative to various cancer hazards and afflictions leading to a whole spate of government and private contracting ties.

of approval, a go-ahead and getting the funds earmarked in the next 5-year plan—then implementation. The timing had to be staggering, the coordination of effort preposterous. And once on the way that technological adventure was required to run unchanged. It would finally be delivering a product which was out of date but newly produced. This made it seem better only because it compared well with whatever antiquity was previously used to perform that function.

Free competition, he told Basov, had a way of speeding up decisions. No technology could endure, as is, in the West unless it was perpetually being freshened. Technology had to be built on, improved, prodded and poked into desired and often unforeseen avenues magnetic and utilitarian enough to cause the compulsion to ownership. That ownership could be by an individual or any sized needing entity all the way up to a government—for a price it would be willing to pay. It was always more exciting to be killed off in the marketplace, Thornton said, or to win a market share by such things rather than die at the hands of a bureaucrat, a safe player, or an envious colleague strategically placed who could block the imaginative innovator. At Litton, Thornton told Basov, the ears at the top were available to everyone. The go-aheads for a technology were almost casually given once the statistics were lined up favoring the move and the leadership's intuitions had gauged the talent and the stamina of the proposer.

First out of the gate from Electron Tube in San Carlos, in an important way was the potential of the microwave for entry into the home. San Carlos had people who had worked with microwaves in several mediums. The microwave inhabits that portion of the electromagnetic spectrum in approximate frequencies of 100 to 300,000 megacycles per second with wavelengths from one meter to one millimeter. This is known as the "microwave region." Before a microwave oven was to become a fact for Litton, there were many other than technological and money considerations. Money? Yes, indeed.

Dr. Norman Moore, once Charlie Litton's company became the Litton root, was having spells of prickly heat sensing other opportunities. He fretted. He walked up and down. He pushed to get a charter to head into Litton's first consumer, or domestic presence—the American kitchen. In a company such as Litton, there was no time for engineers entertaining and playing to an audience of other engineers. They, no matter how sharp, had to be housebroken into a profit relationship as quickly as possible. The Thornton-Ash picture of such efforts was in the clear perspective of usefulness and marketability. While Academician Basov specified that only 70% of his jurisdictional responsibility was so pinned down, Litton wanted to be as close as possible to 100% pointed to product derivatives. They never even had to be first, just participatory. Raytheon, struggling for years with Perry Spencer's microwave oven, had known big frustrations and bigger losses.[2] Dr. Norman Moore's experience of a hard time and close questioning spun off the Raytheon troubles and to determine whether he had thought things through. Had he been less enthusiastic and irrepressible by nature he would surely have given up.

The Thornton-Ash reservations were calculated over broader cloth, how deciding to go all out would be interpreted by the host of "Litton watchers."

When Joseph Imirie came on the corporate headcount to run the company's Industrial and Professional Group, how much weighting to give this action which was answerable to him occupied him, too. None among them was disinterested, but all were calculating. Was the time right, and how consumed was Moore and how determined about

---

2. Perry Spencer was not alone in the knowledge that the magnetron generated heat, but he took an important next step. He got a bag of popcorn and placed the kernels in front of the hornlike waveguide whose face was notepad size. The popcorn instantly danced into fluffy flakes. Next he tried an egg and netted another discovery. The egg cooked so quickly its shell exploded. Cooking by "radio" it was first called, the agent which caused it all being the microwave. Spencer, with colleagues Laurence Marshall and Fritz Gross believed it necessary to imprison the microwaves in a closed, shielded space, an oven-resembling niche or cavity where the food could be placed. From the very start they sought to restrict radiation leakage. Their first enclosed space was a common garbage can in which when the magnetron was turned on, water boiled. A trip through the supermarket was made to get packaged cake, muffin and biscuit mixes. These were given varied times and amounts of magnetron exposure for different sized batches. Their lab so reeked of the sweetish odors of gingerbread which they used most often in their experimentation, they never liked gingerbread for as long as they lived after that. Otto L. Scott, in his book, "The Creative Ordeal," spotted at once the difficulty which tempered their enthusiasms: "In microwave cooking . . . no customer was either at hand or visible on the horizon. Who would sell the oven? How would salesmen he selected and organized? How would the oven be distributed? Finally, to whom would it be sold?" By the time Perry Spencer died at 76 in 1970, Litton was already proving Roy Ash right in not having to be first to do well. Litton's ovens were in 10,000 restaurants, more than 50,000 food centers, and Litton was predicting 1,000,000 of its ovens in use in another five years.

seeing it to fruition? There was no doubt of microwave technology's versatility. It could serve in many ways. In its several military versions it was already doing so. For Litton, given its magnetron, excellence, and course record, getting to an oven which would work well was not nearly as standoffish as the change of attitude that must be brought about among kitchen inhabitants.[3]

The Litton dilemma was based on whether there could be a quick mass acceptance for this first real change in the classical approach to cooking in centuries. The best item in the world which would sell slowly if at all hardly charmed the Litton leadership, nor the shareholders who were almost "cultish" in their admiration for the company. It was an "in" thing to be a holder of Litton securities. People often tried to one-up each other in claims of investment canniness by comparing dates of first ownership of the high flyer's stock. The decision to place the bet on this first example of technological extension—the microwave oven—and push it to a technical and profitable maturity by entering the commercial mainstream was not lightly taken. It could just be the proof of the contention that the original Charlie Litton enterprise was just as Wall Street-smart as it was an opportunities grab bag from which Litton could grow up and out. In-

---

3. A young America had been built around cooking fires historically, as it was in perpetual movement with life lived in the open. Wild game and fish were staples of sustenance. It wasn't until the 19th century that the cook stove, made of cast iron with an oven for baking took victuals warming from the fireplace. Cooking gas acceptance was so slow that by 1859 there were less than 100 users. In 1876, with ham 17¢ a pound and eggs 15¢ a dozen, pies baked in a gas fueled oven at Philadelphia's Centennial Exposition were considered oddities. A crusty old Charlie Goodnight was the frontier novelty as he introduced the "chuck wagon" ("Chuck" was his nickname). He fed trail drives, roundups and horse-breakings with things which came over his wagon's end gate to his nearby fire over which pots and spitted meats were exposed to the heat. The electric range was a 1910 development but it was really not until WWII was consigned to the past that research and production of appliances related to food and its preparation came on with a rush. An entire new generation of kitchen appliances emerged and was displayed in sleek color layouts in page after page of women's magazines. Some scenes in popular movies took place in that part of the house, the star usually getting a duplicate of the set in her own Beverly Hills mansion—with the studio granting the manufacturer the right to advertise either an individual appliance or the whole kitchen design as the product of a given company. Such tie-ups required the company to name the film and under such glamorous sponsorship the food freezer, electric frypan, mixers and blenders made that cuisine center one of the most exciting rooms in a house or apartment.

ternal strengthening from a reworking of microwave and magnetron expertise could, if successful, provide another important ingredient, confidence.

It's hard to say what was most important when such an exploration is initiated. People, surely. Some are early, and some come later. For Joe Imirie, they were easy to count off. Norm Moore, Vin Carver, Robert Bruder, William George, Wayne Bledsoc, Cal Hagberg, Harold Anderson, Pete Daly, Verna Ludvigson, Dwayne "Bud" Haagenson, Al Heathfield, Verle Blaha, Leon Loos—they were all vital at one stage or another.

Most agree, though, that it was a thought which awakened Bud Haagenson in the middle of the night which let some air into the big puzzle which turned the corner. Everyone had thought from the beginning that the magnetron should be water-cooled. This led to overheating and burnouts resulting in oven destruction and little progress. The idea Haagenson came in with was that there should be six small holes cut for air to be admitted through each waveguide, the holes to be in a small circle over the tube's antenna so air could be passed over and around the magnetron. The overheating problem was solved. Predictability and assurance were emphasized in the presentations before customers after that. But the oven size was greater than could be accommodated in most homes.

This led to the first major sale, the so-called "airborne oven." TWA had a test-prototype on board one of its flights, one which had been developed by Cal Hagberg. TWA, when the newness wore off, decided to pass for a few years, perhaps to come back in the picture later because they liked the distinctive status symbol it gave them. Airlines hungered for such things. The first actual sale was to BOAC, the British carrier, just as 1968 was waning. They installed it at Heathrow airport outside London for training and meal preparation for BOAC flight crews. Considering that 1968 was the start of Litton's difficult decade, small sale it may have been, but it was a sale. Something cracked in the barrier that every microwave oven manufacturer was encountering. Continental was next after Litton had installed one of the ovens in Bob Six's home, he being the Continental AirLines founder. He liked it and it went on Continental. TWA then returned with renewed interest. And then there was a startling request for installation of Litton's microwave ovens in the Air Force ONE and some of the other plush planes in the Presidential fleet. That was in President Johnson's time, he a man of long memory including of those Saturdays when he and Thornton were young in Washington, fresh from their lean and hungry Texas beginnings.

The airborne ovens were profitable but had many difficulties. With TWA, it was a nomadic nightmare when the New York-Milan, Italy leg was selected as the test route. Long before the late Rod Serling wrote that TV script about how commercial carriers could be hijacked and this aloft-equivalent of holding up the overland stage caused marshals to ride "shotgun" on board, there was a "microwave marshal" system instituted. Oven experts could be handy to answer questions and do emergency repair. That transatlantic trio that logged thousands of miles and never really caught up with its baggage included Al Heathfield, Pete Daly and Leon Loos. They comprised, sympathized and improvised at 30,000 feet.

It was the money which came out of their limited commercial intrusion on high which kept what was the Atherton division of Litton afloat financially. TWA told its first class passengers on their menus that with this ultramodern microwave cooking equipment it was no longer necessary for them to be fed wham-bam as though in a cattle car. They could have a hot meal and entree choices whenever they were hungry. To a small degree, it was a reinforcement of Bob Bruder's firm belief that microwave ovens would wend their way into homes if there was some intimate relationship with people in an environment where they could lay hands on the items. This would provide a personal sales seduction. Passengers, with all that sky time, came to look and marvel. They talked the ovens over among themselves.

When TWA had their prototype installation, the airlines collected a group of high level executives at Club "21" in New York. Getting them well lubricated; they flew them over the Lindbergh route to the Paris Air Show at *LeBourget*, celebrating the 40th Anniversary of his 1927 New York-to-Paris nonstopper. Before the flight was completed at *LeBourget* the passenger list had access to seven entrees and an ample wine cellar's array of liquid augmentation. The only real gastronomic similarity to Lindbergh's exploit was the use of a gallon of drinking water.

Behind the fun and games, the airlines began to like one feature very much—they could pay for the ovens rather quickly in savings on food costs. Health laws required that food be offloaded at destination. It could not be reboarded unless it was frozen. TWA found merit in an entirely new food provisioning system—frozen—which could use the microwave ovens for defrosting and only defrost what was actually needed for the varying numbers of the ticketed and present. Prior to this, hundreds of dollars worth of edibles had to be thrown out at each turnaround. Transatlantic or transoceanic flights made the airborne oven sensible.

It had snob appeal as it was only used for the first class section to augment the leisure and luxury atmosphere. Startup moneymaker though it was, it had to be the institutional, hotel, restaurant and eventually the home which would make or break Litton's Atherton division.

From Norm Moore's[4] day he always figured the microwave oven could be given the same demonstration-in-the-neighborhood party approach as Tupperware, or could be sold door to door. That was pedestrian in more ways than one. A sales person plodding about the suburbs was lucky to make a sale a day, or ten in a week, and that was cause for elation. The Minneapolis assembly line coughed up fifty ovens a day. Demographic studies indicated that people who had money enough to own boats, from medium to the yacht variety, had "buy" tendencies. Litton accorded them special consideration—a small Galley Master model for boats. Another pitch was to real estate developers talking them into including built-in microwave ovens in the kitchen of each unit. In Canada, the Canadian Pacific had them on their transcontinental trains. But the penetration which really counted was the Bob Bruder-directed entry into company snack bar usage. This allowed great numbers of people to tinker with the ovens, experiment and operate them with various combinations of food preparations. Subtly, it began to occur to women in offices that this could

---

4. After all his tilting at technological windmills as it some latter-day Don Quixote, when Dr. Norman Moore left Litton there was speculation as to where he'd wind up. It was not long before the energy crunch sent the world reeling. Finding alternate energy sources was the pressing mood of the time. Where else, then, for Moore to be but the President of U.S. Windpower, Inc., that found him planting windmills over landscape swept by persisting high velocity air currents. Converting air in motion to energy generation made just as much sense to him as adapting radar's magnetron component to a cooking role.

simplify the other side of their distaff coin—the one when they went home to the housewifely chores of feeding a brood.

"We made the key judgment in the early '70s," said Pete Daly. "That was to go with the microwave countertop self-contained units which we thought we did best. Specialty manufacture would take away from this, so we declined the offers to get into custom and exotic fields until we had made the most of consumer opportunities we saw in mass marketing."

Verna Ludvigson, who had been employed in the natural gas and public utility arena in their customer services, came into Atherton in 1968. She really knew the nature and the reactions of Atherton's potential customers. She, with Pete Daly and Rolf Engstrom, put together the rudiments of a one-on-one sales force. They decided to do test marketing exercises in Atlanta, Dallas and in their hometown, Minneapolis. When Dan Cavalier (recruited from General Electric) signed on, he was given the goal of having Litton microwave ovens in national distribution in one year.

Atherton had to come out of its old brand name associations such as Sears, Montgomery Ward, Admiral and Tappan. Atherton was no longer—that borrowed designation from Norm Moore's hometown in California—now it was Litton Microwave Cooking Products. Cavalier accomplished what they assigned him in that one year. Verna Ludvigson stayed in close touch with that growing list of users and plumbed for the basic questions asked enroute to the "buy" decision—those sales resistance reasons such as whether microwave ovens were only for defrosting, for reheating, for melting. Were they dangerous to glassware and dishes? Would it violate family customs and habits? Was there a requirement to completely relearn how to cook? It was through the sensitivities and perceptiveness of Verna Ludvigson that the engineers were oriented on what the oven would do better than ever for the one who owned it. It was this that would sell the oven more than the newness of the technology. The advertising line became the tell-all: "Litton–Changing the Way America Cooks"! Many of the engineers who had been proud of their Raytheon time where the microwave oven was invented now defected to Litton where they felt the microwave oven had been perfected. Litton had more of the market at one time than any of the other 28 manufacturers. A technology acquired in that little side-of-the-road San Carlos facility had now ballooned into the biggest public identification with that still mysterious Litton. "What does Litton do?" was the most asked question in the company's fledgling years. Now people said: "For one thing, they're the company that makes all those microwave ovens." It was only a small part of what Litton did, but it gave the public a handle on the bucket.

It was new, though, and anything new and remarkable attracts rumors and rumors of rumors. Such things, even if never proven, were menaces to sales.[5] Just as the simple match, struck and bursting into flame in a southern mansion in the 1830s caused women to faint, believing themselves in the presence of a sorcerer, microwaves have their days and nights as scare inducers. Thomas Edison had to instruct people not to try to blow out the electric light bulb in the same way as a kerosene lamp or candle, but to use a switch on the wall. For the microwave oven, there was the specter of "dangerous radiation." "Perhaps" and "maybe" it introduced some hidden hazard into the kitchen. The industry, for want of government guidelines at the oven's inception, took for its own safety standards the U.S. Military analysis of radiation. Post-WW II the Army and Army Air Force Medical Services began interesting themselves in research involving radio frequency and microwaves. Clinical studies as early as 1943 examined exposure of lab personnel to radar and high frequency radio waves and possible eye effects. None of those findings had produced concern. Two years later they focused on blood and its production system. For a short time, the U.S. Navy had cognizance for all the services for the interaction covering radio frequency energy. After 1954, the U.S. Air Force was the inheritor of this responsibility. None

---

5. Public concern about possible radiation dampered sales in 1970. In August, 1971, Bruder made 28-year old William George executive vice president, and the decision to enter the consumer market with the Litton brand name. The biggest concern was whether it could compete with powerhouse General Electric. In quickstep, a new plant was built in Plymouth, a Minneapolis suburb and opened in 1975, and in March 1977, a second countertop plant bowed in Sioux Falls, S.D. Fred O'Green had toyed with taking it into Mason City, Iowa, his hometown, but Sioux Falls won it when a delegation headed by no less than Governor Richard Kneip flew to Minneapolis to talk to Bill George. The 700-800 level of employees in high season made it the third largest employer in Sioux Falls and 10th in size in South Dakota. It was Sioux Falls plant's Earl Birk, an engineer, who came up with the flexible door which adjusts to and closes tight on any surface which finally answered the radiation leakage concerns.

of this research, revealed increased microwave usage caused any official safety concern as long as the rules were observed. The Veterans Administration once checked 1,945 men being treated for cataracts and 2,134 who did not have them, all with comparable occupational histories in the presence of microwave radiation. No evidence was found that such employment had anything to do with eye afflictions. The microwave oven industry, on its own, backed off additional distance from military allowable tolerance level settling for ten milliwatts per square centimeter as safe for industrial, occupational and general civilian exposure to microwave radiation. On October 6, 1971 after hearings before the Department of Health, Education and Welfare and its Bureau of Radiological Health, there was a further reduction to five milliwatts per square centimeter.

Despite TV talk shows, radio conversations and newspaper and magazine features worrying about whether there "could be" hazards, consumers voted their approval in mammoth numbers and ran microwave oven sales higher and higher.[6]

The original Thornton tenet that a Litton on the course he laid for it would have to be in military contracting to pick off technologies developed there which could be beneficial consumer projections was proven right in this, the very first instance. The British writer, C.P. Snow, who had had both scientific and literary bright minds among his associates, once declared sadly that technology had become a *pejo-*

---

6. Litton used to laugh loudest when some sensation mongering interviewee viewed the potential "microwave radiation" with alarm and cited how much more rigorous the Soviet Union was than the U.S. in policing microwave radiation tolerances. On his trip to the U.S.S.R. in August 1969, "Tex" Thornton took a Litton Microwave oven with him which was given to Prime Minister Aleksei Kosygin. It was tested three full days and in every way by the Soviet Ministry of Electrical Industries before it was placed in Kosygin's apartment. Kosygin, a widower after his wife died in 1966, had his daughter Lyudmilla perform as his official hostess after that. She, married to Dzhermen Gvishiani, the Vice Chairman of the State Committee on Science and Technology, lived in the apartment next door to Kosygin. On all those nights when he had friends in, or late working sessions, whenever a snack was called for, she turned to the Litton oven for its preparation. Litton was able to defuse the fear-and-dreaders claims by citation of Soviet safety requirements having been met. Such countering material served to the disturbed interviewees often left them with mouths agape and a requirement for quick subject change. After all, Kosygin was then No. 2 man in the Kremlin and the Litton oven use was not considered too risky for him nor for members of his family.

rative word. "Escaping the dangers of applied science is one thing," he once observed, "and doing the simple and manifest good which applied science has put in our power is another, more difficult, more demanding of human qualities and far more enriching to us all."

The go-go '60s were frequented by many people who only seemed to brush surfaces as dragonflies do the water in summer. Sloganeering in big type on placards became the editorials of the time. Outrage about highly complex and complicated aspects of Man's affairs were only worth bothering with if they could be packaged in a kind of staccato shorthand capable of being mouthed in unison or shouted in cadence as football teams were once exhorted to do. There was so much noise that decibels seemed to have been substituted for deliberations. Professional adversaries wore the Viet Nam experience as penitents' hair shirts rather than seeing it for the passing fever blister it was on the international body politic, or that some things had come from it in a technological way which would be a boon to the human race. Litton was the applier of one of them and was quick to see there were far more sobering, bigger truths with which to reckon than rifle fire from and in the rice paddies.

Whole industries were crying for plant replacements. Equipment and facilities in America, overused and tired from both the demands of war and inputs made to help with economic restorations abroad, were ancient. The industrial base in other parts of the world was more often bright and new, making the U.S. dowdy by comparison. At the same time that so much affluence was so visible, it was making western and northern nations envied by substantial portions of the world which were hungry, unskilled and denied hope. In such lands were great resources in more than 20 strategic materials of the earth, which meant the traditionally richer countries had to deal with the frustrated and the angry. Access once so automatic in the colonial period was now obtained only by sufferance.

Litton's applicable technology was readymade and demonstrably a significant means of dealing with that rising and sticky dilemma. Its credentials went back many years. Negotiating land relationships with the newly created national entities, however embittered now, was not insurmountable. Litton had the means of narrowing choices of probable location of minerals, oil and gases, and underground water. Energy in its many forms was what was called for everywhere wheels needed to turn, including what the United Nations labeled "emerging" or "less developed countries." What Litton could do in a technological way was often the means by which a country found it could get others by the political forelock, thus assuring them a hearing. It caused all the world to come knocking at the doors of Litton's Western Geophysical (foremost in seismic exploration) and Aero Service (oldest in use of the airborne magnetometer); within those two were the capabilities to open the lock on the secret hiding places of the earth's treasures.[7] One of America's least comprehended statistics is that about one in every 20 jobs is tied in some way to less developed countries.

From Viet Nam's utilization for reconnaissance of SLAR (Side Looking Airborne Radar), a product of Goodyear Aerospace, came an adaptation for commercial use. Dr. Homer Jensen, who had seen the

---

7. In the National Library of Australia in Canberra a "Cook cannon" stands in a place of honor. The plaque states these words of Capt. James Cook, British Royal Navy: "We not only started (taking) water, but throw'd overboard our guns, iron and stone ballast, casks, hoops, stores, oylejars etc. . . ." That was June 11, 1770 that his *H.M. Bark Endeavour* snagged a coral outcrop. Six months earlier on that voyage, January 26, Cook raised the British Union Jack at Botany Bay claiming that great Australian "island continent" for the British Empire. That cannon and five others were finally recovered in January, 1969, through an expedition organized by and with the help of the U.S. Academy of Natural Sciences in Philadelphia. It had enlisted the aid of Dr. Virgil Kauffman, the founder of Aero Service. He turned to old colleagues in the AERO Service division. It was then in the midst of fulfilling an exploration contract along the Great Barrier Reef. Once the exact location was determined by Aero where that desperate ditching had occurred, the rest was relatively easy. All six of the cannon rescued were turned over to the Australian government. The first was presented in a full scale ceremony to "the people of Australia" by (then) Prime Minister, the Right Hon. J.G. Gorton, M.P., March 17, 1970. The inscriptions on that cannon and the others do not mention Litton, or Aero Service, but Australia does remember Litton's geophysical teams for identifying its Bass Strait's great petroleum promise. They confirmed that a wealth of such resources must lie in those waters which separate the Australian mainland from Tasmania, the latter being much more famous as the birthplace of Merle Oberon and Errol Flynn. Besides Canberra, the other five cannon are on view at the National Maritime Museum (Greenwich), London, England; Capt. Cook's Landing Place Historic Site Museum (Kurnell), Sydney and the Capt. James Cook Museum, Cooktown, Queensland in Australia; Peabody Museum, Salem, Mass., on "deposit" by the National Academy of Natural Sciences, Philadelphia; and the National Museum of New Zealand in Wellington. It was a mere detour for a Litton technology, but a first class find for posterity.

magnetometer for the crucial role it could play with Aero Service, was quick to bring about a tie with Goodyear once the technology was sprung from the classified state where it had been militarily isolated since 1962. It could bring a 20-mile wide strip of land 40,000 feet below the Caravel, an aircraft in which cameras recorded it on 5-inch film. It could penetrate clouds, haze and vegetation. It put locations on the earth's surface within 50 feet of actuality on the resulting aerial mosaics for maps and charts. It was a long, long way from Virgil Kauffman's battling with the U.S. Army Corps of Engineers to get in their considerations for mapping in the '20s.

More important, Litton's geophysical arm was as nomadic as any desert Bedouin. It didn't have to even pitch a tent for long, and it needn't stay. It did its work and never tarried around enough for a political thrust to be made at it. It was often accommodating to the point of painting out its logo and company markings and chameleon-like appear to be a part of the national scene where it was momentarily for hire. Sometimes it was a few aircraft. Other times, a few ships, and still others large land vehicles for which there was no such word as inaccessible.

When Litton Resources Systems was brought into being, the geophysical Litton community could invite in offshore delegations, teach them to use the equipment they manufactured and sold to them. They could return to their own countries and probe and explore. Source of replacement packets and parts was Litton Resources Systems, of course.

On March 25, 1965, Aero Service issued a 159-word press release in Philadelphia. It had only been with Litton 15 months. It was a fateful one in terms of the future which was rushing down the calendar. It said: "A 375,000 square kilometer (144,000 square miles) airborne magnetometer survey of the North Sea will be performed for participating oil companies—ten companies have subscribed—believed to be the largest over water aerial survey ever undertaken. Several oil companies are considering participation and may commit before the flights begin April 15—field operations will be completed in six months—participation costs are $75,000 per company—delivery of the first reconnaissance maps for approximately one-third of the survey area will be made to all participants on April 10th—the new aeromagnetic record traces and isomagnetic maps will be delivered periodically to all participants."

Western Geophysical had seismic pieces of the action promised once the geologists got their hands on those early readings. Ultimately more than 40 oil companies bought the chart which, when finished, measured 8.382 meters (27 and a half feet) wide and 7.467 meters (24 and a half feet) long. The project manager, E. Charles Hoefsmit, and Chief Pilot George Miller mostly used an old B-26 with an extended tail boon mounting for the magnetometer. It had to start on a line at the Straits of Dover. As each flight was made across the water, the plane moved north exactly two miles and flew back in parallel to that previous line. Miller, in the 275-mile-an-hour plane, droned over and back with the help of Litton's LN-3 inertial navigation until finally reaching a line from Stavanger, Norway to Edinburgh, Scotland. He had been based part of the time at Schiphol airport near Amsterdam, and the rest of the mission at Odense in Denmark, Hans Christian Andersen's hometown.[8]

The charts fingered Dogger Bank in the United Kingdom-Netherlands markoffs of the North Sea as most promising, although such surveys only indicate where to look rather than sure reward for doing so. One Littonite[9] wrote, once it was completed, that "The implications in NATO, should these drillings reward the borers substantially, would be considerable. The political aspects if Western Europe were to become less dependent on the Middle East for its crude oil ton-

---

8. It would have been hard to make a casual observer believe Aero Service was an "American company." Charles Hoefsmit was born in Naarden, Holland. Dr. Homer Jensen, who had supervised 5,000,000 land miles of aerial exploration from the North Slope of Alaska to Australia, and from Mozambique to the Guatemala rain forests, was a first generation American of Danish parentage. The Eriksens, Garlen, a co-pilot navigator, and his wife, Toni, mapping draftsman, were Danes, too. Arthur Devlin, data technician and geological field analyst was born in Scotland and Kenneth Fraser, a pilot, was from Canada.

9. More important, though, was that this knowledge of United Kingdom energy-self-sufficiency enabled British Foreign Secretary Sir Alec Douglas-Home to come closest to all-out support of a united consuming countries' front as proposed by the U.S. to counter the OPEC cartel onslaught. Japan, UK and Ireland, plus 11 energy dependent European countries conferred on this crisis in Washington in 1974. France was asking for an anti-coalition, each country for itself tactic, but the U.S. suggestion carried. OPEC was jumping per-barrel prices every time the membership convened— and they were meeting often.

nages, could be felt on every continent by the reorientation of marketing which would be made to compensate." That was in 1966, and it
was said to be "smoking opium." In England in 1974 Fleet Street and
BBC news were full of "first petrol from the North Sea going into
automobiles all over Great Britain today."[10] What a difference that
tiny B-26 war-surplused aircraft, equipped with its airborne magnetometer, had made in Britain's history. And Denmark and Norway
too.[11] The Litton presence was practically never mentioned, but Litton knew how important Western Geophysical and Aero, Service and
its inertial navigation had been. It was paid well, and increased its
international reputation for being extremely good at things of this
kind. This paved the way to other contracts and more business.

When Side-Looking Airborne Radar was broken out of its military straitjacket, Homer Jensen literally trembled about what this
could mean to Aero Service and to emerging nations. In its F-4C
"Phantom" aircraft mounts in Viet Nam and Western Europe, SLAR
revealed the enemy and his works on the ground and indicated what
he might be about. The commercial applications on the Aero Service
Caravelle found it dealing with an even more insidious enemy in back-

---

10. The article appeared in NATO 15 NATIONS, PUBLISHED in AMSTER-
DAM Holland, and was written by Col. Barney Oldfield, USAF (Ret). Branded an
"opium smoker" by some of his colleagues, Oldfield happened to be in London in
1974 and saw vindication of BBC News. The magazine was circulated to government
officialdom in NATO and more than 50 other countries. The title: BEST UNKEPT
SECRET OF THE NORTH SEA is still sought in reference libraries.

11. Norway, relying on fish oil for centuries, turned petroleum producer and exporter of its derivatives as it was getting oil from the North Sea in quantities at least
six times what it could use domestically. Its natural gas from its continental shelf is
marketed in Western Europe and even the U.S. As the Federal Republic of Germany
had to develop an *Ostpolitik* to deal with the Eastern Countries, Norway, so long
remote and "out of it," found itself having to come up with its own *Nordpolitik* to deal
from its newfound economic strength. In that one respect, Great Britain was a have-
not nation no longer. Ultimately there were 66 oil concerns based in Aberdeen and
Edinburgh in Scotland alone and by 1980 pumping from the British North Sea sector
amounted to 1,700,000 barrels daily—the equal of the Persian Gulf's Kuwait! For at
least twenty years, always noisy and critical British Anthony Wedgewood Benn said
his country would never have to spend a pound sterling for Middle Eastern oil. Litton
was being increasingly contacted and contracted as a migrant magician which could
pass its magnetometers, lasers and seismographic instruments over both earth and sea
revealing clues to secrets hidden there which were the makings of national wealth and
upward economic mobility.

ward and struggling countries as well as developing nations ignorant of the locations, types, and possible worth of oil, natural gas, minerals, water table characteristics and all those other wonders which electronics could isolate and point to in the inscrutable earth. Whatever was there belonged to the peoples indigenous to the region and could be revealed to their benefit. If properly developed, this could aid their advancement within reach of greater expectancies.

Perhaps none was more fantastic than the appeal which came to Aero Service from Brazil and Venezuela.

The Ministry of Public Works in Venezuela for the Development of the South (CODESUR), its Cartographic Institute, and its Ministry of Mines as a forward-looking trio for Venezuela, were matched by Brazil's National Development of Mineral Production. The latter assigned to LASA Engineering, S.A. (an important resource developer and engineering concern in that vast country which lay on both sides of the Amazon), the colossal task of mapping the great river basin. Venezuela wanted the same thing done with its Orinoco. The objective of all this, as stated by both countries, wasn't just to locate likely resources but also to find a way to get out raw materials undoubtedly present. This made soil structure of prime interest as roadbeds and rail spurs had to figure in the realization of the visions of both South American powers.

The Caravelle took off from airfields in Caracas and Belem for 2,500-mile roundtrips, the outgoing and the incoming courses each covering swaths 20 miles wide. Pulse signals transmitted were recovered by the aircraft cameras after they bounded off the surface of the earth. Variations in the cathode ray tube signals were recorded as distinctive gray tones on the fine grain, blue sensitive film. As soon as the Caravelle landed, the 750 feet of film was developed through several processes to eye-readable form. The fast handling insured that coverage was complete. Once that preliminary action was behind the field crews, off went the footage for further interpretation to the Aero Service scientific and technical staffs in Philadelphia. Topographical maps with appropriate earth resources overlays were assembled for return to the contracting country. "Not only could we identify in detail different kinds of vegetation," Victor L. Bellerue, the Aero Photogrammetry director, said, "Our geologists were trained to check the aerial photos to provide clients such things as rock structure composition and the probability of discovering different minerals in certain locations."

Venezuelan President Rafael Caldera moved in the early '70s to reserve for the state the "Cerro Impacto" region which lies in the Manapiare Valley between Bolivar State and Amazon Territory. His geologists, Pablo Colvee and Jorge Gamba, acting on Aero Service promptings, were able to assure him that the "Cerro Impacto" contained "rich deposits of iron, manganese, thorium, niobium and radioactive minerals."

Brazil learned so much about itself that Aero Service was asked to do aerial mapping and charting of the whole country! Not only did both countries benefit, but in reassurance that within their own borders lay billions in monetary wealth. The North Sea and the Orinoco-Amazon projects in one decade would be enough by any standards, but Litton's geophysical expertise had been at one time or another in 100 countries over the same period. The long reach of geophysical technology was well-established in ministries devoted to natural resource discovery, but little known elsewhere, including the rest of Litton Industries. Considering all the capabilities it had to perform where needs were so great, it was no wonder that it became the leading profit producer of the company. Dislocations due to energy dependence alone, and the shifting allegiances caused by this development, wreaked havoc all over the globe.[12] The welcoming latchstring nevertheless was always out for Litton's geophysical know-how and those

---

12. Long before most of the American business preoccupation out of the U.S. some concerns which were turned by merger into Litton divisions knew a lot about the world's chokepoints. They had worked them and their neighborhood—Suez, Malacca Straits, Gibraltar, the Bosporus, the Skagerrak and Kattagat, the Panama Canal and the Strait of Hormuz. Litton lost a Western Geophysical seismic vessel and all its crew in a still unexplained event in the Red Sea off South Yemen. During the Iran-Iraqi war, another of its ships wandered too close to Iran and was seized. One was stuck in the Mouth of the Zaire River off Point Noir, requiring pull-off by a tug, and passing tugs are not all that frequent along that part of the African coast. Aero Service gave Women's Lib an extreme statistic to consider in that Amazon River survey. It was necessary to have navigational beacons, or SHORAN (Short Range Navigation) installations on high points in the midst of thick jungles. Aero's president, Gale Livingston, O.K.'d a man and wife being parachuted in. All their sustenance during the project was airdropped to them. He said they shared equally in everything—bugs, mosquitoes, snakes and other reptiles, ferocious jungle animals in search of a good meal and not choosy.

Litton divisions with extraordinary credentials. This was true even in the Communist-block countries.

One of Litton's most demanded and demanding technological turns surfaced for two important reasons. The heritage of Floyd George Steele was vital in each. One was Litton's steep commitment for modernized shipbuilding and the supporting infrastructure. The other was for the international needs in refurbishing plants and assembly lines the world around. Numerical controls furnished and multiplied capabilities to meet these enormous tasks. The main staple for all this lay in machine tools, for they, as is the case with Man himself, are capable of reproducing themselves. They have been and continue to be the sinews provider by which industries can be started, developed, modernized and renewed. At the same time, Dr. Norman Moore was finding the microwave ripe for a technological jump from vacuum tubes to ovens, Jack Connolly, a gifted and brooding engineer, was assigned to chase computer opportunities for Litton. In his earliest musings and meditations, he started finding logic in welding machine tools and numerical controls, in which the computer would tell the machine tools how long, how wide, how deep, how many, what pattern and where to place the finished product for its designed role. He was reinforced in this by the aroused numerical controls sentiment when the Machine Tool Builders Convention in 1955 met and talked of the next step their closely knit fraternity would have to take.[13]

It was a tragic automobile accident rather than the best strategy that moved Litton finally into that enclosed industry. The interest was there of course, and heightening all the while. The suddenness with which it happened was another matter.

Machine tools in America were a part of the early migrations from England to the Colonies. People came out of the Huddersfield

---

13. Several primitive versions of numerical controls were exhibited at the 1955 Machine Tools Show in Chicago. Back in the 18th Century, there had been cards used in France as guides for operation of textile looms. The 1890 U.S. Census employed antique ancestors of the "punch card." Applications first suggested for machine tools were on rolls with holes cut into them such as made the player piano function. Film strips with clear spots to trigger, or direct tools were written about in the trade journal, *American Machinist* in 1920. This was used in cutting gears on a gear-shaper. Dr. Fred W. Cunningham wrote extensively about this coming relationship in that magazine in February of 1953, Litton's natal year.

and Yorkshire environs where the industrial revolution began; others came from Europe. Many settled in New England to work in textile mills. As the Ohio river was what passed for a liquid Interstate Highway of the 19th Century, many industrial products were manufactured in sites along its banks. Cincinnati, truly the gateway to the west and south, was from earliest times a machine tools concentration point.

Franklin Frick Landis, for his era a well-educated farm boy, got into machine tools at the age of 17. He had tired of following what agriculture considered high technology—the walking plow. It was in 1862, and America was struggling to keep itself a single country which could accommodate extreme differences of opinion. A great amount of the battling was along that very Antietam Creek where he had grown up. Once the war was over, Landis found himself a surprising ally of the U.S. Patent Office. It required models to be submitted with all the inventions being registered with it. Landis became a frequent port-of-call for those who needed models constructed. From that he expanded into life sizes and the building of steam engines particularly those which were the power element for threshing machines.

Landis seemed a classic case of how it was possible to take the boy out of the country, but not the country out of the boy. Later his horizons were expanded and the locale which appealed to him was Waynesboro, Pennsylvania. There the Landis enterprise was purchased by the Geiser Company in order to get Franklin's brother, Abraham, who was 9 years younger and a smart designer. It was Abraham who had the idea that the grinders would work much more satisfactorily if water were allowed to flow over the area of the grinding. When that was proved right, Landis began to get the lead it was never to relinquish.[14] The Landis Brothers spun themselves off from Geiser and in 1889 were on their own.

While it seemed totally unrelated to Litton's new technological direction-seeking insofar as anyone though then, some Cornell University students were eagerly planning and looking forward to their annual spring break. It had been a miserable winter in Ithaca, the chill

---

14. According Landis "world-wide respect" is not a debatable statement. Litton was eventually to be in every industrialized country with its machine tools. It had quality going for it in every one. "You charge too much for those Landis machine tools," Soviet Ministry of Foreign Trade negotiator, Vladimir Sushkov once told Roy Ash, "but they always work, so we will pay what you ask."

air blowing strongly across those broad Cayuga's waters and people seeing their breath a lot. Florida, they all thought, was the place to head for. By taking turns driving, they could go straight through to give themselves maximum time in the sun and on the sand. One of them had worked all the past summer in the yard at Landis. His cited reason for leaving had been "return to college." He was a top student in engineering, an interest which had persisted from his first toy blocks. Since the day of his birth, July 28, 1940, there had been a future for him at Landis. But all that changed abruptly.

Asleep in the back seat of the car heading for Florida, he was killed when it was "totaled" in a terrible crash near the journey's end. The Associated Press account was modest, but when the news and his obituary appeared in Waynesboro, it was to affect hundreds of people, each in his own way. His name was Milburn A. Hollengreen, Jr. His father Metz had come to Landis in 1926. By his canniness, he had won for it the sobriquet of "the Cadillac of the machine tool business." There was another son committed to a law career and had no interest in his father's field. Without the younger Hollengreen, Landis which had facilities in the U.S., in England and France,[15] and a worldwide standing which brought people from all over to the tiny 10,000-population Waynesboro, changed all future projections. Metz Hollengreen was a towering figure in every way, more than six feet tall. None ranked higher in the esteem of the machine tool industry. He had once headed their association. Now he was literally crushed. It was not only the loss of his son but the shambles in his planning which confronted him. There was his "other family" too—his hundreds of loyal employees. Having no knowledge of any of this, Tex Thornton and Roy Ash pored over the collected information of Jack Connolly and Seymour Rosenberg. They decided that there were many subtleties in

---

15. Landis included in the U.S., Gardner Machine in Beloit, Illinois; Landis-Lund in Cross Hills; Keightley in Yorkshire in northern England, the very cradle of the 16th Century industrial revolution; Landis-Gendron in Lyon, France, in the Rhone Valley, a picturesque city of silks, the University of Lyon, and a divertissement known as the world-class restaurant of Paul Bocuse. On the wall outside the backgate of Landis-Gendron was a big lettered smear of black paint, a leftover from a French Communist party protest against the American presence: "Yankee-Go Home!" In time, the advice would be taken. Metz Hollengreen, who had gone international in the European reconstruction and Marshall Plan days, was finding France less and less attractive as a place of business.

machine tools, those old and proud clans with generations of cross-marrying and tradition. Connolly ran into that problem in the first sashay and was rebuffed. To get anywhere, there was need for romancing and some honey. Above all, there had to be a sensitive appreciation of how wrenching it was going to be for those old concerns to leave "independence" and "join" something completely foreign to them. All things considered, there seemed to be only one way to go, and it was taken. Litton designated Glen McDaniel, its corporate general counsel and chairman of its executive committee, to pursue the establishment of a machine tools group.

The idea from the first was to have a spread rather than a concentration. It was well known that machine tools were subject to wild cyclical swings, largely because firms had grown up around a single product. One mild change or sudden leap in a technology could make it hard for all others in the same line. Therefore, Litton was first of all to be counter-cyclical—half aimed at capital goods, half at production of consumables. In machine tools there were the cutting varieties which were used in the capital goods. While not as glamorous, the consumables could erect a stabilizing bridge linking the peaks of the business without having to ride out those deep valleys of occasional glut and purchasing agent disinterest. Litton thought there was a way out of its being a prince and pauper industry and elected to prove it. McDaniel was convinced that it not only made sense, but being a lawyer to boot, he knew what was tolerable in the eyes of antitrusters in the Department of Justice.

To avoid the antitrust pitfall, McDaniel carefully drew up a matrix of seven types of machine tool companies. Under columns for each category, he wrote the names as a shopping list from which likely candidates could be selected. Conversations could be had. If all went well, negotiations, then by merger, membership in the Litton fold. McDaniel wanted each to be clean of any appendages which might have them intruding on another in terms of product similarity. This could cause that "tilt" sign to flash indicating a taboo by Washington standards. In, the law firm of Covington & Burling, he knew Joel Barlow represented not only Landis Tool in Waynesboro but the whole Machine Tool Builders Association, too. Barlow knew Glen McDaniel and was comfortable with him. Just as the action was about to begin, and McDaniel had word of the tragic plight of Metz Hollengreen after the loss of his son and heir, McDaniel was himself beached for six months by a heart problem.

Working with his assembled portfolio about Landis, Tex Thornton and Roy Ash had innumerable talks with Hollengreen on both coasts and in Waynesboro. Hollengreen was alternately listless and numb and then driven to bring about a good solution for everyone. The Littonites were patient when he was not psychologically ready to talk about it, and stood by to be ready when he was. Hollengreen was always the great gentleman, but he was granite-like also.

He was finally convinced that Litton was the move for him to make. He signed the agreement to merge on October 26, 1967, and the final closing document on January 16, 1968. About $130,000,000 in Litton Industries stock at that day's value completed the transaction. The Litton shares were exchanged for Landis' authorized 2,000,000 shares[16] of which 1,688,117 were issued and outstanding in the hands of 2,800 holders.

McDaniel returned to full-time harness after his heart ailment had improved. He was ready to resume the rest of the machine tools group task. He now had Metz Hollengreen as an ally and counselor.

The skies over Litton were darkening even as Hollengreen's signature was drying on that October 26th agreement. Litton had been up to $120.375 that day on the New York Stock Exchange, and closed at $120,125. In another part of Litton, William E. McKenna was checking out of the Business Systems and Equipment Group. Tempers were as short as the shortcomings beginning to be in evidence. That all-time high was good news to the 75,000 shareholders in the company. They were used to these up, up, and away characteristics, so didn't

---

16. Because the Landis shares paid a $2 dividend, Litton created a new issue of 4,500,000 Series B convertible preferred stock which could be traded one-for-one for Landis and paid a $2 annual cash dividend. Landis shareholders who wished to have the regular Litton shares were permitted that option on a value ratio against the market price of that common. Beyond Landis, the $2 issue could be useful in other acquisitions where a cash dividend was in use and would not be interrupted. This would lessen uneasiness among the owners of the old paper they were required to surrender. The convertibility cued on the value of the Litton regularly declared 2½% stock dividend. In 1974 as the common stock price bumped along its bottom, that value was such a splinter fraction, the convertibility aspect ceased.

cheer. After that so-modest start at 10-cents a share in 1953, there had been ten years of 2½% stock dividends and three stock splits.[17]

In January, when Hollengreen made it final, it was barely a week to the time Litton was going to have to blush publicly about the disarray in which it found itself.

Nowhere was the long reach of technologies so dramatically in hand as in Litton, nor was there anywhere which would need them so urgently as a bulkwark against the abundance of threats.

---

17. The Litton formula for a stock split two-for-one Tex Thornton said, required that each of the resulting shares after the action had to earn as much or more as the unsplit share was accruing a year before.

SPECIAL SITUATION #16

DRACHMAE, ESCUDOS AND SO FORTH

A paperback novel needed no better setting.

The Belgian leaning against the Minos Beach Hotel bar on the Mediterranean Island of Crete was Pierre Alphonse Guillaume. He could sell anything. Himself. Or, a newly popped idea. Or, whoever might be listening as he embroidered it. A charming conversationalist, suave in his social movements, a connoisseur of wines, and a gourmet diner, he represented Litton-Benelux, S.A. He made business development forays from its offices in Brussels, Belgium.

He didn't need the ouzo in the glass before him to loosen his tongue, nor heighten his zeal. Elias Sothrchos, the Greek, was giving him full attention. As Greeks will, he "knew somebody" in Athens. He had promoted and developed Minos Beach, an expanse of lovely cabanas strung along milkwhite sands that went down to meet the lazy, deep blue water. The two men were so engrossed they ignored the wealth of visual satisfaction out there in the blazing sun. Dozens of holidaying Scandinavian AirLines stewardesses were giving their Nordic charms bikini brevity with minimal concealment.

Two items in his mail spurred Guillaume. One was a memorandum written by John Rubel; the other a speech recently delivered by Roy L. Ash at Mt. St. Mary's College in Los Angeles. Rubel's memos were many and long in those days—the mid-60s. They were exciting reading to some but sowed disquiet in others. In this particular one, he declared there was an integrated systems management approach to socioeconomic and socio-political problem solving. Ash in his remarks said this could actually be a more effective means than the halfhearted and unimaginative methods employed by governments and their agencies. In his speech he stated it to be completely rational to let contracts to businesses and businessmen who could apply their expertise.

The management of great numbers of traditional governing activities was seldom handled well in even the most sophisticated of states. It was often woefully bungled in more primitive societies. It was so sensible to outline the nature of the required service, the time needed depending on the size of the engagement and its goals, and to make a cost analysis. Then with the approving nod, proceed. It was so logical, and if one were to pursue logic to its ancestral roots, where else should one look but to the land of Plato and Aristotle? It was a management update on the mercenaries of old—hirelings of a sovereign state to subdue or circumvent an adversary.

The enemy in emerging or developing countries was sparseness of employment, of economic mobility, of opportunities or the means to get foreign exchange. Once the dimensions of such an effort were known and mutually agreed upon, a company could take up a development alliance with a government. The amount of reimbursements could be computed and an allowance made for profits commensurate with efforts and risks.

It was this theme that Guillaume had come from Brussels to expound. Litton could very well be such an interested company, and a talented partner candidate, he said, for a country such as Greece.

Guillaume knew Western Europe as well as his oldest necktie. Greece and Portugal were the continent's two poorest countries. Each had big eyes on the European Common Market yearning for membership. The roads ahead for each were almost impassable. Portugal had one of the longest running dictatorships headed by Dr. Antonio Salazar. Greece had so many military governments since 1843 they were about as common as the safety pin and often the same automatically reached for emergency device. There had been five coups in Athens since 1922. Greece had a shaky reputation in international monetary circles for its tendency to repudiate obligations of previous regimes. It had stiff tariff barriers protecting Grecian special interests. But Guillaume had decided to sound out Greece first because he figured if there was ever a country in need of a crutch salesman, it had to be that ancient, beautiful, historic and troubled land. Litton Industries, he reasoned, was just the prop the Hellenes needed.

The proposition? An economic development contract in which Greece would enlist Litton Industries to put it on the way to financial respectability.

In the *Area Handbook for Greece* compiled by the American University in Washington, Litton is mentioned twice. Once in the index, and in the text with a single sentence: "Two major industrial development schemes, one promoted by Litton Industries, and the other under the aegis of Aristotle Onassis . . . foundered for lack of investment support". If ever there was a skipping rock over a vast expanse for roiled political waters, that understatement has to be it!

For one thing, Litton was a "foreigner". That made it a convenient target for any charge or claim or the butt of any joke. There is no different word for "foreigner" and "stranger" in the Greek language. The truth is, they are mostly comfortable with incomers as "tourists". *Politicus* is one of their words, though, and a sense of the political is inborn in every citizen. The Greek is good at it, never without it, and can be absolutely lethal in his use of politics. Emotional, too.

Onassis was an international swinger with side sweep including boats, banking and boudoirs. Athens was home turf to him. He had started there as a pistachio nuts salesman, hawking them by the bag to tourists. His favorite beat was the array of tables strewn around Syntagma (Constitution Square). Litton's offices-to-be overlooked that same Square of sun-shielding umbrellas. Under their shade were coffee and *aperitif* quaffers, animated chatterers, and girl watchers. Unlike Onassis, Litton was only a rumored giant, mysterious and ten times zones removed. Onassis, in Greece, was an established, fabled achiever with an airline, a fleet of tankers plying the seven seas, and now the latest husband of Jacqueline Kennedy, widow of the slain American President. But who, was asked often, was this Litton Industrics, anyway? The going would hardly be easy, but it was also possible, Sothrchos said.

He explained to Guillaume how Greece worked. A highly placed sponsor was an absolute necessity. Each Greek, he said, believed himself wiser than any Oracle of Delphi, which had long since been relegated to package tours and postcards. A modest Greek by his observation, one without an opinion of his own which became his unvarnished truth, was as rare as an iceberg at the Equator. *Hybris*, that Greek word anglicized to *hubris*, is cyrillic alphabet shorthand for overweening self-confidence. It is Hellenic custom, to assign it to others designated as worthy of its wearing because Greeks all knew its standard ingredients so well. Cooperation is very difficult for a Greek, he declared. It implied heeding or seeking help, which always translates into an outright admission of weakness. Ancient and modern Greece had never known long absence of troubles. Name the kind, and that rocky, mountainous, arid nation whose meandering coastline gives it 15,000 miles of water's edge, has known it. Hunger, oppression, invasion, occupation, moments of wild and delirious freedom, downtrodden humiliation in defeat, occasional statesmen and often scoundrels alternating in power. It had bred philosophers who were said in their time to have advanced dangerous thoughts and who died for them, but who are today idolized for their reason and good sense. Their devotion to the Greek Orthodox Church and observance of its rituals is equaled only by the country's idolatrous worship and pursuit of foreign exchange. The author Leslie Finer explained it well when he said Greece was a "nation of villages of which Athens is the largest."

Into this Athens hub and setting Pierre Alphonse Guillaume was ushered by Sothrchos. Driving in from Hellenikon[1] airport, Guillaume thought idly of Litton and its success with navigation. It was the nearby Greek islands, stretching to the east and south which had taught the first navigators. They treated the islands as mileposts or beacons while sailing out from the port of Piraeus, then guiding on them in reverse order to get safely back to homeport. Ahead of his taxi, Guillaume saw the ageless Parthenon which had withstood centuries of clandestine souvenir stone chippers and still looked down on that old Mediterranean metropolis as if to say: "What else is new?"

Guillaume had an appointment with Deputy Prime Minister Stefanos Stefanopoulos. The word was that he was finding his relationship with prime Minister George Papandreou galling. Some said he stood so well with young and handsome King Constantine that he might be tapped as Papandreou's replacement; the King was tiring of Papandreou. It was almost a solid bet, or as nearly as one could approach such things in the Aegean area that someone might be asked to form a new government. The King, though, had told a visiting journalist that to call on Stefanopoulos for a chore of this size would be like trying to build a Parthenon out of wet macaroni. But in the murky world of the international marketer today's pariah can be on tomorrow's pinnacle and vice versa. Guillaume's way was well prepared as he went straight to Stefanopoulos' office. There were no preliminaries, no time wasting, and their conversation was agreeably cordial and responsive. Guillaume talked to Beverly Hills that night

---

1. The final *n* has been dropped since. Helleniko, they now call it.

and said it was his impression that an economic development contract could be drawn up at once.

There was almost high blood pressure in California, and a long luncheon in Litton's executive dining room with Roy Ash, George Scharffenberger, and John Rubel. It sounded too pat, so good as to be suspicious. The proponents for this kind of engagement being a proper one for Litton had been taken at their word. They did decide, though, that if they were going to go ahead with it, it was too much of a commitment for the company to be left entirely to a marketer's judgment and a salesman's enthusiasm. Rubel, caught with having one of his brainstorming memos taken seriously and one which had gone so easily into his dictaphone to be typed by Grace Davis, found himself on a TWA flight to Athens. It was one thing to read in the corporate office, but here was a development assuming international proportions—and a loaded Pandora's Box of implications. As he flew along, he kept telling himself that he didn't think Greece was the most practical place in the world to try out this integrated systems management idea he had so blithely authored. But Ash was high on it—a trial balloon setting for one of his speeches which had hooked a nibble. The cork was bouncing invitingly. "Go over and look at it yourself," Ash had said. And there he was at 35,000 feet.

Guillaume was waiting for Rubel in the chaotic Athens baggage heap just off the Hellenikon Passport Control positions. He had the gear picked up and loaded. He talked all the way into the city. As soon as Rubel was registered in his hotel, Guillaume squired him to Stefanopoulos.

It was true Eastern Mediterranean. The outer office was awash in relatives, hangers-on, and a passel of civil servants trying to get the main man's attention long enough to hear a Yes or No, that being the grease of bureaucracy. Stefanopoulos greeted the Litton twosome warmly. Then as a farmer does with chickens on his doorstep, he shooed all the others out, killing most of them, male and female alike. Could they speak French, he asked, motioning them into chairs before his desk? Rubel, always anxious to practice his own, nodded.

'*Alors*," said the Minister, rubbing his hands together. "Tell me about Litton Industries." Rubel waxed eloquently on the subject.

"All of Greece needs help," the Minister said. "Two regions especially." On the map on the wall of his office, he outlined their problems saying their configurations and locations seemed to make them most resistant to relief measures and attempts to improve the quality of life. One was the Western Peloponnesus, that half which shoulders itself out against the Adriatic Sea. It enclosed Olympia, the site of the first Olympic Games in 776 B. C. The whole area cried out for agricultural, touristic and industrial development. The other target for treatment was to the south of Athens an hour by air, or as an all-day or all-night trip by ship—the Island of Crete. These two sectors accounted for 15% of the Grecian landmass, and 12.5% of the country's 9,000,000 population. Crete, was 160 miles long and at its widest, 36 miles. The per capita income of the two sectors was about $350 annually. "If we can work things out," Stefanopoulos said with a grand sweep of his arms, "we can make a later arrangement for all of Greece."

Rubel and Guillaume had been in his office less than a half-hour. Rubel was a little shaken by it all, but quiet until they were once more in the street. Glancing first to his right and then to his left, checking to see if anyone looked as though he understood English as if fearing they might be followed, he zeroed in on Guillaume.

"What is this?" he demanded somewhat testily. "Here we have been with this Minister who listens to me a little bit about Litton. Then he says all Greece can be ours. It doesn't sound right to me; it's crazy." In his head that old adage was circling about bewaring of Greeks who came bearing gifts. But nowhere could he recall that there had ever been a proffered gift of the country itself! But he was in it and had to find out more about it. He plunged on. This meant taking two of the wildest rides of his life with Greeks at the wheel in both instances.

On Crete, invoking St. George at every hairpin turn, the driver never slowed down, only had one hand on the wheel and fed himself with the other while going at fearsome speeds. If any crumbs dropped to the floor, he took his eyes off the road until they were retrieved and popped into his mouth. On a map, Western Peloponnessus appears to nuzzle right up to Athens, but it's a daylong excursion because of poor roads. Through it all, Rubel was thinking of Murphy's Law—if anything can go wrong, it will. By the time he left Greece, he was sure that admonition had not come directly from Ireland. It had to have been pirated from somebody who had migrated from Athens and shortened his name from Murphilopoulos. After all, it was well known in the Eastern Mediterranean that the Greeks "invented everything." They even lay claim to having been the "cradle of democracy", but neglect to point out that their original concept had it resting on the broad and strong backs of slaves, some of whom rocked the cradle and others did the heavier work. They equated the systematized thought processes of Plato and Aristotle and attributed to Plato's dialogues four centuries before Christ the root of Rubel's "integrated systems management" approach. That avant garde buzzword of American industry was considered by some as their own oral household icon.

Greece through all its ages and eras, including the 400 years of Ottoman rule, was now down to a government headed by wily old George Papandreou of the Center Union Party. It was a mixed bag of barely warm leftovers from his old Liberal associates and others whose leftist leanings made him antsy. Papandreou, for one thing, wanted to break the Army ties to the Throne. He was of the mood and mode of the country's previous strongman, namely roughhewn Eleutherios Venizelos. Both courted cult-like followings, trod heavily on their opponents and rolled over any independently minded adversaries. They enjoyed adoration of the masses. Under rules of the Greek Monarchy, it could never openly talk with or try to influence the press. The politicians could on whim summon protesting partisans into the streets for mob scenes and rioting.

Papandreou had a son, Andreas. He hadn't graduated from Athens University, that important first step in linkage with the "the old boy network". He did get an M.A. and a Ph.D. at Harvard in the U.S. where he was first an instructor, then moved to similar posts at the University of Minnesota and University of California in Berkeley. On that last campus, he was made a full professor and headed its department of economics. When Andreas came back to Athens, he brought with him at least three strong mental persuasions in addition to the baggage he cleared through customs in Hellenikon airport—great respect for U.S. corporate know-how in managerial techniques which got complicated things done, a far greater tolerance for the political left than his father had and that he didn't need his father's sun to bask in any longer—*ergo* that he was Prime Minister material himself and ruthless enough to bump his illustrious parent off his perch. For the moment though, he was fresh from that America that all Greeks so admire as long as it stays where it is on the globe and is an unfailing conduit of money from Greek émigrés and U.S. Aid programs. For the place to bide his time, he chose to become one of his father's Ministers.

Andreas Papandreou, first a Litton proponent and later a Litton thorn, was an eager, ambitious, can't-wait son of his father. In his rush for the ladder and a constituency to hold it for him, he was strongly tied to the so-called ASPIDA Affair, a leftist Army Officers' group bent on booting the Monarchy and its resident symbol, King Constantine. When it failed, the Prime Minister tried for the King's permission to get the Defense Ministry portfolio, but he saw how easily a political father could shield an erring political son from disclosures in a Defense-run investigation. Papandreou, sure of himself and his political muscle, invoked crisis and resigned. It had been under his tumultuous wing that initial Litton talks about economic development started. His opposition criticized him for toying with making Greece a financial plaything for foreigners such as Litton Industries and the likeminded investors it would attract to "despoil the sacred soil of Greece". If the country had gone into an election he had counted on, he probably would have won. The King did not call an election, but told Panayiotis Kannellopoulos he was the new Prime Minister and to form a government.

When Rubel, somewhat dizzied by all this, went back to Beverly Hills, he found Ash still in a GO state for contract talks. He believed what was going on in Greece between King, Cabinet and Parliament was politics as usual. That portion of critical opposition of yesterday now in power, he thought, would opt for economic development. He was right—but the Papandreous who had once applauded, now turned on Litton with a barrage of oratorical abuse. Politicans in the Eastern Mediterranean fear success when out of power as it tends to reflect favorably on those in the saddle. That conract was being rewritten, redirected, reviewed and rephrased every 24 hours.[2]

---

2. The Littonites in the contract action in New York were Bemelman Adrian of Hewitt-Robin's and Rubel. In Zurich, there were inputs from Monauni Hano, Charles Kolar, and Kurt Mueller of Litton World Trade. Other shots were being called in the Litton Benelux Brussels office by Pierre Guillaume and his staffers, Guy Weestrerman, Peter Buchanan, Carman Dayg, George Dupont, Charles French, Mathew

The LITTON Adventure That Was

The drafts made Litton a hunter-and-seeker of companies for plants to locate in Greece, investments of all kinds, and there was also a massive Litton obligation to assume with fixed money mile-posts running over 12 years of the agreement's proposed life.

The Greeks had studied the political situation carefully and knew Tex Thornton and President Lyndon Johnson to be old friends. Richard Nixon, who was sounding more like the probable replacement every day, knew Litton's toppers very well. Their records showed that Johnson often asked Thornton to serve on difficult commissions such as the one looking into the Air Force Academy cheating scandal and the Governor Kerner group studying the origins of civil disorders and means of their correction. As they wrote their scenario, it was perfectly reasonable to the Greeks to have by this contractual tie someone they could turn to in a crunch which might be coming down their road such as Turkey, their traditional sore point just over the Aegean. As they were always crowding them on Cyprus, making that island a bone of contention which could turn to bloodletting at any moment, perhaps an economically minded friend at court wouldn't be bad.

They were well up on the U.S. Congress's growing intolerance for foreign aid appropriations, and how difficult it was for an elected representative to return to West Virginia or New Mexico or wherever and explain "How come"? he had voted in favor of it. It was already in the records that at the first Conference of the United Nations on Trade and Development in Geneva, Switzerland in 1964, up jumped those 77 "have-not" nations who made their declaration that they were as bad off as they were because of "colonial exploiting powers." They were still being frustrated at every twist of the trail when they tried bettering themselves. There were only 28 fully affluent, sophisticated, industrialized nations in all the world. Unless they and their business colossuses did something drastic, the 77 complainers were destined to drop back almost a year for every day that dawned on them. Their shortcomings made them unable to keep the others in sight. Washington was in the act from several directions as was the United Nations. Many business leaders were sensing a clutch at their lapels urging

---

Lord, John Kimbrough, Eberhard Rongen, Jean Schaeller, Zephyr Tamba, Thomas Walk and Dr. Paul Zukin. The Author was made a Vice President of the Litton International Development Corporation spending half his time in Athens and half in Beverly Hills.

them to take up part of this burden by inserting themselves in local and regional projects offshore. Wouldn't it make more sense, Litton reasoned, to try a developing country first, one that had some experience with nationhood over centuries, but was technologically backward, rather than step into some barely emerging country trying to find a way off its flatwheel status? Litton considered all those things and Greece seemed right.

The contract lurched and caromed along. The Greek Prime Minister situation was an every morning eye-opener. When the King dismissed Papandreou, he chose the appointment route rather than election for his replacement to form a government. Two men, Navas and Tsirimokis, not only failed to get Parliamentary approval but were not on the job long enough for Litton to get acquainted. His third pack, Stephanos Stefanopoulos, was approved and Littonites breathed a sigh of relief, especially Rubel and McDaniel who had made his acquaintance earlier on. But he served very briefly and was replaced by Panayiotis Kannellopopoulos, and even as he was barely warming his chair, a new figure began to hover over the scene—the well-regarded Constantine Karamanlis. King Constantine called for a May, 1967 election. Meantime, those migratory names who had first sought the contract with Litton, now "out of power", fought the contractual tie with Litton. Each in their periods of rising power curves thought it attractive to have Litton place itself as a respected fiscal entity between the Greek government and sources of money and possible multinational corporate expansion planners, international bankers and investor syndicates. The ultimate beneficiaries, in order, would be the sponsoring political leadership, the Government of Greece, and the Greek people.

As Rubel explained it: "The desired economic goals included for Greece (1) a one-time investment of foreign capital in projects to be developed (2) long term foreign exchange to come through the completed ventures, (3) increased employment and per capita income, (4) social benefits through improvement in health, education and welfare, (5) reorganization and revisions in government procedures and regulations, (6) provision of an improved base for rapid and competitive economic development, (7) training of government personnel—and, (8) assisting the Greek government to achieve full membership in the

346

European Economic Community, or Common Market (their situation at contract negotiations time was that of an "associate member").

Litton was also required to identify probable investment opportunities to serve both the Greek internal and export markets, to prepare feasibility studies and make research assessments enabling clients to draw precise investment surmises and to make appropriate decisions. Where necessary Litton was to be the way-paver agent expediting investment applications, a picker-of-the-way through the reefs and shoals of a layered, entrenched and genuinely lethargic civil service.

Karamanlis declared earlier that as much as $200,000,000 in gold was being hoarded throughout Greece by people who had no faith in the paper drachmae. Interest rates had been known to reach 45% or more. Investment inclinations had dried up. The public attitude in Greece was distrustful and debilitating.

Nowhere inside Greece was there as much pessimism about the country's future as that prevailing among moneymen abroad. Greece might well be a land with from 90 to 120 days more sun annually than the rest of Europe, but it was depressingly cloudy and had a dreary effect on bankers. To them it was a modern monstrosity and every bit as real as were the mythological stables of King Augeas of Eli. They had to be cleaned up in one day as "the fifth labor of Heraklies (Hercules)." The official accumulation which faced that legendary strong man was only 30 years in the piling up. The financial morasses of the Greece of King Constantine and his Ministers had been a-building much longer.

In addition, there was the inheritance from the four centuries of the Ottoman Empire, that old Turkish custom of *Rousfeti*. It would come out "bribe" in English and down through the centuries it changed coloration only slightly translating into promises made by a politician seeking favors to hand off favors to those who supported him in victory. It denies any chance of equality before the law. The "who do you know?" factor is crucial. It was this among other things which made of Greece a member of the "walking wounded" as it entreated for inclusion in the European Economic Community. Favors tend to deemphasize productivity and Greece was about 50% as productive as other EEC members.

All these distress signal flares were there as the Litton contract palaver staggered on. Each session added new Frankenstein aberra-

The Western Peloponnesus Kid (My Zorba the Greek period (1965-69), Col. Barney Oldfield, USAF (Ret), Vice President, Litton International Development Corporation, based in Beverly Hills, California, but working everywhere else which would evolve into East/West trade. This photo was taken when Patras, Olympia and Kalmai were producing story opportunities by the dozen. The typewriter and raincoat were a 'badge of office' then, as drenching showers were sudden and often. On this particular occasion we were working on establishing an 'Olympian Arlington' on the site of the initial ancient Olympic Games, and every Olympian who had been awarded a medal would be entitled to burial there. Applications were coming in from all over the world—but our development contract was terminated and it never happened!

tions. King Constantine finally called for an election for May of 1967. Litton's legal battery of Glen McDaniel, Robert Berry and Rudy Ernst were by then so badgered, bewildered and blinded they saw no chance that the ballot box would clear the air. They capped their fountain pens so long poised for signing and left Athens.

They were barely home when on April 21, 1967, the Greek Army moved in as it had many times before, sickened of the politicians, of rioting in the streets and of the leftish tinge of affairs of state. Twenty officers, the highest ranker being bald, brusque old tank commander, Brig. Gen. Stylianos Pattakos, born in a small village on Crete, in one night took over the government in a bloodless coup. The rest were colonels and lieutenant colonels. The "cradle of democracy" which had been made messy by the professional politicians became a government of "the colonels" or "the junta" depending on the polemicist in residence, whether that residence was within or safely beyond Greece' borders. Desiring as quickly as possible to be seen as not only in power and restorers of stability, but also as progressive and decisive, there appeared to be one decision the new leadership could make immediately.

Every shade of Parliamentary government for more than two years had waxed and waned about "economic development". It was at once an urgent and emergency imperative, but also the target for opposition outcries. Now that Col. George Papadopoulos as Prime Minister and Col. Nickolaos Makarezos as Minister of Coordination were installed, there was a phone call to Guillaume in Brussels to return to Athens at once. There was no opposition now; signatures on the document were all that was needed—and the new government had pens in hand.

The Beverly Hills corporate office of Litton was a little benumbed by now because of the on-again, off-again Greek matter but did not wave Guillaume off.

William Berry, Litton's treasurer just recently appointed, had come into the picture late. He had been seeking some outside advice and guidance as he had been mostly in U.S. military government contracting until tapped to take on the shepherding of Litton's monies. The very thought of presenting himself to banks in that position with him being the neophyte he was, kept him shy until he'd had some talks with AT&T's treasurer. That had given him a quick course about the methods of cash management systems. This speed-reading showed him how it was computerized, how funds were moved mercurially into overnight investment opportunities and associated protective measures which treasurers had to know to perform money affairs well. A fast learner, Berry was proud of his record in raising the number of banks extending lines of credit to Litton from five to 29.

He had barely time to smile smugly while shaving one morning when the full import of the Greek contract's Litton involvement hit him. He went to Harry Gray, then Litton's Senior Vice President for Finance and Administration. He was agitated.

"This is dangerous for Litton," he said. "I'm totally opposed to it. I've talked with a couple of banks in New York. They tell me this kind of thing can never succeed. Greece doesn't even have the infrastructure to be industrialized. They need roads, railroads, utilities— because they're power starved. They don't have bridges in the right places even. . ."

It was purely postcard, sunning, hiking, artsy-craftsy, touristic country-side. The very things which made it attractively quaint for the migrant campfire backpackers was its worst obstacle to development along modern lines. Within that bronzed, hairy-legged, sandled and giftshop oriented international set there was a ferocious and vociferous uproar brewing against any changes at all.

Harry Gray tried to comfort Berry by saying he thought financing would come from Europe and the Middle East oil sheiks and perhaps the Orient. Berry went right out of Gray's office, headed for the airport and took a plane for Europe to poll some of the big merchant bankers. Everyone of them chilled his veins with the same refrain— that they would not lend a shilling, franc, pfennig, lira or krone for development in the part of Greece assigned to Litton by the contemplated contract.

"Is it because of the present military government?" This question was put by Robert M. Allan, Jr., newly made President of the Litton International Development Corporation (LIDCO).[3] LIDCO was to be

---

3. Because of my NATO experiences, as General Dwight D. Eisenhower's advance man when he returned to Europe, in 1951 and where I'd helped establish each of NATO regional Headquarters, LIDCO President Robert Allan to whom I'd been assigned, announced intent to make me one of his Vice Presidents. It caused consternation in Litton's PR office where I was carried as Corporate Director, Special Mis-

Litton's leading edge in probing for carrying out such economic development contracts not only in Greece, but in other countries as well. Greece was the test case.[4]

"I lend money to Franco in Spain and to the Soviet Union," said Rothschild in London. "Money has no conscience politically. We want to be sure only that we will be paid back. But where industry is concerned we don't want to lend money for what looks like foolish ventures." In the bankers' minds were all those documented experiences with Greece's debt repudiation. An elephant has no attention span or memory at all compared to a burned banker. The country that was Greece cried for credibility.

Ash still believed in the project. Just because it was sure to be rocky going did not mean it was unsolvable. Greece yearned for Litton's financial respectability to give it respectability, too. On May 15, 1967, in Athens, the contract was signed between the two parties. It was exactly 24 days after the military coup. It was the first major decision and commitment by the new government. Greece, only slightly better off than the so-called *Tiers Monde* (Third World), and barely ahead economically of Portugal, Europe's poorest state, had signed up what it hoped was a modern Hercules to sluice away the smelly past and bring the money changers into harmony with their temporal realm.

The document which Guillaume signed stated that all the action was to be audited by Greek certified public accountants since it was a cost reimbursement agreement. While Roy Ash was enthused about this new Litton avenue, he was sharp enough to insist that Litton

---

sions & Projects. Then VP Ralph O'Brien opposed it, and at a meeting of the VPs, Allan, exasperated, took O'Brien to Roy Ash. He and I had worked together on each of his trips to Athens. Allan wanted the VP thing OK'd and told Roy. "I thought it was settled," Roy said. "What's holding it up?" O'Brien was embarrassed, said lamely: "There is a policy that no corporate employee can be an officer of a subordinate division. . ." Roy broke in: "Ralph, why do we have a policy? It is so we can break it when it's in the best interests of Litton. This is in Litton's interest." One learns as one goes along, and Litton was a sporty environment then.

4. In Ralph O'Brien's first foray as Litton's liaison with the investment community, 14 of the U.S. brokerages in the City of London joined him at the Dorchester Hotel for breakfast. He was stunned when the White-Weld rep before putting his fork to his scrambled eggs, asked: "What on earth is Litton doing in Greece? That's been a disaster area for 2,000 years!" Comments were similar in Brussels, Frankfurt and Zurich, which he reported to Roy Ash on his return.

351

would always be operating on "their money". If the relationship foundered for whatever reason, it would be negotiable as to how much of what Greece had advanced to Litton would be given back to the givers. Litton was to be paid $1,200,000 the first year, the rate steadily increasing to $3,600,000 by the 48th month. There was an incentive that 11% of Litton's actual costs would stay in Litton's treasury plus the availability of extras paid on a sliding scale as Litton-induced foreign capital was brought in. The agreement was projected to have a 12-year life, produce $120,000,000 in investments by the 24th month, and $240,000,000 by the 48th month. The most revealing aspect of the voluminous paper pile was that it stretched its time over a dozen years. That indicated how difficult everyone on both sides of the table thought the going would be. The tone on signing day was one of celebration; if there was fear anywhere, it was well hidden.

The excitement of new adventuring was general, not confined to the back room where the signatures were collected. Litton's man put all his names on the line—Pierre Alphonse Guillaume. It had been a long trek from that early Minos Beach conversation. The Greek signers were Col. Nikolaos Makarezos, the Minister of Coordination and No. 3 in the new regime's pecking order, and Constantine N. Georgiades, the official translator in the Ministry of Foreign Affairs. That document, reproduced in both Greek and English, became an immediate best seller throughout that old country. More than a million copies were printed in the Greek language. With Athens the population center of nearly 2,000,000 people, the news kiosks[5] had long queues of customers who waited for hours to get and then devour their copies.

LIDCO's Robert Allan fresh from Cyprus Mines Corporation on site on that fevered and often wretched island with its Grecian inclinations and blood feuds with the Turks, was hastily required to put the Litton-Greece unit together. No corporate honcho in his right mind would have even started on that while the seesawing was going on and an outcome much in doubt. Ultimately settled on for the Litton-Greece helmsman was Gordon Pehrson, who had been the most highly placed civil servant in America's POLARIS missile program. The

---

5. Those kiosks were always supposed to be operated and owned by Greek war veterans. That had not been so until the junta had taken power. In August and September of 1967, the Greek language copies of the Litton contract outsold PLAYBOY on those newsstands.

fact that he had helped make an underwater launching pad function under one set of circumstances was not too much of an environmental change from the one he found himself in now. While much of the POLARIS was classified and only spoken or written about in overall and general ways, the world audience watching him now—and Litton—was of the same texture as the sometimes hysterical fans who gather to watch a bullfight, not caring too much about who might win, but wanting to miss none of the action.

There were two impending events in Athens which lay across the Litton path and could help speed the visibility. One was the American Society of Travel Agents (ASTA) annual convention, and the other, the Athens gathering of the United Nations Industrial Development Organization (UNIDO). The Litton task was to engage in development of tourism, agricultural and industrial projects. Even with that long and halting route to the signatures, these two door-step coincidences were handled at the same time Litton was opening its office in the American Express building on Syntagma. From the UNIDO meeting alone, Litton was able to sound the great Third World hunger for assistance. More than 20 countries' representatives visited the Litton Hilton Hotel suite talking about their own dreams of development back home.

There were some mine fields and time bombs out there, and some obvious booby traps. Under the contract heading, *Article 5, Obligations of Litton*, was the biggest booby trap. The very first lines said: "Litton is a privately established, non-political business enterprise. Therefore, Litton shall refrain from any active participation in political activities in Greece." One of the soon-to-be-exploded potentials for making that nonsense was then being detained in Hotel Pikermi, the fiery Melina Mercouri.

For her actressish outbursts at the regime, she was deGreeked by the junta, disowned and made a non-citizen of her homeland. Made additionally famous for her role as a harlot in "Never on Sunday", she became the dais darling for assemblies for attacks on the "colonels" from whatever country. When the junta released Papandreou, they became the noisy duo of protest.

The problem of keeping the "Political" out of any contract with any government is impossible. Any investor prospect approached by Litton about taking risks in a certified-as-fractious region always asked an informed opinion about how stable the area was—the most natural of inquires when he wonders how much time he has to work his way to a profit. If the agent, or Litton Industries as one, answers either way, it has to be a "Political" judgment. The oral outrage and printed commentary heaped on the regime by its "exiles" ranted at every gesture, effort or statement constructively made and denounced each as "supportive of the junta". Litton was cast as the villain to the point that when LIDCO head, Bob Allen, was addressing an audience in Copenhagen, Denmark, he said he didn't think much of the highly raucous rhetoric and remarked: "and who are these people who give advice on economics? One is an agitating professor out of work, and the other, an aging actress without a play!" When Allen and some of his staff were threatened if Litton persisted in going on with the contract that "something may happen to you. . ." it was obviously a gloves-off situation.

Littonites tended to glance over their shoulders at times in Athens although the prejunta turmoils in the streets had quieted. How to adhere to the contract was prickly enough. It was written, explained Jacques Warshauer, one of the senior staffers, in "both English and Greek". Neither was its official language. "This meant it was Greek to us and English to them" he said. There was nothing facetious intened. Example: There is no Greek word for "incurred", and an English speaking accountant can hardly function without it. The Greeks wanted handwritten receipts for everything and wouldn't accept photocopies of cancelled checks used for payments. Warshauer set up and ran a seminar attended by more than 30 Greek accountants which lasted for three hours. It went all the way from a profile of the U.S. Federal Reserve Banking system to the conclusion that a perforated cancelled check was the best proof of payment one could have. The Greeks were profuse in their thanks, agreed absolutely and said they would be perfectly happy to accept the perforated cancelled checks as proof ". . . as long as they are accompanied by the original signed receipts."

Litton entered their world of the paper blizzard and ended up doing it the Greek way. Not only did the paper pile up, the Greeks loved this add-on to their already mountainous files of studies and charts which had been accumulating through the years and gathering dust. It was the usual mistaken impression that in bureaucratic bustling something was getting done, when the very bustle was part of the obstacle to that being so. A chart received most enthusiastically and with sage nods of approval carried no obligation to pursue an objective via such a schematic diagram.

The Greek system was typical of old geography strewn with the tracks of conquerors and occupiers who held power for short and long periods. Their adjustments to defeat and subjugation gave them trappings stolen from other procedural forms. Some of what Greece had was borrowed from the French and from the British. There was Turkish mishmash flavoring it. But one thing was sure, never had a sovereign government of its own volition signed an accord delegating to a foreign business firm entire responsibility for development planning in much the same fashion that government agencies are usually organized and chartered to do.

The hunt for investment interest was the main thrust.

Gordon Pehrson assembled the Litton-Greece staff every Monday morning. He invited and encouraged ideas to be thrown about freely, whether projects or investment sources. One of the hottest from the first, identified by a German staff member, Günter Hutten, was the Frankfurt-based Henninger brewing enterprise. That German firm knew a lot about Crete. Hitler's paratroopers had landed there in WWII and German brew came with them.[6] Henninger forward planners thought there were several Eastern Mediterranean market areas for their brand. Heraklion, on Crete, was the site they liked.

Another courting quarter was FIAT, the great Italian complex in Torino. They believed there was merit in having one of their auto assembly plants in Patras, the Western Peloponnessus port city just across the narrow Adriatic from Italy. This forecast positive action in each Litton zone.

Litton was a combination chamber of commerce, project developer, financing finder, way clearer with the Greek government when an investor surfaced, fixer, explainer, friend-at-court, the traditional but plenipotentiary middleman. Litton ran headlong into a basket of annoyances. Site selection, for instance. Generations of Greek fami-

---

6. In fact, the Henninger firm had one of those paratroopers in line to manage the Heraklion plant. He was Dr. Otto Bolz, who had first come to Crete by parachute in 1942!

lies had parceled and fragmented land ownership through each generation of offspring. This meant small, irregularly outlined plots in random hands, many of whom exercised absentee ownership. The records of some of the holders were in the musty archives of the Greek Orthodox Church which had shielded the names from the Turks. Others were in government documents, but disputed. When ownership was not forthcoming, Litton often used the simple ploy of a stake and a maul. The Litton hand went on the property of interest and began noisily to drive the stake into the ground. Rather soon, this produced a Greek peasant who might only be curious. More often than not, he would ask the stake-driver what he was doing "on my land." If he could prove it by hidden documentation, only then could a deal be struck.

The FIAT people, for all their initial enthusiasm, never did come to Greece. Jacques Warshauer, who was initially Litton-Greece' "marketer", went to Torino many times. Eventually he returned to Athens with FIAT's "Power of attorney" to arrange for the assembly plant. For 13 months the application languished in the Ministry of Coordination and was never acknowledged as being there! One could easily conclude that what was already in being in an automotive way in Greece was considered "sufficient" by some people with power who could encourage an endlessly dilatory attitude. The potential investor was entitled to ask the question that if it was going to be this difficult getting in, how much more so would it be when committed and in there? And many did. FIAT was no fly-by-night, after all.

At the start, Bob Allan had decreed after consulting with Roy Ash that Litton would not come into the Grecian picture as an investor, or plant locator. This was considered as probably detrimental and that Litton would appear to be grabbing all the best possibilities for itself from its privileged position. In no time, Litton found quite the opposite rumors around to the effect that if Greece was all that great an investment haven, how come Litton was standing aside and playing some cagey Judas goat?

Ash encouraged Arnie Kaufman of the Litton components Group to survey Crete for one of his electronics plants. Crete had all those nimble fingered women who engaged in weaving exotic patterns in blankets and bedspreads and drapes from Mt. Ida's sturdy sheep's

356

wool. They could easily convert to the bread-board assembly work, so proximity to Heraklion was also suggested.

Ash told Joe Imirie, the head of the Professional Services Group, that his Stouffer's Restaurants and Inns division should think about going international. There was a promising hotel development opportunity in Khania along Crete's northwest coastline.

Kaufman didn't want to say NO, but he was considering Singapore for a Kester Solder facility. Ash was cheerful about it and told him to go for both! Kaufman sent James Pandapas, whose Poly-Scientific had been recently sold into Litton divisional status, as a friendly reconnoiterer. He was a Greek-American and nimble with the language.

A most reluctant Stouffer's was far from thrilled about the Khania hotel proposal. They had just come into Litton's big world and had to feel their way. Bob Allen left Beverly Hills for one of his many transatlantic "shuttle runs" to Athens. He felt sure in his mind that he had these two quick examples of Litton "puts". As he was making the press conference announcement in Athens, the reorganizational convulsion hit Stouffer's in Cleveland. All the stubbornness about going international returned and the Khania project being promised was dead as a smelt. This was when Jim Stouffer, Vernon Stouffer's son and heir who he couldn't put at the head of the family enterprise, bailed out after his brother-in-law, Jim Biggar, had been chosen.

There was trouble trying to get the Heraklion land for both the Henninger brewery and the Litton electronics plant locations, but that was solved when brass-knuckled Greek Gen. Pattakos, a Cretan by birth, called the appropriate official in Heraklion and said cryptically:

"Either clear that land for this plant construction, or I'll send in some tanks!" Suddenly that land ownership matter simplified. It was a hard league, hard ball and hard doing, all the time.

Twice LIDCO President Bob Allen had been taken off airplanes with heart condition flare-ups which were frightening, the result of the pressurized life he was leading. Besides Greece, he had Dr. F.H. "Ted" Haner, recently recruited from the University of Southern California, working on an economic development proposal for Portugal and one for the west of Ireland.

The way into Portugal had been on another lead furnished by Guillaume. The Portugal idea was to provide a sophisticated marketing structure in that country to plan the planting and synchronize the harvests of fruit, vegetables and other farm products of the Alentejo region—nearly a million acres of land lying just east, and to the north and south of Lisbon. The plan covered the processing of these products and their marketing in the United Kingdom and Northern Europe. The Portuguese were phased to acquire 10% of the concept each year for ten years. Then it would all be in the hands of Portuguese nationals. Litton would be out of the picture. It was wallowing inconclusively because the ailing and elderly dictator, Dr. Antonio Salazar, could only agree that it made sense but wasn't about to be hurried into it. He had been in power for more than three decades. He was depending on his Treasury Chief and his Economics Minister to work it out. The money czar was a tightfisted resister of new ideas and believed an escudo saved was an escudo earned. The Economics Minister was much younger, a charming bachelor and bon vivant. They disliked each other so intensely they would not willingly be in the same room, nor would they agree on anything. Salazar had no wish to enter as a referee, or appoint someone to head the project, which if successful might, make a public hero of that individual. It could almost amount to picking his political successor. He had obvious reticence about wanting to stage a cockfight at that time of his life.

One day Ted Haner was sitting in the sun idly watching automobiles go over the great Salazar bridge which crossed the river Tagus. The young Portuguese sitting with him mused:

"Do you know how long ago the talks began about building that bridge?" "No," Haner said. He was told it was in 1936. Did he have an idea when the first car had crossed it? Haner shook his head. "It was 1966," the young man said. Thirty years, thought Haner, and Litton, so big, so widespread, was only half that old. He began to have misgivings.

The reports from Ireland where Litton was prepared to invest in development projects and secure other likeminded entries in such an overall effort were that Irish Finance Minister Charles J. Haughey was finding the local political currents difficult wading. Over in Turkey, Tom Pearson was the Litton on-scene coordinator. The Turks often cued on Greece, as the Greeks did on them, neither wanting to be outshone. The Turkish government offered tentatively for Litton development planning that portion of their homeland fronting on the Mediterranean from Izmir (once Smyrna) eastward to Iskenderun and inland from 50 to 75 miles. The tourism possibilities were grand as it included Ephesus, and its legendary mountain eerie where the Virgin Mary was said to have lived out her final years after the Crucifixion. It was also the home ground of the Bishop of Myra in Antalya who became St. Nicholas, and one of the ancient manmade wonders of the world, the temple of Diana.

Turkey was edgy politically, and anti-Americanism was in the air making it hard for a rickety government to openly affiliate with or enlist a U.S. company and be charged with having given it *carte blanche* (whether it did or not) to wheel and deal.

The remaining economic development tie involved the Kingdom of Morocco, particularly the Tadla, the Haouz and the Abda Doukkala sectors with the hope of bridging them economically to the countries of affluent Western Europe.

Bob Allen, ailing and spent from his exertions, found his LIDCO spread thin and under siege. He took Gordon Pehrson off the Litton-Greece project. He replaced him as the managing director with Jacques Warshauer who was thought to have a better personal rapport with all the potential investors and the Greek government as well. Then Litton replaced Allan with Gordon Murphy,[7] who had recently vacated the principal's chair at Litton's Data Systems division. All this was happening when Litton was reeling from disclosures of its other management problems.

Murphy, the one who said a call from Roy Ash always made his palms moist, had inherited a buzz saw. He was walking into puzzles aplenty as Litton International Development Corporation was shown

---

7. Component Group's Jack Connolly wanted no part of an electronics plant on Crete. Being a corporate gamesman of some stature, he came well armed for a meeting between himself and LIDCO president Robert Allan in Roy Ash's office. He had compiled not a few, but 200 questions for Ash to work from, all of them hard. They forced Allan to say "don't know" too often. The session ground on for three hours. Ash, always the "numbers" man, closed off the inconclusive conversation by saying: "This is a $2,000,000,000 company. I have 2,000 hours a year, or an hour for every million of that action." He looked at Bob Allan. "You used up three years of your time with me today." Bob Allan resigned as LIDCO's head the next day. Litton never did put its components plant on Crete. That's the way Litton was then.

to him in a dead run briefing. One thing that caught his eye was the Greek contract proviso which said either party to it at the 24-month mark could signify the wish to renegotiate the accord into a more workable form, or signify desire to drop it.

The second anniversary of the military coup of Greece' takeover was just ahead of Murphy on April 21, 1969. Groundbreakings were scheduled for the Henninger brewery and the proposed Litton Electronic components plant outside Heraklion as part of the celebrations. Dr. Wilhelm Nuber, member of the Board of Directors of Henninger Bräu, KgaA, out of Frankfurt, and Litton's Augerinos "Rino" Sotiriou, slated to be managing director of Cretan[8] Electronics Manufacturing, were to be the visible incomers. Squat Brig. Gen. Stylianos Pattakos, Deputy Prime Minister and Minister of Interior for Greece, was the Government's face card. He had just come from representing the Government of Greece at former President Eisenhower's funeral in Washington. He knew from the kind of press he and his associates were getting in the U.S. some good news was needed. To avoid getting in the way of the big April 21st revolutionary anniversary plans, the earth turning in Crete was set for April 19th.

As Pattakos spoke that day, Murphy was waiting his podium summons. He remembered that the very ground they were standing on had been secured under threat of force in the form of Army tanks. No matter how positive Pattakos was, most of the press attending didn't even bother to take notes. Projects being implemented, Pattakos said, represented total investments of $3,350,000 of which $1,650,000 was foreign money. It was a start. He went on to say that project applications had been approved worth $17,217,000, with $8,417,000 of that coming from foreign sources. Applications for which approval was still pending amounted to $5,900,000 of which $3,400,000 was offshore money. Projects for which investors had been found, but their applications were still being considered totaled $4,500,000 with more than half of that coming from abroad. Other ventures still being analyzed and evaluated that looked promising to the government of Greece, he declared, stood at the $75,000,000 level and $48,000,000 of that would come from out-of-country treasuries.

---

8. It's an eastern Mediterranean "funny" that one can say his father is a Cretan and his mother a Lesbian and he's talking geography rather than physical aberration, a kind of phonetics entrapment.

Murphy's speech was in his pocket. It would be translated for him during the luncheon program which followed the ground breading. Costos Hadziotis had gone over the English several times to get the sense of it, and to provide the idiom. In it, after all the opening graciousness and politeness, were these words:

"We are both a great deal wiser as fits two years of experience. . . both sides have been considering possible changes in our contracts to determine how we can make Litton's efforts more cost effective for Greece. We expect to enter into negotiations with representatives of the Government. These negotiations will result in modifications to the direction specified and to the incentives. . ."

Pattakos sat there stonefaced. He didn't like the tone. Word was passed that any press accounts should not use the Litton words "renegotiate" or "modifications". As is the case with all governments, the Greeks would have preferred to have been first to state publicly being aggrieved. It was being shellacked outside its borders by the "exiles" claiming when they came back to power one day, they would repudiate any contracts or obligations undertaken by the junta. Now this from Litton. As governments will always manage to do, though, theirs is the biggest platform from which to make announcements. While sensing the handwriting on the wall, and the bloom being off Litton's rose, it would be the Government which would state the termination on its own calendar. Nowhere in Greek language newspapers were those Litton uttered words "renegotiate" or "modifications" to surface. But Litton did mange to get the figures as enunciated under Government auspices in English and French in *Hellas* magazine in Athens, that magazine being widely circulated abroad. What Litton had been able to do was there in the Government's own utterances, on the record—and in the archives.

When Gordon Murphy went to Ankara, Turkey, it was for more hard-nosed talk. He insisted on seeing Turkish Prime Minister Suleiman Demiral personally. He told him he needed some positive movement toward the contract. He even said his job was "on the line" if some solution wasn't immediately forthcoming. That might have sounded like strong medicine to Murphy, but he was in a country which often terminated political careers with jailings. The founder of modern Turkey, Mustapha Kemal Ataturk had once hanged all his Parliamentary opposition to lampposts along a main thoroughfare.

They dangled there and were viewed by all the resident diplomatic corps homeward bound from a reception he hosted. He wanted their dispatches to home foreign offices to show him as unwilling to brook any watering down of his goal for his country. Demiral, an engineer by profession, had worked in the U.S. from 1949 to 1951. After a short time home, he returned to America as an "Eisenhower Fellow", one of the first. Even so, he couldn't understand how Murphy would think the loss of some non-Turk's job was a very strong argument for the contract. It didn't move any faster.

Shortly after that, Murphy went on to the greener meadows of Cerro Wire and Cable Co. His short course in unstable governments with Litton was a good preparatory for his new task. Copper riches never considered what kind of zany humanity might one day hold domain when the ore chose its locations spottily around the globe. Litton's winder-upper for this particular economic development try was Gale Livingston. He was the last man in line for the Ash thesis that all such operations should be on "their money". To Livingston was left the chore of contract conclusion and how much, when terminated by its sponsors, Litton would give back.

The Greek Government finally let the other shoe drop, and set October 15, 1969 as the official date that the contract with Litton would end. On that day, Jacques Warshauer's summary showed Litton-Greece engaged in 58 projects which involved $263,000,000 of estimated funding requirements with $131,000,000 the foreign capital infusion. Of these 40% were related to actions approved by the Government or in the process of being OK'd. In that 40% foreign investors had been identified and the monies allocated.

The nightmares of the title problems were about to be where Litton found them—such as one 2 1/2 acre plot right in the middle of a proposed marina development, which was owned by six Greek citizens and a 11/30th by the Ministry of Agriculture! Four of the Greeks were in Athens, one in the U.S. and the other nowhere to be found. There was the lady from Boston who was "left hanging" because she had a small parcel of land in the Western Peloponnessus area she hoped would appreciate in value. She told Andreas Sinopolos of the Litton-Greece staff that if she could improve the worth of her dowry by that much, she could get a "better looking husband." Left to the pondering of historians was that grand plan to refurbish the Olympia site, where the Olympic Games originated nearly eight centuries B.C. Ever since the games were revived by French Baron Pierre deCoubertin in 1896, the Greek delegation had marched in the lead as competitors from all over the world parade in the Olympiad's opening ceremonies.[9]

In early 1970, Litton International Development Corporation went into "parking orbit" as was said of company units no longer functional. Litton cleared Greece, Turkey, Ireland, Portugal, Morocco, a fish-processing project in Newfoundland, and discontinued its attempts to set up a banana road in Ecuador and wood-pulp manufacturing in Guyana (had that one gone ahead, Litton would have been a near neighbor of the later ill-fated Jonestown cult and its final suicidal, bloody conclusion). In each instance, Litton learned that the world's environmentalists have consistently overlooked the most lethal environmental problem of all—not nasty water, not pollution, not air befouled, not land eroded, but the various political environments in which business enterprise may try its best, but even a best effort cannot succeed.

Litton's flagship experience was in Greece. The "Colonels' regime" which signed them in, ran from 1967 to 1974. Had Litton's contract still been rolling (as it was to go until 1979) it would undoubtedly have been cancelled summarily. The "exiles" had said over and over that once they were restored to power they would repudiate

---

9. Greece' only gold medal ever went to King Constantine for a yachting event, George Voubanis, a relative of the Skourases who were so big in 20th Century-Fox and theaters, went to UCLA and learned to pole vault in world class style and decided to compete for Greece at Melbourne in 1956. He won a bronze medal and became a *bona fide* Hellenic hero. King Constantine told Voubanis that when he died, he would be buried at Olympia with his "head sticking out" as a kind of national monument! Bob Allan invited Olympian gold winner Mal Whitfield, the 800-meter man, teaming him with Voubanis. He sent the pair of them to Olympia to give him some ideas about how to develop it with special atention to the athletic elite's views of the hallowed vale. They saw it as a place to instill and cultivate the Olympic ideal in sports clinics, hotel and touristic facilities, stadium and a museum. They suggested a kind of "athlete's Arlington" where Olympians from all over the world might rest forever in a special cemetery. Near there the Olympic flame is kindled each four years and starts its long relay of runners to light the blaze which burns for the life of the Games in the principal stadiums in whatever world capital is hosting. Litton conducted a survey of coaches attending the Mexico City 1968 games and men from 75 coutnries, for both communist and western teams, reported themselves as enthusiastic about seeing the idea pursued. But it was not to be under Litton supervision.

all the junta-born agreements. The signers on the Greek side were jailed. One of the trial outcomes could have been death, and certainly would be prison. Prison, it was to be. The whole concept lived on as a collegiate focus viewed in both politcal science and international marketing classes as a case study. Litton, contrary to popular impression, actually made money—not big, but some. Its losses were in face rather than fiscal.[10]

In the case of Portugal, there was another side to it. When that country suffered its wrenching political upheaval after Dr. Salazar died and felt the communist grip at its throat, if Litton had had its contract there still in force, it would have been ending at a most fortuitous moment. As it was, one of Litton's Sweda managers, Karl Zimmerman, was kidnapped by his own Portuguese employees and held for ransom—the ransom being the amount of fringe benefits monies and severance pay. Sought was $3,000,000 to be in the form of a cashier's check made out to the Bank of Portugal. Litton's negotiator was its time tested warhorse, Grady Warwick. He wouldn't go for the cashier's check, but said he'd leave all of Litton's "accounts receivable" in Portuguese hands if the Government would assume the employee liabilities under the social contract provision. The manager was freed.

The principal ministerial backing in Ireland for the Litton proposal died of a heart attack. It was at the boundaries of the lands earmarked for Litton development that the Earl of Mountbatten was later assassinated. Each of the territories which opened before Litton, or sought to do so, was closely interwoven with political instability and economic discontent. It illuminated just how much corporate courage has to be invested beyond money before even starting to wrest solutions from age-old and entrenched backwardness, demagoguery, and outright chicanery.

---

10. The pyrotechnics of Greek politics were further illumined on October 18, 1981 when Andreas Papandreou became Prime Minister. Melina Mercouri celebrated her 58th birthday by retaining her Piraeus constituency seat in Parliament. Incidentally, in addition to Prime Minister, Papandreou assigned himself the Ministry of Defense portfolio, too. Melina became the Minister of Science and Culture. It was exactly 12 years after the Litton contract with Greece was terminated. Papandreou gained his high office by saying he would opppose continuance in NATO and membership in the Common Market. He called the same Army which had once imprisoned him "guardians of integrity"! *Politicus* is a Greek word, after all.

Most important of all, Litton was not driven off from its concern about economic development assistance internationally, but pointed into a safer mode for its accomplishments—that represented by the search and find capabilities of its Western Geophysical and Aero Service divisions. They could perform their special high technology tasks and then leave to the countries covered their own decision making in terms of ties with other concerns able to exploit what appeared to be profitable prospects. They were mobile, too, could perform their function and leave those which made them less vulnerable to the firebrand nationalist who attacks outlanders who come to stay—and achieve enough success to be attractive for expropriation or nationalization.

But the import of this Litton move was read in many ways. It was a company not likely to be dismayed, no matter how formidable the challenge. It would make the good try. It was savvy enough to know what it meant to be asked in for a tough one. If there was any other way of solving it, it probably wouldn't have had an invitation to join forces. It was another case so often evident around Litton that one could learn by doing, maybe, if only learning which way or ways wouldn't work. Litton, at least, sat down at the world's economic development table and played the cards dealt to it. Not many corporate entities could say that. As far as the critics are concerned, a business enterprise learns quickly to understand how outsiders view its power by the decibels they expend on howling it down.

Many of the things started by Litton in Greece have since been found reasonable, workable and have matured, even if to no credit for Litton. Litton, when LIDCO was shelved, had some real losers on its hands which would eclipse it by far, but the pain of it persisted as there was a degree of emotional involvement well beyond bookkeeping. It attracted writers, professors, engineers, doctors, historians, specialists in antiquities, movie makers, polemicists, artists, dietitians, generals, congressmen, an American vice president, oil tycoons, intellectual think-tanks and even tourists seeking an explanation about it. There was something in it, truly, for everybody, but not enough in it for a company such as Litton, nor fast enough for a transient government such as the junta.

A wise Greek once said that their mythological Zeus was worshipped because he never came down from Olympus. It was Litton's error that it did. Some would agree, but not all. There was never a moment before or after it that was quite like it—a Litton unique.[11]

---

11. Some former Litton-Greece alulmni were gathered around a Beverly Hills restaurant table in 1980 when the truncated Olympics was being staged in Moscow. Litton's Greece contract would have concluded 7 1/2 months before the Soviet Union exploded into Afghanistan leading to the boycott of Moscow by more than 50 countries including the U.S. There had been Litton plans for a stadium at Olympia in the misty, romantic Peloponneses. A Gallup Poll, masterminded out of Princeton, N.J. said 62% of Americans responding favored a permanent site in Greece for the Olympic Games of future. In May, 1980, almost on the anniversary of Litton's old contract start 13 years before, the Government of Greece offered the International Olympic Committee an agreement by which Olympia could become a neutered zone, politically. What started in Greece 27-plus centuries ago could return to permanent residence in the land of the Hellenes. The outgoing head of the IOC, Lord Killanin, said he did not believe it could be possible before 1992. The IOC member assigned the survey, Louis Guirandou-N'-Diaye of Africa's Ivory Coast, considered it "perfectly feasible" to make the move. The Litton-Greece alumni noted that the idealists saw this as a perfect solution to an Olympic Games every fourth year more beset by world politics as it moved from one sponsoring country to another. A move to Greece to *escape* politics? *Politicos* everything. To house the Olympic Games in Greece as a safe haven from politics was what was being talked about seriously. "Ho, ho, ho," said the Litton-Greece alumni.

SPECIAL SITUATION #17

ENTER THE VILLAIN, TPP! (TOTAL PACKAGE PROCUREMENT)

Had there been poll-takers then, 99.44% undoubtedly would have said Noah was nuts!

Some of the votes might have come from his own family. He was sure he was right. The source of this intelligence leading him into all that hammering and hewing of wood was indisputable. The purposes of the exercise to which he addressed so much effort, while being roundly jeered by onlookers, were as fanciful as they were questionable. His decision to go ahead with the building of the Ark was vindicated. In that most republished Book in all the world, the Bible, Noah's name is mentioned repetitively; none of those who scoffed his enterprise is so honored.

There is no record of debate at the gangplank about the wisdom of admittance of some of the pairs of arriving loathsome creatures holding their rainchecks of eligibility. Noah's instructions were that representatives of very living thing be boarded, no matter if it made sense or not in the short run. How was a Noah, who had been *selected* rather than *elected* to his office, to know what products might be developed later?

Corporations would be formed for termite lease-termination and roach assassination. Laboratories that milked water moccasins' venom converted to serum might make the difference between living and dying from some of Man's afflictions. On reflection, one could almost say that the base reference point for what emerged in America's '60s as TPP (Total Package Procurement) was Biblical in origin as there were so many similarities.

The creeping barrages of profanities and obscenities hurled by both sides in contractual relationships assigned the evils principally to bureaucracy. It was in some quarters a "holy Hell" of an experience, one of those being Litton Industries. Litton drew more barbs and sneers than Noah, and unfortunately, it took more than 40 days and nights of heavy rain for Litton to be proven right.

For Tex Thornton who had brought Ingalls Shipbuilding into the company, it did not seem extraordinary. He sincerely believed it made sense while all the rest of aerospace was charging into the Cosmos for

367

there to be some modern facility which could respond to rising international maritime and military requirements. The price had been right. Got it for a song, really. The need for new ships extending down through the rest of the century and well into the next was verified. America, in ship production, ranked about 14th, or "even below Yugoslavia," as he often said. There was good reason to believe that more than half the cost of future ships would be for the electronics they enclosed both below and above decks. Litton already had a halter on many of the electronic components and systems that were in immediate demand and in the future forecasting. There were able people at Ingalls, men who had worked and learned under its exacting and querulous founder, Robert Ingalls himself. Cost saving was his obsession bracketed with pride that his family's name was a guarantee for integrity and quality in the vessels produced. In any crunch, he gave most weight to preservation of that reputation. He might verbally abuse those who erred, but he would dig deep in-pocket however grudgingly, to make up for misjudgments. His old hands had accomplished miracles on that tiny 55 acres which accommodated four "ways" on the east bank of the Singing River at Pascagoula, Mississippi.

Before Litton, Ingalls Shipbuilding had built 189 ships. They included merchant and passenger ships, cargo liners, atomic-powered submarines, anti-submarine net layers, refrigerated stores ships, troop transports, oil tankers and amphibious dock transports. There were 28 types of seagoing specimens on the "ways" or in adjacent waters when Roy L. Ash announced in 1965 that it intended to enter the competition for an upcoming Navy program, the Fast Deployment Logistic Ship.

The FDLS was projected as a probably 40-ship package. The appetite-whetting aspect was that the first increment to be awarded a winning proposal would be a contract for more than $1,000,000,000! He knew and Ingalls knew if it did win it would have a tough problem on its hands. That Singing River on which it depended as its conduit to the Gulf of Mexico and the oceans was shallow. The "ways" were too narrow to provide the roominess for construction in the bigger dimensions in ships being envisioned by both maritime and Naval strategists.

A professional dramatist could never develop a better or more suspenseful script than the situation at that moment for Litton Industries and the way it would turn. It was all there—a collection of characters who were not only real with genuine parts to play, but who ranged widely. It included business leaders, Senators and Congressmen, a controversial Secretary of Defense who shed orthodoxy for innovation, a conceptualizer who was equal to any imagination-demanding occasion with modern medicine show touch, a governor who would "see the light" and remake his whole portrait for historians to ponder as a contemporary Saul-to-Paul conversion enroute not to old Damascus but on the road from Oxford to Jackson, Mississippi.

It was a time of America preoccupied with picking at its bellybutton lint. Her cities were beginning to resemble arsonists' convention sites, combinations of flaming statement-making and applications of the torch. The campuses were politicized to the extent that students were busy painting and carrying protest signs, and classes were a bore. Varying college degrees for shades of near-nihilism were available as rewards for negative and rebellious attitudes. Who had the right to wear "white hats" and be the "good guys" wasn't crystal clear and was debated in city halls, the home, the governors' offices, the presidency and whatever regime was in power in whatever country. It was enough for some to pose the difficult question and then turn a deaf ear to an unappetizing answer no matter how on the mark it might be. It was every day more painfully obvious to the few engaged in global strategy positioning that the realities of the earth's warts, boils and leprous ailments gave little evidence that humanity was on the brink of "one world" yet.

"Wars of national liberation" had become the productive ploys for spreading influence of aggressively-minded ideologies now that the superpowers had seemingly reached their nuclear standoffs. A current not-so-laughable quip was about the Soviet Union citizen who was asked what kind of transportation he used, and he said: "When I go work, I go Metro. When I go Leningrad, I use train. When I go abroad, I go by tank!" The communist-bloc played have-not nations like a flute, patiently probing and pushing. There was generous opportunity for them to add geographical real estate by sorting through the shambles and despair in wake of regional clashes. All one had to risk was aid and advisers, and if its side won, collect IOUs in the aftermath.

With geography went the people in residence whose sympathetic or cooperating leadership made of them captive servants for whatever political evangelism the carpetbaggers were carrying. In international forums there were railings against interference in the internal affairs of sovereignties. The prevailing wisdom was that the gift of a tank needed an accompanying adviser on methods and mechanics of its operation, appropriate target selection, with the tank being driven by an indigenous national. The key to it all was insuring dependence philosophically by means of loaned expertise that helped national goal-setting. This could be made to serve some greater international purpose, with skill training, scholarships for proper political orientation in the aiding country, and of course, spare parts.

In this game, plan-oriented governments have advantages which go with deliberate choosing of time and place to strike. Democracies depend heavily on their electorate's emotions as a catalyst. Each of the strong but wavering defenders accuse others of shortcomings which bring them to some precipice or another. Litton's backdrop was the still throat-parching memory of Soviet missiles in Cuba, and the rising involvement in Southeast Asia. Cerebral exercises of all kinds were the vogue in State Department and Pentagon corridors as well as in Congress. How could there be some American means of showing presence and deep concern near seething and potentially explosive parts of the world?

One statistic loomed—there were 135 coastal nations around the globe which could be reached via oceans and seas!

Military ships which could endure extended time at sea seemed logical. Properly pointed at this mission, they had to be a kind of "floating island," provisioned and armed, and able to spend long and indefinite periods in international waters, but near conflagration-vulnerable spots. If there could be a variety of such shipping, bulging with special forces materiel and manpower, it could be a significant factor in deterrence regionally. If stakes proved so urgent that commitment of troops and materiel became necessary, such ships could disgorge at any troubled site a stabilizing force, or help restore order if incidents had ballooned out of hand.

The LITTON Adventure That Was

The rightness of this kind of questing to be fielded by Litton[1] was a combination of the company's characteristics by then. Acquiring of companies and knitting them together is indeed a special art. It also resembles a jumping paratrooper in that no matter how exciting it might be to get from the plane to the ground, it's on the ground where he must use his weapons and engage in the resulting battle. Where the hostilities await, that's where the real test occurs. Acquisitions take a modicum of diplomacy, imaginative processes, supreme confidence and an inventory of talents and technologies in hand make a tired property hum with renewed vigor.

Litton had what might be called an "attitudinal edge." It was not only new to shipbuilding, it had new ideas about it. Being listless and phlegmatic were intolerable. There was the goading of shipyards abroad, too. After having suffered strafing gunfire, ship-to-shore barrages, bombings and minings and in some cases, carefully plotted sabotage raids which had been effective, facilities were now being freshly rebuilt incorporating all the trendy innovations they could lay hands on. As America was in a coasting or back-pedaling state, shiny new and versatile manufacturing complexes were coming into being in the swept up ruins of the Federal Republic of Germany, the Netherlands, as well as in Sweden and Japan. All were incorporating computer

---

1. There were 5,777 U.S. Navy ships produced in American yards in WW II. Reckoning from that experience and because so many assembly lines had done this so well was the possibility of switching to a production format for shipyards rather than staying with the traditional construction approach. There had been many refinements of tools and facilities over the millennia, but the hand-work aspects of getting a ship from its keel-laying into the water were not all that different from primitive methods, used by Arabs on their lateen-rigged dhows or the Chinese flat-bottomed junks. Liberty and Victory ships, those much vilified and ridiculed WW II seahorses which carried cargo to all compass-points of conflict, had broken with many ancient ways. Such cargo carriers were squeezed down their skids with the neatness and slickness of link sausages. The commonality of the models gave pleasing dividends in cost-saving and production speed. There was a great deal of the assembly-line mode in their building, but nothing like what was possible post-war with numerical controls. Trouble was that with the war over, the U.S. went big into the "mothball" business. The peace-glut of those until recently so necessary war-fighting "bottoms" found them enclosed in mammoth cocoons and anchored cozily in tethered flotillas in every available nook and inlet along either coast. U.S. shipyards languished because the number of moth-balled ships overrode public consciousness that the ships were merely survivors. They had few of the modern appointments now available and urgently needed.

controls and complementary precision instrumentation and the "automated shipyard" was the dominating chit-chat of the trade.

Part of the Thornton-Ash assurance that they were on the right heading was their surmise that age and rust were doing more damage to U.S. Navy posture than had all the skirmishes of the Axis powers during World War II. It had been a Navy tip, after all, which had gotten Litton's attention when the Ingalls SOS flag was flying in the wind and the smell of disaster was in the air. Not lost on Litton was that Ingalls had on its record that it had once bid well under-cost for a five ship increment of LSTs. Monro Lanier had been determined to prove Ingalls could meet Navy specifications and deliver a quality high seas performer for the most exacting and demanding customer. The first of the five LSTs inflicted a sea of red ink on the Ingalls treasury, but by the time the fifth LST was batted across the prow with its christening bottle, the story had a happy ending profit. Ingalls had learned its production lessons well. The more experienced its labor force became, the more cost reductions it toted up. The effort had been substantial, wearing, and at times suspenseful, but it was strong support for the idea that series production in a single shipyard had the best chance of being a bargain for monies expended.

Litton Industries, with the decision to enter the Fast Deployment Logistic Ship competition, had to do some gutsy things. The Ingalls East bank 55 acres had never been assaulted or bombed by an enemy, but if Litton was going to pursue seriously that FDLS rabbit over the obstacle course, there had to be a new ship construction site either there in the old neighborhood or somewhere else along the Gulf or East Coast.

Before there had even been a Litton Industries, the military services had done their own kind of a three-for-two split. On September 18, 1947, six years ahead of Litton's birth, the separate U.S. Air Force was established. Co-equal with the Army and the Navy, the legislation said, it was also much lighter of foot and freer of the barnacles of tradition. The Army had its proving grounds and arsenals, the Navy its Bureau of Ships. In them, long-in-the-tooth civil service employees and uniformed transients tried to mesh future battle needs with available budgets. They showed understandable reluctance to leave behind too quickly old weapons with which they'd served and whose capacities had been demonstrated in the last big war. Air Force horizons were seen in a farther out perspective natural to flight. It was said that different types of minds and thought processes tended to be attracted to aeronautics and astronautics. They thought nothing of making incredible and wild, or bold demands in their military specifications. Their aerospace orientation led them to believe having licked gravity anything was possible given funds and encouragement. The Air Force had to lean heavily on America's industrial base for its weaponry, and it contracted to "think-tanks" for research and development. Those who wore the Uxbridge Blue seemed to have, or assumed they had some kind of special ticket to explore some of Man's oldest mysteries and theories about means of unleashing itself from earthly shackles.[2]

Visionary firms, once given the perimeter within which to suggest means of mission accomplishment, were inclined to strain the known resources of their company profiles to the maximum. There was even contract encouragement to recruit brainpower to fill whatever gaps firms knew or thought they had. This centered groups of various intelligences and disciplines under specific industry umbrellas, a resource "fix" such as the country had never known before. An Air Force Assistant Secretary, Robert Charles, once an executive vice president of McDonnell-Douglas, said it made sense to give a prime contractor "the whole thing." This was because in part the Air Force usually made contract awards which called for large numbers of items, seldom under 100. The AKC-135 contract to Boeing costing the Air Force around $9,000,000 a copy could transition into a com-

---

2. They were almost a page from that 1901 kind of "foolishness" which had Kaiser Wilhelm II in Germany arranging for the old Barnum & Bailey Circus to tour the Fatherland for one season. He didn't care whether the audience enjoyed it or not, but exacted the single privilege that 30 members of the German General Staff travel with that tented enterprise. He wanted them to learn two things—the system by which the Circus loaded its trains so quickly over the ends of its flatcars rather than over the side as the German Army did after which heavy equipment had to be turned about and manhandled which was time consuming, and how the rolling kitchens were operated. From this most unusual source, Germany learned well and could get its heaviest equipment aboard and fully make up three 22-car trains in an hour. And those kitchens could serve troops hot meals wherever the force materialized. That "lightning strike" capability of its time almost brought France to its knees in the first few August days of 1914! There were lots of things to be picked up outside military enclosures, no matter if Napoleon himself had once said: "Any man who thinks is my enemy."

mercial version called a 707 going to the airlines for as low as
$4,000,000 apiece. It was the "learning curve" which over time made
the difference. With the Lockheed win of the huge C-5A task, TPP
came to military life—Total Package Procurement.

This was a "cradle to grave" concept. The contractor's commitment was to conceptualize, design, cost analyze, build, train crews,
guarantee fits to stated roles and missions, plus caring for rehabilita-
tion and repair functions for the entire service life of whatever weapons system was involved.

It was literally breath-taking in the sweep of it. The Air Force
ran with it. Not so easily generated was enthusiasm for the changes it
would enact in the older uniformed services. Secretary of Defense
McNamara was strong for "commonality"—procurement of all like
items for all services rather than separately. The Navy had been accustomed to certify as required a number of ships of a certain class,
then give fractions of the total to several shipyards. This gave every
shipyard a start-up formula to arrive at, and shortened the benefits of
the "learning curve" as each shipyard had to have one.

There was appeal in this idea for a new Navy Assistant Secretary
named Graeme Bannerman. He'd started in Navy procurement, knew
it well, and then wandered off into other roles offering him advance-
ments in money and enhancement in status. By the time of his recla-
mation by the Navy in 1965, he had worked a great deal with Air
Force opposite numbers. He believed that a portion of new procurement ideas could be borrowed as well as some of fresh perspectives on
contract fulfillment. Why not bundle up several years of contracting
obligation, he reasoned, and deposit it all on one shipbuilder's doorstep?[3] Bannerman was completely enamored of such things as sys-

---

3. One in the Pentagon who made a favorable impression and had real rapport
with Secretary of Defense McNamara was a relatively obscure Navy 2½ striper, Lieutenant Commander Charles DiBona. A Rhodes Scholar at Oxford, he'd become engrossed in economics, and marine economics especially. Not normally an entrancing
subject among his "sail 'em & sink 'em" colleagues, on returning to duty he found
himself in the systems analysis group at the Department of Defense. He was appalled
about ships' costs having become unreasonably high. His careful research satisfied
him that where a great number was involved, a contract to a single shipyard for the
whole series made sense while the penny-packeting tactic would up dollar-dismaying
every time. He was a proponent of larger, or total awards by contract to one company
insuring its labor force would become more adept, resourceful, cost-cutting and would

tems analysis, computerized controls and design and it seemed elementary good sense to him to pick a properly configured concern with known capabilities and "give it the business." It was in industry, he thought, were the high IQ heads, the capacities for imaginative leaps and the practical professionals, all in harness. Bannerman found this irresistible.

On the Litton side of the outreaching arch was its Vice president for Technical Planning, John Rubel. He'd been through the ropes, a California Institute of Technology graduate who had gone with General Electric and Hughes Aircraft, then succumbing to the Washington of Camelot days when President John F. Kennedy appointed him Assistant Director for Research and Engineering in the Department of Defense. In that assignment, his mental roaming had been on the general subject of long range, strategic strike forces and the design of actual strategic weapons systems. He had tangled with the Air Force regularly. He was a lightning bug, flashing here and flashing there, never at loss for words, buzz or otherwise. Surely he was a long-looker as advance planners were called, often more inclined to want to sketch concepts against the world he hoped for than the one likely to be out there to meet him. He was a concept dreamer-upper, and also abrasive. His coming to Litton was described in Air Force circles as a "wash." ("Either Litton will never get another Air Force contract because he's there," it was said and in no way a joke, "or they'll get a big one just for getting Rubel out of the Pentagon and their hair . . .").

This was the Navy, however, and in Navy circles somebody who was hard on the brashness of those in "the upstairs business" possessed a certain charm. The Navy said it wanted the Fast Deployment Logistic Ship. Among other things, while Rubel was in the Defense Department he had fathered the military procurement procedure known as *project definition* and later *program definition* when such matters got more complicated and were more all-encompassing than a mere piece of hardware. Who better to put on FDLS than the one who had invented the rules for the game in contract seeking? For the design and concept phase for the FDLS, President Roy L. Ash named Rubel as Litton's Director for the Fast Deployment Logistic Ship project.

---

shorten time of ship delivery—money outlays per ship would decline as the series progressed to its end.

Late in 1965, the Navy invited the shipbuilding industry and its supporting vendors to a Pentagon briefing. The auditorium was jammed with 850 company representatives that day, part of them with interests in the whole package, and others in parts of the package. The meeting with its questions and answers was barely over when the Navy found itself with startling knowledge on its own drawing boards—there were only 12 of the firms who had attended who had established and reliable competence to take on an obligation of such tremendous magnitude! There was further review, and the number shrank to five. Two were the longtime ship-building giants, Bethlehem and Todd. The other three were Lockheed, General Dynamics and Litton Industries. Whether it was because all the other old-line shipbuilders ignored the proceedings, or that they smelled perils ahead of a size they didn't want to tackle, Todd and Bethlehem scratched. What had happened was the unthinkable. This new direction of the Navy's procurement not only didn't spread small slices of the cake around the ancient and honorables in the ship business, these aerospace giants had reached gluttonous hands into their trough.

The unions were quizzical, having a new cat among their old chickens. The maritime industry had vocal misgivings. After all, here was the Navy thinking of perhaps 40 ships for which the most apt description was that they would be "floating warehouses" or "seagoing supply depots." Their carrying capacities would be fully loaded and ready to set sail on order.

Congress was irked because it was well known that the shipbuilding industry had a kind of muscular dystrophy affliction from being chronically short-rationed, and here was a blatant signal for yet another and new shipyard. The Navy had hoped to work its way down to three finalists, yet in hardly a fortnight after its initial briefing there by self-elimination, or by default of the rest who elected not to play.

Rubel was as happy as a hummingbird in flowers. There was much in the FDLS for Litton's own in-house and considerable arsenal. He saw Subcontracts for Alvey-Ferguson (Litton Unit Handling), and Hewitt-Robins, the conveyor systems suppliers which would be so necessary for loading and unloading FDL ships. They were already in U.S. Navy Supply Centers in Oakland and Long Beach, California.

Litton's Mellonics,[4] specialists in systems engineering, had on their records a diversity of activities such as satellite command and control communications, operations analysis, celestial controls, cost effectiveness studies, logistics and inventory controls, medical data processing and data fitting methods, as well as computer selection and amplification.

Rubel could be a great romancer when the mood was on him, and as a kind of technological Tom Sawyer he knew no peer his equal in making prospects alluring to such as TRW for contributions in configuration management; Peat, Marwick & Mitchell for management information and weapons systems acquisition processes; J.J. Henry & Co., a firm renowned for cost reduction design practices, preparations of final construction plans for new ships (J.J. Henry, in fact, brought in the first automated steam propulsion plant, a fully automated cargo vessel, a highly automated oil tanker and an automated container ship); and the Ralph M. Parsons Co., an organization well-thought of for its facility engineering in many agencies of government such as the Air Force, National Aeronautics and Space Administration (NASA), the Atomic Energy and Maritime Commissions.

The first task for Rubel was, of course, a design phase program definition proposal. It guided on a schematic he formulated himself when on the receiving side in the Pentagon and frustrated about how each military service tended to use what he called the "sacramental wine" approach to increase funding. This was the designation of some program as having the greatest priority, then asking for increased budgeting by appeals before appropriate Congressional committees. These supplementals he found at times to out-distance original cost estimates double and more. It had been his thesis that by going this *program definition* first step, which was a competition funded by the procuring service, the outline would come in so precisely that a fixed-

---

4. Mellonics systems Development, nestled among those other "Silicon Valley" exotics in and around Sunnyvale, California, was a natural "way in" for Litton in practically the whole of the aerospace scene and had other applications as well. It was a near neighbor and by proximity familiar with more than 50% of guided missile and space vehicular manufacture which was in its front yard, along with 42% or so of semi-conductors and a quarter of the computer equipment serving America's needs. Its president, Frank Druding, swapped it for about 45,000 shares of Litton stock then selling at around $66 a share. The agreement was dated May 23, 1964 and finalized later that year.

fee contract could be entered into to which there would be absolute adherence by both parties. He saw some reason even in his sense of ultimate righteousness for cushioning allowances for judgmental errors, or for interference from unexpected quarters.[5] The Canadians always called that "the Jesus factor," which was maneuver room when on some course only God can predict the outcome, but He isn't telling. There could always be lots of bumps and deflections. And human errors, too.

"Flexible response" was new in military terminology. FDL ships were to have a part in that. The Air Force was well along with the mammoth C-5A. It had already achieved the journalese handy cliche "troubled." It had more critics than rivets. This air transport was asked to carry 220,000 pounds of cargo, or about 350 fully combat-rigged troops.[6]

The program definition exercise had to bracket all the known realities and intangibles. Along carnival midways, the men who ran the gambling games always said: "Awright, now, ah'll tell you what we're gonna do . . ." And then they did just that, always with the hand being quicker than the eye. In government the numbers are greater, procurementese used bigger words and more cumbersome sentence structures, and made grander promises—but with the same aim—to convince the money to go along. It is always a big wagering atmosphere.

Program definition calls for the evolvement of a preliminary design and outline. With the "go" signal, or signatures, it's possible to set out the details with the confidence of almost knowing what's expected and wanted. Those details include settling on specifications, performance objectives, schedules and preliminary model construction

---

5. Rubel, and surely some others, believed the Navy could never be counted on for full acceptance of TPP. How much it would interfere and make changes after the contract was let to a winner, would add a lot to the final cost. How right he was!

6. The C-5A was a substantial upgrading from the 225 C-54s in the 1948-49 Berlin Airlift, which could manage but ten tons each on 800 to 900 Berlin-inbound flights daily. However many ready-to-fight men the C-5A could disgorge in some hostile area over the horizon, without their unit equipment they had only the accoutrements they came with to do battle. With a C-5A and an FDL ship unloading in close proximity to their drop or air-landing, it meant heavy materiel, ammunition, fuel, spare parts and all the instrumentation of command and control would be there to establish unit integrity for effective, coordinated action.

heading the contract with more assurance to a fixed-fee with an agreed-upon margin for the contractor and no more. Program definition, as Rubel explained it, is "putting an extra long barrel on a rifle to improve the accuracy with which a target may be hit . . ."

The Navy had three programs in line—FDLS, LHA (Landing Helicopter Assault) for the Marine Corps, and the DDs (Spruance Class destroyers). An informal but understood goal was that U.S. shipbuilding needed more modern facilities. This had to be in the overall approach.

In parallel with the proposal making, the Litton hunt for a new shipyard locale was undertaken. There were initially 50 places on the list. This was quickly narrowed to four: The west bank of the Singing River at Pascagoula; Tampa and Jacksonville, Florida, and the out-of-business New York Shipbuilding site in Camden, N.J. The employment impact was forecast as sizeable, between 5,000 and 7,000 jobs at least to be added on the 10,000 already in Pascagoula if that was the choice. Pascagoula made the most sense from the first if the State of Mississippi could be inspired to go along. It was a tense time there, in no way did it want to see this plum get away.

President Roy Ash was set up for a meeting with Mississippi Governor Paul Johnson. They both converged on Pascagoula at the urging of the State Research and Development Agency. Ash was armed with all the "can't lose" statistics the company could provide, and so was the Governor. Johnson was from Hattiesburg, which was at the very outer edge of the probable affected portion of the state, so he wasn't politically vulnerable in any way on this issue. The study showed, in fact, that the whole state would share in dollars which would turn over two or three times in its economy.

Four moves had to be made to keep the action in Mississippi. They were: (1) Allowing the state to float a bond issue in the amount of $130,000,000; (2) raise the interest rate on state obligations to 5%; (3) permit the state to purchase 611 acres of West bank land from Jackson County; and (4) an enactment by the legislature which gave the state the right to negotiate a contract with a subsequent leaseholder for the construction of the facility itself.

Governor Johnson said he would call a special session of the legislature which would authorize the issuance of a category of bonds for the shipyard which would be tax-free-general-obligational securities.

The shipyard itself was to be built to Litton's design, then leased to the company with the provision that the lease rental would be sufficient to meet monetary payments when due. Those bonds were even to pay one percentage point less interest than the prevailing rate. Giving an almost Christmas-tree lighting effect to the whole thing was that the state's ownership of the land freed it from *ad valorem* taxation annually amounting to nearly $2,000,000. Mississippi was down in the books and records as anti-business in the first half of the 20th Century. It had bared its teeth with laws against corporate ownership of even paltry acreages of the kind which had so enriched Louisiana in jobs and investments by being a welcoming alternative. Mississippi made a remarkable switch in attitudes and cooperating gestures.

Although Governor Paul Johnson, son of an early '30s former governor, was talking with Ash, he was sensitive about the invitation to political mischief the whole matter represented. As soon as he had the Ash assurances of Litton's serious intent to go ahead and that Mississippi was favored, he immediately convened in the Governor's Mansion in Jackson the five gubernatorial and eight lieutenant governor candidates lining up for the next election. He asked them to refrain from making this matter so important for Mississippi and the state's future into a short-term whipping-post. That promise, miraculously, was kept.

The necessary papers putting everything in motion were signed on September 27, 1967 for Litton and for Mississippi. If there had been deliberation and pro-and-cons pondering before, everything took on a new urgency now. Financial institutions were lining up and getting the prospectus as well as the bonds printed. The tension heightened because only one law firm in the U.S. and one member of that firm that had the necessary respect of bond underwriters above all others when municipal and state obligations were coming out—Nixon, Mudge, Rose, Guthrie, Alexander & Mitchell.[7] The Nixon

---

7. The Mitchell performance at a called "do diligence" meeting to establish the General Obligation Port Development Bonds rating was an experience for George Howell, Ingalls' longtime legal warrior and worrier. There had been some misunderstanding that the bonds' interest payments were totally dependent on Litton as the leaseholder, when the securities had not only that but the full face and credit of the State of Mississippi. Mitchell met the Mississippi delegation at his office door, took them to the street, hailed a cab and they all piled in. Out came the Mississippi Code, and he was read pertinent portions of the state's constitution and the legislation which

would become President in 1968 and John Mitchell would be his attorney general. As a corporate and municipal bond lawyer, Mitchell had no peer. He knew the Mississippi stance as to prior financing, promptness and capacity to pay and the state's prospects for economic growth. With his carefully worded and oratorical blessing before the board of convened experts, none rated the offering with less than an "A."

There was a catch to it all, though.

Litton won the design phase competition. This was for an 848-foot long Fast Deployment Logistic Ship, 104 feet wide, speed of 24 knots, displacement 40,000 tons with an endurance of 8,000 miles while carrying 10,000 tons of cargo. The introductory program called for issuance of a $1,000,000,000 contract on July 20, 1967.

The catch? The U.S. Congress decided against funding the FDLS program!

Litton was committed "all over Hell's half acre," as one analyst put it. It had won what the trade called ". . . a leather medal." Those traditional shipbuilders whose noses had been bent out of shape by aerospace companies getting into their act were twitting Litton in its discomfort and saying ". . . welcome to the club!" Ingalls Shipbuilding President Fred W. Mayo had been warning Rubel that it would be better if they were sharing FDLS action with someone—he preferred Todd. Rubel had scorned the advice. Mayo found some pleasure in the discomfort in Beverly Hills.

Ash had a palace revolution of sorts on his hands. When the bulk conveyor Hewitt-Robins had been spliced into Litton, the company picked up a languishing project for a six-to-eight feet wide belted movement of Mesabi Range iron ore from Lake Erie docks to steel mills inland. The right-of-way requirements were a quagmire. Besides, Hewitt-Robins strategists were outlanders and the old neighborhood around Cleveland thought their concept was outlandish, too.

Jack Cogan got Litton into one leg of the ore movement picture by acquisition of the eleven ore boats of Wilson Marine Transit Company in January of 1967 from a Pittsburger named Henry Hillman and

---

applied. With that cab ride briefing, Mitchell quoted from all the sources given him in the taxi, and the stature of the bonds was increased appreciably in money circles. "He didn't use a note," Howell said. The bonds were sold Dec. 1, 1967.

its President, E.T. Binger. The thinking was that having gotten the ore that far toward the blast furnaces, a tie into a conveyor system would make sense and the remaining transportation more efficient.

It was eyeball deep in politics.

Cleveland's slum areas, even though no environmental impact statements were then required, would be where the condemnation actions were necessary for the long conveyors to be built. No matter, Jack Cogan brought on E. Laurence "Larry" Gay from his now defunct post of Hewitt-Robins treasurer and secretary and made him president of a four-man unit grandiosely titled Litton Great Lakes Corporation. This planning body was to deal with smooth means of ore boat offloading and transfer of cargo to the mills. This was to be the end-of-the-line tie with the Wilson ore boats capable of 25,000 tons capacity—as well as 50,000 tonners which were to be built. The rationale led naturally to an ore boat production facility somewhere on Lake Erie which would manufacture these newer, more ponderous toting monsters.

Ultimately the site picked was at Erie, Pennsylvania. Cogan had a nimble wit when it came to deals, a trait Ash admired, except that much of the direction he kept tightly confined in his own head, revealing sparingly if at all and capable of quick amendment for the occasion. Had Cogan lived in Dodge City or Tombstone in the Old West and been a euchre sharpie, he would have been in that group described as playing ". . . close to the vest."

There was occasional talk along the corporate corridors about a "transportation group." It could include shipyards, conveyor systems manufacture, ore boats and anything added which was thematically attuned. As is always the case, rumors were circulating that if such a circumstance were to come about, what names would be management-compatible to pull together such a broad commitment? Rubel was one, and also Cogan, Ellis Gardner who was Ingalls-bound, and that dark horse, Austin Goodyear. Some press interest began to ferment and a memo was circulated asking who would at that stage be the "spokesman"[8] for the "transportation group concept"? Rubel was

---

8. As there was so much military impact and involvement as the longest timer in military public relations, war and peace, plus experience with joint service enterprises and mission oriented commands, Ash had assigned me as the Litton spokesman and coordinator. Mine was the memo which asked who among all the Litton "face cards"

summoned suddenly by Ash and asked if he would see any problem in Cogan being elevated to a vice presidency and to head a Transportation Group of Litton Industries.

There it was. Rubel didn't like it. He not only said so, he enumerated his reasons in withering detail. Rubel, for one thing, was already a winner with the Navy even though Congress had held back the money for FDLS. He was topping Litton's Advanced Marine Technology division in Culver City, California and was head-long into readying the company's LHA competition entry. The prize for this was a nine-ship contract in the $1,000,000,000 range. It would make up for the FDLS loss. Rubel was also working with Navy people who had been his associates in the Pentagon, who both know and had respect for him. In contrast, what Cogan was sighting for was a combination of the barge and ore boat business. The very idea of having as the senior man a barge and ore boat type overseeing these distantly related fields would make the Navy go seasick and throw up as it was chasing future technologies. Rubel told Ash that his proposal which was engaging 200 top experts and specialists which would require 25,000 pages in 68 loose-leaf binders, and in 100 complete sets— 6,880 documents in all—would go forward to the Navy with his signature attached. If that was not to be the case, and Cogan's was to be the responsible signature, Rubel was at the end of his line with Litton.

"You can run or organize Litton anyway you wish," said Rubel, with a cottony sensation in his mouth. "That's your prerogative. What I'm telling you is what I can live with professionally."

That face off ended abruptly, the atmosphere in Ash's office as frigid as the North Pole. Rubel went home and told his wife that he had probably "blown it." The first plateau of his stock options was near when he would be given unrestricted ownership of the first 2,000 shares. As he was driving home that night, he had calculated the cost of speaking his mind as $140,000, the market value of those shares.

Ellis Gardner, the Little Rock, Arkansas-born fellow KP potato peeler who had impressed Austin Goodyear, replaced Fred Mayo as

---

should be the quoted, or interview source and explainer. Rubel came storming into my office, red-faced, angry, and it showed. "That's," he said, "none of your damned business." From that came the Ash-Rubel Saturday breakfast face-off which was so tense it was not an Ash "come to my office," but a Rubel "you know where I am" so it was in an obscure fast food in Culver City near where Rubel worked.

the high honcho of the Ingalls Shipbuilding division. On him was placed responsibility for the conversion of the added 611 acres into what he liked to call ". . . the shipyard of the future." He was aggressive, an intent manager who had a passionate love affair with the competitive challenges of marketing. For two such highly charged individuals, it was remarkable that they got along so well and were so complementary.

Rubel had tired of Mayo as one who always felt it wiser to run with the traditional shipbuilding crowd rather than the maverick role relished by Rubel. Rubel was thinking it was all academic anyway. After his confrontation with Ash he went back to Culver City and the complex where his team was putting together the LHA proposal. He wasn't one to take back what he'd said, but he was uncertain about his future. The Culver City climate was tolerable when the feisty Rubel was only irascible, but it was a thornbush now for sure. Everyone was hunkered down.

Rubel, in one of his scowling black moods, said there would not be one paragraph in those proposals written in the passive voice; all sentences had to be assertively positive, active voice. He wrote the preface to every one of the 63 documents himself. If a professional proposal writer tampered with his work or the tense, the explosion from Rubel must have made the engineer who wrote the first proposal and dull manual, spin like a dervish in his dust. There was romance in ships and shipbuilding. It was there in the very physical makeup of the audience who would judge the merits of what Litton was suggesting. That would be the kind of music to which they would all march—and they did. It got to be a good idea to call his secretary, Grayce Davis to find out whether it was safe to say "Good Morning!" to him. Chances were, it wasn't. Not if the hired help was polled. To get his exercise, he would race them in the halls. The prevailing wisdom was that the staffer, like an exercise horse, was not supposed to win the race and none did. It was better that way.

No doubt about it, Ash knew how to make people perspire. Things rocked along. Then his call to Rubel came. Could they talk? Rubel considered his Litton future short but he'd changed jobs before. Trouble was, as so often was the case at Litton, he loved what he was doing. He asked Ash since he was immersed in directing the project and the staff if they could have the chat at lunch on Saturday. Then, most of the people except the workaholics such as himself would be off enjoying being out of reach of his temper. Ash agreed, and on the appointed day, they went to a small Culver City restaurant.

As they picked up their menus, Ash said: "John, we have a problem in this Transportation Group matter . . ."

"That's not right." Rubel said, peering over the top of his menu. "YOU have a problem. It can easily go anyway you want it to go. I have only told you my position, my conditions."

In contrast with what was facing Tex Thornton and Roy Ash then, it was all small potatoes. Rubel had excellent credentials, the expertise, the entree, the touch and had that $1,000,000,000 contract bet riding with his continuance. The prospects in the Lake Erie area were getting cloudier by the minute, with delays, irritations and indecisions abounding. The profit projection was tentative because of unforeseen shortfalls. The "Shipyard of the Future" was looming as a bigger and bigger inroad on the treasury. There were commitments all over the place, all kinds of corrections called for, and the corporate cup in truth was in a "runneth over" mode with a bitter taste to it.

Fred W. O'Green, whose Defense and Space Systems Group was grinding on making profits as always, put it in his bare bones way. "We're in deep yogurt," he said. There was no need to amplify. But as Ash was engaging Rubel, he appeared to be pushing toward the Transportation Group idea just as resolutely as ever with Cogan out front. Rubel, the acid count in his stomach higher than the Washington monument, listened glumly. He restated his view that Cogan was inappropriate for the audience of blue-suiters to which he was playing, which was where the real money and real shipyard business lay. Ingalls was being revived as the No. 1 contender. It was a long and labored lunch which Rubel left thinking the only plus was that Ash had picked up the check. Back in his office, Rubel thought it had a lifeless hue about it. Not a typewriter was going, no voices, and all at once, he found himself absently cleaning out his desk. He was about to get on with what the trade calls "career planning"—getting out resumes or calling headhunters to announce availability. But he didn't.

In the end, there never was a Transportation Group. The LHA proposal went forward and Rubel told the Beverly Wilshire hotel "office party" that he knew Litton's proposal would win. "It weighed 1,100 pounds more than our nearest competitor," he said.

Cogan had his hands full with Wilson Marine Transit and its rusty "bottoms." He got the Erie Marine shipyard into modular production of the Great Lakes ore boat giants which were to be thousand-footers in length. They had to be equipped with right-angled thrusters—sort of built-on miniature tugboat metaphors. They made it possible to hula their way through the squeeze points or narrows which were the linkage of the various larger bodies along the winding waterways.[9]

In Ellis Gardner's Ingalls domain, cement was being poured with steel reinforcements added and his "Shipyard of the Future" took shape. There was a West Bank groundbreaking on January 11, 1969. The air was charged with foreboding, but in the manner of old Admiral Farragut in Mobile Bay more than a century earlier, he was paraphrased: "Damn the cash flow, full speed ahead!"

The one thing missing from it all and never publicly admitted by those in position to know better than anyone—the U.S. Congress and the U.S. Navy—was that had it not been for Litton Industries' bullet-biting resolve after the debacle of the denied Fast Deployment Logistic Ship contract, neither the United States nor the U.S. Navy lost a day of the shipyard construction. The readying of that automated, ultra-modern West Bank facility continued unabated, to be ready when and if the agencies of government made up their minds what was

---

9. The first 1,000-foot ore boat produced at Erie Marine was a series of 48-foot long modules welded together, but the prow and stern were built in far-off Pascagoula at Ingalls. For the long seaward trip, this fore-and-aft section was assembled into a configuration aptly called "Stubby," and the crew painted a dotted line from the water to the deck with instructions to "cut here." It went out of Pascagoula into the Gulf of Mexico, up the east coast, into the mouth of the St. Lawrence and through the locks to Erie. It was separated on that line and electrically sutured at each end. At launch time, it was christened the STEWART J. CORT and delivered May 1, 1972 to Bethlehem Steel Corporation. Built to carry taconite iron ore pellets from Taconite Harbor, Minnesota to the Bethlehem mill in Burns Harbor, Indiana, it was 105 feet wide with cargo-carrying capacity of 52,000 long tons at 16 miles an hour. The Hewitt-Robins 10-foot wide conveyor on board was the world's largest. It doubled the tonnage delivered per trip over the largest then existing ore boat, and one of its taconite loads produced enough steel to make 15,000 automobiles. The Sault Ste. Marie locks were only five feet wider than the CORT. More than 20,000 people turned out along shore to watch it negotiate the narrows and cheered its triumphal passage as crowds do a football team. But again it was one of those instances when Litton was ahead of its time—and the market. It has since been vindicated, however.

wanted for the nation's security. It was the most gutsy thing in American industry to that time.

On May 1, 1969, after what seemed an interminable waiting period, the Navy announced the award of the General Purpose Assault Ships (LHA) contract to Litton's Ingalls Shipbuilding division. The money figure attached was $1,012,000,000 for nine of this class. The LHAs were made to order to increase readiness and effectiveness of the Navy and Marine Corps seaborne forces. It was described as a fixed price, incentive agreement.

The Pascagoula establishment set out to accomplish it in its new ship production plant which incorporated the world's most advanced marine manufacturing technology. As the West Bank of the Singing River appeared at the time of the contract news flash,[10] one had to have a good imagination to conjure that assembly line at water's edge the LHA was scheduled to tower 20 stories high. Each weighed in as the largest movable man-made object on earth at 19,500 tons—820 feet long and 106 feet wide. Once in the water, with additions, it would displace 39,300 tons. Only the most major of modern aircraft carriers were larger. Where the FDLS idea had been one of warehousing materiel afloat only, LHA was to accommodate a full Marine combat team of 2,000 with its full complement of equipment, from logistics to firepower support, all in one package. LHA living on board included pleasant individual berthing, storage facilities, shower bathing, messings in areas with attention to decor, a small PX, ice cream bars, a TV studio for production of programs aboard or instructional use, and acclimatizing air conditioning systems to get the attack force in a match with the weather of the destination.

Rubel, who had thought his statement of position so vehemently in the Transportation Group matter would give him the heave-ho, received a raise and the Advanced Marine Technology division was taken by him right into the third plum competition—the DD-963, Spruance Class, a 30-ship series of multi-mission destroyers. They

---

10. Litton's Data Systems division which grew out of the early decision to head into specialized computers and applications of them in numerical controls found Ingalls to prove that heading correct. At the peak, more than 200 Data Systems people were lodged at the Ingalls facility seeing to those very applications.

were named for one of the Navy's most revered heroes, shy, intellectual and thoughtful Admiral Raymond A. Spruance.[11]

The shipbuilding trade betting was that Litton's string had run out, that its "Shipyard of the Future" was still to be realized, and because of all the start-up difficulties attending the LHA, they suggested facetiously it should be renamed "the shipyard with no future." At least, in a competitive sense, it was thought the Navy would want to go elsewhere.

The Navy was asking a lot for the destroyers it wanted in this series. The ships had to have capabilities of shore bombardment, surface warfare, of providing the platform for the launch of short-range missiles for defense against airborne threats, with deck facilities to permit helicopter landings and takeoffs, and all the apparatus of electronic warfare detection over the horizon. Making the aerospace backgrounds of Rubel's AMTD group seem even more correct than ever, the Spruance Class was in line to be the first of major warships in the Navy to use gas turbine power plants for their propulsion, an outgrowth of the jet engines which had put thunderbolt speeds in aviation—and the Navy wanted each ship to run with fewer crew members than ever before!

---

11. Spruance had been sent in as a substitute for his ailing, longtime friend, WW II's Admiral William F. "Bull" Halsey, and up-ended Japanese plans for Southwest Pacific domination at the decisive Battle of Midway. There are no Navy names more highly regarded, no better records for relentless pursuit and attack of an adversary, and no ships whose command is more zealously coveted than these in the Spruance Class. When Navy Lt. Commander Thomas Buell wrote the book about him, "Quiet Warrior," Litton had 30 copies leather-bound and autographed given to each crew, both as the first book to officially enter each destroyer's library and to travel with that ship throughout its operational life. After arranging the Buell book commitment, I called Universal studio in Universal City, California, which was producing "MIDWAY," starring Henry Fonda as Admiral Nimitz, Robert Mitchum as Admiral "Bull" Halsey and Glenn Ford as Spruance, all of them on location down the Gulf Coast at Pensacola. "What are your plans for the exploitation of "MIDWAY" I asked them. "BIG, BIG," they said, "It will be the movie industry's give to the Centennial!" Did they know about the oncoming USS Spruance at Pascagoula? No. We talked and Glenn Ford did a recording for us telling the Spruance story. Copies of that recording were given every crew member when he boarded at Pascagoula, and Glenn Ford, when asked by US NAVY recruiters for something from him as incentive awards, sent them that record. Every admiral then serving the U.S. Navy got one, as well as every Mississippi Senator, Congressman, and Mississippi legislator. The media had dropped "troubled shipyard" from its cliche list.

The priority aim was a sound, seaworthy warship design capable of taking on a variety of weaponry still in experimental states. This adaptable platform, along with those "learning curve" lessons, was expected to minimize cost as the program went along. Litton, casting itself as a prime contractor candidate, had 70 major subcontractors. "The ships must lend themselves to less costly modernization and conversion," was the way R.H. DuBois, the Litton destroyer project manager, put it. Not only minimum cost but minimum time out of service. The reduction of personnel to 270 officers and crew was of great significance as this was about 80% of the manpower required for similar-sized ships that would lessen operational costs by $500,000 per year per ship.

Ellis Gardner, a Litton Senior Vice President and heading Litton's Marine Group, had Ned Marandino bossing the East Bank in Pascagoula and Dr. Robert L. Roderick, the West Bank. Marandino had his part humming along.

Roderick,[12] on the other hand, was having to run hard just to stand still. It is well known that no matter how long a government agency may dawdle on its way to decision, once the decision is made and the contract signed, some kind of hull outline is expected to be visible shortly.

When the time came for the competing companies to make their presentation, Litton found itself last on the podium. Later this suspense factor was revealed for what it was—shipbuilding bid presentations were normally dull, plodding and seemed to be awarded in equal parts on merit and on audience fatigue.

All the factual base was in the Litton offerings, but with Rubel and Gardner there was some old-fashioned medicine show and Barnum & Bailey to provide occasional relief. It was the stimulating and enlivening of the proceedings which they contributed that made it an almost festive affair, attention arresting, and even exciting. For those

---

12. Dr. Robert L. Roderick was picked by John Rubel to be president of Litton's Advanced Marine Technology division which was the proposal-making facility in Culver City, California. He transitioned to the presidency of Litton Ship Systems at Pascagoula during the West Bank startup. It didn't work out. He was brought to Litton corporate to become the developer of East/West Trade. He came to Litton from Hughes Aircraft in 1968, and was back at Hughes in 1973. He won the prestigious American Machinist award in 1970 for "distinguished contributions to manufacturing." He had that to comfort him, anyway.

hung up on ships as romantic, worthy of song and story, and not just steel plates and rivets and superstructure with a prow which would split water, there was all of that and more in Litton's presentation.

On June 23, 1970, Litton Industries accomplished the incredible. Still categorized as an aerospace-oriented firm, it won the 30-ship Spruance Class, DD-963 destroyer contract!

"Litton will award subcontracts worth more than 60% of the dollar value of each ship to hundreds of companies in 45 states," Ellis Gardner said with exultation in his voice. That was an economic impact statement all its own, affecting a wide area and of substantial heft as the ceiling price for the 30-ship packet was $2,140,000,000.

There were several tailings which passed almost unnoticed.

Governor Paul Johnson, who had master-minded that $130,000,000 Mississippi Industrial Development bond issue which made the Ingalls West Bank 611-acre automated shipyard adjunct possible, had made a major political turn on the road. When Ross Barnett had been Governor and Johnson his lieutenant governor, it had been Johnson he sent to stand in the entrance door of sainted Ole Miss (The University of Mississippi) in Oxford attempting to deny entrance to James Meredith, a black man, in 1962. About 6% of the Ingalls Shipbuilding employees which Litton acquired that same year were black. Soon 35% were from minority resources. Johnson, when he became governor, handled a whole series of political footballs one after another during his regime, and the Litton-assisting bond issue the least troubling. Through him, though, his state legislated the Mississippi Educational Television Authority, eliminated racism in the State Highway Patrol, and stepped on the notorious White Citizens' Council as if it were a bug. Yet it had been his stance against Meredith at Ole Miss which had had most to do with his being elected in the first place. Once in Jackson, his whole perspective changed. His leadership among his own people brought Litton in to become the biggest free enterprise employer in Mississippi. The Litton training program made minority Mississippians employable as they were recruited raw from 20 southern counties of that state and 15 of the nearby Alabama Counties. Fully 95% of employees were locally recruited and trained, and then stayed there.

As Mississippi had long been daubed with the tar brush of such as Senator Bilbo, it was now being written about in such sophisticated financial publications as *The Bond Buy* which said of the state: "The $130,000,000 industrial bond issue . . . is remarkable as an innovation in the frontier land of finance that looks too good to be true. It should be noted that the bonds were authorized at an extraordinary session of the Mississippi Legislature to present on a state level a financing device that had been available on the local level for 30 years. Further, the bonds were made full faith and credit obligations of Mississippi even though the credit of the great Litton complex would appear to have been more than sufficient security for bondholders. . . . Yes, there seems to be something in this Mississippi deal for everybody— taxpayers, bond buyers and holders, commercial bankers and investment bankers, local government, Washington, private enterprise and even American shipping. Surely one for the book. Why then the reservations?"

A good and proper question, as they say. A good question, indeed!

And there was an answer, but it was going to be hard to come by, take a long and worrisome time and have a happy ending for everybody. To get to that happy and vindicated ending, Litton's leadership and its believing and faithful shareholders would experience their severest test. They stood together, and they stood alone, but they stood up to what faced them without giving or asking quarter.

SPECIAL SITUATION #18

WHERE THE SPECTACULAR WAS COMMONPLACE

There was no place quite like outer space for Litton Industries to show the range of its versatilities, and the rightness of its concept of readiness and ability to do almost anything asked of it. This was only one illustration. There were many more.

Yet, as was the case so often, it made no particular effort by publicity and breast-beating to put itself in such a frame of reference.

It's only now, on reflection, that one sees that Litton was far more than the "multinational conglomerate" it was claimed to be. That was just the worldly appraisal of it in the business press. It was a company, in fact, which was not unacquainted in the universe itself. That it could *say* this was one thing, but the *fact* that it did demonstrate with performance after a short corporate life bordered on the incredible.

Almost day and date with the November 2, 1953 beginnings of Litton, Alexander Nikolaevich Nesmeyanov, an organic chemist who was then President of the prestigious Soviet Union National Academy of Sciences, made a declaration. He said it was now possible to send a stratoplane to the Moon, or that an artificial earth satellite could be put in orbit. There was an avalanche of Soviet literature immediately afterward about rockets, man-made earth circling instrumented packets and mind-boggling discussions of how to go gallivanting among the planets. It was a calculated learned literary underscoring of his remarks.

At that time Tex Thornton and his associates were trying to get a company together which would ride as an outrigger on his concepts. Last of all would he have thought that he would be the first capitalist industrialist who would be asked to be an "official guest" of that same Academy of Sciences. Or, the outrageous improbability that Litton could eventually claim to be the only company in at the very start of the "space race" in both the U.S. and the U.S.S.R!

This was only one among many things around Litton where the unusual was ordinary. What was otherwise thought ordinary was often asked into imaginative applications making the impossible attainable. Both Nesmeyanov and Thornton, though they were never to know each other, shared the common conviction that on the advanced technologies would the fates of nationhood be determined and maintained. Sovereignties have long been proclaimed, accepted in international affairs, and their later violations considered serious enough to induce threats of or actual conflict. Among the many posturings about what constitutes the skeletal structure by which countries stand erect and are assessed for true power, it was the Science Council of Canada which gave this succinct explanation: "A nation can be said to be sovereign when it has the ability to develop and control technological capability to ensure economic and hence its political self-determination."

None ever said Litton could walk on water, not even in its palmiest days of its early promissory rhetoric—but walk into that future with audacious and idolatrous appreciation of the advanced technologies it would and did.

At its quarter century milestone, barely pausing for breath from all the exertions, the people who were with Litton still and those along the way who had left the fold for their many reasons, could hardly believe it all. Litton had assisted Man to feel his way along the deepest darkest floors of oceans, had mapped and surveyed regions hitherto inaccessible, had accurately fingered probable locations of oil, natural gas, minerals and subterranean water tables, had known the Moon and Mars[1] and helped others to know them, had dealt with a whole range of sociological problems, had participated in "nation building", had accomplished considerable smartening of the world about itself and had benefited in some way—including learning its limitations—from all these actions.

The whole idea from the first had been to be ready for anything, to anticipate needs and how to meet them, to gather technical capabilities, to exploit the enduring values of its technologies. It had to be carefully selective and wary about seductions and tantalizing mirages which glimmered temptingly but not profitably in such profusion out

---

1. For the Viking probe to Mars, Litton's Guidance and Control Systems division was asked to build the Gas Chromatograph Mass Spectrometer. This small "lab" was to "spade" up some Martian soil, put it in its "oven" and cause actions to determine whether some form of life was detectable on that far off planet. Litton's Datalog's digital imagery recorders beamed all those photographs of the Martian landscape across 230,000,000 miles of space into "hard copy" computer-enhanced photos for all the world to see and marvel.

there. Not everything Litton touched was to turn to gold, but there was something golden about the atmosphere of the place because of its willingness to make the good try. It depended on how one looked at it from the inside. Many seemed to value the experience of Litton more than any riches it might offer and they were the ones over time who tended to wind up well off in both.

Who would have thought anything extraordinary would come of the acquisition of that electronics division with which General Mills in Minneapolis was uncomfortable? Litton took it over in August of 1963 for a pittance of 23,530 shares of Litton then valued at $2,550,000. That old Aerospace Research and Engineering Department of General Mills was renamed the Litton Applied Sciences Division. One of its products, a two man deep submersible submarine called Alvin, was to hold a world enthralled and anxious for 40 days and nights. It was to be the only memorable bright spot in terms of product, but it bequeathed Litton some engineering talent who had much to do with its microwave oven[2] development and the successful launching of Litton in that direction.

While Greece may assign them totally to mythology, Mercury and Apollo in their reincarnations for the American space program became a showcase for Litton. Astronaut Neil Armstrong, on returning from the Apollo 11 mission with his fellow spacemen, Cols.

---

2. The "old boy network" was at work for that General Mills willingness to spin off what Litton got, Brig. Gen. Ed Rawlings, who was at Wright-Patterson Air Force Base where procurement centered, in 1945 had made up his mind to join the investment firm of Herbert Walker in New York. There had been a call from Tex Thornton asking him to come to Washington for an interview because Tex had recommended him to General Eaker to become a "first" — the first Air Force Controller, the money handler. Rawlings spoke of his intentions to leave the Air Force, and his four boys he had to educate, and how any officer such as he had been without combat experience would be relegated to the dustbin in the post-war military picture. He had to get that release from a then Under-Secretary named Stuart Symington. When Symington heard of the promise to Herbert Walker, he said he could square that as they had been at Yale together. A momentarily dismayed Rawlings found his exit blocked, but he did become the first Air Force controller, did become a 4-star General, and on retirement was recruited to head General Mills. Rawlings always believed that Thornton phone call was the most fortuitous thing that ever happened to him. That Applied Sciences addition to Litton brought with it Verle Blaha and Harold Anderson, both engineers who transitioned to microwave oven research and had a lot to do with that success story. Anderson, in fact, had been in the Maryland Electronics acquisition before that.

Edwin "Buzz" Aldrin and Michael Collins, addressed pointed and special sentimental remarks to all the 400,000 workers in aero-space-related companies: "Through you", he said, "we touched the moon!" More than 12,000 of Litton's people were included in his editorial "you" as he embraced all the assembly line stalwarts whose care and precision artistry had made that long and potentially perilous ordeal one that was accomplished without flaw or fault.

There were at least 200 different kinds of participations by Litton Industries in equipment, expertise and services in NASA's Apollo missions.

As early as 1963, on a wild idea which had awakened Crosby M. Kelly at 4 a.m. one day and in which Tex Thornton concurred, Litton decided to expand the number of languages in which it printed its annual reports. It had been doing them in English, German and Italian because of the growing number of facilities in those countries and the likelihood that there would be more. The decision which intrigued Kelly so much was that Litton would transition into the never-never land of the Cyrillic alphabet and publish a version in the Russian language. The vague thought then was that it could be a document which would show off Litton both as a company and its philosophy as a free enterpriser and see what response, if any, would result.

The climate could not possibly have been worse. U-2 Pilot Gary Powers had been shot down three years before and had been used by Khrushchev as an excuse to kill a summit conference. He had been released a few months later. It was not the first step Litton had ever made among nettles. It was intriguing to toy with what the Soviet leadership, the trading organizations of the state, polytechnical institutions and their professors, and frivolously, the stars of the Bolshoi and sports would think when confronted by the same Litton documentation it used to explain itself to shareholders. Litton thought they could read and judge for themselves. About one quarter of Litton's employees were enrolled in the company's stock purchase plan. This seemed a way to boot the old communist cliche that capitalism exploits the worker. It clearly illustrated those participants had a chance to profit over and above their wages in the firm's success. Litton found it was not only the first company to do this, but a whole basket of novelties surfaced of which it was unaware before. One was that in its acquisition of Rust Engineering,[3] none other than Nikita Khrushchev himself, had actually been an employee of Litton's family tree!

Litton was one story after another like this, but its focus was on what seemed choice acquisitions, their merits, their promise, their effect on earnings. Much of the excitement of Litton's substance and contributions to history in the making were lost in the shuffle of hastening lawyers and accountants and their paper flurries. When Harry Gray headed the Components Group he was always bugging the public relations hirelings to get on with a magazine piece about how many ways he was in the action with the space program. He was humored in the conversations, but got little in way of action. But he was sniffing at a good one and he knew it. What better way was there to show the many sides of Litton Industries as the probable answer no matter how staggering the puzzle might be?

The Soviet ICBM in August, 1957 didn't make this much of a stir, but the Sputnik satellite launched in October did. But they were professional worrywarts anyway. Some of them believed when that happened it was not only exceedingly dangerous to the West and the U.S., but was the near twin of the Pearl Harbor debacle 16 years earlier. There were no pictures of battleships, bottoms up, or smoking ruins of a great port, and morbid casualty lists. Political soul searching was the order of the day. It seemed better politics for America to remain technologically becalmed and leisurely in its attitude rather than it assume a crisis posture with no visuals other than word pictures to support it. The popular tactic was to say that the Soviets were ahead because America had captured "the wrong Germans". This was a reference to the sorting over of Hitler's celestially oriented resources from the rocket tests at Peenemuende, some of whom came to America, and others went east to Moscow.

The difference was that the Soviets were urging theirs full speed ahead to make good on their Academy of Sciences' President Nes-

---

3. Rust Engineering, along with the Belgian Coppee-rust, and Coppee-Great Britain, came into Litton for $11,000,000 or 103,226 Litton Preference shares. It was negotiated by Ludwig T. Smith for Litton, and with the beneficiaries of four E.M. Rust Trusts, including S.M. Rust, Jr., Alice M. Scheetz, Mary R. Gillies, George M. Rust, Patty Rust Benedict, H. Lee Rust, Louise Rust Gillespy and Mary H. Rust, with its principal offices in Birmingham, Ala. and Pittsburgh, Pa. The agreement was signed February 10, 1967, and the transaction completed in 1972. It was Coppee-Rust which provided the tie to Khrushchev.

meyanov predictions five years earlier. When that trailblazing rocket lit up the sky and imaginations around the globe, Litton Industries had at least 35 divisions with significant roles to perform when the U.S. decided to shake off its lethargy.

"We have set sail on this new sea" John F. Kennedy said almost four years later, "because there is new knowledge to be gained and new rights to be won, and they must be won and used for the progress for all people. For space science, like nuclear science and all its technology, has no conscience of its own. Whether it becomes a force for good or ill depends on Man, and only if the United States occupies a position of prominence can we help decide whether this new ocean will be a sea of peace, or a new terrifying theater of war."

One of the earliest asked into the space catch-up was Litton with its contract for the "Mark I, U.S. Air Force Model: Extra-Vehicular and Lunar Surface Suit". This became the venerable first ancestor of the technology which evolved through many stages until finally worn by the astronauts on the cheerless, airless and bleak surface of the moon. The birth of the National Aeronautics and Space Administration (NASA) on September 30, 1958 had made it possible for it to call from inventory all the findings and research in flight medicine from the Army, Navy and Air Force. It also got Dr. Hubertus Strughold, and Air Force "house asset". He had been the first to study the Luftwaffe-discovered characteristics of the phenomenon called "weightlessness". NASA could also summon the imaginations and equipments of industry. The Soviets had a lead and a momentum and the U.S. had to come off a standing start, or nearly so, and begin to roll with contributions from whatever quarter. The public captivation was with the astronauts. NASA concentrated the expertise of America's work force, making it dedicated to and bent on insuring that it would be "all system GO" when the time came. These special painstakingly selected human beings would have their courage matched with as much safety, care and attention as each could give them.

Everywhere the astronauts cast a glance, Litton cast a shadow. There was a constant need-to-know requirement as to their health and wellbeing. The Profexray division of Litton Industries in Des Plaines, Illinois provided its 300 MA 125 Diagnostic X-Ray for the NASA Manned Spacecraft Center in Houston. These X-Ray devices went over the Mercury and Apollo astronauts periodically and in great detail. Profexray had come into the Litton enclosure almost by accident, when Ted Vatz called on Seymour Rosenberg and Frank Slovak. He had heard of Litton's long ago original six areas in which the company wanted to be, one of them X-Ray. It hadn't worked out. Perhaps there was a sliver Litton wanted to get rid of that would match with what he had. Litton had been studying the rising health consciousness of government. It had gotten into the medical products field with its Fritz Hellige acquisition in Germany. Rosenberg said Litton was buying, not selling. Would Profexray be interested in joining Litton? He checked with his colleagues, and they were favorably inclined. All 1,100 of Profexray's people had hands on part of the moon expeditionary project. They had gotten used to the idea that they would probably always be small, and even a dead end. Now they were addressing the universe itself.

Preparations of the astronauts for the flight included hours and hours in simulators duplicating with detail the lunar approach, landing, takeoff and on return, splashdown at sea. For NASA's LMPS (Lunar Module Procedure Simulator), two special CRT (Cathode Ray Tubes) had to be designed and constructed by Electron Tube, that very first Litton acquisition and one more validation of its being a futures technology resource. That San Carlos, California facility had all of its 1,260 employees either looking in or actually engaged in some of the tasks which produced those CRTs. They were mounted covering the triangular shaped windows of the LMPS which was an exact duplicate of the real Lunar Excursion Module. It was that last lap unit to touch down on the moon, and the first step off the moon toward rendezvous with the orbiting Command Module. Those Cathode Ray Tubes were programmed to present the Moon as it would be seen by the astronauts to resemble sighting it from 50,000 feet. From that height, the astronauts were cued through the various procedures to descend. The Moonscope was amended for detail and reality as their proximity increased.

Another important Litton inclusion was arrived at circuitously. North American Aviation had the contract to deliver by 1965 a full color 6-feet-in-diameter sphere which was a model of the earth itself. This carefully conceived ball gave dynamic visual impressions of the earth as it was being orbited by a space capsule. The *earth* the astronauts saw on their TV replica was this reproduction exactly as it would appear from 100 miles off. On this globe there were 230 different geographic identifications with which the astronauts had to be familiar. The whole of its preparation was handed to Litton's most geographically knowledgeable division, Aero Service, whose 362 employees were in Philadelphia. On their talent pool and its known accuracy in such matters, NASA paid its respects by making Aero Service the sole source producer of film graphics which projected the views orbiters would see before them in flight. It was elaborate. It included eight full spins around the earth and ten possible landing sites as seen by a spaceship approaching the Moon. By the time Armstrong, Aldrin and Collins were seated in the Command Module, Aero Service had been able to give them the advantage of photographic passes which had been made on previous non-landing Moon-orbiting missions. NASA respected the quality of the Aero Service product so much by then, that the contract stayed there, and five more touchdown locales were fed by it into the simulator, precise to a gnat's eyelash.

Launch Complex No. 39, the Cape Kennedy starting point for all the Mercury and Apollo blastoffs, was fat with more than 200 Monroe Calculating Machines serving all the computing requirements of the Kennedy Space Center. The Monroe Epic 3000 programmable calculating devices were in easy astronaut reach at their Training Command assisting with all the complicated numbers which were a part of their simulator time. Monroe rotary and printing calculators helped in the spacecraft assembly and all the figure work which proceeded each launch, including that eye-popper, Apollo 11. The 735 Monroe employees in New Jersey never had Cape Kennedy long off their minds in the preparatory phases just from knowing this was probably the most historically dramatic association they would ever know.

The majestic Saturn V rocket, eyed so often before each takeoff by the astronauts, stood 374 feet tall. It was towered over by the Rust Engineering-built LC-39 Mobile Service Structure. It was the largest man-made, movable land object up to that time. For it all the technicians who had to toil during readiness and monitor at every level were able to reach out, touch, and fix whatever needed their attention and correction. No one who remembers whose fiery departures can ever forget that big, brotherly, brooding presence, so sturdy and comforting, and which, when all systems were announced as "GO!" would pull itself ponderously back as if to say: "It's all yours!"

As part of it, Litton's Louis Allis[4] division in West Allis, Wisconsin was contracted to design and build eight drive systems (two for each launch pad on LC-39). The biggest of them—giant 2,500 horsepower Louis Allis Adjustable Speed Drive machines—forced and controlled the pumping of 1,000,000 gallons of liquid oxygen into the rocket at the rate of 10,000 gallons per minute. As liquid oxygen becomes quickly gaseous, speed control was vital. Smaller 200-horsepower Louis Allis Motors did the topping off and held until the last moments before liftoff. It took some effort of Rust Engineering's 1,288 people in Birmingham—all of them—to build the 400-foot Mobile Service Structure which had to stand there upright as the catalyst for all pre-flight support activities. The Louis Allis complement of 3,618 in Wisconsin tailored all those motors which performed critical readiness measures for what became Man-on-the-Moon.

Litton's Potentiometer division in Mount Vernon, New York, that early $44,000 1954 buy, had its 437-payroll roster manufacturing the devices which helped the control and telemetering of the liquid oxygen fuel and its hydrogen components. Its relationship began in 1960 with the Saturn V rocket, and Potentiometer stayed the demanding course.

Litton's Litcom division in Melville, New York, was asked by NASA to fabricate cable harnesses, operational intercom systems, terminal boxes, cable-potting and wave guides, and to install and check these out as they served in Launch Complex No. 39. Litcom also sup-

---

4. Louis Allis founded the company wearing his name March 15, 1901. One of his early patents was filed in 1913 as a "fly swatter". Somebody built a better one, so he switched it to the role of type cleaner for typewriters and this evolved into a perfect wire brush for jazz band drummers. It was quickly into off-the-shelf electric motors, and then to industrial motors in the range of from one to 10,000 horse-power, AC and DC, standard and engineered drives to specifications and systems, totaling and solid state adjustable alternators, generators and screw compressors. It had 686,031 shares outstanding and came under the Litton flag on a one-for-one trade of those securities for shares of Litton preference stock valued at $54 a share. Agreement was signed November 3, 1966 to merge with Litton. Later, one of America's most trying international experiences would ricochet on Louis Allis. Kevin Hermening, one of the 52 hostages held by Iran for 444 days (November, 1979 January, 1981) was the son of Richard Hermening of the Louis Allis Production Control Department and his wife, Pauline, a former Louis Allis employee.

plied its Weather fax Recorders (RJ4) which received continuous weather data from the U.S. Weather Bureau as well as from the U.S. Air Force Weather Transmitting Network. In all the detail with which the New York Times treated the space experience, it had no print to claim a bit of credit for itself in the matter. It was Litton's acquisition of Times Facsimile Corporation and Time fax Corporation in March of 1959 from the Times which contributed to this capability which Litcom's 550 employees made possible.[5]

The Advanced Circuitry division of Litton in Springfield, Missouri had its 614 people turning out multi-layer circuit boards, depended on heavily by NASA, which had need of their close tolerance and precision printed circuits, and single sided and multi-layer back panels.

Just up the road in quiet Olathe, Kansas, 147 of the townspeople there who worked for Litton manufactured 1,200 bipods for use on the Saturn VJ-2 engines, a cluster of six such engines being required for each Apollo launch, and eight more such bipods, called for each time as part of the engines' linkage controls. This was Twin City Tool, which was also a NASA purchasing point for 18 special fittings made from blocks of titanium. These were part of the housing for the Lunar Excursion Module (that LEM which lowered the astronauts to the Moon, then bounced them back up again to rejoin the mother ship, Columbia, when it was time to return to earth). The crucial moments of docking hundreds of thousands of miles in space gave jangled nerves to that Olathe 147 who had engaged in this production. None was more relieved than them that these parts on which they'd labored functioned well. Having performed, they were left as part of that growing accumulation that is called "space junk".

The Winchester Electronics[6] division in Oakville, Connecticut made the series connectors (SRE) and (SREC) which were key ele-

---

5. This was yet another bow to the Austin Cooley-developed process by which photos were moved by wire. Apollo 11's call on Datalog for help with around-the-world weather reporting was merely a new extension of the old story of that technology. Already coming into focus was Joe Verruso's Datalog direction called Policefax which was so useful in high speed fingerprint transmissions with clarity. It was the darling of the FBI and more than 200 state and local law enforcement agencies. Rising crime rate statistics made this an unexpected growth area for Litton!

6. Winchester Electronics and Pyne Molding came to Litton February 1, 1963, a maker of electronic and electrical connectors for computers as well as other industrial,

The Great, Great Grand-Daddy Mark 1 USAF Model Litton
moon suit with the author.

ments of the Apollo computers used in navigation and guidance instrumentation. The Winchester Electronics payroll of 453 men and

---

commercial and military uses. It had Horatio H. Burtt at its head. The price was
$4,300,000, broken down into 43,214 shares of Litton common as well as 3 1/2%
convertible subordinated debentures.

women also provided connectors for the Lunar Module Procedure Simulator.

It was the Clifton Precision Products division of Litton, 331 people in Colorado Springs, Colorado, that produced dozens of its respected synchros. These electromechanical electromagnetic components discipline power transmission and were updated from their long-time traditional participation in aircraft to equal importance in spacecraft.

Perhaps it was Litton's Amecom division in College Park, Maryland that supplied a kind of linkage with which the world could most identify. Its 451 employees on the outskirts of Washington, D.C., assembled the 4 S-band quartz antenna discs which were attached to the greatest circumference area of the Apollo 11 Command Service Module, *Columbia*, as backup for the high gain antenna system. They were called into action throughout the mission for live voice, tracking and telemetry information such as critical performance, navigational data and bio-medical statistics. Over those S-band routes to Mission Control in Houston could come moment-by-moment details on how astronaut body temperatures registered, as well as their oxygen consumption rates and their blood pressure readings. When Neil Armstrong's boots stirred their first powdery dust of the Moon's surface and he said: "That's one small step for Man, a giant leap for Mankind!" Amecom's contribution made redundantly sure he had the world by its ears!

If, as Mission Control claimed at the time, everybody there was about to bust their blood vessels and have coronaries while awaiting confirming word that ". . . the Eagle has landed!", the suspense was far from over. There were three mighty hurdles still—getting off the Moon, docking, in tandem the lunar orbiter Lt. Col. Michael Collins with the *Columbia*, and the splashdown in the Pacific. Those Amecom S-band elements insured constant communications if all others might blank out on re-entry of the earth's atmosphere.

Litton's Encoder[7] division was to figure in the watery sequencing, too. That small group of 200 in Chatsworth, California, well off the beaten path, had been asked for six Gallium Arsenide Optical En-

---

7. Encoder, a Chatsworth, Calif. . . . unit, was an early internal growth example within Litton, having been foaled out of Guidance Control Systems division. On the books it was a $151,137 transaction. It was by description a "shaft encoder" manufac-

The LITTON Adventure That Was

NASA bonanza for Litton. Request was sent to the divisions to let it be known if they had contracts of any kind which were related to APOLLO 13, the mission to the moon. More than 200 surfaced, the largest being the stories high launch gantry, and the most imaginative, Stouffer Foods, contracted to provide food services, had a national ad campaign the moment the three astronauts plopped in the Pacific. Headlines that big said: *Everybody who's been to the moon is eating Stouffer's!* A film clip, *Cooking: Stone Age to Space Age* was played repeatedly on 39 of the world's broadcasting networks.

coders for installation in the U.S. Navy's Flexure Monitor equipment. Superstructures of ships flex, and it is not determinable by the naked eye. This can cause a degree of error in fixing the exact location at a given moment of a fast moving space vehicle. To compensate for this flexing, the first measuring was done by laser optical systems con-

turer, that item providing shaft angle positions to interface with digital computer circuitry or computers in military, industrial or commercial systems.

tained in the Flexure Monitor. Litton encoders translated this into digital form, the results being a real-time, reliable and accurate fix of the spacecraft.

After the watery dunk of their return, the Astronauts had a symbolic question mark, or plague sign on them. None knew whether the Moon encounter had been as sterile as hoped or might have stirred up lethal bacteria to be loosed on earth after coming in as stowaways in their gear, or if breathed in might be in the digestive or circulatory systems of the spacemen. It was science-fiction, possibly, but not surely. The answer was to insert them in a 21-day quarantine—first, in their mobile quarters flown from the recovery site to Houston, and afterward they were placed in the Lunar Receiving Laboratory along with the Moon rocks which returned with them.

Litton was present in this aftermath phase, too. The 21-day quarantine menu had been constituted by NASA's dietitians at the Manned Spacecraft Center and in Solon, Ohio in the Stouffer Foods division where 563 employees had been engaged in the preparation, processing, and packaging. More than half of what the astronauts ate during quarantine came from Stouffer's. Neil Armstrong spoke admiringly of its palatability to his taste for a year afterward.[8] The food was cooked in Litton Microwave ovens which were assembled by 220 people employed in their manufacture in Minneapolis, Minnesota.

That first U.S. Air Force Mark I Model, "Extra-Vehicular and Lunar Surface Suit", had *not* received the final contract for the garb worn by the astronauts on the Moon, although its technology threaded its way through all the development staircase. In the lunar Receiving Laboratory, NASA did ask Litton's Space Sciences Laboratory in Beverly Hills to design, develop and produce 17 one-atmosphere or

---

8. The Stouffer Foods association with the astronauts provided a merchandising bonanza. Their ad agency, Ketchum, McLeod & Grove's hep copywriter, Rita Franklin and account executive Richard Weber came up with an ad to go with splashdown in 50 major markets under the whopper headline: "EVERYBODY WHO'S BEEN TO THE MOON IS EATING STOUFFER'S." Stouffer's restaurants offered free copies of the astronaut's menus and more than 600,000 were picked up in one month. Sales of the 14 main and side dishes of Stouffer's which were used in the Lunar Receiving Laboratory confinement doubled in the supermarkets. A film by Larry Mascott for Litton on Joseph Imirie's urging, FOOD PREPARATION: STONE AGE TO SPACE AGE, was used as a filler on 39 national networks and state-operated broadcasting systems abroad.

vacuum glove systems to handle the rocks which were brought back from the Moon. These lunar rocks were placed in an F-201 Sampling Chamber, sterilized and depressurized to simulate as nearly as possible the vacuum conditions native to the Moon. They had to be designed with three major characteristics in order to work with the lunar materials: Strong enough to withstand the normal atmospheric pressure of earth, at least 14.7 pounds per square inch at sea level; the material covering the metal gloves from fingers to shoulder had to shield the wearer from either earthly or lunar bacteria; and the entire Litton one-atmosphere vacuum glove system had to have maximum mobility. Litton delivered all three, the handiwork of a dozen scientists of that small staff. Litton's Electra Motors division[9] was asked under subcontract to the Atomic Disposer Company for special 7 1/2 horsepower motors for the grinders through which some of the Moon rocks passed to break them down into more reasonable sizes for tests, and 277 of the work force was caught up in that.

Although nothing was said of it publicly, all the human body wastes, liquid and solid, of the three pioneering Moon men were sacked individually and sent to Litton' Bionetics Research Laboratories in Kensington, Maryland for exhaustive checks to determine space flight effects such as sustained weightlessness on healthy human bodies. It wouldn't have been appropriate for Litton to have said it was in the space business from cradle to grave, as that script is open-ended, but it could say from start to stool, as Litton was right on!"[10]

---

9. The pooled $400 of Edward and Franklin Merriman on the outskirts of Boston at the turn of the 19th century to get them in the fog warning business in the city's port area eventually had an outer space application, too. They graduated to block-and-tackle for yachts (and sailed on every America's cup race from the 1913 Resolute to the 1958 Columbia), and parlayed the durability of the blocks into dam gate bearings, which found them in business all the way from Boulder Dam to the Thames River Tidal Barrier. NASA uses Merriman bearings for the giant rotary bridge which moves the payload change out room to the space shuttle for loading. They are designed to withstand a vertical pressure of 1,870,000 pounds in case of hurricane. Merriman was first bought by Union Twist Drill in 1963, and UTD brought it into Litton with it in 1968.

10. When Roy Ash, during his official guesting in the U.S.S.R. in 1971, showed Soviet Minister Konstantin N. Rudnev a picture of their Cosmos Center and the Litton electrocardiograph and pulse-monitoring equipment in use during Gagarin's first earth orbit, Rudnev was very excited. As he was a highly honored and renowned pioneer in the Soviet space program himself, he asked abruptly: "If we have been in this kind of

Probably the combined cash total of all this was insignificant, but the implications were not. Litton, by all these products and capabilities, had established itself as a place for the puzzled to turn to for solutions, large and small. There was another saltier side, which was learned much later. The Litton acquisition in West Germany of Fritz Hellige & Co., GmbH, had its own special ingredient to add. In the same 1957 of the Soviet's SPUTNIK I, it already had many customers in the Socialist or Eastern Bloc countries, one of them the Hungarian People's Republic to which it had sold some electrocardiograph machines and pulse monitoring medical electronic units. All this action was running in close parallel with the Litton atmosphere-free pressure chamber construction in Beverly Hills which led to the "Moon suit" contract. The Soviets badly needed just such high technology inclusions as Hellige sold the Hungarians.

Once it was inside the Socialist fraternity, it was easy to transship a part of the order to the Baikonur cosmodrome east of the Aral Sea. Nearby was the industrial city of Magnitogorsk where in that newly mushroomed boomtown suburb of Tyura Tam lived one diminutive Russian, Major Yuri Gagarin. Tyura Tam was a U.S.S.R. counterpart of Florida's Cocoa Beach and the nearby complex of Cape Canaveral—Patrick Air Force Base. Gagarin, almost small enough for a jockey at 154 pounds was to capture the imagination and admiration of all earthlings when at age 27, he went up, and out and around the world in a 108-minute ride in VOSTOK I. By telemetry, those Fritz Hellige instruments clung to him. They traced his minute-by-minute heart action and blood pressure, and the pulse beat's rhythm was magnified in the cosmodrome, all by that gadget placed almost like a vase so casually on the TV monitor which showed Gagarin's face.[11] It was

---

thing together, why are we not doing more business today?" Taking a cue from that I had a walnut wood backed plaque made showing US Test Pilot Capt. Ivan Kincheloe in Litton's space suit, and the Soviet Space Center with Hellige's electrocardiograph consoles and pulse monitor on the TV with Maj. Yuri Gagarin's face on TV as he was in orbit. A great many Soviet Ministers had it on their walls as a reminder of a Litton delegation visit. Rudnev, was the one who asked Svenska-Data Register AB to make a proposal for a cash register manufacturing plant in Ryazan.

11. Electra Motors came to Litton September 23, 1965, when the president of the Anaheim, California unit, Allen Arval Morris, OK'd the offer of $1,571,240 in Litton Industries $3 A Convertible Preferred stock, and James Kilbridge signed off on it for Litton.

as though some time-beating metronome was counting him through his gravity-escaping exercise which had been declared possible centuries before by old Sir Isaac Newton in his assertion that centripetal forces were the orbital "glue" which held planets on courses. With Fritz Hellige & Co., GmbH as a "manufacturer of scientific and medical apparatus" coming into Litton with this recent sale on its books, its managing director, Franz Morat, bequeathed to the new ownership the right to a fascinating claim—Litton could say its family of assembled companies and internally grown off-shoots had placed it at the very start of the space and cosmos competition between the superpowers of the era.

This was done not by treaty, not by government-to-government trade agreements, not by high level diplomacy, but by the oldest variety of international relationship on earth—the pursuit of commerce. It is doubtful that any company could claim a like achievement. It was done a full 15 years before politics would get around to establishing as respectable such a rapport between the East and West.

And if Litton could be "far out", it could also be "far down".

No matter how often or in how many specialty areas Litton had seemed appropriate to space minded governments and their agencies, it also found a place in the U.S. Navy thought processes in Washington that contended ". . . the bottom of the sea ought to be just as interesting as the backside of the Moon. . ."

The Woods Hole Oceanographic Institution in Massachusetts had a scientist named Allyn C. Vine. Litton's deep water direction started from an idea he had for a chubby, 2-man submersible vehicle which could take a pair of scientists into the ocean depths some 6,000 feet or more. This could mean that Man would no longer have to depend entirely on undersea camera operated by remote control, or underwater coring equipment and even trawls and dredges to do their samplings for them. From such a submersible with pressure-resisting windows, observers could actually view the deep ocean scenes from intimate positions. They could be selective by sight of rocks that looked interesting, types of sediment, and marine life in its own deepest, darkest habitat. Vine was a gifted writer.

He did such an eloquent dissertation on the promise of such an amphibious vessel that the Office of Naval Research let a contract to the General Mills Aerospace and Engineering Department. On the sale of that division to Litton, the unfinished contract became a part of the acquisition baggage. Under General Mills, it was doing experiments in upper atmosphere physics, in communications sciences and metallurgy and minerals—most of them space-related.

The submersible had a pet-like appearance about it, being fat and short-coupled. It was appropriately and sentimentally named ALVIN (those two syllables plucked easily from the name of Allyn C. Vine). Considering how widely it would range in the international waters the name could not have been better. Alvin is an old, old one found in many languages. The earliest trace of it shows in high German, and it transitioned from there into Anglo-Saxon to become Elvin, or "elf friend". In French, it was Alouin and in Italian and Spanish, Alvino. From selective bits of Allyn C. Vine's name it might have come, but events were to show that it would touch in some way all of those countries and their interests and would know various answers to questions and solutions to dilemmas.

It left Minneapolis almost unheralded. It wore Litton's logo right up to the last day on its premises at the Applied Sciences Division. Once in the Navy's hands which had spent $500,000 on the project, Litton's logo came off quickly. The Office of Naval Research and its brand went on one side of the conning tower and Woods Hole Oceanographic Institution was on the other. Just below on each side in 10-inch high letters was ALVIN. The submersible went immediately to its test site at Tongue-of-the-Ocean off Bermuda. Prior to doing anything with a crew on board, ALVIN was let down in a trench-like watery abyss to a level of 7,500 feet. Brought up again it was checked over closely to determine how well it had fared beneath the crushing, smashing weights when so far down and at the mercy of such overhead tonnages of water. Then and only then, the test crew had been satisfied that it had shouldered all those burdens satisfactorily. It was sent back down to the 6,000-foot depths with a crew. It had just been through this testing of all the initial requirements, but something happened far away that yanked it from scientific anonymity forever. That this little ALVIN would become a household word had to be against odds greater than 1,000,000 to one. Most gamblers would be hard put to remember any such outrageous outside chances at a racetrack starting gate, let alone that it could have anything to do with the first nose at the wire when the race was run.

The LITTON Adventure That Was

The year 1966 was but 17 days old when the event occurred.

A U.S.A.F. Strategic Air Command B-52 was on a routine airborne alert patrol with four hydrogen bombs on board. Not far from the Spanish base of Torrejon near Madrid which was used by SAC, a jet-refueling KC-135 tanker edged up to rendezvous at 37,000 feet. It was an often repeated, commonplace variety of exercise which gave SAC those necessary long legs for sustained proximity to preselected targets in Eastern Europe should a retaliation strike be ordered. Routine it may have been, but something went amiss and the two aircraft crashed into each other. The sky was suddenly filled with an angry, boiling ball of flame as thousands of gallons of flammable liquid were ignited along the southeast coastal region of the otherwise sleepy Iberian peninsula.

The principal concentration of debris struck in the vicinity of a drowsy Spanish village called Palomares, home to less than 1,200 people. The littering was over fewer than 250 acres. Even though some of the breakup of the planes produced heavy blocks of material, no one on the ground was hurt. All of the four KC-135 aircraft crewmembers were killed, as were three of the B-52's roster. Three, unbelievably, survived. But the concerns quickly switched from casualties to the whereabouts and conditions of the four hydrogen bombs. They caused international jitters. Three of these most fearsome weapons fell to earth where they were roped off and retrieved. The fourth, apparently the last to spring out, landed offshore in the Mediterranean. It wasn't bad enough that one of the H Bombs was lost and hidden under the serenity of the deceptively tranquil sea. That sea lapped against such world-famous stretches of sand as the French and Italian Riveras, Costa Brava and Costa del Sol.

All over North Europe brochures were just coming off the presses with color pictures and dreamy prose inviting tourism to those very beaches *en masse*, and there in Madrid's authoritative newspapers, *El Alcazar*, were headlines black and high about *LA BOMBA*. Variations of this were repeated around the globe in all languages. The U.S. Navy's Sixth Fleet in the Mediterranean, the principal contribution to the marine side of the North Atlantic Treaty Organization, was on station. What was in those waters was its responsibility. Rear Admiral William S. Guest was immediately given command of a hastily organized Task Force 65 to conduct the search and salvage mission. The greatest hunt sequel to the attempt to find a needle in a haystack was on!

Admiral Guest, born in Rome, Georgia, had never thought he'd see Navy service like this. As he set out for the quest, he made a quick checklist of things to do. They included fixing the direction and draft of the falling wreckage with help coming from the line of the three H-bombs which had fallen on land being extended seaward. They had to make allowances for the fact that the bombs fell through a roaring 100-miles-an-hour jet stream, that high altitude wind which goes west to east around the world constantly. Also, the Mediterranean Sea floor off Palomares had spiny mountains which come down to Europe's waters' edges. He needed to know the resources he could call for from the U.S. Navy to help him.

Over crackling Navy communications, he asked urgently for three known crafts. He didn't care where they might be in their respective test patterns, what they were doing at the moment, or what arbitrary limitations had been written into their original specifications. He was in need, dire need. His SOS order book asked for the Ocean Services, Inc. in Florida for its PERRY CUBMARINE, and the Reynolds International ALUMINAUT. The ALUMINAUT was a 60-footer, almost thrice the size of the 18-foot CUBMARINE. And he asked the Woods Hole Oceanographic Institution for its ALVIN, the Litton new kid in town. The ALUMINAUT had been proven seaworthy at 6,250 foot-depths. The ALVIN had managed several such dives unscathed. It all depended on where the missing H-bomb lay in the water—high, or halfway down a slope, or at the very bottom of some watery canyon.

ALVIN already had a fan club. One of the most articulate among its membership was the Deep Submersible Research Vehicle Project's James W. Mavor, Jr. at Woods Hole. He had written a paper just published in February which said the ALVIN was ". . .the first deep-diving submarine" as contrasted with the vertical traveling bathyscaph. He said it had completed a 6-months show of capacities during which the vehicle and its support equipment experienced real ocean environment. This had been preceded by a 4-month test period and a 6-months refit respite. He said the ALVIN crew of William Rannie, Jr., Marvin McCamis and Valentine P. Wilson was dedicated and ready for anything. It was "show and tell" time now, for sure. As both ALVIN and CUBMARINE were air transportable, they were flown immediately to join Task Force 65. Mavor when writing his paper about the suitability of ALVIN to a variety of challenges had no idea how quickly the 29,960-pound vehicle was going to have not only the chance but urgent necessity to demonstrate that he was right—and visibly so.

The undersea search began on February 14th just short of a month after the midair collision. Admiral Guest said: "I would prefer combat to this anytime." The suspense was weighty and constant. There were miles of newspaper columns and tens of thousands written of words or worried commentary being broadcast daily. While the submersibles were being assembled, Admiral Guest had used the intervening time well. Getting the "fix" hadn't been easy as most of the ground onlookers at the time of the crash had been excited and fearful that their lives were in jeopardy. While the Palomares people on land had run about, hither and yon, the fishermen who came from the villages and were out to sea tended to hold reasonably close to one spot. There was added confusion as to whether the floating incoming parachutes were carrying crewmembers or the H-bombs. The Admiral had finally developed a 2-mile wide path stretching 25 miles from the shore out over the water. Somewhere along it he felt sure the missing H-bomb had to be. His assurance was bound up in one unflappable fisherman, Francisco Simon-Ortiz. He said he was certain LA BOMBA lay on the bottom of the Mediterranean about 12 miles from the beach—and a circle three miles in diameter was outlined for intensive search.

Each of the specialty subs was given 1,000-meter squares. Each was told to go over the assigned sector in careful inspection looking for the 12-feet long, 2-feet around 20-megaton weapon. In that relatively small package was enough explosive power to obliterate any capital city of any country whose shores touched the Mediterranean, with area destructiveness and lethal fallout well beyond that. The weapon was not armed, but even so it was a hairy sub-sea encounter mission and in inky darkness such as attends great depths.

It was a rough and rugged sea floor to traverse. All those rivers which emptied into the Mediterranean carried the silt and refuse of the ages to its bottom where it mixed with the remains and skeletons of ships wrecked and sunk since antiquity. No wonder it took days, then weeks, and almost a month before that tenacious team of McCamis and Wilson in the ALVIN found their necks prickling on spotting what appeared to be the trail of something dragged across the sea floor before them. They were about 2,500 feet down and any place touched sent up a flurry of view obstructing sediment. As they interpreted the track it was as if some tumbling, awkwardly heavy object had gone that way. ALVIN at the time was mincing along the edge of a precipitous 70-degree slope.

Suddenly, right there before them was the H-bomb!

It was a foot deep in the mucky, slimy mud. The find was a tribute to the unerring eyesight of Simon-Ortiz, the fisherman. It lay right on the outer edge of the circle which he had outlined as its probable resting place.

The ALUMINAUT quickly left its assigned patrol and placed itself on the watch alongside ALVIN. The only way ALVIN could point its finger at the H-bomb was by staying with it, not quite the most comforting companionship. It squatted there in the crevasse on the edge of which the deadly weapon was so tentatively perched still attached to its parachute. The Navy's MIZAR, a research ship, hung onto ALVIN with its sonar-transponder which nailed down depth, distance and bearing. Finally, ALUMINAUT gave up and surfaced leaving tiny ALVIN lonely and staring and held there by dog-tired and strained McCamis and Wilson for an eight full hours. All that explosive power, a potential Krakatau undersea volcano, was close enough for them to touch. The plutonium content of it alone had about 24,400 years of life. ALVIN stayed there until a refreshed ALUMINAUT and crew returned for its relief. As ALVIN had submerged, it was with the most forlorn of hopes and had no indicated promise at all. When it surfaced this time, it was world-renowned and a flashbulb and TV-lighted bonanza of a news story.

Shortly thereafter the huge destructive monster weapon was brought up and laid on the deck of Admiral Guest's Task Force 65 command ship. It was a press field day. The so called "atomic shape" had been one of the military's most highly classified secrets, and photographs had never been allowed before. But in the interests of tourism on the Rivieras, Costa del Sol and Costa Brave, it became imperative to refute a Soviet-inspired whispering campaign that

414

Americans would claim they found it, even if they hadn't. Governments could fall if such rumors were allowed to go unrefuted.

Now Madrid's EL ALCAZAR on April 1, 1966 had a full front page paragraph and accompanying explanatory headline: "HE AQUI LA BOMBA!" The 400 members of the press who had haunted Palomares for the more than 40 days of the hunt were doing their own variations on the same theme.

At no point then was any reference made to Litton, the builder. All credit flowed to the Woods Hole Oceanographic Institution under whose auspices it had been funded.

Once each year, the Navy League has its convention which is customarily addressed by that services Secretary. On such occasion he gives a status report and "points with pride". Navy Secretary Paul Nitze barely was under way with his speech in Los Angeles that year — only 150 words — when he was saying:

"The successful recovery of the nuclear weapon lost off the coast of Palomares, Spain dramatically demonstrated to the nation and to the world a feat previously assumed not feasible. Undaunted by the lack of previous capability designed to accomplish such a mission, the corporate effort of this nation produced an international manifestation of American know-how and perseverance. The response of the scientific oceanographic community, American industry, the Navy's research and development laboratories and the operational Navy was instantaneous and spontaneous. The recovery of the lost nuclear weapon must be regarded as a significant milestone in our national security long range plans. The name of ALVIN known only to a few in the oceanographic field was flashed to the world proclaiming it a hero at Palomares."

Nitze never said so, but there were hundreds in Fred O'Green's Defense and Space Systems Group who had provided the careful and expert hands which had built ALVIN. *They* knew what they had done but were sophisticated enough to know that as always is the case with the urgently summoned industrial base, the spotlight goes inevitably to the user, not the maker. The exception is when a program is troubled in which case the industrial partner not only has to handle his assigned task, it must also lend itself to identification as the culprit and bare its back to the whip.

August 1969, Col. Barney Oldfield, Litton Founder Tex Thornton, and Soviet Academician Gheorgi A. Arbatov in Leningrad.

But Litton was too busy to mourn. In that 1966 fiscal year, it had acquired 19 new companies, 11 of them in the period of the H-bomb quest — Alvey Ferguson, Everett-Waddey, Maverick-Clarke, McCray Refrigerator Co. Inc., in the U.S. and McCray Refrigerator Co. of Canada Ltd., Willy Feiler Zaehl-und-Rechenwerke, GmbH, Louis Allis Co. and Louis Allis Control Center, Fenix Manufacturing, and Institute of Computer Management of Baltimore, Cleveland and Pennsylvania. Some 36% of Litton's revenues that year were generated by business equipment and supplies, 35% by the defense and space systems sales and 29% by industrial and professional products and services. ALVIN was a contract long since performed and delivered by Litton and in its past. There was no cash flow continuance that made it an accounting brush-aside. Only a grateful world released from its terrors was unaware as to whom it should be appreciative, and Litton couldn't bank that.[12]

---

12. National Oceanic and Atmospheric Administration in Washington announced in 1981 the discovery of an immense undersea ore deposit of copper, silver and other

The LITTON Adventure That Was

Tex with his interpreter inside the Kremlin.

That same year Litton stopped something begun four years before — its annual report in Russian.

It appeared a dead end, going nowhere and milked dry. None had taken seriously the fact that Soviet Minister K.N. Rudnev had come to the Svenska Dataregister booth at that year's exposition in Leningrad. He asked why Litton's Swedish division had never made a proposal for his Ministry of Instrument Building, Means of Automation and Control Systems about the design, tooling and installing of an assembly line somewhere in the U.S.S.R. for a cash register manufacturing facility?

How little Litton knew then of the impact of what it had been doing and was now discontinuing! Starting in 1963, the decision had been made to extend the Litton annual reports into the Russian language. The 1963, 1964, and 1965 and 1966 annual reports had been given that treatment. PRAVDA had been outraged and said so. In

---

minerals worth billions of dollars in international waters 350 mile west of Ecuador, near the Galapogos Islands — and the discovery was accomplished by the deep diving research submarine, ALVIN! About 10% of the find was copper, 10% iron, and other types included Molybdenum, vanadium, zinc, cadmium, tin and lead. The copper is ten times richer than that found in land mines.

Litton Founder & Chairman Tex Thornton, Academician Gheorgi A. Arbatov and interpreter outside the Europeskaya Hotel in Moscow, August 1969.

those days Litton used the annual reports to expound on its leadership's philosophy. The preface of the 1963 document said Litton was ". . . dedicated to utilizing the discoveries of modern science by converting them into useful goods and services — products which bolster the Free World's vital economic base and defend the inflexible ideal of human freedom. . ."; in 1964 was declared ". . .the body corporate, be it political, economic or social in character is but the manifestation of its individual leaders. A free society reflects in every facet the dedication, the sense of responsibility and the moral convictions of the men and women who direct its endeavors. If it is to be vigorous, the corporate structure must remain simply the opportunity and vehicle for expression, not the master of the individual. . .", in 1965, the Litton word was that ". . .leadership in the marketplace is hard won and stoutly defended. Those who have earned and retained it have contributed greatly to the improvement of Man's standard of living and the protection of his freedom. . .", and in 1966 Litton asked the celebrated and respected historian, Allan Nevins, to do the lead page and he chose at one point to say: "The timeless ideas in politics from

The LITTON Adventure That Was

Tex and tourists at the auto entrance of the Kremlin.

Pericles to Churchill have been those of liberty, tolerance, integrity and responsibility." Well said for reading outside the Communist bloc, such little aphorisms infuriated PRAVDA and some of the Soviet literary gazettes. They had their say in column after column, fulminating about Litton as a preaching "was monger" and "weapons builder", a NATO prop, guilty of warlike prose and purveyor of unwelcome capitalistic pronouncements.

Kremlinologists, were delighted by all the stir the presence of a small number of Litton annual reports caused. How they had gotten there was a bait of philatelic gamesmanship. No marketer could safely carry in such things in bulk lest he become a connoisseur of *gulag* cuisine. The U.S. Embassy could not undertake handing out such materials. It was Mary Ann Wassmuth, a secretary in the public relations office who asked innocently: "Why don't you mail them"' This jogged my memories of the first Soviet appearance in 1952 in the international competition of the Helsinki, Finland Olympic Games. All Eastern country competitors literally stormed the main stadium's philatelic window buying commemorative stamps. I vaguely recalled being told then that there were three times as many members of philatelist societies and clubs in the U.S.S.R. as there were chasing this

Everywhere Tex went, he was asked technical questions.

hobby in the U.S. The appetite was made even more acute because the ordinary citizen was forbidden to receive from or mail to anyone outside the communist wall. The Helsinki trip was sanctioned and official, hence the mass of buying to send the Olympic commemoratives home to appreciating relatives and friends.

At Litton, work began sorting through every published document that could be found which contained Russian names and identified them with some agencies, polytechnical institutes, plants, renowned physicists, chemists, engineers, the whole Politburo, the roster of Ministers, heads of the trading organizations, well known athletes, journalists and just for fun, Bolshoi ballet stars. This brought into being an original, first time mailing list of 1,850. It was the time of the 5-cent stamp. The Beverly Hills post office said it would cost 65-cents each to mail by surface means an annual report to any address inside the Soviet Union. The Beverly Hills postmaster was asked for 1,850 each of 13 different commemorative U.S. postage stamps. Every envelope used for mailing was plain with no return address, and left Litton a positive rainbow of color rivaling a field marshal's tunic bosom after waging a successful war. How silly, the wise sophisticates said around Litton, as there was no known buzzword for "stamp". Would such a ploy work? Work, it did, indeed!

The PRAVDA blast which "welcomed" Litton's literary intrusion on the Moscow scene was the work of its commentator, Yuri Zhukov, and generous. Paragraph after paragraph poured from his typewriter, covering the same amount of space as a party congress. He summoned every communist cliche and used each several times, and noted that he had received *five* copies when he didn't even want one. As PRAVDA was published in 40 cities daily and had more than 9,000,000 circulation it was a formidable barrage of chastising artillery indicating that the disturbed higher-ups had no way of knowing how general the mailing had been. Using their party guidance organ, they wanted there to be no doubt that in their view this Litton litany about free enterprise and its rewards was to fall on deaf ears, be greeted by dogmatically blinded eyes and was a conversational no-no.

Kremlinologists in the West were titillated. It indicated the annual reports were probably being handed about surreptitiously, were the subject of admiring chit-chat and this was about as popular as a tin of pure bubonic plague virus. Surely there was an open door via the post office. After all the fancy footwork and cocktail hour intellectual exercises about reaching "hearts and minds", simplicity had something going for it. The Litton mailing list grew to more than 4,000 in 1964, and rose to 6,200 in 1965 and 1966. Everything worked well except in 1964 because corporate life always had to reckon with the "efficiency expert" and cost effectiveness, and the numbers people.[13]

In the subsequent years of 1965 and 1966, the mailings were done from nine European countries using the commemorative stamps of the several nations. The ploy was based on Litton's belief that the

---

13. Their intrusion was for the 1964 annual report mailings which they rationalized thusly: The printing of all Litton's foreign versions was done in Antwerp, Belgium and sent to European points from a mailing house in Amsterdam so why not save postage costs by having the same Dutch handler take care of the Russian version as well? All but 400 were sent that way, metered with the required postage and were trucked to a single border transmission point. They were never delivered, never heard from — and it was again only the Beverly Hills 400 for the principals of the Politburo, trade groups, Ministries and some plants sent with commemorative stamps which penetrated the barriers. As often happens, the "efficiency expert" had a short term cost saving, but in terms of the reason for the action, his suggestion could be written off as a total loss.

ones receiving each packet would be in ages that gave them grandchildren or children or those of friends who were engaged in stamp collection. No clerk in an outer office would dare intercept such a prize, hence the addressee indicated would get it.

Litton could hardly believe its success. It had become a highly visible and curiously interesting company within the operational and political superstructure of the Soviet Union. It was demonstrably a capitalistic, private enterprise mechanism of substantial achievement. The leadership was easily identifiable and was no way an amorphous committee or bureaucratic body. It separated its adolescents from its adults by asking for high trapeze and wire performance without a safety net, rewarded its winners and freed its losers to go elsewhere. Those who left usually did well and were successful because of lessons hard-learned. But with the issuance and posting of the 1966 annual report, Tex Thornton, being pestered by those who said it was "going nowhere" and the money spent on it was "wasted", decided to draw the line and said there would be no 1967 Russian version.

All this was done just as Minister Rudnev made his call on the booth of Svenska Dataregister. How about a proposal for a cash register manufacturing plant, he had asked?

The Soviets, considering the climate in which they live politically, always have a hovering cloud of conspiracy present or imminent in the affairs with which they live. They take steps almost instinctively to protect themselves should its outcroppings draw near them. There was no Litton mail in 1967. They missed it. They assigned something ominous to it, even if it was only the closing of its wide open door which gave them a yearly look in the parlor, bedroom and bath of a leading American industrial concern. As 1967 ended, two widely separate events occurred. One was in the U.S.S.R. and one was in Los Angeles.

In Moscow, Leonid Brezhnev was consolidating his hold on the Politiburo, the ruling political mechanism of his vast country. He wanted a better, truer assessment of North America and the United States particularly. The old system wherein Soviet masters had depended on reporting apparatus which reinforced their preconceived notions, prejudices and positions did not appeal to him. He had a trusted associate who had toiled at his elbow in the Communist Party of the Soviet Union Secretariat, Prof. Georgi Arbatov. He removed

Arbatov from his acolyte role at the CPSU and ordered him to establish and head the Institute of U.S.A. and Canada Studies as part of the Academy of Sciences. He wanted it to reflect more correctly the probable directions of and reasons for U.S. and Canadian policies and their reactions to Kremlin moves on the world stage.

Litton President Roy L. Ash in Red Square, Moscow, May Day (May 1, 1972) heading a Litton delegation two weeks prior to President Nixon's historic visit to start Détente.

One of those who had puzzled over Litton's Russian language annual reports, Arbatov had a first priority. He wanted to bring Tex Thornton to Moscow as a renowned technological mountain climber with established credentials. He pictured this as exactly the kind of launch mechanism his Institute needed and which would show it as a serious forum or exchange device for airing East/West opinions freely. His people would get a feel of the U.S. pulse. And he knew that while political leadership was pervasive in the Soviet Union, the men who made America roll with such relentlessness were its business and industry movers and shakers. Litton Industries was not only one of those companies, it was still headed by the man who founded it.

Viktor Ivanov (here before Lenin Mausoleum with Litton president Roy L. Ash) told me when he was stationed at the UN in New York that he and other espionage colleagues would go to the top of the Empire State Building on New Year's Eve and, at midnight sharp, bottoms up their vodka glasses to Communism's sure and inevitable triumph over all capitalistic nations.

However much he wished to have Tex Thornton in Prince Volkonsky's old home,[14] he was also cautious enough not to expose

---

14. Arbatov's Institute went in motion in late 1967 when he and his deputy, Dr. Evgeny Shershnev, took over a rather shabby building at Khlebniy (Bread Street) not far from the Kremlin walls. For all its rundown exterior, the building is a historic Moscow landmark. It was the old home of Prince Volkonsky, who often entertained as a houseguest the revered Mikhail Kutuzov, who had chased Napoleon out of Moscow a century and a half before. It was under the general wing of the Academy of Sciences, then headed by the brilliant Mstislav Vsevolodovich Keldysh, a mathematician and mechanical engineer. He liked what Arbotov had in mind for his Institute — bringing to it and making available to his staffers Western political and business leaders, the latter being the holders of all those technological "gold mines". The Institute of U.S.A. and Canada Studies was eventually to grow to 400 researchers, and to be the haven for sons and daughters of Soviet leaders on their way to sophistication in world affairs and probable high level careers of their own. In small world category, Dr. Shershnev's daughter was later in the Soviet Embassy's visa office in Washington D.C., and I never had to wait for passport and visa matters as she insisted on handling the papers and issuances herself.

himself to rejection personally if the Thornton reaction was negative. He used a stalker. The selection was Valentin Zorin, who was part of his small startup staff, but was often referred to as ". . .the Walter Cronkite of the Soviet Union. . ." He was a respected and trusted and party line hewing spokesman on the U.S.S.R. All-Union Radio and Television. He was coming to America in 1968 to cover the two political conventions.

Litton first knew of it when Marshall Berges, the TIME bureau chief, called. Would Tex Thornton talk with Zorin in that hiatus of a month between the two political conclaves? While the only thing he had to go on was the vitriolic press reaction to the annual reports, and somewhat puzzled, he agreed to see him. He had been amused by previous Zorin writings which alluded to starving people begging at the "barbed wire fence" which he said surrounded Litton, and his reference to Litton's founder as ". . .one of the uncrowned kings of the United States. . ." As the Thornton experience had been to grow up in the unfenced expanses of Texas, he hadn't seen very many such barriers in all his life and there were surely none at Litton. None had ever offered to fit him for a crown lately, either, and the only headgear he had was a 7 1/2 gallon, beat-up and floppy broadbrim which he wore at the ranch on weekends. When Zorin came, he explained his "errors" in writing about his host attributing it to press clippings and incomplete reference materials. Then he changed the subject abruptly by his surprise statement that he ". . .was empowered by my government to invite you, Mr. Thornton, to be the first American industrialist to be an official guest of the Soviet Union under the auspices of our Academy of Sciences!"

Taken aback by this level of interest in him and the company he headed, Tex Thornton said he would have to think about it and passed him along to me, for further conversations to amplify what was going on. I pointed out quickly that it wouldn't be useful for Litton or the U.S.S.R. if a Tex Thornton were given the usual cultural exchange treatment, endless toasts, tourism type gadabout excursions and the like — but it would be helpful to both countries if he were allowed to meet and talk at length with the Ministers and significant Committee Chairmen who ran the Soviet industrial enclaves, as well as institute chiefs whose research led them toward practical product applications. After all, Zorin was told, it was not a one-way street because when a

Enter the "how to" man president Roy L. Ash — make a deal, that is.

In 1971, when the author escorted Litton president, Roy L. Ash, he was taken deep into Siberia to Novosibirsk, 'Science City.' By executive order, one-quarter of the members of the prestigious National Academy of Sciences were ordered there to study plans for developing the resources — rich, but largely unknown vast territories. Oil and natural gas being two resources, and Litton a premier geophysical capability, it led to commercial ties. But primitive it was. When we checked into our hotel, we signed the register, were each issued two blankets, two sheets, a pillow case, and we had to make our own beds. Plus we slept in our clothes, except shoes, as it was 30° below zero outside.

man of Thornton's stature returned, all of his associates on the Business Council would want his impression as a basis for corporate judgments of their own, and they were the 100 leading industrialists in America. He was also a friend of the U.S. Presidents, past and present, who would surely ask for soundings from another point of view in that milieu where political leaders work.

426

The LITTON Adventure That Was

Litton president Roy L. Ash and wife Lila.

Zorin shrank back. He couldn't promise such high level treatment, but he said his colleague who was coming to America soon could do that. The colleague: Prof. Georgi A. Arbatov.

When Arbatov arrived in Los Angeles in February, 1969, he reaffirmed the official guest invitational status and asked for a list of the people Tex Thornton wanted to see. That August Tex made the trip and with the one exception of Prime Minister Kosygin[15] who was holidaying in the Caucasus, he saw them all.

---

15. He was hosted by Deputy Prime Minister Vladimir A. Kirillin, Chairman of the State Committee on Science and Technology; K.N. Rudneve Minister of Instrument Building, Means of Automation & Control Systems; V.D. Kalmykov, Minister of Radio Industries; A.I. Shokin, Minister of Electronics Industries; Vasilly Kazakhov, Deputy Minister of Aviation Industries; Academician and Nobel Prize Winner N.G. Basov, of the Lebedev Institute of Physics;President M. Keldysh of the U.S.S.R. National Academy of Sciences and key members of his staff; Aleksei Tupolev, designer of the TU-144 Supersonic Transport, and Edouard Ellijan, its chief test pilot. He was the first American taken to Togliatti, the industrial city thrown up overnight near Kuibyshev on the Volga where FIAT built their Volga Auto Works to produce what the Soviets call their Zhiguli car. That whole visit had milestone significance because American Ambassador Jacob Beam had been finding the diplomatic atmosphere colder than Siberian winter and when he hosted an Embassy reception for Tex Thornton; all the Soviet leaders who had been talking with him attended. Lesser

After signing the first ever protocol agreement between the USSR (a sovereign government) and an American Industrial corporation, Litton Industries President, Ash celebrated by playing tourist at Zagorsk, the religious center, with his wife Lila.

The Soviets were puzzled when Tex Thornton never brought up the subject of trade. Minister Rudnev, holder of several Lenin prizes for his pioneering in the space effort, was the one picked by the Kremlin to lay their interests on the table.

"If you wish," he told the man from Haskell, Texas, "I will arrange for exhibit space as large as you need to you can display for us all the things Litton Industries might wish to show us in the interest of

---

Soviets there said it should be considered a change of attitude, a "starting point", as they put it. As a farewell party joke, Host Arbatov and his staff told Thornton they wanted to make him an "honorary member of the Communist Party". He didn't say NO, only that he would have to reciprocate and give each member of Arbatov's Institute a share of Litton stock. The matter was dropped — but Arbatov did make him a "consultant" at one ruble a year! From where Thornton came from, even a facetious Communist Party affiliation would be politically hazardous, but for the Soviets to own shares in a capitalist enterprise was ideological "original sin." My suggested Kosygin gift was a Litton microwave oven as a consumer product evolved from a military root. A widower, his daughter Ludmilla, lived across the hall and cooked for him. It became a hard to beat example of penetration of a government at the highest level.

trade." Thornton expressed appreciation, but said he might have problems with that. What problems? He cited the Soviet record for dragging out negotiations so interminably, for long and expensive waiting periods, causing heels to cool in corridors. Thornton said that, based on the interest of Rudnev, Litton had gone seriously about the cash register proposal and that here three years later, an agreement and contract seemed no closer. There were troubles about Litton's New Britain-AMTEC machine tools acceptance for the Volga Auto Works. Unless the pace could somehow be quickened, it was the Tex Thornton belief he would not find much enthusiasm among his divisions to pursue trade expansion. Rudnev said he would look into it and suggested it would be a good idea to have some Litton follow-on delegations make presentations under the joint umbrella of the Academy of Sciences and the State committee on Science and Technology.

There was a last, poignant feature of the Thornton[16] time in Moscow and Leningrad, in that everywhere he visited — Ministries, Committees, Institutes, plants — each showed him what they considered to be a prize reference — copies of each of the four annual reports of Litton Industries in Russian which had been read, reread and retained at each place received. He was also shown that in official publications and technical dictionaries, they had used Litton terminology and definitions — all taken from those annual reports. PRAVDA to the contrary, it was being said that in the hostile and almost poisonous political climate of that time, the annual reports in Russian had been the best possible direct mail advertising campaign any company could have mounted and carried out!

Two years later, the invitation came again to Litton, this time for Roy Ash to come to Moscow as an "official guest" as well. The Litton acquaintance was renewed with Kirillin and Rudnev, and in addition, Chairman Nikolay Baybakov, of GOSPLAN (the 5-year plan agency); Nikolay Patolichev, Minister of Foreign Trade; Dr. Boris Pe-

---

16. Tex Thornton on his visit left Kosygin a Litton microwave oven. Minister A.I. Shokin's Electronics Industries staff put the oven through series of exhaustive tests before it was passed on to the Prime Minister. At one point, Tex Thornton himself had to bake an apple as part of the demonstration. Afterward, Tex often joked at my expense that when James Bond did his Soviet spy intrusions, very beautiful women came through the windows and doors and some stayed overnight, but he knew for a fact that my first three nights in the Hotel Rossiya, I had slept with a microwave oven at the foot of my bed awaiting its test!

trovskiy, Minister of Public Health and Dzhermen Gvishiani, Vice Chairman of the State Committee of Science and Technology and the husband of Lyudmilla, Prime Minister Kosygin's daughter; and A.V. Sidorenko, Minister of Geology. Ash decided to spring an idea which if OK'd would lessen the chances that Litton proposals would wander off into marginal and unproductive regions, costing money and time.

To Novodyevichi Cemetery, only the great do go. Including a not so great prophet or so. When Soviet leader Nikita Khruschev visited Los Angeles in 1959, he said: "We will bury you." Litton president Roy Ash and the author in Moscow in 1971 took each other's photo at his gravesite to show who was buried first!

It was a "protocol agreement" between a company and a country, rather than country-to-country. Chairman Kirillin did not warm to the idea at first saying there should be more commercial action than there was. I let Arbatov know that Ash felt it was a dead-end for the building relationship if such an arrangement couldn't be made. On the last day of his stay, October 18, 1971, with Gvishiani signing for the State Committee and Roy Ash for Litton, the protocol became a fact. It stated the areas of interest in Litton to be geophysical exploration, business machines and equipment and systems, medical electronics, electronic components, chemical processing plants and specialty paper. After the protocol was signed, Ash visited Moscow's Novodyevichy cemetery where the Soviet Union buries all the famous in its history. One of the newly heaped-up graves was that of Nikita Khrushchev, who had once boasted to capitalist America that ". . . we will bury you!" Ash never said whether it occurred to him, the capitalist, to note their relative positions that day.[17]

The spectacular was common place at Litton, and while the company was being roughed up in the late '60s and '70s, there were so many remembered unbelievable events it was on such that Littonites clung as assurances of brighter days. Other companies might have to do with one or so, but at Litton they were all around.

Getting to the Moon had been a long, preparatory and demanding exercise. The U.S. Air Force School of Aviation Medicine had depended heavily on animals in research such as marmosets from Cen-

---

17. The chemical processing plants action, if any, would have been Copper-Rust, the Belgian, and that of Litton's Rust Engineering. Contained in that acquisition was a charming human interest feature which dated from 1912. It surfaced unexpectedly when Nikita Khrushchev was trying to get Josip Broz Tito to come back in the Communist Bloc. It was during his trip to Belgrade. Tito took the occasion to show Khrushchev off to the Belgrade diplomatic corps at a reception. As ambassadors came along to shake hands with his ebullient guest, one was tiny and very correct Robert Rothschild of Belgium.

Khrushchev was in bumptious good spirits and loudly declared he was glad to meet the representative of that ". . . small satellite of the United States and one of your countrymen still owes me money!"

Rothschild was furious and matched the rudeness of the remarks with some of his own. Khrushchev, next day, saw him again and apologized and explained that old Baron Evence Coppee in Brussels had an 1880 invention of his grandfather which made it possible to retrieve byproducts from coke oven gas. His customers then were looking for ways of financing. In Czarist Russia between 1900 and 1914, Coppee secured contracts to construct 50 such coke ovens in the Donetz basin representing two-thirds of the entire Russian capability in this field. Coppee's contract asked that for the construction he have rights to all byproducts for ten years, and beyond that all rights to sell them as the Czar's agent.

The Czars' labor "recruiters" loaded up Ukrainians and hauled them to the Donetz to work the plants where the odors were frightful. One of those workers refused to stay, walked off and didn't collect his day's pay — one ruble! Nikita Khrushchev. The Brussels Foreign Office checked with Coppee and the records showed it to be true. Coppee was going to have fun with it, taking one ruble from 1912 with interest, and cost of living increases, visit the Kremlin and pay Khrushchev. All preparations were made and in October, 1964, Khrushchev was ousted from power, becoming an un-person and pensioner, so he died with Litton — technically — owing him a day's pay.

Col. Barney Oldfield at the Khruschev gravesite
photo taken by Litton president Roy Ash.

tral and South America and the Rhesus pale brown monkeys from India, as well as the Philippine varieties of the same breed. "Sam" the marmoset, rode the "Little Joe-2" rocket on December 4, 1959 and when that experiment took it to 100,000 feet under full power and its second stage giving it a coasting trajectory of 280,000 feet (about 53 miles). "Sam" made it back without harm except for the landing impact and the discomfort of six hours laced up in a pseudo astronaut mode in a capsule. A Navy destroyer hunted for him as he bobbed about in the drink off Wallops Island.

There was a "Miss Sam", a Rhesus type, for another such shot. And there was "Ham", the astronaut chimpanzee who was given a ride on a centrifuge to test how much excess gravity pull he could safely take. "Ham" then rode on Mercury-Redstone missile off Cape Canaveral becoming the true link between required propulsion and Man's tolerance for participation in such antics.

Everything conceivable that could go wrong did. During the countdown his cramped quarters overheated. He was well trained, an amiable animal who seemed to shrug it off and did what he was supposed to do. It took longer than programmed to get all systems "GO".

432

This endangered the project because it could end the mission; the nighttime would make it hard to find "Ham" and his floating capsule. When "Ham" took off, his angle was steeper. He had to endure 17 times gravity. He picked up an unexpected 52,000 pounds of thrust which threw him forward at 7,540 feet per second, a full 1,000 feet faster than ever intended. Ultimately he was going 6,857 miles and hour and 40 miles longer than scheduled and 132 miles farther out to sea than had been calculated. He was weightless seven minutes. When he came back into the atmosphere he pulled 14.7 negative gravity landing in a choppy sea with the nearest recovery ship 60 miles away. Was there a Litton division beckoning in all that? Yes, there was.

Who's to Breakfast in Beverly Hills, California, at Litton's corporate headquarters? Litton's second chairman, Fred O'Green, is here hosting a delegation from the USSR headed by Mikhail Schkabardnya, who was about to be made USSR Mikhail Gorbachev's chief of staff, head of the USSR Council of Ministers. The author was his escort from coast to coast, and Schkabardnya wore his red hat all the way.

Once "Ham" was on deck and released from his topsy-turvy experience, he took an apple and ate it and half an orange, too. He was telling onlookers loads of things which were Man-applicable.

He gave some of the witnesses an idea that there could be a company that could engage in animal research seeking answers to more things than space flight. One evolvement was called Bionetics Research Laboratories which had addresses on Jefferson Street in Falls Church, Virginia and in Kensington, Maryland. It grew from the belief of its organizers — Francis E. Miller, Richard Guttmacher, Arthur J. Pallota, Carlton Maxwell, Joseph D. Casolaro, Robert L. Loeb and L.P. Gray III — that there were ways animal research could ease the way for humanity, whether astronauts or not.

On June 25, 1968, almost a decade after the original heroics of the marmoset "Sam", Fred O'Green engineered this Bionetics Research Laboratory entry into Litton as a division. The "buy" was through exchange of 11,002 Litton common shares for the 536,508 shares of Bionetics. Tiny marmosets, as well as chimpanzees, apes and other primates became assets of Litton, making it the largest single private owner of primates in the U.S.[18] This made the division a hand-maiden of the National Institute of Health, the National Cancer Center and when the Soviet Minister of Public Health, Dr. Boris Petrovskiy, made his exploratory tour of the American countryside he asked especially to have Bionetics on his itinerary that lead to many cancer-tumor-blood afflictions studies in reciprocal exchange. A whole new business developed to work pre-introduction of new products to determine whether they had carcinogen inducing properties.

---

18. Not Ringling Brothers or Barnum & Bailey, not any municipal zoo can compete with Litton Industries in terms of primate ownership. Wild it may have seemed when Dr. William Jacoby, an engineer, found himself running what was called Litton's Economic Development Division. It was suggested that the sunbelt across America's south might be profitably sown with natural walled acreages in which African, South American and related animals were allowed to run free as sight-seeing enterprises. There was a right and wrong side to it. Litton didn't develop the tourist-variety of preserves, but they did through Litton Bionetics become big in apes, monkeys, and baboons. Just a few miles from the U.S. Marine Corps' Parris Island reservation in South Carolina is something called the Yenassee Primate Center, and it has a satellite called Morgan Island on which more than 1,500 rhesus monkeys jump, climb, chatter and lead the good, loose life until called to the lab. At no time was Litton's primate population smaller than 5,000, the largest privately owned collection in the United States. Art Hall was the monkey manager of Yenassee, and Dave Taub, the Morgan Island *mayor* with a huge monkey constituency. Only to outsiders was this considered odd, because the reason was to search for an answer to the deadly killing affliction colon cancer.

434

The LITTON Adventure That Was

That "crazy" idea that Crosby M. Kelly had in 1963 which led to those Russian annual reports may have aroused the ire of PRAVDA for its free enterprise preachments, but it led finally to the American Embassy in Moscow stating that Litton people had probably met more of the Ministerial (operational) level of the Soviet Union than any other American company. It found itself on the itineraries of Soviet delegations of all sizes and kinds who came to the corporate headquarters as well as individual divisions, only those however that the Department of Commerce Offices of Export License Control would permit to consider trade relationships.[19]

Roy Ash[20] made good on Litton's promise to Minister Rudnev to bring an array of Litton experts for face-to-face talks the first fortnight

---

19. Inertial navigation jumped the Great Wall of China for Litton, as it was not about to be left behind now that the Communist countries were opening to the West a little, and selectively. Their Tsui Huan-Min, high in their National Machinery Import and Export Corporation came to Beverly Hills in July, 1973. He wanted LTN-51 inertial navigation systems for the Peoples Republic of China's newly bought Boeing B-707s, particularly for the 7th, 8th, 9th and 10th of the aircraft to be delivered under that purchase. Chairman Mao, deity, father figure and formidable presence, was still alive and said his country should only buy what it had money to pay for as he was against credits. Sitting with Tsui was a 20-year career captain, Liu Chang-fu, who headed the Peking Regional Office of the PRC Civil Aviation Administration. When President Nixon had come to Peking for his gates-ajar gesture, Liu Chang-fu, had been taken on Air Force One by its chief pilot, Col. Ralph Albertazzie and had been shown the LTN-51s on that plane. He reasoned quickly that what was good enough and dependable enough to be trusted by an American President, was what he wanted on those B 707s the PRC intended to use on international flights. The Chinese sat patiently as Litton briefers talked of the company's marine capabilities such as ship's communications, geophysical exploration and cancer research. They sat up when Joern Joop, Litton's international finance man, mentioned casually that Litton had 1,350 accounts in more than 400 banks around the world and could deal easily in 35 to 40 currencies. The previously imperturbable and bland Tsui Huan-Min lit like a Chinese lantern. Could the PRC buy in any of several of those currencies? They could — and negotiations proceeded with Litton's Aero Products' President Charles "Chuck" Hofflund and his marketing chief, Lute Eldridge.

20. The Roy Ash led delegation from Litton in May, 1972, included Count G.A. "Ibo" Douglas, international marketing chief for the Business Systems and Equipment Group; John Grado, president Fitchburg Paper; Dr. Homer Jensen, chief geophysicist technical development of Aero Service; J. Robert Fries, international vice president of the Machine Tools Group; Richard Simon, product and market planner for advanced retail systems; Carl M. Savito senior vice president for technology for Western Geophysical; Donald Graf, director of marketing and planning, Monroe International; Andre DuBois, electronic engineer of Litton Systems (Canada), Ltd.; Dr. Johann

in May, 1972. All doors swung wide. It was an historic time to be there as President Nixon and his entourage were but 14 days behind Litton when that first detente move was made. The Minister of Geology made nothing of concerns about the coming energy crunch, but he, A.V. Sidorenko, said his Ministry had 11,000 energy search units in the field that day stretching from the Baltic to the Bering Sea, from the Arctic to the Black Sea and wanted Litton help.

In the Ministry of Machine Tools & Tool Building, the announcement that New Britain Machine was a Litton division was a minor bombshell, causing a great hubbub on the Soviet side of the long conference table. Deputy Minister Chepburakov explained that everyone with him in that Ministry had studied in technical schools where the illustrations in all their books had been New Britain Machines. This was as startling to the Litton people as none knew that in the early '20s, Lenin, the Bolshevik firebrand, had asked for assistance in getting the new country going on the wreckage of Czarist Russia, and it had been to New Britain that he had turned. A Lenin validation made those text-book illustrations required reading. Litton by then had about $25,000,000 worth of machine tools in the Togliatti Volga Auto Works, another $12,000,000-plus in the Kamaz River Truck complex and on September 8, 1973 signed an agreement with the Soviets to furnish design and tooling, and to erect an assembly line in Ryazan for the manufacture of Sweda mechanical cash registers, a sale in the $18,000,000 size.

Litton was at ease with it all — the Volga Auto Works to pour forth around 800,000 Zhiguli models for Soviet citizenry able to afford them; the Kamaz River trucks were a part of the 24th Party Congress goal of allocating more than 50,000,000,000 rubles for road building, making regions accessible that were not reachable by canals,

---

Schaedert general manager, Fritz Hellige & Co., GmbH; Werner Herbst, director of manufacturing, Triumph-Adler Werke, Nuremberg; Pol Baeken, chemical process engineer of Coppee-Rust, and Dr. Robert Roderick, Litton vice president for East/West Trade, and myself. How mercurial the switches in attitudes could be. After all those denunciations showered on Litton's annual reports in Russian, Roy Ash was asked officially to have the 1971 edition in a Russian language version, but to let them distribute it only to those who "had need to know." There were 2,500 copies of that document circulated in the USSR. Times had indeed changed as Academician Georghi Arbatov sent his chauffeur and car to make the deliveries to all interested Ministries!

rivers, or railways, and would permit, according to GOSPLAN Chairman Baybakov, wider distribution of more prevalent consumer goods. Those cash registers called OKA[21] rather than the Sweda and named for the river which runs through Ryazan, were in a volume of 80,000 annually. Half their sales were in the U.S.S.R. and the other half in other Socialist countries, which indicated a rise in retailing and broader availability of consumer goods and the good life.[22]

When the Woods Hole Oceanographic Institution celebrated its half century of existence on 1980, it had a performing star — ALVIN, the 2-man Litton-built submersible which was still covering itself and its home base with one exploratory glory after another. On January 15, 1980, ALVIN did its 1,000th dive as kick-off of the Golden Jubilee Year for what is now called a National Research Facility. It is supported by such prestigious organizations as the National Science Foundation, the Office of Naval Research, and the National Oceanic and Atmospheric Administration. That little incompletely tested AL-

---

21. It was on that same OKA river that a 10-year old Vladimir K. Zworykin was allowed to play with the pushbuttons which flashed signals to the engine rooms on his father's fleet of boats. With that early electronic interest, he came to the U.S. and his invention of the iconoscope in 1923 was the first primitive step to television. He was so appalled by what was programmed on TV, though, he would never allow his grandchildren to watch it. Shortly before he died he went to the Jet Propulsion Laboratory to see TV Transmissions from Mars; "That's what television is for," he said.

22. Litton's Ludwig T. Smith was the final negotiator of the Svenske Dataregister contract with the Soviet trading organization, *Prommashimport* to build the cash register manufacturing assembly line in Ryazan. That was Aleksandr Solzhenitsyn's old hometown. Also, it was where Major Yuri Gagarin's brother lived and wrote the family history of the world's first cosmonaut. The *Prommashimport* negotiator was a lawyer named Madame Kobsova, whose husband managed a cement plant. A very attractive woman, she was also an iron maiden, clause by clause. Smith's instructions were firm as to price and areas of responsibility. At one point the Soviets said his stubbornness gave them no other choice than to declare him *persona non grata*! In New York, the trading unit, AMTORG, was headed by President Victor I. Bessmertnyi. He was sent to Beverly Hills to complain. Smith told his counterparts in Moscow that all they were doing was insuring he would get a bonus and a raise when he returned home for "following my instructions". The Soviets wanted to whittle $2,000,000 of the price. Smith shook his head and cooled his heels. The last week in Moscow, Smith came to the table one morning and said he knew what their trouble really was and laid it facetiously at the feet of Madam Kobsova declaring ". . . she has obviously fallen in love with me!" The lady negotiator blushed, withdrew and never rejoined the talks which finally ended at Littons price. They said Madame Kobsova had "an allergy", but in the U.S.S.R. a little suspicion can go a long way.

VIN was flown into the emergency of the Palomares H-bomb hunt. It had since been found capable of operating at depths of 12,124 feet (4,000 meters). That 1,000th dive had ALVIN communicating with Woods Hole from an intersection in the Equator rift and two fracture zones which are undersea mountain structures just north of the Equator in the Pacific Ocean. Its performance had been so impressive since the steel-shielded personnel sphere was upgraded with a titanium version in 1973, that all its users were so enthralled with its credentials that they provided an annual operational budget for its activities four times greater than Litton was paid for it.

ALVIN remains a family affair among biologists, geologists and other scientific related disciplines. Its name, that elision of two parts lifted from Allyn Vine's has the additional sentimental touch of having a mother ship named LULU, in honor of Vine's maternal parent.

As all pervasive as the Litton presence was in so many novel ways, there was probably no equal in being far-fetched than the coincidence of NASA's purchase of two stepper motors. These are the kind which kick 45 degree revolutions for each movement. One motor was priced at $929 and the other at $980. The manufacturer and seller was Clifton Precision Products in Clifton Heights, Pa. The pair of stepper motors was for SKYLAB.

In 1979 the forecasting began that SKYLAB was about to come tumbling out of orbit and disintegrate on reentry. A whole segment of the earth's population under its orbital path became taut with concern. The celestial littering eventually occurred over the Indian Ocean and Australia. Enterprising editor Reg Murphy of the San Francisco Examiner quickly offered $10,000 to anyone who first showed up at the newspaper's 901 Mission Street address with an authentic bit of SKYLAB debris.

Some of those fragments clattered on the tin roof of the "outback" home of a 17-year old Australian boy. He overcame his shyness and the many intervening miles by splicing together a hitch-hike — to Perth to consult a chemist, then a speeding car followed by a loaned Learjet and a sympathetic airline. Within the 72-hour deadline after SKYLAB was declared "down" by NASA, he delivered his dozen "bits" in San Francisco. Whether his collection included the burned and melted Clifton stepper motors or not will never be known.

The LITTON Adventure That Was

Litton's Tex Thornton admired resourcefulness and determination like that and thought when he was younger and living in Haskall,
Texas had SKYLAB ended there he would have done the same. The
Aussie got five times as much out of SKYLAB as Litton's Clifton
Precision Products did, but they both shared in the excitement of a
special era. There was further "relativity" in the "outback" Australian
teenager. His name was Thornton, too — Stan Thornton.

While Litton was in its ten-year diet of discontent, it was a spirit-
lifter to have memories like these on which to subsist — many Littonites believed they would see their like again.

Book II

That Difficult Decade

SPECIAL SITUATION #19

THE IDES OF JANUARY

Custom requires that dates be assigned momentous events.

More often than not, the date has nothing to do with when they occurred. It's just when they are noticed officially, or go public. Snow, for instance, can pile on a rooftop a flake at a time, and then, when its accumulation can no longer be borne, the roof caves in. A tire tread can go along for miles, and then blows when a driver is in the fast lane of the Interstate in heavy traffic.

For Litton Industries, it's put there as January 22, 1968. It took the form of a confessional shareholders letter.

Julius Caesar was warned in antiquity to beware of the Ides of March. Events were working their way toward him over months and years. For Litton, there had been a kind of invulnerability, a can't-stop-us assurance, a churning momentum which seemed to feed on itself and could swallow whatever errors there were without breaking step. Litton's Ides of March became the Ides of January.

When Litton's time arrived, it knew its strengths quite well, but was a very long time finding out how deep-seated were its frailties and how long it would take to get rosy cheeked again.

In construction circles, there is a term called "cut and cover". William E. McKenna had used acquisitions to cover, or at least, give him time to make a big high stakes play, and take the corrective actions the Business Systems and Equipment group needed.

He had picked up on the hints dropped among operational people that they had nobody to talk to about their problems at the corporate headquarters. Tex Thornton had always been pleasant, but he wasn't a nitty-gritty man. He had the vision, was the strategist, the keeper of the dream of what Litton was to be — that "broadly-based, blue chip company" he had promised the Lehman Brothers when they gave him that grubstake money. Normally, the point of the contact seemed to be President Roy L. Ash, but he didn't like to entertain the details of problems. He tended to philosophize and ask those uncomfortable penetrating questions. The latter seemed more to determine whether the one who sought him out was the man to continue the job, or whether he should be replaced. The way McKenna pictured it; the company needed a designated No. 3 man, a true chief operating officer. Having thought of the idea and charmed by its merits in his own mind, he thought it quite logical that he should fill that position.

He decided that the time had come to confront the Board Chairman with his views and step himself up in power.

His timing was as bad as it could be.[1]

There was Litton with its "shipyard of the future" being built and nary a contract in hand to justify it. Prospects, yes, but one can't put prospects in any bank or meet a payroll with them. The Parks Job Corps Center, while a very profitable commitment in terms of monetary return, was getting the company all kinds of bashing by the press, as was Litton's contract with the government of Greece for economic development in that country. Tex Thornton had just served on a passel of the U.S. Government commissions and boards, the latest being the Governor Kerner-headed National Advisory Commission on Civil Disorders so things added up to disarrays, foreign and domestic. And as McKenna sat there in his office, there were disturbing flashes coming in from the field about the overall plight of the Business Systems and Equipment Group. It wasn't all that pleasant to come home to as the Board Chairman and his disappointment showed through when McKenna suggested he should be the Litton No. 3, the operational pivot for the whole company.

His supporting arguments were in no way positioned on strength, or accomplishment, or as the stats were showing, anything like a hopeful future for his Business Equipment Group on which Litton depended so heavily for both balance and the balance sheet.[2] There was acrimonious exchange in Thornton's office, the air getting so blue that McKenna flashed out his trump card — that none knew the Group as well as he, and where it needed repairs and Band-Aids. In his eyes, he

---

1. The Business Systems and Equipment group was widespread and international by then including by years of acquisition: Monroe, 1958; Svenska Dataregister, 1959; Kimball, London Office Machines, Simon Adhesive, Cole Steel and Eureka, 1961; Advance Data Systems, Fitchburg Paper, Streator, American Tag, M & M Manufacturing, A. Carlisle and Atlas Stationers, 1964; Royal Typewriter, Papeterie Versoix, Newport Printers, Leopold Co., Plimpton's, and Lehigh Furniture, 1965; Everett-Waddey, Maverick-Clarke, Sturgis-Newport, Imperial Typewriter, 1966; Saphier, Lerner & Schindler, 1967, and Brand-Worth, 1968.

2. Litton was among the first five firms to set up its own computerized cash management control system. This made it literally the banker for its divisions, starting in 1967.

was the indispensable man. He said he would resign. It didn't play at all the way he thought or hoped it would because Tex Thornton accepted the resignation just as McKenna was finishing the sentence.[3] That big reliance point, Business Systems and Equipment Group, which had grown so widespread in capabilities, so big and international in scope, was temporarily headless. It was late October, and the Litton leaves were also turning color.

Just how bad was it? At that moment, Litton had more than 106,000 employees. In late 1967, 26 new manufacturing facilities had been completed. The company was doing business in 35 countries in 219 plants and laboratories, and 1,508 other facilities. It was generating more than $100,000,000 yearly in cash internally, and had $115,000,000 available under a revolving credit agreement with 29 banks. That, combined with some $457,000,000 in working capital, gave it secure foundations on which to stand while performing remedial actions indicated to be necessary. Only the Defense and Space Systems Group under Fred W. O'Green did more for the Litton treasury than the Group McKenna left behind him.

McKenna was still clearing his desk when Harry J. Gray, that bundle of ambition and energy just down the corridor from him, was pulled out of his Finance and Administration function and hustled into the breach. Almost at a dead run, he was sent to search and survey for the skeletal truth about his new responsibilities, and report back what his findings were *post haste*. Gray didn't want the job they'd given him, as he, too, had big eyes for that No. 3, or operational slot McKenna had envisioned. If he came up with a solution, though, it would look well on his credentials.

---

3. Old Thornton notes indicate that the "People factor" was always the toughest of all the problems. The differences were rooted in turf, status, reward and even he was actually the target of a palace guard attempt to unseat him in the early days. The granting of option shares was the first upsetting factor, Thornton getting them in a 60-20-20 rate to Ash and Jamieson, which Lehman Brothers thought fair and relative to the importance of the people involved. As to early operational procedure, he jotted in his own handwriting that Ash, Jamieson and Myles Mace, plus Crosby Kelly, were the only ones to report directly to him. At one juncture, the heat was becoming intense, and he wrote if things could not be worked out, "I will leave the Company." They did work out, the dissenters realizing he was better glue to hold the company together than they could see any one of their number at the top given the Thornton responsibilities.

The slate was not pretty. There was a strike in progress at Royal Typewriter. He inherited along with that a McKenna $55,000,000 profit forecast. The first thing he found was that the office copier machine segment was running at about a $300,000 monthly loss rate. Having been the Litton financial officer where he thought he knew all about the dollars, he quickly concluded that he did not. "I don't believe any of the figures," he told Thornton and Ash. He immediately initiated a series of financial reviews in each of his divisions.

The annual meeting of the shareholders was behind them in December of 1967 when he came in with his summary to lay before the Litton leadership. They were flabbergasted and reluctant to believe Harry Gray. That so often mentioned strut in the Litton fuselage—autonomy—grinned and mocked at them. They knew instinctively that the company was strong, well-positioned, but isolated in that moment of its history as if it were suddenly without oxygen at 70,000 feet where a man's blood would boil away. Harry Gray was sent back to scan the prospects once more and report back. He first gave full time to settling the Royal strike and on New Year's day, 1968 began a 21-day microscopic appraisal of the Business Equipment Group's profit potential. He had thought that perhaps $5,000,000 of the previously promised group $55,000,000 was attainable.

"We can't even make that $5,000,000," Harry Gray declared in mid-January. "We're going to be lucky to break even!" Litton at the top trusted Gray, that he would bust a gut trying if given his head and he was. Whatever the emotions within them, "Tex" Thornton, a terribly disappointed man, was determinedly in command. Ash gave off a cool exterior whatever was going on inside him. They thought Litton was holding a good hand of cards, even if a case of the blight had suddenly struck a member of the family. Glen McDaniel was there and after the pros and cons reminded them that the Securities and Exchange Commission had a legal need to know of this altered profit course. Litton wasn't going to show a loss in its just finished 1968 second quarter; it was just not going to continue its upward projection as promised.

The Sunday of reckoning came. A statement had to be prepared admitting that the Litton rocket had momentarily peaked at the end of 57 spectacular quarters. The 58th was to be blah, the waters muddy and beyond that a disconcerting haze.

Thornton was in his richly appointed office. It was early. That was no problem for him as he hadn't slept well or long the night before. Roy Ash came in, his yellow-ruled tablet in hand and pencil poised. The writing and re-writing that day was bound to be extensive. Glen McDaniel, a master with wordage when it came to legal phraseology, arrived almost as if to the funeral of a dear friend who tried to think of nice and soothing things to say. Joseph T. Casey, up from Touche, Ross, the accounting firm, and on whom Gray relied as his money man, had more numbers combinations going in his head than a 7-rollered Las Vegas slot machine. The appointed clerk-typist, who never used more than two fingers at the keyboard, was Ludwig T. Smith, one of McDaniel's lawyers. He thought it especially poignant that he had to use a Litton typewriter of the Royal brand name to convey all this bad news onto the paper of the communiqué. There were people across the corridor on call—William Berry, then the Gray Group controller, and his corporate counterpart, Paul Brunton.

It was tortured paragraph after tortured paragraph all day. At 8 p.m. that Sunday evening, Casey emerged with the latest Smith-typed draft. At that moment, Roy Ash was reading a copy of it over the phone to Harry Gray who was in his Waldorf-Astoria hotel room in New York. He was talking late into the night with Count Ibo Douglas about the Sweda cash register part of the problem.

"We're going with a press release on this turndown in earnings," Ash told him, and then read it to him.

Gray registered mild shock as he thought the statement was too long by 70%," and should not include some of what he called "damning words." The ones which made his hair stand erect attributed Litton's troubles to "certain earlier management deficiencies." *Management* had been the very lock on Litton's chastity belt, a mark of distinction and the mystique which altogether had created Litton as a technological Holy Grail.

"Forecast the turndown, Roy," he pleaded, "but just state it's due to this or that division, which it is. It's a big mistake to lay it on past errors on the part of management."

"The best brains at Litton," Ash said, "have worked on this for the past ten hours. This is the way it's going out." That was that. Gray, reflecting on it later, said that obviously it was the desire of honest people at the top to hold nothing back. They were also unsure as to whether they had a handle on the whole story yet so any attempt to let down easy might well be even worse.[4]

When Casey read it to Berry and Brunton, Berry felt a prickling sensation at the back of his neck when he heard ". . . certain earlier management deficiencies" roll by. He thought they sounded louder in the Casey monotone than everything else in it. When he, too, suggested to Casey that it could be put differently, Casey said everyone who could rule on changes had gone and that the release would stand. There were two other calls he had to make.

A surprised Bob Sohngen was one of them, awakened at home in Pennsylvania, he was the head of Litton's News bureau in New York, and an hour's train ride from his office. There, barefooted and in his pajamas, hair-tousled, he copied the release in long hand as it was read to him.

"Catch the earliest train to New York," he was told. "Hand carry the release to Dow Jones." This meant he had to be there with the "night people" picking their way to wherever they lived to sleep away the daylight. He had to get to that eerie 30 Broad Street address, the ancestral home of not only the Dow Jones wire, but the Wall Street Journal, too. He was leaning against the door when the bureau chief

---

4. The letter to Litton's shareholders which went in the mail on January 22, 1968 said there were "unexpected delays in completing the final engineering work on the all-electric portable typewriter planned for introduction in the spring, necessary price reductions of present portable electric's pending introduction of the completely new machine, volume variances in the plan in two other business equipment products (steel office furniture and calculators), the continued amounts charged to current expense in entering the office copying machine market, and labor strikes at three major Litton division plants have contributed significantly to the variance from expected levels of profitability." As words of reassurance, the letter followed this discussion of profitability sinking-spell's with "The new all-electric portable typewriter, especially designed for one of the most rapidly growing of consumer markets, is now being tooled for volume production. The addition of the new Royfax 1700 book copier to our copy machine line is expected to add considerably to the field population of Royfax copiers and thus to revenue received from copy paper sales. These products are expected to become profitable during the next fiscal year . . . (and) while the sales volume and profit of calculators did not decline from earlier periods, they did not reach the growth goals planned. Five new calculators introduced last month—two electric and three electromechanical—are expected to regain our growth rate. Two of the labor strikes are now over, and the other is expected to be settled in the next quarter . . . During the quarters, also, we are setting aside $8,000,000 to offset special costs relative to our marine technology programs."

showed up, very startled to see him at such an early hour. When he read the release, he understood.

A second call went to Ralph O'Brien which awakened him at 2 a.m. in New Jersey. He had just been appointed Litton's Vice President for Public and Shareholder Relations and had been home to help with the packing for the family's imminent displacement to Los Angeles. He was told the release was being made and the timing. It was then read to him.

The new appointment which had seemed so soaring and wonderful when he had gone to bed now gave him a greenish feeling in his stomach. He had all the Litton shares he owned there in the house as he expected to hand carry them with him to California. When he hung up the phone, he put on his robe. Gathering up the stack of securities in his arms, he walked into the living room of the darkened house. He plopped down in the armchair which had always been so comfortable before.

"My Gawd!" he said softly into the night. It was his welcome to the Big Leagues.

James Cleaveland didn't know why, or what would be in it, but the action for him started earlier than most. He was chief of Litton's Shareholder Services, and on the Saturday night before the corporate gathering to write the release, he was attending a typical drink-out at the Bel Air Hotel hosted by the Sorg printing firm which specialized in financial publishing. The Bel Air room was filled to the windows and transoms with corporate lawyers and secretaries, all of whom watched each other with special suspicions which are native to Wall Street people.

One phone call was nothing, of course. If anyone had several, it was read as a "signal". Cleaveland had several that evening from the corporate Vice President and Secretary, George Fenimore. That was serious enough, but he suddenly stopped drinking—and he didn't leave the party. His watchers translated this as meaning he had to have his wits about him, pay attention to whatever the caller said, and to be somewhere where there could be a line to him.

"We're going to have a big mailing on Monday," Fenimore said. "That's January 23rd. About 200,000 envelopes will go to our shareholders." Cleaveland said he was new on the job, which he was, but he knew he didn't have that much stationery backup. "Get them," said

Fenimore. He told him all the Top Secret character of what he was doing.

Cleaveland jockeyed the Sorg man into a corner and placed the order. This required the interception of two huge Kenilworth 18-wheelers coming along an Interstate which had the exact sizes of required mailers. By the time all this was completed, the rest of the Sorg guest list was zeroed in on Cleaveland like prairie dogs peering from their holes at an intruder.

"You won't believe this," Cleaveland said, shamefacedly, "but one of our Litton security guards has found that the safe is missing from my office. Another security guard has found a safe in another office he's never seen before. It's my safe, which I asked to be moved this weekend, but I forgot to tell Security about it." His audience looked at him, with his face so red, and somehow believed it was the kind of dumb thing that could happen in a company headquarters.

Cleaveland ordered another drink, which he resisted sipping and saw the party through to the end. When the rest of the partygoers saw the Dow Jones tape n Monday, he got more calls than he could take congratulating him on his Academy Award performance as an actor. He had lulled them and kept the company's secret.

He was too busy getting out all those letters to take a bow for his kudos.

SPECIAL SITUATION #20

AS THE SPARKS FLY UPWARD

An equilibrist is one who does his act in unnatural positions with hazardous movements at great heights and without a protective net.

Depending on how much altitude, how considerable the courage quotient from the norm and how many discernible dangers are evident in his performance, watchers cringe and applaud. For Litton Industries in the wake of the January 22, 1968 stockholders warning of profit projection shortfalls, its hero worshippers of yesterday turned into common scolds.

Security analysts who had fawned over and favored the company with approving phraseology became verbally ferocious. Other so-called conglomerates moaned aloud and upbraided Litton for daring to put on paper the public acknowledgment of "management deficiencies." They felt several points of their own stock price rode on assumption of conglomerate "management mystique." If a Litton could be so brash as to admit such things were possible, and it was the recognized patriarch of the "loose rein" idea, it could spook all of their securities' holders, too—and they were right.

Those who lolled in brokerage offices coast-to-coast and abroad chasing the ticker tape quotes with their eyes were especially waspish. Tex Thornton found himself suddenly being anointed as a failed modern day Moses. He was scored for falling short in leading them to their "promised land" of perpetual appreciation for their Litton share prices. In their assessments he seemed about to drown in his very own Red Sea, the kind made of crimson ink. One publisher who hobbied as a hot air balloonist and thought it takes one to know one had made reference in the past to "Roy Ash's chain-letter," his way of describing the basis for Litton's ebullience on the stock exchanges. He and others now readied their editorial sawed off shotguns to do more than chortle ". . . I told you so!"

Ash himself had often talked of the "psychology of the market place," its susceptibility to trends, "in" things and generally how capricious it could be. He now had a vivid example. It was much too close!

Harry Gray had guessed to Bill Berry that the price might slide all the way down to "about 35 times earnings" as the most extreme development. He had found himself right in one week's time!

That January began with Litton's common stock at its high of $104.75 the first trading day of the new year. By the end of that month it was down to $70.50.

The five trading days before the letter went out recorded only 227,000 of Litton's 22,000,000 shares going to new ownership. During the week following the letter and the Dow Jones wire's confirmation of its contents, 1,326,800 changed hands. Vicki Johnson, the Litton receptionist, always kept the daily stock price on her notepad. It could be easily seen by the incoming executives. Once it had been the morning pick-me-up as the New York trade was usually one and sometimes two hours old when the West Coast work force showed up; now it was a morning sickness to see the shrunken values of what they held. It put lead in their shoes and clouded the sun.[1]

Yet Litton was no latter-day Pompeii hit by its own kind of Vesuvius. That 70 A.D. natural temper tantrum had buried the ancient city in lava and ash. Nothing like that had happened to Litton except that it had gone public with documentation of its plodding sectors. James Russell once wrote:

". . . once to every man and nation comes the moment to decide;
in the strife of Truth and Falsehood, the good or evil side."

There was no alternative but to lay it all out there—let everybody know what had to be fixed and fix it. After all, for those 57 upward spiraling quarters Litton had made good on every promise. What it was now saying was not that suddenly it had become a loser, only that its appreciation and profit would not be as great as was its custom. Though a 4% gain was far from its usual spectacular, there were many other companies that year that did not do as well. Perilous as the position and the performance seemed, there was still a great deal of

---

1. Ludwig T. Smith, the lawyer who had two-finger typed the stockholders' letter, had borrowed money to exercise his stock options, a Litton executive custom of the period. He now found the bank selling his shares as rapidly as they became unrestricted which ultimately cost him $85,000. Two others who saw their paper worth disintegrate were Bob Bruder and Al Strogoff, but the suffering and pain was general throughout the shareholding family.

protective padding for the company's continued operations while corrective measures were being taken. Clearly though, the days of homage paying to Litton, the idea and its ideals, were over, and it was now a time for carping.

Wall Street began to contort, and grieve, tear its hair and act as though it had stood hog-tied to a tree and witnessed a Little Red Riding Hood deflowered. The easy way, the "Chinese money" days of increasing share prices with which to barter, had been interrupted. As Wall Street cringed at what it thought it saw, Litton had to see itself for all it was. Its basic strength had to correct the weaknesses which were now embarrassing it.

The mechanism that was Litton Industries was on no cleared track and highballed to run by itself. Tex Thornton began to say NO to spreading himself too thinly by accepting advisory roles on committees and commissions at government request. He became resistant to showers of attractive invitations for him to serve on other corporate boards of directors.[2] His availability for speeches diminished to zero. He and Roy Ash would finish whatever commitments they had made. Beyond that they would both devote their time to the decisions which had to be made in Beverly Hills. The telephone link was no longer enough. There had to be face-to-face discussions with those who had major responsibilities. Thornton had to look them in their eyes when they told him what Litton really had to do. He had to make on-site inspections. He could then tell whether the problems had been clearly identified and analyzed and could be brought to solution by incumbents, or whether they were so overwhelmed by them their paralysis

---

2. Thornton's directorships included United California Bank (now Wells Fargo), MCA, Inc., Western Bancorporation, and Trans World Airlines. He had been a special consultant to the U.S. State Dept. and U.S. Air Force (1946-47)l member of the President's Commission on the Patent System (1965-66) consultant to the Secretary of the Air Force to review programs at the Air Force Academy (1964-65) consultant to the Secretary of the Navy on educational requirements (1962); member of the President's National Advisory Commission on Civil Disorders (1967-68); member, American Revolution Bi-Centennial Commission (1966-69); member, special committee of businessmen of the President's Commission for Observance of the Human Rights Year (1968); member, Air Force Academy Advisory Council (1966-71), member, Air University Board of visitors (1969-72). There were his other obligations stemming from his membership on the Business Council, the Emergency Committee for American Trade, the National Executive Committee on Crime and Delinquency and Junior Achievement.

indicated they had to exit in favor of replacement. He had to judge what was blustering excuse making, and what was teeth-gritting resolve to mend and once more assume the climbing direction.

Tex Thornton was more the "people to people" man than Roy Ash. He knew how much easy access to him had meant to them all in those early years, and how the men who worked for him wanted to please him. This had been the very grease on which Litton's wheels had turned. He now knew that for any member of his crew to feel he had failed him was a kind of flop-sweat inducer with accompanying dryness in the throat making it hard to swallow. He counted on all that. It was what the charisma of leadership is all about, which could ask for extra distance, for extra staying power, for extra determination. Those who could cut it and from their knowledge and experience help in the turnaround would hear him say he had faith in them. Those not up to it would reveal themselves as found wanting and would have to go.

Don McMahon of Monroe used to say he "felt sorry" for Tex Thornton during the opportunity reviews which caused him to sit through all those introspective presentations by division heads. Litton's chairman knew that they were worth their weight in gold as each presenter had to get to know what he in truth had and what its promise was. That was what Litton needed now, a kind of corporate executive physical exam as to the health of each part of the enterprise. Roy Ash was no longer the Michaelangelo of the multiples. He became a restrained and patient explainer that Litton's now measured, slower cadence was only momentary and for catching its breath. It was a time of intense introspection, pulse-taking, bedrock estimating anew, diagnosing and finding remedies.

Running down the corporate "tick list," Litton was healthy in most of its extremities, vibrant in some. In others, it had licked earlier annoyances, or was on the verge of doing so. Geophysical exploration was in worldwide demand. Insiders in the energy camp were already sensing the bind on the horizon and were contracting out feverishly to hunters of new sources. Litton had more different kinds of participation in getting Astronauts Neil Armstrong, Edwin "Buzz" Aldrin and Michael Collins ready for their conquest of the moon than any other company. Litton's heavy experience in inertial navigation was rapidly making it the world's capital for that technology while everyone else was being given bare sustenance type contracts. This was to keep them from fading out of the picture entirely which would turn Litton into the one and only, that government contracting anathema—single source. In food services the Stouffer Foods and Litton Microwave Cooking Products combination were vigorous, challenging all comers. It was getting more than its share, with prospects of doing even better.

On the other hand and as visible as a naked woman at the beach, there were two confrontations with corporate catastrophe unless dealt with quickly. One was the Ingalls Shipbuilding construction of the new West Bank facilities on the Singing River at Pascagoula, Mississippi running in parallel with two huge, likely-to-be Navy contracts. The other was the Business Systems and Equipment group which was one-third of Litton's business.

The Navy wanted from Litton initially nine, later reduced to five, LHA (Landing Helicopter Assault, or general purpose amphibious assault) ships configured especially for the roles of the U.S. Marine Corps. It also wanted the DD-963 "Spruance Class," a series of 30 sleek destroyers. There was a little time, but precious little, for the whole Ingalls matter to develop and flower.

The Business Systems and Equipment Group was over-extended, suffered a lot from oversights, and was crying out for quick stabilizing actions. McKenna was gone with accompanying fire and brimstone accusations. He brooded over what he'd left behind him as he signed on with Norton Simon.

Harry Gray, a business adaptation of a basketball court rebounder, had more on his hands than he had hands but he came on strong as McKenna's replacement.

There were optimistic statements about Automated Business Systems. It was a computer-tied invoice processing producer useful in making a daisy chain of varied operations to bring off sums at a central point, and be helpful to small businesses. It was too early to tell what the market response was going to be.

Roy Ash was there when Eureka dedicated its new $10,500,000 printing plant in Scranton. He was listened to more when he talked of electronics which was where Litton had started than he was about the printing of trading stamps, catalogs and other premium and promotional materials. It was high technology in its way, but not too Litton-exciting was this speed imprinting of color and glue and tear-here perforations produced in the millions.

The Cole Steel and office desk and other products had been partially derailed. Its old dealer assemblage was in confusion because of introduction of a new management philosophy which brushed them off in favor of the office product centers. It was a big difference from the time of Tony Scheinman and his catalogs. Over it all, like some threatening jungle Gargantua gone berserk, the typewriter involvement was the unresponding dead weight across the corporate back.

Harry Gray put Bill Berry into a crash appraisal mode for the whole market sector including manufacturing quality control aspects. Obviously, both Royal and Imperial languished under a technological malaise from a bread and water diet of research and development effort. One halfhearted move had been made in the direction of an electric model with the acquisition of the German Willy Feiler Zaehl and Rechenwerke, GmbH, in Berlin, but it neither jelled nor helped. Gray muttered and chafed when he saw the mounting evidence of the short *R* and *D* ration of Royal as attempt was made to get a customer pleasing and high quality electric typewriter. That old bugaboo that forever lurks there had too long tempted hotshot managers to starve the future to fatten the figures for the present quarter's summaries. Royal had the manual office typewriter which once was everybody's favorite, but when a motor was grafted into its innards it was not a good machine. By a super promotional effort, it sold well and even made money in 1966 and 1967. There was now noisy caterwauling choruses among the poorly served and unhappy customers which was growing in size every day. With it, there was increasing sales resistance. Nowhere in all this searching for a short term way onward and upward was there time to consider that oncoming single element machine—the one with a ball carrying all type characters and sizes—in either the Royal or Imperial future.

Berry thought he glimpsed hope offshore. His way out for the quality portable market led him to an association with Silver-Seiko in Japan. It was one of the arms of the 20 or so industrial empires in that country with which Litton had affiliations. Royal had sales of $50,000,000 in the 1968 fiscal year, but a loss of about $15,000,000 was laid against it. The one winning flat portable in the product line was Silver-Seiko's. True, there was an equally acceptable model being manufactured in Springfield, Missouri, but its production costs were prohibitive. Litton had to face the portable typewriter clout of SCM (Smith-Corona-Marchant), as it did the power of IBM who dominated the office electrics. Berry fussed and courted Olivetti, Smith Corona, Hermes and others, but he always came back to the gate Orhan Sadik-Khan, McKenna's acquisition seeker, had found bolted against him.

The address was in Nuremberg in the Federal Republic of Germany. It was part of the private preserve of Grundig Mechanische Fabrik. It was an industrial island built by hand from the rubble of the Third Reich after its unconditional surrender. In a shed-like garage, short and tough Max Grundig and his mother had wrested incredible success from the raw wounds of national devastation. Grundig grew to his formidable entrepreneurial stature by having shrewdly assessed that with Germany's newspapers in ruins and in the hands of the occupier victors, radio was the only quick way people morbidly curious about what was going on around them could learn the news. From the refuse of a lost war, he collected vast amounts of no-longer-needed Wehrmacht radio receivers. He resold them both through barter and for money and profited generously because of the junk prices he paid for them. Mightily positioned now, he was in television, radio and typewriters. He plainly liked the world of television most of all.

Berry, who by Harry Gray's decision, had replaced Earl Tiffany as Royal's executive head, wrote Grundig a letter.

He said he would like to talk with him about making a block purchase of 50,000 electric typewriters annually which could be sold under the Litton brand name. If that didn't interest him, Litton would like to buy the Triumph-Adler[3] part of Grundig Mechanische Fabrik, or his whole company. Berry was startled when Grundig invited him to come to Nuremberg to confer with him. He ran for the next plane.

Berry spoke German well. He was excited as he flew over the Atlantic. If he could find some alternative which would interest Grundig, he felt that no matter how deep the sag might be at Royal and Imperial, the technological transfusion needed to raise their heads

---

3. Adler, besides being an old typewriter brand name in Germany, was a part of folklore, too. When in 1921, Adolf Hitler set up his Munich office on Corneliusstrasse, his first piece of equipment was a used Adler typewriter bought on the installment plan.

was there in the hands of that redoubtable German in Nuremberg. Regardless of the towering esteem and accolades paid him as a German businessman—self made, autocratic, monarch absolute of all he had—Grundig was a small man physically. Berry was expecting to see someone as big as his reputation. When he was admitted to his spacious office on the top floor, the first thing he saw was Grundig behind his desk which was on a raised platform in a far corner. The Cardiff giant—alive—could have come to call and Max Grundig could look down on him, too.

There was another reason for this perch. The building which housed his corporate headquarters was an enclosure surrounding a small Bavarian cottage. From his window he could look at it any time he wished. Grundig had been born in that little house six decades earlier. His mother, Frau Grundig, the one who had worked side-by-side with him as they dug themselves out after Germany's unconditional surrender, still lived there. This was his way of watching over her. The two of them, starting in the small shelter, had given the great Grundig Mechanische Fabrik its very foundation. When Frau Grundig came out each summery day to look after her flowers, she could glance up at his glassed-in corner and wave. It was a gesture he seldom missed and he never failed to wave back. They were once close in the harshness required to survive; they were still close in his success.

He and Berry engaged in some introductory light banter, Grundig obviously pleased that he had an American in his presence who spoke his language. Berry eased into the business at hand. He said he'd like to talk with him seriously about making that block purchase of 50,000 electric typewriters a year. Was Grundig interested in this? Grundig looked out of his window seeing his mother moving about as caringly industrious as always among her beds of blossoms. She might be down there in person, but she was also up there with him in his mind at this moment.

"When a man gets to be 60 years old in Germany," Grundig said as if ignoring the question, "it's the custom for him to gather around him his closest advisers and members of his family to discuss his life—and what to do with the rest of it. Your letter arrived just after I had done this."

Berry had been bracing himself for dealing with a brittle and imperious tradesman who would probably make outrageous demands. He was surprised by the warmth, the frankness and the totally relaxed attitude of this old Bavarian. He didn't know whether to be pleased or not that the timing of his correspondence had been so on the mark with this crossroads conference. He was about to say something but only nodded and smiled deciding to let Grundig play out his thoughts. Then a chill struck him when he heard Grundig saying he was not at all interested in the 50,000 typewriter package sale. Berry had seen acceptance of that as the way to make the next proposal, the bigger share of the Grundig company. Here he was pinched off before leaving the starting gate—or so it appeared.

"I have been advised by my associates," Grundig said, "to do some liquidating. I need some money to put into television operations. I wouldn't want to sell everything, though—what would I do then? If we can agree on terms, I'll sell you my Triumph-Adler typewriter properties. That way, you can have what you want and I'll have what I want."

Berry could hardly believe what he was hearing. It was as if there were technological spas also, where one could go and "take the waters." In this case, it was a way to come afresh into the marketplace with renewed resolve and vigor and a product which could really compete. It would also save the company's institutional reputation and the jobs of hundreds of employees. After some of the usual amenities and assurances of Grundig's positive declarations, Berry shook Grundig's hand and left. Once out of the door, he cautioned himself to balance off those elations he felt with another real concern he had.

He had no doubt that Harry Gray would go along with him, would be gung-ho to go, in fact. But what kind of a reaction was he going to get from Thornton and Ash? They already had bought three typewriter concerns, each of them with horror stories and disappointments. Their conditions were worsening by the day.

Back in Beverly Hills, he found he had diagnosed Harry Gray's enthusiasm for the deal correctly. He was additionally heartened that Thornton was agreeable as it made sense to him, and it offered prospects of solution without wasting time. Time as always was that one commodity with which he could never be profligate. He did want it cleared with Ash though, and he was in Athens, Greece, looking into progress of Litton's contractual involvement with the Hellenic government for economic development of its Western Peloponnessus and the Island of Crete. If they had their marching orders from Ash, they could stop in Nuremberg on the way back and put the acquisition wheels in motion.

Gray, Berry and their retinue flew off on the red-eye TWA flight to Athens. They confronted Ash as he came down to breakfast in the lobby of the Grande-Bretagne on Syntagma Square. Ash, after the usual innumerable questions had been answered to his satisfaction, flashed the green go-ahead light.

On August 1, 1968, it was agreed that a portion of Grundig Mechanische Fabrik so laboriously put together by Frau Grundig and her son, Max—Triumph-Adler and its attachments worldwide—went into Litton Industries.[4] Going with the sales was Grundig's No. 1 associate, Gerd Weers, an executive very much at home in the marble halls of governments from Western Europe to Australia. He was also smooth among the business barons of German commerce.

It was a time in which American-owned firms were prone to cosmetics in what passed for sophistication in international circles and would occasionally name indigenous executives abroad to pseudo company officer status. They were usually eunuch-like in that they could attend social functions and have their names on business cards with titles. They had little voice, or none in actual world strategies for their enterprises. Litton saw in Gerd Weers a finely honed operator who could be made into a company officer co-equal with all the others in Litton Industries. Gerd Weers earned it, too, so it was no act of

---

4. The Grundig spun-off packet included 98.4% of the typewriter manufacturing company, Triumph-Werke Nuremberg AG, 82% of Adlerwerke on Fleyerstrasse in Frankfurt-Main, 95% of the real estate company, Triumph Werke Wohnungsbau, GmbH, as well as offshore operations in Sydney, Australia; Paris, France and New York devoted to sales and distribution abroad. The erratic behavior of Litton's shares on the stock market had nothing to do with the sale as Grundig wanted cash and got it, $61,500,000. If it could stop the flow of Litton's corporate blood in this one troubled quarter, it would be worth every penny of it. There was yet another barrier, as Litton had had some glares from the U.S. Federal Trade commission on some of its previous mergers. It seemed best to let the FTC know of this planned move, and get its blessing. FTC was not pleased and said so. When it appeared there would probably be an announced negative position stated from that quarter Litton closed with Grundig and braced to fight it out. It seemed the better part of valor to argue from *fait accompli* than to seek a blessing not ever likely to be granted.

hollow diplomacy. He had the makings of the good doctor for the Litton growing list of typewriter ailments which were rapidly growing to epidemic proportions. After all that domestic U.S. talk with cambers of commerce and trade associations and the Congress about technology transfer being a "one-way street"—from the U.S. to Western Europe and the Orient—Litton showed it up for the 4th of July oratory it was. The sole hope Litton had for the salvation of its typewriter dilemma was coming from German and Japanese sources!

Harry Gray and Bill Berry had but a short time for exultation. The Federal Trade Commission persisted in its flagellation of Litton when it filed the charge that the Triumph-Adler acquisition had been an act to reduce competition. Litton insiders and those generally knowledgeable in the trade knew there was no chance that Royal and Imperial could be kept alive with their dwindling clientele, nor could their labor forces be continued in employment without Triumph-Adler. It was Grundig himself who had opted to get out of the typewriter business and focus his effort on television which he liked better.

FTC said the step taken by Litton was ". . . an alternative to original research and to developing a suitable machine based on the present state of the art." FTC, in its loftiness, could make such a statement and try to make a case, it did, but the backs of Harry Gray and Bill Berry were to the wall. Gray told Berry to make all speed to strap on as much of the newly acquired electric typewriter technology as rapidly as possible. He and Litton's appointed and feisty legal eagle, Ted Craver,[5] took on the FTC with oral and written fusillades based on IBM's having more than 80% of the office electric typewriter market. They said unless the Triumph-Adler acquisition was allowed to stand, become mature and final with minimal lost time, IBM would have no appreciable competition at all. The way Litton pictured it

---

5. Ted Craver was to have three of Litton's biggest antitrust legal tussles besides this. The suit against the Chessie System (SX), Norfolk & Western, Bessemer and Erie Railroads for blocking the Hewitt-Robins plan to erect ore boat unloading and transporting conveyors from Cleveland docks to steel plants up the Cuyahoga River; the LITCOM spin-off of a Business Telephone Systems which would have given Litton a big lead in the interconnect field, and XEROX for certain obstacles in the copier machine arena. He won almost $12,000,000 from XEROX. He proved to court satisfaction that AT&T muscle thrown against the Business Telephone Systems destroyed it and won a $274,000,000 judgment against Ma Bell. Craver is often referred to by his colleagues as the "legal profit center."

from its nearly supine position, the marketplace was about as one-sided as the Roman Coliseum's Christians tossed in among the lions could expect a fair fight. Craver had the demeanor of a professional gunslinger, cornered, faced by some hometown hotshot backed by friends rooting him into a fight as a leg-up on a reputation.

First, Craver needed time, and second, he had the big wish that good reason would prevail. This began a protracted struggle which severely impeded the totality of the needed Triumph-Adler reinforcements. It interrupted the orderliness with which the typewriter technology upgrading could be absorbed. This provided a kind of high altitude race with pylons on two continents and an island kingdom where about 16,000 employees were worried and involved onlookers.

Berry thought the only sense making strategy was to get Royal typewriter production out of ancestral Hartford, Connecticut. It had been there ever since 1908 when Edward B. Hess and Lewis C. Myers had picked that state capital as the starting point for Royal's route march into the future. Royal was always plagued with strikes. It was in the midst of one when Litton was acquiring it. In 1969, the Springfield, Missouri plant which manufactured those portable electric typewriters at such prohibitive cost, decided to hit the streets again with ON STRIKE placards aloft. That one was no child's play affair; one of the supervisors was shot in the head. The Allied Industrial Workers of America Local No. 469 harangued for a termination settlement including pension benefits, health and life insurance, vacation pay and sought preferential hiring status for the jobless to come. They were on a losing wicket, a really no win situation for both employees and employers as the plant's product was not competitive.

Litton closed that plant, and consolidated that manufacturing in Hartford. It sold the tooling to a company in Portugal from which it contracted for the machines needed from that offshore assembly line. The next action moved everything in a manufacturing way out of Hartford and into the Imperial plants in Leicester and Hull in England's mournful midlands. The 60 cents an hour differential in the pay scales spread over time seemed to promise to cover the moving costs. The British Isles, the Commonwealth and the Common Market countries all were promising trade territory in contrast to the odds against Litton's typewriter lines in America. The dispositions were

460

close to Triumph-Adler with its modernizing array of talents plus a strong marketing base.

The grim and forbidding midlands of England contained the two Imperial manufacturing sites. Old Roman ruins clustered here and there, bleak reminders of how long the area had known intruders from abroad. There were still existing benchmarks of the industrial revolution which had begun not far away. Hull had the lesser skilled labor force, about 500 of them, and the output was 600 machines weekly. The relocation from Hartford to Hull, if all went along scenario lines, meant that Hull plant was to swell by more than 1,000 additional jobs. Leicester, with about 800 employees, was one of those browned, sooted, frowning and tired old cities where Roman Legions had rested to stage adventure and depredations and other forays into the north country of both England and Scotland. The quality of the labor was better, the higher skills being more plentiful. The projected expansion to 1,800 or more there was not a problem.

The British Government, much beleaguered because of all its promises and tasks assumed in behalf of an electorate which contained about 13,000,000 union members, was rubbing its hands in anticipation. All this was happening right before its eyes—an American company branded by that fearsome word "multinational" not going in the direction forecast by socialist theoreticians and detractors in the United Kingdom and Western Europe. In adversity, such companies were supposed to retreat into the country of the corporate home address. Here was this Litton Industries wooing a fading beauty of yesteryear with as much ardor as a new young Lochinvar out of the west offering posies at the door, not only holding to the level of employment at acquisition time, but with intentions of doubling it! If the welfare statists found this to be a shocking rebuttal to their hallowed concepts, they could live with it and wait for a first flaw.

Two years after the incoming Triumph-Adler and with the FTC still gnawing away, Litton made the decision that manufacture of its office electric machines would also exit Hartford for Hull and Leicester, and it was done. By early 1973 all the assembly lines in Connecticut were stilled. The entire rhythm of Litton's typewriter production was on the other side of the Atlantic—a substantial part of it back in England where old Queen Anne 260 years before had granted Henry Mill that patent for ". . . an artificial machine for the impressing or transcribing of letters singly or progressively one after another as in writing." Some was also transferred to the Nuremberg and Frankfurt plants of Triumph-Adler.

Financial summaries were now showing that fully 35% of the Litton Business Systems and Equipment Group was outside of the U.S. The timing of the Hartford closeout in favor of the United Kingdom coincided day and date with the January, 1973 entry of Great Britain, Denmark and Ireland in the Common Market. It had been the attractiveness of this prospect which had goaded William McKenna to take the risky Imperial step. Triumph-Adler had not been at all interested then in joining Litton, preferring to stay behind its own safe and prosperous moated enclave with its drawbridge up.

Hull's plant payroll rose to 1,400 and was in its own way what the typewriter story had been all along—bonanza for the employment of women. Leicester grew to that 1,800 level in terms of work force. Fully 60% of the production for the Business Systems and Equipment Group by then no longer was in the United States. The less complicated manuals for the Canadian and American markets poured out of Hull as well as some of the electric machine parts; in Leicester, the electric machines were built. The British Government continued to applaud in its own special way by allowing the production line from Litton closures in Hartford and in the Netherlands to pole vault tariff and customs barriers enroute to the midlands for installations and plant upgrading. The British trade unions Amalgamated Engineering, Association of Scientific, Technical and Managerial Staff, and the big Transport and General Workers Union (TWGU)—were all delightedly reasonable at this stage, showing toothy smiles and their relations with the Imperial plants were especially good.[6]

---

6. In May a year later, a British version ethnic dispute about hiring practices for grades of jobs, for promotions and incentive payments came to a head in an unauthorized work stoppage involving nearly 400 of Asian ancestry. They said they were upset with both TWGU and Imperial. Litton found itself caught in a race relations investigation after having made the move to rid itself of craft orientation for the work force to open it to those very Asians who were barely qualified technically. The investigation board reported out that ". . . if management recruits immigrant labor, it had a responsibility to itself, to the indigenous labor force, to the immigrants and to the community as a whole to take action to ensure these problems are resolved," but it did admit there was no unlawful discrimination as was claimed. The typewriter for all its ubiquitousness in the business world seemed to have a quicksand quality, no matter

The LITTON Adventure That Was

The other major Litton concern had been growing in parallel. Now that it appeared that the Business Systems and Equipment Group was seeing occasional glimmers of light ahead, Harry Gray was taken off the course correction task for that even bigger brow furrower, the Ingalls Shipbuilding division and related activities on the Great Lakes.

"But I'm only part way through," Gray said. He was told it was well enough along that a reach could be made again for that often dipped into well, the personnel bank that was Monroe. The election to come in behind Gray was Ralph O'Brien, a master salesman and marketer who had a reputation for making his quotas quicker than any of his peers, but he was a question mark as to his ability to manage diverse entities. As a hockey player he had learned to skate fast over bad ice and subdue obstacles with stick and bump techniques. His instincts told him that the Group's ailments dictated continuance of the effort to renew the health of the product lines, or customer displeasure would continue to swamp him. He girded himself with swashbuckler's sword and prepared to do battle with the action he understood best—sales. He quickly found that it was more than a marketing matter.

Harry Gray surveyed that new picket fence which he had to hop ruefully. In that long ago meeting in Birmingham, Alabama, Tex Thornton made such a dazzling impression on Mrs. Ellen Ingalls that she agreed to sell the Pascagoula shipbuilding unit. It had been the Thornton lighter that was decorated by the Stars and Bars of the Confederacy which when clicked on played "Dixie" that had broken the ice and the merger proceeded. People asked Tex Thornton where he got the lighter. He always said, "I forget who gave it to me." Whether he did or not, as he was not big in forgetting anything, there was no mystery as to who had handed it to him in Harry Gray's mind.

It was a fellow named Harry Gray.

That innocent souvenir lighter which had breached a lady's defense found him, the giver, now rewarded as inheritor of Litton's biggest can of worms.

---

what was tried. Litton was not alone with this impression as besides Imperial, the United Kingdom had extensions of Italy's Olivetti trying for a share of its market and coming up short by about $7,000,000 annually; Germany's Olympia, too, IBM and Remington had given up their units in Scotland deciding to lob in whatever product required from their offshore points.

SPECIAL SITUATION #21

HARD FACTS AND HARD TIMES

One of the dire forecasts of the ancients was that he who lives by the sword will probably have one thrust through him—in the end.

In modern times it has been paraphrased that any company which takes the New York Stock Exchange to bed with it, fondles it, has its way with it, then finds itself tiring of it can be summarily thrown out of it. The interest wanes in direct ratio to how yesterday's swains see their onetime companion as damaged goods. Litton Industries in 1968 found itself not only thrown out of bed, but considered a faithless floosie after having reigned so long as the fairest flower of them all.

Prevailing opinion inside Litton was that while it had some dubious enterprises that stayed stubborn resisters to profit, they were not thought to be incurable situations. The big time requirements lay immediately in the typewriter dilemma, which Harry Gray thought he had solved with Germany's Triumph-Adler, and the rising needs of Ingalls Shipbuilding.

There were all kinds of indications that segments of the West's industrial base were in for major changes. One thing was sure, no kind of industry which engages in manufacturing could alter its directions or products without retooling. Machine tools were similar to components in that they had to be in the action, or there was no action. Any nation which rests on great industrial power and expertise has as ravenous an appetite for machine tools as a man-eating tiger after a 40-day hunger strike yearns for red meat.

Regardless of the acknowledged Litton problems in the January letter to shareholders, life had to go on. Corporate life, Litton life, did that. It was quickly evident that it would no longer be as effortless. The vaunted momentum was menaced with each day's devaluation of Litton securities at home and abroad. The greatest unfilled hand around the Litton table was machine tool capabilities, so carefully balanced by Glen McDaniel and Metz Hollengreen. It was adjudged a great future area to be in before the January confession of inability to maintain the upward profit pace. It was still believed to be one. It provided another degree of strength added to the main Litton structure.

McDaniel had to leave because of a heart problem just as Landis Tool became the focus. Tex Thornton and Roy Ash, together and separately, spent time on both coasts with Metz Hollengreen. Hollen-green was allowed to go at his own pace as he was numbed by the tragedy of the loss of his son and his desire in the aftermath to do the right thing for his family of Landis employees. He finally drove him-self to concentrate on that, and on October 26, 1967, he signed the agreement to merge with Litton Industries. For about $130,000,000 in Litton Industries stock measured in the values assigned by the mar-kets, the transaction was sealed.[1] It was a busy time for Thornton and Ash, as they had just gotten Stouffer Foods after long haggling.

Litton had started at the very top in putting its machine tools drive under way. None ranked higher anywhere than Landis Tool. It was the premier maker of grinding machines and discs, circulating pumps, and fine boring equipment. Professionals from all over the globe came to out-of-the-way Waynesboro, Pennsylvania just to see the plant and how it operated.

The merger was closed on the very day the crest was reached for Litton's stock price. The first flashes of disappointing performance in the Business Machine and Equipment Group were beginning to come in. As the ink was drying on the Hollengreen signature on the October 26th agreement to merge, Litton closed on the New York Stock Ex-change that same trading day at $120.125 per common share. It cheered the 75,000 holders of Litton, but they were used to perpetual good news then. That was the peak of the long rise over 57 quarters, three stock splits and a long parade of 2½% annual stock dividends from the 10¢ a share start. When Hollengreen put his name to the final document on January 16, 1968 it was six days before the word that the 58th quarter would find Litton plateauing. None was then reading the extent of the tremor nor guessing the length of the slide, nor was the company deflected from continuance of its spread and growth, internally and externally.

---

1. In 1967, Wilson Marine Transit, Cleveland; Jefferson Electric, Bellwood, Ill.; American Book and McCormick-Mathers publishing, in New York; Fester Solder, Evanston, Ill.; Saphier, Lerner & Schindler, New York; Chicago Solder Co., Chicago; Marine Consultants & Designers, Cleveland; Ditran Corporation Newton, Mass.; Rust Engineering, Birmingham, Pittsburgh and Brussels, Belgium; Indiana Display Promo-tions and Streater Store Fixtures, Albert Lea, Minn.; in addition to Stouffer's, all be-gan their march under the Litton flag. The final closing on Landis Tool merging it with Litton occurred on January 16, 1968.

The LITTON Adventure That Was

What Hollengreen had done had been watched and talked about, pro and con, by his peers. Because of his having headed the Machine Tool Builders Association, they knew him and how his mind worked. They had elected him to lead them in their association's affairs. Whether they were inclined to follow him now as he came to his solution of his own peculiar and personal problem was far from automatic, but what Hollengreen would do and why he did it carried substantial weight among his colleagues. He and McDaniel counted on that, but there was some skittishness among their prospects about conglomerates. McDaniel was one of the smoothest and cleverest and politically astute of corporate lawyers. He had written substantial parts of the so-called "book" on government contracting. He was acutely sensitive to anything which might cause "tilt" lights to flash warnings of antitrust vulnerability, the taboos by Washington standards. Hollengreen knew the machine tools fraternity from family backgrounds to personal piques. He was one of the most admired and best known in the field both in America and abroad. If there was a way to proceed carefully, break through amiably, as a duo they had both the prestige and push to be believed before their selected audiences. If anyone could, they could fabricate a machine tools group for Litton which would have balance enough to avoid and cyclical hazards.

In the Washington law firm of Covington & Burling, attorney Joel Barlow represented not only Landis Tool but the Machine Tool Builders Association. He knew everyone in the trade well, their fears and their thought processes. It would be no more than natural that when Litton shifted into "high" gear that Barlow was selected as the catalyst. It was in his Florida home during the Association's convention in May of 1968 that McDaniel was introduced around by him. It was obvious that there under the Barlow roof and at social ease were all the heads of those enterprises McDaniel had drawn up in his matrix of companies. Taken together, they would augment, support and complement each other under the Litton tent. The conversations even indicated that many of the companies, if they were to survive, were confronted with having to bring some others into their circle. That might have short term merit, or they could merge with some bigger industrial entity which would offer both compatibility and financing. Hollengreen, having committed his Landis Tool to Litton, meant the largest manufacturer of precision grinders was within the corporate gates of a conglomerate. If he could live with it, others would surely be moved to think it a sensible route to take. Their reasons might differ from the emergency which had caused him to hitch his horse to another wagon, but they had other compelling reasons to find some solution.

The two most immediately attractive to McDaniel and Hollengreen were Union Twist Drill (UTD) in Athol, Mass., a leading producer of metal cutting tools such as drills, reamers and hobs, all those accessories that are the working elements in machine tools operations, and the New Britain Machine Company. New Britain had taken its name from the Connecticut town where it was formed under the name of J.T. Case Engine Company. It had opted for a name change in 1893, long before Litton's time. It had gained stature every year as a source of multiple spindle automatic turning systems, numerically controlled profilers, boring, milling and drilling machines.

When Litton began its first tentative probes toward machine tools which Jack Connolly had identified so promptly as a reasonable target for computer controls, he had approached Julian "Jude" Pease at New Britain[2] on July 8, 1966. Seymour Rosenberg accompanied him.

---

2. New Britain was like a walk-through of America's past. It had its own monuments just like an old battlefield. Its adaptability to fast changing and demanding new directions was well documented. Its early engines had powered and lit the tents of the old Barnum & Bailey circus and Buffalo Bill's Wild West Show. It was a New Britain engine on the tender that supplied the light used by the sea diver who investigated the sunken U.S.S. Battleship MAINE, which on being blown up had set off the Spanish-American War. The diver by that light proved that the ship's plates were blown inward showing that exterior attack had been the cause rather than some interior explosion. This caused an entire country to rally around the slogan: "Remember the Maine!" Having gone from J.T. Case to New Britain in 1893 that kind of participation in a telling American exercise entitled it to honor and kudos. In 1927, New Britain's sales manager, Edward Steinle, established sales offices in England, France, Belgium and Germany and David O. Swanson was appointed European sales boss a year later.

At the depression's "bottom", 30 New Britain machines were sold to the Soviet Union via AMTORG in New York (six-spindle chucking, single spindle chucking, and six-spindle screw machines). The purchase required that a set-up man go along. Gus Ahlquist, so fascinated the Russians on sites in Volvograd and Kharkov in the Ukraine he was extended ten months to get all the plants on line! A further contribution of New Britain to USSR industrialization was its licensing agreement with Poland in 1936 for machine tools for their arsenals, which required all drawings pertinent to manufacture and assembly to be furnished to the Polish government. When Germany and the Soviet Union pounded on Poland in 1939, Soviet engineers carefully copied

Barely ten days before, Pease, the board chairman and president had huddled with Angus MacDonald of the business brokerage house, Braxton & Company; Joel Barlow, the lawyer; Robert Fisbie and Palmer McGee, who were New Britain staffers. Pease let them all know rather flatly that he felt the future of the industry and his part of it rested on keeping it "within the family", i.e., the machine tools brotherhood. The indications were it was better to marry first cousins than to take up with strangers from out of town. The strangers before him that day were from Beverly Hills, California. What could they possibly know of machine tools? Barlow and McGee counseled him against being too quickly a door-slammer. At least, he should hear out any interested parties, whether they knew anything technically of machine tools or not. They just might be helpful in other ways. With no more than a little distaste and much less than enthusiastic endorsement of going along, this was the Pease demeanor when Connolly and Rosenberg walked in.

If he was ever to be warmed up, they immediately knew they were not the ones to do it. He gave them such a cool reception, they would have been more comfortable in parkas than in their sporty California clothes. They "looked the part" of the conglomerate manners and mannerisms his own mental stereotyping had led him to expect. They reinforced his prejudices. Clearly, for this kind of an undertaking for Litton Industries, no amount of fawning FORTUNE and BUSINESS WEEK articles would constitute credentials. Someone the industry knew and found believable had to be the contact, the cajoler and the convincer.

Metz Hollengreen had grown up with Pease and knew him as if they had attended the same schools and were next-locker at the same club. Hollengreen knew how adamant the Pease stand was against conglomerates. He advised a bypass of New Britain for the moment while they tried elsewhere. Pease, he thought, would be unlikely to be pleased by any other suitors either so the clock could safely run insofar as he was concerned. This turned the Litton spotlight on UTD.

Union Twist Drill was an inheritance for its head, Stanley L. Holland. A tall and handsome man with athletic frame, he was an *affic-*

---

the component designs for New Britain Models 60 and 61, set up the Kiev Machine Works and manufactured more than 400 of that variety of machine tools—before being overrun by Hitler's deep penetration that took Kiev.

cionado of the ancient sport of curling. Nimble as he was while whisking his broom back and forth across the ice in front of his curled goosenecked stone as it slid along, he was phlegmatic and not considered a scintillating operator. There was no doubt that he ran his company, though. Those who agreed with him absolutely got along fine. Those who didn't got lost. But he did bring on some high quality management types who served well for years. He was sufficiently a presence to have made a deep impression on his employees. When people who visited UTD asked why they did something in a certain or special way, the answer was not that it made sense, but that Holland wanted it done that way. Holland, Glen McDaniel found, was more amenable to a game of curling than he was to merger.

McDaniel was surprised one evening at his Bel Air home by the visit of a UTD board member. He was making contact on the basis of their long ago Navy service. As the conversation shifted to the present, he said he was really there because he was dissatisfied with Holland's management of the company. This put McDaniel in a quandary; from his position he could only deal with a firm's top man. He told his informant frankly that he would have to disclose on approaching Holland that it was a board member's dissatisfaction which was the root of their meeting. The board member had no objections, but it set up an extremely hostile environment for the negotiations. Holland was miffed about how and why McDaniel was at his door. He wasn't about to agree with anything his complaining board member favored. Holland also know how to play the merger game, particularly the wisdom of having more than one suitor to see who brought the biggest box of chocolates. He said coolly that he had other interested aspirants for his hand.

There was one in the midwest, Sundstrand. It was a company with about 52% of its earnings coming from power transmission systems, the rest from contracts subject to extensive renegotiations, quicksand at best. While appearing both pained and yet gracious for having to resort to such tactics, McDaniel expended some of his most persuasive prose. It was this single and endangered narrow view which had driven Holland to set up his own mini-conglomerate.[3] If he

---

3. UTD included what had once been separate firms named Contromatics Rockville, CT.; Reed Rolled Thread Die Company, Holden, Mass.; Union-Card Division, Athol, Mass.; Butterfield Division, an enterprise of dual nationality in Derby Line,

were to go with Sundstrand, McDaniel said he would be walking into another problem area rather than in the direction of relief—joining a company already hard-pressed at the very moment of trying to escape. On the arm of Litton Industries, the way Glen McDaniel painted it, it would be a march down the aisle with strength which would make UTD's 3,700 stockholders with their 1,551,791 shares feel they had married the "king of the hill" rather than just another attractive corporate commoner, however poor and honest it might be.

Machine tools was such a small nest that it was generally known that a significant and decisive difference of opinion floated around Sundstrand. A rocky road was revealing itself ahead over the Chairman and President's desire to undertake a heavy commitment to build a highly sophisticated machine. It would take metal bars at entry point and deliver them finished and with assembled components at exit almost as a magician produces phalanxes of rabbits from hats. The executive vice president viewed this computer-controlled, intricate wonder worker capable of such a multiplicity of outputs as suitable for some manufacturers engaged in filling military requirements. He thought industry as a whole was not a market quite ready for it yet. That difference led to the executive vice president's resignation which was propitious for Litton Industries two ways: It made Litton more attractive to Holland, and the resigned executive, Burnell Gustafson, was available and Litton was rightly impressed with him. Litton hired him.

Union Twist Drill's agreement[4] to merge was formalized June 13, 1968. The whole UTD package was valued at $69,800,000 in Lit-

---

Vermont and Rock Island, Que., the two nations boundary line running right through the facility, and Merriman Division in Hingham, Mass. There was also a Union-Butterfield plant in Gaffney, SC, known as the Straight Line Division (one school of thought claimed it was called that because it was a straight line style of manufacturing facility, and another was that the S and L derived from the Stanley L. portion of Holland's name).

4. There was one stipulation—UTD should take immediate steps to sell off its West German twist-drill manufacturer, R. Stock & Co. Its addresses in Germany rang of an old 8th Air Force targeting folder—Berlin-Merienfelde, Dusseldorf, Bielefeld, Hannover, Bremen, Munich, Stuttgart and Mannheim. UTD had gotten it in 1956 after most of its properties had been rebuilt since all had suffered bombing at one time or another. One of its problems was that it needed 28 different processing steps to achieve its finished items. Its assembly line was snail-like in pace and inefficient. There was another warning flag in that 90% of the employees were in the metal work-

ton shares exchanged for those of UTD. UTD holders could elect either Litton's preference stock which grew in value by formula to more than two common shares by 1989, or the Litton $2 B dividend paying convertible preferred.

With both Landis and UTD in, McDaniel and Hollengreen pulled New Britain Machine up, front and center. Its first products had been a chainsaw mortising machine capable of cutting only one mortise at a time. These were grooved to fit woods or metal strips. Once this was designed into a multiple-spindle rig, it was able to jump production to eight or ten mortises simultaneously. For a growing and building America, its role was not insignificant. By 1911, a line of automatic chucking machines was added. Two years later, automatic bar and screw machines came into its capabilities quiver. The lines grew both by innovations within the company and through its acquisitions. New Britain was an acknowledged leader of consequence.

Post World War II, the surging automobile industry and Henry Ford's assembly lines plus those of General Motors and others gave machine tools a mighty conversion role taking them out of the armaments business and into consumer products. It was easy for a "Jude" Pease to ask what a Litton Industries could possibly do for him. On that humid May night in Joel Barlow's home in Florida where there was a cocktail rump session on the main Machine Tool Association, McDaniel and Pease had met for the first time. In spite of all he'd said before,[5] something sparked between himself and McDaniel and they agreed to meet in June for further talks.

---

ers union. There was already talk in the air about "codetermination", or having union members in the management structure. People such as farseeing Fred O'Green were concerned that outside the U.S., in the Federal Republic of Germany, Litton had its biggest offshore payroll. Co-determination smacked of being dangerously close to the capital investor losing control of his investment. Its full implications were as yet unknown but there was no use asking for it, particularly with such a marginal facility as R. Stock & Co. When that deletion was completed, UTD was a sparkling prospect, both in the quality of its managers and product lines.

5. Julian "Jude" Pease, New Britain's chairman and president, was a tough customer who had made statements about "conglomerate companies" which were unfavorable, and also said he would never be acquired by anybody. He was an acquirer of some proportions himself including the Gridley Machine Co. of Hartford (1929) a name so respected in the automatic bar and chucking field that its imprint is carried on some models to this day; Storms Drop Forging of Springfield, Mass. (1949); Lucas Machine Co. of Cleveland (1949) (Koehler Aircraft Products of Dayton, Ohio (1955);

"We're listening to two others," Pease said. He identified them as Houdaille Industries and Brown Sharpe. "They're quite compatible with us." He didn't say Litton wasn't, but he wanted the record to show he had other options. Pease was intrigued by now as the trade publication, METALWORKING NEWS, had headlined two weeks earlier the problems of the Ballard Company after its acquisition by White Consolidated. Some 98 people had been separated as an "economy move" and included among them was Francis Dabney, the president of their Association! That article had been kind, though, to Litton, and this had not been lost on Pease. He was standing firm against the whole idea and he didn't want any formal proposals from Litton, saying he'd like to wait a month to see what would happen in the other quarters with which he was in the midst of a flirtation. He was writing friends in the meantime telling them: "Metz Hollengreen is working on me constantly to join Litton."

Barlow suggested a new tack. A letter to Pease should be sent by McDaniel making so high a bid, he would have to bring it out of his office and to the attention of his board. This was done, and it loosened him up appreciably when he saw Litton was offering a $20 margin over New Britain's stock exchange price—this being a matter of staggering import to possessors of 1,032,000 New Britain shares. Tex Thornton joined the proceedings at that juncture, listened to what Pease had to say that would make him happy. On August 8th, the pot was sweetened with an offer to exchange for each New Britain share a market-priced $65 share of Litton's $2 convertible preferred, or 9/10th plus $10 for each Litton preference. The day the final price tag was to be arrived at was December 6, 1968. At New Britain's shareholders' meeting the place was a-buzz with excitement and when the vote was taken, 48,272 of the shares took the combination offer and 992,485 took the Litton preference. New Britain was in the door.

Xcel Mold & Machine, North Canton, Ohio (1955) H. Boker & Co., Maplewood, N.J. (1965); Atlas Vac-Machine Corp. of Rochester, N.Y. (1965); Lund Manufacturing Co. of Biddeford, Maine (1968) Carlson & Son, Metuchen, N.J. (1967) and Osley & Whitney, Inc., Westfield, Mass. (1968) In France, there were New Britain facilities, AMTEC, in both Nanterre, a suburb of Paris, and in Lyon. The H. Boker & Co. provided Litton with a significant personnel milestone in Anne Kilgallon who came with it—later to be the first Litton employee to reach the 50 years of service level, no small attainment when she commuted some 100 miles each day more than half those years.

In that 1968 of ultimate stock market rudeness to its securities, Litton had filled out its machine tools hand with aces. Its scope was formidable, being in grinding machines, cutting tools, metal cutting machines, metal and special products, and plastics forming.

Welding it all into a group was assigned first to a recruit from the Pentagon E-Ring, Tom Morris, then to Robert Stewart, but each had his difficulties because they were outsiders and the clannishness of those inside plus the association with the corporate bigness of Litton caused a kind of covered-wagons-in-a-circle to form. Litton, having hired Burnell Gustafson, put him first at the top of New Britain, with New Britainite, Nathaniel "Bud" Howe in the next chair to provide support. After a time, Gustafson himself mounted the group saddle and Litton was a power in machine tools from that day forward. It had all kinds of other prowess. In spite of its being nipped at constantly and there were negative appraisals as to what the company's future might be. In machine tools it was modern, capable and would never be out of the top ten in the field.[6] Litton's summary of its fiscal year 1970 said one third of its machine tool sales were made by Landis Tool, another third by the UTD and Garner Machines divisions, and the rest by New Britain. [7]

---

6. Lucas Machine in Cleveland, part of the New Britain collection, was a pioneer in introduction of new technologies for control and accuracy of multiple axis machining systems. It was an inheritance from founder Henry Lucas who in 1901 manufactured the first horizontal boring mill, one that could be moved up, down, side to side over the metal being bored, rather than decrease precision by moving the metal being worked. Although not the first with numerical controls applications, in 1958 Lucas was the initial firm to utilize it for point-to-point positioning of axes to assure precision in repeatable operations.

7. It was an interesting sidelight that New Britain's President Nathaniel "Bud" Howe used the Litton merger and aftermath in a panel presentation at MIT. His paper was called "The Experience of a New England Company in the Fold of a Conglomerate." Litton corporate didn't like the way he painted the picture, but he had only gone public with how an often-hoped-for merger marriage can sour the incomers. Machine tool stocks, invariably low, he said, caused company managements to fear being taken into an unhappy partnership, but the time had come for movement into a chosen firm which offered financial assistance into needed electronic developments required, and access to new technologies which could help the unit into its future more competitively. Litton was chosen, and it was immediately turbulent. A small, family company, he said, relies on its people, knows them, keeps their interests in mind. A large one immediately introduces sophisticated management information systems, requires projections or plans and reviews them for their legitimacy periodically, makes adjust-

The LITTON Adventure That Was

The Japanese Government had approved a licensing agreement and the purchase by Litton of a 20% interest in Nippei Industrial Company, a grinding machine manufacturer in Japan. It was admittance of Litton into the very first equity position in an existing Japanese machine tool concern for an American company. Barely into that market, the Litton divisions had fared better in a down period than the rest of the industry, and were poised to lead in the upturn to come.

This all was related to that carefully designed matrix approach to the acquiring effort. It had worked well in avoiding antitrust harassment by ducking encroachments and overlaps in capabilities. It was spread over consumables and capital equipment in such a way that it was a hedge against cyclical tendencies of the trade.

Litton was in the U.S.S.R. Volga Auto Works by "inheritance", so to speak. George Lopato, a retired French Army officer who'd served in the French *Etat Major* Russian section, was an avid student of Russian language, literature and culture. As WW II ended, Germans held thousands of French POWs in their *stalags* well to the east making it difficult for them to escape. These prisons were overrun by the advancing Soviet Armies, causing the French captives' internment to continue. Lopato was sent to negotiate for their release. He had a full quota of salesman's finesse and charm which speeded many a Frenchman home. Once his uniform was hung away, he went back into his old profession where he was highly regarded in France— machine tools. He began managing New Britain's AMTEC division with operations in Nanterre (that Paris suburb which has voted Communist faithfully in every election) and in Lyon.

---

ments, and quite often those adjustments result in executive replacements and layoffs. The result in his opinion was employee distraction from the jobs being done, greater tendency to rely on union defenders of job security rather than trusting management as in the "family ownership" days. Initially, he said, Litton "investigated in detail the operational activities of all personnel and analyzed the organizational structure in depth, operational methods and style were scrutinized, accounting procedures audited, all leading to recommendations for major changes." He also said morale had slipped when New Britain employees had received Litton stock in exchange for New Britain at $59 a share and saw it go down to $3.50, the original New Britain paper having been accrued with "hard-earned money." There was a predictable result: the top management resigned, but Litton had learned one valuable lesson by then—it sought its new executive leadership from inside and critic "Bud" Howe was the one.

France and Italy both had bilateral trade treaties with the Soviets. When New Britain was threaded into the Litton necklace, not only AMTEC came along—but with it by subcontract to FIAT a requirement to build and equip a 2-mile long assembly line for the Moscow-desired model of their small car to be called the Zhiguli. Lopato included a machine tool order for 400 multiple spindle automatic bar and chucking machines, vertical precision contour boring and turning machines. He was assured extension of 150 to 250 more a year for a decade. That huge assembly line on the Volga at a new city, Togliatti (named for Italy's longtime, faithful Communist leader), was eager for AMTEC machine tools; the first car had to come off the assembly line April 21, 1970—the Centennial of Lenin's birth.

Lopato gloried in the deal he described as ". . one of the largest contracts ever negotiated in the history of sales of that particular product." The then head of the machine tools group, Bob Stewart, didn't like what he saw in the spread of Litton's obligations and, uneasy with the go-go tactics employed by Lopato, told Burnell Gustafson then heading New Britain to catch up with Lopato wherever he was and dismiss him. Gustafson argued against it, but Stewart was adamant, Gustafson thought that Lopato, given time, could have worked out the loose and flapping ends. Relations with the Soviets became tense. All the follow-on orders went to Japanese and German manufacturers. In making a super try to meet the deliveries on time, there was a splurge in Litton machine tool employees in France up to more than 700 people. In taking on Frenchmen, hirings get workmen but also cause the French government to throw out more tentacles than an octopus—as letting an employee go, or making layoffs is an experience not to be relished. Litton had reason to remember the Mark Twain admonition: "A man who has a bull by the tail knows seven or eight things other men do not."

The company was introduced to *reglement judiciare* (anglicized, controlled bankruptcy) which runs over five years requiring payment of all social contract guarantees to employees. It cost Litton substantially. AMTEC was finally severed at a giveaway $3,500,000, but could have been kept alive if the labor force had been taken down to 300. Litton's deck did not clear of this taint until July 31, 1980. It was still in France—but not in machine tools.

The LITTON Adventure That Was

The *Chicago Daily News* on January 3, 1969 hit the streets with its financial page headlining: 1968's WINNERS AND LOSERS.

The "leading losers", it said, were ranked from largest decline and were in order—United Air Lines, Freeport Sulpher, Avco, Boeing, Bendix and Litton Industries. A selection of four photos rode with a supporting streamer: MEET SOME OF 68's MARKET MILLIONAIRES, and two of them were Charles B. Thornton and Roy L. Ash. The reason they were included was a new experience for them and for Litton, as they were listed under the subhead: LOSERS, 1968!

"Litton's biggest loser (and perhaps the nation's biggest, too)," the story said, "was the giant Los Angeles conglomerate's founder and chairman, Charles B. Thornton. He took a $33,832,485.75 loss on the common stock." At year end, it was acknowledged that his 1,033,053 shares were still worth $74,379,816. Some loser!

The story had Roy Ash losing $10,195,664 but still holding $22,414,896 in his family sugar bowl. They had gotten Ash on the phone, and he said that he followed the stock from the view of the business operations, not his personal investment; he had no concern about performance in any one year as long as the long term trend was up.

The newspaper wrote about the Litton plight for about one sixth of its paragraphs. Vernon Stouffer, who had boarded the Litton express in October of 1967, had done so just in time to qualify for a $3,571,649 sag in his stocks worth, and his wife's share was off $1,606,911. George F. Monroe, the one who had maneuvered Monroe into Litton, saw his holdings down $4,630,326 from the previously January. Glen McDaniel, who had labored like a beaver all year getting the machine tools elements together, tallied and found himself less well off on paper by $1,463,794. Henry Salvatori had been on the long slide, too, and was down $1,323,034 in his worth.

Wall Street viewed it as blood running in the streets, and discounted the blood in the eyes of the Litton leadership about righting the situation. Through 1969 and 1970, there were other acquisitions, but they were relatively small to fill in requirements still open in some groups.[8] Assessments were being made about dead weight elements,

---

8. In 1969, Litton brought in that single big one, Triumph-Werke/Adlerwerke after the August, 1968 agreement to merge had been processed. In order then came

not having responded by then, or likely to do so ever, and to sell them off. There were closures and consolidations. Frank Slovak, the hand which had reached for so many of what were now Litton divisions, was about to become one of Litton's busiest as he looked for buyers who would pay favorable prices for the units earmarked to be handed off.

There were lean years ahead, or as Fred O'Green so earthily put it, "deep yogurt" years.[9]

Topics Publishing, out of Cowles Communications, VEAM, the components firm, and G. Pandozy & Figli, both in Italy; Hanscom Eliot, Nechin & Beveridge, Inc.; ATAL, the furniture house in France; Medical Arts Supplies Company, El Dorado Tool manufacturing in Milford, Connecticut; Houston X-Ray Corporation; Southern Dental Supply, Inc.; Delmar Publishers; William R. Niedelson Company; Paul's Woodcraft Company, and Dumont Aviation Associates, which made Nat Dumont a major Litton shareholder.

9. In 1970, Reinhold Book Corporation was added, plus Xcel Mold & Machine Co.; Sterimed, GMbH; Steriplast, GmbH; N.V. Etikettenfrabriek Gebr; Mijnhardt N.V.; Checkmaster, Inc.; Valentine Pulp & Paper Company, that "Cajun" converter of sugar cane stalks into special paper; the joint venture with Japan's Royal-Seiko for typewriter manufacture; Parker-Hannifin Corporation; Landis Optics & Coating; Digital Systems, Inc.; C. & B. Corporation, and the Fulton Company, and in December, Raypar Electronics. It was at that point that the outward bound, sell-off traffic was established

SPECIAL SITUATION #22

CHANGING THE GUARD

What will happen to a company such as Litton Industries if Tex Thornton or Roy Ash both leave?

The question was often phrased by analysts and financial pundits. The company was rather sparing about having other executives being quoted in the national and international media outlets, and particularly in the business press.

The strategy was in the thought processes of the Thornton and Ash duo. To all the other executives it seemed better that way. They had operational things to do, and holding press conferences, except at trade shows, were limited occurrences. It did cause the suspicion to grow that Litton was some sort of revolving door, where people came and went in the middle ranges of management, like so many battered tennis balls crossing and re-crossing a net.

There were the LIDOs, of course, those much touted Litton Industries Dropouts, who sent up signal flares as to their availability, cited Litton learning and took off. Some of them made it big, but the fact that they departed helped sow the disquiet about whether Litton had any management "depth." The company saw them officially as distinguished graduates, and as evidence of the Litton moxie adaptable anywhere vibrance was needed.

For nearly two decades of Litton's life, the fact of the blockage at the doors of the company's two principal offices often made the eager beavers who were group heads restive. William E. McKenna thought he had a solution if the company would enlist a certified No. 3, or purely operational executive, which would make him a part of a troika at the top. That didn't work, and McKenna went off on his march through top executive posts with other major companies. There was always that guessing about who *really* was the ". . . third most important man at Litton."

In the Pentagon, they guessed it was George Scharffenberger. When Harry Gray was doing all that bounding around from one group to another in his trouble-shooting roles, there were those who would have bet on him. Insofar as the pinnacle of the executive suite was concerned, if asked they would have answered "none of the above."

He was there all right, and his name was Glen McDaniel.[1] He was the corporate general counsel, of course, but he had to handle some of the hottest potatoes the firm had and was a known deliverer. In the by-laws there was eventually an amendment which made him Chairman of the Executive Committee. It empowered him to be in the chair for meetings of the Board of Directors in the absence of Thornton and Ash. He is probably the first man to have stated publicly that he thought he knew long before the eventuality who would be the successor to them both. He had to wait ten years to be proven right—and it would be McDaniel who was told to deliver the "word" to that upcoming candidate to ready himself as the time was near for the fateful step upward.

In 1966, after Litton had been at it for 13 years, Roy Ash was asked to summarize the Litton management philosophy and he made a statement suitable for all occasions. It ran widely enough to be included in the Congressional Investigation of Conglomerates Corporations. There it was for reference to be read by anyone who cared to, and it said, ". . . we elect to manage by not managing. We have one rule—there is no rule. Our policy is we have no firm policy. What is there left for management to do? The management of capital. We are decentralized, period. We grew up decentralized. We have acquired companies alone because it is ridiculous to make everything conform to one pattern. You destroy everything that was there. We have closer cooperation between managers than any corporation I know of because they are not running scared. We tell division and group leaders 'You make the decision, we'll back you.'" Obviously he believed that.

The assessment of Ash always was that he was a "numbers man," not people-focused at all. But it was dawning on everyone in the middle '60s that with that rainbow of more than 100 accumulated companies by merger turned into divisions, and by internal growth the spawning of many others, Litton had gone beyond a centralization of bookkeeping with its every enterprise more or less given its head.[2]

---

1. Litton's prospectuses annually listed Glen McDaniel's name among the Board of Directors showing his alignment with the company payroll as ". . . a director of the corporation since 1953, except for the period, April 15, 1954 to July 9, 1957."

2. The company was becoming more introspective by the minute. On May 1, 1972, Litton Industries became the first company to qualify under Rule #496, NYSE,

The LITTON Adventure That Was

The allure of Washington dawned later than most for Roy Ash. He had relished the power base of the executive suite, and Washington seemed to be a kind of ultimate in terms of strength. He had made speeches in which he'd said government could well contract out to business for better performance of some of its functions. He thought it left a lot to be desired because other than assigning managers for some of its programs, it didn't seem to equate management with the budgeting activities. In early 1969, President Nixon was seeing the national government processes in need of overhaul as there were all the cabinet heads as well as those of agencies and commissions and boards, about a hundred in all, who could claim a right to his ear. They loved that Oval Office access as much as the perquisites of their jobs. Nixon took the usual Washington steps in such things—and established his President's Advisory Council on Executive Organization. He also picked Roy L. Ash to be its chairman. The period of this involvement ran well into 1971 before the Council's findings were finally drafted and published. The period of the Council's work coincided precisely with the beginnings of the Litton hotfoot being felt at the highest level.

Some acquisitions were having to be concluded at high cost. Because they were brought in with an exchange of Litton stock for the shares of the incoming company, there were sometimes provisions for paying the purchase price in two installments of Litton Industries securities. This was done because Litton considered the shares under priced. That led to the hope and expectation that fewer shares would be delivered in the second installment, as the stock prices would surely increase in the interim. Roy Ash believed this, and Thornton concurred, but they miscalculated and had to pay added shares.[3] The

which decreed that it was unnecessary to have a stock co-transfer agent in New York City. This pull-a-way from Morgan Guaranty Trust cut payments by Litton to that bank for such service by $250,000 a year. It wasn't all a Litton saving, as the company had to staff to handle it. It was a net saving to Litton, says James Cleaveland to whom the responsibility shifted, of about $5,000 monthly. Many companies have since followed Litton's lead.

3. Nat and Valerie Dumont's Dumont Aviation became one of the classic cases of Litton's stock price decline in what was paid in Litton paper from closing date November 19, 1969 to "subsequent payment average price" which had to be made by December 31, 1971. The 1,000,000 Dumont shares, 975,000 issued and 25,000 in the treasury, were to come to Litton for an initial price of $2,300,000 in Litton common. There was optimistic expectancy that by subsequent payment date a $4,200,000 valuation would be reached, or Litton would compensate with additional shares. The price

Ingalls obligations were mounting until they would soon reach a point of being a major part of the Litton Industries investment.

An undercurrent began to develop among the outside members of the Board of Directors.[4] They sensed the day-to-day bundle of operational pains being laid at the Ash doorstep were intruding on the aloofness he would have preferred. Some say it finally popped out of either George Monroe or Joe Thomas, as they were long-timers. It could also be in part the misgivings of Ransom Cook and Henry Salvatori. Surely Cook and Salvatori were concerned about the amount of debt the firm had and the high interest costs to service it.

The fingers all pointed to the shipbuilding commitment which they thought were bad contracts. They were always asking for explanations about how the Litton so-called Total Package Procurement obligation was different from the pioneering one with Lockheed for the C-5A. The difference was scary. Litton had agreed to get going when the designing was in a preliminary stage, not yet frozen, therefore there was no adequate way to proceed with charges for requested changes by the Navy when the ships were in the building process. It was all open ended, like unplumbed depth in a swamp.

Their first move was of a kind the Litton boardroom had never known before. They sought enlargement of the Executive Committee to include Litton board members. Cook and Salvatori said they needed some assurance that Litton's leadership would make no future

---

at closing was $51.725 which led to the Dumonts getting 38,666 shares and 5,800 were put in escrow. By the time of final settlement, the Litton shares were down to $21.875, whereupon the Dumonts received 153,334 additional shares of the Litton common. This made them one of the biggest of Litton holders. Now called Litton Fastening Systems in Lakewood, California, from a 1946 start as a war surplus marketer of aviation nuts, bolts, screws and other components for military and commercial aircraft, helicopters, missiles and launchers, it employed about 300 people. It produces 50,000,000 units annually of structural fasteners for aircraft wings, fuselages, tails and other body components, 95% of its market aerospace and 5% industrial and Commercial.

4. In the late 1960s, a series of court actions and decisions caused extensive revisions in Delaware General Corporation Law. Boards of Directors were made increasingly responsible to shareholders as well as to many government regulatory agencies. Outside directors demanded and got more in-depth information than before, and in committee assignments probed more deeply into company affairs. Litton is a Delaware Corporation.

moves in a big obligational way without a vote of that Executive Committee. There it was, a Litton first. Anyway one read it, it was a vote of no confidence in Litton's management!

In the spring of 1972, it began to roll out on the table. There was a familiarization meeting in Connecticut on the premises of New Britain Machine, a relatively new acquisition and in the New England town which had given the company its name. Joe Thomas, up from Lehman Brothers in New York; George Monroe, out of Kalamazoo, and Jayne B. Spain, in from Washington, were at one table, eating and talking. When the coffee was poured at the end, George Monroe blurted out to Thomas that he had to see Tex Thornton personally and alone and talk to him about their belief that the time had come. Hurtful or not, there was the harsh fact of Litton becoming an endangered species unless there was a sleeves-rolled up, involved, truly managing overseer at the company's top.

Salvatori was all for it, and thought there was a solution which had plusses in it for everybody—and Litton Industries. The Ash Council's report was out, and it contained the recommendation that there should be abolition of the old Bureau of the Budget and in its place an Office of Management and Budget. Salvatori was sure that there would be a search for someone to head it. Who better for the job than the one who had chaired the Council and was conversant with its aims, or could articulate it better than Roy Ash? He said he would check it out.[5]

---

5. The CONGRESSIONAL QUARTERLY of September 18, 1970 said ". . . twenty four of the 25 top (DOD) Department of Defense contractors had officers and directors who made political contributions in 1968. Hughes Aircraft, number 24 on the list, was the lone exception. Republicans got six dollars for every one by the Democrats. The military contractor executives donated $671,252 to the Republican party, and $110,000 to the Democrats. Litton Industries which ranked 14th on the DOD contractor list in 1968 led the givers with a total of $156,000. Eleven of Litton's 29 officers and directors made donations. The Republican party got $151,000, the Democrats nothing. . . . miscellaneous committees received $5,000. Litton executives were among the most generous donors. Mr. and Mrs. Henry Salvatori contributed a total of $60,000 to Republicans and $5,000 to miscellaneous committees."

Salvatori was described as a ". . . wealthy Californian who supported Sen. Barry Goldwater for the Presidency in 1964." He was always making personnel appointment suggestions. He always got a polite hearing—and action, when it made good sense as this did.

When Joe Thomas did get the Board Chairman alone, it was just one more progression of events which had been dogging Litton's head ever since those first flash reports in late 1967 which led to that January 22, 1968 shareholder's letter announcing the reduction in profits. Would that phrase never go away, that one about "certain earlier management deficiencies"? Joe Thomas posed the chilling possibility that were the Ash removal not done, there was even doubt that Tex Thornton himself would stay when the road ahead worsened, as it surely would and become bumpier, as it had to before any noticeable improvement could set in.

If the Chairman had known it was coming and that the options would be so few and dreadful, he could never have dreamed of it this way. None could have blamed him for the wishful thinking that it couldn't happen. Here was his original choice of Roy Ash as his second-in-command around whom the storm was brewing. When he'd made the selection, Litton was much simpler, and a numbers man was what was needed. Even if that had cost him some of his talented early mainstays in the company, he was sure they would have left anyway as they had too many ambitions stewing to have been hangers-on for long. But now, the man they were finding vague, not responding directly when tough questions were asked, was the one who had been his main reliance for so long. He could almost tell what Roy Ash was thinking while he was thinking it. He knew him as one who could phrase his answer so beautifully.

Ash sensed the Thornton gut reactions as a palmist does lines in a client's hand. How many times Thornton had said to so many that he only had one employee, Roy Ash, and everybody else at Litton worked for Roy? Dozens and dozens of times he'd said it. The outside members of the board were now telling him that his earlier judgment had run out of runway, and Ash didn't have the executive capacity to fly Litton through this upcoming merciless examination. There were nearly a hundred thousand people on Litton's payrolls, and twice that many holders of the company's stock. They all had a stake in this.

After Joe Thomas had gone, Tex Thornton sat there alone. He had that one characteristic which so many had admired him for, his capacity for devoted loyalty to someone who had been on his team, had pulled his weight, had loved the game of building causing small things to become big, multiplying capabilities—and the whole of what could take place from such an effort was there, Litton Industries. Ash had always been indefatigable. He never committed himself sparingly. None could fault him for his devotion to the Litton ideal. It was in that uncharted "management relationship" sea that he appeared wanting in the eyes of these critics. There were those who said Ash had always been cold, and perhaps he was, but there had been a special bridge and trust between them. It was bitter brew for Thornton to drink.[6]

No action was taken immediately, but it was there on the Thornton lap all the time. Arthur Choate of Clarke-Dodge, the one who had pushed 45% of those original 50 packets of Litton bonds and stocks, called him one day from New York for an appraisal of the company's condition. "They're trying to take the company from me," Choate quoted the Chairman as saying to him darkly. Choate said he called him personally to get a reading because he couldn't always follow Roy Ash and his answers. There was a hint to Choate that Ash was under pressure, on the front burner, and the gas was being turned up.

Toward the end of summer, Glen McDaniel convened Henry Salvatori and Ransom Cook, who came down from San Francisco, for lunch at the Los Angeles Country Club. Other people were outside the windows teeing off for no bigger problems than 18 holes into which to sink small balls. McDaniel had to activate them for a special meeting in Litton's executive dining room where they would lay the situation cold turkey before Ash with the firm instruction that he would have to go. There were discussions about the Office of Management and Budget position. No one wanted any public outcry, nothing demeaning or ungracious, no move which would be reputation-destroying because, after all, the Ash credentials in certain areas were of the highest caliber.

A little earlier, at a dinner, in the same room when the Board was in town, Joe Thomas had excoriated Ash in front of everybody. It had

---

6. Even with all the years in between, it was still like yesterday in his mind when he was hailed by Bill Jamieson outside old Bldg. "C," the combination Ramo-Wooldridge lab and machine shop at Hughes Aircraft to tell him about Charlie Litton's electron tube plant and how he wanted to see it into good hands somewhere. The future was so murky then. Roy Ash was flirting with a job at Ford but didn't want to move to Detroit. What would the story have been had he done so?

been embarrassing as well as brutal. None wanted more of that. The other thing Glen McDaniel had to do was deliver in another quarter a quite different message—that the office occupant who now headed one of the three of Litton's groups should hold himself in readiness to assume the Litton Presidency. That selection agreed on by all the board members was Fred W. O'Green. This was the same man Mc-Daniel had intuitively felt was a successor at the very Litton top when he had first met him ten years before.

The drafts of the Chairman and President's letter to the share-holders for the opening pages of the 1972 annual report were being done and redone. The opening paragraph seemed to stay essentially in the same form. "Fiscal year 1972 was both a difficult and decisive year for Litton Industries," it read. "A number of significant manage-ment decisions were made and actions taken to reverse the decline in Litton earnings and to strengthen the overall market position for the company. These primarily involved the consolidations, discontinu-ance of unprofitable product lines, relocations and other one-time spe-cial expenses which have impacted on earnings."

Ah, and what an impact. The earnings amounted to a meager $1,118,000 against $50,003,000 for the previous 12 months. This wasn't enough to pay the preferred cash dividends, and it added up to 14¢ a share loss.

From the first annual communication in 1954 these carefully drawn documents, so well phrased, had been signed only by Charles B. Thornton. The one for 1961 changed that. Side by side with the text was a formal photo of a seated Ash with a standing Thornton symbolically behind him. The signatures then became a cemented-in tradition, Thornton's first, and Ash immediately below it. Even though the national elections would fall a full week after the 1972 annual report was dropped in the mails, the odds against there being a change in White House occupancy were heavy. Ash was scheduled to lead the transition of the new White House staff that the incumbent would form. It was a heavy hand that Tex Thornton used to put his name on the accustomed line. Whatever emotions Ash attached to his last inking of that document, he kept them to himself in his usual cool detached way. There was only one other major document left for him to sign. That was his official resignation dated to take effect Decem-ber 9, 1972—the day of the Litton annual shareholders' meeting.

486

The Ash focus swung more and more to Washington.[7] The votes were barely counted when word was passed to him that "some time around thanksgiving"—actually it was December 2nd—he was expected to attend a special breakfast at the Transition Team site, the Hotel Pierre, on 5th Avenue in New York. He was scheduled to address the cabinet as the Office of Management and Budget Director-designate.[8]

He returned for his swan song, the Beverly Hills High School conclave of the disappointed and concerned Litton shareholder family. They wished him well. He saw Fred O'Green, his replacement, introduced. There was always a "postmortem" buffet luncheon for the Litton Board and staff, and Lila and Roy Ash attended and talked of the excitement they were sure was in the offing in Washington. It was a sentimental moment, forever fixed for so many reasons in the minds of those who were there. It went off without a wrinkle showing. Suddenly, the Thorntons and the Ashes withdrew, and went to the B-1 level of Litton's Plaza South where the executives park their cars. They tried to say their good-byes in a "we'll see you in Washington" vein.

Except, Tex Thornton's voice and the hand he shook his goodbye with, trembled. He had never envisioned quite what it would be like when such a time would come for whatever reason. Now he knew. It had been worked out with care and consideration. What could have

---

7. Those Navy contracts dogged Roy L. Ash all the way into his White House Office of Management and Budget post. Gordon Rule charged that Litton was a favorite of both the White House and the Department of Defense, and he was smarting from Litton's charges that the so-called overruns were the fault of the Navy. He even surfaced the Eisenhower quotes about the "dangers" of the "military-industry complex," but the Ash appointment stood.

8. Roy Ash, as head of the Office of Management and Budget in the White House, was only six months away from being a participant in a similar drama at the highest level of government. But as an insider spectator, not the principal. On April 30, 1973, he with the rest of the senior staff of Henry Kissinger, Charles Shultz and John Ehrlichman assembled in the conference room of Presidential Chief of Staff, H.R. Haldeman. It was then that Haldeman told them that he was resigning his post in the Watergate-swamped administration of Richard Nixon. Haldeman had been with Nixon a decade, less than half the time Ash had been so intimately intertwined in Litton's executive suite, but he probably understood the Haldeman traumatic crossroads better than anyone else present.

been highly uncomfortable and bitter was not that way at all. Only sadness was there.

But Litton Industries was now on a long road to renewal. Who knew and with what cost what other hairy adventures would come? The man Tex Thornton would go to work with the next Monday morning had not been wasting time. The traditional Fred O'Green attitude was that he was going to win. It was the thought line he had to convey to everyone—fast.

In saying goodbye to Roy Ash, Tex Thornton had also said farewell to a phase—going from a Litton on the make to a Litton that would be a blue chip.[9]

---

9. FORTUNE, which once hung on his every word, dismissed Ash with its appraisal as ". . . utterly abstract in his view of business, he enjoyed to the hilt exercising his sharp mind in analyzing the most sophisticated accounting techniques. His brilliance led him to think in the most regal of ways: Building new cities, creating a shipyard that would roll off the most technically advanced vessels the way Detroit builds automobiles. . . ."

The 1973 annual report pictured 15 faces along the corporate shelf. Over the next months, six more were gone. Ralph O'Brien went to Mohawk Data Sciences, Orion L. "Orie" Hoch was wooed into ailing Advanced Memory Systems in Sunnyvale, Calif., which needed a turnaround doctor badly, and he "doctored" it well. James R. Mellor was lured to the Presidency of AM International by Roy Ash, which was to turn out badly for him. Ned Marandino left Litton's Marine Systems operations, as Ingalls' condition was listing dangerously. Crosby M. Kelly, who had been with Litton early, came back as a retread, then again gypsied off to Rockwell International. Ludwig T. Smith stayed around longest, but went with the Triumph-Adler sale to Volkswagen.

Of all the departures, one turned into a kind of "business sabbatical," that being Dr. Orion Hoch. He had accumulated 17 Litton years, hired on by Dr. Norman Moore at Electron Tube in 1957. He became Electron Tube's President in 1966, a Components Group VP in 1968 with Advanced Circuitry, Airtron and Electron Tube under his wing. He was brought into the executive suite in 1970, a corporate vice president for investor relations and public affairs to which labor and industrial relations were added. He then moved on as O'Brien's deputy in the Business Systems and Equipment Group. It was there that Advanced Memory Systems came for him with attractive opportunities. He left, but unlike the others, he would be back. And come out best of all.

SPECIAL SITUATION #23

THE JEKYLL-HYDE SIDE OF WASHINGTON, D.C.

Whatever else may be said of Litton Industries, Washington, D.C. both looked at it and to it a great deal. Curiously, in hope, desperately and sometimes vindictively, or so it seemed to the firm's insiders.

Wherever and whatever it was up to and doing in the world, there was some Washington address that seemed to be interested.

Washington sought Litton, invited it in, entertained it, sued it, arbitrated over it, laid its critical whip on it, yet never ceased expecting miracles from it, or that it would rise to more calls than almost any other company.

Mythology is an unborn idea crying from its womb in search of reality. One of the ordeals of Hercules in the Greek fantasies was directed against Hydra. She was the serpent who quickly grew two heads when each old one was destroyed. She had nine to start with! The Romans had their legendary Janus. He was a portal keeper capable of looking fore and aft and became a symbol for falsity and deceit. He was remarkably suited for aligning himself on any side as a weathervane accommodates itself to the wind. And in the works of Robert Louis Stevenson, there was the pre-Haight-Ashbury hophead who vacillated as the elegantly handsome and professionally mannered Dr. Jckyll who could quaff some evil test tube brew that converted him into a brutish Mr. Hyde. Each of these could exude menace, evoke fear, and represent danger in all manner of unpredictable ways.

They all knew a kind of reincarnation—Washington, D.C.

The nation's capital was allocated 61 square miles generally north, and west of where the Potomac River is about to get "too big for its britches." Before long, it becomes something else, the Chesapeake Bay. Historically, people elected go there to undergo a similar transition. They use their powers to beget commissions, committees, boards, and study groups, all with supporting appendages—enough to make Hydra curl up and die of envy. Washington, that started as a bedroom community to which some would repair to govern the new United States began to sniff the drug of power early. The cost of supporting this addiction to power became tremendous, growing, and perpetual. Everyone was asked to pay—the pusher of record being the Internal Revenue Service.

No country in the world does tax collection better than the instrumentalities of Washington. No country distributes that piled up mountain of money more widely, or with as much inventiveness. No world capital equals Washington in universal appeal to kings and knaves, prime ministers and princes and businessmen. Only the latter, however, are never quite allowed in the game until and unless everyone else has made a mess of something.

So-called statesmen misguess the degree of hostile intentions of other leaders, then go to war because of the miscalculation. This requires someone to build weapons, either to deter or fight, deterring making the most sense. It is always the hardest capability to justify. Businessmen or industrialists who are asked to perform are sitting ducks for later political potshots. Social "ills" can go overlooked or sparsely addressed for decades until politicians discover that those who constitute the "ill" also vote. This causes the undertaking of costly programs which tend to imprison those targeted within the "ills," while businessmen and industrialists are employers, vocational trainers and providers of economic mobility. This is a role they have always played.

The old aphorism that those who can, do; those who can't, teach, has a Washington paraphrase. Those who little understand or care about the processes or about those who can bring about productivity, love to strangle by regulation and restrictions those who do and can. Because they are organizers and problem solvers by instinct and experience, tycoons only get whistled off their benches and into Washington when situations are about as bad as they can get. When a problem is diminished, the businessman who was beseeched to help reverts to his status of pariah, probably to be the first to know suspicious inquiry or Congressional investigation. This is especially true if there's the potential of a headline in it, or the makings of sternly voiced commentary on the nightly news on TV.

The industrialist is somewhat like the earnest country boy up from the farm with cow manure still on his shoes, who can only throw strikes one after another, or when he comes to plate can hit a ball so hard it will land in the suburbs. He knows how to count, the difference between profit and loss, and has much more severe judgmental rules by which he must play. It is his paradox that to survive he had to spend as much time getting to the bottom of things as he does maintaining a clear view from the top of whatever domain is assigned to him.

Politicians can string together a series of purely expedient actions when they present themselves for re-election. The businessman or industrialist has to project himself and make decisions in terms of decades rather than two, four and six year terms of office. These two quite different perspectives converge in Washington. The bulk of the money which wends its way there via taxation comes largely from corporations or from their employees. How it will be spent is decided by those who are elected. Will Rogers once mused in an understandable state of puzzlement: "Why does that man hate me? I never did a thing for him in my life!" Many a businessman, equally baffled, has asked himself why Washington treats him and his colleagues as it does when they have responded in every way asked of them.

Litton Industries was on Washington premises so much precisely because it was capable of so many things that translated into multiple areas of vulnerability. It wasn't just because of its constant listing among the 20 leading defense contractors. The excellence of its militarily useful equipment and manufacture was there from the first.

Charlie Litton's vacuum tubes were key elements in radar, the kind on the rim of the Arctic Ocean called the Distant Early Warning (DEW) line stretching from the Aleutian Island chain across the Canadian north via Greenland to Iceland. Charlie Litton was exasperated with the Washington tendency to pester him in spite of his high quality workmanship and his efficiency in production. It moved to punish him for excellence and reduce his profits by re-negotiation. This had been the principal goad persuading him to sell his baby, Litton Industries of California, to Tex Thornton in the first place.[1]

---

1. Litton's legal staff found immediately after Charlie Litton had made his sale to Thornton that even though he had profited heavily, he had been able to produce those highest quality electron tubes so well, he had brought pricing of all other manufacturers down. That fact caused the government side in the renegotiations to allow the new owners to keep those profits! The Renegotiation Act of 1951 might be an anathema to a lover of the lab, but in the hands of the legally skilled it could be made into a persuasive case—and was.

When Joseph P. Kennedy pulled back from putting his money into the Thornton proposition, it was because of Kennedy's knowledge of the way Washington worked. He knew where his investments could be coupled detrimentally to become a hazard to the quickening political career of his son, John. How anything can be made to "look" or could be speculated upon, or lend credence to an accusation was as much a part of Washington as vote counting, lobbying, "perks" and the political junket.

Washington is the No. 1 coiner of acronyms and also, pejorative words. These lend themselves to headlines—"escalate," as in conflicts and costs; "overrun," which describes bringing program tabs up to their real size rather than lesser amounts offered as probable price tags to get program's feet in the Congressional door; "viable" as not only denoting workability, but with the possibilities of development and growth, and of course, those two hoary staples, "crisis" and "scandal." All by overuse have become tattered cliches in media streams in which they swim. Most of the time they conceal truth, leave readers and hearers with false impressions, but they do the work of Washington very well.

The Washington bureaucracy runs on the same set of wheels as the old-time fire-eating evangelist who has tasted the gutter, known sin and finds rebirth by changing portfolios and profiting from the errors of his way. The bureaucrat reaches an overripe old age by getting out-of-towners "on the hook" with his making them convenient patsies for shortfalls and blame when obstacles develop. They are granted minimum credit where success is achieved. The preacher declares himself as a penitent, a healer and giver of the Word. A Washington habitue becomes a "Beltway bandit" because he knows his way around. He has qualified himself by being an intimate of the system, which knowledge he will share for a price. He had advantages over the evangelist who deals in the hereafter; he is the consultant in the here and now, or what is called "ongoing programs."

Tex Thornton knew Washington long before he knew Litton. Roy Ash was a later comer. It was the first Thornton base, when he started from that clerk level at $1,260 annually. Working his way along had made him relaxed in any office where he had to talk. Ash, on the other hand, came in chairing the President's Advisory Committee on Executive Organization in 1970-71 during the Nixon first term.

He went into his second administration as the Director of the Office of Management and Budget (OMB). Both of the Litton toppers were roughed up on occasion. Ash was given the scalded cat treatment on the Washington scene which caused him to remark ruefully to newspaper columnist Jerry terHorst[2] that the biggest mistake he'd made in switching residence from one coast to the other was that ". . . I didn't bring my own supply of blood plasma with me."

He had not worked his way up through low and medium seats, and his intentions toward those who occupied them were feared by all who currently sat in them. Washington often asked Litton for help with ideas, for services on commissions and task forces; it would send for Litton for proposals for contractual involvements especially when addressing unmapped trouble zones, and it would ask for its executives for important appointments.[3]

It would condone and encourage it in economic development adventures which might lessen the sting administrations and congressmen suffered before the electorate for persisting in foreign aid appropriations.

Every other government in the world where Litton was, walked hand-in-hand with its business community, and snared its management and marketing talents to generate exports and foreign exchange. Washington for the most part, persistently questioned and challenged business and industry. It assumed various postures adversarially in nature and made what sports and gaming refer to as "judgment calls."

There were in Litton's case Congressional hearings ranging from antitrust fishing expeditions into the role of multinationals and on into the great brouhaha about shipyards.

The Federal Trade Commission attempted to block and kill outright a merger which was the company's only hope for staying competitive in a field where one firm alone, IBM, had more than 80% of

---

2. terHorst was later President Gerald Ford's press secretary. He resigned the post when Nixon was pardoned by Ford.

3. Typical of this was the recruitment of Mrs. Jayne B. Spain, a Litton division president and member of its Board of Directors, who became Vice Chairman of the Civil Service Commission; of Robert Berry, who headed the Washington office, tapped to be General Counsel of the Department of the Army; of John Rubel who was in the "war on poverty" group which became the Office of Economic Opportunity; and of Tom Cheatham, an Assistant Secretary of Defense.

the electric typewriter market. The interpretation by FTC was that Litton had made the acquisition to *lessen* competition!

The Office of Export License Control in the Department of Commerce was a hurdle which had to be jumped in any trade with the Eastern or Communist bloc countries by Litton's domestic divisions. Litton technologies sent to its divisions and plants offshore had a much less restricted time of it as long as they were in tune with more lenient national policies and bilateral treaties in effect—trade and otherwise—with the sovereign governments where such facilities and labor were.

When the manufacturer of microwave ovens began and that whole industry had acted responsibly in setting very demanding standards to lower the levels of acceptable radiation, it fell to Litton to be thrown neck deep into controversy just as it was coming on strong enough to dominate the market. It had to spend days, weeks and months of legal tussling with the Department of Health, Education and Welfare and its Bureau of Radiological Health. Reason: After paying little or no attention or bothering to compliment a whole industry for having acted with caution and care about safety, HEW, looking over its shoulders at all those roving bands of "consumer interest" groups who needed scareheads to insure funding and staying alive, stiffened the standards still further. The industry—and Litton— welcomed the new guidelines and set about building to them, but Robert Bruder who was Litton's microwave oven man-of-the-moment, naturally didn't relish having to reach out and back, tracking down old owners, to bring those previously bought ovens up to the new standards. This, on an agency whim, would require Litton to suffer the expense of the testing, the locating of possessors, the hiring of hundreds of people to perform both the survey and tests—all seeming ridiculous when there had never been a proven, recorded instance of a microwave or radiation casualty from any Litton oven.[4]

---

4. Those hearings were in the regime of Dr. Jesse Steinfeld as Surgeon General, he having come from being deputy director of the National Cancer Institute and therefore very sensitive to the nuances of radiation and its tolerable limits. Being a scientist of some standing as well, when no denunciation of the microwave oven was forthcoming, the public was reassured. As 1981 began, there were more than 15,000,000 microwave ovens in use in homes and restaurants in the U.S., and all of the Litton models had been built in compliance with the rigid standards specified by the Bureau of Radiological Health. No known documented injury was recorded as the

The LITTON Adventure That Was

Litton, for having the courage to attack a needing country's economic development, enlisting its company name, reputation and clout, found Amnesty International lobbying the U.S. Department of Justice for Litton to be registered as ". . . an agent of a foreign power"![5] It never happened, but it induced much hassling and Washington time all because Greece, the country concerned, happened to have an unpopular military junta in power. Regardless of whether Litton had negotiated with three favoring previous regimes, or whether the junta was the Government of Greece at signing time, sophisticated peoples know that politics take strange directions. Governing falls into peculiar hands sometimes, but there are still the populations of whatever countries that hunger for and deserve betterment of their plights no matter who rules them. A healthy economy is usually the key to that happening. Politicos out of power, and often out for good reason, beat their own self-serving drums. They try to drown the voices of the people they say want them, when what is really desired is stability, known and dependable monetary values, and freedom and security of home and family.

Washington, no less prone than any other capital to shelve those portions of American history which don't read too well because a page here and there has innocent blood on it, can often masquerade as Unctuous Sam and does to an insufferable degree. The trouble with that is that other nations have read how our states became "united" and how

---

result of microwave oven leakage. This is not the same as to say that there were no suits which made such claims, but then, there were also suits to force teaching that the earth is flat! "Radiation" is one of the easiest words to spook laymen. There are so many encounters with degrees of radiation in everyday living, sunlight being one, it can be easily raised to fearsome dimension by being piggybacked on a new or mysterious technology. The microwave oven became a handy, but maligned tool of such spookers.

5. The Foreign Agents Registration Act puts a requirement on individuals or concerns to register with the Department of Justice if performing at request or under direction and control of a foreign principal in any one of the following ways: Engage in political activities for or in the interest of a foreign principal, acts as PR counsel, engages in the transaction of money for that foreign principal or represents the interests of a foreign principal before any U.S. government agency or official. The contract inclusion of the statement that it was not political, nor would the Litton obligation carry with it purely political activities was there to head off the requirement to register. One exception to the need to register under this Act are those engaged in the sale of Israeli bonds.

some shaky moral characters distance in time have been canonized in history books.

Stretched across the 850 sales and service points in 130 countries, Litton conducted its business affairs in economies of less developed, emerging, and on up to affluent nations. In them, what would go and what would not, and how, and what were the entrenched customs in trade not to be whimsically or profitably changed, and what were the forms, rituals and traditions to be observed did not always mesh with the latest fashion on the banks of the Potomac. It was sometimes laughable and even weird abroad.

After Fred W. O'Green became Litton's President and chief Operating Officer, he explained:

"While our Litton Industries policies and procedures apply equally in domestic and foreign operational units, we are very careful about making certain that our foreign activities *nationalize* our guidelines. The national flavor . . . or influence . . . is important because it would be very unwise to expect offshore elements of a firm to be in all ways identical to what we expect in the U.S. Our government seems to have thought otherwise at times and to have thought such similarities absolutely appropriate. They have suffered political bruises because of this."

Litton's leadership from the start valued all those indigenous managements which came with so many of the acquisitions. They brought with them varying degrees of expertise, absolute familiarity with their own national backgrounds as to marketing practices and operational environments, which included local political situations. They had quantities of intuitive poise which goes with being born in certain geography, with being educated in its schools and with comprehension of the facts of day-to-day on-the-scene relationships. Washington will always send generous party givers to winning candidates to posts abroad as Ambassadors, certified as duly acceptable and socially "right" for the kind of trust and reportage expected of them. Neither they nor their inherited staffs abroad are ever as likely to know the trade idiom as well a born-there plant manager insofar as his manufacturing or service sector might be concerned. Litton, as did other companies, preferred its own "horse's mouth" when it came to reading indigenous facts of life—not just because that was the more reliable end of the horse, but because it spoke with the tongue and "body language" of country or province.

The multi-headed Hydra symbolism of Washington became intensely real for Litton Industries at a worst possible moment. The company was ear-high in the corrective actions resulting from faltering in its steady climbing a year before when there was urgency to do something about its typewriter problems.

On February 19, 1969, the House of Representatives Anti-trust Subcommittee sent for Litton as one of six companies[6] to participate in its ". . . investigation of mergers and acquisitions by conglomerate corporations asking it to produce information which would throw light on the legal and economic effects . . ." of ventures by such labeled business organisms. Litton not only agreed to be present, but sent in bags and boxes of materials while readying itself for its days and time before that Congressional body. Then, an arm of that same Congress, the Federal Trade Commission, on April 11th, challenged the acquisition of the German typewriter manufacturer, Triumph-Werke Nuremberg, A.G. and Alderwerke, A.G. (which Litton called its Triumph-Adler division). It was stated to be a violation of the Celler-Kefauver Act having to do with antitrust.

The Litton stance of that moment found it stating that it had made 106 acquisitions through 16 years, 89 of them domestic and 17 abroad. The company was ranked among sales leaders in office calculating machines, manual and electric typewriters, cash registers, power transmission equipment, A.C. electric motors, seismic exploration, store fixtures and refrigeration equipment, medical x-ray devices, and elementary and high school textbooks. It was the second largest builder of commercial and military ships. Litton printed about 90% of all the trading stamps of all companies engaged in that merchandising premium business, as well as postage stamps and government paper for money and securities for 26 countries. It was Western Geophysical

---

6. The six companies asked to appear before the Congressman Emanuel Celler House Subcommittee on Anti-Trust, besides Litton Industries, were International Telephone & Telegraph, Ling-Temco-Vought, Inc., Leasco Data Processing Equipment Corp., National General Corp., and Gulf & Western Industries, Inc. Both ITT and LTV had *court* actions pending, as differentiated from FTC investigations challenging company actions.

which was first in its type of seismic exploration. Ingalls was the shipbuilder.

Svenska Dataregister was second in cash register manufacture. Westrex led in sales of recording equipment and already took pride that some 250 of the nominees in the "best sound" category for Academy Awards had gotten there aided by Westrex technology.

Glen McDaniel put on the submission papers that 80% of Litton's acquisitions had involved companies with annual sales of less than $10,000,000, and that 50% of those had actually done less than $5,000,000. It had mostly fished for minnows which could never get to be whales without the capital and expertise that someone such as Litton Industries could offer. Litton was what Roy Ash liked to call a "structured conglomerate" in contrast to so many which were only "arithmetic conglomerates" or collections of enterprises which had scant if any relationship or central theme.

Congressman Emanuel Celler, who headed that House Subcommittee on Antitrust,[7] licked his chops in anticipation of having Litton before his group. It was almost tailor-made for a keel-hauling during which he could erect an old populist style bugaboo, the fear of bigness. In his script, it now was the death knell for all those wonderful old "mom-and-pop" small business which would be erased from Americana, and artists such as Norman Rockwell would have nothing to paint anymore. He carried in his head the notion of that older America disappearing, its so-called "little people" to be cast into the streets and country roads to wander and beg their way to the poorhouse and adjacent cemetery. It was his kind of a "straw man" and he loved it.

The truth was that Litton had showered benefits and had been almost the only solution in most cases for many small family companies that had elected to join it. Tex Thornton had said over and over, and it was a fact, that Litton had never engaged in raids or forced takeovers and had rarely used debt or debentures. The company had

---

7. Besides Celler, the Antitrust Subcommittee was composed of Peter W. Rodino of New Jersey, Byron G. Rogers of Colorado, Harold W. Donohue of Massachusetts, Jack Brooks of Texas, Don Edwards of California, William M. McCulloch of Ohio, Clark MacGregor of Minnesota, Robert McClory and Tom Railsback of Illinois, Richard H. Poff of Virginia and Edward Hutchinson of Michigan. Litton had something in way of plants and manufacture in every state they represented.

always striven to be the most attractive alternative for all the incomers up against some difficult decision.

Litton was getting more fish to fry than it had pans. It had a big bone in its throat and marshaled its battery of legal tacticians headed by Glen McDaniel. Tex Thornton took them all before the Committee to introduce them himself. Besides McDaniel on that June 4, 1969, there were Ted Craver as the inhouse expert on antitrust; Robert Berry, who besides his considerable understanding of government contract law was the head of the Litton Washington office, and Wallace Adair, who was especially hep on the Federal Trade Commission beat. The bone? McDaniel stated it flatly: "This Triumph-Adler suit has allegations which bring into issue all Litton's past acquisitions and therefore will be covering the same ground that is involved in this investigation."

He was rightfully fearful, he thought, that with FTC being an appendage of the Congress, it could sneak-feed on the Antitrust Subcommittee findings as an additional informational repository. Not kosher in such matters, he maintained stoutly.

Ted Craver, slight and of brooding countenance, was eager and anxious to get into the fray. He was once described by McDaniel as some kind of alloy which derived from the genes which produced a combination of the appearance and character of a General Robert E. Lee in that he never considered any cause lost, and that renegade Valdosta, Georgia dentist, "Doc" Holliday, who turned from pulling teeth to being quick on the draw as a frontier gunfighter. Holliday survived against all contrary odds to die in bed rather than in some saloon brawl. When Bob Lentz had urged McDaniel to hire Craver, he was so high on him he said Craver "could really make water run up hill." In this arena he would have his chance. If Litton was expected to defend itself on both fronts, Celler's Committee and the FTC, McDaniel claimed that Litton was entitled to a fair and impartial hearing at the FTC on the merits of its charged erring, that and no more. Litton already knew the FTC panel was "loaded for bear," particularly when one of the group declared herself as a "registered Republican," but who never voted for a member of that party in her life. An appointee of President Lyndon Johnson, she was known to have a strong antibusiness bias. Her name was Mary Gardiner Jones. It appeared more and more to be a restaging of the shootout at the OK Corral in

Tombstone. Craver was the man assigned the FTC face-off, which meant for this he was in the camp of Harry Gray. Gray, as the head of the Business Systems and Equipment Group, was the one who had brought the Triumph-Adler packet into Litton. Gray, pugnacious as always, wanted it said quickly that it was ludicrous that the acquisition was painted by the FTC as "lessening" competition when it was the one and only "save" move available to Litton. He wanted to go all out.

McDaniel never lost his cool. He set out with soft-voiced, but put-upon manner, to give the Subcommittee and its staff his version of how Washington had been organized under the Constitution with its Executive, Legislative and Judicial branches and the reason why it had been arranged that way. It was his, and the Litton claim, that it should be excused from the conglomerate hearing before the Celler Subcommittee if the FTC inquisition was to proceed. He said the FTC was an instrument of the Congress, funded by it, with its membership approved by that body. He said that FTC Counsel John V. Buffington's letter to the Subcommittee contained "half-truths" when it contended FTC saw no conflict of interest and therefore, no reason why Litton should seek to be excused before the Subcommittee. As lawyers will, McDaniel smelled backroom odors of something cooking in the FTC kitchen, the origins and indications being that FTC was reaching out for far more than knowledge of Triumph-Adler. It wanted an additional conduit to Subcommittee discovery for Litton's history of motivation, its decision making processes, profit and loss records before and after acquisitions, costs and management efficiencies or lack of them. The published findings of the House Subcommittee's sweeping overview could be very helpful to FTC, and perhaps, detrimental, at least bothersome, to Litton. When it was said that two other called-up conglomerates were also engaged in court actions, but would appear anyway, McDaniel pounced on that. The Federal Trade Commission being a Congressional captive, he asserted, could in no way resemble a court action and for it to be assumed so could result in any conclusions from the hearing being repudiated if relief in court was later sought.

"We are losing $6,000,000 every year attempting to compete with a monopoly," McDaniel declared, referring to the IBM[8] hold on the office electric typewriter market. "We are going to use every resource of our company to defeat this foolish case which has been brought by the FTC which promotes monopoly." He added the footnote that Litton had by then a $100,000,000 investment in Triumph-Adler, and it was in jeopardy. It was easy to comprehend why Litton was in this dukes-up, backed into a corner posture ready to do battle. The Subcommittee kept assuring him that it was not hostile and that if Litton was found to be in the clear that everyone on the panel was willing to sign off so stating. There were also non-reassuring pooh-poohing statements that McDaniel's description of Litton's desperate typewriter plight was exaggerated. He reiterated that the FTC action was "foolish."

His fencing was to no avail. Litton had to appear in both places, although the Congressional Subcommittee portion was delayed to March 4, 1970. Net result: Celler's Subcommittee took Litton to its woodshed and spanked it publicly merely for being so good at what it did.[9] Celler wanted to use Litton, the granddaddy and patriarch of the

---

8. The reason pushing Litton toward this last ditched pitched battle was that IBM's chokehold on the electric typewriter field was up in eight years from 62% to more than 80%. Litton was No. 2, that's true, but it was almost an imperceptible splinter in the total, 7.5%. FTC took the position that Litton had sufficient R & D capability to have made its own technology updating rather than taking Triumph-Adler into its barn just when it was rumored interested in trying for the American market on its own. Grundig's own reasons for selling to the Littonites were ignored, it being his wish to lighten his load and concentrate on TV which was more to his liking. Litton reminded FTC that when Royal had been diverted into fuse manufacture in WWII, IBM had been directed to continue as the sole electric typewriter manufacturer. That helped IBM significantly in establishing its leadership in the field.

9. Just how good Litton was at the merger art was shown in two instances—the straight triangular merger, and the reverse triangular merger. The first involved setting up a subsidiary into which was placed a sufficient number of Litton shares to meet the transaction specifications and the sought company was then brought intact into the subsidiary, but retained its corporate entity intact. The reverse triangular tactic called for erecting the subsidiary, allocating it the needed shares, that subsidiary being telescoped into the acquired company. The latter was the ploy used for both American Book and Stouffer Foods. Reason: American Book had contracts with its authors which would otherwise have to be renegotiated in each instance, a cumbersome if not impossible dragging out of the acquisition. Stouffer's had many restaurants and inns which had liquor licenses in various states. Litton outright ownership would have compelled the company to go before all state and local liquor licensing

glamorous go-go conglomerates movement as the basis for his follow-on proposal to charter a whole new government agency to monitor conglomerates. The mythological Hydra was indeed alive and well. But Celler's wish never got off the doodle pad on his desk.[10]

The Federal Trade Commission changed its mind—three and one half years later—and found Litton should be allowed to keep its Triumph-Adler division after all. More than a ton of Litton records had to cross the continent, be selected from and sorted at both ends of the line. There were reports written and presses run. Time consuming and unproductive it was, and the whole affair which McDaniel had labeled as "foolish" going in, and which was restated over and over by Craver, was finally borne out to be exactly that.

It was no isolated instance, though. There were many more. It was revealing just how far the ripples rolled out from such a center of action. The American Embassy in Bonn had to field all kinds of questions about mergers in process or being contemplated which involved German companies coming into other U.S. based firms. The Federal Republic of Germany couldn't understand this kind of role-playing by U.S. agencies, whose goals they thought mischievous. If Litton had given up on the FTC after the Subcommittee seance, its alternatives would have been from the stark to nil—cut the losses, close down, let it impact on the employees in four countries, or fight. Litton fought and won the day. If it had refused to flare its porcupine quills, Triumph-Adler would have fallen back on Max Grundig, sure to have

---

commissions and via individual hearings get renewals. The legal skills of Litton so awed onlookers that at one time there were 15 corporate legal counsels of NYSE-listed companies who had gone through the Glen McDaniel "school for boys."

10. The Cellar Committee report was issued September 1, 1971, more favorable than unfavorable to Litton, which couldn't be said for all the scrutinized and queried companies. It was merely a staff report, the Cellar Committee neither signing nor endorsing it. In such matters, the best one can expect is not to be mentioned. Under headings and chapters which criticized accounting practices, Litton was not mentioned. On subjects concerning insiders and their relationships with other industrial firms and their banks to acquisitions were surveyed, Litton was left out. Overall result was that there was no substantiation or call for major legislation, only a recommendation that greater corporate disclosures be made. The general tone was that some conglomerates were well-managed, and structured to do well in the competitive marketplace. When a Congressional committee cannot be negative, it's said, it can be reluctantly and hesitantly positive. That is the Capital Hill equivalent of a father's blessing given his pregnant daughter at a shotgun wedding.

resulted in international court action. Litton had been busily peering into and adapting its applicable and needed technologies to its own typewriter shortcomings all the while the matter was floating along with the outcome undetermined. The exercise by Ted Craver of ploys and counter ploys was skillful demonstration of foot dragging. It was, nevertheless, destructively costly in delays, annoyances and difficulties in absorption of the needed electrical typewriter upgrading. Strain and distraction and a beadstring of unknowns pervaded Litton's word processing sector. It was pure Washington harassment, a specialty of the house among regulatory agencies. It aroused the Litton resolve to somehow, some way, siphon enough know-how into Royal-Imperial to give it a chance to stand erect and once more breathe in the marketplace.

In the end, though, it changed nothing except for the worse. It excessively hobbled Litton at a time of corporate diagnosis as being on the "critical list." It extended into months and years. It caused the company to struggle with a major problem with one hand trussed tightly behind its back. It cast a shadow, a blanket of uncertainty over every member of its work force. FTC, more than anything else even including the declining share prices, effectively put a block on Litton's long-running major merger and acquisition drive. With Triumph-Adler in, finally, it had solved more than a single conundrum because it got a super executive in Gerd Weers, a German who knew how to lay curative hands on if a cure was possible.[11]

---

11. FTC Hearing Examiner Walter R. Johnson ruled that the Triumph-Adler acquisition "has been pro-competitive." He ordered dismissal of the complaint challenging the acquisition ending a 6-year turmoil and losing Litton critical time in making the most of the German company's technological strength. He said that without Triumph-Adler, Royal could never be a substantial competitor as "every reasonable effort had been made to revitalize Royal. Litton acquired it below book value for $29,000,000 in 1965, made cash advances of more than $26,000,000 and by 1971 had accumulated losses of $37,500,000. All its efforts to develop quality electric typewriters failed." If Triumph-Adler were divested, he said, there was no reason to believe that Royal would ever have had the capability of developing quality electric typewriters. "The record supports the testimony of responsible Litton officials," he concluded, "that if it were to divest Triumph-Adler, serious consideration would have to be given to closing the Royal operation. "As Litton had contended—IBM with 69% of the office typewriter market and 86% of the heavy duty machines, and SCM with 57% of the portable manual and 78% of the electrical portable market—Litton was far to the rear, and the evidence it presented was accepted showing "conclusively

Litton's longest presence on the Washington scene was a brutal, demanding epidemic of corporate aches and pains induced by the two high price contracts with the U.S. Navy. One was initially required to deliver nine LHA (Landing Helicopter Assault) general purpose, amphibious combination mini-aircraft carriers, that could take into their interiors a whole U.S. Marine Corps combat team and equipment to sail off to deter or to do battle anywhere in the world. The other called for 35 super destroyers, DD-963, 30 of them for the U.S. Navy and the others slated to go via the U.S. Navy to the Government of the Shah of Iran.[12] They were called the "Spruance Class," the Navy naming it in honor of the late Admiral Raymond A. Spruance.

It had all been so rhapsodic going in, it was almost as though the legendary Three Rhine Maidens had been booked to help with the seduction ritual. Everyone who had ever furled a sail, pulled on a hauser rope or laid a keel from the most obscure marine relationship to the biggest shipyards came to hear the Navy's presentation about what it had in mind. When the Navy looked over all those familiar and some not-so-familiar names signing in, it decided that some were there for a crumb or two. Others were fit for substantial subcontracts, and a very few could take the whole ball and run with it. The Navy was making noises about breaking with the past to try the new tactic of awarding major series production to one shipbuilding firm rather than spread it around several such facilities. Determining who had proper credentials wasn't hard, but the Navy also wanted shipbuilders with the intestinal fortitude to get into anything so untried and demanding, and who would be the prime contractor.

There was such a magnificence about it when Litton's Ingalls Shipbuilding was selected, so flattering to have this kind of certification and implied faith and confidence, but it was also a trap—it was loaded with all that Washington syndrome. There was the Jekyll of propriety in one quarter and Hydes waiting in crevasses all over the

---

that the acquisition by Litton has not lessened competition nor does it have any probability of lessening competition." FTC had allowed Litton and some 16,000 employees to twist in the wind for a costly and debilitating overlong time.

12. The U.S. Navy was not about to allow Iran to have this Shah-committed five especially built top of the line destroyers go to the de-Royaled Navy. It kept them in the U.S. fleet as the Kidd Class named for the Admiral, but in the fleet it was labeled by jokesters as the "Ayatollah Class."

place, and there was the Janus arm of government playing lip service to Total Package Procurement, but not about to pull the teeth of all the vested interest who would be allowed to intrude.

Litton was the manufacturer. As a producer of items large and small, it had an established record for taking on hard challenges. All such companies tend to see Washington similarly. Indisputably the largest cluster of bureaucracy in this country, this means it has more of what entrenched bureaucracy produces—inertia and obstacles. Anything which menaces the established prerogatives of bureaucracy will discover barriers can be erected faster than an Olympic high hurdler sees popping up ahead of him after he leaves his starting blocks. When Litton won those two contracts, both awarded by the U.S. Navy, this meant it was dealing with the most tradition-minded of all the military services. One of its satraps is its Bureau of Ships. From the time the charter was given by the signers of the American Constitution that mandated U.S. presence on the high seas, BuShip's had everything to say about design and construction of Navy equipment that included providing platforms for weapons, aircraft and rocket launches and the crews to employ them. The LHA TPP contract had gone to Litton, over concerns in several quarters, and ill-concealed hostility in some of old BuShips friends, allies and beneficiaries. Of course, Secretary of Defense Robert S. McNamara had laid down before the admirals that TPP was "in," and to get on with it.

But people like Tex Thornton and Glen McDaniel had done "Washington time." They knew better than to be too sanguine about a directive. They were well aware of how a directive can appear to be conformed to, but how a contractor once committed can be niggled at, endure amputations in contract length, and that requests for "adjustments" or large and medium changes can come in every mail and high level visit. There can be calculated slowness in reaching decisions on key requirements which can make assembly lines tardy. Litton had to build that totally new shipyard to accommodate not only the LHA, the DDs, but also future follow-ons. There were suggestions about that, too.

The trap in the Navy's contract for Litton was the Navy's desire for fixed price with an allowance of 18.4% above that for the ceiling price. If the company reached that ceiling because of its own delays, that was one thing, but if the Navy imposed pace-slackening demands, or there were rising labor and materiel costs, there could be no profit. It was an extension of what John Rubel had set out to get when he was in the Department of Defense and on his crusade to police contractors, and which was now a hazard to the two contracts awarded to his current employer. His hope, as was the case with everyone, was to get a handle on the swelling costs which were getting out of reach.

The Navy's motivation in this was natural. While it wanted everything it could get, it had to face those Congressional Appropriations people who blanched noticeably when they saw the pricing that accompanied the Navy's requests. To go in for approvals citing the lowest possible levels of expenditures with the hope of coaxing up corrective supplemental funds later was more attractive and tolerable than to toss out top figures before commitment to programs.

Litton had been through that one meaningless "win" when it had been the final choice for the Fast Deployment Logistic Ship, when Congress later turned pockets out showing it empty of enthusiasm. The LHA, nine ships in the original order, dwindled to five.[13] This was to be a monsterish quintet, each more than 800 feet long and 20 stories high. The tortured course from keels to commissionings was to make an inevitable couplet which media types so adore—in this case, it was not just the Ingalls Shipbuilding division of Litton, but Litton's "troubled shipyard."

Both houses of Congress had members who shouldered their press release machines to produce and aim volleys and barrages of complaining diatribes and how questionably and how costly Litton was going about it. These were lobbed into the handy racks of the National Press Club, marked *hold for release* for Monday mornings. That being dull news time, it virtually assured longer versions, as hard news is tough to come by on weekends. Wally Knief and later, Bob Knapp, became known for picking these up as qualified messengers to be shot for bringing bad news. Washington in addition to all its other

---

13. Changing one's mind in Navy contract terms can be expensive. When the Navy had Litton Ingalls Shipbuilding contractually committed for nine LHA, then cut back to five, it caused an item of $109,700,000 to appear in the Fiscal Year 1972 Navy budget. It was to cover the contract cutback and was due Litton. Of course, this meant that right at the point where production sought learning curve savings for the last four LHAs, they could never be realized. The five surviving LHAs were the U.S.S. Tarawa, SaiPan, Belleau Wood, Nassau and Peleliu, all serving with the U.S. Marine Corps.

charms includes not only monuments with pigeons to splatter them, but institutions and programs on which the media performs the same function. The capital has more bureaus, more competing columnists, and more commentators in daily search for a story peg or angle than any other seat of government in the world. A news story with the Washington dateline hanging whatever's said on a quotable name, rides out of town as a platoon of Chicken Littles. This is true whether the one quoted knows what he's talking about or not. Competence in the subject matter isn't necessary as long as there's a typist and a source.

But that's the way it is. It's basic Washington to be suspicious that it's being had by the outsider at every turn, and the outsider tends to be just as sure he's being had by Washington. It's a sort of "courtship of Belle Starr" affair, she being that frontier boudoir easy mark who arranged for those who didn't perform well in her bed to die off!

Litton's Ingalls facility ultimately had all the contracted LHAs on its ways. At that point it was into its own money by more than $100,000,000 with prospects of doubling that. When, at the top of this precarious spending ridge with wolves at its heels and what seemed an alkali dry desert before it bereft of potable drinking water, Litton again elected to stand its ground and take on its harriers.

When Fred O'Green came to work on Monday, December 11, 1972[14] the only thing new for him was his office. The title was now President and Chief Operating Officer, but the in-basket was loaded with old and trying situations. He had one big advantage. Roy Ash

---

14. It was a skimmed milk diet that previous Saturday and a whole new world for holders of Litton securities, as it was for the Board of Directors seated in full view. Even the dim light couldn't hide the questioning sea of faces, and everyone had been uncomfortable. In 1971, the earnings had been $50,003,000 and a year later they were down to $1,118,000. When preferred holders were paid, every Litton share was assessed a 14¢ loss. It really didn't do much for those in the audience to hear the company declaring itself to be in sound financial position with a new current ratio of 2.2 with net worth of more than $809,000,000, with cash in hand of $92,000,000 and with unused bank credit of $130,000,000. The Ash departure was a considerable scenery change for them to swallow. Some wondered aloud if his going to Washington would help the company, and would he come back in some role later? On the dais, though, they knew he would not and right then and there—as was the case everywhere else within Litton—Fred O'Green knew he had to take charge, quietly, firmly, reassuringly, and he had done that.

had thought well of and advanced Ralph O'Brien as his candidate to succeed him. O'Green was the Thornton choice. It made a lot of difference when the going was bumpy to know he had been chosen by the staying rather than the departing leadership element. Even so, he felt the swamp waters waist high and rising, and he knew there were alligators in it circling him. He had had about three months of going at a dead run to introduce himself to the "big picture." Not nearly enough, anyone would have said, but he couldn't ask for any more now because he might wish had been overtaken by events. His carefully chosen title—"chief operating officer"—was where he had to show big and company-wide improvement. Management and production had been his main thrust all his professional life, and it was in that quarter that much of the fixing had to take place.

Litton's annual reports, traditionally glowing accounts of how the company had the future by its whiskers, had become a kind of penman's purgatory. How to say it all honestly and not have it feel as though one's fingernails were being pulled one by one with a pair of Inquisition pliers was not a charming prospect. The 1972 version went to press, the final one bearing the Ash signature, as it was known internally that he was on the way to Washington and the Nixon White House. O'Green's elevation had not yet gone public.

Royal Typewriter production had been moved to England's midlands saving $2.40 an hour labor cost, but the transfer had cost more than Ralph O'Brien had estimated and became one of those "one-time special expenses."

Rust Engineering joined the developing outward bound traffic as a Litton sell-off[15] when it went to Wheelabrator-Frye for quick cash in

---

15. It was a rueful Thornton who admitted Litton had gotten into some things that it never should have, but in its breakneck pace it was understandable. The selling off really began in 1970. That October Eureka Specialty Printing, the trading stamp and premium house, went to Danforth Press Ltd. In November, Inter-West Industries, Inc. and All-Ocean Products Holdings, Ltd., bought Litton's Marine Technology, Inc. December saw Rust Engineering disposing of its Painco-Rust to General American de Mexico, S.A. In January, 1971, Litton Business Systems separated out its Automated Business Systems Computer Services which went to Automatic Data Processing, Inc.; International Fisheries & Fishmeal, Ltd. was taken by Marine International Corp.; a portion of Applied Sciences was bought by Sci-Med, Inc. and the Skyphone division went to GTE Sylvania. In 1972, the pace accelerated as well as the size. Marine Consultants and Designers became the property of John Souris, Carlton Tripp and

the amount of $18,000,000, more than Litton had paid in its stock to get it in 1967. The idea had been with all the Hewitt-Robins range of conveyors and those especially sophisticated ones of Alvey-Ferguson (now Litton Unit Handling) that structures to house them could make a single package contract. It just hadn't worked. Buyers didn't think in such overall terms yet. Litton was hurting for more cash and the bankers were having grander ideas of interest every time Joe Casey talked to them. He especially welcomed this infusion. In July, 1972, Rust had waved goodbye, and Dr. Robert L. Roderick, then Litton's East/West trade developer, had to write a so-sorry letter to Vladimir Sushkov, the key negotiator for the Soviet Union's Ministry of Foreign Trade, telling him that the continuing talks for a turnkey fastener plant in his country would have to be under Wheelabrator-Frye auspices rather than Litton.

As Litton's 1973 fiscal year arrived, the aging ore boats of its Wilson Marine division sailed off to American Shipbuilding and George Steinbrenner and Kinsman Marine Transit. All of the Litton electric motor manufacture was lodged at Louis Allis in Milwaukee; the Evansville, Indiana plant that had previously been its address was shuttered. These had been Tylenol-sized headaches for Harry Gray, who at one time or another had asserted Litton was going to make them all work. When he left Litton in September 1971 to pump up ailing United Aircraft, the scope of Fred O'Green's Defense and Space Systems Group had been enlarged by adding Marine Systems. He had been living with Ingalls Shipbuilding, Wilson Marine Transit, and the Litton-built modular construction site for ore boat manufacture for the Great Lakes, Erie Marine, in Erie, Pennsylvania. There was little comfort in being well acquainted with them, he found.

John Suehrstedt in April, and in May, the Environmental Systems product line became a XONICS property. These minor league rehearsals done, Litton sold its stock of Rust Engineering to Wheelabrator-Frye that July. Litton's Power Transmission went to Jeffrey Collins, Inc. in February, 1973, for $16,500,000 and assumption of certain of its liabilities (This was a John Rubel decision, regretted later). In March there was the exit of Stouffer's to Nestlé Alimentana, S.A. for $105,000,000. It was in February, 1975 that Litton Leasing Corp. sold its fleet of 21 containerships to Reynolds Leasing for $23,500,000 cash and a 3½ Convertible debenture worth $6,071,000. There was a political plus in the 1973 April sale of Hewitt-Robins Africa to Envirotech, and that July's marketing of African Aero Service to Kenting Africa Resource Services, Ltd., which took Litton out of South Africa.

Because they had come to Litton almost the same day in 1962 and had always worked together, O'Green sent his trusted trouble-shooter, Grady Warwick, into one of these situations after another. There was first a year on site at Ingalls, where he watch-dogged that criticized 168-acre conventional and nuclear submarine construction portion, and the adjoining, newer 611-acre plant specializing in modular techniques for series production of surface ships. What Grady Warwick saw and reported led to the determination to state neither profit nor loss for Ingalls while the high decibel arguments were going on between Pascagoula, Beverly Hills and Washington. They were about interminable differences over unresolved pricing for the lead contract, the LHA program.

The Washington obligation, or the shipbuilding contract, was sucking money from every quarter of Litton. Frank Slovak who had ushered so many companies into Litton and was flushed by the Rust Engineering sale and its fresh money, didn't ask or tell anyone about the next idea he had. He set off after it quickly, and secretly, too. Stouffer's, which had ended its "family company" character in Cleveland by joining Litton in 1967, had a total of 52 restaurants and ten very attractive motor inns in operation in 1972. It was consistently profitable all of its Litton years and had just rung up $125,000,000 in annual sales.

That was good enough for Slovak. He put a figure up there in his head of $125,000,000 for which he would sell Stouffer's to somebody for cash. He contrived an audience with Marion C. Sadler, vice chairman of American Airlines. "Our Stouffer hotels are in all of American's best stops," Sloval told Sadler, and that it would be both a comfortable and natural ownership for his carrier. When he mentioned $125,000,000 in cash as the necessary lubrication, Sadler's interest cooled noticeably, but as he escorted Slovak to the door he said he would ". . . think about it." Slovak said that if so much as a whisper leaked out about their chat, Litton would deny the whole thing.

As such things will, however, Sadler went golfing that weekend with a relative who just happened to work for Lazard Freres, the investment bankers. Forgetting being sworn to secrecy, he mentioned that it was his belief that Stouffer's was available. The Lazard Freres man was sure that United Airlines would be interested. And when the rumors started darting around, Slovak was aghast. One thing which made him grow white around his gills was that Vernon Stouffer was on the United Airlines board of directors! Another was that he hadn't told anyone at Litton what he was doing. Now he had to, so he hurried to Tex Thornton. There instead of the rebuke he expected, he found enthusiasm for him to press on with his "feelers." Word got to Jim Biggar, the Stouffer son-in-law who had opposed going into Litton in the first place and resented the constant draw on his till to hold up another part of Litton's playpen. Now the Stouffer's president, he wanted to go to banks and raise the money to buy it back. He made some probes, but nothing was going fast enough.

A telephone call came to Tex Thornton from Nestlé Alimentana, S.A., the Vevey, Switzerland chocolate people.[16] Two of the company's toppers, A. Fûerer and Pierre Vogt, were to be in Florida and had set aside three hours in case Thornton could join them. Could he? He could and was on the Litton plane in a finger-snap. They offered $105,000,000 in good, hard currency Swiss francs. In less than three hours, Stouffer's departed its Litton home and was the biggest U.S. face card of Nestle's. Litton had fresh sustenance which it heeded so badly to carry it along while the Washington and Navy argument spaced out inconclusively. Mother Mahala Stouffer's celebrated recipe for Dutch Apple pie had been a substantial factor in keeping Litton afloat.[17] Biggar found himself with more independence than even his

---

16. At one point, Merrill Lynch expressed interest in being the underwriter should Stouffer's be allowed to emerge as its own separate, public company. The initial worth was to be $85,000,000, but Merrill Lynch felt a chill, and backed away to $80,000,000. A further complication was that Nestle's had picked up whiffs of antitrust litigation sure to stalk them, but the team of Robert Lentz and Ted Craver produced an analysis so convincing to Nestle's that even if sued, they would win, they gambled. When Thornton got that $105,000,000, Litton lit up like the proverbial Yuletide tree and his legendary negotiations and sales prowess glowed again. Nestle's did have that antitrust encounter, but as the Litton lawyers had said they would, they won.

17. If Ben Franklin's Poor Richard's Almanac could list as a "maxim" that line "For want of a nail, the shoe was lost, etc.," it is proper here to list Mahala Stouffer's recipe for Dutch Apple Pie: Her homemade crust was by combining flour and salt in a mixing bowl, cut lard into mixture with a pastry blender (or by using two knives) until pieces are the size of large beans. Ingredients: 1 cup, all purpose flour, 1/2 teaspoon salt, 1/3 cup lard for shortening, 2 1/2 to 3 tablespoons ice water. Filling: 4 cups Jonathan, Winesap or McIntosh apples only, peeled, cored and cut into 3/4 inch cubes. 1/8 teaspoon cinnamon. 1 3/4 cups granulated sugar. 1/4 cup all purpose

father-in-law had allowed him. Litton still had its microwave ovens which could cook any firm's frozen foods, not just Stouffer's. The hitherto pale and wan treasury had been fattened internally. That March 6, 1973 day when it was concluded, it went on the Litton books as a most pleasing plus, and with a sigh of relief.

Fred O'Green found himself in quandaries mindful of the fabled "old, bold pilot," the one who said the air above and the runway behind were no help at all. That wasn't quite valid in his case. While he may have had only three months to get ready for the move into the No. 2 post, he had a decade of the Litton runway behind him, and he'd never been blind to its soft spots. He had seen the company waltz around with the analysts when it was Wall Street vogue to shy away from companies with too much military or government contract dependence. Never during his responsibility for the company's defense and space systems, until the shipbuilding, or the marine units had been assigned to him, had it not been a substantial profit producer. Nor had it changed now with James Mellor occupying his old chair. Unlimited runway seemed ahead for all electronic systems and technologies.

His strategy was to take the shipbuilding involvement with him into his new front office by having it report directly to him. This took away that erosion of time and talent from his old Group, and put him where he would be on top of all the D.C. and Pascagoula popoffs. Most of the air above Litton was as rich an arena to apply Litton's product excellence and systems as it had ever been, and he wanted nothing to interfere with that. It had been O'Green's lifetime skill to be a "how-to" expert, a program manager. That had been what had

---

flour. 1/2 teaspoon salt. 3 tablespoons milk. 6 tablespoons coffee cream. Instructions: The added ice water to be mixed lightly with a fork, pastry being moist enough to hold together but not sticky. Chill thoroughly. Roll chilled dough to 1/8 inch thickness and line pie pan, lifting and smoothing to remove air bubbles. Do NOT stretch dough. Flute edges and trim pastry even to pan. Spread cubed apples evenly in pie shell, sprinkle with cinnamon. Mix sugar, flour and salt together, add milk and cream. Beat mixture 8 to 10 minutes at medium speed with electric mixer. Pour evenly over apples. Bake in 375-degree Fahrenheit oven for 1 to 1-1/4 hours. Serve warm. NOTE, said Mrs. Stouffer, "This pie is very juicy. If juice runs over during baking, clean rim and loosen crust while juice is still hot. Use the point of a silver knife wrapped in a clean, wet cloth.

Mrs. Mahala Stouffer not only made a family commercial empire possible with that simple gastronomic pleaser, she helped save Litton Industries after she was dead and gone.

brought him to Litton in the first place. When the Litton board, so frustrated for so long, asked him an operational or production question, he jumped at the chance to explain it. He did so with a special brand of confident eagerness. What he said not only made sense but smelled of the positive and the possible. Now one after another, he found himself in pursuit as a whippet lopes after dog track rabbits, except that he was determined none of his quarry would get away. What had to happen would be genuinely corrective rather than brushed-over solutions. That strategem of having the bilious and sickly report to him directly found Grady Warwick sent here and yonder, searching for whys and wherefores. It was always said of O'Green that he was quick to get to the heart of a problem. At least one of the reasons this was so, he freely admitted, was because he usually had available to him a Grady Warwick assessment.

In the flurries of preoccupations with Washington and its tendrils, one part of the Thornton-O'Green incoming conversations was tabled and almost forgotten, because there was so much activity in the transition. That was the part where Tex Thornton had said that ". . . after a couple of years or so . . ." he wanted to shed his own long standing designation as Chief Executive Officer, give the charter to O'Green, and retain for himself only the Chairman of the Board portion. As the shadows lengthened over all the rearranging and fixing which had to come about quickly, it made sense for each to be exactly where he was, doing precisely what he was doing, constituting the greatest stabilizing factor of all. With his "operational" scepter in hand, O'Green noted that the combination of "downers" in business equipment and systems, shipbuilding, materials handling and electric motors had together accounted for $1.07 of the earnings per share drop in 1971. This was a trend only partially countered by machine tools and professional publishing—which though profitable—were 24¢ off from the previous year. Defense, geophysical exploration, and components were strong. They helped tote the wearier, the lame and the halt.

Tracking the money was an urgency—its sources and quantity were laid out. He made Grady Warwick controller, but absolved him of none of his trouble-shooting housecalls for diagnosis and prescription. That prevailed for a year and the Warwick eyeballs were beginning to be permanently inflamed from those "red eye" all night plane flights. Finally he asked O'Green to put Wayne Grosvenor in the controller function and free him for full time poulticing and bandaging. For months, his wife, Connie, knew she was married to somebody named Warwick, but he was mostly a picture she kept by the telephone to remind her of what he looked like when he called her from somewhere.

In Medical Systems, part of Joe Imirie's Professional Services and Equipment Group, substantial amounts were being spent on product development. In fact, the company was advancing $100,000,000[18] or more in each of its fiscal years on Research and Development to be sure of its future. In Medical Systems, manufacturing improvements and sales were on the way upward in all types of healthcare merchandise, especially in the higher performance X-ray and film processing categories. In spite of Washington's frowns and umbrage in other quarters, Litton's Bionetics Research Laboratories, headed by Dr. James Nance, drew a contract to manage the Fort Detrick, Maryland conversion from its bizarre biological warfare stance into a National Cancer Center. The "monkey business" so scoffed at by detractors who saw high technology only in wonder widgets, had come on line along with all those other space age derivatives. Litton had never given up on its early commitment to the health field which was now beginning to shine more brightly and in unanticipated ways. An opportunity area, Litton was well placed technologically to reach for its many kinds of business development possibilities. As it had been O'Green who had gone after Bionetics originally, he took particular satisfaction in that.

The world's appetite for new sources of metals and minerals in less developed countries, a deep Washington concern since so much of what the U.S. needed to maintain its lifestyle was in short domestic supply, found pilgrimages to Western Geophysical and Aero Service to rattle their doorknockers for audience—and to line up in compacts of one kind or another to roam the earth.

Jim Mellor's defense and space-oriented lieutenants—Joseph Caligiuri at Guidance and Control Systems division and Charles

---

18. "Difficult decade" it was, but Litton never let go of its determination to once more grab the future. The more than $100,000,000 Litton laid out for all research and development annually became a ritual, and in 1977 rose to $140,000,000 and in 1978 to $183,000,000. The tabs were $181,000,000, $211,000,000 and $251,000,000 in 1979, 1980, and 1981, more than a third of that being company sponsored.

"Chuck" Hofflund's Aero Products division in Woodland Hills and John Freitag at Data systems division in Van Nuys, California were gathering in substantial business for both navigation and command and control systems, all jostling for ever larger pieces of real "Pie-in-the-sky." The two most visible programs—the B-1 bomber for military roles and the British-French Concorde (their supersonic commercial transport) both wanted Litton's inertial navigation systems, Litton was known to be hands down favorite for whatever company might become the prime contractor for the cruise missile.

In the Federal Republic of Germany, Dick Hopman's Litton Technische Werke in Freiberg was picked as designer and developer of the central computer for the new Multi-Role Combat Aircraft (MRCA), which was an open-ended invitation to NATO's British-German-Italian joint production of that new weapons system.

Freitag's Data Systems, with Tom O'Donnell, the onetime marine, monitoring it every step of the way, delivered for initial tests a much-desired TACFIRE for the U.S. Army. It was a means of coordinating a firing plan for widely separated artillery units doing in minutes what had required hours and even days in earlier battle situations. DSD's Tom O'Donnell was always close behind sales of I-HAWK and Hercules missile systems offering TSQ-73 Litton-built command and control "missile minders" for battalion headquarters. He, with colleagues Tom Wilmers, and Jim Thomas, had been to Iran where seven of the TSQ-73s, were needed and as long as they were in the neighborhood, they elected a "what the heck" stopover in Saudi Arabia. They thought another three TSQ-73s might be saleable there. They met Prince Khalid, a young captain in the air defense section, son of the Minister of Defense. He was interested in their TSQ-73, and as it turned out—in a great deal more as well. It would take six years and 60 Tom O'Donnell trips to Jedda, but it produced a thriving Litton Data Command division in Agoura, California and transformed the cash-poor Litton of 1973 into a mini-world bank.

Meanwhile, back in Singing River country along the Gulf Coast, the LHAs were lightning rods. The other program, the DDS, or destroyers, was proceeding well. In engineering and early production phases it had come on line as projected and fabrication was indicated to begin a full six months ahead of schedule. Every milestone was being met, but this was obscured by the heckling headlines and hectoring Congressmen who fixed their press release lances and charged. The total work force had grown to about 18,000 with perhaps 1,000 more to be added over the next 12 months. It was the biggest single concentration of Litton employees.[19] While there was some comfort in this, there was little time for taking bows for what was working right.

O'Green and Warwick went to England in 1973 to examine the now desperate plight of Royal-Imperial typewriter production. The Federal Trade Commission's dilatory pressing for the divestiture of Triumph-Adler had assessed its toll. Even with having the move from Hartford in the U.S. completed, and with closures planned for Holland to consolidate everything outside Germany on a United Kingdom base, it was a more than usually dismal "midlands" they saw. Somber and forbidding in the best of times, the labor situation was racially explosive. Three times as many of the employees were Asians as Caucasian. There was a roiling of the waters by their insistence that both Imperial and the Union were guilty of discrimination and bias with such things as job specialties, who got upped in grade and where bonuses went. About 400 of the Asians were threatening to strike, and even though unauthorized, it bedeviled the Leicester plant for three months.

The forecasts for flattening the steep downhill direction of Imperial by a dose of U.S. technological medicine from Royal just hadn't helped. What had been figured to be a loser for two years or so before new vigor would set in became instead a worsening victim of a kind of chronic and incurable malady, mainly because of out-of-date and noncompetitive products. From 1966 when the Litton phase started for Imperial to the time O'Green and Warwick came in for their determination seven years later, it was all down, down, down.

Litton had to take a rap on the treasury jaw of $20,000,000 for the transfer of production from Hartford. In the seven years since the acquisition, it has spent about as much to position it for better market prospects in the British Isles. O'Green and Warwick were now told

---

19. Ingalls became one of the biggest Indian employers in Mississippi. It used Sam Kinsolving, great grandson of the Apache chieftain, Cochise, as its recruiter. He worked 47 reservations west of the Mississippi. Indians had no fear of high work.

that another $7,000,000 or so was needed in the coming year. The once cheaper labor now chorused endless demands for increases in hourly rates. Raw materials were becoming gold-plated in price. Each Royal-Imperial typewriter came off the assembly line double the cost when Litton had first bowed in on the U.K. turf. The Japanese were on the march, too. Their typewriters were not only good merchandise but much less a bite to the buyer, which pushed Royal-Imperial's product into non-saleable shelf life. And while all this was sounding so hollowly, the early flashes for the 1974 fiscal year accurately forecast what became a fact, a Litton company-wide loss of $39,806,000.

O'Green told Ralph O'Brien to get on with his own variety of corporate "body search" to spot what lines he could terminate quickly to hasten the Business Systems and Equipment Group out of all electromechanical and as soon as possible into electronics. He was also told that no matter how painful it might be to the Litton coffers to put aside $77,220,000 in his "grouch bag," or in more polite accountant jargon "in reserve" to cover all the come-uppance in prospect.

The 106,500 Litton employees and its 160,330 shareholders had their own fever chart to watch as the patient worsened, namely the daily NYSE tallies of stock action in the newspapers, or flashing by on brokerages' tapes. The share price stumbled along like a drunken cripple in leg irons. It weakened from 6 to 5, tried for awhile to hold at 4, then sank to the 3s, with fractions. Would it never stop? Litton, which had merged more than a hundred companies, now began to look good as a takeover itself. November of 1974 was being watched as a canary is mesmerized by a snake. November 8, it was—that sorriest day to remember. On one transaction that day on the New York Stock Exchange. Litton shares went from one owner to another for $2! That was the all-time low, the deepest pit by far that the shares had known since going public. Folks who played "penny stocks" found once mighty Litton within reach. Some bought, not big, and a few held for the odd reason that they forgot about owning it. How shattering, how humbling could things get? A Litton security being held because it had become so inconsequential it could slip one's mind!

Then, on January 17, 1975, came another dark day for Litton, Britain, that country's foreign trade, and for 3,000 employees. The word was given that 30 days later, the two plants in Leicester and Hull would close. It will be debated forever, probably, what the six years of uncertainty caused by the FTC in Washington about whether Triumph-Adler would have to go or could stay had to do with this development. It surely didn't help. Nor was it to be orderly and tidy and done in 30 days.

The British Parliament had outsiders (foreigners) to take its lash. Employees had sit-ins in both plants. There was an attempt to keep both Leicester and Hull under some sort of Labour Government support mechanism. In a very short time, their survey team reported back that the market prospects were as limited as Litton contended. Predictably, Peter Grant, the "midlands" representative of the Transport and General Workers Union (TGWU) blustered that the closing was being opposed because it was ". . . against the right of a multinational company to walk away from Britain like this . . . ." By then he had forgotten or found it inconvenient to mention as did the outraged Parliamentarians that Litton had extended the jobs nearly a decade by making its good try as the plants would have closed in 1966 had they not been acquired. At the finish more than twice as many were on the payroll as when Litton had arrived. Every "fix" then known to Man and management had been attempted to make Royal-Imperial survive and prosper, even consolidating in Britain at the expense of jobs in the U.S. and The Netherlands. In the end, no solution had worked. In mid-July, the last lingering "employee" gave up and cleared the premises. He left behind a macabre souvenir in the Hull plant, a coffin adorned with the acronym LITTON. On closer viewing, which the TV cameras obligingly did, it was found to stand for Lost In The Turmoil Of the multi-National.[20]

Yet another Business Systems and Equipment unit had by its geography (Sweden) and its politics (socialist) and its slowness to adapt to the market (going for electronics rather than staying with electromechanicals) had become non-competitive. The Sweda line in the U.S. and elsewhere, as result of its manufacturing in New Jersey, had a chance. It was well beyond cash registers alone and into two generations of Point of Sale systems and stand-alone electronic sales regis-

---

20. Royal was to bring out its last manual typewriter in 1982, and the price gone up to $400—with no takers.

ters. One of the POS types was designed for general merchandise stores and the other, more complicated, to serve a ". . . broad cross-section of retailers in Europe and other international markets." That new stand alone sales register was the very first Sweda electronic product directed at what was considered a huge market made up of smaller retail businesses. Its reception had not only been promising, but was exciting as well. But the so-called "welfare state" demands on the company operations in Sweden were gross in their emphasis on job guarantees for employees without tying their jobs and their durability to production of a competitive product, attractively priced. It was well beyond the Litton free enterprise concept and was an unworthy drag on the already struggling company. Litton effort was concentrated there on how to relieve itself of this growing burden yet preserve the Swedish plants in some form of ownership to continue as much employee security as possible.

The device was to form an independent Swedish firm, Svenska Kasseregisteraktiepologet, which with government funding assistance could become a separate business operated by Ake Johansson and the managerial staff. The first requirement was that it continue to produce electromechanical cash registers for sale wherever there might be an existing market, as well as spare parts for the Svenska Dataregister's present product line in place in many countries. As an aid to all this, Sweda International would buy certain of its POS and related equipment requirements from the new Svenska Kasseregisteraktiebologet for some years. This made possible the sale of the 129,000 square feet of cash register plant in Varberg, Sweden, and it extended the employment of its 300 people under a new banner. In Solna, a Stockholm suburb, the changeover saved the 500 jobs at stake there. Fred O'Green took some sentimental satisfaction in this solution, which served everybody well. His Swedish ancestry showed a little in the Litton promise to continue to market the Svenska Kasseregister-aktiebologet products and parts as ". . . it will be a great advantage to us and our worldwide customers that these products will still carry the quality mark 'Made in Sweden' . . . ." The 17 years of Svenska Dataregister as a Litton division, had ended.[21]

---

21. It had been Glen McDaniel, the one who had conducted the weeks-long negotiations to get Svenska Dataregister in 1959, who was sent in 1975 to Stockholm to deliver the bad news. Litton, he told Ake Johansson and his associates, the head of

Strangely, it was a bureaucrat, one of those procurement maver-
icks, who began to be most listened to on Capitol Hill by Congressmen on the Navy dispute with its shipbuilders. He was an ex-Navy
Captain named Gordon Rule, who had elected on retirement to become a double-dipper and continue as a civil servant. At first, he was
a table pounder about Litton's conduct of its Navy affairs and obligations under its contracts. Then it began to occur to him that the Navy
itself was far from blameless. He was cerebral, crusty, but also fair,
possibly always had been hard to face down or accept compromise.
That made his admiral's broad stripes unlikely. If he had not
kowtowed in uniform, why should he now? He loved the Navy, and
wanted what was best for it and served it well. Because of his frankness and willingness to discuss where the patches were on the Navy's
bellbottoms, he became a kind of Congressional darling. Litton didn't
send him on, but the company was very appreciative of his straight-
forwardness and for his occasional declarations that Litton had some
reasons for standing erect. He helped balance things out.

For more than a year, George Howell, at Ingalls; Herb Fenster, an
outside legal counsel in Washington, and Bob Lentz had been urging
the tactic of stopping all work at Ingalls until the Navy began to pay.
Fred O'Green was most reluctant to resort to this tactic, and continued
to negotiate with the Navy in Washington. It was in the office of the
Secretary of Defense that the Navy attendees stung him with scornful
comment that he should be gone, that he "had no case." At that moment, Fred O'Green changed direction.

Litton decided to go for broke.

First, the Navy was informed that Ingalls wouldn't continue
unpaid.

---

the union, and the banks, had tried to find a new home for their Swedish operations,
but had been unable to do so. Therefore, Litton would have to close the plants unless
another solution could be found. The penalties to close a plant under the social contract were so great, it made sense for Litton to give the employees the plant for $1,
which was far less punitive than the penalties for outright closure would have been.
Through a combination of private financing and government aid, the deal was struck.
McDaniel, talking with a leading banker, asked him why Sweden had ever allowed
itself to be taken so far into the social contract swamp as it had always wanted to stay
competitive with Germany and Holland. He said that ". . . fortunately those countries
are as stupid as we are and are adopting the same social contract abominations."

That meant that all those started but unfinished ships would have no one working on them and the labor force most knowledgeable about LHA expertise would promptly melt away looking for new affiliations with another shipyard. The experience gained in series building which the Navy had bought as a means of scaling down costs over time would be lost, and restart monies would be horrendous and wasteful. The Navy had few enough modern ships at sea as it was. Ingalls was where the most advanced and significant facelift was under way. The haranguing covered everything, including costs, ordered changes, and differences of opinion about the size of the billings. Tex Thornton believed it was neither Litton's nor its shareholding family who should be in effect subsidizing and upgrading the Navy out of their own pockets.[22]

Such legal tiffling is seldom staged in the Washington area. McDaniel was aware by long acquaintance that whoever the Washington or government litigant might be, it seemed to win in the District of Columbia neighborhood. He took the Navy away out of town, starting the Litton action before Judge Cox in the U.S. District Court for the Central District of Mississippi in Jackson. The charge he leveled against the Navy: Breach of contract. The prospect of laying out more than $300,000,000 of Litton's money just to keep going was too much. While Thornton and McDaniel were in this stand-tough frame of mind, Fred O'Green, more market-oriented, was uneasy as to whether it was a good idea to label a customer who was going to be around a long time with "breach of contract." It was only a short hesitation for him, though. He joined in their being repelled by the very thought of the company, in effect, financing the continued betterment of U.S. Navy capabilities. All of them thought the Navy, for all its arrogance, was more than a little to blame for this situation. O'Green signed the notice that work would stop at the Ingalls Shipbuilding division in 30 days. He cited a dozen or so of the most blatant contract violations.

---

22. That charge of financing the U.S. Navy was not just rhetoric. One of the most painful acknowlegements Litton's chief financial officer, Joe Casey, had to note in the 1974 annual report was that our interest costs for the year totaled $68,000,000, a 45% increase over the previous year. Most of this greater expense was due to the prevailing high interest rates on the company's borrowings rather than to the expanded use of credit." Litton was having to carry the Ingalls payroll on its own back, while the Navy dawdled and withheld payments.

McDaniel reasoned that the Navy had too much to lose and would not respond only by using some of its more terrorizing options. He knew they could conceivably order some other shipbuilder to continue the unfinished Litton ships. They could sue Litton for the difference in cost. This could be as much as $1,000,000,000 or more. He counseled himself that the Navy could ill afford many more setbacks. Sending down some "enforcer" in an Admiral's uniform wouldn't make too charming a picture, either. Martial law, yet. He thought they would merely go into court for an injunction requiring that Litton continue the shipbuilding. The fat was in the fire.

'Twas the night before Christmas, December 24, 1975 that something happened. On almost the last trade of that listless day, First National Bank of Chicago as a "nominee" placed a BUY order for 9,100 shares of Litton Industries common. It was picked up for $6,625. It didn't cause any Littonites to go to bed that night with any sparked visions of sugar plums. On the 29th, right on the eve of the New Year, the same buyer came in for 41,000 shares. On January 5, 1976, the pickup was 50,000 shares; on January 7th, 20,000 and January 9th, 10,100. The repetitiveness hung in there in the large numbers. It didn't subside. On March 15th there was a BUY of 196,000 and the price was up to $14.875. Big blocks followed, 195,900 on the 18th and on the 19th, 147,000 shares more.

The "nominee" was then revealed[23] to be a buyer for United Insurance, Argonaut, Trinity Universal and UIC Investments, all of them subsidiaries of Teledyne, Inc. UIC alone by the end of June, 1977, when it made its last purchase, had a total of 3,811,337 common shares of Litton. All these holdings had come to Teledyne under $15.50.

Of course, it was all business. Teledyne's Dr. Henry Singleton was indisputably one of the world's greatest entrepreneurs and wise businessmen. But for those to whom sentiment means something, he to this day remembers that time when funding for one of his first tries to get Litton an inertial navigation system was cancelled. It was a

---

23. The revelation that it was Teledyne as the force behind the nominee was when a large envelope landed on the desk of James Cleaveland, of Shareholder Services at Litton. It contained the 13-D form required by the Securities & Exchange Commission that the true buyer of shares be disclosed when ownership reaches 5% of the outstanding shares of any company.

man named Tex Thornton then who continued to believe in him when nobody needed a vote of confidence more, and Litton could ill afford the money he was draining from its meager treasury. He now, in the stark language of branding Litton a good investment, had expressed his own kind of confidence and had placed a substantial "bet" on Litton Industries. An act of faith is an act of faith. Whoever needs it and gets it when he needs it can be excused if his heart is touched. Tex Thornton's surely was, and his resolve renewed. And sometimes, as in Singleton's case, it could all be done—and the price can be right.[24]

The time came during the Navy controversy when the House Subcommittee on Defense wanted Litton's President O'Green to testify before its committee on appropriations. They set a date, March 23, 1977. Glen McDaniel, plus Ingalls President and former Navy Captain Len Erb with his staffers, George Howell and Archie Dunn, massaged the wordage over and over to be sure it was zeroed to every mark and that it was leak proof. O'Green was to have it all with him on the hearing table when he was sworn in. By that time, he had been over that potholed and stoney road so often, the written statement was merely a reference prop on occasion. He told the Congressmen so. He said he wanted to talk to them directly, look them in their eyes and give them the same privilege as they followed what he was saying.

"Our marine sales last year were $690,000,000, or 20% of our total," he stated. "We have 25,000 employees in our shipyard in Pascagoula. The principal programs there are the LHA and the DDS, plus the submarine overhaul and repair that we do. Our shipyard has expanded in response to the Government's desire to upgrade U.S. shipbuilding capabilities during the period of the 1960s. As of January 1977, our company had a cash investment of $437,000,000 in the shipyard and there are outstanding obligations against it of $166,000,000—that more than $600,000,000 being the principal part of the investment in our corporation."

He continued on. He observed that after all the tumultuous years, Litton now faced a near-term under-utilization of the shipyard. De-

---

24. Litton's 1981 prospectus had the four Teledyne insurance units holding 10,196,258 of the company's common shares, for which the October 1st 2% stock dividend added 203,922 more. This constituted 25.9% of the firm's ownership. The stock had traded in the $55-57 range. When Litton declared its first cash dividend in 1979, more than $2,000,000 had gone to the Teledyne coffers.

cline in the backlog of business was worrisome. He covered how going the Total Package Procurement route had presumably assigned
everything about the ships and their systems to the discretion and responsibility of the contractor. That had been set aside along the way
and such decisions were now the Navy's handiwork. The record of
the shipyard, he declared, was that it had produced ships of quality
and that under TPP Litton would have had a greater degree of control
over its own destiny than it did when the roles had been separated out
into two camps. What was learned on the LHA made the "Spruance
Class" destroyers a smoother program, more satisfactory to both parties to the contract. But, and he said it was a big "but," once the TPP
concept was broken and there could be *directed changes* in the ships'
construction, the paperwork alone required for renegotiations had cost
Litton $20,000,000. He twitted the arrangement which was a sock to
the Litton midriff when it had had to extend $135,000,000 of its cash a
year earlier. To carry on to completion could run as high as
$450,000,000 more.

Congressmen who heard him said the O'Green performance was
impressive.[25] The points he made stuck with them. And with that,
McDaniel's wisdom in taking Litton's court action out of Washington

---

25. O'Green not only had the U.S. Congress on his hands, but a disquieting development abroad—the Bundestag enactment in Germany of the Codetermination Act of
1976. It was a substantial gain for labor unions in the Federal Republic. Speaking at
the winter commencement of Pepperdine University's School of Business and Management on April 16, 1977, he said bluntly: "Perhaps the most serious problem encountered by business in Germany is in the law of codetermination which is now in
effect. It requires membership of a board of directors to consist of an equal number of
representatives from management and from labor unions. A voting standoff is pre-
vented by giving two votes to the chairman of the board, who, at the present time is a
member of management. In event there is an absence from the board's management
team, the chairman is denied his two votes. Discussions took place when this law was
passed that included the possibility that the chairmanship might be rotated between
management and labor under this system the capital investor is dangerously close to
losing control of his investment. The law of codetermination does not stop in Germany. It has been extended to other countries and will become law in those nations as
it moves forward." He concluded by the sobering statement that restrictions that were
imposed prohibit the necessary flexibility required for a free enterprise environment.
Investors in those countries were looking for other places to put their money—the
U.S. highest in their estimation. It was a signal in its way that Litton was looking for
a way to reduce its payroll presence in Germany, but there was no suggestion yet of
its having Volkswagen in its future.

paid off. The Navy went for the injunction. It had no pro-government court on its hands. In the State of Mississippi, Litton was a most visible employer. that Judge Cox ruling was like an Easter sunrise after a long and dark and depressing rainy season. The Judge viewed the tremendous pressure which was on Litton to settle for only 65% of the costs which would have amounted to a mammoth company loss as unconscionable.

He ruled that the U.S. Navy would ante up 91% of those costs, and at once!

McDaniel ran for the nearest pay telephone booth in Jackson to call Thornton.

"I'll never forget how it hit Tex when I told him we had been awarded 91%," McDaniel recalled. "If he could have reached down that phone, I think he would have kissed me."

"This is absolutely wonderful," the long beleaguered Board Chairman kept saying to McDaniel. It was almost as if he had been buried for six months in a cave in coal mine listening for reassuring sounds, but when heard they seemed so far off, help could never come in time. Now the debris was cleared, and he was out in the light. There was no getting him to hang up, he wanted McDaniel to go over it all in minute detail. It was as though he feared if he hung up he would think his ears had played tricks on him.

That 91% payment meant Litton could catch up on all the towering incurred costs. They could begin to realize some of Ingall's profit potential. No work stoppage was necessary anymore to make a point. No time was lost by either of the Navy shipbuilding programs—and best of all, serious pursuit of final settlement could begin. It had dragged on so long, Congress had become embittered about the Navy's tactics and wanted clearer sailing ahead.

As the Jackson court action had been one watershed, in another Congressional act of 1977—the confirmation of a new Secretary of the Navy, Graham Claytor, was another. He was told by the now disenchanted Congress that those outstanding Navy claims involving General Dynamics, Newport News Shipbuilding and Litton's Ingalls had to be solved—now.

McDaniel had known Claytor as a Covington & Burling lawyer with machine tool connections. He had gone to head Southern Railway and make it one of America's five best-run companies. His action was to appoint someone who would work that one particular problem—the dispute with the shipbuilders. He was Edward Hidalgo, out of Columbia University and Holy Cross. Hidalgo and McDaniel had lived in the same dormitory for three years as students. Later Hidalgo's Mexico City law firm had been retained by Litton. He knew the company and its people. Also of importance was that he was a courageous type who couldn't be intimidated by any tin of worms, even if grown to a nest of snakes.

The way it came out made Litton have to take a deep breath, bite its bullet, and sustain a big onetime loss of $333,000,000 in the 1978 fiscal year ($200,000,000 of that was described as a benchmark loss based on the existing estimates of what it would require to complete the contracts. The remaining $133,000,000 represented unrecovered startup expenditures, but with no prejudice to continuing litigation whose purpose ultimately would be to recover all or at least a part of that wrangled over amount).

The Litton Board was convened in Washington. Tex Thornton was still outraged. For Litton to take this kind of financial punishment was a choking sensation to him after all the company had been through. It was the youngest board member then, William Banowsky, Chancellor of the University of Oklahoma, who broke the jam. Pedagogue style, he went to a blackboard and did a comparison of what the other two shipbuilders had to eat which showed Litton had come off very well. And there were allowables here and there, some of the debated charges still open to negotiation and there were recovery provisions in the future.[26]

---

26. The fine print of the agreement said Litton's Ingalls Shipbuilding contracts for the two Navy programs were to be increased $447,000,000, which included an immediate initial cash payment to the company of $97,000,000. These figures meant that the Navy had decided to honor $265,000,000 of the $312,000,000 Litton claimed was due, less $47,000,000 which had previously been paid. And there was allowance for Litton's loss taking to be reduced by as much as 80% of any savings in the estimated tab for completion of the contracts. That $200,000,000 was an "exposure," or a benchmark number. If the loss was to exceed that figure, the first $100,000,000 of such loss would be shared 50/50 by the Navy and Ingalls; if it came out more than $300,000,000, it would all be borne by Litton. If less than the $200,000,000, Litton and the Navy shared 80/20 on money not expended. By this time, the Litton efficiencies learned in the series production node saved so much money, no part of the $200,000,000 loss had to be assessed. It became a dual vindication, for series production contracts and for the Litton management.

526

"Our decision to accept these terms came after a rigorous evaluation proved that the settlement would be in the shareholders' interest," said a relieved Tex Thornton. He reasoned that excessive and protracted litigation and the unpredictability of a 5-to-10-year delay in bringing it all to a final head would be ". . . unproductive of management's time and energy." He also wanted to get that adversary relationship out of Litton's dealing with the Navy. "We welcome an end to nine years of controversy," was the way he put it. "Litton now looks forward to the undistracted use of its advanced shipbuilding capabilities as a key national asset in producing the fleets the Navy needs to maintain the nation's security."

Litton's first nine months in 1978 showed operating profits 30% improved over a year earlier, but he had to say ruefully that this would result in a substantial loss for the full 12 months. It was the last twinge of pain from a long Washington-inflicted ailment, and now it was over. That judgment cleared at last the major dark cloud of uncertainty which had hung over Litton, persisting almost a decade. It was the first bright sky sighted after the tedious, long and brimstone-tinged umbrage which had passed between Litton and Washington's formidable apparatus. All during those perilous ten years it was never possible to state with any credibility what the Litton financial position really was. There was always the caution in the annual reports insofar as shipbuilding was concerned. The Ingalls watchers and accountants refused to book either profits or losses pending the final outcome, whichever way it went. Now it was out there in the open at last.[27]

Litton had, as of September 30, 1977, ten of the 35 ships being built under two programs delivered and in the hands of the U.S. Navy, and 12 more were in the water after having been christened. Nine additional vessels were in some stages of modular production. The

---

27. Booking of neither profit nor loss led to a later Securities and Exchange Commission charge that Litton had improperly held loss information from its shareholders. As its admission would have ". . . substantially reduced Litton's reported net income," so said SEC. The charges filed in the U.S. District Court by SEC said Litton had committed violations of disclosure regulations between 1971 and 1978. When Litton settled, it neither admitted nor denied the charges, but agreed to be guided by the SEC disclosure regulations in the future. The SEC aim was at the bookkeeping relative to the LHA military and the 8-ship commercial contract to build vessels for American Presidents and Farrell Lines. Judge Adrian G. Duplantier, U.S. District Court jurist in Mississippi, eventually dismissed the fraud charges against Litton in January 1983.

last four were in preliminaries of construction. The Navy had lost nothing—not time, not a hard-working partner, nor any of its goal in modernizing the fleet to the extent of those two contracts. The company had gambled with what seemed ever so long ago to have been favorable odds when it engaged in building the country a most up-to-date ship production center. It had continued when it won that first, then unfunded, Fast Deployment Logistic Ship award. It had taken all the long risks, paid all that exorbitant interest on bags of borrowed money as the Navy had gambled nothing while making up its mind at a leisurely pace. It knew all the while that when it did give the GO signal, the Ingalls facility would be there awaiting it. None of those in the Congress who were so critical of the programs when they were initiated by Litton found neither type nor voice to record official utterances to the effect that Litton had done what was expected of it, and more. It had served the national security interest of the United States well.

At sea, where it really mattered, and where our defenses are drawn up, the view of Litton was quite different. Commander George E. Sullivan, skipper of the Litton-built U.S.S. Paul Foster (DD-964) said: "This ship without qualification is the finest surface platform for anti-submarine warfare in the U.S. Navy!" Out there on all those stations lies the final judgment of product quality which takes its perspective from lives being on the line. That's where the whole thing really adds up. It is far from Washington where uniformed crews are sent to bring about an American "presence." At that moment, about 70% of the modern Navy was Litton product.

When Fred O'Green became Litton's President and its Chief Operating Officer and Roy L. Ash left the company to take his high level Washington post, O'Green set his jaw and said: "Our attitude is that we're going to win. We are going to continue to run this company on the basis that we will win."

There were those who thought it was mighty brave talk when he said that. Litton had just been whacked twice—the Federal Trade Commission action to force divestiture of Triumph-Adler, and the Navy's announcement it would pay only $946,000,000 of the LHA's mounting costs, far short of the requirements. But now at the very end of Litton's most difficult decade which was ushered in with 1968, and ended in 1978[28] with the Navy agreement, what he'd said was no small boy's whistling in the night as he passed a country graveyard to screw up his courage. By marshalling all Litton behind him, he'd stated a simple truth.

---

28. There was a media poignancy to Litton's turnaround in 1978. The Chicago Daily News carried the January 3, 1969 headline: "1968's Winners & Losers" wherein its financial editor, Dick Griffin, had written that Tex Thornton's paper loss of $33,832,485.75 on his 1,033,053 common shares made him "the year's biggest loser." The Chicago Daily News closed its doors March 4, 1978 causing 600 people to lose their jobs. It wasn't around to note the difference between short-term losers and longer term survivors. Litton had 94,000 on its payroll with future prospects brighter than ever. As a "media event," it wasn't much, but to that 90,400 it was what leadership is all about. Griffin had a couple of years with FORTUNE's Chicago office, and when last heard of was writing a novel in the mountains near Grand Junction, Colorado.

Book III

The Baton Passes

SPECIAL SITUATION #24

KING OF THE HILL

There was no doubt about it. Litton Industries was right side up, and solidly so, and its upside prospects were improving with every minute.

From 1979, when Tex Thornton first became sure of it, he'd been listening to lots of suggestions and ideas about how the company could plunge on again. He just didn't seem interested — not just yet, anyway. He wanted to catch his breath and savor it for awhile. He was not in any hurry. As long as he lived and was feeling well, he was determined to have an office at Litton to come to and a reason for doing so. Less active, less involved, sure; but Litton had been and still was his life. A monument inseparable from him, he was as married to it as he was to Flora. Litton, that long-held dream realized, had been a tangible built around him. What he was having to wrestle with mentally now was that big adjustment, that he had to accept that it was more important to him than he was to it. He was entertaining the same dilemma he had encountered so often in Litton's building — how to and how much authority and to whom over what period of time to surrender it or, thinking more positively, had off to someone else what fractions of authority. Max Grundig, who had put Grundig Mechanische Fabrik together in Germany, had said he wanted to keep and run the part that would remain after held sold Litton his Triumph-Adler segment. "If I sold it all," he asked, "what would I do then?" From the comfortable Thornton perspective, with a management sense he was holding nothing but face cards in that biggest of trumps — a carefully groomed and trusted successor in Fred O'Green.

The move which he rolled around in his mind was one he'd put off almost too long. It was logical and what he could live with. It was to shed his mantle as chief executive officer while retaining the title of chairman of the board. He could enclose as much or as little within that chairmanship as would please him. He could be sure that he would never be denied the courtesy of a part to play in consultations before major decisions. To bracket the CEO responsibilities with the presidency involving O'Green was a natural move and overdue.

He realized some of the ricochets it would produce. One would be the signal it sent to all the financial analysts and other money managing nabobs who called Litton "skim milk thin in management depth." He'd always insisted that Litton had a wealth of talents to summon into any breach even when it was so young that none had much mileage on him. O'Green had joined Litton in 1962. He'd done everything asked of him anywhere he'd been in the company. None could dub him as an "expert by appointment". Step by step he'd been made into a rounded and tempered top executive. Thornton knew that other companies had tried to get him. O'Green had always been there like a rock, physically strong and pugnacious enough to pile hour on wakeful hour in both advance preparations or in holding the line in negotiations until others around him sagged from sheer exhaustion. O'Green was never a word mincer, nor one of those glib semantics spouters who, as pitchers with fancy windups, threw everything but a hard-to-hit ball. He stated things baldly, exposed, laid open. He isolated problems and gave them high visibility, stating what he thought had to be done. Sometimes he was audacious. He was usually right. They had been a remarkable combination at the Litton pinnacle for nine of O'Green's 19 years. They had occupied offices next door to each other, O'Green, president, chief operating officer, less a No. 2 and more nearly a shared No. 1. They both thought of themselves as a "blue chip" company's leadership even if the financial newsletters and brokerage house assessments hadn't yet conferred that distinction on Litton. Well, no matter — they'd been wrong before.

As the Thornton 67th birthday went by in July, 1980, he was in good spirits, relaxed, but not yet ready to be tagged as an "elder statesman". He was thinking it was right to get on with what he and O'Green had conversed about in terms of timings of other things beyond his elevation to the Presidency. Thornton was sure that the 1981 fiscal year was going to be Litton's biggest and grandest ever. Joe Casey, his financial officer, was often telling him so, volunteering rose-tinted realities instead of having to be sent for to explain some new financial blip forecasting a hair-raiser on the horizon.

The BUY urge for Litton shares hadn't developed quickly, but none of the insiders was disheartened by that. In Litton's 25th anniversary year, the New York Stock Exchange range was from a January 2nd high 14.50, closing at 14.375, and on December 29, 1978, the high was 19.875, Low 1925, Closing at 19.625. The Litton fiscal year ended July 31, and in the next 94 days leading to the actual quarter-century milestone, the company practically exploded with a new out-look turning it away from its low calorie diet in public esteem to smooth sailing on a sea of cream.

"From the outset," Thornton had hand-written on November 30, 1954, "the company's management planned to first establish a profita-ble base of operation."

Not only had that text been fulfilled, but Litton had known both amazingly good days and indescribable discouragements. Two years later the stock had gone to 38.875 going into the New Year's Eve still buoyant. More than a billion in cash was in hand, or as Butcher & Singer, the investment researchers put it, $25 for every share that might be used for a major acquisition." The "Chinese money" time seemed long, long ago when the struggle was for that higher-than-high Price/Earnings ratio to make the stock a currency on its own to barter for other properties. It was fat with real money now.

O'Green was a major factor in that golden glow. If Thornton, as he reasoned it, were to make the move during the final moments of the fiscal year and against all that bountiful and expansive frame of refer-ence, it would parallel so well with the way he was feeling — king of the hill. The magic of his leadership was restored, marveled at and admired once again. What if Litton in his so recent past had been more of a bucking bronco than a rocking chair? He was snug in the saddle now, as much so as if he were on old Prince, his Hidden Valley ranch Tennessee walking horse. He was not quite ready yet, for any porch swing and contemplation of sunsets. He enjoyed his reflections. Who had earned the right to them more than he had? After all, Babe Ruth had struck out 1,330 times during his career. He was fantasti-cally well-remembered for a little more than half that number of hit balls which sailed out of the ballparks.

There were adaptabilities of Litton versatilities all over the place. He'd always contended that there would be a way this would happen when in those first years he'd take either the back of an old envelope or a paper napkin from a table to sketch a T in a circle's center, that T standing for Technology. Then he'd draw lines from various locations on the circle's circumference to other points illustrating how a tech-nology could serve in more than one application, or way, and comple-ment another. Ever since 1977 when Dr. Charles Bridge was made Litton's Chief Scientist, he'd had his aide, Clint Burdick, setting up annual Litton Technology conferences to air such things. It was working better every year.

Ingalls Shipbuilding! Imagine what was happening there? Once the despair of insiders and outsiders and the target for broadsiders, it was now a shining precious stone in the Litton foundation. President Len Erb was in the midst of that promising, long running "Spruance Class" sequel — the CG-47 Class of Aegis Guided Missile Cruisers, and there was a lot more.

The leadoff U.S.S. Ticonderoga barely completed, Erb and his eager minions had scouted up several additional involvements. For one thing, Ingalls had tumbled to the idea that the inside of a steel railway car was not very much different from the interior of a ship's hull. This caused the 55-acre original East Bank works of the shipyard to ease into production of railcars for the North American Car Co., a division of Tiger International.[1] The railcar production line was running two busy shifts and humming along at a 20-cars-a-day pace. This meant that Ingalls' employees were using more steel each fortnight than had been necessary in the building of each of the LHA general-purpose amphibious assault ships.

While Ingalls had once seemed out of the way down *beyond* New Orleans, it had a geographic advantage now. There were few locations in U.S. manufacturing where there was an American advantage over the Japanese, but Ingalls was one of them. When the Gulf of Mexico was sprouting oilrigs and drilling platforms, Ingalls began fabricating them. It was only a short Singing River Channel distance from the shipyard to the emplacements at drill sites. Similar paraphernalia produced in Japan incurred at least $2,000,000 in towing charges to arrive in the same neighborhood. Once one of the most far-fetched and improbable bridgings of all — Western Geophysical, the preeminent seismic explorer, and Ingalls, the shipbuilder — became the most natural of allies when it began to make good sense to mount a system on a barge which was able to convert normally wasted "flaregas", those bright, billowing oilfield throwaways to methanol. As the oil companies marched venturesomely farther and farther out into deeper

---

1. This produced a coincidence of sorts, as on the Tiger International board was William E. McKenna, who had accompanied Thornton that day when they'd talked with Mrs. Ellen Ingalls, and she agreed to sell the shipyard to Litton 20 years before.

waters along the continental shelves in their energy hunts, the oilrigs needed became more complex. Their price ballooned, starting with $25,000,000 as the cost per item. The newer ones ranged upwards beyond $100,000,000.

While this was going on, the U.S. showed signs of turning inward. It was pained by the fact that of the 5,000 ships engaged in hauling dry bulk cargos, or around 80% of the ore, coal, grain and commodities, less than 20 were American bottoms. Most of those should have been in a maritime version of an old sailor's home. Ingalls' president Len Erb was ready for any turn in the road with his procedural "musts", a simple but religiously adhered to 1-2-3 — make schedule, make budget, and deliver a quality product. As far as he was concerned, the Ingalls show had just opened.[2]

A gourmet delight to the Thornton taste buds was the contract Litton's Data Command Systems had drawn from the Government of Saudi Arabia. Came to a sparkling, money-jingling $1,640,000,000, it did. It asked that Litton provide that far-off desert Kingdom with a command, control, and communications system — the requirements for modern air defense of a whole nation. About $585,000,000 of that amount was forked over in advance. That bonanza was now in the Litton barrel and fermenting gaily in one of those jumbo interest accounts begetting more than $70,000,000 each year.

It was the kind of happening Thornton enjoyed thinking about, all those roots in so many unrelated events, or so they had all seemed when they were in the making. There was first that 800,000 miles of Aero Service flown aerial photography in Saudi Arabia between 1949 and 1958. The Middle East got into oil drilling in 1908, a full half century after the U.S. beginnings in Titusville, Pa., so it was way behind. Although Aero Service put friendly aircraft over such places as Jedda, Taix, Dhahran, Dammon and a number of other oil fields, they were foreign and seemed lightning fast to the worried camel and goat herd population gathered around oasis campfires at night.

---

2. In 1982, Ingalls Shipbuilding signed a contract to provide technical services, manufacturing technology and materials procurement for construction of drill rigs with the Peoples Republic of China, the work to be done in China by Chinese. Ingalls had five U.S. companies for which it had delivered six such rigs, the series to continue indefinitely, of its L-780 jack-up types. The PRC agreement, ongoing and open-ended, resulted from two years of negotiations.

Westrex was subcontracted to Commonwealth Services International soon after for maintenance and operation of the communications center at Dhahran airport, which showed how vital such services could be.

But it was that time in 1966, when President Johnson had hosted the Saudi Monarch, King Faisal, on his State Visit to the U.S. that Thornton himself found he was hitched to high drama. New York's Mayor John Lindsay buckled under political pressure and withdrew from participation in any social or other events during the King Faisal days and nights in Gotham where he went to the United Nations and attended to other affairs. Johnson hastened in his old Texas friend, Tex Thornton, asking him to act as surrogate for the President filling in for the lack of official Manhattan graciousness. Thornton hosted a Metropolitan Club luncheon.[3]

Even though King Faisal had passed on, the memories lingered in consonance with a rising sense of Middle East vulnerabilities. When veteran Litton marketer Tom O'Donnell had been on a Data Systems selling mission to Iran, a side trip to Jedda started what became this great money tree. All he'd known then was that in King Faisal's time, his government had contracted with the Raytheon unit in Lexington, Mass., which manufactured the I-HAWK missiles, to engage in site construction including housing, barracks and supplies of incidental equipment. Where HAWKS went, O'Donnell's "missile minders" were usually welcomed. He found that the Saudis warmly remembered Litton all the way back to New York courtesies. Saudi Arabia wanted the means of protecting itself, its people and its oil from the instability seething around it. The talks were immediately and eagerly begun to explore what a Saudi air defense system would require. That was in 1973 when Litton was in a strained and tortured state, the same year the OPEC nations jumped oil prices first in October, then doubled them two months later.

---

3. In foreign affairs events can take odd turns, Litton found. One of the early Middle East helpers at the Metropolitan club luncheon was Saudi Arabian Adnan Khashoggi, tycoon, entrepreneur and big time operator. When divorce action was filed against him seeking a $2,500,000,000 split, his wife Saraya mentioned several corporations in her deposition — one of them Litton. She claimed to have been present when Khashoggi conferred with Thornton and Ash. Case No. 293734 in Los Angeles Superior court with the notorious "palimony" legal paladin, Marvin Mitchelson riding shotgun, was settled out of court in January, 1982.

The LITTON Adventure That Was

Both Thornton and O'Green while dealing with Litton's plentiful vicissitudes often looked over their shoulders hoping that it would all eventually materialize into something important. O'Donnell logged many round trip flights to Jedda, and in April of 1979, all the signatures had gone on the appropriate lines and the contract was in force.

To deal with something of this magnitude, a whole new division was chartered, Data Command Systems, with O'Donnell as president and based in Agoura, California. It read stud heritage to a horse fancier such as Thornton — Data Command Systems out of Data Systems Division out of an early commitment stemming from an after-the-borscht course conversation with George Kosmetsky when Litton was very young. As Thornton thought about it now, it was a fine example of how somebody's idea of bad politics could be someone else's very good business — and that the little things of yesterday could mean a lot tomorrow.[4]

As Litton waded into its second quarter-century, it would hardly go so far as to say that it was trying to prove the aphorism "crime does not pay" wrong, but it was certainly true that in criminal bafflement

---

4. It was such a surging cash flow contrast to other "high joltage" financial considerations Litton had to ride out in the '70s. These had included more than $100,000,000 in a massive international borrowing of Swiss Francs, German Deutschemarks and Dutch Guilders in the early period and that urgent cash sale of Stouffer's for $105,000,000 in 1973, the 1974 nose-to-the-buzz-saw requirement to set aside a reserve of $77,200,000 in anticipation of the Business Systems and Equipment Group obligations, the 1978 settlement of the U.S. Navy's contractual imbroglio calling for the company to take that whopper $333,000,000 loss before taxes, the 1979 Triumph-Adler disposition which was Litton's largest foreign subsidiary. That was also the year when the cash dividend of $1 annually was inaugurated and the stock dividend reduced from 2 1/2 to 2%.

By 1980, momentum was developing highly favorable to Litton. Out of the May, 1979 sell-off of Triumph-Adler to Volkswagen of part of the Litton interest, there was a gain of $42,197,000 ($26,009,000 after taxes), and in January, 1980, the final increment for $21,764,000 ($14,037,000 after taxes), the company immediately moved to repay all it owed in Swiss Francs, half of its indebtedness in Deutschemarks, and most of the Dutch Guilders encumbrances. As the dollar had been much abused, had this payout been necessary in U.S. currency, Litton would have had to pay back almost double what it had borrowed. That offshore money played a significant role in easing the financial pain. The 10-year period had seen Litton make a January 29, 1970 listing on the Frankfurt *Börse* and at the period's end, the company was dealing in 35 foreign exchange areas. The Saudi Arabia agreement stood flagpole high over the rest of money movements.

several Litton divisions found themselves in high cotton. The rising phenomenon of the neighborhood and commercial district marauder and the hoodlum population saw Litton units being asked into this sorry and costly and frightening picture to make electronic and other efforts to reduce dangers to citizenry and property in homes and places of business.

Airtron, back in 1969, had risen to that most glamorous and fabled emergency of all. That was when the insurance company holding the theft policy on Elizabeth Taylor's $1,300,000 plus Cartier diamond given her by Richard Burton had insisted on having a 69.42-carat artificial duplicate made. The real one was the 56th largest diamond in all the world, and one of very few in such size privately owned. Airtron produced the copy, thus bewildering muggers and cat burglars who could never know for sure they would get the real or the false gem. That lowered Burton's insurance coverage premium substantially.[5]

---

5. Saudi King Faisal's brother, Crown Prince Khaled had a heart ailment and came to Cleveland Clinic late in 1971 for a checkup. In February, 1973, he had open heart surgery there which coincided with the O'Donnell odyssey — and set up another unlikely ricochet for Litton. Another brother, Price Sultan, Saudi defense minister, had a son, Capt. Khaled ibn Sultan ibn Abdul-Aziz, who was being carefully prepared to be Director Plans & Projects for Saudi armed forces. At the U.S. Army's Air Defense school at Ft. Bliss, Texas and the Command and General Staff College at Ft. Leavenworth, Kansas, he sensed immediately that all weapons purchases previously made could not effectively operate in the desert kingdom environment without command and control systems, with radar, communications, training schools and logistics support. The size of such a commitment meant higher placed Saudis and Littonites had to meet. Data Systems chief John Freitag and Prince Khaled dined at a restaurant in London. The evening did not go well until Freitag digressed to his favorite sport — shark fishing! No business school teaches such things can be important in international marketing, but in Prince Khaled's consuming curiosity about shark fishing, they finished the evening warmly and left the restaurant, arm in arm.

Thornton got in the action later, throwing a western style party complete with a ten gallon hat for each one in the royal entourage at his Hidden Valley ranch. There was strong protocol advice against such raw doings for the regal, but the Thornton instincts about their desert and horsey origins proved correct. The Saudis had a great time.

Later, on Oct. 3, 1978, now King Khaled (he succeeded Faisal in March, 1975) had six hours open heart surgery at Cleveland Clinic. During his recovery, he was visited by Secretaries of State and Defense, Cyrus Vance and Harold Brown. Quietly at the royal request, Litton's Tex Thornton also came. It was then that the royal blessing was put on the huge contractual commitment. When Thornton congratulated

The LITTON Adventure That Was

Litton had long service in the field of electronic countermeasures for military applications which led to a fattening of the order books because of law enforcement measures dictated by an ever more sophisticated criminal element on the loose.

Poly-Scientific which had been born so obscurely in the small university town of Blacksburg, Virginia, was known mainly as a spawning from a 5-man lab headed by its founder, James Pandapas. The slip rings which were its specialty were mysterious to the townspeople, a product which had to be shipped off somewhere to be useful. Those brush-like rotating electronic connections were integral parts of aircraft, gun turrets and offshore oilrigs. Started the same year as Litton, it was merged into it in 1962. While considered important to the components mix, it was always described as a "nuts and bolts" thing. Under Al Bowman and his marketer, Phillip Reed, it was one of those technologies which never lost its original market and was always adding to it.

It grasped at the opportunity crime gave it, and found itself in a leading position with security alarm systems. Anyone trying to breach a wall, window, gate, fence or door could be detected and easily foiled, and it was nearly impossible for the systems to be tripped into registering false alarms. This had graduated into a whole Security Facilities Management Systems approach, which led to Litton's Energy Control Systems being in it. It was found that financial houses, high rise structures and other complicated enterprises frequently asked for not only crime prevention capabilities but energy monitoring of temperatures. Unless computer-watched, water pipes bursting and other mundane but damaging developments could occur, so Litton could marshal a package appealing to any customer.

Litton's Datalog, later enclosed within the Amecom division, developed *Policefax*. It was an outgrowth of the original technology bought for a song from the New York Times, called Times Facsimile in 1959, hitherto used for photo transmission. Policefax provides the means of instant fingerprint transmission country-wide with the potential of ties to the 40-nation crime fighting cooperative called Interpol. Crack salesman Joe Verusso was sent to haunt federal, state, county

---

him on the educational preparation of the young Saudi captain for his role, the King said much was expected of him.

and city law enforcement agencies. He demonstrated the technique before panels, talked to governors, mayors and police academies. More than 200 such points were convinced by him of the value of this instant accurate identification capability.

Streator, the display and showcase manufacturer, found itself being asked for tough glassed-in doors for the items hitherto out in the open for merchandise presentation. These were thief-proof, providing a barrier against the quick fingered shoplifter or after hours intruder.

Gerald Pokorny's Electron Tube plant in Tempe, Arizona — just north of historic old Tombstone and its OK Corral — lent its expertise in night vision devices for crime detection.[6] This Viet Nam sniper assisting technology was converted into identifying and photographing individuals engaged in crime perpetration in inky darkness. Drug traffickers were apprehended and other law enforcement measures helped.

That favorite Thornton contention that ". . . people are more important than things . . ." had surely been certified to him. He had never known greater riches in management nor had he felt more right in that conviction.

O'Green had never been very impressed with graduates of business schools. He thought they had little more than entry level skills when it came to a company composed of many highly different and specialized entities such as a Litton Industries. He'd never bought the thesis ". . . that if a man's a manager, he can manage anything." The Litton O'Green had had to correct and redirect tended now to be entrusted entirely to the hard rather than to the bubble heads.

---

6. When Don LePore, a young AIRTRON engineer then, had been working with lasers and became enthralled at how atrium Aluminum Garnet (YAG for short) could be grown in a lab and when highly polished would become an artificial diamond, he went first to Sears, then Saks Fifth Avenue. Both cheered him on. Rumors were out in jewelry marts that something was afoot. But it was Cartier's, that elegant stonepile at 52nd and Fifth Avenue, which sold Richard Burton the 56th largest diamond that produced an insurance problem for him. Cartier's preferred to deal through a second party when an "artificial diamond" was needed. On that dreary 40th anniversary of the great stock market crash, October 29, 1969, Cartier's wrote Voucher No. 23125 which asked in long-hand that Saks consider it ". . . Order: I Diamonair, PS — to match exactly the 69.42 ct. Cartier diamond. Confirmation (price), Approx. $3,500. . ." The work of LePore, Roger Belt, Richard Putbach and Joseph J. LoSchaivo had bounced into the big leagues.

The LITTON Adventure That Was

If Thornton had claimed, but not too many believed, that Litton was awash in submerged talents that had only to be bidden to present themselves front and center, there was ample proof now in who was heading and running divisions and from whence they'd come.

Long ago and into folklore was that period when Litton appeared to be hemorrhaging, and the glitter went with the so-called LIDOs (Litton Industries Dropouts), those bright mercurial management meteors who had jumped the fences to much greener grass in new pastures. Several did indeed flourish; some foundered. Now was the time of the LETS (Littonites Electing To Stay). Only occasionally did the company engage an executive search agency to poach other premises and bring in a "savior" from the outside. The stayers had come into their own.

O'Green himself had learned that lesson. Coming behind Dr. William Jacoby at Guidance and Control Systems, he'd brought in three short-term outsiders at Guidance (Allan Grant, Dr. Donal Duncan and Joe Smith), then began to pick from insiders who'd been on the premises: Dr. Harold Bell, Joseph Caliguiri and Roland Peterson. Caliguiri was tapped after Jim Mellor to head the Group when O'Green was Litton president. He told Chris Christofferson once that he'd found "if the man comes from inside, everybody wants him to succeed; if he comes from the outside, nobody cares." Those who were running Litton now had almost to a man been unnoticed when their smaller company had joined Litton — in the lab, maybe an engineer or a marketer, or a program developer. They tended to know what their enterprise did best, what the logical extensions could be, what possibilities were worth probing, and where the promising mail drop boxes were for proposal submissions. Not only were insiders applauded, valuable time was often lost bringing strangers into an acquaintance level while trying to retain momentum. The stayers knew where the potholes and soft spots were and then were more inclined to frankness when asked for remedies. Litton considered it anathema to have on board those who wrote memos by the yard and plans as thick as a best seller. Some thought of themselves as wizards with the balance sheets but were only marginally acquainted with the product and the league in which they were expected to play. In no time they were revealed as false prophets — and even worse, losers. It was one of the enduring legends around Litton that when the business school atmosphere was thick on the corporate shelf, one of the MBAs had casually asked O'Green what his ROGA was (return on gross assets). "What's a ROGA?" O'Green asked. He was a say-what-you-mean type who was always more sure of his business than any of those who buzz-acronymed their way through a conversation.

Thornton was comforted by evidence of the O'Green hand all over Litton.

O'Green had each lame calf cut from the roundup herd. One could watch an animal run that way, and decide whether he could get through the winter, or lag behind to be eaten by the wolves. The big O'Green move early was to make an island of the Business Systems and Equipment Group's parts which were ailing and needed intensive care treatment. He chose to separate the elements which were running well, or had run well once, and his instincts had him believing that they could again.

He had plenty of "old reliables" on which to depend at the top. The dependability bellwether and patriarch of all his "groupies" was indisputably Arnold "Arnie" Kaufman.

He might have bowed his neck stubbornly against coming aboard with the UTRAD in 1956, but he'd grown up and out and thrived on it. He'd even gotten rich from it — and so had Litton for having him where he was. The stable, stay-put people such as Kaufman began to be in evidence midway along the Litton course. He was the kind none had fingered as exciting or even too promising in the GO-GO days. Kaufman had consistently impressed everyone with the quiet way he'd taken components and made every element within it sneeze money. What happened to him became O'Green's annual meeting joke as he was introduced to the shareholders: "He's got the longest title in the company," Fred would say and that was right. The once-cheered Ball State University tight end was carrying on under a wordy designation even the smartest quarterback could hardly have mouthed — Executive Vice President, Components, Industrial Systems, Office Products and Furnishings Group. It was claimed, but not true, that he was the reason none of the titles at Litton were on office doors as there'd never been enough room for his. If one did have a perplexing jurisdictional question, it was considered elementary good sense to walk in on Kaufman for an answer as it might just be one of his activities.

The LITTON Adventure That Was

Both Thornton and O'Green were happy with Kaufman and what he'd done with what he had. He was surely not surrounded with new boys and strangers to the Litton scene. Alex Owen, who came with Clifton Precision and its Servomechanisms, was a 20 year man; Gordon Palmer, a long-timer in unit handling; Charlie Gallagher, once bench mechanic at Airtron now head of Winchester Electronics, had swelled.[7] Phil Lynn, with magnetics after having seen first Litton light as an industrial relations expert in labor law; Jule Vetter, a power transmission production expert and Rolf Klasterer, Kaufman's international marketer who attended to Western Europe and its environs.

Kaufman, in fact, was in a well manned and organized situation — a sort of corporate tree house overlooking a many-sided mini-empire which appeared bigger and better every morning. Even in times when others along the corporate corridor had rocky days and money squeezes, he never seemed to have that problem. Other horizons could be bleak, his were always in the black.

As is usually the case, when one is well organized, he is often assumed not to be overworked. While O'Green was standing all those entities up for scrutiny, he wanted the fixing to be generally shared. Painless for Kaufman, he thought, could be the divesting of the Litton Office Products Centers from the Business Group to him. There was a people angle to it, too. When Harry Gray had been the Components boss, he'd identified a sharp executive ability in Justin Oppenheim while he was with Potentiometer. When Gray went to the Business Group, he thought Oppenheim seemed right for the enfeebled office products centers. After the various hands had been laid on that hoary old "one step shopping" theory about Litton readiness to provide show room access anywhere a potential business office furnisher or outfitter could come for what he needed, and display before him furniture and other pertinencies, Oppenheim had made it work. When Monroe joined in 1958, it had all seemed so logical that this could be a progression from their in-place 350 sales and service locations that had

---

7. Night vision equipment was requested by the Atlanta police investigating the murder of the 28 young blacks. These consisted of camera mounts which were located at several points along the Chattahoochee River into which the bodies had been thrown. Atlanta had been an early buyer of Policefax. The night vision goggles also helped West Phoenix police nab a rapist just before he was set to assault a young woman, and the arrest was made. His potential victim was unharmed.

only to be enlarged. A lot of angles had been used, and a lot of picks had been broken. But Oppenheim had an eye for the right kind of personnel, systems and a plan, and he'd made it thrive. A super-salesman and corner cutter, he'd brought the product line up competitively by hiring Dick Tierney to see to it.

Oppenheim had more than just Litton products in those centers, too. While there was nothing high technology about it, the profit margin was substantial. It spread the reach of Litton as it was originally envisioned. O'Green knew that Kaufman's idea of "smarts" was nothing to do with an IQ, but a healthy respect for the P and refusal to countenance the L as in P&L. In 1974, O'Green splintered Oppenheim and his Centers off to Kaufman. It was a homecoming of sorts. Oppenheim, a components' prodigal son, was the one who had sense enough when coming back into the family to do so rich and getting richer. It was a "love match" insofar as Don Drueger, Kaufman's money man, was concerned. It also gave Kaufman a kind of corporate secret to keep from Thornton who was straight-laced about certain things.

There was more to come. It was almost as though Kaufman was playing tight end again, and the only one in the clear to receive a quarterback's toss.

When John Rubel vacated Litton premises for the bizarre Billy Jack Enterprises, the anti-Establishment film-maker and guru of the acne set, what he left behind was facetiously referred to as Rubel's "Kennel Klub" — all "dogs".[8] Rubel was often one long oral overrun, and when within kissing distance of a dictating machine, could cause

---

8. In addition to the Product Centers, the Oppenheim responsibility included Cole Steel, York, Pa.; Streater Industries in Albert Lea, Minn.; Lehigh-Leopold in Burlington, Iowa and ATAL in Paris and Laon, France. ATAL, with its manufacturing plant in Laon and showrooms all over France, was acquired in 1969 and became second biggest in Common Market office furniture share. The product was good, but it also had the most talked about advertising campaign. Oppenheim always said a furniture manufacturer had the most legitimate excuse to look speculatively and appreciatively at a girl's *derriere* as statistics could prove she had to put it some 74 places a day. Therefore, it was logical for the furniture maker to fabricate whatever would fit the commercial part of the 74 daily accommodations. ATAL's ads always used models in the buff sitting at its desks and on its furniture, filing in its cabinets, or at its credenzas. Oppenheim never claimed to have inspired this campaign, but he never tired of the task of reviewing "Sales strategy studies" as each new season's output was unveiled with naked gamboling nymphs in provocative array among the

memos by the kilometer if in Europe, or by the mile in an English speaking country. He installed droves of accountants. He made so much Holy Writ of a plan, and "meeting plan", he once had a division which started the year with a plan which would come in half a million dollars short — and he awarded a cup to that division because it came closest to plan. He was a graphic example of how executives exceedingly good at one thing can be less so in others. All those old Hewitt-Robins units, and their add-ons, he would have liked to box up and ship off somewhere because solutions to their plights constantly eluded him.

O'Green presented this groggy and reeling contingent to Kaufman. In severe contrast to Rubel, Kaufman wrote sparingly. He signed checks, or jotted down a name of someone who was assigned something to deal with and preferably would come in or phone him when it was satisfactorily done. He would settle for the figures of a division handwritten on a single sheet of paper, as long as it squared with the truth. In his uncomplicated mind, he reasoned that all the divisions had been good once and had even amassed respectable international reputations. If they could start with that, and were turned around, it wouldn't be the first time that better backroom preparations to compete by a knowledgeable handler had taken a "dog" to a blue ribbon. One thing for sure, he had to get them out of their back alley of despond where they were when given to him.

Kaufman quickly beckoned for cob-rough Alex Owen at Clifton Precision. He was given a "medicine man" type of charter to go among and sort over the prostrate and the "walking wounded". His recommendation after investigation immediately gave O'Green and Kaufman some grounds for optimism. Owen, for one thing, fed on grim situations and they made his adrenaline jump. Out of all the head bumping and boisterousness he'd known, he'd emerged the victor and was a profit producer. He hadn't found it too much trouble in the tussle and tumble. He could even will himself ear-plugs during harangues, concentrating on what he was doing while appearing to be listening and paying attention. When Kaufman tagged Owen so precipitously to run a thorough check on the materials handling business, there was no other person who seemed to possess credentials as

---

merchandise of ATAL. He talked a lot about visibility, and with ATAL he surely got it!

exact as he did to bring about a revival. At least, behind him was the 1974 action ceasing the struggle for that ancient Hewitt Rubber Company the elder Robins had bought. Loss of slightly more than $29,000,000 had to be taken before taxes. The aim was to get that sure and chronic loser shorn away to allow focus on elements for which the prospects were more favorable.

Owen found that superstructure had been encouraged to grow like jungle vines do in the vicinity of an elephant manure pile. They in turn were populated by layers of people who generated paper for each other to read. It was 180-degrees from the infant Litton which had hated memos with passion. With Hewitt-Robins and Litton Unit Handling, the shop and marketing effort appeared to have been placed far back to make room for something similar to that curse of academia — "publish or perish". Owen sent his trusted and capable Poly-scientific's Al Bowman on tour to give his new possessions a careful once-over, and out of that fact finding a whole new face began to show. Accountants and MBAs went out, and new heads were appointed. It was like the old Czarist times' admonition for dealing with a backward Army recruited from peasantry: "Never change orders to a guard. Change the guard!"

Kaufman and Owen both liked the product planner at Litton Unit Handling. He'd been one of those "out back" since 1966 when he'd come in as a new hire by Jayne Spain, and had grown as one of the old Alvey-Ferguson stalwarts. He'd observed the series of floundering directions, front office fascination with balance sheets and disregard of the product, personnel reduction and other acts of desperation which restricted effectiveness and how it had all depressed moral and marketplace respect. He was Gordon Palmer.

Kaufman and Owen ticked off what they called their ABCs of managing by their yardsticks. They didn't call it ROGA as the MBAs did, but SG&A — sales, general and administrative expenses. "Get that down under 14%," Owen told Palmer. "When you've figured costs, raise your price." They were betting on Palmer for the excellent reason that he knew the technology and the market for it, and he appreciated the "people factor" relationship to proficiency and product excellence. These repairs introduced, the newly skeletonized accounting department would be assured substantial improvement in the figures they toted up. Where people had been jumped about as checkers on a board, Palmer was expected to get them back into areas for which they were best suited and could again achieve quality workmanship.

In the waning hours of that hard 1973, Gordon Palmer took over a somewhat bedraggled Litton Unit Handling in the Industrial Park of Florence, Kentucky. It was one of the first major management change bets OK'd by Fred O'Green as Litton's president, and it was a good one. Probably most startling about it was that customers who had been turned off by price cutting they considered too drastic were now reassured when they were charged more as long as the product merited it, and it did. In the 15 years Jayne Spain ran the place it had always been profitable. Kaufman considered that in the hands of knowledgeable direction it could be true again.

Immediately all that trade talk of automated warehouses and benefits which could be introduced by storage and retrieval technology[9] started drawing Litton Unit Handling 7 and 8 digit contracts ranging all the way from major post offices to an Israeli Air Force supply depot outside Tel Aviv, from Sara Lee baked goods inventories to a meat and vegetable cold storage facility in County Cork in Ireland.

Endless possibilities surfaced including subcontract ties to major firms going into the People's Republic of China. This unit carried Gordon Palmer to its presidency and his election as corporate vice president. It was back to basics: By focus on product priced correctly, profits followed naturally. One of the "dogs" had escaped its grubby alley, was cocky and well fed again, drew deserved respectful attention and could bark with the best of them.

Owen, once he'd turned Palmer loose on his problem, became equally attentive to the Hewitt-Robins "inheritance". He used that old "visibility" technique again. He didn't like the interlocking and wanted each element to stand alone to be studied for its ability to survive on its own merits. Viewing each performance singly, he fer-

---

9. Under Rubel, the units assigned him dropped from about $100,000,000 as an annual sales pace to $80,000,000 by the time he departed. He urged the sale of Hewitt-Robins Power Transmission division, including Electra Motors. Frank Slovak protested but was overruled, whereupon it went to Jeffrey Gallon, Inc. It netted about $16,500,000, but it was like removal of a key finger from the H-R hand. It went out of H-R in late January, 1973, shortly before Rubel left — and was considered by him an achievement. That view was not widely shared in the corrective aftermath.

reted out overhead and unnecessary staff, reduced paper flow, concentrated on marketing efforts. Each of them began to turn for the better. Owen acted as though he were a tree pruner as he sought to reinvigorate roots — production — while cutting back dead branches — overhead.

In doing this it was not just new broom and sweep it out. He also identified some comers, one of them a young Patrick Forster. He'd started at the corporate pinnacle in advance planning, but sensed he needed line experience if he were to ever to bloom fully. Forster had elected Hewitt-Robins; there he caught Owen's attention when he was cauterizing some of the open wounds. Owen put Forster over Hewitt-Robins Conveyor Equipment in Passaic, N.J. It was the manufacturer of the conveyor idler that still had its key initial patent, as well as mine and bulk conveyors and their parts. Owen told him the place had just shipped $12,000,000 in sales, and netted $151,000, which he wanted improved. The next year the action was up 30%, and Forster was on his way. He became a corporate subgroup head four years later.

John Cernek was mounted on Robins Engineers and Constructors in nearby Totowa, N.J. He placed Litton's mark widely and in many unexpected places.[10] Spencer Latham, with the Hewitt Robins Vibrating & Crushing Equipment plant in Columbia, S.C. was surely Litton's best example of going for new but never abandoning an old market — some of his manufactured equipment was used in Santo Domingo mining which had been started originally by Columbus on his third voyage to the Americas in 1500 A.D.!

Owen called all this Industrial Systems, which is how that got added to Kaufman's Group title. It read almost like a Wall Street law firm when he counted off his dependables — Oppenheim, Vetter, Palmer, Owen, Gallagher, Klasterer, Lynn. They all relished the

---

10. Not only did Litton Unit Handling Systems come back, it bought land from the Ford Motor Company near Hebron, Kentucky to build a 285,000 square foot materials handling center. With that early 1983 announcement, Fred O'Green said: "We see Litton UHS as a leader in meeting the industrial productivity challenge with our turnkey automated storage and retrieval systems. We're investing $15,000,000 in this new center in addition to a $6,000,000 expansion completed last September at Florence, Kentucky." Considering what happened to the U.S. economy then, all this and the promise of 300 added jobs was not bad reading. In making that announcement, O'Green also noted that Gordon Palmer had a ". . .background of more than 20 years in materials handling management posts."

Kaufman-provided atmosphere and its freedom to run as long as Don Kruger had his palm properly crossed with silver as promised at each quarter's end. As Thornton and O'Green assessed Kaufman he was exactly opposite that renowned and roistering musician, Bix Beiderbecke. When Bix died, someone asked what he'd died of and was told: "He died of everything!" Kaufman had learned to live with everything Litton threw him — and very well, too.

When the shipbuilding log-jam had finally been blown, it receded in memory as time went by. Although it had been concluded during the faltering Presidency of Jimmy Carter when defense appropriations were skimpy, stretched out and decisions delayed, the Reagan White House placed Litton in a quite different perspective. One appraiser said Litton was ". . . strongly positioned as a beneficiary of the Reagan commitment to increase military preparedness." The validation given this reasoning was Litton's lead in navigational and control systems, as well as its being a builder of destroyers, cruisers, submarines and amphibious ships for the Navy. The electronic aptitudes of Litton had always been in military, space and related activities domestically and abroad. It had been true in the Group during the time of George Scharffenberger, of O'Green, of Jim Mellon and still was with Joe Caligiuri running it. Caligiuri had a certain advantage — he'd come from another navigational camp, Sperry, back in 1969 when he showed up at Litton's Guidance and Control Systems division as its VP for engineering. When Mellor left the Group throne room to be No. 2 to Roy Ash and president of AM International, Caligiuri replaced him. For all those years it had been Defense and Space Systems, then had Marine Systems added. Finally its scope and possibilities were more extended than those specific words implied. Caligiuri transitioned it into a newer, more encompassing, flexible and explanatory body of capabilities he chose to call Advanced Electronic Systems Group. If Arnie Kaufman had a collection of management "solids", so had he.

There in his old office at Guidance and Control was Roland Peterson, who'd gone through the Sperry navigational action first as he had, before signing in with Litton as a major project engineer in 1960. Peterson and Bob Lentz, the corporate counsel, were about the only ones at Litton who could sing the Brooklyn Polytechnical song, but theirs had been one ladder rung after another of advancement, which meant they had time to pause and learn on the way up. Peterson had hosted a special ceremony in mid-April of 1979 when the AN/ASN-130 system was presented to McDonnell for fitting into the U.S. Navy F-18 Hornet combat tactical aircraft. That was no ho-hum business as usual day as that was the 15,000th inertial navigation system, and there were some eyes damp at the corners when he said that ". . . much has happened since Litton delivered the first system for operational use in 1957. "J. Ray Donahue was there both days, and being an Irishman, it got to him a little. All four of the U.S. military services, several NATO and Allied air forces and more than 100 of the world's airlines that had grown fully within the company." Navy Captain G.W. Lenox added the clincher: "We can't do without it. We're striving for an aircraft that is more accurate and has better overall weapons delivery than anything we have today." He wasn't there, but Donahue remembered with affection that lone Air Force Col. Gordon Graham who had given inertial navigation a whole new reason for serious consideration — the role it could perform in more accurate weapons delivery. Long lookers, as they're called, are so seldom remembered when they're right, but once in awhile it happens. It's only fair, but also infrequent, and Litton's Thornton and O'Green could vouch for that.

Aero Products, a spring off Guidance and Control and worn like a bouquet from its first divisional status day by Charles "Chuck" Hofflund, was still in his hands and bustling. Hardly anywhere in the world was there an airline pilot who didn't have, or didn't wish he had a Litton commercial inertial system on board. It saved time, required less fuel expenditure, and shortened routes.

Caligiuri had beefed up Amecom division by giving it Datalog which strengthened the Litton expertise in electronic warfare, radio communications systems, ultra high speed digital printers and facsimile equipment. Who was running it? Charles Fink, that's who. He had been there with a small, 5-man engineering research group in the lab of old Maryland Electronics manufacturing when a young Turk named Thornton had come by to shake hands with all the employees when the place was acquired in 1956. There had been some misfits and not-quite-up-to-it leaders for Amecom over the intervening years, but Charlie Fink kept moving upward until he was ensconced at the decisional hub. It was under him that the commercial side of the enterprise flourished like a well watered greenhouse plant.

Charles Holmquist, who had left the U.S. Air Force in 1957 for Data Systems division where he was first assigned work on an Airborne Tactical Data Systems which could be in a Constellation aircraft, had a manager's head on him. He helmed Mellonics with its space and other ties. When sent for to come in behind a departing John Freitag at Data Systems, he left Mellonics to Dick Baker who had a fair hunk of Litton time on him, too.

Ron Keating, at Litton Systems (Canada) Ltd., was in the counting house when Litton made its first move in position itself outside the country with manufacturing facilities — and he was still there.

Offshore, Richard "Dick" Hopman seemed almost to be a part of the woodwork at Litton Technische Werke (LITEF) in Freiburg im Breisgau in West Germany. He easily held the house record for an American heading a Litton action abroad, the only one who made what appeared to be a life's work of it. His German was so flawless, he was thought to be one. There were not many such commercial chameleons of his kind who melted so completely into a culture and tongue.

In Hamburg, C. Plath continued its world renowned status as a marine navigation instrument maker bossed for more than a decade by Dr. Norbert Klieman.

It was only at Litton-Italia, s.P.a., LITAL, in Pomezia, that Caliguiri had a new but able Marcello Corradetti. A quality technologist, he was also a sophisticate on the Roman scene of constantly shifting political sands. Ministerial portfolios changed hands as often as the in-and-quick-out Governments.

Demand continued for inertial and other systems. Litton was recognized as the best at producing them not only for aircraft and missiles, but also ships, torpedoes and even vehicle-mounted, land-based weapons systems. What had won for Litton first — miniaturization of its devices to fit them into smaller and smaller spaces — still enhanced its attractiveness. Litton had become the primary supplier of air defense and interceptor control apparatus whether for artillery fire coordination, close air support, platoon level and short range air defense making it almost able to duplicate the claim of an old country auctioneer whose calling card reminded that there was ". . . no job too large or too small."

In 1981, Litton had no need to be backward, nor reluctant to say it was ". . . one of the largest defense electronics contractors in the U.S." This was a historic business commitment. It was also a necessity for a nation's military preparedness. It had been a constant growth area even before the firm was formed. Litton was in a different America, a far cry from the '60s and '70s when activists roamed the land and political position takers deluged Litton with mail about refusing to buy Litton products ". . . unless Litton ceased to manufacture weapons." The Litton answer then was that it had started out responding to declared defense needs, would continue to do so, and if any holder was uncomfortable with his investment, Litton recommended that ". . . the shares be sold." Now the Caliguiri clan could be everybody's best selection for a cruise missile guidance system. A more realistic generation, sensing the reason for a stronger America as well as its allies, saw in Litton technologies the means to address such honesty.

Overseers of the destinies of the Litton machine, cutting and specialty tools group were among the least surprising when it came to lasting retention. Those who made commitments tended to be non-wavering about the trade as a place of employment. Most grew to maturity in families already at work in some phase of the industry. Around dining tables they heard tales of their fathers' jobs, and were fed into this lasting career orientation almost by osmosis. This was true at the lower skill levels and all the way to the top. Veteran Burnell Gustafson could lay down his day-to-day supervision, as he did in August 1981 with nary a worry about what he'd worked so hard to tie together, and how expertly it would run after him.

The Gustafson replacement was Nathaniel "Bud" Howe, who had the attitude if not the inclination of a professional basketball player. He'd gotten his first check from New Britain in 1946, almost the same day Tex Thornton had been shown his new office on the 16th floor, or "mahogany row", of the Ford Motor Company. Considering how much executive geography hopping and restlessness was common in the post-World War II era, Litton machine toolers were really stick-in-the-muds. "Bud" Howe was only one of the many such examples —

and one thing about them all, they had made Litton machine tool family compile a profit margin record not equaled anywhere in the trade.[11]

The mini-conglomerate that constituted the Joe Imirie preserve was in the hands of the lone recruit from the Pentagon E-Ring who adapted, contributed and developed into a long-timer. His was a heavily diversified collection which rode under the description of Professional Services and Equipment Group. It might be hard to explain in terms of relationships, but never in income. It had a way with treasure, plumbing inaccessible regions of the earth for hard-to-come-by resources in energy and minerals. It strolled improbable paths technologically and realized unexpected bonanza potentials. If ever there was a corporate benign leader, Imirie exemplified it best. Diminutive in stature, he was always at ease with those who thought about and did big things. Even when he was being critical of shortcomings, he smiled a lot at one of those who needed prompt correction without being unpleasant about it. Having walked among Washington's politicians as much as he had before Litton, he had picked up some of their arts of persuasion and was a near miracle worker in terms of the revered "bottom line". Everyone along the executive row might be taller than he, but he didn't mind having to stand on a stool to reach the rising direction of his premises as he drew graphs at plan meetings. Geophysical exploration, medical electronics, educational publishing, microwave cooking products, frozen foods, restaurants and inns, paper products with all their coated and electronics-added derivatives, and medical research laboratories were all his at one time or another.

One of the best executive performers in geophysical matters joined Henry Salvatori in Western Geophysical just as Tex Thornton was landing his $1,260-a year civil service job in Washington in 1936. Out of Kingston, Oklahoma, Booth Strange was an honor graduate of the University of Oklahoma School of Engineering. Salvatori made him his supervisor of seismograph operations. He became Western's president in 1965 after it had been in Litton five years and Salvatori wanted to be off and about his own personal interests. (He especially

---

11. Data Systems Division was headed in order by Dr. George Kosmetsky, Jack Connolly, Gordon Murphy, James Mellor, Dr. Nicholas Begovich, John Freitag — then Charles "Chuck" Holmquist.

enjoyed being a skilled and energetic fund-raiser for political campaigns.)

Booth Strange was found by world history and Litton to be in precisely the right spot, with abundant experience and expertise, when in 1973 the OPEC cartel jumped oil prices. If there was to be a last holdout for the "loose rein" Litton management philosophy, it had been preserved by Imirie for this geophysical, or Resources Group part of the company. The Imirie "holding" of this sterling strange sector was next to imperceptible, because it worked that way better than it could have otherwise. This included not only the huge Western Geophysical, the recognized foremost seismic explorer in all the world, but also Aero Service, Litton Resources Systems, and Litton Energy Systems.

Booth Strange had worked in all its management positions, moving from supervision of all seismic operations to vice president and director status in 1950, a full 10 years before Salvatori decided Western Geophysical could have a grander future with Litton. Strange was important enough in Western's affairs by then — he was one of the six who had to be compensated in the Litton buy. Under Strange, the Resources group was a gushing coin shower into the Litton treasury, more than 35 times greater than at the time of its Litton entry. Now that there was urgency to get the U.S. more self-sufficient, all those previously considered marginal, or cost prohibitive areas were deserving of further look. The panorama of opportunities for contracts both at home and abroad were numberless. None was more at home among the petroleum potentates than Strange and the man he'd picked to step into the presidency behind him, Howard Dingman. Seasoning has always been a careful requirement in the energy field. Strange had 46 years on him, and Dingman, his junior by 12 years, had 34, not Johnnies-come-lately to the exploration scene in either case.

The Imirie cluster was first called the Industrial Group, but Ash hadn't cottoned to that. It became the Professional Group because it either made high technology technical products for professionals or it rendered a professional service. Because the annual reports seldom gave their accounting tallies by executive pigeon-holes, it never really mattered as long as there was a corporate executive who could respond at question time.

Boxes, and lines drawn linking them to the biggest box at the top, had always been worrisome to Thornton. It annoyed him if he even thought somebody might have a schematic hidden in his desk. He operated somewhat on the Eisenhower scale, the General having once said: "None can ever chart a personal relationship." Thornton often likened his crown princes to pastured blooded horses. "Thorough-breds are born to race," he would tell interviewers. "It's the same with people, something inborn." Where such temperamental steeds were fenced didn't matter as long as they felt free, and were massaged and hayed. Performance did.

Imirie managed to do well most of the time except in some fields which were cyclical. The whole of what Imirie had was in the low group in sales in 1973 when the energy crunch came, $371,745,000. As the hunger for new energy sources surged, so did what Strange had to offer. By 1981 earth resources activities almost doubled that number.

Dr. James Nance and his staff had made great strides with the Litton Bionetics Research Laboratories. What's more, he'd shifted it from almost total dependence on government contracting. It grew as a pre-introduction checkpoint for new consumer products by providing a test center to determine whether any new entries were carcinogen-prone. He also had the medical research and products operation, including not only Bionetics, but also the Hellige division in Freiburg im Breisgau in West Germany, and its American extension in Elk Grove, Illinois.

Litton was able to describe itself as a major presence in bio-medical research, laboratory products and testing. It served pharmaceutical, chemical, food and health care agencies of the U.S. government. Since 1972, it had managed the National Cancer Institute's Frederick Maryland Cancer Research facility. It had become a showplace frequently toured and inspected by other nations. The Hellige contributions to patient monitoring, diagnostic and testing systems were recognized as world class.

John Grado's Specialty Paper, Printing and Forms in the U.S., Canada, Mexico, Switzerland and Belgium tended to run copycat alongside the economy; when booming, it boomed, and when stalled, it slowed, too. It was the cyclical part of Imirie's house.

Wayne Bledsoe's Litton Microwave Cooking Products, which had done so much to bring the glamour and utility of new technology into the kitchen, had also led to about 40 different manufacturers who offered customers a jillion models from which to choose. Having done so much to establish the microwave as a household servant, Litton now saw consumers lured to other brands and bargains. Bledsoe often felt as had the late General George Custer when overwhelmed by Little Bighorn ethnics whose numbers were greater than expected in the neighborhood. Litton was still in the big three, but its market share was down a bit. Thornton had never been happy with that other Imirie extension, Litton Educational Publishing, even though the magazine part of it was a gold mine. Originally, the educational direction had seemed to forecast the higher technology of teaching machines, and that hadn't worked. With the O'Green urge to be a more readily identifiable high technology company, that sell-off had made everyone feel better.

Grady Warwick, the veteran warhorse of so many challenges charged into dark places on the Litton landscape, was finally allowed to climb down and tie his horse to a manger — he was given what was left of the Business Systems and Equipment Group. At least now he didn't have the typewriter burden any longer. A lot of print was being given to how the old American names in typewriter manufacturing were all gone as if to some elephant graveyard. Only Smith Corona had survived. What a mighty fight Litton had made of it technologically as inventor of the portable electric and the cartridge ribbon, but it was having competitive troubles with the Japanese. He was glad to be out of that one, and even Volkswagen, who'd bought Triumph-Adler, was making unhappy noises.

He had Robert Kane, a Monroe hand since he'd started in the Pittsburgh office in 1948.[12] Monroe Systems for Business was in full stride with two microcomputers for office use, a Japanese plain paper copier of top-of-the-market quality wearing the Monroe brand, and ultra low-priced lines of business calculators in profusion. The Monroe sales force was the focus and the old reliable once more, still

---

12. Of all the different actions reporting to Joe Imirie, the Resources Group had become so huge as a profit producer, decision was made to bring it up to the corporate group level with Booth Strange as the Senior Vice President and overall executive.

with the Monroe pride and still formidable against any competition encountered in the field. It was brave enough to forecast it would double the sales in the next few years.

The slowness with which Svenska Dataregister had approached electronics by staying overlong with electromechanicals in its Sweda line had given National Cash Register time to recover. NCR was now sticking out its tongue at the U.S. Sweda line, which had to be changed.

Even Westrex, so long the film studios sturdy dependable for quality sound-on-film, had seen its leadership dissipated, but Warwick had that making competitive noises again.

From the top, Thornton was more than pleased with O'Green's handiwork. With the world economy as uncertain as it was, most of the corporate horror stories had shifted to the doors of those who had watched Litton's miseries in the recent past. But how right Litton was for the "now" world in which it found itself! If industries had to retool, and most of them did, Litton had the means to help them do that. If new energy sources were desired, and they were, Litton had expertise to ferret them out. If health care, no matter how managed, was to continue to be a concern, Litton had some of the needed key capabilities. If America and her allies were going to have stronger defenses, the salient ingredients to upgrade the security requirements were in high numbers and qualities within Litton. Over and over, the former nettle patch was now a bed of roses.

There was one simple statistic floating around that had its roots in the Thornton-pencilled first annual report text in 1954 when he referred to the "plan" as aiming to ". . . establish strong proprietary product values and a broad base on which to grow." In mid-1981, Litton owned 5,213 U.S. and foreign patents. Nobody had ever placed an inventory price tag on them as they were "negotiable", or could be when licensing agreements were made. They were usually complicated, and specialized. Each in its own time could be vital to progress itself. The Litton breakdown included 2,087 in the U.S., with 232 applications pending, and 1,982 foreign, with 911 applications pending.

There was an underscoring of the startup Thornton wisdom in having to participate in military contracting to gain benefits of such technological advances from which there could be adaptations useful for the consuming public as well. These included cancer research and a range of medical products, and the jump from electronic warfare to crime fighting gadgetry.

Being right is heady stuff. It's even more pleasant when the people and the leadership who pulled it off are there when it happens. Of the compensations and rewards that men and women dream of and seek, having taken a correct course that wins against all odds is the highest return. To see it on those faces only multiplies the satisfaction and assurance needed to take on the future. Of the nearly 50,000 Litton employees who were eligible to take part in the company's stock purchase plan, more than 12,000 were in the action as Litton's fiscal Year 1981 closed. They'd seen everything happen, but they were the LETS.

SPECIAL SITUATION #25

THE ANCHOR MAN

Saul Cooper, of Los Angeles, bought his first shares of Litton common on June 23, 1969.

He had added to them. He'd suffered the long downswing in share price. In 1980, in the Beverly Hills High School auditorium where the company annual meeting was held, he liked everything he was hearing. Good tidings were pouring out like water from a boot about Litton's position and prospects. He didn't like what he was seeing, though.

Something bothered him, and he fidgeted. Finally, he waved his hand in the air. Dick Thiel approached him with one of the mobile hand microphones when the Chairman recognized him. If the Chairman had known what he was going to say, perhaps he would have ignored his raised hand and looked somewhere else.

"Mr. Chairman," Cooper said hesitantly. "I don't know how to put this because it's personal. This is said from a good, serious heart. I have been a shareholder for many years . . . am beginning to do well. I would like to see your stewardship go on so I will do better. Now, this is the personal part of it. I have been observing that one of our key men has been a chain smoker." The big auditorium stilled noticeably.

Cooper cleared his throat and went on. "Inasmuch as I am selfish in this respect, I think a little control on the intake—because the person I am alluding to is eating them—will be for the benefit of the corporation and for everybody and particularly for him who I would like to see here for many years to come."

There was strong applause when he finished and sat down. Joe Imirie and Bob Lentz on the lower dais, and at the podium, Tex Thornton, self-consciously stubbed out their cigarettes. Thornton said that while he was "touched by the remarks—we have great depth in the management of Litton Industries and I don't think anyone is indispensable."

None knew it then, but Saul Cooper had inadvertently put his words and phrased them in such a way that everyone in the audience would remember that moment and would say later that he or she "was there that day." The stopwatch was being held on Tex Thornton. He had but 11½ months to live. It was his last annual get-together with the shareholders. Fred W. O'Green sitting beside him was about to be the leadership inheritor. In all the ways he had dreamed that it would come to him and he had hoped it would, he would have given everything he had rather than have it passed to him from the founder's dying hands. Saul Cooper, more perceptive than all the rest, sensed the biggest event of all rushing toward Litton Industries—the finale of an epoch signaled by the demise of the company's visionary, spiritual and actual leader from its Day No. 1.

Anyone who had ever been in the Thornton office during those hassling Navy contract and FTC-harassing years recalled a stack of cigarette butts in his ashtray by mid-morning. And a pyramid of them by the time he left in the evening. He consumed a lot of them, no doubt about that, and especially in tense times when the pressure was on. He tried to kid himself he was cutting down by only puffing each one to the half-way point, but he always lit another. The executive dining room had his brand available just in case he left the pack he was working on back on his desk when he came to lunch. Willie Hardy, his long-time chauffeur, was sometimes rebuked if Thornton ran out along the way and there was no replenishment in the glove compartment. Willie in his unperturbed manner occasionally lectured him about his habit.

While none expected his curtain was to be drawn so quickly, it was understandable because there were so many distractions.

It was Joe Imirie who was on the corporate mind then. He was talking about relieving himself of some of the day-to-day chores anyway. O'Green had been streamlining the company for months, getting it more on that high technology plane. He wanted to pull back from the incredibly deep involvements he'd known during those nine chief operating officer years. He saw the group heads as able to take more responsibilities. It fit his mode of operating that they do so. As he and Thornton talked of ways of accommodating Imirie's wishes, O'Green began having misgivings about something else he saw.

In Litton's 1981 final quarter incredible developments were taking place behind Litton's outer facade. It involved not only Joe Imirie, a group head, but Tex Thornton, the chairman. In May, both became ill. The spotlight was on the planning about Imirie, as none suspected how serious the Thornton plight was.

560

The LITTON Adventure That Was

The Litton Educational Publishing portion was gone.[1] What Imirie had left could be parceled to other group leaders, and he could get on with what he had to do. He'd been around long enough so he'd earned the right to call some shots, pick and choose what should be left to him to do, as little or as much as he wished. This resulted in a kind of "homecoming" ritual, activities coming back into orbits they'd long since departed.

Dr. James Nance, whose sweep included healthcare also embraced scads of electronic technology; it had constant engagements in government contracting. The greatest concentration within Litton of that expertise in a marketing sense was surely in Joe Caligiuri's Advanced Electronic Systems. When O'Green had been at Guidance and Control, he had gotten well acquainted with Fritz Hellige and its spin-off, Litton Technische Werke in Germany. That had been the door opener for inertial navigation manufacture, overhaul, and repair in the Federal Republic.

O'Green as the group head had gone after and shepherded into Litton the Bionetics, Research Labs, so there was a familiarity in the Caligiuri camp which would be helpful in the assimilation. It had been 21 years since Hellige had joined Litton. While it had helped other electronics things to happen in its neighborhood, it had stayed directionally true to being a top flight electronic medical systems health care house. Dr. Johann Schaeder, who'd been with Hellige nearly three decades, had retired in 1973, and had been followed by Wolfgang E. Schaer. Schaer had never allowed the respect for Hellige in medical products to abate. It was considered a prime source for medical electronics systems in Sweden, France, Italy, Austria and The Netherlands. American awareness of its product line for research labs, clinics, hospitals and doctor's offices was growing. That was one Imirie element take away and it was put in Caligiuri's good hands.

---

1. International Thomson Organization, Ltd. of Toronto and London, acquired Litton's entire Educational Publishing collection in March, 1981, including the Medical Economics division, Van Nostrand-Reinhold, D. Van Nostrand, Delmar, American Book Co., McCormick-Mathers and all related U.S. and foreign subsidiaries. It was a Litton gain of $9,438,000. Consolidated sales for the three years previous were in the $82,635,000 (1979), $89,328,000 (1980), and $60,903,000 (first 8 months of 1981) range.

Arnie Kaufman's components kit contained Litton's ancestral root, Electron Tube, that first of all the acquisitions which had been bursting with microwave technology. Out of it all those years ago had marched Dr. Norman Moore with his tail afire about how the magnetron could be harnessed to a bright new wagon—the microwave oven. It was history now, but the success that grew on the slip of an idea had been one of Litton's bigger internal growth stories. If there would be a natural home for Litton Microwave Cooking Products as Imirie let it go, where better for it to come to rest than with Kaufman? The microwave oven was one of Component Group's most illustrious progeny that had made an impressive commercial product with consumer appear and had ". . .changed the way America cooks." It provided one of those rare times in advertising when the slogan had been arrived at after the fact. Raytheon's Amana, Tappan, and Litton shared the pioneering credit. Litton had become the one to watch as it went after a major share of annual microwave oven sales. In all that bush-beating for customers and price cutting, those best able to survive the feuding and extend product penetration always included the Litton brand. There was even talk that with a chip or two added, the small screen fronting each oven could be converted into a TV image supplier so the cook with so little to do in way of food preparation could kill time with her favorite soap or news program.

Paper was another returning to the original hearthside. It had been one of those extensions Fred Sullivan believed necessary for the Business Systems and Equipment sector. Paper could go so many ways in commerce. One could start with the traditional stationery, order books, forms and checks and run all the way up through sophisticated coated and electronically treated versions. Even transfers of printed patterns to cloth were possible, some of it almost magical. It was a bit upsy-downsy in the beginning until John Grado and his staffers worked on what had been mostly theory.

One of them, John Holman, had come with McBee. He had the subgroups called Litton Business Forms that embraced Kimball Systems, Sturgis-Newport, McBee in the U.S. and Canada, plus Litton Security Graphics which was the umbrella over check printing and

Kimball M & M, the credit card manufacturer.[2] McBee did its manufacturing in Ogden Utah; Damascus, Virginia and Athens, Ohio.

Grado's group was labeled Specialty Paper, Printing and Forms,
and apart from the Holman-assigned areas, he had Fitchburg and
Decotone in the U.S. and Belgium, Papeterie de Versoix in Switzerland, and the onetime sugar cane stalk converters to bagasse, Valentine in Louisiana, plus Carolina Gravure in South Carolina.

The O'Green decision was to relieve Imirie by presenting these
operations to Grady Warwick. He was now the main man for what
Litton called its Business Machines and Retail Information Systems.

All these moves freed Joe Imirie to give himself full time to his
doctors. It gave O'Green an opportunity to fasten more of the managing on the group heads and himself more maneuver room which he
needed. He had been in that mode of ". . .when in trouble, report
directly to O'Green" for so long now that he could do with less of that.
He was generous with time for them all to work out how each of the
absorptions was to take place. Everyone knew O'Green had something going on next door which was momentous in its implications.

Tex Thornton was making up his mind fast that he must take
himself out of the corporate picture.

There were rumors, and some apprehensive wonderment first.
There was no doubt something serious was afoot when he wrote a
letter to the Board of Directors that for the first time since there had
been a Litton Industries he would not be able to attend the scheduled
meeting on July 16, 1981 at Litton Systems (Canada), Ltd., in
Rexdale, Ontario.

At the time O'Green convened that body, Thornton was in Houston where he was given extensive tests at the M.D. Anderson Clinic.[3]

---

2. In February, 1982, Litton's check printing capability—those old names such
as Ritter-Ardes, Checkmaster, and checkprinting aspect of what was once Eureka/
Carlisle, along with the security and credit card manufacturer, Kimball M & M—all
went to Canadian Consolidated Graphics Limited of Toronto for $6,500,000. The
plan was to add it to their U.S. subsidiary, Interchecks, Inc.

3. The M.D. Anderson Hospital and Tumor Institute, established in wake of legislation in 1941, was a gift in the memory of that prominent Texas cotton-broker,
Monroe Dunaway Anderson. It is part of the University of Texas System Cancer
Center. The Center serves as the official state agency for care of Texans with cancer,
for training and research in cancer and for activities related to prevention of the
disease.

It was determined there that cancer that had started in one lung had metastasized to his shoulder. Prospects were not reassuring. It was a stunning and somber Thornton household to which he returned. He determined to move quickly at the crest of Litton's biggest year. He announced on August 4th that O'Green on October 1st would become President and Chief Executive Officer, with Thornton to retain the Board Chairmanship as long as he lived.

It was a long reach through time from that day at Lehman Brothers in New York when their lawyer, Ray Rusmisel, wouldn't allow Thornton to go out of their One William Street front door with those two checks for $1,465,000 until he had written that "If I die" letter. At that time there was concern if this new company was anywhere but locked up in the Thornton head, or if it could be carried out without some written blueprint if Fate were to incapacity him after their backing money was committed.

Now, with a simple press release, the O'Green succession was made official, the founder's blessing conferred. The way ahead for O'Green was cleared for him to exploit all the opportunities he identified as conceptual bedfellows. Lehman Brothers might have been unsure initially, but no such thoughts bedeviled Thornton about O'Green. With that press release Thornton slipped off the last bridle and O'Green was free to run.[4]

Thornton was not through with his focus on the future. If he could be vulnerable so totally and so unexpectedly, so could O'Green. Almost in the next breath, he began talking privately with O'Green and McDaniel. Once the O'Green elevation had been dealt with, Thornton charged O'Green with making up his mind who he should have in that office next to him, who in turn would be shaped as his successor. There were several names they sorted over, but the two most often discussed were James R. Mellor and Dr. Orion L. "Orie" Hoch. They were both favorites, though momentarily "off the Litton reservation", so to speak.

---

4. Attending the last Thornton-chaired board of directors meeting were William S. Banowsky, Wallace W. Booth, Ransom Cook, M.A. Hollengreen, Glen McDaniel, Don G. Mitchell, Fred W. O'Green, George T. Scharffenberger, Jayne B. Spain, Dr. Norman Topping, and James O. Wright. Advisory directors I. Edward Lundy and Arjay Miller were also there.

Mellor was at AM International. The crystal ball on that future was clouding fast.

Hoch had taken off like a comet and achieved success first with Advanced Memory Systems in Sunnyvale, California, to which he had added Intersil, Inc., called that whole semiconductor enterprise Intersil, Inc. He took them from a stumbling state into a formidable competitor among the Silicon Valley habitues. General Electric had just bought them for cash the previous February.[5]

In either case, no critic could say Litton had to "go outside the company". Both had been at Litton longer than anywhere else in their professional lives. Little by little, the Hoch candidacy began to cast the longer shadow. O'Green knew Mellor was highly regarded by General Dynamics, but even so, he came to feel more firmly that Hoch was his man.

For several years, because of the multiplicity of O'Green operational decisions and executive choices, there was no reason for this

---

5. In February, 1981, for $235,000,000 giant GE bought Intersil, Inc., made by canny "Orie" Hoch's combination of two wobbly semiconductor concerns. GE was so excited about what it had done, it included Hoch in its presentation before the New York Financial Analysts at the Hotel Pierre on April 2nd. Executive VP James A. Baker told them that GE sensed it had "missed the boat in microelectronics especially productivity and energy-related products using microelectronics—that we would truly become an aging wonderboy of the electromechanical age." Whatever it all was as a catch-up and enhancement of GE's already major position in integrated circuit manufacture worldwide, it was a monumental tribute to Dr. Orion Hoch.

In six years, he had taken the rickety enterprises to 4,000 employees, sales bounding upward 25% per year. The half billion sales mark was not far off. It caused quite a ripple among all the Litton flock as they took a kind of ricocheting pride in how one of their own, tempered in those 17 upsy-downsy Litton years, was running in a kind of parallel. Litton's third quarter showed the way ahead so promising that the cash dividend was raised from 30¢ to 35¢. The quarterly report used such words as "record operating performance" to describe it. There were some at Litton who said that GE had read up on Litton's old acquisition formula because the GE buy of Intersil, Inc. tied Hoch into the package as a GE division president for a year, and some months beyond that as a consultant.

It was at the Litton board meeting in December, 1981, that O'Green first surfaced before that body the name of Hoch as his choice to be his successor as President and Chief Operating Officer of Litton Industries when Hoch's last shackles to GE were to be severed on June 3, 1982. And that was the way it happened. The public announcement was made after a Board familiarization meeting at Winchester Electronics, April 19, 1982. It was the kind of story often used across town in the movie studios.

turn of events to signal any big changes. The company's position overall was in remarkably good health. Both Thornton and O'Green were always prone to mention with pride the numbers of scientists and physicists Litton employed. While Tex saw them as the fabricators of Litton's outreach for applicable products to meet all those futures challenges lying in wait, O'Green actually liked to rattle around in the labs and discuss with them about how they were attacking each situation. Hoch was of the same cut of cloth, having been in research as his first job. There was no direction that chitchat or shoptalk could lead where O'Green couldn't hang a Litton involvement of some kind on it. He was up on artificial diamonds, cancerous monkeys as research aids, where the Litton-constructed 2-man submersible ALVIN might be engaged in exploration of some deep oceanic floor, the long trail of frustrations from a component sent in quest of a microwave over application, especially tailored computers, night vision goggles originally designed for the battlefield and their myriad possibilities for public use by those with eye trouble as well as for apprehending of criminals, machine tooled robots for manufacturing, and if there was a scale of one to ten to show where O'Green stood in terms of the clutch his job held for him, he would have been an easy 11. Thornton had been used to having people around him all his life who had some of the tendencies he saw distilled within O'Green. He'd never known a single individual as deeply and totally wrapped up in the scope of his job as this new CEO.

By the time of O'Green's actual assumption of the chief executive officer promotion, it was obvious that another responsibility was going to descend upon him quickly—much more rapidly than anyone would have imagined when that date had been selected. The Thornton health was in steep decline, and just before midnight on November 24, 1981, he died.[6]

---

6. The day the Thornton funeral cortege converged on Arlington, the U.S. Navy dispositions around the world spoke eloquently of what he'd meant to a nation's security. Ingalls-built, all, the DD-963 (Spruance) was operating out of Guantanamo, Cuba; and out of Pearl Harbor DD-948 (Norton), SSN-682 (Tunny); in the Pacific, DD-964 (Forster) DD-976 (Merrill); in the Western Pacific, LSD-33 (Alamo), LSD-35 (Monticello), DD-683 (Parche), SSN-647 (Pogy); off the U.S. West Coast, DD-965 (Hewitt), DD-967 (Elliot), DD-971 (Ray), DD-973 (Young), DD-984 (Leftwich), DD-985 (Cushing), DD-986 (Hill), DDG-33 (Parsons), SSN-680 (Bates) SSN-596 (Barb), SSN-607 (Dace), SSN-261 (Haddock), SSN-590 (Sculpin), SSN-581 (Blueback); in

The LITTON Adventure That Was

On December 11, 1981 Litton's Board of Directors elected Fred O'Green to the additional office of chairman of the board. The fear expressed by shareholder Saul Cooper at the last annual meeting had been prophetic.[7]

In the first quarterly statement for Fiscal Year 1982, the baptismal one for O'Green to sign alone, he said: "From the very beginning, Tex Thornton planned on developing a major industrial company built on a cornerstone of high technology. Litton has grown from a tiny electron tube company to the dynamic Litton Industries of today—a worldwide organization of 77,000 employees strong with an annual sales rate in excess of $5,000,000,000. Tex Thornton's dedication to making Litton a major high technology company led directly to his unfailing commitment to research and development. He believed in technological leadership and imbued in Litton's management team a drive to develop a constant stream of new products which placed the company in preeminent positions in many strong and growing markets. New products for new markets and new products to replace older ones in markets already served, became a well-known Thornton philosophy."

Then he shifted the attention gently to the positive, the future, that place Thornton had always tried to target, and he did it with remarkable accuracy. He had been with him when he had made his toughest decision, the one to take himself out of the lineup as the game he had played so long was not his to join any longer.

---

the Atlantic, DD-969 (Peterson) DD-970 (Caron), DD-974 (Comte de Grasse), DD-977 (Briscoe) DD-987 (O'Bannon, DD-980 (Moosbrugger), DD-983 (Rodgers) LSD-32 (Spiegel Grove), LSD-34 (Hermitage); out of Subic Bay, in the Philippine Islands, DD-972 (Oldendorf, DD-975 (O'Brien), SSN-652 (Puffer); in the Caribbean, DD-978 (Stump), DD-98 (Hancock), DD-982 (Nicholson), DD-968 (Radford) in the Persian Gulf, DD-979 (Connolly); in the Mediterranean, SSN-592 (Snook); in the Indian Ocean, SSN-639 (Tautog) and off Cockburn Sound, Australia, SSN-648 (Aspro). None of the shipyard's critics came to the Thornton funeral—they thought they'd buried him years before. They'd written him and Litton off too soon.

7. When Tex Thornton died, the Litton shareholder family stood at 107,336. Common shares were held by 98,337, 1,854 still had not converted their preference securities and 256 of the Series A $3. The $2 B preferred was in the hands of 6,839. The records showed 10,629 having the common, 1,029 with the preference, 35 with series A and 48 with Series B were "lost holders". Some of those were the buyers who had picked up a few shares when the stock was in the pits.

"We in Litton will miss Tex Thornton—both as a leader and a man," O'Green stated. "He left us a great business legacy in place: We have the resources, the people and the confidence to build in the future the company that he set out to create 28 years ago. If institutions can be monuments, then the strength of this company and its world-wide leadership stand as a reflection of his vision."

He opened the 1981 annual meeting on December 12th with a statement in the same vein telling them that Thornton had left behind him ". . .a company of great strength . . . great capability, made up of the people of Litton Industries. We fully understand his objectives and goals and we're confident that we have the ability to extend Litton on the course that he so clearly stated and so well established."

And with this, the new leadership got down to the business just as Tex Thornton would have wanted.

Litton may well have once been considered the ultimate conglomerate but O'Green's instincts drove him toward a pronounced emphasis on high technology and a strengthening of that perspective for the company.[8] Many of the businesses which had gone out the Litton door in the "tidying up" during O'Green's tenure were now with more sympathetic company environments, where their continuance under the Litton banner could only have limited or no-growth prospects at best. Now, in their departure, the Litton step had been lightened and strides lengthened.

O'Green told the shareholders not necessarily to expect big mergers, but perhaps small ones which were going in the technological directions that by Litton diagnosis were promising. No more barnacles

---

8. The original Thornton belief that to be a high technology company, Litton had to be in military contracting was born out in the 1981 annual meeting in a way which was a more dramatic tribute than what was said about him personally. Arthur Bronson, a representative of the Retinitis Pigmentosa International, saluted Gerald Pokorny and his staff at Electron Tube in Tempe, Arizona for a derivative of their military nigh vision goggles. A commercial version, he said, was very helpful to sufferers of degenerative eye disease which afflicts about 400,000 people. Immediately after the meeting, with Los Angeles Mayor Tom Bradley in attendance and Screen Star Charlton Heston as presenter, a set was given to a 12-year old Georgia boy, Todd Cantrell. He had recently returned from a fruitless emergency trip to the Soviet Union for corrective treatment. This propelled the Litton Tempe plant into international prominence, and was one more bit of evidence about how right—and visionary—Thornton had been. Through the Litton goggles, Todd Cantrell told Bronson he had seen the stars at night for the first time.

on the Litton body, but rather smooth splices into its weave is the way O'Green pictured it. The very last Litton quote attributed to Thornton in the year-end financial statement had him as steadfast at the end as he had been at the start when he stated: ". . .continuing investments at increasing rates in research and development of new proprietary products along with plant expansion and modernization for increased productivity provide the basis for my confidence in continued growth of Litton."

O'Green had given the formal and deserved tribute to Litton's founder, but the rest of what he said would have counted most with Thornton. He ticked off leadership examples in various markets and over comparable industrial competitors—ability to reach 30,000 feet down in seismographic support of oil drilling at such depths, laser gyros appropriate to the cruise missile navigational needs, the Spruance Class destroyers[9] coming back at around $15,000,000 each for overhaul and repair as well as new and big follow on ship construction programs where Litton was best positioned and most capable for such contracting, and that the company's defense, energy-related and productivity-oriented reputation had been many times demonstrated and was well recalled in those markets.

"We have an invaluable asset," O'Green said, "in a highly capable and stable work force." The state of Litton Industries with O'Green now running it was good and rich, too. He was the anchorman, smoothly passed baton in hand.

In business no less than in entertainment and sports, there are superstars. They are bigger and more lasting than the financial reports, box office grosses, and box scores they caused. Their names mean something. People muse forever and marvel about what made them different and special. A kind of aura accompanies them into conversations, or when it's recollection time. Mention the name, and everyone present summons his own picture for instant reference. While nearly all of them come from nowhere, in the end they are known everywhere.

---

9. On February 22, 1982, the Ingalls-built U.S.S. Caron, DD-970, became a 3-column front page photo for the New York Times when it relieved the electronics surveillance ship, the U.S.S. Deyo, DD-989, also a Pascagoula product, on station in El Salvador's Gulf of Fonseca.

Will Rogers once told Cecil B. DeMille at the premiere of "King of Kings" that he'd ". . .make a better picture when you have a better subject." DeMille directed Hollywood's first full-length movie called "The Squaw Man" in December, 1913. It grossed about $225,000, made Hollywood the film capital of the world and DeMille eminent enough to have his name above the film's titles because it guaranteed the ticket buyer spectacle and grandeur and sweep. Yet when he was gone, the movies went on without him.

Iron man Lou Gehrig, who played in 2,130 consecutive baseball games, a record which stood 51 years until that bead string was matched by Carl Ripken of the Baltimore Orioles who stretched it to 2,632 in 1993 before a home crowd in the season's finale. Gehrig was only 37 when, stricken by amyotrophic lateral sclerosis, asked to be taken out of the lineup in Detroit May 2, 1940. He'd played poorly at home against Washington on April 30th, which had been that game No. 2,130. On July 4th between a double-header in which the Senators won the first game, there was a Lou Gehrig tribute. He stood there wasting in the Bronx sun that sad afternoon saying how proud he was to have been in that batting order which was called "murderers' row" which had terrorized American League pitchers and that he considered himself ". . .the luckiest man in the world." He heard the crowd roar one more time as he painfully picked his way to the dugout and the tunnel leading to the locker room. Behind him, he heard Plate Umpire Bill McGowan call the traditional order: "Play ball!" The Yankees won that second game. The team and baseball went on without him.

The immortal Vince Lombardi's widow said he had made football players of many men, and even men of some football players. He was intense, concentrating, driven to excel. He once surprised sportswriters on the eve of the Green Bay Packers quest of a third national championship in 1967 by telling them he guided on one of the Epistles of St. Paul. He quoted it in great seriousness and with attention to every word: "Know ye not that they which run in a race run all, but one receiveth the prize? So run, that ye may obtain!" The blasé pressbox habitues looked at each other and grinned and when he was gone scoffed saying it was ". . .the Gospel according to Lombardi." But one of their number was a careful man named Red Smith. He checked his motel Gideon Bible. There it was—Corinthians, Chapter 9, Verse

241. Lombardi would go to any length to make his point and to be correct on whatever assertion he made. It's no accident that the Super Bowl Trophy bears his name.

All these men truly were indomitable. Tex Thornton belongs in their company. He'd made managers of men who never guessed the sizes of the enterprises they'd be called upon to run. He'd made millionaires by the hundreds. He made time for individuals and their problems. He gave a lot. He'd gotten magnificent rewards. Like them, he was demanding and confident. In banding others with him, no mountain was too steep or high to climb—and banded together, they achieved—record makers and breakers all.

What Fred O'Green said in tribute at the annual meeting of Litton was recognition in that vein. The shareholders stood there a moment in honor of the departed founder, each thinking her or his own thoughts. The Litton Industries Tex Thornton left behind him had long since been able to run without him. He'd seen to that. He had been honest in his statement that he had never thought anyone was indispensable, surely not himself, just as he had told that Los Angeles shareholder, Saul Cooper. Litton would never forget him, though. None needed to award him any posthumous corporate goodbye gold watch. He'd become a golden memory.

And his band played on.[10]

THE END

---

10. The author used to joke about Litton's trio of "S" men—Tex Thornton who schemed it, Fred O'Green who saved it, and Dr. Orion "Orie" Hoch who split it.